D0852634

WHAT SO PROUDLY WE HAIL

WHAT SO PROUDLY WE HAIL

The American Soul in Story, Speech, and Song

edited by

Amy A. Kass, Leon R. Kass, and Diana Schaub

Wilmington, Delaware

Copyright © 2011, editorial matter by Amy A. Kass, Leon R. Kass, and Diana Schaub

All rights reserved. No part of this publication may be reproduced or transmitted in any form or by any means, electronic or mechanical, including photocopy, or any information storage and retrieval system now known or to be invented, without permission in writing from the publisher, except by a reviewer who wishes to quote brief passages in connection with a review written for inclusion in a magazine, newspaper, broadcast, or online publication.

Library of Congress Cataloging-in-Publication Data

What so proudly we hail : the American soul in story, speech, and song / edited by Amy A. Kass, Leon R. Kass, and Diana Schaub.

    p. cm.
    Includes bibliographical references.
    ISBN 978-1-61017-006-2

    1. National characteristics, American. 2. National characteristics, American—Literary collections. 3. United States—Civics I. Kass, Amy A. II. Kass, Leon. III. Schaub, Diana.
  E169.1.W414 2011
  973—dc22

                2011005117

Published in the United States by:

ISI Books
Intercollegiate Studies Institute
3901 Centerville Road
Wilmington, Delaware 19807-1938
www.isibooks.org

To Our Students

For additional materials and opportunities for comment,
readers are invited to visit our website:
www.whatsoproudlywehail.org

Contents

Introduction

This is a book about America for every American. More precisely, this is a book about American identity, American character, and American citizenship. Addressing hearts as well as minds, exploiting the soul-shaping powers of story, speech, and song, it is designed to make Americans more appreciatively aware of who they are as citizens of the United States. Its ultimate goal, stated without apology, is to produce better patriots and better citizens: men and women knowingly and thoughtfully attached to our country, devoted to its ideals, and eager to live an active civic life.

Although we are committed to the goal of producing thoughtful patriots and engaged citizens, the editors have no partisan political agenda or ideological intentions. The patriotism we seek to encourage is deep, not superficial; reflective, not reflexive; and, above all, thoughtful. This anthology addresses liberals and conservatives, Democrats and Republicans and independents, employers and employees, rich and poor, young and old, and Americans of every race, religion, and ethnicity, for all Americans have a stake in the well-being of our nation.

Thoughtful Americans have a stake as well in the questions explored in this book: Who are we? How do we identify ourselves, as individuals and as a people? What do we look up to and revere? To what larger community and ideals are we attached and devoted? For what are we willing to fight and to sacrifice? How can America produce citizens who are knowledgeably attached to their country and their communities, and who possess the character—the attitudes, sensibilities, and virtues—necessary for robust civic engagement? How do *we*—parents, teachers, and community leaders—form good citizens?

Challenges for American Identity and Citizenship, New and Old

These enduring questions are again timely, indeed urgent, as current circumstances present new reasons to be concerned about America's future. Numerous studies have documented the cultural and historical illiteracy of today's youth, even among graduates of our best colleges. Knowledge of American history and government has declined, in part because these subjects are no longer centerpieces of public education. Very few colleges require students to take even a single course in matters American. Studies show that, despite volunteering more for community service, today's young people, compared with those of generations past, are less interested in public affairs, less likely to vote regularly, and less likely to stay informed about politics and current events. The reigning ideology that welcomes immigrants to our shores no longer calls for their assimilation into our "melting pot" but instead celebrates their diversity, multiplicity, and cultural distinctiveness; the political "*unum*" of America is lost amid the focus on the multicultural "*pluribus*." Ironically, although recent immigrants (and their children) usually know from fresh experience how their lives have improved by coming to the United States, the well-off children of the native-born, knowing little of history or of current political alternatives around the globe, take for granted the privileges of American citizenship and prosperity. Increasingly, leading intellectuals, opinion leaders, and politicians talk of globalization and the need to regard ourselves as "citizens of the world." Between such cosmopolitan universalism and ethnic and racial "tribalism," *national* pride and attachment are often disparaged, and in some quarters regarded as obsolete.

But national identity and citizenship in America face deeper and more permanent challenges, some linked to the special character of our liberal democratic republic. Citizenship in the United States is legally defined, by the Fourteenth Amendment to the Constitution, in this minimalist way: A citizen is any person "born or naturalized in the United States, and subject to the jurisdiction thereof." The Constitution speaks of our *rights* as citizens; it never mentions any of our *duties* or what it takes to defend those rights. To be sure, becoming a citizen by naturalization requires passing certain tests, again rather minimal. For most Americans, however, citizenship is in no way earned; it is bestowed by the mere accident of birth within our borders.

Yet the American Republic was founded as—and remains—a nation not of birth, lineage, or inherited ways but of ideas. It was the first nation to define itself in terms of certain teachings and aspirations, what may be thought of as the American creed—the equal rights to life, liberty, and the pursuit of happiness; freedom of religion and religious toleration; majority rule; minority rights; and the rule of law. To exaggerate but slightly, anyone who embraces these universal ideas can become in spirit an American.

But for this reason, attachment to the United States cannot easily rely on patriotic emotions arising from familial, tribal, and religious ties or from traditional bonds to place, language, music, and inherited cultural norms. America, according to a patriotic song, may be the "land where our fathers died," but we never refer to it as the fatherland (*patria*) or motherland, as do Germans or Russians regarding their native land. What takes the place of such deep sentimental attachments? Is acceptance of certain basic political or philosophical principles enough to make citizens willing to serve and sacrifice for their country in time of need?

Complicating the difficulty is the fact that America embraces people from all over the world, who come with different ways, speak different languages, and practice different religions. We have never had an established national church or even an articulated national morality. Our tolerance, and even encouragement, of ethnic and religious pluralism is a great national strength, but it also poses a challenge for creating a deep national bond and spirit. As a result, our emotional ties to our separate ways and beliefs often exceed ties to our common national whole. Our identification as Americans seems at best to be "hyphenated," not unqualified.

National attachments may be harder to sustain also because America celebrates the individual, not the collective. The state, according to our creed, exists to protect the rights of individuals; the individual does not exist to promote the power or glory of the state. Our individual rights encourage our *private* pursuit of happiness and prosperity—within the limits set by law, but not necessarily with a view to what would promote the *common* or *public* good. We jealously guard our freedoms and our privacy; save in times of national emergency, we are deeply suspicious of encroachments upon them, especially by the state. Making public-spirited citizens out of a nation of individualists has long been a challenge.

America's embrace of science, technology, and other forms of progress paradoxically poses another challenge. The United States Constitution, silent on the all-important matter of educating citizens, speaks up in favor of progress in science and the useful arts: the first and only right mentioned in the original Constitution of 1787 is the right of authors and inventors to their writings and discoveries. But a people that looks largely to the future and that loves and rewards novelty is less likely to have reverence for the past or to care about preserving our institutions and mores. Our spectacular energy and enterprise and our penchant for innovation and improvement—traits made possible by the freedoms guaranteed under our Constitution—render tenuous our sentimental attachments to the gifts and traditions that we have inherited. This long-standing difficulty becomes more severe in the age of cyberspace and instant communication.

America is, by design, a commercial republic; according to the *Federalist Papers*, the multiplication of competing interests and the encouragement of trade were indispensable to protecting against majority faction, previously the bane of democracies and a threat to liberty. Yet while commerce and prosperity contribute to our freedom, this freedom can be put solely in the service of the accumulation of wealth—the means becoming the end. The love of gain, encouraged by our polity, can produce a materialism that deadens the souls of its citizens and keeps them from thinking about life in other than economic and self-interested terms. Further, our high geographic mobility, created and demanded by the modern transnational economy, weakens ties to place and opportunities for long-term local civic engagement. What kind of continuing community life is possible where children leave home never to return, where the most successful people move off to greener pastures, and where municipal institutions and local concerns lack cosmopolitan glamour?

Our economic successes thus challenge our sense of national unity and civic devotion. Thanks to technological progress and democratic capitalism, the average American worker today enjoys a higher standard of living and a longer, healthier life than did dukes and duchesses but a century ago. Yet expectations have risen as well, meaning that gratitude to the Republic for these blessings has not increased proportionately. Indeed, as inequality between rich and poor has increased, we see greater resentment, alienation, and complaints of social injustice among the have-lesses and their advocates. Addressing these inequalities, governmental entitlement programs, first enacted by the welfare state to provide safety nets for the poor, have been expanded to benefit the middle class, encouraging many citizens to think more about what their country can do for them, less about what they can do for their country.

The Importance of Citizenship

Why, you might ask, does any of this matter? What difference does it make whether the next generations of Americans identify with their country, admire its institutions and ways, and devote themselves to robust civic participation? Can we not continue to enjoy our civil rights to life and liberty and our blessings of prosperity and private happiness, however great or small our civic attachments and involvements?

Up to a point, perhaps so. The genius of our liberal democratic form of government allows most of us happily to tend our own gardens and mind our own business, inattentive to the problems that our nation faces. We are spared the often turbulent and bloody consequences of living in countries where politics is all-important and omnipresent, especially those whose illiberal regimes compel service to the state and punish deviance from official orthodoxies.

But our freedom not to care comes at a price, precisely because we live in a polity in which the people are sovereign. It is we the people who must elect the representatives to govern on our behalf, defend our nation in times of crisis, and shoulder our responsibilities in times of peace—at the very least, by upholding the law, voting in elections, paying our taxes, and serving on juries. How well will we judge, how wisely will we choose, how firmly will we stand if we don't know who we are as Americans and why the blessings we share are worth defending and perpetuating, or if we lack the affections for our country that can move us to act in public-spirited ways?

Citizenship in the United States is only partly a national matter, for we live in a federal republic, with various levels of government—national, state, county, and local—responsible for different aspects of our common life. We depend on local schools, hospitals, transportation, libraries, colleges, museums, parks, police and fire departments, and departments of sanitation and public health—many of which require civic support and citizens' attention. Our life together comprises also the myriad voluntary, *non*governmental associations—from religious institutions to Little League, from soup kitchens to nature-preservation societies, from the Red Cross and the United Way to friends of the symphony and the PTA—where, through our own active participation, we give meaning to our lives and strengthen our communities, which in turn enrich our existence. How vibrant will our communal life be, how rich will our human associations be, if we think only of ourselves and our immediate families and our own pursuit of happiness? Can we have communities worth joining if we lack public spirit, civic attachment, and the character needed for active and effective civic participation?

The Importance of Character

What, then, *is* the character needed for American citizenship? Character, it should be stressed, goes deeper than temperament or personality, deeper also than one's moral beliefs and principles. It is a disposition of soul, not merely a state of mind. It is more than the sum of the rules and commandments—the "thou shalts" and the "thou shalt nots"—to which we give assent or the moral maxims to which we intellectually subscribe. People may hold decent opinions or support "right values" without incorporating them into the grain of their being: Thought alone cannot guide action. The source of our conduct is always a matter of the heart as well, embodied in the state of our desires, the shape of our wishes, and the direction of our intentions. Character, then, is the established disposition of our *power of choosing*, a most peculiar fusion of heart and mind that reveals itself in the choices we make and the deeds we do.

The excellences of character we call "virtues"—their opposites, "vices"—and we name them according to the specific domains in which they show themselves: courage in relation to fearful things; generosity in relation to wealth; self-command in relation to temptations and passions; civility and justice in dealings with others; compassion and charity with regard to suffering; respect and reverence in relation to things deemed worthy and holy. In freeing a person from passions and desires that might otherwise enslave him, the virtues both perfect the individual and facilitate his pursuits and aspirations, also making him a responsible member of the community. In shaping a person's attitudes and dispositions toward other people, the virtues elevate relations among fellow citizens and give rise to public-spirited acts and activities.

The virtues of character are largely the product of rearing and habituation, acquired through practice and training, and reinforced by praise and blame, reward and punishment, from parents, teachers, clergy, and other members of the community. Even if human nature is everywhere more or less the same, different ways of life will encourage different virtues—and contribute to different vices. A polity like ours, which celebrates individual liberty, commerce, and progress, is likely to produce a character different from that produced by a polity that celebrates service to the state, piety, and strict adherence to tradition. And the character and virtue (or vice) a polity tends to produce may not be the same as the character it *needs* in order to flourish.

What, in the American Republic, will keep liberty from producing scofflaws and libertines? What will keep the pursuit of gain from destroying generosity and charity? What will keep free speech civil, religious freedom tolerant, and the love of progress grateful for blessings received? What will enable a rights-loving nation to produce citizens who will choose gladly to do their duty—to their offspring, their neighbor, their community, their nation?

The Importance of Identity

Citizenship is a legal and political status, relating each citizen to the body politic, conferring privileges and immunities, and assigning or implying responsibilities and duties. Character is an ethical condition, shaped partly by the polity, but with virtues and vices that are not finally regime-specific (self-command, generosity, and courage in battle are universally available, and we recognize them even among our enemies). But deeper than citizenship, and separable from character, is our national identity: that which makes us Americans, both in fact and in our self-understanding. Our character helps to distinguish us—as human being, rather than animal; as civilized, rather than barbarian; as virtuous or decent, rather than vicious or indecent. But our national identity helps to unite us. Only through identifying with our nation—its ideals, its ways, its story, its aspirations, its institutions—will we care enough to take an active role in promoting its well-being.

"National identity" names both an objective fact and a subjective state of soul. The objective aspect of national identity is familiar to anyone who has traveled abroad: even those fellow countrymen who feel little affection for the United States are immediately recognized as Americans, not only from the distinctive way we speak but also from myriad subtle manifestations of having been reared in our midst. But for present purposes, it is each person's *internal* sense of belonging to the nation that matters most. For how will anyone be willing to pull his civic oar if he cares little for city or country? What kind of robust civic life is possible for a citizen who lacks patriotic attachment?

As it happens, American identity is important not only for civic life. Paradoxically, it is also important for personal self-fulfillment. In this age of global economics and the World Wide Web, it is tempting to dismiss as outdated or dangerous the significance of *national* identification for personal identity and personal happiness. One can choose to identify oneself as belonging to the party of humanity or even imagine oneself as a citizen of the world. But that is a dream contrary to fact, because citizenship is a political category, tied to membership in a *specific* political and legal system. National identity is unavoidable; it is also desirable. For the plain truth of the matter is that, for the vast majority of human beings, human life *as actually lived* is lived parochially and locally, embedded in a web of human relations, institutions, culture, and mores that define us and give shape and meaning to our lives. One's feeling for global humanity, however sincere, is based on an abstraction, hard to translate into the concrete and meaningful expressions of interest and concern that lead neighbor to care for neighbor, Chicagoan for Chicagoan, Texan for Texan, and American for American. We are not talking about shallow jingoism or the psychic boost we give ourselves by yelling "USA, USA" at the Olympics. We are talking, rather, about the genuine elevation of our lives made possible by belonging freely and feelingly to something larger and more worthy than our individual selves.

Other nations, of course, can and do lay claim to similar attachments and loyalties—appropriately so. But for us Americans, there are special reasons to promote and celebrate our national identity. For we are the heirs of a way of life that has offered the blessings of freedom and dignity to millions of people of all races and religions, and that extols the possibility of individual achievement as far as individual talent and effort can take it. The universal ideas set forth at the founding of the American Republic were embodied not in some universal nation of humankind united, like the biblical city of Babel, but in a particular nation—well-founded, stable, orderly, decent, and given always to self-critical efforts to bring its reality ever more closely in line with its ideals. To belong to such a nation is not only a special blessing but also a special calling: to ensure that, in Abraham Lincoln's words, a nation "conceived in liberty and dedicated to the proposition that all men are created equal" will long endure, and "that government of the people, by the people, for the people shall not perish from the earth."

Making Citizens: Educating Hearts and Minds

Recognizing the importance of American citizenship, character, and identity is relatively easy. Knowing how to produce them is difficult, especially given the obstacles, old and new, that we face today. Active and attached citizens of good character are not born, they are made. Their making depends partly on explicit instruction, partly on habituation in character-shaping activities—in homes, schools, houses of worship, community organizations, youth groups, voluntary associations, branches of military service, and the like. How all these influences work and coalesce is, in truth, something of a mystery, especially if we remember that making citizens involves more than correcting people's ignorance or refining their opinions. It requires, above all, the shaping of the central attitudes, sensibilities, and concerns of their being. It is precisely to address these deeper, and often neglected, aspects of making citizens that we have assembled this volume.

Many people in the United States, concerned about the state of civic literacy and national identity, have been developing new programs of instruction that emphasize American history, political thought, and civic institutions. These worthy efforts are largely cognitive: they seek to correct our abysmal ignorance by providing knowledge. But such knowledge will not by itself produce love of country or desires to do something in its service. *Knowing* the good, while necessary, is not sufficient for *doing* the good.

Another recent approach to improving civic participation emphasizes learning by doing. Called "service learning," this approach sends students out into the community to perform mandated services for others, in the hope that the students thereby develop the habit of serving. But these worthy humanitarian activities are usually framed in social services' language of "client" and "provider," or the cosmopolitan language of compassion and care, rather than in the political and polity-specific language of American citizenship. And they are rarely accompanied by the sorts of study and discussions that could inform the sentiments employed or make the students more thoughtful about the character and purposes of the polity in which they live and serve.

Developing robust and committed American citizens is a matter of *both* the heart and the head. Like all building of character, it requires educating our moral imaginations, sentiments, and habits of heart—matters displayed in but also nurtured by great works of imaginative literature. As has been known at least since Homer and Plato, it is the poets, not the philosophers and historians, who shape the loves and hates of souls and cities. Today as well, works of fiction speak most immediately, engagingly, and movingly to the hearts and minds of readers of all ages. For these reasons, we have adopted a literary approach to making citizens, an approach centering on stories.

The Power of Stories

By furnishing our imaginations with well-drawn characters confronting concrete difficulties in well-defined circumstances, a well-crafted story can shed light on our national character and civic practices. By enabling us to identify and sympathize with the characters and the situations in which they find themselves, the story invites us to reflect also on ourselves and our own personal and civic experiences. For a practically minded people like us, not generally given to deep philosophical inquiry or long epic sagas, the short story is a perfect vehicle for generating fruitful self-examination and self-knowledge. In fact, it may well be *the* supremely American literary form, whose "nervous, formal, concentrated, brief, and penetrating" literary character, as Wallace Stegner has said, best "expresses us as a people." Many of us love to tell stories, and most of us love to hear them. But to hear—or read—and discuss the best stories told by the best storytellers is more than a way of passing time. It is a way of deepening time, by taking us to the profoundly humanizing truths contained in the ordinary surfaces of our experience. With the help of a great storyteller, we can see in the commonplace the things that really matter. Yes, stories are entertaining, but at their best they inform and reform us by dramatizing belief and rendering feeling thoughtful.

Short stories—most of them fictional, some autobiographical, and all written by American authors, living and dead—form the majority of the selections in this anthology. Supplementing the stories are important public speeches, by noted American statesmen and civic leaders, that shed light on our commitment to freedom and equality or give voice to our enduring aspirations for national and civic improvement. The speeches not only illuminate some past circumstance; thanks to their rhetorical power, they enable us today to feel more fully our lives as American citizens and to recognize which dispositions and practices enhance (and which undermine) republican self-government and ordered liberty. Carefully considered, the feelings and reactions aroused by both the speeches and the stories can be thoughtfully attached to principled opinions. And the cumulative experience of such reflective reading and discussion can foster a deeper sense of American identity and contribute to forming the character needed for robust American citizenship and public life.

The American Republic, despite its grandeur, is not simply a success story. And the American character is not simply a picture of unalloyed human excellence. The honest treatment of our subject, therefore, does not allow for chest-thumping, self-congratulatory tales. Thoughtful and engaged citizenship cannot be had by simple indoctrination into the American creed. But it can be fostered by looking into the multiangled mirrors our finest authors provide, and by discovering in our reflections the richness and worth of American identity, character, and citizenship.

The Structure of This Book

One of the virtues of an anthology is that readers are free to pick and choose what they wish to read, skipping around in no particular order. Yet there is method in our ordering, and we think there is additional advantage in following the text straight through. Chapter One, "National Identity: Why Should It Matter?" explores the nature and significance of national identity in general and of American identity in particular.

Chapter Two, "The American Creed," lays out the major ideas and ideals of the American Republic: freedom, individual rights, and government by consent; equality; enterprise and commerce; freedom of and for religious worship; and religious toleration. Taken together, the five selections also invite reflection on how, as Tocqueville observed, America manages marvelously to combine the spirit of freedom and the spirit of religion, which elsewhere often war against each other. Mindful of our nation's founding principles and ideals, readers will be ready next to reflect on the character of citizens likely produced under such a polity.

Chapter Three, "The American Character: Individuals Free and Equal," comprises seven short stories, each of which examines different traits of the American character. The stories explore the strengths and weaknesses of American individualism and independence, the implications and limits of our love of equality, the condition of virtue in a democratic society devoted to gain and reputation, and the assets and liabilities of religious devotion and religious toleration. These portraits of the American character do more than celebrate life lived under our principles. They also point out the deficiencies and excesses to which we Americans may well be prone precisely because we are privileged to live our lives as free and equal individuals, pursuing happiness as each sees fit.

Alerted by seeing how our honored virtues are linked to our potential vices, the reader is ready to consider what is needed to protect us from vices, and which virtues are requisite for robust American citizenship. The selections of Chapter Four, "Toward a More Robust Citizenry: The Virtues of Civic Life," are divided into five sections, each devoted to a different set of virtues, each targeting a different domain of civic attention and responsibility: the virtues of individual self-command and self-respect, without which neither personal flourishing nor fruitful civic engagement is possible; the elementary civic virtues of lawabidingness and justice; courage and self-sacrifice, virtues for critical times, not only in battle but in other difficult situations as well; civility, tolerance, and compassion, virtues required toward our neighbors; and, finally, public-spiritedness, charity, and reverence, virtues and responsibilities regarding larger public goods.

While Chapter Four deals with the virtues Americans need for an active and flourishing civic life, Chapter Five, "The Goals of Civic Life," explores the basic question: What should civic life be for? What *are* the goals to which we as engaged and responsible citizens should devote ourselves? Beyond the fundamental goals of lawabidingness, public order, and national security—implicit in the virtues discussed in Chapter Four—is a wide array of possible purposes. Some civic activities are directed toward *lifting the floor* for those who suffer near the bottom of society, whether owing to poverty and injustice, racial discrimination, lack of education, or inadequate family life. Other civic activities are directed toward *elevating the ceiling* of human possibility and achievement, whether in the fine arts, athletics, statesmanship, or bold adventure, enterprise, and exploration. Still other civic activities are focused not on change but on *perpetuating and preserving* our traditions, institutions, and ways of life. About these differing goals there is often public contention, less about their goodness than about their relative importance and urgency. Rarely do we take the time to reflect carefully on any of them, seen in the company of the others. Accordingly, the three sections of Chapter Five are devoted to these three kinds of goals, seeking to give each its due.

After the explorations of civic virtues and civic goals, we are still left with the question of national identity with which we began: how to make one out of many? What can counter our centrifugal and privatizing tendencies, resulting from our devotion to (our own) life, liberty, and the pursuit of happiness? What can attach the hearts and minds of our citizens—each of us an individual and family member with his or her own interests and concerns, each of us a member of this or that ethnic, racial, or religious subgroup, each of us a citizen also of this or that neighborhood, town, or metropolis—to the American Republic as a whole? Chapter Six, "Making One Out of Many," considers three aspects of national unity and identification: assimilation and integration of immigrants, especially in relation to a common public language; American patriotic songs for free men and women; and the great symbols of the American republic—the Great Seal of the United States, the American eagle, and the American flag.

The centrality of the songs in the last chapter deserves a further word. In encouraging national identification, songs target not our character as much as our sentiments and attachments, our *feelings* of love, reverence, and devotion. Song—the singular combination of moving speech set to stirring music—is everywhere employed in shaping hearts and souls, and the capacity of song to inspire is part of its power. Yet if focusing *only* on principles and ideas risks a thin and heartless attachment of the intellect, focusing *only* on music risks a thoughtless surrender to roused emotion and jingoistic fervor. The approach to the songs in this anthology seeks to avoid both dangers, by inviting attention to the meanings of the words and self-conscious reflection on the feelings aroused by singing them.

The Spirit of Reading and Thinking

The three editors of this volume have been engaged in teaching high school and college students for a cumulative total of more than a century. In our teaching, we have relied mainly on the great writings by the best authors, whether living or dead, for we have found them to be the best companions for thought and the richest materials for enlarging the horizons, stimulating the imaginations, and challenging the intellectual complacencies of our students. Thus, we rely most heavily on stories by America's finest writers, including Nathaniel Hawthorne, Herman Melville, Mark Twain, Henry James, Stephen Crane, Willa

Cather, Flannery O'Connor, Ralph Ellison, Wallace Stegner, Saul Bellow, and John Updike, and on speeches by America's great statesmen and civic leaders, including George Washington, Benjamin Franklin, Thomas Jefferson, Abraham Lincoln, Frederick Douglass, Booker T. Washington, W. E. B. DuBois, Theodore Roosevelt, and Martin Luther King Jr. Authors such as these help us not only to understand the phenomena about which they write but also to experience them. By giving powerful voice to profound experiences, their writings allow us access to those mysterious aspects of human affairs that are graspable not by outward description alone but by educated feeling.

We offer these works not because they are authoritative, and we chose these authors not because they are old or great or "canonical." Rather, we offer them in the spirit of wisdom seeking rather than wisdom delivering—as writings that make us think, challenge our unexamined opinions, expand our sympathies, elevate our gaze, and introduce us to possibilities open to citizens in our everyday American life that may be undreamt of in our philosophizing.

On a subject this complicated and massive, there can be no pretense of representing all important points of view. There are other civic virtues and other national goals that we have not considered. There are important authors that we have overlooked; there are stories that might be better than those we have included—and in fact we welcome readers' suggestions. In the end, we have gone with readings that we know and have taught or that were recommended to us, that we think valuable for addressing the questions about American identity and citizenship, and, of course, that we ourselves admire and enjoy.

As any teacher knows, most good books do not teach themselves. We are all frequently lazy readers, who skip over what is puzzling or unfamiliar, and, even worse, who fail to see the depth in what is familiar and congenial. Moreover, in delicate political subjects, our prejudices get in the way, and our inexperience blinds us to crucial subtleties and nuances. Accordingly, we have tried to introduce each reading with some observations and questions designed to make for more active and discerning reading.

The readings in this anthology impose no particular moral, political, or religious teaching. Indeed, they impose nothing; they only propose. They propose different ways of thinking about different aspects of our shared lives as American citizens. Some of these proposals will almost certainly "impose" themselves upon the reader's mind and heart as being more worthy than others. But they will do so not because they offer simple abstractable principles or suggest procedures for solving this or that problem of public life. They will do so because they strike the thoughtful reader as wiser, deeper, and truer. We ourselves have had this experience with our readings, and we hope you will also. For the American life you examine in these pages is—or could become—your own.

1

National Identity:
Why Should It Matter?

The Man without a Country

Edward Everett Hale

Edward Everett Hale (1822–1909), Unitarian minister, antislavery activist, and for a time chaplain in the United States Senate, was also a prolific author of essays and stories, of which this one—written in 1863, the year of the Emancipation Proclamation—is the best known. The plot of the story is straightforward: Seduced by Aaron Burr, young, ambitious Philip Nolan, an artillery officer in the "Legion of the West," becomes a Burr accomplice and is later convicted of treason. Asked after his conviction whether he wishes to declare his loyalty to the United States, he cries out, "Damn the United States! I wish I may never hear of the United States again!" His judges, half of them Revolutionary War veterans, give him precisely what he asks for. From that moment, September 23, 1807, until his dying day, May 11, 1863, Nolan "never but once again" hears the name of the United States, spending the rest of his life literally and figuratively at sea. [*]

Why is Philip Nolan so quickly seduced and enlisted, "body and soul," into the service of Aaron Burr? What causes him to change his attitude and feelings toward his country? Is Nolan's eventual appreciation of his country simply the love of his own—his family, his country, his flag, his mother—or is it tied instead to something peculiarly American, such as our principles

---

[*] *The story is purely fictional, though it has echoes of historical events: After Aaron Burr left the vice presidency in 1805, he did make two trips down the Mississippi; he and his accomplices were tried for treason; and he was accused, among other things, of a conspiracy to steal Louisiana Purchase lands away from the United States and to crown himself king or emperor. Hale, years later, reported that the story, at least in part, was "testimony" against the election of 1863, in which Clement Vallandigham (1820–1871), an ardent antiwar, pro-Confederate, anti-"King Lincoln" Ohio Democrat, was running for office from exile in Canada, and who, at his own earlier treason trial, like the fictional Nolan, asserted that he did not want to belong to the United States.*

of freedom and equality? What does Nolan—what do we—learn from the emancipated slaves' desire to return to their native lands?

Hale hoped that his story would contribute "towards the formation of a just and true national sentiment, or sentiment of love to the nation." Does it do so for you?

I suppose that very few casual readers of the "New York Herald" of August 13th, 1863, observed, in an obscure corner, among the "Deaths," the announcement,

"NOLAN. Died, on board U. S. Corvette Levant, Lat. 2° 11′ S., Long. 131° W., on the 11th of May, PHILIP NOLAN."

I happened to observe it, because I was stranded at the old Mission-House in Mackinac, waiting for a Lake-Superior steamer which did not choose to come, and I was devouring, to the very stubble, all the current literature I could get hold of, even down to the deaths and marriages in the "Herald." My memory for names and people is good, and the reader will see, as he goes on, that I had reason enough to remember Philip Nolan. There are hundreds of readers who would have paused at that announcement, if the officer of the Levant who reported it had chosen to make it thus:—"Died, May 11th, THE MAN WITHOUT A COUNTRY." For it was as "The Man without a Country" that poor Philip Nolan had generally been known by the officers who had him in charge during some fifty years, as, indeed, by all the men who sailed under them. I dare say there is many a man who has taken wine with him once a fortnight, in a three years' cruise, who never knew that his name was "Nolan," or whether the poor wretch had any name at all.

There can now be no possible harm in telling this poor creature's story. Reason enough there has been till now, ever since Madison's Administration went out in 1817, for very strict secrecy, the secrecy of honor itself, among the gentlemen of the navy who have had Nolan in successive charge. And certainly it speaks well for the *esprit de corps* of the profession and the personal honor of its members, that to the press this man's story has been wholly unknown,— and, I think, to the country at large also. I have reason to think, from some investigations I made in the Naval Archives when I was attached to the Bureau of Construction, that every official report relating to him was burned when Ross burned the public buildings at Washington. One of the Tuckers, or possibly one of the Watsons, had Nolan in charge at the end of the war; and when, on returning from his cruise, he reported at Washington to one of the Crown-inshields,—who was in the Navy Department when he came home,—he found that the Department ignored the whole business. Whether they really knew nothing about it, or whether it was a *"Non mi ricordo,"* determined on as a piece of policy, I do not know. But this I do know, that since 1817, and possibly before, no naval officer has mentioned Nolan in his report of a cruise.

But, as I say, there is no need for secrecy any longer. And now the poor creature is dead, it seems to me worth while to tell a little of his story, by way of showing young Americans of to-day what it is to be A MAN WITHOUT A COUNTRY.

Philip Nolan was as fine a young officer as there was in the "Legion of the West," as the Western division of our army was then called. When Aaron Burr made his first dashing expedition down to New Orleans in 1805, at Fort Massac, or somewhere above on the river, he met, as the Devil would have it, this gay, dashing, bright young fellow, at some dinner-party, I think. Burr marked him, talked to him, walked with him, took him a day or two's voyage in his flat-boat, and, in short, fascinated him. For the next year, barrack-life was very tame to poor Nolan. He occasionally availed himself of the permission the great man had given him to write to him. Long, high-worded, stilted letters the poor boy wrote and rewrote and copied. But never a line did he have in reply from the gay deceiver. The other boys in the garrison sneered at him, because he sacrificed in this unrequited affection for a politician the time which they devoted to Monongahela, sledge, and high-low-jack. Bourbon, euchre, and poker were still unknown. But one day Nolan had his revenge. This time Burr came down the river, not as an attorney seeking a place for his office, but as a disguised conqueror. He had defeated I know not how many district-attorneys; he had dined at I know not how many public dinners; he had been heralded in I know not how many Weekly Arguses; and it was rumored that he had an army behind him and an empire before him. It was a great day—his arrival—to poor Nolan. Burr had not been at the fort an hour before he sent for him. That evening he asked Nolan to take him out in his skiff, to show him a canebrake or a cotton-wood tree, as he said,—really to seduce him; and by the time the sail was over, Nolan was enlisted body and soul. From that time, though he did not yet know it, he lived as A MAN WITHOUT A COUNTRY.

What Burr meant to do I know no more than you, dear reader. It is none of our business just now. Only, when the grand catastrophe came, and Jefferson and the House of Virginia of that day undertook to break on the wheel all the possible Clarences of the then House of York, by the great treason-trial at Richmond, some of the lesser fry in that distant Mississippi Valley, which was farther from us than Puget's Sound is to-day, introduced the like novelty on their provincial stage, and, to while away the monotony of the summer at Fort Adams, got up, for *spectacles,* a string of court-martials on the officers there. One and another of the colonels and majors were tried, and, to fill out the list, little Nolan, against whom, Heaven knows, there was evidence enough,—that he was sick of the service, had been willing to be false to it, and would have obeyed any order to march any-whither with any one who would follow him, had the order been signed, "By command of His Exc. A. Burr." The courts dragged on. The big flies escaped,—rightly for all I know. Nolan was proved guilty enough, as I say; yet you and I would never have heard of him, reader, but that, when the president of the court asked him at the close, whether he wished to say anything to show that he had always been faithful to the United States, he cried out, in a fit of frenzy,—

> "D——n the United States! I wish I may never hear of the United States again!"

I suppose he did not know how the words shocked old Colonel Morgan, who was holding the court. Half the officers who sat in it had served through the Revolution, and their lives, not to say their necks, had been risked for the very idea which he so cavalierly cursed in his madness. He, on his part, had grown up in the West of those days, in the midst of "Spanish plot," "Orleans plot," and all the rest. He had been educated on a plantation, where the finest company was a Spanish officer or a French merchant from Orleans. His education, such as it was, had been perfected in commercial expeditions to Vera Cruz, and I think he told me his father once hired an Englishman to be a private tutor for a winter on the plantation. He had spent half his youth with an older brother, hunting horses in Texas; and, in a word, to him "United States" was scarcely a reality. Yet he had been fed by "United States" for all the years since he had been in the army. He had sworn on his faith as a Christian to be true to "United States." It was "United States" which gave him the uniform he wore, and the sword by his side. Nay, my poor Nolan, it was only because "United States" had picked you out first as one of her own confidential men of honor, that "A. Burr" cared for you a straw more than for the flat-boat men who sailed his ark for him. I do not excuse Nolan; I only explain to the reader why he damned his country, and wished he might never hear her name again.

He never did hear her name but once again. From that moment, September 23, 1807, till the day he died, May 11, 1863, he never heard her name again. For that half century and more he was a man without a country.

Old Morgan, as I said, was terribly shocked. If Nolan had compared George Washington to Benedict Arnold, or had cried, "God save King George," Morgan would not have felt worse. He called the court into his private room, and returned in fifteen minutes, with a face like a sheet, to say,—

"Prisoner, hear the sentence of the Court. The Court decides, subject to the approval of the President, that you never hear the name of the United States again."

Nolan laughed. But nobody else laughed. Old Morgan was too solemn, and the whole room was hushed dead as night for a minute. Even Nolan lost his swagger in a moment. Then Morgan added,—

"Mr. Marshal, take the prisoner to Orleans in an armed boat, and deliver him to the naval commander there."

The marshal gave his orders and the prisoner was taken out of court.

"Mr. Marshal," continued old Morgan, "see that no one mentions the United States to the prisoner. Mr. Marshal, make my respects to Lieutenant Mitchell at Orleans, and request him to order that no one shall mention the United States to the prisoner while he is on board ship. You will receive your written orders from the officer on duty here this evening. The court is adjourned without delay."

I have always supposed that Colonel Morgan himself took the proceedings of the court to Washington City, and explained them to Mr. Jefferson. Certain it is that the President approved them,—certain, that is, if I may believe the men who say they have seen his signature. Before the Nautilus got round from New Orleans to the Northern Atlantic coast with the prisoner on board, the sentence had been approved, and he was a man without a country.

The plan then adopted was substantially the same which was necessarily followed ever after. Perhaps it was suggested by the necessity of sending him by water from Fort Adams and Orleans. The Secretary of the Navy—it must have been the first Crowninshield, though he is a man I do not remember—was requested to put Nolan on board a Government vessel bound on a long cruise, and to direct that he should be only so far confined there as to make it certain that he never saw or heard of the country. We had few long cruises then, and the navy was very much out of favor; and as almost all of this story is traditional, as I have explained, I do not know certainly what his first cruise was.

But the commander to whom he was intrusted—perhaps it was Tingey or Shaw, though I think it was one of the younger men,—we are all old enough now—regulated the etiquette and the precautions of the affair, and according to his scheme they were carried out, I suppose, till Nolan died.

When I was second officer of the Intrepid, some thirty years after, I saw the original paper of instructions. I have been sorry ever since that I did not copy the whole of it. It ran, however, much in this way:—

"*Washington*" (with a date, which must have been late in 1807.)

"SIR,—You will receive from Lt. Neale the person of Philip Nolan, late a Lieutenant in the United States Army.

"This person on his trial by court-martial expressed with an oath the wish that he might 'never hear of the United States again.'

"The Court sentenced him to have his wish fulfilled.

"For the present, the execution of the order is intrusted by the President to this Department.

"You will take the prisoner on board your ship, and keep him there with such precautions as shall prevent his escape.

"You will provide him with such quarters, rations, and clothing as would be proper for an officer of his late rank, if he were a passenger on your vessel on the business of his Government.

"The gentlemen on board will make any arrangements agreeable to themselves regarding his society. He is to be exposed to no indignity of any kind, nor is he ever unnecessarily to be reminded that he is a prisoner.

"But under no circumstances is he ever to hear of his country or to see any information regarding it; and you will especially caution all the officers under your command to take care, that, in the various indulgences which may be granted, this rule, in which his punishment is involved, shall not be broken.

"It is the intention of the Government that he shall never again see the country which he has disowned. Before the end of your cruise you will receive orders which will give effect to this intention.

"Resp'y yours,
"W. Southard, for the Sec'y of the Navy."

If I had only preserved the whole of this paper, there would be no break in the beginning of my sketch of this story. For Captain Shaw, if it was he, handed it to his successor in the charge, and he to his, and I suppose the commander of the Levant has it to-day as his authority for keeping this man in this mild custody.

The rule adopted on board the ships on which I have met "the man without a country" was, I think, transmitted from the beginning. No mess liked to have him permanently, because his presence cut off all talk of home or of the prospect of return, of politics or letters, of peace or of war,—cut off more than half the talk the men liked to have at sea. But it was always thought too hard that he should never meet the rest of us, except to touch hats, and we finally sank into one system. He was not permitted to talk with the men, unless an officer was by. With officers he had unrestrained intercourse, as far as they and he chose. But he grew shy, though he had favorites: I was one.

Then the captain always asked him to dinner on Monday. Every mess in succession took up the invitation in its turn. According to the size of the ship, you had him at your mess more or less often at dinner. His breakfast he ate in his own state-room,—he always had a state-room,—which was where a sentinel, or somebody on the watch, could see the door. And whatever else he ate or drank he ate or drank alone. Sometimes, when the marines or sailors had any special jollification, they were permitted to invite "Plain-Buttons," as they called him. Then Nolan was sent with some officer, and the men were forbidden to speak of home while he was there. I believe the theory was, that the sight of his punishment did them good. They called him "Plain-Buttons," because, while he always chose to wear a regulation army-uniform, he was not permitted to wear the army-button, for the reason that it bore either the initials or the insignia of the country he had disowned.

I remember, soon after I joined the navy, I was on shore with some of the older officers from our ship and from the Brandywine, which we had met at Alexandria. We had leave to make a party and go up to Cairo and the Pyramids. As we jogged along, (you went on donkeys then,) some of the gentlemen (we boys called them "Dons," but the phrase was long since changed) fell to talking about Nolan, and some one told the system which was adopted from the first about his books and other reading. As he was almost never permitted to go on shore, even though the vessel lay in port for months, his time, at the best, hung heavy; and everybody was permitted to lend him books, if they were not published in America and made no allusion to it. These were common enough in the old days, when people in the other hemisphere talked of the United States as little as we do of Paraguay. He had almost all the foreign papers that came into the ship, sooner or later; only somebody must go over them first, and cut out any advertisement or stray paragraph that alluded to America. This was a little cruel sometimes, when the back of what was cut out might be as innocent as Hesiod. Right in the midst of one of Napoleon's battles, or one of Canning's speeches, poor Nolan would find a great hole, because on the back of the page of that paper there had been an advertisement of a packet for New York, or a scrap from the President's message. I say this was the first time I ever heard of this plan, which afterwards I had enough, and more than enough, to do with. I remember it, because poor Phillips, who was of the party, as soon as the allusion to reading was made, told a story of something which happened at the Cape of Good Hope on Nolan's first voyage; and it is the only thing I ever knew of that voyage. They had touched at the Cape, and had done the civil thing with the English Admiral and the fleet, and then, leaving for a long cruise up the Indian Ocean, Phillips had borrowed a lot of English books from an officer, which, in those days, as indeed in these, was quite a windfall. Among them, as the Devil would order, was the "Lay of the Last Minstrel," which they had all of them heard of, but which most of them had never seen. I think it could not have been published long. Well, nobody thought there could be any risk of anything national in that, though Phillips swore old Shaw had cut out the "Tempest" from Shakespeare before he let Nolan have it, because he said "the Bermudas ought to be ours, and, by Jove, should be one day." So Nolan was permitted to join the circle one afternoon when a lot of them sat on deck smoking and reading aloud. People do not do such things so often now; but when I was young we got rid of a great deal of time so. Well, so it happened that in his turn Nolan took the book and read to the others; and he read very well, as I know. Nobody in the circle knew a line of the poem, only it was all magic and Border chivalry, and was ten thousand years ago. Poor Nolan read steadily through the fifth canto, stopped a minute and drank something, and then began, without a thought of what was coming,—

> "Breathes there the man, with soul so dead,
> Who never to himself hath said,"—

It seems impossible to us that anybody ever heard this for the first time; but all these fellows did then, and poor Nolan himself went on, still unconsciously or mechanically,—

> "This is my own, my native land!"

Then they all saw something was to pay; but he expected to get through, I suppose, turned a little pale, but plunged on,—

> "Whose heart hath ne'er within him burned,
> As home his footsteps he hath turned
> From wandering on a foreign strand?—
> If such there breathe, go, mark him well."

By this time the men were all beside themselves, wishing there was any way to make him turn over two pages; but he had not quite presence of mind for that; he gagged a little, colored crimson, and staggered on,—

> "For him no minstrel raptures swell;
> High though his titles, proud his name,

Boundless his wealth as wish can claim,
Despite these titles, power, and pelf,
The wretch, concentred all in self,"—

and here the poor fellow choked, could not go on, but started up, swung the book into the sea, vanished into his state-room, "and by Jove," said Phillips, "we did not see him for two months again. And I had to make up some beggarly story to that English surgeon why I did not return his Walter Scott to him."

That story shows about the time when Nolan's braggadocio must have broken down. At first, they said, he took a very high tone, considered his imprisonment a mere farce, affected to enjoy the voyage, and all that; but Phillips said that after he came out of his state-room he never was the same man again. He never read aloud again, unless it was the Bible or Shakespeare, or something else he was sure of. But it was not that merely. He never entered in with the other young men exactly as a companion again. He was always shy afterwards, when I knew him,—very seldom spoke, unless he was spoken to, except to a very few friends. He lighted up occasionally,—I remember late in his life hearing him fairly eloquent on something which had been suggested to him by one of Fléchier's sermons,—but generally he had the nervous, tired look of a heart-wounded man.

When Captain Shaw was coming home,—if, as I say, it was Shaw,—rather to the surprise of everybody they made one of the Windward Islands, and lay off and on for nearly a week. The boys said the officers were sick of salt-junk, and meant to have turtle-soup before they came home. But after several days the Warren came to the same rendezvous; they exchanged signals; she sent to Phillips and these homeward-bound men letters and papers, and told them she was outward-bound, perhaps to the Mediterranean, and took poor Nolan and his traps on the boat back to try his second cruise. He looked very blank when he was told to get ready to join her. He had known enough of the signs of the sky to know that till that moment he was going "home." But this was a distinct evidence of something he had not thought of, perhaps,—that there was no going home for him, even to a prison. And this was the first of some twenty such transfers, which brought him sooner or later into half our best vessels, but which kept him all his life at least some hundred miles from the country he had hoped he might never hear of again.

It may have been on that second cruise,—it was once when he was up the Mediterranean,—that Mrs. Graff, the celebrated Southern beauty of those days, danced with him. They had been lying a long time in the Bay of Naples, and the officers were very intimate in the English fleet, and there had been great festivities, and our men thought they must give a great ball on board the ship. How they ever did it on board the Warren I am sure I do not know. Perhaps it was not the Warren, or perhaps ladies did not take up so much room as they do now. They wanted to use Nolan's state-room for something, and they hated to do it without asking him to the ball; so the captain said they might ask him, if they would be responsible that he did not talk with the wrong people, "who would give him intelligence." So the dance went on, the finest party that had ever been known, I dare say; for I never heard of a man-of-war ball that was not. For ladies they had the family of the American consul, one or two travellers who had adventured so far, and a nice bevy of English girls and matrons, perhaps Lady Hamilton herself.

Well, different officers relieved each other in standing and talking with Nolan in a friendly way, so as to be sure that nobody else spoke to him. The dancing went on with spirit, and after a while even the fellows who took this honorary guard of Nolan ceased to fear any *contre-temps*. Only when some English lady—Lady Hamilton, as I said, perhaps—called for a set of "American dances," an odd thing happened. Everybody then danced contra-dances. The black band, nothing loath, conferred as to what "American dances" were, and started off with "Virginia Reel," which they followed with "Money-Musk," which, in its turn in those days, should have been followed by "The Old Thirteen." But just as Dick, the leader, tapped for his fiddles to begin, and bent forward, about to say, in true Negro state, "'The Old Thirteen,' gentlemen and ladies!" as he had said, "'Virginny Reel,' if you please!" and "'Money-Musk,' if you please!" the captain's boy tapped him on the shoulder, whispered to him, and he did not announce the name of the dance; he merely bowed, began on the air, and they all fell to,—the officers teaching the English girls the figure, but not telling them why it had no name.

But that is not the story I started to tell.—As the dancing went on, Nolan and our fellows all got at ease, as I said,—so much so, that it seemed quite natural for him to bow to that splendid Mrs. Graff, and say,—

"I hope you have not forgotten me, Miss Rutledge. Shall I have the honor of dancing?"

He did it so quickly, that Shubrick, who was by him, could not hinder him. She laughed, and said,—

"I am not Miss Rutledge any longer, Mr. Nolan; but I will dance all the same," just nodded to Shubrick, as if to say he must leave Mr. Nolan to her, and led him off to the place where the dance was forming.

Nolan thought he had got his chance. He had known her at Philadelphia, and at other places had met her, and this was a Godsend. You could not talk in contra-dances, as you do in cotillions, or even in the pauses of waltzing; but there were chances for tongues and sounds, as well as for eyes and blushes. He began with her travels, and Europe, and Vesuvius, and the French; and then, when they had worked down, and had that long talking-time at the bottom of the set, he said boldly,—a little pale, she said, as she told me the story, years after,—

"And what do you hear from home, Mrs. Graff?"

And that splendid creature looked through him. Jove! how she must have looked through him!

"Home!! Mr. Nolan!!! I thought you were the man who never wanted to hear of home again!"—and she walked directly up the deck to her husband, and left poor Nolan alone, as he always was.—He did not dance again.

I cannot give any history of him in order: nobody can now: and, indeed, I am not trying to. These are the traditions, which I sort out, as I believe them, from the myths which have been told about this man for forty years. The lies that have been told about him are legion. The fellows used to say he was the "Iron Mask"; and poor George Pons went to his grave in the belief that this was the author of "Junius," who was being punished for his celebrated libel on Thomas Jefferson. Pons was not very strong in the historical line.

A happier story than either of these I have told is of the War. That came along soon after. I have heard this affair told in three or four ways,—and, indeed, it may have happened more than once. But which ship it was on I cannot tell. However, in one, at least, of the great frigate-duels with the English, in which the navy was really baptized, it happened that a round shot from the enemy entered one of our ports square, and took right down the officer of the gun himself, and almost every man of the gun's crew. Now you may say what you choose about courage, but that is not a nice thing to see. But, as the men who were not killed picked themselves up, and as they and the surgeon's people were carrying off the bodies, there appeared Nolan, in his shirt-sleeves, with the rammer in his hand, and, just as if he had been the officer, told them off with authority,—who should go to the cockpit with the wounded men, who should stay with him,—perfectly cheery, and with that way which makes men feel sure all is right and is going to be right. And he finished loading the gun with his own hands, aimed it, and bade the men fire. And there he stayed, captain of that gun, keeping those fellows in spirits, till the enemy struck,— sitting on the carriage while the gun was cooling, though he was exposed all the time,—showing them easier ways to handle heavy shot,—making the raw hands laugh at their own blunders,—and when the gun cooled again, getting it loaded and fired twice as often as any other gun on the ship. The captain walked forward by way of encouraging the men, and Nolan touched his hat and said,—

"I am showing them how we do this in the artillery, Sir."

And this is the part of the story where all the legends agree: the commodore said,—

"I see you do, and I thank you, Sir; and I shall never forget this day, Sir, and you never shall, Sir."

And after the whole thing was over, and he had the Englishman's sword, in the midst of the state and ceremony of the quarter-deck, he said,—

"Where is Mr. Nolan? Ask Mr. Nolan to come here."

And when Nolan came, the captain said,—

"Mr. Nolan, we are all very grateful to you to-day; you are one of us to-day; you will be named in the despatches."

And then the old man took off his own sword of ceremony, and gave it to Nolan, and made him put it on. The man told me this who saw it. Nolan cried like a baby, and well he might. He had not worn a sword since that infernal day at Fort Adams. But always afterwards, on occasions of ceremony, he wore that quaint old French sword of the Commodore's.

The captain did mention him in the despatches. It was always said he asked that he might be pardoned. He wrote a special letter to the Secretary of War. But nothing ever came of it. As I said, that was about the time when they began to ignore the whole transaction at Washington, and when Nolan's imprisonment began to carry itself on because there was nobody to stop it without any new orders from home.

I have heard it said that he was with Porter when he took possession of the Nukahiwa Islands. Not this Porter, you know, but old Porter, his father, Essex Porter,—that is, the old Essex Porter, not this Essex. As an artillery officer, who had seen service in the West, Nolan knew more about fortifications, embrasures, ravelins, stockades, and all that, than any of them did; and he worked with a right goodwill in fixing that battery all right. I have always thought it was a pity Porter did not leave him in command there with Gamble. That would have settled all the question about his punishment. We should have kept the islands, and at this moment we should have one station in the Pacific Ocean. Our French friends, too, when they wanted this little watering-place, would have found it was preoccupied. But Madison and the Virginians, of course, flung all that away.

All that was near fifty years ago. If Nolan was thirty then, he must have been near eighty when he died. He looked sixty when he was forty. But he never seemed to me to change a hair afterwards. As I imagine his life, from what I have seen and heard of it, he must have been in every sea, and yet almost never on land. He must have known, in a formal way, more officers in our service than any man living knows. He told me once, with a grave smile, that no man in the world lived so methodical a life as he. "You know the boys say I am the Iron Mask, and you know how busy he was." He said it did not do for any one to try to read all the time, more than to do anything else all the time; but that he read just five hours a day. "Then," he said, "I keep up my note-books, writing in them at such and such hours from what I have been reading; and I include in these my scrap-books." These were very curious indeed. He had six or eight, of different subjects. There was one of History, one of Natural Science, one which he called "Odds and Ends." But they were not merely books of extracts from newspapers. They had bits of plants and ribbons, shells tied on, and carved scraps of bone and wood, which he had taught the men to cut for him, and they were beautifully illustrated. He drew admirably. He had some of the funniest drawings there, and some of the most pathetic, that I have ever seen in my life. I wonder who will have Nolan's scrap-books.

Well, he said his reading and his notes were his profession, and that they took five hours and two hours respectively of each day. "Then," said he, "every man should have a diversion as well as a profession. My Natural History is my diversion." That took two hours a day more. The men used to bring him birds and fish, but on a long cruise he had to satisfy himself with centipedes and cockroaches and such small game. He was the only naturalist I ever met who knew anything about the habits of the house-fly and the mosquito. All those people can tell you whether they are *Lepidoptera* or *Steptopotera*; but as for telling how you can get rid of them, or how they get away from you when you strike them,—why Linnæus knew as little of that as John Foy the idiot did. These nine hours made Nolan's regular daily "occupation." The rest of the time he talked or walked. Till he grew very old he went aloft a great deal. He always kept up his exercise; and I never heard that he was ill. If any other man was ill, he was the kindest nurse in the world; and he knew more than half the surgeons do. Then if anybody was sick or died, or if the captain wanted him to on any other occasion, he was always ready to read prayers. I have remarked that he read beautifully.

My own acquaintance with Philip Nolan began six or eight years after the War, on my first voyage after I was appointed a midshipman. It was in the first days after our Slave-Trade treaty, while the Reigning House, which was still the House of Virginia, had still a sort of sentimentalism about the suppression of the horrors of the Middle Passage, and something was sometimes done that way. We were in the South Atlantic on that business. From the time I joined, I believe I thought Nolan was a sort of lay chaplain,—a chaplain with a blue coat. I never asked about him. Everything in the ship was strange to me. I knew it was green to ask questions, and I suppose I thought there was a "Plain-Buttons" on every ship. We had him to dine in our mess once a week, and the caution was given that on that day nothing was to be said about home.

But if they had told us not to say anything about the planet Mars or the Book of Deuteronomy, I should not have asked why; there were a great many things which seemed to me to have as little reason. I first came to understand anything about "the man without a country" one day when we overhauled a dirty little schooner which had slaves on board. An officer was sent to take charge of her, and, after a few minutes, he sent back his boat to ask that some one might be sent him who could speak Portuguese. We were all looking over the rail when the message came, and we all wished we could interpret, when the captain asked who spoke Portuguese. But none of the officers did; and just as the captain was sending forward to ask if any of the people could, Nolan stepped out and said he should be glad to interpret, if the captain wished, as he understood the language. The captain thanked him, fitted out another boat with him, and in this boat it was my luck to go.

When we got there, it was such a scene as you seldom see, and never want to. Nastiness beyond account, and chaos run loose in the midst of the nastiness. There were not a great many of the negroes; but by way of making what there were understand that they were free, Vaughan had had their hand-cuffs and ankle-cuffs knocked off, and, for convenience' sake, was putting them upon the rascals of the schooner's crew. The negroes were, most of them, out of the hold, and swarming all round the dirty deck, with a central throng surrounding Vaughan and addressing him in every dialect and patois of a dialect, from the Zulu click up to the Parisian of Beledeljereed.

As we came on deck, Vaughan looked down from a hogshead, on which he had mounted in desperation, and said,—

"For God's love, is there anybody who can make these wretches understand something? The men gave them rum, and that did not quiet them. I knocked that big fellow down twice, and that did not soothe him. And then I talked Choctaw to all of them together; and I'll be hanged if they understood that as well as they understood the English."

Nolan said he could speak Portuguese, and one or two fine-looking Kroomen were dragged out, who, as it had been found already, had worked for the Portuguese on the coast at Fernando Po.

"Tell them they are free," said Vaughan; "and tell them that these rascals are to be hanged as soon as we can get rope enough."

Nolan "put that into Spanish,"*—that is, he explained it in such Por-

---

* The phrase is General Taylor's. When Santa Aña brought up his immense army at Buena Vista, he sent a flag of truce to invite Taylor to surrender. "Tell him to go to hell," said old Rough-and-Ready. "Bliss, put that into Spanish." "Perfect Bliss," as this accomplished officer, too early lost, was called, interpreted liberally, replying to the flag, in exquisite Castilian, "Say

tuguese as the Kroomen could understand, and they in turn to such of the negroes as could understand them. Then there was such a yell of delight, clinching of fists, leaping and dancing, kissing of Nolan's feet, and a general rush made to the hogshead by way of spontaneous worship of Vaughan, as the *deus ex machina* of the occasion.

"Tell them," said Vaughan, well pleased, "that I will take them all to Cape Palmas."

This did not answer so well. Cape Palmas was practically as far from the homes of most of them as New Orleans or Rio Janeiro was; that is, they would be eternally separated from home there. And their interpreters, as we could understand, instantly said, *"Ah, non Palmas,"* and began to propose infinite other expedients in most voluble language. Vaughan was rather disappointed at this result of his liberality, and asked Nolan eagerly what they said. The drops stood on poor Nolan's white forehead, as he hushed the men down, and said,—

"He says, 'Not Palmas.' He says, 'Take us home, take us to our own country, take us to our own house, take us to our own pickaninnies and our own women.' He says he has an old father and mother, who will die, if they do not see him. And this one says he left his people all sick, and paddled down to Fernando to beg the white doctor to come and help them, and that these devils caught him in the bay just in sight of home, and that he has never seen anybody from home since then. And this one says," choked out Nolan, "that he has not heard a word from his home in six months, while he has been locked up in an infernal barracoon."

Vaughan always said he grew gray himself while Nolan struggled through this interpretation. I, who did not understand anything of the passion involved in it, saw that the very elements were melting with fervent heat, and that something was to pay somewhere. Even the Negroes themselves stopped howling, as they saw Nolan's agony, and Vaughan's almost equal agony of sympathy. As quick as he could get words, he said,—

"Tell them yes, yes, yes; tell them they shall go to the Mountains of the Moon, if they will. If I sail the schooner through the Great White Desert, they shall go home!"

And after some fashion Nolan said so. And then they all fell to kissing him again, and wanted to rub his nose with theirs.

But he could not stand it long; and getting Vaughan to say he might go back, he beckoned me down into our boat. As we lay back in the stern-sheets and the men gave way, he said to me,—"Youngster, let that show you what it is

---

to General Santa Aña, that, if he wants us, he must come and take us." And this is the answer which has gone into history.

to be without a family, without a home, and without a country. And if you are ever tempted to say a word or to do a thing that shall put a bar between you and your family, your home, and your country, pray God in His mercy to take you that instant home to His own heaven. Stick by your family, boy; forget you have a self, while you do everything for them. Think of your home, boy; write and send, and talk about it. Let it be nearer and nearer to your thought, the farther you have to travel from it; and rush back to it, when you are free, as that poor black slave is doing now. And for your country, boy," and the words rattled in his throat, "and for that flag," and he pointed to the ship, "never dream a dream but of serving her as she bids you, though the service carry you through a thousand hells. No matter what happens to you, no more matter who flatters you or who abuses you, never look at another flag, never let a night pass but you pray God to bless that flag. Remember, boy, that behind all these men you have to do with, behind officers, and government, and people even, there is the Country Herself, your Country, and that you belong to Her as you belong to your own mother. Stand by Her, boy, as you would stand by your mother, if those devils there had got hold of her to-day!"

I was frightened to death by his calm, hard passion; but I blundered out that I would, by all that was holy, and that I had never thought of doing anything else. He hardly seemed to hear me; but he did, almost in a whisper, say,—"O, if anybody had said so to me when I was of your age!"

I think it was this half-confidence of his, which I never abused, for I never told this story till now, which afterward made us great friends. He was very kind to me. Often he sat up, or even got up, at night to walk the deck with me, when it was my watch. He explained to me a great deal of my mathematics, and I owe to him my taste for mathematics. He lent me books, and helped me about my reading. He never alluded so directly to his story again; but from one and another officer I have learned, in thirty years, what I am telling. When we parted from him in St. Thomas harbor, at the end of our cruise, I was more sorry than I can tell. I was very glad to meet him again in 1830; and later in life, when I thought I had some influence in Washington, I moved heaven and earth to have him discharged. But it was like getting a ghost out of prison. They pretended there was no such man; and never was such a man. They will say so at the Department now! Perhaps they do not know. It will not be the first thing in the service of which the Department appears to know nothing!

There is a story that Nolan met Burr once on one of our vessels, when a party of Americans came on board in the Mediterranean. But this I believe to be a lie; or rather, it is a myth, *ben trovato,* involving a tremendous blowing-up with which he sunk Burr,—asking him how he liked to be "without a country." But it is clear, from Burr's life, that nothing of the sort could have happened; and I mention this only as an illustration of the stories which get a-going where there is the least mystery at bottom.

So poor Philip Nolan had his wish fulfilled. I know but one fate more dreadful; it is the fate reserved for those men who shall have one day to exile themselves from their country because they have attempted her ruin, and shall have at the same time to see the prosperity and honor to which she rises when she has rid herself of them and their iniquities. The wish of poor Nolan, as we all learned to call him, not because his punishment was too great, but because his repentance was so clear, was precisely the wish of every Bragg and Beauregard who broke a soldier's oath two years ago, and of every Maury and Barron who broke a sailor's. I do not know how often they have repented. I do know that they have done all that in them lay that they might have no country,—that all the honors, associations, memories, and hopes which belong to "country" might be broken up into little shreds and distributed to the winds. I know, too, that their punishment, as they vegetate through what is left of life to them in wretched Boulognes and Leicester Squares, where they are destined to upbraid each other till they die, will have all the agony of Nolan's, with the added pang that every one who sees them will see them to despise and to execrate them. They will have their wish, like him.

For him, poor fellow, he repented of his folly, and then, like a man, submitted to the fate he had asked for. He never intentionally added to the difficulty or delicacy of the charge of those who had him in hold. Accidents would happen; but they never happened from his fault. Lieutenant Truxton told me, that, when Texas was annexed, there was a careful discussion among the officers, whether they should get hold of Nolan's handsome set of maps, and cut Texas out of it,—from the map of the world and the map of Mexico. The United States had been cut out when the atlas was bought for him. But it was voted, rightly enough, that to do this would be virtually to reveal to him what had happened, or, as Harry Cole said, to make him think Old Burr had succeeded. So it was from no fault of Nolan's that a great botch happened at my own table, when, for a short time, I was in command of the George Washington corvette, on the South American station. We were lying in the La Plata, and some of the officers, who had been on shore, and had just joined again, were entertaining us with accounts of their misadventures in riding the half-wild horses of Buenos Ayres. Nolan was at table, and was in an unusually bright and talkative mood. Some story of a tumble reminded him of an adventure of his own, when he was catching wild horses in Texas with his brother Stephen, at a time when he must have been quite a boy. He told the story with a good deal of spirit,—so much so, that the silence which often follows a good story hung over the table for an instant, to be broken by Nolan himself. For he asked, perfectly unconsciously,—

"Pray, what has become of Texas? After the Mexicans got their independence, I thought that province of Texas would come forward very fast. It is really one of the finest regions on earth; it is the Italy of this continent. But I have not seen or heard a word of Texas for near twenty years."

There were two Texan officers at the table. The reason he had never heard of Texas was that Texas and her affairs had been painfully cut out of his newspapers since Austin began his settlements; so that, while he read of Honduras and Tamaulipas, and, till quite lately, of California, this virgin province, in which his brother had travelled so far, and, I believe, had died, had ceased to be to him. Waters and Williams, the two Texas men, looked grimly at each other, and tried not to laugh. Edward Morris had his attention attracted by the third link in the chain of the captain's chandelier. Watrous was seized with a convulsion of sneezing. Nolan himself saw that something was to pay, he did not know what. And I, as master of the feast, had to say,—

"Texas is out of the map, Mr. Nolan. Have you seen Captain Back's curious account of Sir Thomas Roe's Welcome?"

After that cruise I never saw Nolan again. I wrote to him at least twice a year, for in that voyage we became even confidentially intimate; but he never wrote to me. The other men tell me that in those fifteen years he *aged* very fast, as well he might indeed, but that he was still the same gentle, uncomplaining, silent sufferer that he ever was, bearing as best he could his self-appointed punishment,—rather less social, perhaps, with new men whom he did not know, but more anxious, apparently, than ever to serve and befriend and teach the boys, some of whom fairly seemed to worship him. And now it seems the dear old fellow is dead. He has found a home at last, and a country.

Since writing this, and while considering whether or no I would print it, as a warning to the young Nolans and Vallandighams and Tatnalls of to-day of what it is to throw away a country, I have received from Danforth, who is on board the Levant, a letter which gives an account of Nolan's last hours. It removes all my doubts about telling this story.

To understand the first words of the letter, the non-professional reader should remember that after 1817 the position of every officer who had Nolan in charge was one of the greatest delicacy. The Government had failed to renew the order of 1807 regarding him. What was a man to do? Should he let him go? What, then, if he were called to account by the Department for violating the order of 1807? Should he keep him? What, then, if Nolan should be liberated some day, and should bring an action for false imprisonment or kidnapping against every man who had had him in charge?

I urged and pressed this upon Southard, and I have reason to think that other officers did the same thing. But the Secretary always said, as they so often do at Washington, that there were no special orders to give, and that we must act on our own judgment. That means, "If you succeed, you will be sustained; if you fail, you will be disavowed." Well, as Danforth says, all that is over now, though I do not know but I expose myself to a criminal prosecution on the evidence of the very revelation I am making.

Here is the letter:—

"*Levant*, 2° 2′ S. @ 131° W.

"DEAR FRED,—I try to find heart and life to tell you that it is all over with dear old Nolan. I have been with him on this voyage more than I ever was, and I can understand wholly now the way in which you used to speak of the dear old fellow. I could see that he was not strong, but I had no idea the end was so near. The doctor had been watching him very carefully, and yesterday morning came to me and told me that Nolan was not so well, and had not left his state-room,—a thing I never remember before. He had let the doctor come and see him as he lay there,—the first time the doctor had been in the state-room,—and he said he should like to see me. Oh, dear! do you remember the mysteries we boys used to invent about his room in the old Intrepid days? Well, I went in, and there, to be sure, the poor fellow lay in his berth, smiling pleasantly as he gave me his hand, but looking very frail. I could not help a glance round, which showed me what a little shrine he had made of the box he was lying in. The stars and stripes were triced up above and around a picture of Washington, and he had painted a majestic eagle, with lightnings blazing from his beak and his foot just clasping the whole globe, which his wings overshadowed. The dear old boy saw my glance, and said, with a sad smile, 'Here, you see, I have a country!' And then he pointed to the foot of his bed, where I had not seen before a great map of the United States, as he had drawn it from memory, and which he had there to look upon as he lay. Quaint, queer old names were on it, in large letters: 'Indiana Territory,' 'Mississippi Territory,' and 'Louisiana Territory,' as I suppose our fathers learned such things: but the old fellow had patched in Texas, too; he had carried his western boundary all the way to the Pacific, but on that shore he had defined nothing.

"'Oh Danforth,' he said, 'I know I am dying. I cannot get home. Surely you will tell me something now?—Stop! stop! Do not speak till I say what I am sure you know, that there is not in this ship, that there is not in America,—God bless her!—a more loyal man than I. There cannot be a man who loves the old flag as I do, or prays for it as I do, or hopes for it as I do. There are thirty-four stars in it now, Danforth. I thank God for that, though I do not know what their names are. There has never been one taken away: I thank God for that. I know by that, that there has never been any successful Burr. Oh, Danforth, Danforth,' he sighed out, 'how like a wretched night's dream a boy's idea of personal fame or of separate sovereignty seems, when one looks back on it after such a life as mine! But tell me,—tell me something,—tell me everything, Danforth, before I die!'

"Ingham, I swear to you that I felt like a monster that I had not told him everything before. Danger or no danger, delicacy or no delicacy, who was I, that I should have been acting the tyrant all this time over this dear, sainted old man, who had years ago expiated, in his whole manhood's life, the madness of a boy's treason? 'Mr. Nolan,' said I, 'I will tell you everything you ask about. Only, where shall I begin?'

"Oh, the blessed smile that crept over his white face! and he pressed my hand and said, 'God bless you!' 'Tell me their names,' he said, and he pointed to the stars on the flag. 'The last I know is Ohio. My father lived in Kentucky. But I have guessed Michigan and Indiana and Mississippi,—that was where Fort Adams is,—they make twenty. But where are your other fourteen? You have not cut up any of the old ones, I hope?'

"Well, that was not a bad text, and I told him the names, in as good order as I could, and he bade me take down his beautiful map and draw them in as I best could with my pencil. He was wild with delight about Texas, told me how his cousin died there; he had marked a gold cross where he supposed his grave was; and he had guessed at Texas. Then he was delighted as he saw California and Oregon;—that, he said, he had suspected partly, because he had never been permitted to land on that shore, though the ships were there so much. 'And the men,' said he, laughing, 'brought off a good deal besides furs.' Then he went back—heavens, how far!—to ask about the Chesapeake, and what was done to Barron for surrendering her to the Leopard, and whether Burr ever tried again,— and he ground his teeth with the only passion he showed. But in a moment that was over, and he said, 'God forgive me, for I am sure I forgive him.' Then he asked about the old war,—told me the true story of his serving the gun the day we took the Java,—asked about dear old David Porter, as he called him. Then he settled down more quietly, and very happily, to hear me tell in an hour the history of fifty years.

"How I wished it had been somebody who knew something! But I did as well as I could. I told him of the English war. I told him about Fulton and the steamboat beginning. I told him about old Scott, and Jackson; told him all I could think of about the Mississippi, and New Orleans, and Texas, and his own old Kentucky. And do you think he asked who was in command of the 'Legion of the West'? I told him it was a very gallant officer, named Grant, and that, by our last news, he was about to establish his head-quarters at Vicksburg. Then, 'Where was Vicksburg?' I worked that out on the map; it was about a hundred miles, more or less, above his old Fort Adams; and I thought Fort Adams must be a ruin now. 'It must be at old Vick's plantation,' said he: 'well, that is a change!'

"I tell you, Ingham, it was a hard thing to condense the history of half a century into that talk with a sick man. And I do not now know what I told him,—of emigration, and the means of it,—of steamboats and railroads and telegraphs,—of inventions and books and literature,—of the colleges and West Point and the Naval School,—but with the queerest interruptions that ever you heard. You see it was Robinson Crusoe asking all the accumulated questions of fifty-six years!

"I remember he asked, all of a sudden, who was President now; and when I told him, he asked if Old Abe was General Benjamin Lincoln's son. He said he met old General Lincoln, when he was quite a boy himself, at some Indian treaty. I said no, that Old Abe was a Kentuckian like himself, but I could not tell him of what family; he had worked up from the ranks. 'Good for him!' cried Nolan; 'I am glad of that. As I have brooded and wondered, I have thought our danger was in keeping up those regular successions in the first families.' Then I got talking about my visit to Washington. I told him of meeting the Oregon Congressman, Harding; I told him about the Smithsonian and the Exploring Expedition; I told him about the Capitol,—and the statues for the pediment,—and Crawford's Liberty,—and Greenough's Washington: Ingham, I told him everything I could think of that would show the grandeur of his country and its prosperity; but I could not make up my mouth to tell him a word about this infernal Rebellion!

"And he drank it in and enjoyed it as I cannot tell you. He grew more and more silent, yet I never thought he was tired or faint. I gave him a glass of water, but he just wet his lips, and told me not to go away. Then he asked me to bring the Presbyterian 'Book of Public Prayer,' which lay there, and said, with a smile, that it would open at the right place,—and so it did. There was his double red mark down the page; and I knelt down and read, and he repeated with me, 'For ourselves and our country, O gracious God, we thank Thee, that, notwithstanding our manifold transgressions of Thy holy laws, Thou hast continued to us Thy marvelous kindness.'—and so to the end of that thanksgiving. Then he turned to the end of the same book, and I read the words more familiar to me,—'Most heartily we beseech Thee with Thy favor to behold and bless Thy servant, the President of the United States, and all others in authority,'—and the rest of the Episcopal collect. 'Danforth,' said he, 'I have repeated those prayers night and morning, it is now fifty-five years.' And then he said he would go to sleep. He bent me down over him and kissed me; and he said, 'Look in my Bible, Danforth, when I am gone.' And I went away.

"But I had no thought it was the end. I thought he was tired and would sleep. I knew he was happy, and I wanted him to be alone.

"But in an hour, when the doctor went in gently, he found Nolan had breathed his life away with a smile. He had something pressed close to his lips. It was his father's badge of the Order of Cincinnati.

"We looked in his Bible, and there was a slip of paper, at the place where he had marked the text,—

"'They desire a country, even a heavenly: wherefore God is not ashamed to be called their God: for He hath prepared for them a city.'

"On this slip of paper he had written,—

"'Bury me in the sea; it has been my home, and I love it. But will not some one set up a stone for my memory at Fort Adams or at Orleans, that my disgrace may not be more than I ought to bear? Say on it,—

"'In Memory of

"'PHILIP NOLAN

"'*Lieutenant in the Army of the United States.*

"'He loved his country as no other man has loved her; but no man deserved less at her hands.'"

From The Promised Land

MARY ANTIN

America, it is rightly said, is a nation of immigrants. Each new immigrant, in his or her own way, must negotiate the passage to becoming an American. This selection offers an account of what becoming an American meant to a young girl who arrived in the United States from a small town in Russia just before the turn of the twentieth century. She came with her mother, two sisters, and a brother, to join her father, who had emigrated three years earlier out of economic necessity, dreaming of a new beginning. Yet he was unable to earn a steady living, making life in America a continuous struggle. Mary Antin (1881–1949) and her family spent their early years in the United States moving from crowded slum to crowded slum, living in gloomy tenements alongside dark alleys littered with gamblers, junkies, and drunks. But Mary Antin was never fazed. Unlike Philip Nolan, whose love of country grew only when he was without one, Antin appreciated what America offered compared with the life she left behind. True heir to her father's dreams, she embraced her new country, becoming an author and lecturer who addressed the themes of immigration and patriotism. These selections from her autobiography (1912) deal with her early arrival in America.

What impressed Mary Antin about America and produced her enthusiastic affection? What does she mean when she suggests that her father, in delivering his children to the public school, "took possession of America"? How do you understand—and what do you think of—her attitudes toward her impoverished surroundings? Toward her new country? Toward school and education? Toward George Washington? Does she, as an immigrant, appreciate her new country more than those of us who are born here?

Now I was not exactly an infant when I was set down, on a May day some fifteen years ago, in this pleasant nursery of America. I had long since acquired the use of my faculties, and had collected some bits of experience, practical and emotional, and had even learned to give an account of them. Still, I had very little perspective, and my observations and comparisons were superficial. I was too much carried away to analyze the forces that were moving me. My Polotzk I knew well before I began to judge it and experiment with it. America was bewilderingly strange, unimaginably complex, delightfully unexplored. I rushed impetuously out of the cage of my provincialism and looked eagerly about the brilliant universe. My question was, What have we here?—not, What does this mean? That query came much later. . . .

Our initiation into American ways began with the first step on the new soil. My father found occasion to instruct or correct us even on the way from the pier to Wall Street [Boston], which journey we made crowded together in a rickety cab. He told us not to lean out of the windows, not to point, and explained the word "greenhorn." We did not want to be "greenhorns," and gave the strictest attention to my father's instructions. I do not know when my parents found opportunity to review together the history of Polotzk in the three years past, for we children had no patience with the subject; my mother's narrative was constantly interrupted by irrelevant questions, interjections, and explanations.

The first meal was an object lesson of much variety. My father produced several kinds of food, ready to eat, without any cooking, from little tin cans that had printing all over them. He attempted to introduce us to a queer, slippery kind of fruit, which he called "banana," but had to give it up for the time being. After the meal, he had better luck with a curious piece of furniture on runners, which he called "rocking-chair." There were five of us newcomers, and we found five different ways of getting into the American machine of perpetual motion, and as many ways of getting out of it. One born and bred to the use of a rocking-chair cannot imagine how ludicrous people can make themselves when attempting to use it for the first time. We laughed immoderately over our various experiments with the novelty, which was a wholesome way of letting off steam after the unusual excitement of the day.

In our flat we did not think of such a thing as storing the coal in the bathtub. There was no bathtub. So in the evening of the first day my father conducted us to the public baths. As we moved along in a little procession, I was delighted with the illumination of the streets. So many lamps, and they burned until morning, my father said, and so people did not need to carry lanterns. In America, then, everything was free, as we had heard in Russia. Light was free; the streets were as bright as a synagogue on a holy day. Music was free; we had been serenaded, to our gaping delight, by a brass band of many pieces, soon after our installation on Union Place.

Education was free. That subject my father had written about repeatedly, as comprising his chief hope for us children, the essence of American opportunity, the treasure that no thief could touch, not even misfortune or poverty. It was the one thing that he was able to promise us when he sent for us; surer, safer than bread or shelter. On our second day I was thrilled with the realization of what this freedom of education meant. A little girl from across the alley came and offered to conduct us to school. My father was out, but we five between us had a few words of English by this time. We knew the word school. We understood. This child, who had never seen us till yesterday, who could not pronounce our names, who was not much better dressed than we, was able to offer us the freedom of the schools of Boston! No application made, no questions asked, no examinations, rulings, exclusions; no machinations, no fees. The doors stood open for every one of us. The smallest child could show us the way.

This incident impressed me more than anything I had heard in advance of the freedom of education in America. It was a concrete proof—almost the thing itself. One had to experience it to understand it.

It was a great disappointment to be told by my father that we were not to enter upon our school career at once. It was too near the end of the term, he said, and we were going to move to Crescent Beach in a week or so. We had to wait until the opening of the schools in September. What a loss of precious time—from May till September!

Not that the time was really lost. Even the interval on Union Place was crowded with lessons and experiences. We had to visit the stores and be dressed from head to foot in American clothing; we had to learn the mysteries of the iron stove, the washboard, and the speaking-tube; we had to learn to trade with the fruit peddler through the window, and not to be afraid of the policeman; and, above all, we had to learn English.

The kind people who assisted us in these important matters form a group by themselves in the gallery of my friends. If I had never seen them from those early days till now, I should still have remembered them with gratitude. When I enumerate the long list of my American teachers, I must begin with those who came to us on Wall Street and taught us our first steps. To my mother, in her perplexity over the cookstove, the woman who showed her how to make the fire was an angel of deliverance. A fairy godmother to us children was she who led us to a wonderful country called "uptown," where, in a dazzlingly beautiful palace called a "department store," we exchanged our hateful homemade European costumes, which pointed us out as "greenhorns" to the children on the street, for real American machine-made garments, and issued forth glorified in each other's eyes.

With our despised immigrant clothing we shed also our impossible Hebrew names. A committee of our friends, several years ahead of us in American experience, put their heads together and concocted American names for us all. Those of our real names that had no pleasing American equivalents they ruthlessly discarded, content if they retained the initials. My mother, possessing a name that was not easily translatable, was punished with the undignified nickname of Annie. Fetchke, Joseph, and Deborah issued as Frieda, Joseph, and Dora, respectively. As for poor me, I was simply cheated. The name they gave me was hardly new. My Hebrew name being Maryashe in full, Mashke for short, Russianized into Marya (*Mar-ya*), my friends said that it would hold good in English as *Mary*; which was very disappointing, as I longed to possess a strange-sounding American name like the others.

I am forgetting the consolation I had, in this matter of names, from the use of my surname, which I have had no occasion to mention until now. I found on my arrival that my father was "Mr. Antin" on the slightest provocation, and not, as in Polotzk, on state occasions alone. And so I was "Mary Antin," and I felt very important to answer to such a dignified title. It was just like America that even plain people should wear their surnames on week days. . . .

In after years, when I passed as an American among Americans, if I was suddenly made aware of the past that lay forgotten,—if a letter from Russia, or a paragraph in the newspaper, or a conversation overheard in the street-car, suddenly reminded me of what I might have been,—I thought it miracle enough that I, Mashke, the granddaughter of Raphael the Russian, born to a humble destiny, should be at home in an American metropolis, be free to fashion my own life, and should dream my dreams in English phrases. But in the beginning my admiration was spent on more concrete embodiments of the splendors of America; such as fine houses, gay shops, electric engines and apparatus, public buildings, illuminations, and parades. My early letters to my Russian friends were filled with boastful descriptions of these glories of my new country. No native citizen of Chelsea took such pride and delight in its institutions as I did. It required no fife and drum corps, no Fourth of July procession, to set me tingling with patriotism. Even the common agents and instruments of municipal life, such as the letter carrier and the fire engine, I regarded with a measure of respect. I know what I thought of people who said that Chelsea was a very small, dull, unaspiring town, with no discernible excuse for a separate name or existence.

The apex of my civic pride and personal contentment was reached on the bright September morning when I entered the public school. That day I must always remember, even if I live to be so old that I cannot tell my name. To most people their first day at school is a memorable occasion. In my case the importance of the day was a hundred times magnified, on account of the years I had waited, the road I had come, and the conscious ambitions I entertained.

I am wearily aware that I am speaking in extreme figures, in superlatives. I wish I knew some other way to render the mental life of the immigrant child of reasoning age. I may have been ever so much an exception in acuteness of observation, powers of comparison, and abnormal self-consciousness; none the less were my thoughts and conduct typical of the attitude of the intelligent immigrant child toward American institutions. And what the child thinks and feels is a reflection of the hopes, desires, and purposes of the parents who brought him overseas, no matter how precocious and independent the child may be. Your immigrant inspectors will tell you what poverty the foreigner brings in his baggage, what want in his pockets. Let the overgrown boy of twelve, reverently drawing his letters in the baby class, testify to the noble dreams and high ideals that may be hidden beneath the greasy caftan of the immigrant. Speaking for the Jews, at least, I know I am safe in inviting such an investigation. . . .

Father himself conducted us to school. He would not have delegated that mission to the President of the United States. He had awaited the day with impatience equal to mine, and the visions he saw as he hurried us over the sun-flecked pavements transcended all my dreams. Almost his first act on landing on American soil, three years before, had been his application for naturalization. He had taken the remaining steps in the process with eager promptness, and at the earliest moment allowed by the law, he became a citizen of the United States. It is true that he had left home in search of bread for his hungry family, but he went blessing the necessity that drove him to America. The boasted freedom of the New World meant to him far more than the right to reside, travel, and work wherever he pleased; it meant the freedom to speak his thoughts, to throw off the shackles of superstition, to test his own fate, unhindered by political or religious tyranny. He was only a young man when he landed—thirty-two; and most of his life he had been held in leading-strings. He was hungry for his untasted manhood.

Three years passed in sordid struggle and disappointment. He was not prepared to make a living even in America. . . . Wherever the blame for his disabilities be placed, he reaped their bitter fruit. "Give me bread!" he cried to America. "What will you do to earn it?" the challenge came back. And he found that he was master of no art, of no trade; that even his precious learning was of no avail, because he had only the most antiquated methods of communicating it.

So in his primary quest he had failed. There was left him the compensation of intellectual freedom. That he sought to realize in every possible way. He had very little opportunity to prosecute his education, which, in truth, had never been begun. His struggle for a bare living left him no time to take advantage of the public evening school; but he lost nothing of what was to be learned through reading, through attendance at public meetings, through exercising the rights of citizenship. Even here he was hindered by a natural inability to acquire the English language. In time, indeed, he learned to read, to follow a conversation or lecture; but he never learned to write correctly, and his pronunciation remains extremely foreign to this day.

If education, culture, the higher life were shining things to be worshipped from afar, he had still a means left whereby he could draw one step nearer to them. He could send his children to school, to learn all those things that he knew by fame to be desirable. The common school, at least, perhaps high school; for one or two, perhaps even college! His children should be students, should fill his house with books and intellectual company; and thus he would walk by proxy in the Elysian Fields of liberal learning. As for the children themselves, he knew no surer way to their advancement and happiness.

So it was with a heart full of longing and hope that my father led us to school on that first day. He took long strides in his eagerness, the rest of us running and hopping to keep up.

At last the four of us stood around the teacher's desk; and my father, in his impossible English, gave us over in her charge, with some broken word of his hopes for us that his swelling heart could no longer contain. I venture to say that Miss Nixon was struck by something uncommon in the group we made, something outside of Semitic features and the abashed manner of the alien. My little sister was as pretty as a doll, with her clear pink-and-white face, short golden curls, and eyes like blue violets when you caught them looking up. My brother might have been a girl, too, with his cherubic contours of face, rich red color, glossy black hair, and fine eyebrows. Whatever secret fears were in his heart, remembering his former teachers, who had taught with the rod, he stood up straight and uncringing before the American teacher, his cap respectfully doffed. Next to him stood a starved-looking girl with eyes ready to pop out, and short dark curls that would not have made much of a wig for a Jewish bride.

All three children carried themselves rather better than the common run of "green" pupils that were brought to Miss Nixon. But the figure that challenged attention to the group was the tall, straight father, with his earnest face and fine forehead, nervous hands eloquent in gesture, and a voice full of feeling. This foreigner, who brought his children to school as if it were an act of consecration, who regarded the teacher of the primer class with reverence, who spoke of visions, like a man inspired, in a common schoolroom, was not like other aliens, who brought their children in dull obedience to the law; was not like the native fathers, who brought their unmanageable boys, glad to be relieved of their care. I think Miss Nixon guessed what my father's best English could not convey. I think she divined that by the simple act of delivering our school certificates to her he took possession of America. . . .

How long would you say, wise reader, it takes to make an American? By the middle of my second year in school I had reached the sixth grade. When, after the Christmas holidays, we began to study the life of Washington, running through a summary of the Revolution, and the early days of the Republic, it seemed to me that all my reading and study had been idle until then. The reader, the arithmetic, the song book, that had so fascinated me until now, became suddenly sober exercise books, tools wherewith to hew a way to the source of inspiration. When the teacher read to us out of a big book with many bookmarks in it, I sat rigid with attention in my little chair, my hands tightly clasped on the edge of my desk; and I painfully held my breath, to prevent sighs of disappointment escaping, as I saw the teacher skip the parts between bookmarks. When the class read, and it came my turn, my voice shook and the book trembled in my hands. I could not pronounce the name of George Washington without a pause. Never had I prayed, never had I chanted the songs of David, never had I called upon the Most Holy, in such utter reverence and worship as I repeated the simple sentences of my child's story of the patriot. I gazed with adoration at the portraits of George and Martha Washington, till I could see them with my eyes shut. And whereas formerly my self-consciousness had bordered on conceit, and I thought myself an uncommon person, parading my schoolbooks through the streets, and swelling with pride when a teacher detained me in conversation, now I grew humble all at once, seeing how insignificant I was beside the Great.

As I read about the noble boy who would not tell a lie to save himself from punishment, I was for the first time truly repentant of my sins. Formerly I had fasted and prayed and made sacrifice on the Day of Atonement, but it was more than half play, in mimicry of my elders. I had no real horror of sin, and I knew so many ways of escaping punishment. I am sure my family, my neighbors, my teachers in Polotzk—all my world, in fact—strove together, by example and precept, to teach me goodness. Saintliness had a new incarnation in about every third person I knew. I did respect the saints, but I could not help seeing that most of them were a little bit stupid, and that mischief was much more fun than piety. Goodness, as I had known it, was respectable, but not necessarily admirable. The people I really admired, like my Uncle Solomon, and Cousin Rachel, were those who preached the least and laughed the most. My sister Frieda was perfectly good, but she did not think the less of me because I played tricks. What I loved in my friends was not inimitable. One could be downright good if one really wanted to. One could be learned if one had books and teachers. One could sing funny songs and tell anecdotes if one travelled about and picked up such things, like one's uncles and cousins. But a human being strictly good, perfectly wise, and unfailingly valiant, all at the same time, I had never heard or dreamed of. This wonderful George Washington was as inimitable as he was irreproachable. Even if I had never, never told a lie, I could not compare myself to George Washington; for I was not brave—I was afraid to go out when snowballs whizzed—and I could never be the First President of the United States.

So I was forced to revise my own estimate of myself. But the twin of my new-born humility, paradoxical as it may seem, was a sense of dignity I had never known before. For if I found that I was a person of small consequence, I discovered at the same time that I was more nobly related than I had ever supposed. I had relatives and friends who were notable people by the old standards,—I had never been ashamed of my family,—but this George Washington, who died long before I was born, was like a king in greatness, and he and I were Fellow Citizens. There was a great deal about Fellow Citizens in the patriotic literature we read at this time; and I knew from my father how he was a Citizen, through the process of naturalization, and how I also was a citizen, by virtue of my relation to him. Undoubtedly I was a Fellow Citizen, and George Washington was another. It thrilled me to realize what sudden greatness had fallen on me; and at the same time it sobered me, as with a sense of responsibility. I strove to conduct myself as befitted a Fellow Citizen.

Before books came into my life, I was given to stargazing and daydreaming. When books were given me, I fell upon them as a glutton pounces on his meat after a period of enforced starvation. I lived with my nose in a book, and took no notice of the alternations of the sun and stars. But now, after the advent of George Washington and the American Revolution, I began to dream again. I strayed on the common after school instead of hurrying home to read. I hung on fence rails, my pet book forgotten under my arm, and gazed off to the yellow-streaked February sunset, and beyond, and beyond. I was no longer the central figure of my dreams; the dry weeds in the lane crackled beneath the tread of Heroes.

What more could America give a child? Ah, much more! As I read how the patriots planned the Revolution, and the women gave their sons to die in battle, and the heroes led to victory, and the rejoicing people set up the Republic, it dawned on me gradually what was meant by *my country*. The people all desiring noble things, and striving for them together, defying their oppressors, giving their lives for each other—all this it was that made *my country*. It was not a thing that I *understood*; I could not go home and tell Frieda about it, as I told her other things I learned at school. But I knew one could say "my country" and *feel* it, as one felt "God" or "myself." My teacher, my schoolmates, Miss Dillingham, George Washington himself could not mean more than I when they said "my country," after I had once felt it. For the Country was for all the Citizens, and *I was a Citizen*. And when we stood up to sing "America," I shouted the words with all my might. I was in very earnest proclaiming to the world my love for my new-found country.

> "I love thy rocks and rills,
> Thy woods and templed hills."

Boston Harbor, Crescent Beach, Chelsea Square—all was hallowed ground to me. As the day approached when the school was to hold exercises in honor of Washington's Birthday, the halls resounded at all hours with the strains of patriotic songs; and I, who was a model of the attentive pupil, more than once lost my place in the lesson as I strained to hear, through closed doors, some neighboring class rehearsing "The Star-Spangled Banner." If the doors happened to open, and the chorus broke out unveiled—

> "O! say, does that Star-Spangled Banner yet wave
> O'er the land of the free, and the home of the brave?"—

delicious tremors ran up and down my spine, and I was faint with suppressed enthusiasm.

Where had been my country until now? What flag had I loved? What heroes had I worshipped? The very names of these things had been unknown to me. Well I knew that Polotzk was not my country. It was *goluth*—exile. On many occasions in the year we prayed to God to lead us out of exile. The beautiful Passover service closed with the words, "Next year, may we be in Jerusalem." On childish lips, indeed, those words were no conscious aspiration; we repeated the Hebrew syllables after our elders, but without their hope and longing. Still not a child among us was too young to feel in his own flesh the lash of the oppressor. We knew what it was to be Jews in exile, from the spiteful treatment we suffered at the hands of the smallest urchin who crossed himself; and thence we knew that Israel had good reason to pray for deliverance. But the story of the Exodus was not history to me in the sense that the story of the

American Revolution was. It was more like a glorious myth, a belief in which had the effect of cutting me off from the actual world, by linking me with a world of phantoms. Those moments of exaltation which the contemplation of the Biblical past afforded us, allowing us to call ourselves the children of princes, served but to tinge with a more poignant sense of disinheritance the long humdrum stretches of our life. In very truth we were a people without a country. Surrounded by mocking foes and detractors, it was difficult for me to realize the persons of my people's heroes or the events in which they moved. Except in moments of abstraction from the world around me, I scarcely understood that Jerusalem was an actual spot on the earth, where once the Kings of the Bible, real people, like my neighbors in Polotzk, ruled in puissant majesty. For the conditions of our civil life did not permit us to cultivate a spirit of nationalism. The freedom of worship that was grudgingly granted within the narrow limits of the Pale by no means included the right to set up openly any ideal of a Hebrew State, any hero other than the Czar. What we children picked up of our ancient political history was confused with the miraculous story of the Creation, with the supernatural legends and hazy associations of Bible lore. As to our future, we Jews in Polotzk had no national expectations; only a lifeworn dreamer here and there hoped to die in Palestine. If Fetchke and I sang, with my father, first making sure of our audience, "Zion, Zion, Holy Zion, not forever is it lost," we did not really picture to ourselves Judaea restored.

So it came to pass that we did not know what *my country* could mean to a man. And as we had no country, so we had no flag to love. It was by no far-fetched symbolism that the banner of the House of Romanoff became the emblem of our latter-day bondage in our eyes. Even a child would know how to hate the flag that we were forced, on pain of severe penalties, to hoist above our housetops, in celebration of the advent of one of our oppressors. And as it was with country and flag, so it was with heroes of war. We hated the uniform of the soldier, to the last brass button. On the person of a Gentile, it was the symbol of tyranny; on the person of a Jew, it was the emblem of shame.

So a little Jewish girl in Polotzk was apt to grow up hungry-minded and empty-hearted; and if, still in her outreaching youth, she was set down in a land of outspoken patriotism, she was likely to love her new country with a great love, and to embrace its heroes in a great worship. Naturalization, with us Russian Jews, may mean more than the adoption of the immigrant by America. It may mean the adoption of America by the immigrant.

On the day of the Washington celebration I recited a poem that I had composed in my enthusiasm. But "composed" is not the word. The process of putting on paper the sentiments that seethed in my soul was really very discomposing. I dug the words out of my heart, squeezed the rhymes out of my brain, forced the missing syllables out of their hiding-places in the dictionary. May I never again know such travail of the spirit as I endured during the fevered days when I was engaged on the poem. It was not as if I wanted to say that snow was white or grass was green. I could do that without a dictionary. It was a question now of the loftiest sentiments, of the most abstract truths, the names of which were very new in my vocabulary. It was necessary to use polysyllables, and plenty of them; and where to find rhymes for such words as "tyranny," "freedom," and "justice," when you had less than two years' acquaintance with English! The name I wished to celebrate was the most difficult of all. Nothing but "Washington" rhymed with "Washington." It was a most ambitious undertaking, but my heart could find no rest till it had proclaimed itself to the world; so I wrestled with my difficulties, and spared not ink, till inspiration perched on my penpoint, and my soul gave up its best.

When I had done, I was myself impressed with the length, gravity, and nobility of my poem. My father was overcome with emotion as he read it. His hands trembled as he held the paper to the light, and the mist gathered in his eyes. My teacher, Miss Dwight, was plainly astonished at my performance, and said many kind things, and asked many questions; all of which I took very solemnly, like one who had been in the clouds and returned to earth with a sign upon him. When Miss Dwight asked me to read my poem to the class on the day of celebration, I readily consented. It was not in me to refuse a chance to tell my schoolmates what I thought of George Washington.

I was not a heroic figure when I stood up in front of the class to pronounce the praises of the Father of his Country. Thin, pale, and hollow, with a shadow of short black curls on my brow, and the staring look of prominent eyes, I must have looked more frightened than imposing. My dress added no grace to my appearance. "Plaids" were in fashion, and my frock was of a red-and-green "plaid" that had a ghastly effect on my complexion. I hated it when I thought of it, but on the great day I did not know I had any dress on. Heels clapped together, and hands glued to my sides, I lifted up my voice in praise of George Washington. It was not much of a voice; like my hollow cheeks, it suggested consumption. My pronunciation was faulty, my declamation flat. But I had the courage of my convictions. I was face to face with two score Fellow Citizens, in clean blouses and extra frills. I must tell them what George Washington had done for their country—for *our* country—for me.

I can laugh now at the impossible metres, the grandiose phrases, the verbose repetitions of my poem. Years ago I must have laughed at it, when I threw my only copy into the wastebasket. The copy I am now turning over was loaned me by Miss Dwight, who faithfully preserved it all these years, for the sake, no doubt, of what I strove to express when I laboriously hitched together those dozen and more ungraceful stanzas. But to the forty Fellow Citizens sitting in rows in front of me it was no laughing matter. Even the bad boys sat in attitudes of attention, hypnotized by the solemnity of my demeanor. If they got any inkling of what the hail of big words was about, it must have been through occult suggestion. I fixed their eighty eyes with my single stare, and gave it to them, stanza after stanza, with such emphasis as the lameness of the lines permitted.

> He whose courage, will, amazing bravery,
>> Did free his land from a despot's rule,
> From man's greatest evil, almost slavery,
>> And all that's taught in tyranny's school,
> Who gave his land its liberty,
>> Who was he?
>
> 'T was he who e'er will be our pride,
>> Immortal Washington,
> Who always did in truth confide.
>> We hail our Washington!

The best of the verses were no better than these, but the children listened. They had to. Presently I gave them news, declaring that Washington

> Wrote the famous Constitution; sacred's the hand
> That this blessed guide to man had given, which says, "One
> And all of mankind are alike, excepting none."

This was received in respectful silence, possibly because the other Fellow Citizens were as hazy about historical facts as I at this point. "Hurrah for Washington!" they understood, and "Three cheers for the Red, White, and Blue!" was only to be expected on that occasion. But there ran a special note through my poem—a thought that only Israel Rubinstein or Beckie Aronovitch could have fully understood, besides myself. For I made myself the spokesman of the "luckless sons of Abraham," saying—

> Then we weary Hebrew children at last found rest
> In the land where reigned Freedom, and like a nest
> To homeless birds your land proved to us, and therefore
> Will we gratefully sing your praise evermore.

The boys and girls who had never been turned away from any door because of their father's religion sat as if fascinated in their places. But they woke up and applauded heartily when I was done, following the example of Miss Dwight, who wore the happy face which meant that one of her pupils had done well.

In a Strange Country

RALPH ELLISON

Not all native-born Americans have enjoyed equality of opportunity and equal respect, especially the descendants of American slaves. What kind of attitudes might oppressed minorities have toward their American homeland? This question much occupied Ralph Ellison (1914–1994), literary critic, essayist, and novelist, best known for The Invisible Man. *In this poignant story (1944), a black sailor experiences both American racism and Welsh hospitality and patriotism when he goes ashore in Wales during World War II. (Ellison himself had joined the Merchant Marine during the war.) As with Mary Antin, the contrast between life in America and life elsewhere shapes the protagonist's emerging attitude toward, and attachment to, his native land.*

What is it about Parker's experience among the Welsh that moves him so? How and why do his feelings change? In their songs, the Welshmen give voice to both their defiance of England and their loyalty to England. How might this divided attitude affect Parker's attitude toward his native America? The Welshmen seem to combine a universal respect for any human being with a particular patriotic preference for their own land and fellow Welshmen. Are such feelings compatible? How did the music alter Parker's attitudes and sentiments? Did it have the same effect on you?

In the pub his eye had begun to close. White spots danced before him, and he had to cover the eye with his hand in order to see Mr. Catti. Mr. Catti was drinking now, and as the bottom of the glass swung down and tapped the table, he looked into Mr. Catti's pale, sharp-nosed face and smiled. Mr. Catti had been very kind, and he was trying hard to be pleasant.

"You miss this on a ship," he said, draining his glass.

"Do you like our Welsh ale?"

"Very much."

"It's not so good as before the war," Mr. Catti said sadly.

"It must have been very good," he said.

He looked guardedly at the pretty, blue-aproned barmaid, seeing her dark hair shift lazily forward as she drew beer from a pump such as he'd seen only in English pictures. With his eye covered he saw much better. Across the room, near the fireplace with its grate of glowing coals, two men were seeing who could knock over a set of skittlepins. One of them started singing "Treat Me Like an Irish Soldier" as Mr. Catti said:

"Have you been long in Wales?"

"About forty-five minutes," he said.

"Then you have much to see," Mr. Catti said, getting up and carrying the glasses over to the bar to be refilled.

No, he thought, looking at the GUINNESS IS GOOD FOR YOU signs, I've seen enough. Coming ashore from the ship he had felt the excited expectancy of entering a strange land. Moving along the road in the dark he had planned to stay ashore all night, and in the morning he would see the country with fresh eyes, like those with which the Pilgrims had seen the New World. That hadn't seemed so silly then—not until the soldiers bunched at the curb had seemed to spring out of the darkness. Someone had cried, "Jesus H. Christ," and he had thought, He's from home, and grinned and apologized into the light they flashed in his eyes. He had felt the blow coming when they yelled, "It's a god-damn nigger," but it struck him anyway. He was having a time of it when some of Mr. Catti's countrymen stepped in and Mr. Catti had guided him into the pub. Now, over several rounds of ale, they had introduced themselves, had discreetly avoided mentioning his eye, and, while he heard with forced attention something of Welsh national history, he had been adjusting himself to the men in cloth caps and narrow-brimmed hats who talked so quietly over their drinks.

At first he had included them in his blind rage. But they had seemed so genuinely and uncondescendingly polite that he was disarmed. Now the anger and resentment had slowly ebbed, and he felt only a smoldering sense of self-hate and ineffectiveness. Why should he blame them when they had only helped him? *He* had been the one so glad to hear an American voice. You can't take it out on them, they're a different breed; even from the English. That's what he's been telling you, he thought, seeing Mr. Catti returning, his head held to one side to avoid the smoke from his cigarette, the foam-headed glasses caged in his fingers.

"It's a disgrace to our country, Mr. Parker!" Mr. Catti said heatedly. "How is your eye?"

"It's better, thanks," he said, brightening. "And don't worry, it's a sort of family quarrel. Are there many like me in Wales?"

"Oh yes! Yanks all over the place. Black Yanks and white."

"Black *Yanks*?" He wanted to smile.

"Yes. And many a fine lad at that."

Mr. Catti was looking at his wristwatch.

"My, my! I'm sorry, but it's time for my concert. Perhaps you would like to come? The boys at my club are singing—no professionals, mind you, but some very fine voices."

"No . . . no, I'd better not," he said. Yet all music was a passion with him, and his interest was aroused.

"It's a private club," Mr. Catti said reassuringly. "Open only to members—and to our guests, of course. We'd be very glad to have you. Perhaps the boys will sing some of your spirituals."

"Oh! So you know our music, too?"

"Very well," Mr. Catti said. "And since your boys have been with us we've learned that, like ourselves, your people love music."

"I think I'd like very much to go," he said, rising and getting into his seaman's topcoat. "You might have to guide me along though."

"Righto. It isn't far. Just a bit up Straight Street."

Outside, the pale beam of a flashlight revealed the stone walk. Somewhere in the damp darkness a group of adolescent girls were singing a nostalgic Tin Pan Alley tune. Here you go again, he thought. Better go back to the ship, no telling what'll jump out of the darkness next; maybe the Second Avenue El. And suppose someone else brings a Yank? Why spoil the fun? Hell, so let *him* walk out. . . .

Mr. Catti was guiding him into a doorway toward a soft murmur of voices. Maybe, he thought, you'll hear that old "spiritual" classic *Massa's in de—Massa's in de Old Cold Masochism*!

When the light struck his injured eye, it was as though it were being peeled by an invisible hand. He did not know whether to cover it or to let it be so as not to attract attention. What was the use?

Mr. Catti was greeting the men who made room for them at the bar. Looking across the room, where folding chairs were grouped neatly around rows of small tables, he heard a man in a blue suit running brilliant arpeggios upon an upright piano. It was a cheerful room.

"Two whiskeys, Alf," said Mr. Catti to the man behind the bar.

"Right! And a good evening to you, Twm," the man said.

"This is Mr. Parker, Alf," Mr. Catti said, introducing him. "Mr. Parker, Mr. Triffit, our club manager."

"How do you do?" he said, shaking Mr. Triffit's hand.

"Welcome to our club, sir," Mr. Triffit said. "You are an American, I take it?"

"Yes," he said. And with sly amusement he added, "A black Yank."

"I thought Mr. Parker would like the concert, Alf. So I brought him along."

"We're happy to have you, sir," Mr. Triffit said. "I believe you will enjoy it, Mr. Parker. If I do say so myself, our boys are . . . are . . . yes, dammit, they're smashing!"

"I'm sure they are," he said, thinking, He acts like he'd fight over it.

"Here's all the best," said Mr. Catti.

"Your health, sir," said Mr. Triffit.

"To Wales," Mr. Parker said, "and to you both."

"And to America, God bless her," Mr. Triffit said.

"Yes," said Mr. Parker, "and to America."

He could see Mr. Triffit about to mention his eye, and was glad Mr. Catti was moving away.

"Come, Mr. Parker. We'd better select our seats."

They sat near the front, where the singers were grouping themselves to begin. The warmth of the liquor was spreading slowly through him now, and it was with a growing sense of remoteness that he heard the first number announced, a Welsh song to be rendered a cappella. The quiet tuning chord sounded far away. He saw the men set themselves and the conductor raising his hand, then, at the downbeat, the quick, audible intake of breath and the precise attack.

The well-blended voices caught him unprepared. He heard the music's warm richness with pleasurable surprise, and heard, beneath the strange Welsh words, echoes of plain song, like that of Russian folk songs sounding.

"It's wonderful," he whispered, seeing Mr. Catti smile knowingly.

He looked about him. He saw the faces of the listeners caught in a single spell of communication while they sipped their drinks or puffed their pipes or cigarettes. Slowly the hall was filling with friendly swirls of smoke. They were singing another of their songs now, and though he could not understand the words he felt himself drawn closer to its web of meaning. Then the familiar and hateful emotion of alienation gripped his throat.

"It was a song about Wales?" he asked, soothing his eye.

"Exactly!" exclaimed Mr. Catti. "And the other was about a battle in which we defeated the English. Nothing like music to reveal what's in the heart. You don't need lyrics, really."

A warm flush dyed Mr. Catti's face. He's pleased that I understood, he thought. And as the men sang in hushed tones he felt a growing poverty of spirit. He should have known more of the Welsh, of their history and art. If we only had some of what they have, he thought. They are a much smaller nation than ours would be, yet I can remember no song of ours that's of love of the soil or of country. Nor any song of battle other than those of biblical times. And in his mind's eye he saw a Russian peasant kneeling to kiss the earth and rising wet-eyed to enter into battle with cries of fierce exultation. And he felt now, among these men, hearing their voices, a surge of deep longing to know the anguish and exultation of such love.

"Do you see that fellow with the red face there?" asked Mr. Catti.

"Yes."

"Our leading mine owner."

"And what are the others?"

"Everything. The tenor on the end is a miner. Mr. Jones, in the center there, is a butcher. And the dark man next to him is a union official."

"You'd never think so from their harmony," he said, smiling.

"When we sing, we are Welshmen," Mr. Catti said as the next number began.

Parker smiled, aware suddenly of an expansiveness that he had known before only at mixed jam sessions. When we jam, sir, we're Jamocrats! He liked these Welsh. Not even on the ship, where the common danger and a fighting union made for a degree of understanding, did he approach white men so closely.

For that's a unity of economics, he said to himself. And this a unity of music, a "gut language," the "food of love." Go on, fool. Behind that blacked-out eye you can get away with it. Knock yourself out. *All right, I will: Dear Wales, I salute thee. I kiss the lips of thy proud spirit through the fair sounds of thy songs. How's that?* Fine. Slightly mixed in metaphor, but not bad. Give us some more, Othello. *Othello? Indeed, and how odd. But. So: Oh my fair warrior nation, because of thee this little while my chaos is gone again*—Again? Parker, keep to the facts. And remember what they did to Othello. *No, he did it to himself. Couldn't believe in his woman, nor in himself.* I know, so that makes Iago a Fifth Columnist. But what do *you* believe in? *Oh, shut—I believe in music!* Well! *And in what's happening here tonight. I believe . . . I want to believe in this people.* Something was getting out of control. He became on guard. At home he could drown his humanity in a sea of concealed cynicism, and white men would never recognize it. But these men might understand. Perhaps, he felt with vague terror, all evening he had been exposed, blinded by the brilliant light of their deeper humanity, and they had seen him for what he was and for what he should have been. He was sobered. Listening now, he thought, You live on the ship, remember. Down Straight Street, in the dark. And at home you live in Harlem. Quit letting their liquor throw you, or even their hospitality. Do the State some service, Parker. They won't know it. And if these men should, it doesn't matter. Put out that light, Othello—or do you enjoy being hit with one?

"How is your eye now?" Mr. Catti asked.

"Almost completely closed."

"It's a bloody shame!"

"It's been a wonderful evening though," he said. "One of the best I've ever spent."

"I'm glad you came," Mr. Catti said. "And so are the boys. They can tell that you appreciate the music, and they're pleased."

"Here's to singing," he toasted.

"To singing," said Mr. Catti.

"By the way, let me lend you my torch to find your way back. Just return it to Heath's Bookstore. Anyone will direct you."

"But you'll need it yourself."

Mr. Catti placed the light upon the table. "Don't worry," he said. "I'm at home. I know the city like my own palm."

"Thanks," he said with feeling. "You're very kind."

When the opening bars were struck, he saw the others pushing back their chairs and standing, and he stood, understanding even as Mr. Catti whispered, "Our national anthem."

There was something in the music and in the way they held their heads that was strangely moving. He hummed beneath his breath. When it was over he would ask for the words.

But even while he heard the final triumphal chord still sounding, the piano struck up "God Save the King." It was not nearly so stirring. Then swiftly modulating they swept into the "Internationale," to words about an international army. He was carried back to when he was a small boy marching in the streets behind the bands that came to his southern town. . . .

Mr. Catti had nudged him. He looked up, seeing the conductor looking straight at him, smiling. They were all looking at him. Why, was it his eye? Were they playing a joke? And suddenly he recognized the melody and felt that his knees would give way. It was as though he had been pushed into the horrible foreboding country of dreams and they were enticing him into some unwilled and degrading act, from which only his failure to remember the words would save him. It was all unreal, yet it seemed to have happened before. Only now the melody seemed charged with some vast new meaning which that part of him that wanted to sing could not fit with the old familiar words. And beyond the music he kept hearing the soldiers' voices, yelling as they had when the light struck his eye. He saw the singers still staring, and as though to betray him he heard his own voice singing out like a suddenly amplified radio:

> ". . . Gave proof through the night
> That our flag was still there . . ."

It was like the voice of another, over whom he had no control. His eye throbbed. A wave of guilt shook him, followed by a burst of relief. For the first time in your whole life, he thought with dreamlike wonder, the words are not ironic. He stood in confusion as the song ended, staring into the men's Welsh faces, not knowing whether to curse them or to return their good-natured smiles. Then the conductor was before him, and Mr. Catti was saying, "You're not such a bad singer yourself, Mr. Parker. Is he now, Mr. Morcan?"

"Why, if he'd stay in Wales, I wouldn't rest until he joined the club," Mr. Morcan said. "What about it, Mr. Parker?"

But Mr. Parker could not reply. He held Mr. Catti's flashlight like a club and hoped his black eye would hold back the tears.

2

The American Creed

Declaration of Independence

The Declaration of Independence contains the first and most authoritative statement of the American creed. In separating from Great Britain, the united colonies declared not only their independence as a distinct people but also the universal principles of legitimate political order. The birth announcement of the American Republic, on July 4, 1776, grounded the claim to political independence in a teaching about individual human rights—to life, liberty, and the pursuit of happiness—to which rightful freedoms all human beings are said to be equally entitled. In articulating the four self-evident truths (natural equality, inalienable individual rights, government founded on the consent of the governed, and the people's right of revolution) and compiling the list of the king's abuses, Thomas Jefferson (1743–1826) claimed to have done nothing more than "place before mankind the common sense of the subject." "It was," he said, "intended to be an expression of the American mind."

What, according to the Declaration, makes the American colonists a distinct "people," entitled to a "separate and equal station" among the peoples of the world? What is meant by the Laws of Nature and Nature's God, and how are these related to our "peoplehood"? What is a "right," and where do individual rights come from? What is a "self-evident" truth, and in what self-evidently true sense can we say that "all men are created equal"? How does the Declaration understand the relation between the individual and the collective? Between our rights and our responsibilities (or duties)? Do we Americans today still hold these truths (or any truths) to be self-evident?

IN CONGRESS, JULY 4, 1776

The Unanimous Declaration of the Thirteen United States of America

When in the Course of human Events, it becomes necessary for one People to dissolve the Political Bands which have connected them with another, and to assume among the powers of the earth, the separate and equal Station to which the Laws of Nature and of Nature's God entitle them, a decent Respect to the Opinions of Mankind requires that they should declare the causes which impel them to the separation.

We hold these Truths to be self-evident, that all Men are created equal, that they are endowed by their Creator with certain unalienable Rights, that among these are Life, Liberty and the Pursuit of Happiness—That to secure these Rights, Governments are instituted among Men, deriving their just Powers from the Consent of the Governed,—That whenever any Form of Government becomes destructive of these Ends, it is the Right of the People to alter or to abolish it, and to institute new Government, laying its Foundation on such Principles, and organizing its Powers in such Form, as to them shall seem most likely to effect their Safety and Happiness. Prudence, indeed, will dictate that Governments long established should not be changed for light and transient Causes; and accordingly all Experience hath shewn that Mankind are more disposed to suffer, while Evils are sufferable, than to right themselves by abolishing the Forms to which they are accustomed. But when a long Train of Abuses and Usurpations, pursuing invariably the same Object, evinces a Design to reduce them under absolute Despotism, it is their Right, it is their Duty, to throw off such Government, and to provide new Guards for their future security.—Such has been the patient Sufferance of these Colonies; and such is now the Necessity which constrains them to alter their former Systems of Government. The History of the present King of Great-Britain is a History of repeated Injuries and Usurpations, all having in direct Object the Establishment of an absolute Tyranny over these States. To prove this, let Facts be submitted to a candid World.

He has refused his Assent to Laws, the most wholesome and necessary for the public Good.

He has forbidden his Governors to pass Laws of immediate and pressing Importance, unless suspended in their Operation till his Assent should be obtained; and when so suspended, he has utterly neglected to attend to them.

He has refused to pass other Laws for the Accommodation of large Districts of People, unless those People would relinquish the Right of Representation in the Legislature, a right inestimable to them, and formidable to Tyrants only.

He has called together Legislative Bodies at Places unusual, uncomfortable, and distant from the Depository of their Public Records, for the sole Purpose of fatiguing them into Compliance with his Measures.

He has dissolved Representative Houses repeatedly, for opposing with manly Firmness his Invasions on the Rights of the People.

He has refused for a long Time, after such Dissolutions, to cause others to be elected; whereby the Legislative Powers, incapable of Annihilation, have returned to the People at large for their exercise; the State remaining in the mean time exposed to all the Dangers of Invasion from without, and Convulsions within.

He has endeavoured to prevent the Population of these States; for that Purpose obstructing the Laws for Naturalization of Foreigners; refusing to pass others to encourage their Migrations hither, and raising the Conditions of new Appropriations of Lands.

He has obstructed the Administration of Justice, by refusing his Assent to Laws for establishing Judiciary Powers.

He has made Judges dependent on his Will alone, for the tenure of their Offices, and the Amount and Payment of their Salaries.

He has erected a Multitude of new Offices, and sent hither Swarms of Officers to harass our People and eat out their Substance.

He has kept among us, in Times of Peace, Standing Armies without the consent of our Legislatures.

He has affected to render the Military independent of and superior to the Civil Power.

He has combined with others to subject us to a Jurisdiction foreign to our Constitution, and unacknowledged by our Laws; giving his Assent to their Acts of pretended Legislation:

For quartering large Bodies of Armed Troops among us:

For protecting them, by a mock Trial, from Punishment for any Murders which they should commit on the Inhabitants of these States:

For cutting off our Trade with all parts of the World:

For imposing Taxes on us without our Consent:

For depriving us, in many Cases, of the Benefits of Trial by Jury:

For transporting us beyond Seas to be tried for pretended Offences:

For abolishing the free System of English Laws in a neighbouring Province, establishing therein an arbitrary Government, and enlarging its Boundaries, so as to render it at once an Example and fit Instrument for introducing the same absolute Rule into these Colonies:

For taking away our Charters, abolishing our most valuable Laws, and altering fundamentally the Forms of our Governments:

For suspending our own Legislatures, and declaring themselves invested with Power to legislate for us in all Cases whatsoever.

He has abdicated Government here, by declaring us out of his Protection and waging War against us.

He has plundered our Seas, ravaged our Coasts, burnt our Towns, and destroyed the Lives of our People.

He is, at this Time transporting large Armies of foreign Mercenaries to compleat the Works of Death, Desolation, and Tyranny, already begun with circumstances of Cruelty and Perfidy, scarcely paralleled in the most barbarous Ages, and totally unworthy the Head of a civilized Nation.

He has constrained our fellow Citizens taken Captive on the high Seas to bear Arms against their Country, to become the Executioners of their Friends and Brethren, or to fall themselves by their Hands.

He has excited domestic Insurrections amongst us, and has endeavoured to bring on the Inhabitants of our Frontiers, the merciless Indian Savages, whose known Rule of Warfare, is an undistinguished Destruction of all Ages, Sexes and Conditions.

In every stage of these Oppressions we have Petitioned for Redress in the most humble Terms: Our repeated Petitions have been answered only by repeated Injury. A Prince, whose Character is thus marked by every act which may define a Tyrant, is unfit to be the Ruler of a free People.

Nor have we been wanting in Attentions to our British Brethren. We have warned them from Time to Time of Attempts by their Legislature to extend an unwarrantable Jurisdiction over us. We have reminded them of the Circumstances of our Emigration and Settlement here. We have appealed to their native Justice and Magnanimity, and we have conjured them by the Ties of our common Kindred to disavow these Usurpations, which, would inevitably interrupt our Connections and Correspondence. They too have been deaf to the Voice of Justice and of Consanguinity. We must, therefore, acquiesce in the Necessity, which denounces our Separation, and hold them, as we hold the rest of Mankind, Enemies in War, in Peace, Friends.

We, therefore, the Representatives of the united States of America, in General Congress, Assembled, appealing to the Supreme Judge of the World for the Rectitude of our Intentions, do, in the Name, and by Authority of the good People of these Colonies, solemnly Publish and Declare, That these United Colonies are, and of Right ought to be, Free and Independent States; that they are absolved from all Allegiance to the British Crown, and that all political Connection between them and the State of Great-Britain, is and ought to be totally dissolved; and that as Free and Independent States, they have full Power to levy War, conclude Peace, contract Alliances, establish Commerce, and to do all other Acts and Things which Independent States may of right do.—And for the support of this Declaration, with a firm Reliance on the Protection of divine Providence, we mutually pledge to each other our Lives, our Fortunes, and our sacred Honor.

John Hancock

Samuel Chase

Wm. Paca

Thos. Stone

Charles Carroll of Carrollton

George Wythe

Richard Henry Lee

Th. Jefferson

Benj. Harrison

Thos. Nelson jr.

Francis Lightfoot Lee

Carter Braxton

Robt. Morris

Benjamin Rush

Benj. Franklin

John Morton

Geo. Clymer

Jas. Smith

Geo. Taylor

James Wilson

Geo. Ross

Caesar Rodney

Geo. Read

Thom. Kean

Wm. Floyd

Phil. Livingston

Arthur Middleton

Button Gwinnett

Fran. Lewis

Lewis Morris

Rich. Stockton

Jn. Witherspoon

Fra. Hopkinson

John Hart

Abra. Clark

Josiah Bartlett

Wm. Whipple

Saml. Adams

John Adams

Robt. Treat Paine

Elbridge Gerry

Step. Hopkins

William Ellery

Roger Sherman

Saml. Huntington

Wm. Williams

Oliver Wolcott

Matthew Thornton

Wm. Hooper

Joseph Hewes

John Penn

Edward Rutledge

Thos. Heyward Jun.

Thomas Lynch Jun.

Lyman Hall

Geo. Walton

Gettysburg Address

ABRAHAM LINCOLN

The creed of the American Republic, as enunciated in the Declaration of Independence, begins with the claim, offered as a self-evident truth, that "all men are created equal." Yet our embrace of the principle was long embarrassed in practice by the existence of chattel slavery, present at the Founding but greatly increased through the first half of the nineteenth century. Critics of the Declaration openly called human equality "a self-evident lie," and the infamous Dred Scott decision (1857) gave voice to a racist and exclusionary interpretation of the Declaration, insisting that its "all men" referred only to "all white men" who were the equals of British subjects living in Britain. No one did more to oppose this (mis)interpretation than our sixteenth president, Abraham Lincoln (1809–1865), who famously claimed that he had "never had a feeling politically that did not spring from the sentiments embodied in the Declaration of Independence." * Lincoln's most famous defense of equal-

---

* *Throughout his career, Lincoln offered numerous statements about the meaning of the Declaration, calling it "the father of all moral principle" in each subsequent generation of Americans and "the sheet anchor of republicanism." In his speech on the Dred Scott decision, he sought to vindicate the inclusiveness of the Declaration's assertion of human equality:*

> *I think the authors of that notable instrument intended to include all men, but they did not intend to declare all men equal in all respects. They did not mean to say all were equal in color, size, intellect, moral developments, or social capacity. They defined with tolerable distinctness, in what respects they did consider all men created equal—equal in "certain inalienable rights, among which are life, liberty, and the pursuit of happiness." This they said, and this they meant. They did not mean to assert the obvious untruth, that all were then actually enjoying that equality, nor yet, that they were about to confer it immediately upon them. In fact they had no power to confer such a boon. They meant simply to declare the right, so that the enforcement of it might follow as fast as circumstances should permit. They meant to set up a standard maxim for free society, which should be familiar*

ity appears in the Gettysburg Address, delivered on November 19, 1863, in the midst of a civil war whose deepest cause was the institution of slavery. Here Lincoln revisits the Declaration of Independence, summoning the nation to achieve a "new birth of freedom" through renewed dedication to the founding proposition of human equality.

How does Lincoln understand the key terms of the creed, and in particular, the relation between equality and freedom? What is the difference between "holding" equality as a "self-evident truth" and regarding it as a "proposition" to which we are dedicated? What is the difference between the "new birth of freedom," coming from the bloody war, and the original birth of the nation, "conceived in liberty"? What do you think is the meaning of equality today, and what is its relation to freedom?

Four score and seven years ago our fathers brought forth on this continent, a new nation, conceived in Liberty, and dedicated to the proposition that all men are created equal.

Now we are engaged in a great civil war, testing whether that nation, or any nation so conceived and so dedicated, can long endure. We are met on a great battle-field of that war. We have come to dedicate a portion of that field, as a final resting place for those who here gave their lives that that nation might live. It is altogether fitting and proper that we should do this.

But, in a larger sense, we can not dedicate—we can not consecrate—we can not hallow—this ground. The brave men, living and dead, who struggled here, have consecrated it, far above our poor power to add or detract. The world will little note, nor long remember what we say here, but it can never forget what they did here. It is for us the living, rather, to be dedicated here to the unfinished work which they who fought here have thus far so nobly advanced. It is rather for us to be here dedicated to the great task remaining before us—that from these honored dead we take increased devotion to that cause for which they gave the last full measure of devotion—that we here highly resolve that these dead shall not have died in vain—that this nation, under God, shall have a new birth of freedom—and that government of the people, by the people, for the people, shall not perish from the earth.

---

to all, and revered by all; constantly looked to, constantly labored for, and even though never perfectly attained, constantly approximated, and thereby constantly spreading and deepening its influence, and augmenting the happiness and value of life to all people of all colors everywhere.

Federalist *No. 10*

Publius

The Federalist Papers, *originally published in New York newspapers between October 1787 and August 1788, were intended to encourage ratification of the new federal Constitution. The eighty-five essays by Publius (the collective pseudonym for James Madison, Alexander Hamilton, and John Jay) have become a much-respected source for understanding the intentions of the Founders in creating our complex governmental structure. Seeking to achieve stable and energetic government while preserving republican liberty, the Founders developed a new science of politics, relying on such institutional mechanisms as the separation of powers, checks and balances, an independent judiciary, representative government, and something called "the enlargement of the orbit."*

This last innovation, first mentioned in Federalist *No. 9, is the subject of* Federalist *No. 10, the most cited of the essays. Here Publius (in this case, Madison) sketches a highly original solution to the problem of majority faction (when ruling majorities ignore the legitimate rights of the minority). He argues that representative government (as opposed to direct democracy) helps avert majority faction by refining and tempering majority opinion. But beyond mere representation he recommends, paradoxically, more factions. Thus he argues for a large republic rather than a small one, for the larger the republic, the greater the number and types of interests and factions, and the more they will be able to balance and counteract one another. Political struggle will be moderated not by moral and religious instruction aimed at making citizens more moderate and virtuous, but instead by the moderating effects of multiplicity and the requirements of effective commercial activity. By design, America's greatest bulwark against the danger of majority faction is the large commercial republic and competition of rival interests in pursuit of gain and personal advancement.*

What assumptions about human nature inform this ingenious solution? Why is heterogeneity preferable to homogeneity, and what, if any, might be its defects or costs? What sort of human character—with what sorts of passions, virtues, and vices—is produced by a large commercial republic? The Anti-Federalists, who opposed the large federal union, held that freedom can be experienced and preserved only in small communities, in which citizens know one another, are like-minded, and actively participate in public life. Might they have been right? Does our federal system, through its division of authority among national, state, and local powers, manage to secure the advantages of both bigness and smallness? What should we think today about the relation among commerce, freedom, and stability?

To the People of the State of New York:

Among the numerous advantages promised by a well-constructed Union, none deserves to be more accurately developed than its tendency to break and control the violence of faction. The friend of popular governments never finds himself so much alarmed for their character and fate, as when he contemplates their propensity to this dangerous vice. He will not fail, therefore, to set a due value on any plan which, without violating the principles to which he is attached, provides a proper cure for it. The instability, injustice, and confusion introduced into the public councils, have, in truth, been the mortal diseases under which popular governments have everywhere perished; as they continue to be the favorite and fruitful topics from which the adversaries to liberty derive their most specious declamations. The valuable improvements made by the American constitutions on the popular models, both ancient and modern, cannot certainly be too much admired; but it would be an unwarrantable partiality, to contend that they have as effectually obviated the danger on this side, as was wished and expected. Complaints are everywhere heard from our most considerate and virtuous citizens, equally the friends of public and private faith, and of public and personal liberty, that our governments are too unstable, that the public good is disregarded in the conflicts of rival parties, and that measures are too often decided, not according to the rules of justice and the rights of the minor party, but by the superior force of an interested and overbearing majority. However anxiously we may wish that these complaints had no foundation, the evidence, of known facts will not permit us to deny that they are in some degree true. It will be found, indeed, on a candid review of our situation, that some of the distresses under which we labor have been erroneously charged on the operation of our governments; but it will be found, at the same time, that other causes will not alone account for many of our heaviest misfortunes; and, particularly, for that prevailing and increasing distrust of public engagements, and alarm for private rights, which are echoed from one end of the continent to the other. These must be chiefly, if not wholly, effects of the unsteadiness and injustice with which a factious spirit has tainted our public administrations.

By a faction, I understand a number of citizens, whether amounting to a majority or a minority of the whole, who are united and actuated by some common impulse of passion, or of interest, adverse to the rights of other citizens, or to the permanent and aggregate interests of the community.

There are two methods of curing the mischiefs of faction: the one, by removing its causes; the other, by controlling its effects.

There are again two methods of removing the causes of faction: the one, by destroying the liberty which is essential to its existence; the other, by giving to every citizen the same opinions, the same passions, and the same interests.

It could never be more truly said than of the first remedy, that it was worse than the disease. Liberty is to faction what air is to fire, an aliment without which it instantly expires. But it could not be less folly to abolish liberty, which is essential to political life, because it nourishes faction, than it would be to wish the annihilation of air, which is essential to animal life, because it imparts to fire its destructive agency.

The second expedient is as impracticable as the first would be unwise. As long as the reason of man continues fallible, and he is at liberty to exercise it, different opinions will be formed. As long as the connection subsists between his reason and his self-love, his opinions and his passions will have a reciprocal influence on each other; and the former will be objects to which the latter will attach themselves. The diversity in the faculties of men, from which the rights of property originate, is not less an insuperable obstacle to a uniformity of interests. The protection of these faculties is the first object of government. From the protection of different and unequal faculties of acquiring property, the possession of different degrees and kinds of property immediately results; and from the influence of these on the sentiments and views of the respective proprietors, ensues a division of the society into different interests and parties.

The latent causes of faction are thus sown in the nature of man; and we see them everywhere brought into different degrees of activity, according to the different circumstances of civil society. A zeal for different opinions concerning religion, concerning government, and many other points, as well of speculation as of practice; an attachment to different leaders ambitiously contending for pre-eminence and power; or to persons of other descriptions whose fortunes have been interesting to the human passions, have, in turn, divided mankind into parties, inflamed them with mutual animosity, and rendered them much more disposed to vex and oppress each other than to co-operate for their common good. So strong is this propensity of mankind to fall into mutual animosities, that where no substantial occasion presents itself, the most frivolous and fanciful distinctions have been sufficient to kindle their unfriendly passions and excite their most violent conflicts. But the most common and durable source of factions has been the various and unequal distribution of property. Those who hold and those who are without property have ever formed distinct interests in society. Those who are creditors, and those who are debtors, fall under a like discrimination. A landed interest, a manufacturing interest, a mercantile interest, a moneyed interest, with many lesser interests, grow up of necessity in civilized nations, and divide them into different classes, actuated by different sentiments and views. The regulation of these various and interfering interests forms the principal task of modern legislation, and involves the spirit of party and faction in the necessary and ordinary operations of the government.

No man is allowed to be a judge in his own cause, because his interest would certainly bias his judgment, and, not improbably, corrupt his integrity. With equal, nay with greater reason, a body of men are unfit to be both judges and parties at the same time; yet what are many of the most important acts of legislation, but so many judicial determinations, not indeed concerning the rights of single persons, but concerning the rights of large bodies of citizens? And what are the different classes of legislators but advocates and parties to the causes which they determine? Is a law proposed concerning private debts? It is a question to which the creditors are parties on one side and the debtors on the other. Justice ought to hold the balance between them. Yet the parties are, and must be, themselves the judges; and the most numerous party, or, in other words, the most powerful faction must be expected to prevail. Shall domestic manufactures be encouraged, and in what degree, by restrictions on foreign manufactures? are questions which would be differently decided by the landed and the manufacturing classes, and probably by neither with a sole regard to justice and the public good. The apportionment of taxes on the various descriptions of property is an act which seems to require the most exact impartiality; yet there is, perhaps, no legislative act in which greater opportunity and temptation are given to a predominant party to trample on the rules of justice. Every shilling with which they overburden the inferior number, is a shilling saved to their own pockets.

It is in vain to say that enlightened statesmen will be able to adjust these clashing interests, and render them all subservient to the public good. Enlightened statesmen will not always be at the helm. Nor, in many cases, can such an adjustment be made at all without taking into view indirect and remote considerations, which will rarely prevail over the immediate interest which one party may find in disregarding the rights of another or the good of the whole.

The inference to which we are brought is, that the *causes* of faction cannot be removed, and that relief is only to be sought in the means of controlling its *effects*.

If a faction consists of less than a majority, relief is supplied by the republican principle, which enables the majority to defeat its sinister views by regular vote. It may clog the administration, it may convulse the society; but it will be unable to execute and mask its violence under the forms of the Constitution. When a majority is included in a faction, the form of popular government, on the other hand, enables it to sacrifice to its ruling passion or interest both the public good and the rights of other citizens. To secure the public good and private rights against the danger of such a faction, and at the same time to preserve the spirit and the form of popular government, is then the great object to which our inquiries are directed. Let me add that it is the great desideratum by which this form of government can be rescued from the opprobrium under which it has so long labored, and be recommended to the esteem and adoption of mankind.

By what means is this object attainable? Evidently by one of two only. Either the existence of the same passion or interest in a majority at the same time must be prevented, or the majority, having such coexistent passion or interest, must be rendered, by their number and local situation, unable to concert and carry into effect schemes of oppression. If the impulse and the opportunity be suffered to coincide, we well know that neither moral nor religious motives can be relied on as an adequate control. They are not found to be such on the injustice and violence of individuals, and lose their efficacy in proportion to the number combined together, that is, in proportion as their efficacy becomes needful.

From this view of the subject it may be concluded that a pure democracy, by which I mean a society consisting of a small number of citizens, who assemble and administer the government in person, can admit of no cure for the mischiefs of faction. A common passion or interest will, in almost every case, be felt by a majority of the whole; a communication and concert result from the form of government itself; and there is nothing to check the inducements to sacrifice the weaker party or an obnoxious individual. Hence it is that such democracies have ever been spectacles of turbulence and contention; have ever been found incompatible with personal security or the rights of property; and have in general been as short in their lives as they have been violent in their deaths. Theoretic politicians, who have patronized this species of government, have erroneously supposed that by reducing mankind to a perfect equality in their political rights, they would, at the same time, be perfectly equalized and assimilated in their possessions, their opinions, and their passions.

A republic, by which I mean a government in which the scheme of representation takes place, opens a different prospect, and promises the cure for which we are seeking. Let us examine the points in which it varies from pure democracy, and we shall comprehend both the nature of the cure and the efficacy which it must derive from the Union.

The two great points of difference between a democracy and a republic are: first, the delegation of the government, in the latter, to a small number of citizens elected by the rest; secondly, the greater number of citizens, and greater sphere of country, over which the latter may be extended.

The effect of the first difference is, on the one hand, to refine and enlarge the public views, by passing them through the medium of a chosen body of citizens, whose wisdom may best discern the true interest of their country, and whose patriotism and love of justice will be least likely to sacrifice it to temporary or partial considerations. Under such a regulation, it may well happen that the public voice, pronounced by the representatives of the people, will be more consonant to the public good than if pronounced by the people themselves, convened for the purpose. On the other hand, the effect may be inverted. Men of factious tempers, of local prejudices, or of sinister designs, may, by intrigue, by corruption, or by other means, first obtain the suffrages, and then betray the interests, of the people. The question resulting is, whether small or extensive republics are more favorable to the election of proper guardians of the public weal; and it is clearly decided in favor of the latter by two obvious considerations:

In the first place, it is to be remarked that, however small the republic may be, the representatives must be raised to a certain number, in order to guard against the cabals of a few; and that, however large it may be, they must be limited to a certain number, in order to guard against the confusion of a multitude. Hence, the number of representatives in the two cases not being in proportion to that of the two constituents, and being proportionally greater in the small republic, it follows that, if the proportion of fit characters be not less in the large than in the small republic, the former will present a greater option, and consequently a greater probability of a fit choice.

In the next place, as each representative will be chosen by a greater number of citizens in the large than in the small republic, it will be more difficult for unworthy candidates to practice with success the vicious arts by which elections are too often carried; and the suffrages of the people being more free, will be more likely to centre in men who possess the most attractive merit and the most diffusive and established characters.

It must be confessed that in this, as in most other cases, there is a mean, on both sides of which inconveniences will be found to lie. By enlarging too much the number of electors, you render the representatives too little acquainted with all their local circumstances and lesser interests; as by reducing it too much, you render him unduly attached to these, and too little fit to comprehend and pursue great and national objects. The federal Constitution forms a happy combination in this respect; the great and aggregate interests being referred to the national, the local and particular to the State legislatures.

The other point of difference is, the greater number of citizens and extent of territory which may be brought within the compass of republican than of democratic government; and it is this circumstance principally which renders factious combinations less to be dreaded in the former than in the latter. The smaller the society, the fewer probably will be the distinct parties and interests composing it; the fewer the distinct parties and interests, the more frequently will a majority be found of the same party; and the smaller the number of individuals composing a majority, and the smaller the compass within which they are placed, the more easily will they concert and execute their plans of oppression. Extend the sphere, and you take in a greater variety of parties and interests; you make it less probable that a majority of the whole will have a common motive to invade the rights of other citizens; or if such a common motive exists, it will be more difficult for all who feel it to discover their own strength, and to act in unison with each other. Besides other impediments, it may be remarked that, where there is a consciousness of unjust or dishonorable purposes, communication is always checked by distrust in proportion to the number whose concurrence is necessary.

Hence, it clearly appears, that the same advantage which a republic has over a democracy, in controlling the effects of faction, is enjoyed by a large over a small republic,—is enjoyed by the Union over the States composing it. Does the advantage consist in the substitution of representatives whose enlightened views and virtuous sentiments render them superior to local prejudices and schemes of injustice? It will not be denied that the representation of the Union will be most likely to possess these requisite endowments. Does it consist in the greater security afforded by a greater variety of parties, against the event of any one party being able to outnumber and oppress the rest? In an equal degree does the increased variety of parties comprised within the Union, increase this security. Does it, in fine, consist in the greater obstacles opposed to the concert and accomplishment of the secret wishes of an unjust and interested majority? Here, again, the extent of the Union gives it the most palpable advantage.

The influence of factious leaders may kindle a flame within their particular States, but will be unable to spread a general conflagration through the other States. A religious sect may degenerate into a political faction in a part of the Confederacy; but the variety of sects dispersed over the entire face of it must secure the national councils against any danger from that source. A rage for paper money, for an abolition of debts, for an equal division of property, or for any other improper or wicked project, will be less apt to pervade the whole body of the Union than a particular member of it; in the same proportion as such a malady is more likely to taint a particular county or district, than an entire State.

In the extent and proper structure of the Union, therefore, we behold a republican remedy for the diseases most incident to republican government. And according to the degree of pleasure and pride we feel in being republicans, ought to be our zeal in cherishing the spirit and supporting the character of Federalists.

Publius.

Mayflower Compact

While we declared our national independence in 1776 and drafted our new, and abiding, Constitution just a decade later, the founding of the United States of America should perhaps not be taken as the beginning point of democracy in America. Before the Founding Fathers there were the Pilgrim Fathers. That great analyst of American democracy Alexis de Tocqueville (1805–1859) argued in Democracy in America *that the nation's point of departure was really to be found in the ideas and practices of the "pious adventurers" who came to the wilderness so that they might "pray to God in freedom" and, in their own words, "build a city upon a hill" as a beacon to the rest of the world. According to Tocqueville, "Puritanism was not only a religious doctrine; it also blended at several points with the most absolute democratic and republican theories." Evidence of the mixture of high religious purpose with political notions that led to the flourishing of independent township government (especially in New England) can be seen in the Mayflower Compact. Signed aboard ship on November 11, 1620, it became the first governing document of the colonists who landed at Plymouth Rock.*

How do the Pilgrims understand their community? Is "covenant" or "compact" just a synonym for "social contract" and government based on consent? Or does the language of covenant indicate something distinctive about the foundations or purposes of their political union? Tocqueville claimed that the American point of departure was "a product of two perfectly distinct elements that elsewhere have often made war with each other, but which, in America, they have succeeded in incorporating somehow into one another and combining marvelously . . . the spirit of religion and the spirit of freedom." Are these two spirits still present—still compatible, still mutually supportive—in America today? Does it matter whether they are still present and still harmonious?

In the name of God, Amen. We whose names are underwritten, the loyal subjects of our dread Sovereign Lord King James, by the Grace of God, of Great Britain, France and Ireland King, Defender of the Faith, etc.

Having undertaken, for the Glory of God and advancement of the Christian Faith and Honour of our King and Country, a Voyage to plant the First Colony in the Northern Parts of Virginia, do by these presents solemnly and mutually in the presence of God and one of another, Covenant and Combine our selves together into a Civil Body Politic, for our better ordering and preservation and furtherance of the ends aforesaid; and by virtue hereof to enact, constitute, and frame such just and equal Laws, Ordinances, Acts, Constitutions and Offices, from time to time, as shall be thought most meet and convenient for the general good of the Colony, unto which we promise all due submission and obedience.

In witness whereof we have hereunder subscribed our names at Cape Cod, the 11th of November, in the year of the reign of our Sovereign Lord King James, of England, France, and Ireland the eighteenth, and of Scotland the fifty-fourth. Anno Domini 1620.

John Carver
William Bradford
Edward Winslow
William Brewster
Isaac Allerton
Miles Standish
John Alden
Samuel Fuller
Christopher Martin
William Mullins
William White
James Chilton
John Craxton
John Billington
Richard Warren
John Howland
Steven Hopkins
Edward Tilly
John Tilly
Francis Cook
Thomas Rogers

Thomas Tinker
John Rigdale
Edward Fuller
John Turner
Francis Eaton
Moses Fletcher
Digery Priest
Thomas Williams
Gilbert Winslow
Edmond Margeson
Peter Brown
Richard Bitteridge
Richard Clark
Richard Gardiner
John Allerton
Thomas English
Edward Doten
Edward Liester
John Goodman
George Soule

To the Hebrew Congregation
in Newport, Rhode Island

GEORGE WASHINGTON

Developing its unique blend of religion and politics, the American Republic pioneered a novel approach to the problems of religious zealotry and religious conflict that plagued Europe. The United States has no established national church and the Constitution proscribes any religious test for holding national office. But this "separation" of church and state, far from being indifferent to the religiosity of the people, was intended to support liberty of conscience and freedom of worship, privileges until then rare among the nations of the world—and today still precarious in many regimes. President George Washington (1732–1799) offered an early, generous expression of the principle of religious freedom even before the adoption of the Bill of Rights (1791) in this Letter to the Hebrew Congregation in Newport, Rhode Island (1790). Washington wrote many similar letters to other denominations in response to their letters of congratulation upon his election as the nation's first president. The array of these letters illustrates the nation's vibrant and peaceful religious pluralism.

Nonetheless, many questions remain. Does vigorous religious pluralism enhance or diminish national identity and civic attachment? Are there limits to religious toleration? Are there religious sects or beliefs that put in doubt the beautiful image of each sitting "in safety under his own vine and fig tree"? Is liberty of conscience, coupled with disestablishment, a sufficient solution to the problem of fanaticism in politics? Where religious and civic duties conflict, which should take precedence? Is the idea behind religious pluralism also indifferent to the distinction between religion and irreligion—that is, to atheism?

Gentlemen

While I receive, with much satisfaction, your Address replete with expressions of affection and esteem; I rejoice in the opportunity of assuring you, that I shall always retain a grateful remembrance of the cordial welcome I experienced in my visit to Newport, from all classes of Citizens.

The reflection on the days of difficulty and danger which are past is rendered the more sweet, from a consciousness that they are succeeded by days of uncommon prosperity and security. If we have wisdom to make the best use of the advantages with which we are now favored, we cannot fail, under the just administration of a good Government, to become a great and a happy people.

The Citizens of the United States of America have a right to applaud themselves for having given to mankind examples of an enlarged and liberal policy: a policy worthy of imitation. All possess alike liberty of conscience and immunities of citizenship. It is now no more that toleration is spoken of, as if it was by the indulgence of one class of people, that another enjoyed the exercise of their inherent natural rights. For happily the Government of the United States, which gives to bigotry no sanction, to persecution no assistance requires only that they who live under its protection should demean themselves as good citizens, in giving it on all occasions their effectual support.

It would be inconsistent with the frankness of my character not to avow that I am pleased with your favorable opinion of my Administration, and fervent wishes for my felicity. May the Children of the Stock of Abraham, who dwell in this land, continue to merit and enjoy the good will of the other Inhabitants; while every one shall sit in safety under his own vine and figtree, and there shall be none to make him afraid. May the father of all mercies scatter light and not darkness in our paths, and make us all in our several vocations useful here, and in his own due time and way everlastingly happy.

August 18, 1790

3

The American Character:
Individuals Free and Equal

To Build a Fire

JACK LONDON

*American freedom and individuality have often been expressed in, and cele-
brated by, stories of exploration, adventure, enterprise, and the pursuit of
gain: the conquest of the prairie, the settling of the West, the taming of the
wilderness, the gold rush, and the mastery of nature through science, industry, and technology. Jack London's story (1908) offers us a picture of one
such fortune-hunting rugged individual. London (1876–1916) took part in
the Klondike gold rush, and though he failed as a miner, he struck gold with
stories drawing on the places and people he encountered during those hope-
filled and brutal times in the Northwest Territory.*

*In this story, an unnamed man, accompanied by a husky, undertakes a
nine-hour walk along a faint and little traveled trail in brutally cold weather,
in order to scope out the "possibilities of getting out logs in the spring from
the islands in the Yukon." How would you describe his character? Is his self-
reliance an exercise of irresponsibility and folly? Or does he embody an admirable spirit of adventure and enterprise of the sort that tamed the wilderness,
settled the West, and established businesses? What do you think of the old-
timer's advice and the reservations clearly expressed by the dog?*

Day had broken cold and gray, exceedingly cold and gray, when the man
turned aside from the main Yukon trail and climbed the high earth-bank,
where a dim and little traveled trail led eastward through the fat spruce timber-
land. It was a steep bank, and he paused for breath at the top, excusing the act to
himself by looking at his watch. It was nine o'clock. There was no sun nor hint
of sun, though there was not a cloud in the sky. It was a clear day, and yet there
seemed an intangible pall over the face of things, a subtle gloom that made the
day dark, and that was due to the absence of sun. This fact did not worry the

man. He was used to the lack of sun. It had been days since he had seen the sun, and he knew that a few more days must pass before that cheerful orb, due south, would just peep above the sky-line and dip immediately from view.

The man flung a look back along the way he had come. The Yukon lay a mile wide and hidden under three feet of ice. On top of this ice were as many feet of snow. It was all pure white, rolling in gentle undulations where the ice jams of the freeze-up had formed. North and south, as far as his eye could see, it was unbroken white, save for a dark hairline that curved and twisted from around the spruce-covered island to the south, and that curved and twisted away into the north, where it disappeared behind another spruce-covered island. This dark hair-line was the trail—the main trail—that led south five hundred miles to the Chilcoot Pass, Dyea, and salt water; and that led north seventy miles to Dawson, and still on to the north a thousand miles to Nulato, and finally to St. Michael on Bering Sea, a thousand miles and half a thousand more.

But all this—the mysterious, far-reaching hair-line trail, the absence of sun from the sky, the tremendous cold, and the strangeness and weirdness of it all—made no impression on the man. It was not because he was long used to it. He was a newcomer in the land, a *chechaquo*, and this was his first winter. The trouble with him was that he was without imagination. He was quick and alert in the things of life, but only in the things, and not in the significances. Fifty degrees below zero meant eighty-odd degrees of frost. Such fact impressed him as being cold and uncomfortable, and that was all. It did not lead him to meditate upon his frailty as a creature of temperature, and upon man's frailty in general, able only to live within certain narrow limits of heat and cold; and from there on it did not lead him to the conjectural field of immortality and man's place in the universe. Fifty degrees below zero stood for a bite of frost that hurt and that must be guarded against by the use of mittens, ear-flaps, warm moccasins, and thick socks. Fifty degrees below zero was to him just precisely fifty degrees below zero. That there should be anything more to it than that was a thought that never entered his head.

As he turned to go on, he spat speculatively. There was a sharp, explosive crackle that startled him. He spat again. And again, in the air, before it could fall to the snow, the spittle crackled. He knew that at fifty below spittle crackled on the snow, but this spittle had crackled in the air. Undoubtedly it was colder than fifty below—how much colder he did not know. But the temperature did not matter. He was bound for the old claim on the left fork of Henderson Creek, where the boys were already. They had come over across the divide from the Indian Creek country, while he had come the roundabout way to take a look at the possibilities of getting out logs in the spring from the islands in the Yukon. He would be in to camp by six o'clock; a bit after dark, it was true, but the boys would be there, a fire would be going, and a hot supper would be ready. As for lunch, he pressed his hand against the protruding bundle under his jacket. It was also under his shirt, wrapped up in a handkerchief and lying against the naked skin. It was the only way to keep the biscuits from freezing. He smiled agreeably to himself as he thought of those biscuits, each cut open and sopped in bacon grease, and each enclosing a generous slice of fried bacon.

He plunged in among the big spruce trees. The trail was faint. A foot of snow had fallen since the last sled had passed over, and he was glad he was without a sled, traveling light. In fact, he carried nothing but the lunch wrapped in the handkerchief. He was surprised, however, at the cold. It certainly was cold, he concluded as he rubbed his numb nose and cheek-bones with his mittened hand. He was a warm-whiskered man, but the hair on his face did not protect the high cheek-bones and the eager nose that thrust itself aggressively into the frosty air.

At the man's heels trotted a dog, a big native husky, the proper wolf-dog, gray-coated and without any visible or temperamental difference from its brother, the wild wolf. The animal was depressed by the tremendous cold. It knew that it was no time for traveling. Its instinct told it a truer tale than was told to the man by the man's judgment. In reality, it was not merely colder than fifty below zero; it was colder than sixty below, than seventy below. It was seventy-five below zero. Since the freezing point is thirty-two above zero, it meant that one hundred and seven degrees of frost obtained. The dog did not know anything about thermometers. Possibly in its brain there was no sharp consciousness of a condition of very cold such as was in the man's brain. But the brute had its instinct. It experienced a vague but menacing apprehension that subdued it and made it slink along at the man's heels, and that made it question eagerly every unwonted movement of the man as if expecting him to go into camp or to seek shelter somewhere and build a fire. The dog had learned fire, and it wanted fire, or else to burrow under the snow and cuddle its warmth away from the air.

The frozen moisture of its breathing had settled on its fur in a fine powder of frost, and especially were its jowls, muzzle, and eyelashes whitened by its crystalled breath. The man's red beard and mustache were likewise frosted, but more solidly, the deposit taking the form of ice and increasing with every warm, moist breath he exhaled. Also, the man was chewing tobacco, and the muzzle of ice held his lips so rigidly that he was unable to clear his chin when he expelled the juice. The result was that a crystal beard of the color and solidity of amber was increasing its length on his chin. If he fell down it would shatter itself, like glass, into brittle fragments. But he did not mind the appendage.

It was the penalty all tobacco-chewers paid in that country, and he had been out before in two cold snaps. They had not been so cold as this, he knew, but by the spirit thermometer at Sixty Mile he knew they had been registered at fifty below and at fifty-five.

He held on through the level stretch of woods for several miles, crossed a wide flat of niggerheads,* and dropped down a bank to the frozen bed of a small stream. This was Henderson Creek, and he knew he was ten miles from the forks. He looked at his watch. It was ten o'clock. He was making four miles an hour, and he calculated that he would arrive at the forks at half-past twelve. He decided to celebrate that event by eating his lunch there.

The dog dropped in again at his heels, with a tail drooping discouragement, as the man swung along the creek-bed. The furrow of the old sled-trail was plainly visible, but a dozen inches of snow covered the marks of the last runners. In a month no man had come up or down that silent creek. The man held steadily on. He was not much given to thinking, and just then particularly he had nothing to think about save that he would eat lunch at the forks and that at six o'clock he would be in camp with the boys. There was nobody to talk to; and, had there been, speech would have been impossible because of the ice-muzzle on his mouth. So he continued monotonously to chew tobacco and to increase the length of his amber beard.

Once in a while the thought reiterated itself that it was very cold and that he had never experienced such cold. As he walked along he rubbed his cheek-bones and nose with the back of his mittened hand. He did this automatically, now and again changing hands. But rub as he would, the instant he stopped his cheek-bones went numb, and the following instant the end of his nose went numb. He was sure to frost his cheeks; he knew that, and experienced a pang of regret that he had not devised a nose-strap of the sort Bud wore in cold snaps. Such a strap passed across the cheeks, as well, and saved them. But it didn't matter much, after all. What were frosted cheeks? A bit painful, that was all; they were never serious.

Empty as the man's mind was of thoughts, he was keenly observant, and he noticed the changes in the creek, the curves and bends and timber jams, and always he sharply noted where he placed his feet. Once coming around a bend, he shied abruptly, like a startled horse, curved away from the place where he had been walking, and retreated several paces back along the trail. The creek he knew was frozen clear to the bottom,—no creek could contain water in that arctic winter,—but he knew also that there were springs that bubbled out from

---

* Racially charged name of a strong dark chewing tobacco of the period, applied here to large hummocks of earth under the snow that are created by centuries of alternate freezing and thawing.

the hillsides and ran along under the snow and on top the ice of the creek. He knew that the coldest snaps never froze these springs, and he knew likewise their danger. They were traps. They hid pools of water under the snow that might be three inches deep, or three feet. Sometimes a skin of ice half an inch thick covered them, and in turn was covered by the snow. Sometimes there were alternate layers of water and ice-skin, so that when one broke through he kept on breaking through for a while, sometimes wetting himself to the waist.

That was why he had shied in such panic. He had felt the give under his feet and heard the crackle of a snow-hidden ice-skin. And to get his feet wet in such a temperature meant trouble and danger. At the very least it meant delay, for he would be forced to stop and build a fire, and under its protection to bare his feet while he dried his socks and moccasins. He stood and studied the creek-bed and its banks, and decided that the flow of water came from the right. He reflected a while, rubbing his nose and cheeks, then skirted to the left, stepping gingerly and testing the footing for each step. Once clear of the danger, he took a fresh chew of tobacco and swung along at his four-mile gait.

In the course of the next two hours he came upon several similar traps. Usually the snow above the hidden pools had a sunken, candied appearance that advertised the danger. Once again, however, he had a close call; and once, suspecting danger, he compelled the dog to go on in front. The dog did not want to go. It hung back until the man shoved it forward, and then it went quickly across the white, unbroken surface. Suddenly it broke through, floundered to one side, and got away to firmer footing. It had wet its forefeet and legs, and almost immediately the water that clung to it turned to ice. It made quick efforts to lick the ice off its legs, then dropped down in the snow and began to bite out the ice that had formed between the toes. This was a matter of instinct. To permit the ice to remain would mean sore feet. It did not know this. It merely obeyed the mysterious prompting that arose from the deep crypts of its being. But the man knew, having achieved a judgment on the subject, and he removed the mitten from his right hand and helped tear out the ice-particles. He did not expose his fingers more than a minute, and was astonished at the swift numbness that smote them. It certainly was cold. He pulled on the mitten hastily, and beat the hand savagely across his chest.

At twelve o'clock the day was at its brightest. Yet the sun was too far south on its winter journey to clear the horizon. The bulge of the earth intervened between it and Henderson Creek, where the man walked under a clear sky at noon and cast no shadow. At half-past twelve, to the minute, he arrived at the forks of the creek. He was pleased at the speed he had made. If he kept it up, he would certainly be with the boys by six. He unbuttoned his jacket and shirt and drew forth his lunch. The action consumed no more than a quarter of a minute, yet in that brief moment the numbness laid hold of the exposed fingers. He did not put the mitten on, but, instead struck the fingers a dozen sharp smashes against his leg. Then he sat down on a snow-covered log to eat. The sting that followed upon the striking of his fingers against his leg ceased so quickly that he was startled. He had had no chance to take a bite of biscuit. He struck the fingers repeatedly and returned them to the mitten, baring the other hand for the purpose of eating. He tried to take a mouthful, but the ice-muzzle prevented. He had forgotten to build a fire and thaw out. He chuckled at his foolishness, and as he chuckled he noted the numbness creeping into the exposed fingers. Also, he noted that the stinging which had first come to his toes when he sat down was already passing away. He wondered whether the toes were warm or numb. He moved them inside the moccasins and decided that they were numb.

He pulled the mitten on hurriedly and stood up. He was a bit frightened. He stamped up and down until the stinging returned into the feet. It certainly was cold, was his thought. That man from Sulphur Creek had spoken the truth when telling how cold it sometimes got in the country. And he had laughed at him at the time! That showed one must not be too sure of things. There was no mistake about it, it was cold. He strode up and down, stamping his feet and threshing his arms, until reassured by the returning warmth. Then he got out matches and proceeded to make a fire. From the undergrowth, where high water of the previous spring had lodged a supply of seasoned twigs, he got his firewood. Working carefully from a small beginning, he soon had a roaring fire, over which he thawed the ice from his face and in the protection of which he ate his biscuits. For the moment the cold space was outwitted. The dog took satisfaction in the fire, stretching out close enough for warmth and far enough away to escape being singed.

When the man had finished, he filled his pipe and took his comfortable time over a smoke. Then he pulled on his mittens, settled the ear-flaps of his cap firmly about his ears, and took the creek trail up the left fork. The dog was disappointed and yearned back toward the fire. This man did not know cold. Possibly all the generations of his ancestry had been ignorant of cold, of real cold, of cold one hundred and seven degrees below freezing point. But the dog knew; all its ancestry knew, and it had inherited the knowledge. And it knew that it was not good to walk abroad in such fearful cold. It was the time to lie snug in a hole in the snow and wait for a curtain of cloud to be drawn across the face of outer space whence this cold came. On the other hand, there was no keen intimacy between the dog and the man. The one was the toil-slave of the other, and the only caresses it had ever received were the caresses of the whiplash and of harsh and menacing throat-sounds that threatened the whip-lash. So, the dog made no effort to communicate its apprehension to the man.

It was not concerned in the welfare of the man, it was for its own sake that it yearned back toward the fire. But the man whistled, and spoke to it with the sound of whiplashes and the dog swung in at the man's heel and followed after.

The man took a chew of tobacco and proceeded to start a new amber beard. Also, his moist breath quickly powdered with white his mustache, eyebrows, and lashes. There did not seem to be so many springs on the left fork of the Henderson, and for half an hour the man saw no signs of any. And then it happened. At a place where there were no signs, where the soft, unbroken snow seemed to advertise solidity beneath, the man broke through. It was not deep. He wet himself halfway to the knees before he floundered out to the firm crust.

He was angry, and cursed his luck aloud. He had hoped to get into camp with the boys at six o'clock, and this would delay him an hour, for he would have to build a fire and dry out his foot-gear. This was imperative at that low temperature—he knew that much; and he turned aside to the bank, which he climbed. On top, tangled in the underbrush about the trunks of several small spruce trees, was a high-water deposit of dry firewood—sticks and twigs, principally, but also larger portions of seasoned branches and fine, dry, last-year's grasses. He threw down several large pieces on top of the snow. This served for a foundation and prevented the young flame from drowning itself in the snow it otherwise would melt. The flame he got by touching a match to a small shred of birch bark that he took from his pocket. This burned even more readily than paper. Placing it on the foundation, he fed the young flame with wisps of dry grass and with the tiniest dry twigs.

He worked slowly and carefully, keenly aware of his danger. Gradually, as the flame grew stronger, he increased the size of the twigs with which he fed it. He squatted in the snow, pulling the twigs out from their entanglement in the brush and feeding directly to the flame. He knew there must be no failure. When it is seventy-five below zero, a man must not fail in his first attempt to build a fire—that is, if his feet are wet. If his feet are dry, and he fails, he can run along the trail for half a mile and restore his circulation. But the circulation of wet and freezing feet cannot be restored by running when it is seventy-five below. No matter how fast he runs, the wet feet will freeze the harder.

All this the man knew. The old-timer on Sulphur Creek had told him about it the previous fall, and now he was appreciating the advice. Already all sensation had gone out of his feet. To build the fire he had been forced to remove his mittens, and the fingers had quickly gone numb. His pace of four miles an hour had kept his heart pumping blood to the surface of his body and to all the extremities. But the instant he stopped, the action of the pump eased down. The cold of space smote the unprotected tip of the planet, and he, being on that unprotected tip, received the full force of the blow. The blood of his body recoiled before it. The blood was alive, like the dog, and like the dog it wanted to hide away and cover itself up from the fearful cold. So long as he walked four miles an hour, he pumped that blood, willy-nilly, to the surface; but now it ebbed away and sank down into the recesses of his body. The extremities were the first to feel its absence. His wet feet froze the faster, and his exposed fingers numbed the faster, though they had not yet begun to freeze. Nose and cheeks were already freezing, while the skin of all his body chilled as it lost its blood.

But he was safe. Toes and nose and cheeks would be only touched by the frost, for the fire was beginning to burn with strength. He was feeding it with twigs the size of his finger. In another minute he would be able to feed it with branches the size of his wrist, and then he could remove his wet foot-gear, and, while it dried, he could keep his naked feet warm by the fire, rubbing them at first, of course, with snow. The fire was a success. He was safe. He remembered the advice of the old timer on Sulphur Creek, and smiled. The old-timer had been very serious in laying down the law that no man must travel alone in the Klondike after fifty below. Well, here he was; he had had the accident; he was alone; and he had saved himself. Those old-timers were rather womanish, some of them, he thought. All a man had to do was to keep his head, and he was all right. Any man who was a man could travel alone. But it was surprising, the rapidity with which his cheeks and nose were freezing. And he had not thought his fingers could go lifeless in so short a time. Lifeless they were, for he could scarcely make them move together to grip a twig, and they seemed remote from his body and from him. When he touched a twig, he had to look and see whether or not he had hold of it. The wires were pretty well down between him and his finger-ends.

All of which counted for little. There was the fire, snapping and crackling and promising life with every dancing flame. He started to untie his moccasins. They were coated with ice; the thick German socks were like sheaths of iron halfway to the knees; and the moccasin strings were like rods of steel all twisted and knotted as by some conflagration. For a moment he tugged with his numb fingers, then, realizing the folly of it, he drew his sheath-knife.

But before he could cut the strings, it happened. It was his own fault or, rather, his mistake. He should not have built the fire under the spruce tree. He should have built it in the open. But it had been easier to pull the twigs from the brush and drop them directly on the fire. Now the tree under which he had done this carried a weight of snow on its boughs. No wind had blown for weeks, and each bough was fully freighted. Each time he had pulled a twig he had communicated a slight agitation to the tree—an imperceptible agitation, so far as he was concerned, but an agitation sufficient to bring about the disaster. High up in the tree one bough capsized its load of snow. This fell on the boughs beneath, capsizing them. This process continued, spreading out and involving the whole tree. It grew like an avalanche, and it descended without warning upon the man and the fire, and the fire was blotted out! Where it had burned was a mantle of fresh and disordered snow.

The man was shocked. It was as though he had just heard his own sentence of death. For a moment he sat and stared at the spot where the fire had been. Then he grew very calm. Perhaps the old-timer on Sulphur Creek was right. If he had only had a trail-mate he would have been in no danger now. The trail-mate could have built the fire. Well, it was up to him to build the fire over again, and this second time there must be no failure. Even if he succeeded, he would most likely lose some toes. His feet must be badly frozen by now, and there would be some time before the second fire was ready.

Such were his thoughts, but he did not sit and think them. He was busy all the time they were passing through his mind. He made a new foundation for a fire, this time in the open, where no treacherous tree could blot it out. Next, he gathered dry grasses and tiny twigs from the high-water flotsam. He could not bring his fingers together to pull them out, but he was able to gather them by the handful. In this way he got many rotten twigs and bits of green moss that were undesirable, but it was the best he could do. He worked methodically, even collecting an armful of the larger branches to be used later when the fire gathered strength. And all the while the dog sat and watched him, a certain yearning wistfulness in its eyes, for it looked upon him as the fire-provider, and the fire was slow in coming.

When all was ready, the man reached in his pocket for a second piece of birch bark. He knew the bark was there, and, though he could not feel it with his fingers, he could hear its crisp rustling as he fumbled for it. Try as he would, he could not clutch hold of it. And all the time in his consciousness, was the knowledge that each instant his feet were freezing. This thought tended to put him in a panic, but he fought against it and kept calm. He pulled on his mittens with his teeth, and threshed his arms back and forth, beating his hands with all his might against his sides. He did this sitting down, and he stood up to do it; and all the while the dog sat in the snow, its wolf-brush of a tail curled around warmly over its forefeet, its sharp wolf-ears pricked forward intently as it watched the man. And the man, as he beat and threshed with his arms and hands, felt a great surge of envy as he regarded the creature that was warm and secure in its natural covering.

After a time he was aware of the first far-away signals of sensation in his beaten fingers. The faint tingling grew stronger till it evolved into a stinging ache that was excruciating, but which the man hailed with satisfaction. He stripped the mitten from his right hand and fetched forth the birch bark. The exposed fingers were quickly going numb again. Next he brought out his bunch of sulphur matches. But the tremendous cold had already driven the life out of his fingers. In his effort to separate one match from the others, the whole bunch fell in the snow. He tried to pick it out of the snow, but failed. The dead fingers could neither touch nor clutch. He was very careful. He drove the thought of his freezing feet, and nose, and cheeks, out of his mind, devoting his whole soul to the matches. He watched, using the sense of vision in place of that of touch, and when he saw his fingers on each side the bunch, he closed them—that is, he willed to close them, for the wires were down, and the fingers did not obey. He pulled the mitten on the right hand and beat it fiercely against his knee. Then, with both mittened hands, he scooped the bunch of matches, along with much snow, into his lap. Yet he was no better off.

After some manipulation he managed to get the bunch between the heels of his mittened hands. In this fashion he carried it to his mouth. The ice crackled and snapped when by a violent effort he opened his mouth. He drew the lower jaw in, curled the upper lip out of the way, and scraped the bunch with his upper teeth in order to separate a match. He succeeded in getting one, which he dropped on his lap. He was no better off. He could not pick it up. Then he devised a way. He picked it up in his teeth and scratched it on his leg. Twenty times he scratched before he succeeded in lighting it. As it flamed he held it with his teeth to the birch bark. But the burning brimstone went up his nostrils and into his lungs, causing him to cough spasmodically. The match fell into the snow and went out.

The old-timer on Sulphur Creek was right, he thought in the moment of controlled despair that ensued: after fifty below, a man should travel with a partner. He beat his hands, but failed in exciting any sensation. Suddenly he bared both hands, removing the mittens with his teeth. He caught the whole bunch between the heels of his hands. His arm muscles not being frozen enabled him to press the hand-heels tightly against the matches. Then he scratched the bunch along his leg. It flared into flame, seventy sulphur matches at once! There was no wind to blow them out. He kept his head to one side to escape the strangling fumes, and held the blazing bunch to the birch-bark. As he so held it, he became aware of sensation in his hand. His flesh was burning. He could smell it. Deep down below the surface he could feel it. The sensation developed into pain that grew acute. And still he endured it, holding the flame of the matches clumsily to the bark that would not light readily because his own burning hands were in the way, absorbing most of the flame.

At last, when he could endure no more, he jerked his hands apart. The blazing matches fell sizzling into the snow, but the birch bark was alight. He began laying dry grasses and the tiniest twigs on the flame. He could not pick and choose, for he had to lift the fuel between the heels of his hands. Small pieces of rotten wood and green moss clung to the twigs, and he bit them off as well as he could with his teeth. He cherished the flame carefully and awkwardly. It meant life, and it must not perish. The withdrawal of blood from the surface of his body now made him begin to shiver, and he grew more awkward. A large piece of green moss fell squarely on the little fire. He tried to poke it out with his fingers, but his shivering frame made him poke too far and he disrupted the nucleus of the little fire, the burning grasses and tiny twigs separating and scattering. He tried to poke them together again, but in spite of the tenseness of the effort, his shivering got away with him, and the twigs were hopelessly scattered. Each twig gushed a puff of smoke and went out. The fire-provider had failed. As he looked apathetically about him, his eyes chanced on the dog, sitting across the ruins of the fire from him, in the snow, making restless, hunching movements, slightly lifting one forefoot and then the other, shifting its weight back and forth on them with wistful eagerness.

The sight of the dog put a wild idea into his head. He remembered the tale of the man, caught in a blizzard, who killed a steer and crawled inside the carcass, and so was saved. He would kill the dog and bury his hands in the warm body until the numbness went out of them. Then he could build another fire. He spoke to the dog, calling it to him; but in his voice was a strange note of fear that frightened the animal, who had never known the man to speak in such way before. Something was the matter, and its suspicious nature sensed danger—it knew not what danger, but somewhere, somehow, in its brain arose an apprehension of the man. It flattened its ears down at the sound of the man's voice, and its restless, hunching movements and the liftings and shiftings of its forefeet became more pronounced; but it would not come to the man. He got on his hands and knees and crawled toward the dog. This unusual posture again excited suspicion, and the animal sidled mincingly away.

The man sat up in the snow for a moment and struggled for calmness. Then he pulled on his mittens, by means of his teeth, and got upon his feet. He glanced down at first in order to assure himself that he was really standing up, for the absence of sensation in his feet left him unrelated to the earth. His erect position in itself started to drive the webs of suspicion from the dog's mind; and when he spoke peremptorily, with the sound of whiplashes in his voice, the dog rendered its customary allegiance and came to him. As it came within reaching distance, the man lost his control. His arms flashed out to the dog, and he experienced genuine surprise when he discovered that his hands could not clutch, that there was neither bend nor feeling in the fingers. He had forgotten for the moment that they were frozen and that they were freezing more and more. All this happened quickly, and before the animal could get away, he encircled its body with his arms. He sat down in the snow, and in this fashion held the dog, while it snarled and whined and struggled.

But it was all he could do, hold its body encircled in his arms and sit there. He realized that he could not kill the dog. There was no way to do it. With his helpless hands he could neither draw nor hold his sheath knife nor throttle the animal. He released it, and it plunged wildly away, with tail between its legs, and still snarling. It halted forty feet away and surveyed him curiously, with ears sharply pricked forward. The man looked down at his hands in order to locate them, and found them hanging on the ends of his arms. It struck him as curious that one should have to use his eyes in order to find out where his hands were. He began threshing his arms back and forth, beating the mittened hands against his sides. He did this for five minutes, violently, and his heart pumped enough blood up to the surface to put a stop to his shivering. But no sensation was aroused in the hands. He had an impression that they hung like weights on the ends of his arms, but when he tried to run the impression down, he could not find it.

A certain fear of death, dull and oppressive, came to him. This fear quickly became poignant as he realized that it was no longer a mere matter of freezing his fingers and toes, or of losing his hands and feet, but that it was a matter of life and death with the chances against him. This threw him into a panic, and he turned and ran up the creek-bed along the old, dim trail. The dog joined in behind and kept up with him. He ran blindly, without intention, in fear such as he had never known in his life. Slowly, as he plowed and floundered through the snow, he began to see things again,—the banks of the creek, the old timber-jams, the leafless aspens, and the sky. The running made him feel better. He did not shiver. Maybe, if he ran on, his feet would thaw out; and, anyway, if he ran far enough, he would reach camp and the boys. Without doubt he would lose some fingers and toes and some of his face; but the boys would take care of him, and save the rest of him when he got there. And at the same time there was another thought in his mind that said he would never get to the camp and the boys; that it was too many miles away, that the freezing had too great a start on him, and that he would soon be stiff and dead. This thought he kept in the background and refused to consider. Sometimes it pushed itself forward and demanded to be heard, but he thrust it back and strove to think of other things.

It struck him as curious that he could run at all on feet so frozen that he could not feel them when they struck the earth and took the weight of his body. He seemed to himself to skim along above the surface, and to have no connection with the earth. Somewhere he had once seen a winged Mercury, and he wondered if Mercury felt as he felt when skimming over the earth.

His theory of running until he reached camp and the boys had one flaw in it: he lacked the endurance. Several times he stumbled, and finally he tottered, crumpled up, and fell. When he tried to rise, he failed. He must sit and rest, he decided, and next time he would merely walk and keep on going. As he sat and regained his breath, he noted that he was feeling quite warm and comfortable. He was not shivering, and it even seemed that a warm glow had come to his chest and trunk. And yet, when he touched his nose or cheeks, there was no sensation. Running would not thaw them out. Nor would it thaw out his hands and feet. Then the thought came to him that the frozen portions of his body must be extending. He tried to keep this thought down, to forget it, to think of something else; he was aware of the panicky feeling that it caused, and he was afraid of the panic. But the thought asserted itself, and persisted, until it produced a vision of his body totally frozen. This was too much, and he made another wild run along the trail. Once he slowed down to a walk, but the thought of the freezing extending itself made him run again.

And all the time the dog ran with him, at his heels. When he fell down a second time, it curled its tail over its forefeet and sat in front of him, facing him, curiously eager and intent. The warmth and security of the animal angered him, and he cursed it till it flattened down its ears appeasingly. This time the shivering came more quickly upon the man. He was losing in his battle with the frost. It was creeping into his body from all sides. The thought of it drove him on, but he ran no more than a hundred feet, when he staggered and pitched headlong. It was his last panic. When he had recovered his breath and control, he sat up and entertained in his mind the conception of meeting death with dignity. However, the conception did not come to him in such terms. His idea of it was that he had been making a fool of himself, running around like a chicken with its head cut off—such was the simile that occurred to him. Well, he was bound to freeze anyway, and he might as well take it decently. With this new-found peace of mind came the first glimmerings of drowsiness. A good idea, he thought, to sleep off to death. It was like taking an anaesthetic. Freezing was not so bad as people thought. There were lots worse ways to die.

He pictured the boys finding his body next day. Suddenly he found himself with them, coming along the trail and looking for himself. And, still with them, he came around a turn in the trail and found himself lying in the snow. He did not belong with himself any more, for even then he was out of himself, standing with the boys and looking at himself in the snow. It certainly was cold, was his thought. When he got back to the States he could tell the folks what real cold was. He drifted on from this to a vision of the old-timer on Sulphur Creek. He could see him quite clearly, warm and comfortable, and smoking a pipe.

"You were right, old hoss; you were right," the man mumbled to the old-timer of Sulphur Creek.

Then the man drowsed off into what seemed to him the most comfortable and satisfying sleep he had ever known. The dog sat facing him and waiting. The brief day drew to a close in a long, slow twilight. There were no signs of a fire to be made, and, besides, never in the dog's experience had it known a man to sit like that in the snow and make no fire. As the twilight drew on, its eager yearning for the fire mastered it, and with a great lifting and shifting of forefeet, it whined softly, then flattened its ears down in anticipation of being chidden by the man. But the man remained silent. Later, the dog whined loudly. And still later it crept close to the man and caught the scent of death. This made the animal bristle and back away. A little longer it delayed, howling under the stars that leaped and danced and shone brightly in the cold sky. Then it turned and trotted up the trail in the direction of the camp it knew, where were the other food-providers and fire-providers.

A Father-to-Be

SAUL BELLOW

*Like Jack London, Saul Bellow (1915–2005) is interested in American indi-
vidualism and the kind of character produced under conditions of freedom
and equality. His story (1955), set not in the wilderness but in New York
City, examines the solitary, modern individual living in very crowded places.
Rogin, a thirty-one-year-old research chemist on his way to have supper with
his fiancée, falls into a "peculiar state," leading him to unusual reflections
about money, love, happiness, and freedom, prompted by the people he
encounters. Although at first liberated from personal concerns to appreciate
the people around him ("everyone has some weight to carry"), he increasingly comes to view them through his own hopes, fears, and fantasies.*

*What sort of individual is this "father-to-be"? Compared with Jack Lon-
don's miner, where does he stand on the scales of self-knowledge, self-respect,
self-confidence, self-absorption, and self-pity? How does the protagonist's
scientific outlook shape his thoughts and feelings about the world and its
possibilities? What does Rogin want from life? What sort of husband, father,
and citizen is he likely to be—or to father?*

The strangest notions had a way of forcing themselves into Rogin's mind.
Just thirty-one and passable-looking, with short black hair, small eyes,
but a high, open forehead, he was a research chemist, and his mind was generally serious and dependable. But on a snowy Sunday evening while this stocky
man, buttoned to the chin in a Burberry coat and walking in his preposterous gait—feet turned outward—was going toward the subway, he fell into a
peculiar state.

He was on his way to have supper with his fiancée. She had phoned him a short while ago and said, "You'd better pick up a few things on the way."

"What do we need?"

"Some roast beef, for one thing. I bought a quarter of a pound coming home from my aunt's."

"Why a quarter of a pound, Joan?" said Rogin, deeply annoyed. "That's just about enough for one good sandwich."

"So you have to stop at a delicatessen. I had no more money."

He was about to ask, "What happened to the thirty dollars I gave you on Wednesday?" but he knew that would not be right.

"I had to give Phyllis money for the cleaning woman," said Joan.

Phyllis, Joan's cousin, was a young divorcee, extremely wealthy. The two women shared an apartment.

"Roast beef," he said, "and what else?"

"Some shampoo, sweetheart. We've used up all the shampoo. And hurry, darling, I've missed you all day."

"And I've missed you," said Rogin, but to tell the truth he had been worrying most of the time. He had a younger brother whom he was putting through college. And his mother, whose annuity wasn't quite enough in these days of inflation and high taxes, needed money too. Joan had debts he was helping her to pay, for she wasn't working. She was looking for something suitable to do. Beautiful, well educated, aristocratic in her attitude, she couldn't clerk in a dime store; she couldn't model clothes (Rogin thought this made girls vain and stiff, and he didn't want her to); she couldn't be a waitress or a cashier. What could she be? Well, something would turn up and meantime Rogin hesitated to complain. He paid her bills—the dentist, the department store, the osteopath, the doctor, the psychiatrist. At Christmas, Rogin almost went mad. Joan bought him a velvet smoking jacket with frog fasteners, a beautiful pipe, and a pouch. She bought Phyllis a garnet brooch, an Italian silk umbrella, and a gold cigarette holder. For other friends, she bought Dutch pewter and Swedish glassware. Before she was through, she had spent five hundred dollars of Rogin's money. He loved her too much to show his suffering. He believed she had a far better nature than his. She didn't worry about money. She had a marvelous character, always cheerful, and she really didn't need a psychiatrist at all. She went to one because Phyllis did and it made her curious. She tried too much to keep up with her cousin, whose father had made millions in the rug business.

While the woman in the drugstore was wrapping the shampoo bottle, a clear idea suddenly arose in Rogin's thoughts: Money surrounds you in life as the earth does in death. Superimposition is the universal law. Who is free? No one is free. Who has no burdens? Everyone is under pressure. The very rocks, the waters of the earth, beasts, men, children—everyone has some weight to carry. This idea was extremely clear to him at first. Soon it became rather vague, but it had a great effect nevertheless, as if someone had given him a valuable gift. (Not like the velvet smoking jacket he couldn't bring himself to wear, or the pipe it choked him to smoke.) The notion that all were under pressure and affliction, instead of saddening him, had the opposite influence. It put him in a wonderful mood. It was extraordinary how happy he became and, in addition, clear-sighted. His eyes all at once were opened to what was around him. He saw with delight how the druggist and the woman who wrapped the shampoo bottle were smiling and flirting, how the lines of worry in her face went over into lines of cheer and the druggist's receding gums did not hinder his kidding and friendliness. And in the delicatessen, also, it was amazing how much Rogin noted and what happiness it gave him simply to be there.

Delicatessens on Sunday night, when all other stores are shut, will overcharge you ferociously, and Rogin would normally have been on guard, but he was not tonight, or scarcely so. Smells of pickle, sausage, mustard, and smoked fish overjoyed him. He pitied the people who would buy the chicken salad and chopped herring; they could do it only because their sight was too dim to see what they were getting—the fat flakes of pepper on the chicken, the soppy herring, mostly vinegar-soaked stale bread. Who would buy them? Late risers, people living alone, waking up in the darkness of the afternoon, finding their refrigerators empty, or people whose gaze was turned inward. The roast beef looked not bad, and Rogin ordered a pound.

While the storekeeper was slicing the meat, he yelled at a Puerto Rican kid who was reaching for a bag of chocolate cookies, "Hey, you want to pull me down the whole display on yourself? You, *chico*, wait a half a minute." This storekeeper, though he looked like one of Pancho Villa's bandits, the kind that smeared their enemies with syrup and staked them down on anthills, a man with toadlike eyes and stout hands made to clasp pistols hung around his belly, was not so bad. He was a New York man, thought Rogin—who was from Albany himself—a New York man toughened by every abuse of the city, trained to suspect everyone. But in his own realm, on the board behind the counter, there was justice. Even clemency.

The Puerto Rican kid wore a complete cowboy outfit—a green hat with white braid, guns, chaps, spurs, boots, and gauntlets—but he couldn't speak any English. Rogin unhooked the cellophane bag of hard circular cookies and gave it to him. The boy tore the cellophane with his teeth and began to chew one of those dry chocolate disks. Rogin recognized his state—the energetic dream of childhood. Once, he, too, had found these dry biscuits delicious. It would have bored him now to eat one.

What else would Joan like? Rogin thought fondly. Some strawberries?

"Give me some frozen strawberries. No, raspberries, she likes those better. And heavy cream. And some rolls, cream cheese, and some of those rubber-looking gherkins."

"What rubber?"

"Those, deep green, with eyes. Some ice cream might be in order, too."

He tried to think of a compliment, a good comparison, an endearment, for Joan when she'd open the door. What about her complexion? There was really nothing to compare her sweet, small, daring, shapely, timid, defiant, loving face to. How difficult she was, and how beautiful!

As Rogin went down into the stony, odorous, metallic, captive air of the subway, he was diverted by an unusual confession made by a man to his friend. These were two very tall men, shapeless in their winter clothes, as if their coats concealed suits of chain mail.

"So, how long have you known me?" said one.

"Twelve years."

"Well, I have an admission to make," he said. "I've decided that I might as well. For years I've been a heavy drinker. You didn't know. Practically an alcoholic."

But his friend was not surprised, and he answered immediately, "Yes, I did know."

"You knew? Impossible! How could you?"

Why, thought Rogin, as if it could be a secret! Look at that long, austere, alcohol-washed face, that drink-ruined nose, the skin by his ears like turkey wattles, and those whisky-saddened eyes.

"Well, I did know, though."

"You couldn't have. I can't believe it." He was upset, and his friend didn't seem to want to soothe him. "But it's all right now," he said. "I've been going to a doctor and taking pills, a new revolutionary Danish discovery. It's a miracle. I'm beginning to believe they can cure you of anything and everything. You can't beat the Danes in science. They do everything. They turned a man into a woman."

"That isn't how they stop you from drinking, is it?"

"No. I hope not. This is only like aspirin. It's superaspirin. They called it the aspirin of the future. But if you use it, you have to stop drinking."

Rogin's illuminated mind asked of itself while the human tides of the subway swayed back and forth, and cars linked and transparent like fish bladders raced under the streets: How come he thought nobody would know what everybody couldn't help knowing? And, as a chemist, he asked himself what kind of compound this new Danish drug might be, and started thinking about various inventions of his own, synthetic albumen, a cigarette that lit itself, a cheaper motor fuel. Ye gods, but he needed money! As never before. What was to be done? His mother was growing more and more difficult. On Friday night, she had neglected to cut up his meat for him, and he was hurt. She had sat at the table motionless, with her long-suffering face, severe, and let him cut his own meat, a thing she almost never did. She had always spoiled him and made his brother envy him. But what she expected now! Oh, Lord, how he had to pay, and it had never even occurred to him formerly that these things might have a price.

Seated, one of the passengers, Rogin recovered his calm, happy, even clair-voyant state of mind. To think of money was to think as the world wanted you to think; then you'd never be your own master. When people said they wouldn't do something for love or money, they meant that love and money were opposite passions, and one the enemy of the other. He went on to reflect how little people knew about this, how they slept through life, how small a light the light of consciousness was. Rogin's clean, snub-nosed face shone while his heart was torn with joy at these deeper thoughts of our ignorance. You might take this drunkard as an example, who for long years thought his closest friends never suspected he drank. Rogin looked up and down the aisle for this remarkable knightly symbol, but he was gone.

However, there was no lack of things to see. There was a small girl with a new white muff; into the muff a doll's head was sewn, and the child was happy and affectionately vain of it, while her old man, stout and grim, with a huge scowling nose, kept picking her up and resetting her in the seat, as if he were trying to change her into something else. Then another child, led by her mother, boarded the car, and this other child carried the very same doll-faced muff, and this greatly annoyed both parents. The woman, who looked like a difficult, contentious woman, took her daughter away. It seemed to Rogin that each child was in love with its own muff and didn't even see the other, but it was one of his foibles to think he understood the hearts of little children. A foreign family next engaged his attention. They looked like Central Americans to him. On one side the mother, quite old, dark-faced, white-haired, and worn out; on the other a son with the whitened, porous hands of a dishwasher. But what was the dwarf who sat between them—a son or a daughter? The hair was long and wavy and the cheeks smooth, but the shirt and tie were masculine. The overcoat was feminine, but the shoes—the shoes were a puzzle. A pair of brown oxfords with an outer seam like a man's, but Baby Louis heels like a woman's—a plain toe like a man's, but a strap across the instep like a wom-an's. No stockings. That didn't help much. The dwarf's fingers were beringed, but without a wedding band. There were small grim dents in the cheeks. The eyes were puffy and concealed, but Rogin did not doubt that they could reveal strange things if they chose and that this was a creature of remarkable understanding. He had for many years owned de la Mare's *Memoirs of a Midget*. Now he took a resolve; he would read it. As soon as he had decided, he was free from his consuming curiosity as to the dwarf's sex and was able to look at the person who sat beside him.

Thoughts very often grow fertile in the subway, because of the motion, the great company, the subtlety of the rider's state as he rattles under streets and rivers, under the foundations of great buildings, and Rogin's mind had already been strangely stimulated. Clasping the bag of groceries from which there rose odors of bread and pickle spice, he was following a train of reflections, first about the chemistry of sex determination, the X and Y chromosomes, hereditary linkages, the uterus, afterward about his brother as a tax exemption. He recalled two dreams of the night before. In one, an undertaker had offered to cut his hair, and he had refused. In another, he had been carrying a woman on his head. Sad dreams, both! Very sad! Which was the woman—Joan or Mother? And the undertaker—his lawyer? He gave a deep sigh, and by force of habit began to put together his synthetic albumen that was to revolutionize the entire egg industry.

Meanwhile, he had not interrupted his examination of the passengers and had fallen into a study of the man next to him. This was a man whom he had never in his life seen before but with whom he now suddenly felt linked through all existence. He was middle-aged, sturdy, with clear skin and blue eyes. His hands were clean, well formed, but Rogin did not approve of them. The coat he wore was a fairly expensive blue check such as Rogin would never have chosen for himself. He would not have worn blue suède shoes, either, or such a faultless hat, a cumbersome felt animal of a hat encircled by a high, fat ribbon. There are all kinds of dandies, not all of them are of the flaunting kind; some are dandies of respectability, and Rogin's fellow passenger was one of these. His straight-nosed profile was handsome, yet he had betrayed his gift, for he was flat-looking. But in his flat way he seemed to warn people that he wanted no difficulties with them, he wanted nothing to do with them. Wearing such blue suède shoes, he could not afford to have people treading on his feet, and he seemed to draw about himself a circle of privilege, notifying all others to mind their own business and let him read his paper. He was holding a *Tribune*, and perhaps it would be overstatement to say that he was reading. He was holding it.

His clear skin and blue eyes, his straight and purely Roman nose—even the way he sat—all strongly suggested one person to Rogin: Joan. He tried to escape the comparison, but it couldn't be helped. This man not only looked like Joan's father, whom Rogin detested; he looked like Joan herself. Forty years hence, a son of hers, provided she had one, might be like this. A son of hers? Of such a son, he himself, Rogin, would be the father. Lacking in dominant traits as compared with Joan, his heritage would not appear. Probably the children would resemble her. Yes, think forty years ahead, and a man like this, who sat by him knee to knee in the hurtling car among their fellow creatures, unconscious participants in a sort of great carnival of transit—such a man would carry forward what had been Rogin.

This was why he felt bound to him through all existence. What were forty years reckoned against eternity! Forty years were gone, and he was gazing at his own son. Here he was. Rogin was frightened and moved. "My son! My son!" he said to himself, and the pity of it almost made him burst into tears. The holy and frightful work of the masters of life and death brought this about. We were their instruments. We worked toward ends we thought were our own. But no! The whole thing was so unjust. To suffer, to labor, to toil and force your way through the spikes of life, to crawl through its darkest caverns, to push through the worst, to struggle under the weight of economy, to make money—only to become the father of a fourth-rate man of the world like this, so flat-looking with his ordinary, clean, rosy, uninteresting, self-satisfied, fundamentally bourgeois face. What a curse to have a dull son! A son like this, who could never understand his father. They had absolutely nothing, but nothing, in common, he and this neat, chubby, blue-eyed man. He was so pleased, thought Rogin, with all he owned and all he did and all he was that he could hardly unfasten his lip. Look at that lip, sticking up at the tip like a little thorn or egg tooth. He wouldn't give anyone the time of day. Would this perhaps be general forty years from now? Would personalities be chillier as the world aged and grew colder? The inhumanity of the next generation incensed Rogin. Father and son had no sign to make to each other. Terrible! Inhuman! What a vision of existence it gave him. Man's personal aims were nothing, illusion. The life force occupied each of us in turn in its progress toward its own fulfillment, trampling on our individual humanity, using us for its own ends like mere dinosaurs or bees, exploiting love heartlessly, making us engage in the social process, labor, struggle for money, and submit to the law of pressure, the universal law of layers, superimposition!

What the blazes am I getting into? Rogin thought. To be the father of a throwback to *her* father. The image of this white-haired, gross, peevish, old man with his ugly selfish blue eyes revolted Rogin. This was how his grandson would look. Joan, with whom Rogin was now more and more displeased, could not help that. For her, it was inevitable. But did it have to be inevitable for him? Well, then, Rogin, you fool, don't be a damned instrument. Get out of the way!

But it was too late for this, because he had already experienced the sensation of sitting next to his own son, his son and Joan's. He kept staring at him, waiting for him to say something, but the presumptive son remained coldly silent though he must have been aware of Rogin's scrutiny. They even got out at the same stop—Sheridan Square. When they stepped to the platform, the man, without even looking at Rogin, went away in a different direction in his detestable blue-checked coat, with his rosy, nasty face.

The whole thing upset Rogin very badly. When he approached Joan's door and heard Phyllis's little dog Henri barking even before he could knock, his face was very tense. I won't be used, he declared to himself. I have my own right to exist. Joan had better watch out. She had a light way of by-passing grave questions he had given earnest thought to. She always assumed no really disturbing thing would happen. He could not afford the luxury of such a carefree, debonair attitude himself, because he had to work hard and earn money so that disturbing things would *not* happen. Well, at the moment this situation could not be helped, and he really did not mind the money if he could feel that she was not necessarily the mother of such a son as his subway son or entirely the daughter of that awful, obscene father of hers. After all, Rogin was not himself so much like either of his parents, and quite different from his brother.

Joan came to the door, wearing one of Phyllis's expensive housecoats. It suited her very well. At first sight of her happy face, Rogin was brushed by the shadow of resemblance; the touch of it was extremely light, almost figmentary, but it made his flesh tremble.

She began to kiss him, saying, "Oh, my baby. You're covered with snow. Why didn't you wear your hat? It's all over its little head"—her favorite third-person endearment.

"Well, let me put down this bag of stuff. Let me take off my coat," grumbled Rogin, and escaped from her embrace. Why couldn't she wait making up to him? "It's so hot in here. My face is burning. Why do you keep the place at this temperature? And that damned dog keeps barking. If you didn't keep it cooped up, it wouldn't be so spoiled and noisy. Why doesn't anybody ever walk him?"

"Oh, it's not really so hot here! You've just come in from the cold. Don't you think this housecoat fits me better than Phyllis? Especially across the hips. She thinks so, too. She may sell it to me."

"I hope not," Rogin almost exclaimed.

She brought a towel to dry the melting snow from his short black hair. The flurry of rubbing excited Henri intolerably, and Joan locked him up in the bedroom, where he jumped persistently against the door with a rhythmic sound of claws on the wood.

Joan said, "Did you bring the shampoo?"

"Here it is."

"Then I'll wash your hair before dinner. Come."

"I don't want it washed."

"Oh, come on," she said, laughing.

Her lack of consciousness of guilt amazed him. He did not see how it could be. And the carpeted, furnished, lamp-lit, curtained room seemed to stand against his vision. So that he felt accusing and angry, his spirit sore and bitter, but it did not seem fitting to say why. Indeed, he began to worry lest the reason for it all slip away from him.

They took off his coat and his shirt in the bathroom, and she filled the sink. Rogin was full of his troubled emotions; now that his chest was bare he could feel them even more and he said to himself, I'll have a thing or two to tell her pretty soon. I'm not letting them get away with it. "Do you think," he was going to tell her, "that I alone was made to carry the burden of the whole world on me? Do you think I was born to be taken advantage of and sacrificed? Do you think I'm just a natural resource, like a coal mine, or oil well, or fishery, or the like? Remember, that I'm a man is no reason why I should be loaded down. I have a soul in me no bigger or stronger than yours.

"Take away the externals, like the muscles, deeper voice, and so forth, and what remains? A pair of spirits, practically alike. So why shouldn't there also be equality? I can't always be the strong one."

"Sit here," said Joan, bringing up a kitchen stool to the sink. "Your hair's gotten all matted."

He sat with his breast against the cool enamel, his chin on the edge of the basin, the green, hot, radiant water reflecting the glass and the tile, and the sweet, cool, fragrant juice of the shampoo poured on his head. She began to wash him.

"You have the healthiest-looking scalp," she said. "It's all pink."

He answered, "Well, it should be white. There must be something wrong with me."

"But there's absolutely nothing wrong with you," she said, and pressed against him from behind, surrounding him, pouring the water gently over him until it seemed to him that the water came from within him, it was the warm fluid of his own secret loving spirit overflowing into the sink, green and foaming, and the words he had rehearsed he forgot, and his anger at his son-to-be disappeared altogether, and he sighed, and said to her from the water-filled hollow of the sink, "You always have such wonderful ideas, Joan. You know? You have a kind of instinct, a regular gift."

Harrison Bergeron

Kurt Vonnegut Jr.

Central to the American creed is the principle of equality, beginning with the notion that all human beings possess certain fundamental rights and equal standing before the law. Our concern for equality has expanded over the past half century to focus also on inequalities in opportunities, wealth, achievement, and social condition. What good is an equal right to pursue happiness if one lacks the native gifts or the social means to exercise it successfully? In this satirical story (1961), set in a future time in which "everybody was finally equal . . . every which way," Kurt Vonnegut Jr. (1922–2007) challenges our devotion to equality and invites us to consider the costs of pursuing it too zealously.

Does the society portrayed here represent a fulfillment of the ideal of equality in the Declaration of Independence, or rather a perversion of the principle? Does opposing invidious distinctions, envy, and feelings of inferiority require reducing all to the lowest common denominator, and is this the true path to "social justice"? Would homogeneity attained by artificially raising up the low, producing a nation of Harrisons rather than a nation of Hazels—a prospect offered by biotechnological "enhancement"—be any more attractive?

The year was 2081, and everybody was finally equal. They weren't only equal before God and the law. They were equal every which way. Nobody was smarter than anybody else. Nobody was better looking than anybody else. Nobody was stronger or quicker than anybody else. All this equality was due to the 211th, 212th, and 213th Amendments to the Constitution, and to the unceasing vigilance of agents of the United States Handicapper General.

Some things about living still weren't quite right, though. April, for instance, still drove people crazy by not being springtime. And it was in that clammy month that the H-G men took George and Hazel Bergeron's fourteen-year-old son, Harrison, away.

It was tragic, all right, but George and Hazel couldn't think about it very hard. Hazel had a perfectly average intelligence, which meant she couldn't think about anything except in short bursts. And George, while his intelligence was way above normal, had a little mental handicap radio in his ear. He was required by law to wear it at all times. It was tuned to a government transmitter. Every twenty seconds or so, the transmitter would send out some sharp noise to keep people like George from taking unfair advantage of their brains.

George and Hazel were watching television. There were tears on Hazel's cheeks, but she'd forgotten for the moment what they were about.

On the television screen were ballerinas.

A buzzer sounded in George's head. His thoughts fled in panic, like bandits from a burglar alarm.

"That was a real pretty dance, that dance they just did," said Hazel.

"Huh?" said George.

"That dance—it was nice," said Hazel.

"Yup," said George. He tried to think a little about the ballerinas. They weren't really very good—no better than anybody else would have been, anyway. They were burdened with sash-weights and bags of birdshot, and their faces were masked, so that no one, seeing a free and graceful gesture or a pretty face, would feel like something the cat drug in. George was toying with the vague notion that maybe dancers shouldn't be handicapped. But he didn't get very far with it before another noise in his ear radio scattered his thoughts.

George winced. So did two out of the eight ballerinas.

Hazel saw him wince. Having no mental handicap herself, she had to ask George what the latest sound had been.

"Sounded like somebody hitting a milk bottle with a ball peen hammer," said George.

"I'd think it would be real interesting, hearing all the different sounds," said Hazel, a little envious. "All the things they think up."

"Um," said George.

"Only, if I was Handicapper General, you know what I would do?" said Hazel. Hazel, as a matter of fact, bore a strong resemblance to the Handicapper General, a woman named Diana Moon Glampers. "If I was Diana Moon Glampers," said Hazel, "I'd have chimes on Sunday—just chimes. Kind of in honor of religion."

"I could think, if it was just chimes," said George.

"Well—maybe make 'em real loud," said Hazel. "I think I'd make a good Handicapper General."

"Good as anybody else," said George.

"Who knows better'n I do what normal is?" said Hazel.

"Right," said George. He began to think glimmeringly about his abnormal son who was now in jail, about Harrison, but a twenty-one-gun salute in his head stopped that.

"Boy!" said Hazel, "that was a doozy, wasn't it?"

It was such a doozy that George was white and trembling, and tears stood on the rims of his red eyes. Two of the eight ballerinas had collapsed to the studio floor, were holding their temples.

"All of a sudden you look so tired," said Hazel. "Why don't you stretch out on the sofa, so's you can rest your handicap bag on the pillows, honey-bunch." She was referring to the forty-seven pounds of birdshot in a canvas bag, which was padlocked around George's neck. "Go on and rest the bag for a little while," she said. "I don't care if you're not equal to me for a while."

George weighed the bag with his hands. "I don't mind it," he said. "I don't notice it any more. It's just a part of me."

"You been so tired lately—kind of wore out," said Hazel. "If there was just some way we could make a little hole in the bottom of the bag, and just take out a few of them lead balls. Just a few."

"Two years in prison and two thousand dollars fine for every ball I took out," said George. "I don't call that a bargain."

"If you could just take a few out when you came home from work," said Hazel. "I mean—you don't compete with anybody around here. You just set around."

"If I tried to get away with it," said George, "then other people'd get away with it—and pretty soon we'd be right back to the dark ages again, with every-body competing against everybody else. You wouldn't like that, would you?"

"I'd hate it," said Hazel.

"There you are," said George. "The minute people start cheating on laws, what do you think happens to society?"

If Hazel hadn't been able to come up with an answer to this question, George couldn't have supplied one. A siren was going off in his head.

"Reckon it'd fall all apart," said Hazel.

"What would?" said George blankly.

"Society," said Hazel uncertainly. "Wasn't that what you just said?"

"Who knows?" said George.

The television program was suddenly interrupted for a news bulletin. It wasn't clear at first as to what the bulletin was about, since the announcer, like all announcers, had a serious speech impediment. For about half a minute, and in a state of high excitement, the announcer tried to say, "Ladies and gentlemen—"

He finally gave up, handed the bulletin to a ballerina to read.

"That's all right—" Hazel said of the announcer, "he tried. That's the big thing. He tried to do the best he could with what God gave him. He should get a nice raise for trying so hard."

"Ladies and gentlemen—" said the ballerina, reading the bulletin. She must have been extraordinarily beautiful, because the mask she wore was hideous. And it was easy to see that she was the strongest and most graceful of all the dancers, for her handicap bags were as big as those worn by two-hundred-pound men.

And she had to apologize at once for her voice, which was a very unfair voice for a woman to use. Her voice was a warm, luminous, timeless melody. "Excuse me—" she said, and she began again, making her voice absolutely uncompetitive.

"Harrison Bergeron, age fourteen," she said in a grackle squawk, "has just escaped from jail, where he was held on suspicion of plotting to overthrow the government. He is a genius and an athlete, is under-handicapped, and should be regarded as extremely dangerous."

A police photograph of Harrison Bergeron was flashed on the screen—upside down, then sideways, upside down again, then right side up. The picture showed the full length of Harrison against a background calibrated in feet and inches. He was exactly seven feet tall.

The rest of Harrison's appearance was Halloween and hardware. Nobody had ever borne heavier handicaps. He had outgrown hindrances faster than the H-G men could think them up. Instead of a little ear radio for a mental handicap, he wore a tremendous pair of earphones, and spectacles with thick wavy lenses. The spectacles were intended to make him not only half blind, but to give him whanging headaches besides.

Scrap metal was hung all over him. Ordinarily, there was a certain symmetry, a military neatness to the handicaps issued to strong people, but Harrison looked like a walking junkyard. In the race of life, Harrison carried three hundred pounds.

And to offset his good looks, the H-G men required that he wear at all times a red rubber ball for a nose, keep his eyebrows shaved off, and cover his even white teeth with black caps at snaggle-tooth random.

"If you see this boy," said the ballerina, "do not—I repeat, do not—try to reason with him."

There was the shriek of a door being torn from its hinges.

Screams and barking cries of consternation came from the television set. The photograph of Harrison Bergeron on the screen jumped again and again, as though dancing to the tune of an earthquake.

George Bergeron correctly identified the earthquake, and well he might have—for many was the time his own home had danced to the same crashing tune. "My God—" said George, "that must be Harrison!"

The realization was blasted from his mind instantly by the sound of an automobile collision in his head.

When George could open his eyes again, the photograph of Harrison was gone. A living, breathing Harrison filled the screen.

Clanking, clownish, and huge, Harrison stood in the center of the studio. The knob of the uprooted studio door was still in his hand. Ballerinas, technicians, musicians, and announcers cowered on their knees before him, expecting to die.

"I am the Emperor!" cried Harrison. "Do you hear? I am the Emperor! Everybody must do what I say at once!" He stamped his foot and the studio shook.

"Even as I stand here—" he bellowed, "crippled, hobbled, sickened—I am a greater ruler than any man who ever lived! Now watch me become what I *can* become!"

Harrison tore the straps of his handicap harness like wet tissue paper, tore straps guaranteed to support five thousand pounds.

Harrison's scrap-iron handicaps crashed to the floor.

Harrison thrust his thumbs under the bar of the padlock that secured his head harness. The bar snapped like celery. Harrison smashed his headphones and spectacles against the wall.

He flung away his rubber-ball nose, revealed a man that would have awed Thor, the god of thunder.

"I shall now select my Empress!" he said, looking down on the cowering people. "Let the first woman who dares rise to her feet claim her mate and her throne!"

A moment passed, and then a ballerina arose, swaying like a willow.

Harrison plucked the mental handicap from her ear, snapped off her physical handicaps with marvelous delicacy. Last of all, he removed her mask.

She was blindingly beautiful.

"Now—" said Harrison, taking her hand, "shall we show the people the meaning of the word dance? Music!" he commanded.

The musicians scrambled back into their chairs, and Harrison stripped them of their handicaps, too. "Play your best," he told them, "and I'll make you barons and dukes and earls."

The music began. It was normal at first—cheap, silly, false. But Harrison snatched two musicians from their chairs, waved them like batons as he sang the music as he wanted it played. He slammed them back into their chairs.

The music began again and was much improved.

Harrison and his Empress merely listened to the music for a while—listened gravely, as though synchronizing their heartbeats with it.

They shifted their weights to their toes.

Harrison placed his big hands on the girl's tiny waist, letting her sense the weightlessness that would soon be hers.

And then, in an explosion of joy and grace, into the air they sprang!

Not only were the laws of the land abandoned, but the law of gravity and the laws of motion as well.

They reeled, whirled, swiveled, flounced, capered, gamboled, and spun.

They leaped like deer on the moon.

The studio ceiling was thirty feet high, but each leap brought the dancers nearer to it.

It became their obvious intention to kiss the ceiling.

They kissed it.

And then, neutralizing gravity with love and pure will, they remained suspended in air inches below the ceiling, and they kissed each other for a long, long time.

It was then that Diana Moon Glampers, the Handicapper General, came into the studio with a double-barreled ten-gauge shotgun. She fired twice, and the Emperor and the Empress were dead before they hit the floor.

Diana Moon Glampers loaded the gun again. She aimed it at the musicians and told them they had ten seconds to get their handicaps back on.

It was then that the Bergerons' television tube burned out.

Hazel turned to comment about the blackout to George.

But George had gone out into the kitchen for a can of beer.

George came back in with the beer, paused while a handicap signal shook him up. And then he sat down again. "You been crying?" he said to Hazel.

"Yup," she said.

"What about?" he said.

"I forget," she said. "Something real sad on television."

"What was it?" he said.

"It's all kind of mixed up in my mind," said Hazel.

"Forget sad things," said George.

"I always do," said Hazel.

"That's my girl," said George. He winced. There was the sound of a riveting gun in his head.

"Gee—I could tell that one was a doozy," said Hazel.

"You can say that again," said George.

"Gee—" said Hazel, "I could tell that one was a doozy."

Idiots First

Bernard Malamud

If the previous story, "Harrison Bergeron," invites attention to possible excesses of our commitment to equality, the present story invites attention to possible deficiencies. What do we think and how do we feel about those people who appear not quite equal—who are demented, enfeebled, or otherwise handicapped, whether by birth or misfortune? How do we treat handicapped newborns, adults with severe mental illness, or old people suffering from Alzheimer's disease? Do we regard them as having equal human rights and equal human worth?

In this poignant and mysterious story (1961) by Bernard Malamud (1914–1986), a dying Jewish man, Mendel, tries desperately to arrange for his mentally impaired thirty-nine-year-old son, Isaac, to be transferred to the care of his only surviving relative, an eighty-one-year-old uncle. Toward the end, his path is blocked at the train station by the ticket collector, a man named Ginzburg, who has mysteriously been shadowing Mendel throughout the story. Ginzburg, who declares himself a follower of the indifferent "cosmic universal law," denies responsibility for "somebody on one cylinder": "I ain't in the anthropomorphic business."

Who is Ginzburg? What is this cosmic law? What is "the anthropomorphic business"? What happens in the mysterious episode at the end of the story to bring about a change in Ginzburg? What has he seen or understood? Should we put "Idiots First"? How do you regard people who might seem "less than equal"?

The thick ticking of the tin clock stopped. Mendel, dozing in the dark, awoke in fright. The pain returned as he listened. He drew on his cold embittered clothing, and wasted minutes sitting at the edge of the bed.

"Isaac," he ultimately sighed.

In the kitchen, Isaac, his astonished mouth open, held six peanuts in his palm. He placed each on the table. "One . . . two . . . nine."

He gathered each peanut and appeared in the doorway. Mendel, in loose hat and long overcoat, still sat on the bed. Isaac watched with small eyes and ears, thick hair graying the sides of his head.

"Schlaf," he nasally said.

"No," muttered Mendel. As if stifling he rose. "Come, Isaac."

He wound his old watch though the sight of the stopped clock nauseated him. Isaac wanted to hold it to his ear.

"No, it's late." Mendel put the watch carefully away. In the drawer he found the little paper bag of crumpled ones and fives and slipped it into his overcoat pocket. He helped Isaac on with his coat.

Isaac looked at one dark window, then at the other. Mendel stared at both blank windows.

They went slowly down the darkly lit stairs, Mendel first, Isaac watching the moving shadows on the wall. To one long shadow he offered a peanut.

"Hungrig."

In the vestibule the old man gazed through the thin glass. The November night was cold and bleak. Opening the door he cautiously thrust his head out. Though he saw nothing he quickly shut the door.

"Ginzburg, that he came to see me yesterday," he whispered in Isaac's ear.

Isaac sucked air.

"You know who I mean?"

Isaac combed his chin with his fingers.

"That's the one, with the black whiskers. Don't talk to him or go with him if he asks you."

Isaac moaned.

"Young people he don't bother so much," Mendel said in afterthought.

It was suppertime and the street was empty but the store windows dimly lit their way to the corner. They crossed the deserted street and went on. Isaac, with a happy cry, pointed to the three golden balls. Mendel smiled but was exhausted when they got to the pawnshop.

The pawnbroker, a red-bearded man with black horn-rimmed glasses, was eating a whitefish at the rear of the store. He craned his head, saw them, and settled back to sip his tea.

In five minutes he came forward, patting his shapeless lips with a large white handkerchief.

Mendel, breathing heavily, handed him the worn gold watch. The pawnbroker, raising his glasses, screwed in his eyepiece. He turned the watch over once. "Eight dollars."

The dying man wet his cracked lips. "I must have thirty-five."

"So go to Rothschild."

"Cost me myself sixty."

"In 1905." The pawnbroker handed back the watch. It had stopped ticking. Mendel wound it slowly. It ticked hollowly.

"Isaac must go to my uncle that he lives in California."

"It's a free country," said the pawnbroker.

Isaac, watching a banjo, snickered.

"What's the matter with him?" the pawnbroker asked.

"So let be eight dollars," muttered Mendel, "but where will I get the rest till tonight?"

"How much for my hat and coat?" he asked.

"No sale." The pawnbroker went behind the cage and wrote out a ticket. He locked the watch in a small drawer but Mendel still heard it ticking.

In the street he slipped the eight dollars into the paper bag, then searched in his pockets for a scrap of writing. Finding it, he strained to read the address by the light of the street lamp.

As they trudged to the subway, Mendel pointed to the sprinkled sky.

"Isaac, look how many stars are tonight."

"Eggs," said Isaac.

"First we will go to Mr. Fishbein, after we will eat."

They got off the train in upper Manhattan and had to walk several blocks before they located Fishbein's house.

"A regular palace," Mendel murmured, looking forward to a moment's warmth.

Isaac stared uneasily at the heavy door of the house.

Mendel rang. The servant, a man with long sideburns, came to the door and said Mr. and Mrs. Fishbein were dining and could see no one.

"He should eat in peace but we will wait till he finishes."

"Come back tomorrow morning. Tomorrow morning Mr. Fishbein will talk to you. He don't do business or charity at this time of the night."

"Charity I am not interested—"

"Come back tomorrow."

"Tell him it's life or death—"

"Whose life or death?"

"So if not his, then mine."

"Don't be such a big smart aleck."

"Look me in my face," said Mendel, "and tell me if I got time till tomorrow morning?"

The servant stared at him, then at Isaac, and reluctantly let them in.

The foyer was a vast high-ceilinged room with many oil paintings on the walls, voluminous silken draperies, a thick flowered rug at foot, and a marble staircase.

Mr. Fishbein, a paunchy bald-headed man with hairy nostrils and small patent leather feet, ran lightly down the stairs, a large napkin tucked under a tuxedo coat button. He stopped on the fifth step from the bottom and examined his visitors.

"Who comes on Friday night to a man that he has guests, to spoil him his supper?"

"Excuse me that I bother you, Mr. Fishbein," Mendel said. "If I didn't come now I couldn't come tomorrow."

"Without more preliminaries, please state your business. I'm a hungry man."

"Hungrig," wailed Isaac.

Fishbein adjusted his pince-nez. "What's the matter with him?"

"This is my son Isaac. He is like this all his life."

Isaac mewled.

"I am sending him to California."

"Mr. Fishbein don't contribute to personal pleasure trips."

"I am a sick man and he must go tonight on the train to my Uncle Leo."

"I never give to unorganized charity," Fishbein said, "but if you are hungry I will invite you downstairs in my kitchen. We having tonight chicken with stuffed derma."

"All I ask is thirty-five dollars for the train ticket to my uncle in California. I have already the rest."

"Who is your uncle? How old a man?"

"Eighty-one years, a long life to him."

Fishbein burst into laughter. "Eighty-one years and you are sending him this halfwit."

Mendel, flailing both arms, cried, "Please, without names."

Fishbein politely conceded.

"Where is open the door there we go in the house," the sick man said. "If you will kindly give me thirty-five dollars, God will bless you. What is thirty-five dollars to Mr. Fishbein? Nothing. To me, for my boy, is everything."

Fishbein drew himself up to his tallest height.

"Private contributions I don't make—only to institutions. This is my fixed policy."

Mendel sank to his creaking knees on the rug.

"Please, Mr. Fishbein, if not thirty-five, give maybe twenty."

"Levinson!" Fishbein angrily called.

The servant with the long sideburns appeared at the top of the stairs.

"Show this party where is the door—unless he wishes to partake food before leaving the premises."

"For what I got chicken won't cure it," Mendel said.

"This way if you please," said Levinson, descending.

Isaac assisted his father up.

"Take him to an institution," Fishbein advised over the marble balustrade. He ran quickly up the stairs and they were at once outside, buffeted by winds.

The walk to the subway was tedious. The wind blew mournfully. Mendel, breathless, glanced furtively at shadows. Isaac, clutching his peanuts in his frozen fist, clung to his father's side. They entered a small park to rest for a minute on a stone bench under a leafless two-branched tree. The thick right branch was raised, the thin left one hung down. A very pale moon rose slowly. So did a stranger as they approached the bench.

"Gut yuntif," he said hoarsely.

Mendel, drained of blood, waved his wasted arms. Isaac yowled sickly. Then a bell chimed and it was only ten. Mendel let out a piercing anguished cry as the bearded stranger disappeared into the bushes. A policeman came running, and though he beat the bushes with his nightstick, could turn up nothing. Mendel and Isaac hurried out of the little park. When Mendel glanced back the dead tree had its thin arm raised, the thick one down. He moaned.

They boarded a trolley, stopping at the home of a former friend, but he had died years ago. On the same block they went into a cafeteria and ordered two fried eggs for Isaac. The tables were crowded except where a heavyset man sat eating soup with kasha. After one look at him they left in haste, although Isaac wept.

Mendel had another address on a slip of paper but the house was too far away, in Queens, so they stood in a doorway shivering.

What can I do, he frantically thought, in one short hour?

He remembered the furniture in the house. It was junk but might bring a few dollars. "Come, Isaac." They went once more to the pawnbroker's to talk to him, but the shop was dark and an iron gate—rings and gold watches glinting through it—was drawn tight across his place of business.

They huddled behind a telephone pole, both freezing. Isaac whimpered.

"See the big moon, Isaac. The whole sky is white."

He pointed but Isaac wouldn't look.

Mendel dreamed for a minute of the sky lit up, long sheets of light in all directions. Under the sky, in California, sat Uncle Leo drinking tea with lemon. Mendel felt warm but woke up cold.

Across the street stood an ancient brick synagogue.

He pounded on the huge door but no one appeared. He waited till he had breath and desperately knocked again. At last there were footsteps within, and the synagogue door creaked open on its massive brass hinges.

A darkly dressed sexton, holding a dripping candle, glared at them.

"Who knocks this time of night with so much noise on the synagogue door?"

Mendel told the sexton his troubles. "Please, I would like to speak to the rabbi."

"The rabbi is an old man. He sleeps now. His wife won't let you see him. Go home and come back tomorrow."

"To tomorrow I said goodbye already. I am a dying man."

Though the sexton seemed doubtful he pointed to an old wooden house next door. "In there he lives." He disappeared into the synagogue with his lit candle casting shadows around him.

Mendel, with Isaac clutching his sleeve, went up the wooden steps and rang the bell. After five minutes a big-faced, gray-haired bulky woman came out on the porch with a torn robe thrown over her nightdress. She emphatically said the rabbi was sleeping and could not be waked.

But as she was insisting, the rabbi himself tottered to the door. He listened a minute and said, "Who wants to see me let them come in."

They entered a cluttered room. The rabbi was an old skinny man with bent shoulders and a wisp of white beard. He wore a flannel nightgown and black skullcap; his feet were bare.

"Vey is mir," his wife muttered. "Put on shoes or tomorrow comes sure pneumonia." She was a woman with a big belly, years younger than her husband. Staring at Isaac, she turned away.

Mendel apologetically related his errand. "All I need more is thirty-five dollars."

"Thirty-five?" said the rabbi's wife. "Why not thirty-five thousand? Who has so much money? My husband is a poor rabbi. The doctors take away every penny."

"Dear friend," said the rabbi, "if I had I would give you."

"I got already seventy," Mendel said, heavy-hearted. "All I need more is thirty-five."

"God will give you," said the rabbi.

"In the grave," said Mendel. "I need tonight. Come, Isaac."

"Wait," called the rabbi.

He hurried inside, came out with a fur-lined caftan, and handed it to Mendel.

"Yascha," shrieked his wife, "not your new coat!"

"I got my old one. Who needs two coats for one body?"

"Yascha, I am screaming—"

"Who can go among poor people, tell me, in a new coat?"

"Yascha," she cried, "what can this man do with your coat? He needs tonight the money. The pawnbrokers are asleep."

"So let him wake them up."

"No." She grabbed the coat from Mendel.

He held on to a sleeve, wrestling her for the coat. Her I know, Mendel thought. "Shylock," he muttered. Her eyes glittered.

The rabbi groaned and tottered dizzily. His wife cried out as Mendel yanked the coat from her hands.

"Run," cried the rabbi.

"Run, Isaac."

They ran out of the house and down the steps.

"Stop, you thief," called the rabbi's wife.

The rabbi pressed both hands to his temples and fell to the floor.

"Help!" his wife wept. "Heart attack! Help!"

But Mendel and Isaac ran through the streets with the rabbi's new fur-lined caftan. After them noiselessly ran Ginzburg.

It was very late when Mendel bought the train ticket in the only booth open.

There was no time to stop for a sandwich so Isaac ate his peanuts and they hurried to the train in the vast deserted station.

"So in the morning," Mendel gasped as they ran, "there comes a man that he sells sandwiches and coffee. Eat but get change. When reaches California the train, will be waiting for you on the station Uncle Leo. If you don't recognize him he will recognize you. Tell him I send best regards."

But when they arrived at the gate to the platform it was shut, the light out.

Mendel, groaning, beat on the gate with his fists.

"Too late," said the uniformed ticket collector, a bulky, bearded man with hairy nostrils and a fishy smell.

He pointed to the station clock. "Already past twelve."

"But I see standing there still the train," Mendel said, hopping in his grief.

"It just left—in one more minute."

"A minute is enough. Just open the gate."

"Too late I told you." Mendel socked his bony chest with both hands. "With my whole heart I beg you this little favor."

"Favors you had enough already. For you the train is gone. You shoulda been dead already at midnight. I told you that yesterday. This is the best I can do."

"Ginzburg!" Mendel shrank from him.

"Who else?" The voice was metallic, eyes glittered, the expression amused.

"For myself," the old man begged, "I don't ask a thing. But what will happen to my boy?"

Ginzburg shrugged slightly. "What will happen happens. This isn't my responsibility. I got enough to think about without worrying about somebody on one cylinder."

"What then is your responsibility?"

"To create conditions. To make happen what happens. I ain't in the anthropomorphic business."

"Whatever business you in, where is your pity?"

"This ain't my commodity. The law is the law."

"Which law is this?"

"The cosmic universal law, goddamit, the one I got to follow myself."

"What kind of a law is it?" cried Mendel. "For God's sake, don't you understand what I went through in my life with this poor boy? Look at him. For thirty-nine years, since the day he was born, I wait for him to grow up, but he don't. Do you understand what this means in a father's heart? Why don't you let him go to his uncle?" His voice had risen and he was shouting.

Isaac mewled loudly.

"Better calm down or you'll hurt somebody's feelings," Ginzburg said with a wink toward Isaac.

"All my life," Mendel cried, his body trembling, "what did I have? I was poor. I suffered from my health. When I worked I worked too hard. When I didn't work was worse. My wife died a young woman. But I didn't ask from anybody nothing. Now I ask a small favor. Be so kind, Mr. Ginzburg."

The ticket collector was picking his teeth with a match stick.

"You ain't the only one, my friend, some got it worse than you. That's how it goes in this country."

"You dog you." Mendel lunged at Ginzburg's throat and began to choke. "You bastard, don't you understand what it means human?"

They struggled nose to nose, Ginzburg, though his astonished eyes bulged, began to laugh. "You pipsqueak nothing. I'll freeze you to pieces."

His eyes lit in rage and Mendel felt an unbearable cold like an icy dagger invading his body, all of his parts shriveling.

Now I die without helping Isaac.

A crowd gathered. Isaac yelped in fright.

Clinging to Ginzburg in his last agony, Mendel saw reflected in the ticket collector's eyes the depth of his terror. But he saw that Ginzburg, staring at himself in Mendel's eyes, saw mirrored in them the extent of his own awful wrath. He beheld a shimmering, starry, blinding light that produced darkness.

Ginzburg looked astounded. "Who me?"

His grip on the squirming old man slowly loosened, and Mendel, his heart barely beating, slumped to the ground.

"Go." Ginzburg muttered, "take him to the train."

"Let pass," he commanded a guard.

The crowd parted. Isaac helped his father up and they tottered down the steps to the platform where the train waited, lit and ready to go.

Mendel found Isaac a coach seat and hastily embraced him. "Help Uncle Leo, Isaakil. Also remember your father and mother."

"Be nice to him," he said to the conductor. "Show him where everything is."

He waited on the platform until the train began slowly to move. Isaac sat at the edge of his seat, his face strained in the direction of his journey. When the train was gone, Mendel ascended the stairs to see what had become of Ginzburg.

The Man That Corrupted Hadleyburg

Mark Twain

The principles of freedom and equality influence the character not only of individual Americans but also of our communal life, which, in turn, shapes us as individuals. For most Americans, the freedom to pursue happiness becomes a search for prosperity. The ensuing multiplication of economic interests, the Federalist's solution to the problem of majority faction, can affect the character of citizens: benign acquisitiveness can grow into a worship of Mammon, selfishness, envy, and hardening of the heart, and can lead to civic division and class conflict. At the same time, the love of equality can lead toward homogeneity and conformity, through the rule of public opinion and the "tyranny of the majority." *

This story (1899) by satirist Mark Twain (born Samuel Langhorne Clemens, 1835–1910) is a biting commentary on American civic life. In Hadleyburg, Twain offers a microcosm of America as it appeared in the latter half of the nineteenth century, a time Twain dubbed "the Gilded Age." Hadleyburg, a commercial town renowned for the honesty of its citizens, happens to offend a passing stranger—how, we are not told—who, bent on revenge, devises a plan to expose the hollowness of the town's reputed virtue.

Twain's hilarious account sheds serious light on several important phenomena, including the fragility of honesty under the prospect of gain; the tyranny of public opinion and the fickleness of the herd mentality; the gap between reputation and genuine virtue; and the foolish pride in untested

---

* *As Tocqueville remarked, "At periods of equality men have no faith in one another, by reason of their common resemblance; but this very resemblance gives them almost unbounded confidence in the judgment of the public; for it would not seem probable, as they are all endowed with equal means of judging, but that the greater truth should go with the greater number."*

virtue. What is the civic character of the citizens of Hadleyburg, and what is their conception of virtue and goodness? What is responsible for their "corruption": the commercial republic, with its licensing of acquisitiveness; democratic equality; lack of worldly experience with temptation; insufficient or hypocritical piety; "human nature"; prideful "original sin"; the diabolical man—a Satan figure?—who brings about the town's fall from innocence? What can we learn from Twain's exposé? Can laughter at others' pretentiousness or hypocrisy moderate similar tendencies in ourselves? Or does it only make us feel superior to the laughed-at? Can humor provide a bond of society and encourage the virtues needed to sustain it?

I

It was many years ago. Hadleyburg was the most honest and upright town in all the region round about. It had kept that reputation unsmirched during three generations, and was prouder of it than of any other of its possessions. It was so proud of it, and so anxious to insure its perpetuation, that it began to teach the principles of honest dealing to its babies in the cradle, and made the like teachings the staple of their culture thenceforward through all the years devoted to their education. Also, throughout the formative years temptations were kept out of the way of the young people, so that their honesty could have every chance to harden and solidify, and become a part of their very bone. The neighboring towns were jealous of this honorable supremacy, and affected to sneer at Hadleyburg's pride in it and call it vanity; but all the same they were obliged to acknowledge that Hadleyburg was in reality an incorruptible town; and if pressed they would also acknowledge that the mere fact that a young man hailed from Hadleyburg was all the recommendation he needed when he went forth from his natal town to seek for responsible employment.

But at last, in the drift of time, Hadleyburg had the ill luck to offend a passing stranger—possibly without knowing it, certainly without caring, for Hadleyburg was sufficient unto itself, and cared not a rap for strangers or their opinions. Still, it would have been well to make an exception in this one's case, for he was a bitter man and revengeful. All through his wanderings during a whole year he kept his injury in mind, and gave all his leisure moments to trying to invent a compensating satisfaction for it. He contrived many plans, and all of them were good, but none of them was quite sweeping enough; the poorest of them would hurt a great many individuals, but what he wanted was a plan which would comprehend the entire town, and not let so much as one person escape unhurt. At last he had a fortunate idea, and when it fell into his brain it lit up his whole head with an evil joy. He began to form a plan at once, saying to himself, "That is the thing to do—I will corrupt the town."

Six months later he went to Hadleyburg, and arrived in a buggy at the house of the old cashier of the bank about ten at night. He got a sack out of the buggy, shouldered it, and staggered with it through the cottage yard, and knocked at the door. A woman's voice said "Come in," and he entered, and set his sack behind the stove in the parlor, saying politely to the old lady who sat reading the *Missionary Herald* by the lamp:

"Pray keep your seat, madam, I will not disturb you. There—now it is pretty well concealed; one would hardly know it was there. Can I see your husband a moment, madam?"

No, he was gone to Brixton, and might not return before morning.

"Very well, madam, it is no matter. I merely wanted to leave that sack in his care, to be delivered to the rightful owner when he shall be found. I am a stranger; he does not know me; I am merely passing through the town to-night to discharge a matter which has been long in my mind. My errand is now completed, and I go pleased and a little proud, and you will never see me again. There is a paper attached to the sack which will explain everything. Good-night, madam."

The old lady was afraid of the mysterious big stranger, and was glad to see him go. But her curiosity was roused, and she went straight to the sack and brought away the paper. It began as follows:

> TO BE PUBLISHED; or, the right man sought out by private inquiry— either will answer. This sack contains gold coin weighing a hundred and sixty pounds four ounces—

"Mercy on us, and the door not locked!"

Mrs. Richards flew to it all in a tremble and locked it, then pulled down the window-shades and stood frightened, worried, and wondering if there was anything else she could do toward making herself and the money more safe. She listened awhile for burglars, then surrendered to curiosity and went back to the lamp and finished reading the paper:

> I am a foreigner, and am presently going back to my own coun- try, to remain there permanently. I am grateful to America for what I have received at her hands during my long stay under her flag; and to one of her citizens—a citizen of Hadleyburg—I am espe- cially grateful for a great kindness done me a year or two ago. Two great kindnesses in fact. I will explain. I was a gambler. I say I *was*.

I was a ruined gambler. I arrived in this village at night, hungry and without a penny. I asked for help—in the dark; I was ashamed to beg in the light. I begged of the right man. He gave me twenty dollars—that is to say, he gave me life, as I considered it. He also gave me fortune; for out of that money I have made myself rich at the gaming-table. And finally, a remark which he made to me has remained with me to this day, and has at last conquered me; and in conquering has saved the remnant of my morals: I shall gamble no more. Now I have no idea who that man was, but I want him found, and I want him to have this money, to give away, throw away, or keep, as he pleases. It is merely my way of testifying my gratitude to him. If I could stay, I would find him myself; but no matter, he will be found. This is an honest town, an incorruptible town, and I know I can trust it without fear. This man can be identified by the remark which he made to me; I feel persuaded that he will remember it.

And now my plan is this: If you prefer to conduct the inquiry privately, do so. Tell the contents of this present writing to any one who is likely to be the right man. If he shall answer, "I am the man; the remark I made was so-and-so," apply the test—to wit: open the sack, and in it you will find a sealed envelope containing that remark. If the remark mentioned by the candidate tallies with it, give him the money, and ask no further questions, for he is certainly the right man.

But if you shall prefer a public inquiry, then publish this present writing in the local paper—with these instructions added, to wit: Thirty days from now, let the candidate appear at the town-hall at eight in the evening (Friday), and hand his remark, in a sealed enve-lope, to the Rev. Mr. Burgess (if he will be kind enough to act); and let Mr. Burgess there and then destroy the seals of the sack, open it, and see if the remark is correct; if correct, let the money be deliv-ered, with my sincere gratitude, to my benefactor thus identified.

Mrs. Richards sat down, gently quivering with excitement, and was soon lost in thinkings—after this pattern: "What a strange thing it is! . . . And what a fortune for that kind man who set his bread afloat upon the waters! . . . If it had only been my husband that did it!—for we are so poor, so old and poor! . . ." Then, with a sigh—"But it was not my Edward; no, it was not he that gave a stranger twenty dollars. It is a pity too; I see it now. . . ." Then, with a shudder—"But it is *gambler's* money! the wages of sin; we couldn't take it; we couldn't touch it. I don't like to be near it; it seems a defilement." She moved to a farther chair. . . . "I wish Edward would come, and take it to the bank; a burglar might come at any moment; it is dreadful to be here all alone with it."

At eleven Mr. Richards arrived, and while his wife was saying, "I am *so* glad you've come!" he was saying, "I'm so tired—tired clear out; it is dreadful to be poor, and have to make these dismal journeys at my time of life. Always at the grind, grind, grind, on a salary—another man's slave, and he sitting at home in his slippers, rich and comfortable."

"I am so sorry for you, Edward, you know that; but be comforted; we have our livelihood; we have our good name—"

"Yes, Mary, and that is everything. Don't mind my talk—it's just a moment's irritation and doesn't mean anything. Kiss me—there, it's all gone now, and I am not complaining any more. What have you been getting? What's in the sack?"

Then his wife told him the great secret. It dazed him for a moment; then he said:

"It weighs a hundred and sixty pounds? Why, Mary, it's for-ty thou-sand dollars—think of it—a whole fortune! Not ten men in this village are worth that much. Give me the paper."

He skimmed through it and said:

"Isn't it an adventure! Why, it's a romance; it's like the impossible things one reads about in books, and never sees in life." He was well stirred up now; cheerful, even gleeful. He tapped his old wife on the cheek, and said humorously, "Why, we're rich, Mary, rich; all we've got to do is to bury the money and burn the papers. If the gambler ever comes to inquire, we'll merely look coldly upon him and say: 'What is this nonsense you are talking? We have never heard of you and your sack of gold before'; and then he would look foolish, and—"

"And in the meantime, while you are running on with your jokes, the money is still here, and it is fast getting along toward burglar-time."

"True. Very well, what shall we do—make the inquiry private? No, not that; it would spoil the romance. The public method is better. Think what a noise it will make! And it will make all the other towns jealous; for no stranger would trust such a thing to any town but Hadleyburg, and they know it. It's a great card for us. I must get to the printing-office now, or I shall be too late."

"But stop—stop—don't leave me here alone with it, Edward!"

But he was gone. For only a little while, however. Not far from his own house he met the editor-proprietor of the paper, and gave him the document, and said, "Here is a good thing for you, Cox—put it in."

"It may be too late, Mr. Richards, but I'll see."

At home again he and his wife sat down to talk the charming mystery over; they were in no condition for sleep. The first question was, Who could the citizen have been who gave the stranger the twenty dollars? It seemed a simple one; both answered it in the same breath—

"Barclay Goodson."

"Yes," said Richards, "he could have done it, and it would have been like him, but there's not another in the town."

"Everybody will grant that, Edward—grant it privately, anyway. For six months, now, the village has been its own proper self once more—honest, narrow, self-righteous, and stingy."

"It is what he always called it, to the day of his death—said it right out publicly, too."

"Yes, and he was hated for it."

"Oh, of course; but he didn't care. I reckon he was the best-hated man among us, except the Reverend Burgess."

"Well, Burgess deserves it—he will never get another congregation here. Mean as the town is, it knows how to estimate *him*. Edward, doesn't it seem odd that the stranger should appoint Burgess to deliver the money?"

"Well, yes—it does. That is—that is—"

"Why so much that-*is*-ing? Would *you* select him?"

"Mary, maybe the stranger knows him better than this village does."

"Much *that* would help Burgess!"

The husband seemed perplexed for an answer; the wife kept a steady eye upon him, and waited. Finally Richards said, with the hesitancy of one who is making a statement which is likely to encounter doubt,

"Mary, Burgess is not a bad man."

His wife was certainly surprised.

"Nonsense!" she exclaimed.

"He is not a bad man. I know. The whole of his unpopularity had its foundation in that one thing—the thing that made so much noise."

"That 'one thing,' indeed! As if that 'one thing' wasn't enough, all by itself."

"Plenty. Plenty. Only he wasn't guilty of it."

"How you talk! Not guilty of it! Everybody knows he *was* guilty."

"Mary, I give you my word—he was innocent."

"I can't believe it, and I don't. How do you know?"

"It is a confession. I am ashamed, but I will make it. I was the only man who knew he was innocent. I could have saved him, and—and—well, you know how the town was wrought up—I hadn't the pluck to do it. It would have turned everybody against me. I felt mean, ever so mean; but I didn't dare; I hadn't the manliness to face that."

Mary looked troubled, and for a while was silent. Then she said stammeringly:

"I—I don't think it would have done for you to—to—One mustn't—er—public opinion—one has to be so careful—so—" It was a difficult road, and she got mired; but after a little she got started again. "It was a great pity, but—Why, we couldn't afford it, Edward—we couldn't indeed. Oh, I wouldn't have had you do it for anything!"

"It would have lost us the good-will of so many people, Mary; and then—and then—"

"What troubles me now is, what *he* thinks of us, Edward."

"He? *He* doesn't suspect that I could have saved him."

"Oh," exclaimed the wife, in a tone of relief, "I am glad of that. As long as he doesn't know that you could have saved him, he—he—well that makes it a great deal better. Why, I might have known he didn't know, because he is always trying to be friendly with us, as little encouragement as we give him. More than once people have twitted me with it. There's the Wilson's, and the Wilcoxes, and the Harknesses, they take a mean pleasure in saying, '*Your friend* Burgess,' because they know it pesters me. I wish he wouldn't persist in liking us so; I can't think why he keeps it up."

"I can explain it. It's another confession. When the thing was new and hot, and the town made a plan to ride him on a rail, my conscience hurt me so that I couldn't stand it, and I went privately and gave him notice, and he got out of the town and staid out till it was safe to come back."

"Edward! If the town had found it out—"

"*Don't!* It scares me yet, to think of it. I repented of it the minute it was done; and I was even afraid to tell you, lest your face might betray it to somebody. I didn't sleep any that night, for worrying. But after a few days I saw that no one was going to suspect me, and after that I got to feeling glad I did it. And I feel glad yet, Mary—glad through and through."

"So do I, now, for it would have been a dreadful way to treat him. Yes, I'm glad; for really you did owe him that, you know. But, Edward, suppose it should come out yet, some day!"

"It won't."

"Why?"

"Because everybody thinks it was Goodson."

"Of course they would!"

"Certainly. And of course *he* didn't care. They persuaded poor old Sawlsberry to go and charge it on him, and he went blustering over there and did it. Goodson looked him over, like as if he was hunting for a place on him that he could despise the most, then he says, 'So you are the Committee of Inquiry, are you?' Sawlsberry said that was about what he was. 'Hm. Do they require particulars, or do you reckon a kind of a *general* answer will do?' 'If they require particulars, I will come back, Mr. Goodson; I will take the general answer first.' 'Very well, then, tell them to go to hell—I reckon that's general enough. And I'll give you some advice, Sawlsberry: when you come back for the particulars, fetch a basket to carry the relics of yourself home in.'"

"Just like Goodson; it's got all the marks. He had only one vanity; he thought he could give advice better than any other person."

"It settled the business, and saved us, Mary. The subject was dropped."

"Bless you, I'm not doubting *that*."

Then they took up the gold-sack mystery again, with strong interest. Soon the conversation began to suffer breaks—interruptions caused by absorbed thinkings. The breaks grew more and more frequent. At last Richards lost himself wholly in thought. He sat long, gazing vacantly at the floor, and by-and-by he began to punctuate his thoughts with little nervous movements of his hands that seemed to indicate vexation. Meantime his wife too had relapsed into a thoughtful silence, and her movements were beginning to show a troubled discomfort. Finally Richards got up and strode aimlessly about the room, ploughing his hands through his hair, much as a somnambulist might do who was having a bad dream. Then he seemed to arrive at a definite purpose; and without a word he put on his hat and passed quickly out of the house. His wife sat brooding, with a drawn face, and did not seem to be aware that she was alone. Now and then she murmured, "Lead us not into t. . . . but—but—we are so poor, so poor! . . . Lead us not into. . . . Ah, who would be hurt by it?—and no one would ever know. . . . Lead us. . . ." The voice died out in mumblings. After a little she glanced up and muttered in a half-frightened, half-glad way—

"He is gone! But, oh dear, he may be too late—too late. . . . Maybe not— maybe there is still time." She rose and stood thinking, nervously clasping and unclasping her hands. A slight shudder shook her frame, and she said, out of a dry throat, "God forgive me—it's awful to think such things—but. . . . Lord, how we are made—how strangely we are made!"

She turned the light low, and slipped stealthily over and kneeled down by the sack and felt of its ridgy sides with her hands, and fondled them lovingly; and there was a gloating light in her poor old eyes. She fell into fits of absence; and came half out of them at times to mutter, "If we had only waited!—oh, if we had only waited a little, and not been in such a hurry!"

Meantime Cox had gone home from his office and told his wife all about the strange thing that had happened, and they had talked it over eagerly, and guessed that the late Goodson was the only man in the town who could have helped a suffering stranger with so noble a sum as twenty dollars. Then there was a pause, and the two became thoughtful and silent. And by-and-by nervous and fidgety. At last the wife said, as if to herself,

"Nobody knows this secret but the Richardses. . . . and us. . . . nobody."

The husband came out of his thinkings with a slight start, and gazed wistfully at his wife, whose face was become very pale; then he hesitatingly rose, and glanced furtively at his hat, then at his wife—a sort of mute inquiry. Mrs. Cox swallowed once or twice, with her hand at her throat, then in place of speech she nodded her head. In a moment she was alone, and mumbling to herself.

And now Richards and Cox were hurrying through the deserted streets, from opposite directions. They met, panting, at the foot of the printing-office stairs; by the night-light there they read each other's face. Cox whispered,

"Nobody knows about this but us?"

The whispered answer was,

"Not a soul—on honor, not a soul!"

"If it isn't too late to—"

The men were starting up stairs; at this moment they were overtaken by a boy, and Cox asked,

"Is that you, Johnny?"

"Yes, sir."

"You needn't ship the early mail—nor *any* mail; wait till I tell you."

"It's already gone, sir."

"*Gone?*" It had the sound of an unspeakable disappointment in it.

"Yes, sir. Time-table for Brixton and all the towns beyond changed to-day, sir—had to get the papers in twenty minutes earlier than common. I had to rush; if I had been two minutes later—"

The men turned and walked slowly away, not waiting to hear the rest. Neither of them spoke during ten minutes; then Cox said, in a vexed tone,

"What possessed you to be in such a hurry, *I* can't make out."

The answer was humble enough:

"I see it now, but somehow I never thought, you know, until it was too late. But the next time—"

"Next time be hanged! It won't come in a thousand years."

Then the friends separated without a good-night, and dragged themselves home with the gait of mortally stricken men. At their homes their wives sprang up with an eager "Well?"—then saw the answer with their eyes and sank down sorrowing, without waiting for it to come in words. In both houses a discussion followed of a heated sort—a new thing; there had been discussions before, but not heated ones, not ungentle ones. The discussions to-night were a sort of seeming plagiarisms of each other. Mrs. Richards said:

"If you had only waited, Edward—if you had only stopped to think; but no, you must run straight to the printing-office and spread it all over the world."

"It *said* publish it."

"That is nothing; it also said do it privately, if you liked. There, now—is that true, or not?"

"Why, yes—yes, it is true; but when I thought what a stir it would make, and what a compliment it was to Hadleyburg that a stranger should trust it so—"

"Oh, certainly, I know all that; but if you had only stopped to think, you would have seen that you *couldn't* find the right man, because he is in his grave, and hasn't left chick nor child nor relation behind him; and as long as the money went to somebody that awfully needed it, and nobody would be hurt by it, and—and—"

She broke down, crying. Her husband tried to think of some comforting thing to say, and presently came out with this:

"But after all, Mary, it must be for the best—it *must* be; we know that. And we must remember that it was so ordered—"

"Ordered! Oh, everything's *ordered*, when a person has to find some way out when he has been stupid. Just the same, it was *ordered* that the money should come to us in this special way, and it was you that must take it on yourself to go meddling with the designs of Providence—and who gave you the right? It was wicked, that is what it was—just blasphemous presumption, and no more becoming to a meek and humble professor of—"

"But, Mary, you know how we have been trained all our lives long, like the whole village, till it is absolutely second nature to us to stop not a single moment to think when there's an honest thing to be done—"

"Oh, I know it, I know it—it's been one everlasting training and training and training in honesty—honesty shielded, from the very cradle, against every possible temptation, and so it's *artificial* honesty, and weak as water when temptation comes, as we have seen this night. God knows I never had shade nor shadow of a doubt of my petrified and indestructible honesty until now—and now, under the very first big and real temptation, I—Edward, it is my belief that this town's honesty is as rotten as mine is; as rotten as yours is. It is a mean town, a hard, stingy town, and hasn't a virtue in the world but this honesty it is so celebrated for and so conceited about; and so help me, I do believe that if ever the day comes that its honesty falls under great temptation, its grand reputation will go to ruin like a house of cards. There, now, I've made confession, and I feel better; I am a humbug, and I've been one all my life, without knowing it. Let no man call me honest again—I will not have it."

"I—Well, Mary, I feel a good deal as you do; I certainly do. It seems strange, too, so strange. I never could have believed it—never."

A long silence followed; both were sunk in thought. At last the wife looked up and said,

"I know what you are thinking, Edward."

Richards had the embarrassed look of a person who is caught.

"I am ashamed to confess it, Mary, but—"

"It's no matter, Edward, I was thinking the same question myself."

"I hope so. State it."

"You were thinking, if a body could only guess out *what the remark was* that Goodson made to the stranger."

"It's perfectly true. I feel guilty and ashamed. And you?"

"I'm past it. Let us make a pallet here; we've got to stand watch till the bank vault opens in the morning and admits the sack. . . . Oh, dear, oh, dear—if we hadn't made the mistake!"

The pallet was made, and Mary said:

"The open sesame—what could it have been? I do wonder what that remark could have been. But come; we will get to bed now."

"And sleep?"

"No; think."

"Yes, think."

By this time the Coxes too had completed their spat and their reconciliation, and were turning in—to think, to think, and toss, and fret, and worry over what the remark could possibly have been which Goodson made to the stranded derelict: that golden remark; that remark worth forty thousand dollars, cash.

The reason that the village telegraph-office was open later than usual that night was this: The foreman of Cox's paper was the local representative of the Associated Press. One might say its honorary representative, for it wasn't four times a year that he could furnish thirty words that would be accepted. But this time it was different. His despatch stating what he had caught got an instant answer:

"Send the whole thing—all the details—twelve hundred words."

A colossal order! The foreman filled the bill; and he was the proudest man in the State. By breakfast-time the next morning the name of Hadleyburg the Incorruptible was on every lip in America, from Montreal to the Gulf, from the glaciers of Alaska to the orange-groves of Florida; and millions and millions of people were discussing the stranger and his money-sack, and wondering if the right man would be found, and hoping some more news about the matter would come soon—right away.

II

Hadleyburg village woke up world-celebrated—astonished—happy—vain. Vain beyond imagination. Its nineteen principal citizens and their wives went about shaking hands with each other, and beaming, and smiling, and congratulating, and saying *this* thing adds a new word to the dictionary— *Hadleyburg*, synonym for *incorruptible*—destined to live in dictionaries forever! And the minor and unimportant citizens and their wives went around acting in much the same way. Everybody ran to the bank to see the gold-sack; and before noon grieved and envious crowds began to flock in from Brixton and all neighboring towns; and that afternoon and next day reporters began to arrive from everywhere to verify the sack and its history and write the whole thing up anew, and make dashing free-hand pictures of the sack, and of Richards's house, and the bank, and the Presbyterian church, and the Baptist church, and the public square, and the town-hall where the test would be applied and the money delivered; and damnable portraits of the Richardses, and Pinkerton the banker, and Cox, and the foreman, and Reverend Burgess, and the postmaster—and even of Jack Halliday, who was the loafing, good-natured, no-account, irreverent fisherman, hunter, boys' friend, straydogs' friend, typical "Sam Lawson" of the town. The little mean, smirking, oily Pinkerton showed the sack to all comers, and rubbed his sleek palms together pleasantly, and enlarged upon the town's fine old reputation for honesty and upon this wonderful endorsement of it, and hoped and believed that the example would now spread far and wide over the American world, and be epoch-making in the matter of moral regeneration. And so on, and so on.

By the end of a week things had quieted down again; the wild intoxication of pride and joy had sobered to a soft, sweet, silent delight—a sort of deep, nameless, unutterable content. All faces bore a look of peaceful, holy happiness.

Then a change came. It was a gradual change: so gradual that its beginnings were hardly noticed; maybe were not noticed at all, except by Jack Halliday, who always noticed everything; and always made fun of it, too, no matter what it was. He began to throw out chaffing remarks about people not looking quite so happy as they did a day or two ago; and next he claimed that the new aspect was deepening to positive sadness; next, that it was taking on a sick look; and finally he said that everybody was become so moody, thoughtful, and absent-minded that he could rob the meanest man in town of a cent out of the bottom of his breeches pocket and not disturb his revery.

At this stage—or at about this stage—a saying like this was dropped at bedtime—with a sigh, usually—by the head of each of the nineteen principal households:

"Ah, what *could* have been the remark that Goodson made?"

And straightway—with a shudder—came this, from the man's wife:

"Oh, *don't!* What horrible thing are you mulling in your mind? Put it away from you, for God's sake!"

But that question was wrung from those men again the next night—and got the same retort. But weaker.

And the third night the men uttered the question yet again—with anguish, and absently. This time—and the following night—the wives fidgeted feebly, and tried to say something. But didn't.

And the night after that they found their tongues and responded—longingly,

"Oh, if we *could* only guess!"

Halliday's comments grew daily more and more sparklingly disagreeable and disparaging. He went diligently about, laughing at the town, individually and in mass. But his laugh was the only one left in the village: it fell upon a hollow and mournful vacancy and emptiness. Not even a smile was findable anywhere. Halliday carried a cigar-box around on a tripod, playing that it was a camera, and halted all passers and aimed the thing and said, "Ready!—now look pleasant, please," but not even this capital joke could surprise the dreary faces into any softening.

So three weeks passed—one week was left. It was Saturday evening—after supper. Instead of the aforetime Saturday-evening flutter and bustle and shopping and larking, the streets were empty and desolate. Richards and his old wife sat apart in their little parlor—miserable and thinking. This was become their evening habit now: the life-long habit which had preceded it, of reading, knitting, and contented chat, or receiving or paying neighborly calls, was dead and gone and forgotten, ages ago—two or three weeks ago; nobody talked now, nobody read, nobody visited—the whole village sat at home, sighing, worrying, silent. Trying to guess out that remark.

The postman left a letter. Richards glanced listlessly at the superscription and the post-mark—unfamiliar, both—and tossed the letter on the table and resumed his might-have-beens and his hopeless dull miseries where he had left them off. Two or three hours later his wife got wearily up and was going away to bed without a good-night—custom now—but she stopped near the letter and eyed it awhile with a dead interest, then broke it open, and began to skim it over. Richards, sitting there with his chair tilted back against the wall and his chin between his knees, heard something fall. It was his wife. He sprang to her side, but she cried out:

"Leave me alone, I am too happy. Read the letter—read it!"

He did. He devoured it, his brain reeling. The letter was from a distant State, and it said:

> I am a stranger to you, but no matter: I have something to tell. I have just arrived home from Mexico, and learned about that episode. Of course you do not know who made that remark, but I know, and I am the only person living who does know. It was *Goodson.* I knew him well, many years ago. I passed through your village that very night, and was his guest till the midnight train came along. I overheard him make that remark to the stranger in the dark—it was in Hale Alley. He and I talked of it the rest of the way home, and while smoking in his house. He mentioned many of your villagers in the course of his talk—most of them in a very uncomplimentary way, but two or three favorably: among these latter yourself. I say "favorably"—nothing stronger. I remember his saying he did not actually *like* any person in the town—not one; but that you—I *think* he said you—am almost sure—had done him a very great service once, possibly without knowing the full value of it, and he wished he had a fortune, he would leave it to you when he died, and a curse apiece for the rest of the citizens. Now, then, if it was you that did him that service, you are his legitimate heir, and entitled to the sack of gold. I know that I can trust to your honor and honesty, for in a citizen of Hadleyburg these virtues are an unfailing inheritance, and so I am going to reveal to you the remark, well satisfied that if you are not the right man you will seek and find the right one and see that poor Goodson's debt of gratitude for the service referred to is paid. This is the remark: "*You are far from being a bad man: go, and reform.*"

> Howard L. Stephenson.

"Oh, Edward, the money is ours, and I am so grateful, *oh,* so grateful—kiss me, dear, it's forever since we kissed—and we needed it so—the money—and now you are free of Pinkerton and his bank, and nobody's slave any more; it seems to me I could fly for joy."

It was a happy half-hour that the couple spent there on the settee caressing each other; it was the old days come again—days that had begun with their courtship and lasted without a break till the stranger brought the deadly money. By-and-by the wife said:

"Oh, Edward, how lucky it was you did him that grand service, poor Goodson! I never liked him, but I love him now. And it was fine and beautiful of you never to mention it or brag about it." Then, with a touch of reproach, "But you ought to have told *me*, Edward, you ought to have told your wife, you know."

"Well, I—er—well, Mary, you see—"

"Now stop hemming and hawing, and tell me about it, Edward. I always loved you, and now I'm proud of you. Everybody believes there was only one good generous soul in this village, and now it turns out that you—Edward, why don't you tell me?"

"Well—er—er—Why, Mary, I can't!"

"You *can't*? *Why* can't you?"

"You see, he—well, he—he made me promise I wouldn't."

The wife looked him over, and said, very slowly,

"Made—you—promise? Edward, what do you tell me that for?"

"Mary, do you think I would lie?"

She was troubled and silent for a moment, then she laid her hand within his and said:

"No. . . . no. We have wandered far enough from our bearings—God spare us that! In all your life you have never uttered a lie. But now—now that the foundations of things seem to be crumbling from under us, we—we—" She lost her voice for a moment, then said, brokenly, "Lead us not into temptation. . . . I think you made the promise, Edward. Let it rest so. Let us keep away from that ground. Now—that is all gone by; let us he happy again; it is no time for clouds."

Edward found it something of an effort to comply, for his mind kept wandering—trying to remember what the service was that he had done Goodson.

The couple lay awake the most of the night, Mary happy and busy, Edward busy, but not so happy. Mary was planning what she would do with the money. Edward was trying to recall that service. At first his conscience was sore on account of the lie he had told Mary—if it was a lie. After much reflection—suppose it *was* a lie? What then? Was it such a great matter? Aren't we always *acting* lies? Then why not *tell* them? Look at Mary—look what she had done. While he was hurrying off on his honest errand, what was she doing? Lamenting because the papers hadn't been destroyed and the money kept. Is theft better than lying?

That point lost its sting—the lie dropped into the background and left comfort behind it. The next point came to the front: *had* he rendered that service? Well, here was Goodson's own evidence as reported in Stephenson's letter; there could be no better evidence than that—it was even *proof* that he had rendered it. Of course. So that point was settled . . . No, not quite. He recalled with a wince that this unknown Mr. Stephenson was just a trifle unsure as to whether the performer of it was Richards or some other—and, oh dear, he had put Richards on his honor! He must himself decide whither that money must go—and Mr. Stephenson was not doubting that if he was the wrong man he would go honorably and find the right one. Oh, it was odious to put a man in such a situation—ah, why couldn't Stephenson have left out that doubt? What did he want to intrude that for?

Further reflection. How did it happen that *Richards's* name remained in Stephenson's mind as indicating the right man, and not some other man's name? That looked good. Yes, that looked very good. In fact, it went on looking better and better, straight along—until by-and-by it grew into positive *proof*. And then Richards put the matter at once out of his mind, for he had a private instinct that a proof once established is better left so.

He was feeling reasonably comfortable now, but there was still one other detail that kept pushing itself on his notice: of course he had done that service—that was settled; but what *was* that service? He must recall it—he would not go to sleep till he had recalled it; it would make his peace of mind perfect. And so he thought and thought. He thought of a dozen things—possible services, even probable services—but none of them seemed adequate, none of them seemed large enough, none of them seemed worth the money—worth the fortune Goodson had wished he could leave in his will. And besides, he couldn't remember having done them, anyway. Now, then—now, then—what *kind* of a service would it be that would make a man so inordinately grateful? Ah—the saving of his soul! That must be it. Yes, he could remember, now, how he once set himself the task of converting Goodson, and labored at it as much as—he was going to say three months; but upon closer examination it shrunk to a month, then to a week, then to a day, then to nothing. Yes, he remembered, now, and with unwelcome vividness, that Goodson had told him to go to thunder and mind his own business—*he* wasn't hankering to follow Hadleyburg to heaven!

So that solution was a failure—he hadn't saved Goodson's soul. Richards was discouraged. Then after a little came another idea: had he saved Goodson's property? No, that wouldn't do—he hadn't any. His life? That is it! Of course. Why, he might have thought of it before. This time he was on the right track, sure. His imagination-mill was hard at work in a minute, now.

Thereafter during a stretch of two exhausting hours he was busy saving Goodson's life. He saved it in all kinds of difficult and perilous ways. In every case he got it saved satisfactorily up to a certain point; then, just as he was beginning to get well persuaded that it had really happened, a troublesome detail would turn up which made the whole thing impossible. As in the matter of drowning, for instance. In that case he had swum out and tugged Goodson ashore in an unconscious state with a great crowd looking on and applauding, but when he had got it all thought out and was just beginning to remember all about it a whole swarm of disqualifying details arrived on the ground: the town would have known of the circumstance, Mary would have known of it, it would glare like a limelight in his own memory instead of being an inconspicuous service which he had possibly rendered "without knowing its full value." And at this point he remembered that he couldn't swim, anyway.

Ah—*there* was a point which he had been overlooking from the start: it had to be a service which he had rendered "possibly without knowing the full value of it." Why, really, that ought to be an easy hunt—much easier than those others. And sure enough, by-and-by he found it. Goodson, years and years ago, came near marrying a very sweet and pretty girl, named Nancy Hewitt, but in some way or other the match had been broken off; the girl died, Goodson remained a bachelor, and by-and-by became a soured one and a frank despiser of the human species. Soon after the girl's death the village found out, or thought it had found out, that she carried a spoonful of negro blood in her veins. Richards worked at these details a good while, and in the end he thought he remembered things concerning them which must have gotten mislaid in his memory through long neglect. He seemed to dimly remember that it was *he* that found out about the negro blood; that it was he that told the village; that the village told Goodson where they got it; that he thus saved Goodson from marrying the tainted girl; that he had done him this great service "without knowing the full value of it," in fact without knowing that he *was* doing it; but that Goodson knew the value of it, and what a narrow escape he had had, and so went to his grave grateful to his benefactor and wishing he had a fortune to leave him. It was all clear and simple now, and the more he went over it the more luminous and certain it grew; and at last, when he nestled to sleep satisfied and happy, he remembered the whole thing just as if it had been yesterday. In fact, he dimly remembered Goodson's *telling* him his gratitude once. Meantime Mary had spent six thousand dollars on a new house for herself and a pair of slippers for her pastor, and then had fallen peacefully to rest.

That same Saturday evening the postman had delivered a letter to each of the other principal citizens—nineteen letters in all. No two of the envelopes were alike, and no two of the superscriptions were in the same hand, but the letters inside were just like each other in every detail but one. They were exact copies of the letter received by Richards—handwriting and all—and were all signed by Stephenson, but in place of Richards's name each receiver's own name appeared.

All night long eighteen principal citizens did what their caste-brother Richards was doing at the same time—they put in their energies trying to remember what notable service it was that they had unconsciously done Barclay Goodson. In no case was it a holiday job; still they succeeded.

And while they were at this work, which was difficult, their wives put in the night spending the money, which was easy. During that one night the nineteen wives spent an average of seven thousand dollars each out of the forty thousand in the sack—a hundred and thirty-three thousand altogether.

Next day there was a surprise for Jack Halliday. He noticed that the faces of the nineteen chief citizens and their wives bore that expression of peaceful and holy happiness again. He could not understand it, neither was he able to invent any remarks about it that could damage it or disturb it. And so it was his turn to be dissatisfied with life. His private guesses at the reasons for the happiness failed in all instances, upon examination. When he met Mrs. Wilcox and noticed the placid ecstasy in her face, he said to himself, "Her cat has had kittens"—and went and asked the cook; it was not so, the cook had detected the happiness, but did not know the cause. When Halliday found the duplicate ecstasy in the face of "Shadbelly" Billson (village nickname), he was sure some neighbor of Billson's had broken his leg, but inquiry showed that this had not happened. The subdued ecstasy in Gregory Yates's face could mean but one thing—he was a mother-in-law short; it was another mistake. "And Pinkerton—Pinkerton—he has collected ten cents that he thought he was going to lose." And so on, and so on. In some cases the guesses had to remain in doubt, in the others they proved distinct errors. In the end Halliday said to himself, "Anyway it foots up that there's nineteen Hadleyburg families temporarily in heaven; I don't know how it happened; I only know Providence is off duty to-day."

An architect and builder from the next State had lately ventured to set up a small business in this unpromising village, and his sign had now been hanging out a week. Not a customer yet; he was a discouraged man, and sorry he had come. But his weather changed suddenly now. First one and then another chief citizen's wife said to him privately:

"Come to my house Monday week—but say nothing about it for the present. We think of building."

He got eleven invitations that day. That night he wrote his daughter and broke off her match with her student. He said she could marry a mile higher than that.

Pinkerton the banker and two or three other well-to-do men planned country-seats—but waited. That kind don't count their chickens until they are hatched.

The Wilsons devised a grand new thing—a fancy-dress ball. They made no actual promises, but told all their acquaintanceship in confidence that they were thinking the matter over and thought they should give it—"and if we do, you will be invited, of course." People were surprised, and said, one to another, "Why, they are crazy, those poor Wilsons, they can't afford it." Several among the nineteen said privately to their husbands, "It is a good idea; we will keep still till their cheap thing is over, then *we* will give one that will make it sick."

The days drifted along, and the bill of future squanderings rose higher and higher, wilder and wilder, more and more foolish and reckless. It began to look as if every member of the nineteen would not only spend his whole forty thousand dollars before receiving-day, but be actually in debt by the time he got the money. In some cases light-headed people did not stop with planning to spend, they really spent—on credit. They bought land, mortgages, farms, speculative stocks, fine clothes, horses, and various other things, paid down the bonus, and made themselves liable for the rest—at ten days. Presently the sober second thought came, and Halliday noticed that a ghastly anxiety was beginning to show up in a good many faces. Again he was puzzled, and didn't know what to make of it. "The Wilcox kittens aren't dead, for they weren't born; nobody's broken a leg; there's no shrinkage in mother-in-laws; *nothing* has happened—it is an insolvable mystery."

There was another puzzled man, too—the Rev. Mr. Burgess. For days, wherever he went, people seemed to follow him or to be watching out for him; and if he ever found himself in a retired spot, a member of the nineteen would be sure to appear, thrust an envelope privately into his hand, whisper "To be opened at the town-hall Friday evening," then vanish away like a guilty thing. He was expecting that there might be one claimant for the sack—doubtful, however, Goodson being dead—but it never occurred to him that all this crowd might be claimants. When the great Friday came at last, he found that he had nineteen envelopes.

III

The town-hall had never looked finer. The platform at the end of it was backed by a showy draping of flags; at intervals along the walls were festoons of flags; the gallery fronts were clothed in flags; the supporting columns were swathed in flags; all this was to impress the stranger, for he would be there in consider-able force, and in a large degree he would be connected with the press. The house was full. The 412 fixed seats were occupied; also the 68 extra chairs which had been packed into the aisles; the steps of the platform were occupied; some distinguished strangers were given seats on the platform; at the horse-shoe of tables which fenced the front and sides of the platform sat a strong force of special correspondents who had come from everywhere. It was the best-dressed house the town had ever produced. There were some tolerably expensive toilets there, and in several cases the ladies who wore them had the look of being unfamiliar with that kind of clothes. At least the town thought they had that look, but the notion could have arisen from the town's knowledge of the fact that these ladies had never inhabited such clothes before.

The gold-sack stood on a little table at the front of the platform where all the house could see it. The bulk of the house gazed at it with a burning interest, a mouth-watering interest, a wistful and pathetic interest; a minority of nineteen couples gazed at it tenderly, lovingly, proprietarily, and the male half of this minority kept saying over to themselves the moving little impromptu speeches of thankfulness for the audience's applause and congratulations which they were presently going to get up and deliver. Every now and then one of these got a piece of paper out of his vest pocket and privately glanced at it to refresh his memory.

Of course there was a buzz of conversation going on—there always is; but at last, when the Rev. Mr. Burgess rose and laid his hand on the sack he could hear his microbes gnaw, the place was so still. He related the curious history of the sack, then went on to speak in warm terms of Hadleyburg's old and well-earned reputation for spotless honesty, and of the town's just pride in this reputation. He said that this reputation was a treasure of priceless value; that under Providence its value had now become inestimably enhanced, for the recent episode had spread this fame far and wide, and thus had focused the eyes of the American world upon this village, and made its name for all time, as he hoped and believed, a synonym for commercial incorruptibility. (*Applause.*) "And who is to be the guardian of this noble treasure—the community as a whole? No! The responsibility is individual, not communal. From this day forth each and every one of you is in his own person its special guardian, and individually responsible that no harm shall come to it. Do you—does each of you—accept this great trust? [*Tumultuous assent.*] Then all is well. Transmit it to your children and to your children's children. To-day your purity is beyond reproach—see to it that it shall remain so. To-day there is not a person in your community who could be beguiled to touch a penny not his own—see to it that you abide in this grace. [*"We will! we will!"*] This is not the place to make comparisons between ourselves and other communities—some of them ungracious towards us; they have their ways, we have ours; let us be content. [*Applause.*] I am done. Under my hand, my friends, rests a stranger's eloquent recognition of what we are; through him the world will always henceforth know what we are. We do not know who he is, but in your name I utter your gratitude, and ask you to raise your voices in indorsement."

The house rose in a body and made the walls quake with the thunders of its thankfulness for the space of a long minute. Then it sat down, and Mr. Burgess took an envelope out of his pocket. The house held its breath while he slit the envelope open and took from it a slip of paper. He read its contents—slowly and impressively—the audience listening with tranced attention to this magic document, each of whose words stood for an ingot of gold:

"'*The remark which I made to the distressed stranger was this: "You are very far from being a bad man; go, and reform."*'" Then he continued: "We shall know in a moment now whether the remark here quoted corresponds with the one concealed in the sack; and if that shall prove to be so—and it undoubtedly will—this sack of gold belongs to a fellow-citizen who will henceforth stand before the nation as the symbol of the special virtue which has made our town famous throughout the land—Mr. Billson!"

The house had gotten itself all ready to burst into the proper tornado of applause; but instead of doing it, it seemed stricken with a paralysis; there was a deep hush for a moment or two, then a wave of whispered murmurs swept the place—of about this tenor: "*Billson*! oh, come, this is *too* thin! Twenty dollars to a stranger—or *anybody*—*Billson*! Tell it to the marines!" And now at this point the house caught its breath all of a sudden in a new access of astonishment, for it discovered that whereas in one part of the hall Deacon Billson was standing up with his head meekly bowed, in another part of it Lawyer Wilson was doing the same. There was a wondering silence now for a while. Everybody was puzzled, and nineteen couples were surprised and indignant.

Billson and Wilson turned and stared at each other. Billson asked, bitingly:

"Why do *you* rise, Mr. Wilson?"

"Because I have a right to. Perhaps you will be good enough to explain to the house why *you* rise."

"With great pleasure. Because I wrote that paper."

"It is an impudent falsity! I wrote it myself."

It was Burgess's turn to be paralyzed. He stood looking vacantly at first one of the men and then the other, and did not seem to know what to do. The house was stupefied. Lawyer Wilson spoke up, now, and said,

"I ask the Chair to read the name signed to that paper."

That brought the Chair to itself, and it read out the name,

"'John Wharton *Billson*.'"

"There!" shouted Billson, "what have you got to say for yourself now? And what kind of apology are you going to make to me and to this insulted house for the imposture which you have attempted to play here?"

"No apologies are due, sir; and as for the rest of it, I publicly charge you with pilfering my note from Mr. Burgess and substituting a copy of it signed with your own name. There is no other way by which you could have gotten hold of the test-remark; I alone, of living men, possessed the secret of its wording."

There was likely to be a scandalous state of things if this went on; everybody noticed with distress that the shorthand scribes were scribbling like mad; many people were crying "Chair, Chair! Order! order!" Burgess rapped with his gavel, and said:

"Let us not forget the proprieties due. There has evidently been a mistake somewhere, but surely that is all. If Mr. Wilson gave me an envelope—and I remember now that he did—I still have it."

He took one out of his pocket, opened it, glanced at it, looked surprised and worried, and stood silent a few moments. Then he waved his hand in a wandering and mechanical way, and made an effort or two to say something, then gave it up, despondently. Several voices cried out:

"Read it! read it! What is it?"

So he began, in a dazed and sleep-walker fashion:

"*The remark which I made to the unhappy stranger was this: "You are far from being a bad man.* [The house gazed at him, marvelling.] *Go, and reform."* [*Murmurs:* "Amazing! what can this mean?"] This one," said the Chair, "is signed Thurlow G. Wilson."

"There!" cried Wilson, "I reckon that settles it! I knew perfectly well my note was purloined."

"Purloined!" retorted Billson. "I'll let you know that neither you nor any man of your kidney must venture to—"

The Chair: "Order, gentlemen, order! Take your seats, both of you, please."

They obeyed, shaking their heads and grumbling angrily. The house was profoundly puzzled; it did not know what to do with this curious emergency. Presently Thompson got up. Thompson was the hatter. He would have liked to be a Nineteener; but such was not for him; his stock of hats was not considerable enough for the position. He said:

"Mr. Chairman, if I may be permitted to make a suggestion, can both of these gentlemen be right? I put it to you, sir, can both have happened to say the very same words to the stranger? It seems to me—"

The tanner got up and interrupted him. The tanner was a disgruntled man; he believed himself entitled to be a Nineteener, but he couldn't get recognition. It made him a little unpleasant in his ways and speech. Said he:

"Sho, *that's* not the point! *That* could happen—twice in a hundred years—but not the other thing. *Neither* of them gave the twenty dollars!" (*A ripple of applause.*)

Billson. "I did!"

Wilson. "I did!"

Then each accused the other of pilfering.

The Chair. "Order! Sit down, if you please—both of you. Neither of the notes has been out of my possession at any moment."

A Voice. "Good—that settles *that!*"

The Tanner. "Mr. Chairman, one thing is now plain: one of these men has been eavesdropping under the other one's bed, and filching family secrets. If it is not unparliamentary to suggest it, I will remark that both are equal to it. [*The Chair.* "Order! order!"] I withdraw the remark, sir, and will confine myself to suggesting that *if* one of them has overheard the other reveal the test-remark to his wife, we shall catch him now."

A Voice. "How?"

The Tanner. "Easily. The two have not quoted the remark in exactly the same words. You would have noticed that, if there hadn't been a considerable stretch of time and an exciting quarrel inserted between the two readings."

A Voice. "Name the difference."

The Tanner. "The word *very* is in Billson's note, and not in the other."

Many Voices. "That's so—he's right!"

The Tanner. "And so, if the Chair will examine the test-remark in the sack, we shall know which of these two frauds—[*The Chair.* "Order!"]—which of these two adventurers—[*The Chair.* "Order! order!"]—which of these two gentlemen—[*laughter and applause*]—is entitled to wear the belt as being the first dishonest blatherskite ever bred in this town—which he has dishonored, and which will be a sultry place for him from now out!" [*Vigorous applause.*]

Many Voices. "Open it!—open the sack!"

Mr. Burgess made a slit in the sack, slid his hand in, and brought out an envelope. In it were a couple of folded notes. He said:

"One of these is marked, 'Not to be examined until all written communications which have been addressed to the Chair—if any—shall have been read.' The other is marked '*The Test.*' Allow me. It is worded—to wit:

"'I do not require that the first half of the remark which was made to me by my benefactor shall be quoted with exactness, for it was not striking, and could be forgotten; but its closing fifteen words are quite striking, and I think easily rememberable; unless *these* shall be accurately reproduced, let the applicant be regarded as an impostor. My benefactor began by saying he seldom gave advice to any one, but that it always bore the hall-mark of high value when he did give it. Then he said this—and it has never faded from my memory: *"You are far from being a bad man—"*'"

Fifty Voices. "That settles it—the money's Wilson's! Wilson! Wilson! Speech! Speech!"

People jumped up and crowded around Wilson, wringing his hand and congratulating fervently—meantime the Chair was hammering with the gavel and shouting:

"Order, gentlemen! Order! Order! Let me finish reading, please." When quiet was restored, the reading was resumed—as follows:

"'"Go, and reform—or, mark my words—some day, for your sins, you will die and go to Hell or Hadleyburg—TRY AND MAKE IT THE FORMER."'"

A ghastly silence followed. First an angry cloud began to settle darkly upon the faces of the citizenship; after a pause the cloud began to rise, and a tickled expression tried to take its place; tried so hard that it was only kept under with great and painful difficulty; the reporters, the Brixtonites, and other strangers bent their heads down and shielded their faces with their hands, and managed to hold in by main strength and heroic courtesy. At this most inopportune time burst upon the stillness the roar of a solitary voice—Jack Halliday's:

"That's got the hall-mark on it!"

Then the house let go, strangers and all. Even Mr. Burgess's gravity broke down presently, then the audience considered itself officially absolved from all restraint, and it made the most of its privilege. It was a good long laugh, and a tempestuously whole-hearted one, but it ceased at last—long enough for Mr. Burgess to try to resume, and for the people to get their eyes partially wiped; then it broke out again; and afterward yet again; then at last Burgess was able to get out these serious words:

"It is useless to try to disguise the fact—we find ourselves in the presence of a matter of grave import. It involves the honor of your town—it strikes at the town's good name. The difference of a single word between the test-remarks offered by Mr. Wilson and Mr. Billson was itself a serious thing, since it indicated that one or the other of these gentlemen had committed a theft—"

The two men were sitting limp, nerveless, crushed; but at these words both were electrified into movement, and started to get up—

"Sit down!" said the Chair, sharply, and they obeyed. "That, as I have said, was a serious thing. And it was—but for only one of them. But the matter has become graver; for the honor of both is now in formidable peril. Shall I go even further, and say in inextricable peril? Both left out the crucial fifteen words." He paused. During several moments he allowed the pervading stillness to gather and deepen its impressive effects, then added: "There would seem to be but one way whereby this could happen. I ask these gentlemen—Was there collusion?—agreement?"

A low murmur sifted through the house; its import was, "He's got them both."

Billson was not used to emergencies; he sat in a helpless collapse. But Wilson was a lawyer. He struggled to his feet, pale and worried, and said:

"I ask the indulgence of the house while I explain this most painful matter. I am sorry to say what I am about to say, since it must inflict irreparable injury upon Mr. Billson, whom I have always esteemed and respected until now, and in whose invulnerability to temptation I entirely believed—as did you all. But for the preservation of my own honor I must speak—and with frankness. I confess with shame—and I now beseech your pardon for it—that I said to the ruined stranger all of the words contained in the test-remark, including the disparaging fifteen. [*Sensation.*] When the late publication was made I recalled them, and I resolved to claim the sack of coin, for by every right I was entitled to it. Now I will ask you to consider this point, and weigh it well: that stranger's gratitude to me that night knew no bounds; he said himself that he could find no words for it that were adequate, and that if he should ever be able he would repay me a thousandfold. Now, then, I ask you this: could I expect—could I believe—could I even remotely imagine—that, feeling as he did, he would do so ungrateful a thing as to add those quite unnecessary fifteen words to his test?—set a trap for me?—expose me as a slanderer of my own town before my own people assembled in a public hall? It was preposterous; it was impossible. His test would contain only the kindly opening clause of my remark. Of that I had no shadow of doubt. You would have thought as I did. You would not have expected a base betrayal from one whom you had befriended and against whom you had committed no offence. And so, with perfect confidence, perfect trust, I wrote on a piece of paper the opening words—ending with 'Go, and reform,'—and signed it. When I was about to put it in an envelope I was called into my back office, and without thinking I left the paper lying open on my desk." He stopped, turned his head slowly toward Billson, waited a moment, then added: "I ask you to note this: when I returned, a little later, Mr. Billson was retiring by my street door." (*Sensation.*)

In a moment Billson was on his feet and shouting:

"It's a lie! It's an infamous lie!"

The Chair. "Be seated, sir! Mr. Wilson has the floor."

Billson's friends pulled him into his seat and quieted him, and Wilson went on:

"Those are the simple facts. My note was now lying in a different place on the table from where I had left it. I noticed that, but attached no importance to it, thinking a draught had blown it there. That Mr. Billson would read a private paper was a thing which could not occur to me; he was an honorable man, and he would be above that. If you will allow me to say it, I think his extra word '*very*' stands explained; it is attributable to a defect of memory. I was the only man in the world who could furnish here any detail of the test-mark—by *honorable* means. I have finished."

There is nothing in the world like a persuasive speech to fuddle the mental apparatus and upset the convictions and debauch the emotions of an audience not practised in the tricks and delusions of oratory. Wilson sat down victorious. The house submerged him in tides of approving applause; friends swarmed to him and shook him by the hand and congratulated him, and Billson was shouted down and not allowed to say a word. The Chair hammered and hammered with its gavel, and kept shouting,

"But let us proceed, gentlemen, let us proceed!"

At last there was a measurable degree of quiet, and the hatter said,

"But what is there to proceed with, sir, but to deliver the money?"

Voices. "That's it! That's it! Come forward, Wilson!"

The Hatter. "I move three cheers for Mr. Wilson, Symbol of the special virtue which—"

The cheers burst forth before he could finish; and in the midst of them— and in the midst of the clamor of the gavel also—some enthusiasts mounted Wilson on a big friend's shoulder and were going to fetch him in triumph to the platform. The Chair's voice now rose above the noise—

"Order! To your places! You forget that there is still a document to be read." When quiet had been restored he took up the document, and was going to read it, but laid it down again, saying, "I forgot; this is not to be read until all written communications received by me have first been read." He took an envelope out of his pocket, removed its enclosure, glanced at it—seemed astonished—held it out and gazed at it—stared at it.

Twenty or thirty voices cried out:

"What is it? Read it! read it!"

And he did—slowly, and wondering:

"'The remark which I made to the stranger—[*Voices.* "Hello! how's this?"]— was this: "You are far from being a bad man. [*Voices.* "Great Scott!"] Go, and reform."'[*Voice.* "Oh, saw my leg off!"] Signed by Mr. Pinkerton the banker."

The pandemonium of delight which turned itself loose now was of a sort to make the judicious weep. Those whose withers were unwrung laughed till the tears ran down; the reporters, in throes of laughter, set down disordered pot-hooks which would never in the world be decipherable; and a sleeping dog jumped up, scared out of its wits, and barked itself crazy at the turmoil. All manner of cries were scattered through the din: "We're getting rich—*two* Symbols of Incorruptibility!—without counting Billson!" "*Three!*—count Shadbelly in—we can't have too many!" "All right—Billson's elected!" "Alas, poor Wilson—victim of *two* thieves!"

A Powerful Voice. "Silence! The Chair's fished up something more out of its pocket."

Voices. "Hurrah! Is it something fresh? Read it! read! read!"

The Chair (reading). "'The remark which I made,' etc. 'You are far from being a bad man. Go,' etc. Signed, 'Gregory Yates.'"

Tornado of Voices. "Four Symbols!" "'Rah for Yates!" "Fish again!"

The house was in a roaring humor now, and ready to get all the fun out of the occasion that might be in it. Several Nineteeners, looking pale and distressed, got up and began to work their way toward the aisles, but a score of shouts went up:

"The doors, the doors—close the doors; no Incorruptible shall leave this place! Sit down, everybody!"

The mandate was obeyed.

"Fish again! Read! read!"

The Chair fished again, and once more the familiar words began to fall from its lips—"'You are far from being a bad man—'"

"Name! name! What's his name?"

"'L. Ingoldsby Sargent.'"

"Five elected! Pile up the Symbols! Go on, go on!"

"'You are far from being a bad—'"

"Name! name!"

"'Nicholas Whitworth.'"

"Hooray! hooray! it's a symbolical day!"

Somebody wailed in, and began to sing this rhyme (leaving out "it's") to the lovely *Mikado* tune of "When a man's afraid of a beautiful maid"; the audience joined in, with joy; then, just in time, somebody contributed another line—

"And don't you this forget—"

The house roared it out. A third line was at once furnished—

"Corruptibles far from Hadleyburg are—"

The house roared that one too. As the last note died, Jack Halliday's voice rose high and clear, freighted with a final line—

"But the Symbols are here, you bet!"

That was sung, with booming enthusiasm. Then the happy house started in at the beginning and sang the four lines through twice, with immense swing and dash, and finished up with a crashing three-times-three and a tiger for "Hadleyburg the Incorruptible and all Symbols of it which we shall find worthy to receive the hall-mark to-night."

Then the shoutings at the Chair began again, all over the place:

"Go on! go on! Read! read some more! Read all you've got!"

"That's it—go on! We are winning eternal celebrity!"

A dozen men got up now and began to protest. They said that this farce was the work of some abandoned joker, and was an insult to the whole community. Without a doubt these signatures were all forgeries—

"Sit down! sit down! Shut up! You are confessing. We'll find *your* names in the lot."

"Mr. Chairman, how many of those envelopes have you got?"

The Chair counted.

"Together with those that have been already examined, there are nineteen."

A storm of derisive applause broke out.

"Perhaps they all contain the secret. I move that you open them all and read every signature that is attached to a note of that sort—and read also the first eight words of the note."

"Second the motion!"

It was put and carried—uproariously. Then poor old Richards got up, and his wife rose and stood at his side. Her head was bent down, so that none might see that she was crying. Her husband gave her his arm, and so supporting her, he began to speak in a quavering voice:

"My friends, you have known us two—Mary and me—all our lives, and I think you have liked us and respected us—"

The Chair interrupted him:

"Allow me. It is quite true—that which you are saying, Mr. Richards; this town *does* know you two; it *does* like you; it *does* respect you; more—it honors you and *loves* you—"

Halliday's voice rang out:

"That's the hall-marked truth, too! If the Chair is right, let the house speak up and say it. Rise! Now, then—hip! hip! hip!—all together!"

The house rose in mass, faced toward the old couple eagerly, filled the air with a snow-storm of waving handkerchiefs, and delivered the cheers with all its affectionate heart.

The Chair then continued:

"What I was going to say is this: We know your good heart, Mr. Richards, but this is not a time for the exercise of charity toward offenders. [Shouts of "Right! right!"] I see your generous purpose in your face, but I cannot allow you to plead for these men—"

"But I was going to—"

"Please take your seat, Mr. Richards. We must examine the rest of these notes—simple fairness to the men who have already been exposed requires this. As soon as that has been done—I give you my word for this—you shall he heard."

Many voices. "Right!—the Chair is right—no interruption can be permitted at this stage! Go on!—the names! the names!—according to the terms of the motion!"

The old couple sat reluctantly down, and the husband whispered to the wife, "It is pitifully hard to have to wait; the shame will be greater than ever when they find we were only going to plead for *ourselves*."

Straightway the jollity broke loose again with the reading of the names.

"'You are far from being a bad man—' Signature, 'Robert J. Titmarsh.'"

"'You are far from being a bad man—' Signature, 'Eliphalet Weeks.'"

"'You are far from being a bad man—' Signature, 'Oscar B. Wilder.'"

At this point the house lit upon the idea of taking the eight words out of the Chairman's hands. He was not unthankful for that. Thenceforward he held up each note in its turn, and waited. The house droned out the eight words in a massed and measured and musical deep volume of sound (with a daringly close resemblance to a well-known church chant)—"'You are f-a-r from being a b-a-a-a-d man.'" Then the Chair said, "Signature, 'Archibald Wilcox.'" And so on, and so on, name after name, and everybody had an increasingly and gloriously good time except the wretched Nineteen. Now and then, when a particularly shining name was called, the house made the Chair wait while it chanted the whole of the test-remark from the beginning to the closing words, "And go to hell or Hadleyburg—try and make it the for-or-m-e-r!" and in these special cases they added a grand and agonised and imposing "A-a-a-a-*men!*"

The list dwindled, dwindled, dwindled, poor old Richards keeping tally of the count, wincing when a name resembling his own was pronounced, and waiting in miserable suspense for the time to come when it would be his humiliating privilege to rise with Mary and finish his plea, which he was intending to word thus: ". . . for until now we have never done any wrong thing, but have gone our humble way unreproached. We are very poor, we are old, and have no chick nor child to help us; we were sorely tempted, and we fell. It was my purpose when I got up before to make confession and beg that my name might not be read out in this public place, for it seemed to us that we could not bear it; but I was prevented. It was just; it was our place to suffer with the rest. It has been hard for us. It is the first time we have ever heard our name fall from any one's lips—sullied. Be merciful—for the sake of the better days; make our shame as light to bear as in your charity you can." At this point in his revery Mary nudged him, perceiving that his mind was absent. The house was chanting, "You are f-a-r," etc.

"Be ready," Mary whispered. "Your name comes now; he has read eighteen."

The chant ended.

"Next! next! next!" came volleying from all over the house.

Burgess put his hand into his pocket. The old couple, trembling, began to rise. Burgess fumbled a moment, then said,

"I find I have read them all."

Faint with joy and surprise, the couple sank into their seats, and Mary whispered,

"Oh, bless God, we are saved!—he has lost ours—I wouldn't give this for a hundred of those sacks!"

The house burst out with its *Mikado* travesty, and sang it three times with ever-increasing enthusiasm, rising to its feet when it reached for the third time the closing line—

"But the Symbols are here, you bet!"

and finishing up with cheers and a tiger for "Hadleyburg purity and our eighteen immortal representatives of it."

Then Wingate, the saddler, got up and proposed cheers "for the cleanest man in town, the one solitary important citizen in it who didn't try to steal that money—Edward Richards."

They were given with great and moving heartiness; then somebody proposed that Richards be elected sole Guardian and Symbol of the now Sacred Hadleyburg Tradition, with power and right to stand up and look the whole sarcastic world in the face.

Passed, by acclamation; then they sang the *Mikado* again, and ended it with

"And there's *one* Symbol left, you bet!"

There was a pause; then—

A Voice. "Now, then, who's to get the sack?"

The Tanner (*with bitter sarcasm*). "That's easy. The money has to be divided among the eighteen Incorruptibles. They gave the suffering stranger twenty dollars apiece—and that remark—each in his turn—it took twenty-two minutes for the procession to move past. Staked the stranger—total contribution,

$360. All they want is just the loan back—and interest—forty thousand dollars altogether."

Many Voices (*derisively*). "That's it! Divvy! divvy! Be kind to the poor—don't keep them waiting!"

The Chair. "Order! I now offer the stranger's remaining document. It says: 'If no claimant shall appear [*grand chorus of groans*], I desire that you open the sack and count out the money to the principal citizens of your town, they to take it in trust [*Cries of "Oh! Oh! Oh!"*], and use it in such ways as to them shall seem best for the propagation and preservation of your community's noble reputation for incorruptible honesty [*more cries*]—a reputation to which their names and their efforts will add a new and far-reaching lustre.' [*Enthusiastic outburst of sarcastic applause.*] That seems to be all. No—here is a postscript:

"'P.S.—CITIZENS OF HADLEYBURG: There *is* no test-remark—nobody made one. [*Great sensation.*] There wasn't any pauper stranger, nor any twenty-dollar contribution, nor any accompanying benediction and compliment—these are all inventions. [*General buzz and hum of astonishment and delight.*] Allow me to tell my story—it will take but a word or two. I passed through your town at a certain time, and received a deep offence which I had not earned. Any other man would have been content to kill one or two of you and call it square, but to me that would have been a trivial revenge, and inadequate; for the dead do not *suffer*. Besides, I could not kill you all—and, anyway, made as I am, even that would not have satisfied me. I wanted to damage every man in the place, and every woman—and not in their bodies or in their estate, but in their vanity—the place where feeble and foolish people are most vulnerable. So I disguised myself, and came back and studied you. You were easy game. You had an old and lofty reputation for honesty, and naturally you were proud of it—it was your treasure of treasures, the very apple of your eye. As soon as I found out that you carefully and vigilantly kept yourselves and your children *out of temptation*, I knew how to proceed. Why, you simple creatures, the weakest of all weak things is a virtue which has not been tested in the fire. I laid a plan, and gathered a list of names. My project was to corrupt Hadleyburg the Incorruptible. My idea was to make liars and thieves of nearly half a hundred smirchless men and women who had never in their lives uttered a lie or stolen a penny. I was afraid of Goodson. He was neither born nor reared in Hadleyburg. I was afraid that if I started to operate my scheme by getting my letter laid before you, you would say to yourselves, "Goodson is the only man among us who would give away twenty dollars to a poor devil"—and then you might not bite at my bait. But Heaven took Goodson; then I knew I was safe, and I set my trap and baited it. It may be that I shall not catch all the men to whom I mailed the pretended test secret, but I shall catch the most of them, if

I know Hadleyburg nature. [*Voices.* "Right—he got every last one of them."] I believe they will even steal ostensible *gamble*-money, rather than miss, poor, tempted, and mistrained fellows. I am hoping to eternally and everlastingly squelch your vanity and give Hadleyburg a new renown—one that will *stick*— and spread far. If I have succeeded, open the sack and summon the Committee on Propagation and Preservation of the Hadleyburg Reputation.'"

A Cyclone of Voices. "Open it! Open it! The Eighteen to the front! Committee on Propagation of the Tradition! Forward—the Incorruptibles!"

The Chair ripped the sack wide, and gathered up a handful of bright, broad, yellow coins, shook them together, then examined them—

"Friends, they are only gilded disks of lead!"

There was a crashing outbreak of delight over this news, and when the noise had subsided, the tanner called out:

"By right of apparent seniority in this business, Mr. Wilson is Chairman of the Committee on Propagation of the Tradition. I suggest that he step forward on behalf of his pals, and receive in trust the money."

A Hundred Voices. "Wilson! Wilson! Wilson! Speech! Speech!"

Wilson (in a voice trembling with anger). "You will allow me to say, and without apologies for my language, *damn* the money!"

A Voice. "Oh, and him a Baptist!"

A Voice. "Seventeen Symbols left! Step up, gentlemen, and assume your trust!"

There was a pause—no response.

The Saddler. "Mr. Chairman, we've got *one* clean man left, anyway, out of the late aristocracy; and he needs money, and deserves it. I move that you appoint Jack Halliday to get up there and auction off that sack of gilt twenty-dollar pieces, and give the result to the right man—the man whom Hadleyburg delights to honor—Edward Richards."

This was received with great enthusiasm, the dog taking a hand again; the saddler started the bids at a dollar, the Brixton folk and Barnum's representative fought hard for it, the people cheered every jump that the bids made, the excitement climbed moment by moment higher and higher, the bidders got on their mettle and grew steadily more and more daring, more and more determined, the jumps went from a dollar up to five, then to ten, then to twenty, then fifty, then to a hundred, then—

At the beginning of the auction Richards whispered in distress to his wife: "Oh, Mary, can we allow it? It—it—you see, it is an honor-reward, a testimonial to purity of character, and—and—can we allow it? Hadn't I better get up and—Oh, Mary, what ought we to do?—what do you think we—" (*Halliday's voice.* "Fifteen I'm bid!—fifteen for the sack!—twenty!—ah, thanks!—thirty—

*thanks again! Thirty, thirty, thirty!—do I hear forty?—forty it is! Keep the ball rolling, gentlemen, keep it rolling!—fifty!—thanks, noble Roman!—going at fifty, fifty, fifty!—seventy!—ninety!—splendid!—a hundred!—pile it up, pile it up!—hundred and twenty—forty!—just in time!—hundred and fifty!—*TWO *hundred!—superb! Do I hear two h—thanks!—two hundred and fifty!—"*)

"It is another temptation, Edward—I'm all in a tremble—but, oh, we've escaped *one* temptation, and that ought to warn us, to—[*"Six did I hear?— thanks!—six fifty, six f—*SEVEN *hundred!"*] And yet, Edward, when you think— nobody susp—[*"Eight hundred dollars!—hurrah!—make it nine!—Mr. Parsons, did I hear you say—thanks!—nine!—this noble sack of virgin lead going at only nine hundred dollars, gilding and all—come! do I hear—a thousand!— gratefully yours!—did some one say eleven?—a sack which is going to be the most celebrated in the whole Uni—"*] Oh, Edward" (beginning to sob), "we are *so* poor!—but—but—do as you think best—do as you think best."

Edward fell—that is, he sat still; sat with a conscience which was not satisfied, but which was overpowered by circumstances.

Meantime a stranger, who looked like an amateur detective gotten up as an impossible English earl, had been watching the evening's proceedings with manifest interest, and with a contented expression in his face; and he had been privately commenting to himself. He was now soliloquizing somewhat like this: "None of the Eighteen are bidding; that is not satisfactory; I must change that—the dramatic unities require it; they must buy the sack they tried to steal; they must pay a heavy price, too—some of them are rich. And another thing, when I make a mistake in Hadleyburg nature the man that puts that error upon me is entitled to a high honorarium, and some one must pay it. This poor old Richards has brought my judgment to shame: he is an honest man:—I don't understand it, but I acknowledge it. Yes, he saw my deuces— *and* with a straight flush, and by rights the pot is his. And it shall be a jack-pot, too, if I can manage it. He disappointed me, but let that pass."

He was watching the bidding. At a thousand, the market broke; the prices tumbled swiftly. He waited—and still watched. One competitor dropped out; then another, and another. He put in a bid or two, now. When the bids had sunk to ten dollars, he added a five; some one raised him a three; he waited a moment, then flung in a fifty-dollar jump, and the sack was his—at $1,282. The house broke out in cheers—then stopped; for he was on his feet, and had lifted his hand. He began to speak.

"I desire to say a word, and ask a favor. I am a speculator in rarities, and I have dealings with persons interested in numismatics all over the world. I can make a profit on this purchase, just as it stands; but there is a way, if I can get your approval, whereby I can make every one of these leaden twenty-dollar pieces worth its face in gold, and perhaps more. Grant me that approval, and I will give part of my gains to your Mr. Richards, whose invulnerable probity you have so justly and so cordially recognised to-night; his share shall be ten thousand dollars, and I will hand him the money to-morrow. [*Great applause from the house.* But the "invulnerable probity" made the Richardses blush prettily; however, it went for modesty, and did no harm.] If you will pass my proposition by a good majority—I would like a two-thirds vote—I will regard that as the town's consent, and that is all I ask. Rarities are always helped by any device which will rouse curiosity and compel remark. Now if I may have your permission to stamp upon the faces of each of these ostensible coins the names of the eighteen gentlemen who—"

Nine-tenths of the audience were on their feet in a moment—dog and all—and the proposition was carried with a whirlwind of approving applause and laughter.

They sat down, and all the Symbols except "Dr." Clay Harkness got up, violently protesting against the proposed outrage, and threatening to—

"I beg you not to threaten me," said the stranger, calmly. "I know my legal rights, and am not accustomed to being frightened at bluster." (*Applause.*) He sat down. "Dr." Harkness saw an opportunity here. He was one of the two very rich men of the place, and Pinkerton was the other. Harkness was proprietor of a mint; that is to say, a popular patent medicine. He was running for the Legislature on one ticket, and Pinkerton on the other. It was a close race and a hot one, and getting hotter every day. Both had strong appetites for money; each had bought a great tract of land, with a purpose: there was going to be a new railway, and each wanted to be in the Legislature and help locate the route to his own advantage; a single vote might make the decision, and with it two or three fortunes. The stake was large, and Harkness was a daring speculator. He was sitting close to the stranger. He leaned over while one or another of the other Symbols was entertaining the house with protests and appeals, and asked, in a whisper,

"What is your price for the sack?"

"Forty thousand dollars."

"I'll give you twenty."

"No."

"Twenty-five."

"No."

"Say thirty."

"The price is forty thousand dollars; not a penny less."

"All right, I'll give it. I will come to the hotel at ten in the morning. I don't want it known; will see you privately."

"Very good." Then the stranger got up and said to the house:

"I find it late. The speeches of these gentlemen are not without merit, not without interest, not without grace; yet if I may he excused I will take my leave. I thank you for the great favor which you have shown me in granting my petition. I ask the Chair to keep the sack for me until to-morrow, and to hand these three five-hundred-dollar notes to Mr. Richards." They were passed up to the Chair. "At nine I will call for the sack, and at eleven will deliver the rest of the ten thousand to Mr. Richards in person, at his home. Good-night."

Then he slipped out, and left the audience making a vast noise, which was composed of a mixture of cheers, the *Mikado* song, dog-disapproval, and the chant, "You are f-a-r from being a b-a-a-d man—a-a-a a-men!"

IV

At home the Richardses had to endure congratulations and compliments until midnight. Then they were left to themselves. They looked a little sad, and they sat silent and thinking. Finally Mary sighed and said,

"Do you think we are to blame, Edward—*much* to blame?" and her eyes wandered to the accusing triplet of big bank-notes lying on the table, where the congratulators had been gloating over them and reverently fingering them. Edward did not answer at once; then he brought out a sigh and said, hesitatingly:

"We—we couldn't help it, Mary. It—well it was ordered. *All* things are."

Mary glanced up and looked at him steadily, but he didn't return the look. Presently she said:

"I thought congratulations and praises always tasted good. But—it seems to me, now—Edward?"

"Well?"

"Are you going to stay in the bank?"

"N-no."

"Resign?"

"In the morning—by note."

"It does seem best."

Richards bowed his head in his hands and muttered:

"Before, I was not afraid to let oceans of people's money pour through my hands, but—Mary, I am so tired, so tired—"

"We will go to bed."

At nine in the morning the stranger called for the sack and took it to the hotel in a cab. At ten Harkness had a talk with him privately. The stranger asked for and got five checks on a metropolitan bank—drawn to "Bearer,"— four for $1500 each, and one for $34,000. He put one of the former in his pocket-book, and the remainder, representing $38,500, he put in an envelope, and with these he added a note, which he wrote after Harkness was gone. At eleven he called at the Richards house and knocked. Mrs. Richards peeped through the shutters, then went and received the envelope, and the stranger disappeared without a word. She came back flushed and a little unsteady on her legs, and gasped out:

"I am sure I recognised him! Last night it seemed to me that maybe I had seen him somewhere before."

"He is the man that brought the sack here?"

"I am almost sure of it."

"Then he is the ostensible Stephenson too, and sold every important citizen in this town with his bogus secret. Now if he has sent checks instead of money, we are sold too, after we thought we had escaped. I was beginning to feel fairly comfortable once more, after my night's rest, but the look of that envelope makes me sick. It isn't fat enough; $8500 in even the largest bank-notes makes more bulk than that."

"Edward, why do you object to checks?"

"Checks signed by Stephenson! I am resigned to take the $8500 if it could come in bank-notes—for it does seem that it was so ordered, Mary—but I have never had much courage, and I have not the pluck to try to market a check signed with that disastrous name. It would be a trap. That man tried to catch me; we escaped somehow or other; and now he is trying a new way. If it is checks—"

"Oh, Edward, it is *too* bad!" And she held up the checks and began to cry.

"Put them in the fire! quick! we mustn't be tempted. It is a trick to make the world laugh at *us*, along with the rest, and—Give them to *me*, since you can't do it!" He snatched them and tried to hold his grip till he could get to the stove; but he was human, he was a cashier, and he stopped a moment to make sure of the signature. Then he came near to fainting.

"Fan me, Mary, fan me! They are the same as gold!"

"Oh, how lovely, Edward! Why?"

"Signed by Harkness. What can the mystery of that be, Mary?"

"Edward, do you think—"

"Look here—look at this! Fifteen—fifteen—fifteen—thirty-four. Thirty-eight thousand five hundred! Mary, the sack isn't worth twelve dollars, and Harkness—apparently—has paid about par for it."

"And does it all come to us, do you think—instead of the ten thousand?"

"Why, it looks like it. And the checks are made to 'Bearer,' too."

"Is that good, Edward? What is it for?"

"A hint to collect them at some distant bank, I reckon. Perhaps Harkness doesn't want the matter known. What is that—a note?"

"Yes. It was with the checks."

It was in the "Stephenson" handwriting, but there was no signature. It said:

> I am a disappointed man. Your honesty is beyond the reach of temp-
> tation. I had a different idea about it, but I wronged you in that,
> and I beg pardon, and do it sincerely. I honor you—and that is sin-
> cere, too. This town is not worthy to kiss the hem of your garment.
> Dear sir, I made a square bet with myself that there were nineteen
> debauchable men in your self-righteous community. I have lost.
> Take the whole pot, you are entitled to it.

Richards drew a deep sigh, and said:

"It seems written with fire—it burns so. Mary—I am miserable again."

"I, too. Ah, dear, I wish—"

"To think, Mary—he *believes* in me."

"Oh, don't, Edward—I can't bear it."

"If those beautiful words were deserved, Mary—and God knows I believed I deserved them once—I think I could give the forty thousand dollars for them. And I would put that paper away, as representing more than gold and jewels, and keep it always. But now—We could not live in the shadow of its accusing presence, Mary."

He put it in the fire.

A messenger arrived and delivered an envelope. Richards took from it a note and read it; it was from Burgess.

> You saved me, in a difficult time. I saved you last night. It was at cost
> of a lie, but I made the sacrifice freely, and out of a grateful heart.
> None in this village knows so well as I know how brave and good
> and noble you are. At bottom you cannot respect me, knowing as
> you do of that matter of which I am accused, and by the general
> voice condemned; but I beg that you will at least believe that I am a
> grateful man; it will help me to bear my burden.
>
> [Signed] Burgess.

"Saved, once more. And on such terms!" He put the note in the fire. "I—I wish I were dead, Mary, I wish I were out of it all."

"Oh, these are bitter, bitter days, Edward. The stabs, through their very generosity, are so deep—and they come so fast!"

Three days before the election each of two thousand voters suddenly found himself in possession of a prized memento—one of the renowned bogus double-eagles. Around one of its faces was stamped these words: "THE REMARK I MADE TO THE POOR STRANGER WAS—" Around the other face was stamped these: "GO, AND REFORM. (SIGNED) PINKERTON." Thus the entire remaining refuse of the renowned joke was emptied upon a single head, and with calamitous effect. It revived the recent vast laugh and concentrated it upon Pinkerton; and Harkness's election was a walk-over.

Within twenty-four hours after the Richardses had received their checks their consciences were quieting down, discouraged; the old couple were learning to reconcile themselves to the sin which they had committed. But they were to learn, now, that a sin takes on new and real terrors when there seems a chance that it is going to be found out. This gives it a fresh and most substantial and important aspect. At church the morning sermon was of the usual pattern; it was the same old things said in the same old way; they had heard them a thousand times and found them innocuous, next to meaningless, and easy to sleep under; but now it was different: the sermon seemed to bristle with accusations; it seemed aimed straight and specially at people who were concealing deadly sins. After church they got away from the mob of congratulators as soon as they could, and hurried homeward, chilled to the bone at they did not know what—vague, shadowy, indefinite fears. And by chance they caught a glimpse of Mr. Burgess as he turned a corner. He paid no attention to their nod of recognition! He hadn't seen it; but they did not know that. What could his conduct mean? It might mean—it might mean—oh, a dozen dreadful things. Was it possible that he knew that Richards could have cleared him of guilt in that bygone time, and had been silently waiting for a chance to even up accounts? At home, in their distress they got to imagining that their servant might have been in the next room listening when Richards revealed the secret to his wife that he knew of Burgess's innocence; next, Richards began to imagine that he had heard the swish of a gown in there at that time; next, he was sure he *had* heard it. They would call Sarah in, on a pretext, and watch her face; if she had been betraying them to Mr. Burgess, it would show in her manner. They asked her some questions—questions which were so random and incoherent and seemingly purposeless that the girl felt sure that the old people's minds had been affected by their sudden good fortune; the sharp and watchful gaze which they bent upon her frightened her, and that completed the business. She blushed, she became nervous and confused, and to the old people these were plain signs of guilt—guilt of some fearful sort or other—

without doubt she was a spy and a traitor. When they were alone again they began to piece many unrelated things together and get horrible results out of the combination. When things had got about to the worst Richards was delivered of a sudden gasp, and his wife asked,

"Oh, what is it?—what is it?"

"The note—Burgess's note! Its language was sarcastic, I see it now." He quoted: "'At bottom you cannot respect me, *knowing*, as you do, of *that matter* of which I am accused'—oh, it is perfectly plain, now, God help me! He knows that I know! You see the ingenuity of the phrasing. It was a trap—and like a fool, I walked into it. And Mary—?"

"Oh, it is dreadful—I know what you are going to say—he didn't return your transcript of the pretended test-remark."

"No—kept it to destroy us with. Mary, he has exposed us to some already. I know it—I know it well. I saw it in a dozen faces after church. Ah, he wouldn't answer our nod of recognition—*he* knew what he had been doing!"

In the night the doctor was called. The news went around in the morning that the old couple were rather seriously ill—prostrated by the exhausting excitement growing out of their great windfall, the congratulations, and the late hours, the doctor said. The town was sincerely distressed; for these old people were about all it had left to be proud of, now.

Two days later the news was worse. The old couple were delirious, and were doing strange things. By witness of the nurses, Richards had exhibited checks—for $8500? No—for an amazing sum—$38,500! What could be the explanation of this gigantic piece of luck?

The following day the nurses had more news—and wonderful. They had concluded to hide the checks, lest harm come to them; but when they searched they were gone from under the patient's pillow—vanished away. The patient said:

"Let the pillow alone; what do you want?"

"We thought it best that the checks—"

"You will never see them again—they are destroyed. They came from Satan. I saw the hell-brand on them, and I knew they were sent to betray me to sin." Then he fell to gabbling strange and dreadful things which were not clearly understandable, and which the doctor admonished them to keep to themselves.

Richards was right; the checks were never seen again.

A nurse must have talked in her sleep, for within two days the forbidden gabblings were the property of the town; and they were of a surprising sort. They seemed to indicate that Richards had been a claimant for the sack himself, and that Burgess had concealed that fact and then maliciously betrayed it.

Burgess was taxed with this and stoutly denied it. And he said it was not fair to attach weight to the chatter of a sick old man who was out of his mind. Still, suspicion was in the air, and there was much talk.

After a day or two it was reported that Mrs. Richards's delirious deliveries were getting to be duplicates of her husband's. Suspicion flamed up into conviction, now, and the town's pride in the purity of its one undiscredited important citizen began to dim down and flicker toward extinction.

Six days passed, then came more news. The old couple were dying. Richards's mind cleared in his latest hour, and he sent for Burgess. Burgess said:

"Let the room be cleared. I think he wishes to say something in privacy."

"No!" said Richards; "I want witnesses. I want you all to hear my confession, so that I may die a man, and not a dog. I was clean—artificially—like the rest; and like the rest I fell when temptation came. I signed a lie, and claimed the miserable sack. Mr. Burgess remembered that I had done him a service, and in gratitude (and ignorance) he suppressed my claim and saved me. You know the thing that was charged against Burgess years ago. My testimony, and mine alone, could have cleared him, and I was a coward, and left him to suffer disgrace—"

"No—no—Mr. Richards, you—"

"My servant betrayed my secret to him—"

"No one has betrayed anything to me—"

—"and then he did a natural and justifiable thing; he repented of the saving kindness which he had done me, and he *exposed* me—as I deserved—"

"Never!—I make oath—"

"Out of my heart I forgive him."

Burgess's impassioned protestations fell upon deaf ears; the dying man passed away without knowing that once more he had done poor Burgess a wrong. The old wife died that night.

The last of the sacred Nineteen had fallen a prey to the fiendish sack; the town was stripped of the last rag of its ancient glory. Its mourning was not showy, but it was deep.

By act of the Legislature—upon prayer and petition—Hadleyburg was allowed to change its name to (never mind what—I will not give it away), and leave one word out of the motto that for many generations had graced the town's official seal.

It is an honest town once more, and the man will have to rise early that catches it napping again.

Former motto: LEAD US NOT INTO TEMPTATION.
Revised motto: LEAD US INTO TEMPTATION.

The May-Pole of Merry Mount

Nathaniel Hawthorne

With the possible exception of Herman Melville, no American writer wrote more deeply about the complexities of the American character than Nathaniel Hawthorne (1804–1864). In this story (1857), we witness an early version of the culture war, each side representing in extreme form one of two guiding ideas of the American Republic: the pursuit of happiness (see the Declaration of Independence) and the spirit of reverence (see the Mayflower Compact), each unmoderated by the other. The Merry-Mounters, the party of jollity, live carelessly for the pleasure of the moment. The Puritans, the party of gloom, live austerely in fear of Heaven. The story invites us to see both strands as part of the American character, and to ponder whether and how they can be reconciled. In the character of the young couple, Edgar and Edith, the story may be suggesting a third option based on love, at once joyous and earnest, winning the respect even of the most Puritan of Puritans.

What can be said for and against the two dominant parties? Is there really some middle way combining the virtues of each without their correlative vices? Where in the American idea do we find support for the blend of self-sacrifice and self-fulfillment implicit in love, marriage, and family?

There is an admirable foundation for a philosophic romance, in the curious history of the early settlement of Mount Wollaston, or Merry Mount. In the slight sketch here attempted, the facts, recorded on the grave pages of our New England annalists, have wrought themselves, almost spontaneously, into a sort of allegory. The masques, mummeries, and festive customs, described in the text, are in accordance with the manners of the age. Authority on these points may be found in Strutt's Book of English Sports and Pastimes.

Bright were the days at Merry Mount, when the May-Pole was the banner-staff of that gay colony! They who reared it, should their banner be triumphant, were to pour sunshine over New England's rugged hills, and scatter flower-seeds throughout the soil. Jollity and gloom were contending for an empire. Midsummer eve had come, bringing deep verdure to the forest, and roses in her lap, of a more vivid hue than the tender buds of Spring. But May, or her mirthful spirit, dwelt all the year round at Merry Mount, sporting with the Summer months, and revelling with Autumn, and basking in the glow of Winter's fireside. Through a world of toil and care she flitted with a dreamlike smile, and came hither to find a home among the lightsome hearts of Merry Mount.

Never had the May-Pole been so gayly decked as at sunset on midsummer eve. This venerated emblem was a pine tree, which had preserved the slender grace of youth, while it equaled the loftiest height of the old wood monarchs. From its top streamed a silken banner, colored like the rainbow. Down nearly to the ground, the pole was dressed with birchen boughs, and others of the liveliest green, and some with silvery leaves, fastened by ribbons that fluttered in fantastic knots of twenty different colors, but no sad ones. Garden flowers, and blossoms of the wilderness, laughed gladly forth amid the verdure, so fresh and dewy, that they must have grown by magic on that happy pine tree. Where this green and flowery splendor terminated, the shaft of the May-Pole was stained with the seven brilliant hues of the banner at its top. On the lowest green bough hung an abundant wreath of roses, some that had been gathered in the sunniest spots of the forest, and others, of still richer blush, which the colonists had reared from English seed. Oh, people of the Golden Age, the chief of your husbandry, was to raise flowers!

But what was the wild throng that stood hand in hand about the May-Pole? It could not be, that the Fauns and Nymphs, when driven from their classic groves and homes of ancient fable, had sought refuge, as all the persecuted did, in the fresh woods of the West. These were Gothic monsters, though perhaps of Grecian ancestry. On the shoulders of a comely youth, uprose the head and branching antlers of a stag; a second, human in all other points, had the grim visage of a wolf; a third, still with the trunk and limbs of a mortal man, showed the beard and horns of a venerable he-goat. There was the likeness of a bear erect, brute in all but his hind legs, which were adorned with pink silk stockings. And here again, almost as wondrous, stood a real bear of the dark forest, lending each of his fore paws to the grasp of a human hand, and as ready for the dance as any in that circle. His inferior nature rose half-way, to meet his companions as they stooped. Other faces wore the similitude of man or woman, but distorted or extravagant, with red noses pendulous before their mouths, which seemed of awful depth, and stretched from ear to ear in an eternal fit of laughter. Here might be seen the Salvage Man, well known in heraldry, hairy as a baboon, and girdled with green leaves. By his side, a nobler figure, but still a counterfeit, appeared an Indian hunter, with feathery crest and wampum belt. Many of this strange company wore fools-caps, and had little bells appended to their garments, tinkling with a silvery sound, responsive to the inaudible music of their gleesome spirits. Some youths and maidens were of soberer garb, yet well maintained their places in the irregular throng, by the expression of wild revelry upon their features. Such were the colonists of Merry Mount, as they stood in the broad smile of sunset, round their venerated May-Pole.

Had a wanderer, bewildered in the melancholy forest, heard their mirth, and stolen a half-affrighted glance, he might have fancied them the crew of Comus, some already transformed to brutes, some midway between man and beast, and the others rioting in the flow of tipsy jollity that foreran the change. But a band of Puritans, who watched the scene, invisible themselves, compared the masques to those devils and ruined souls, with whom their superstition peopled the black wilderness.

Within the ring of monsters, appeared the two airiest forms, that had ever trodden on any more solid footing than a purple and golden cloud. One was a youth, in glistening apparel, with a scarf of the rainbow pattern crosswise on his breast. His right hand held a gilded staff, the ensign of high dignity among the revellers, and his left grasped the slender fingers of a fair maiden, not less gayly decorated than himself. Bright roses glowed in contrast with the dark and glossy curls of each, and were scattered round their feet, or had sprung up spontaneously there. Behind this lightsome couple, so close to the May-Pole that its boughs shaded his jovial face, stood the figure of an English priest, canonically dressed, yet decked with flowers, in heathen fashion, and wearing a chaplet of the native vine leaves. By the riot of his rolling eye, and the pagan decorations of his holy garb, he seemed the wildest monster there, and the very Comus of the crew.

"Votaries of the May-Pole," cried the flower-decked priest, "merrily, all day long, have the woods echoed to your mirth. But be this your merriest hour, my hearts! Lo, here stand the Lord and Lady of the May, whom I, a clerk of Oxford, and high priest of Merry Mount, am presently to join in holy matrimony. Up with your nimble spirits, ye morrice-dancers, green-men, and glee-maidens, bears and wolves, and horned gentlemen! Come; a chorus now, rich with the old mirth of Merry England, and the wilder glee of this fresh forest; and then a dance, to show the youthful pair what life is made of, and how airily they should go through it! All ye that love the May-Pole, lend your voices to the nuptial song of the Lord and Lady of the May!"

This wedlock was more serious than most affairs of Merry Mount, where jest and delusion, trick and fantasy, kept up a continued carnival. The Lord and Lady of the May, though their titles must be laid down at sunset, were really and truly to be partners for the dance of life, beginning the measure that same bright eve. The wreath of roses, that hung from the lowest green bough of the May-Pole, had been twined for them, and would be thrown over both their heads, in symbol of their flowery union. When the priest had spoken, therefore, a riotous uproar burst from the rout of monstrous figures.

"Begin you the stave, reverend Sir," cried they all; "and never did the woods ring to such a merry peal, as we of the May-Pole shall send up!"

Immediately a prelude of pipe, cittern, and viol, touched with practised minstrelsy, began to play from a neighboring thicket, in such a mirthful cadence that the boughs of the May-Pole quivered to the sound. But the May Lord, he of the gilded staff, chancing to look into his Lady's eyes, was wonder-struck at the almost pensive glance that met his own.

"Edith, sweet Lady of the May," whispered he, reproachfully, "is yon wreath of roses a garland to hang above our graves, that you look so sad? Oh, Edith, this is our golden time! Tarnish it not by any pensive shadow of the mind; for it may be, that nothing of futurity will be brighter than the mere remembrance of what is now passing."

"That was the very thought that saddened me! How came it in your mind too?" said Edith, in a still lower tone than he; for it was high treason to be sad at Merry Mount. "Therefore do I sigh amid this festive music. And besides, dear Edgar, I struggle as with a dream, and fancy that these shapes of our jovial friends are visionary, and their mirth unreal, and that we are no true Lord and Lady of the May. What is the mystery in my heart?"

Just then, as if a spell had loosened them, down came a little shower of withering rose leaves from the May-Pole. Alas, for the young lovers! No sooner had their hearts glowed with real passion, than they were sensible of something vague and unsubstantial in their former pleasures, and felt a dreary presentiment of inevitable change. From the moment that they truly loved, they had subjected themselves to earth's doom of care, and sorrow, and troubled joy, and had no more a home at Merry Mount. That was Edith's mystery. Now leave we the priest to marry them, and the masquers to sport round the May-Pole, till the last sunbeam be withdrawn from its summit, and the shadows of the forest mingle gloomily in the dance. Meanwhile, we may discover who these gay people were.

Two hundred years ago, and more, the old world and its inhabitants became mutually weary of each other. Men voyaged by thousands to the West; some to barter glass beads, and such like jewels, for the furs of the Indian hunter; some to conquer virgin empires; and one stern band to pray. But none of these motives had much weight with the colonists of Merry Mount. Their leaders were men who had sported so long with life, that when Thought and Wisdom came, even these unwelcome guests were led astray, by the crowd of vanities which they should have put to flight. Erring Thought and perverted Wisdom were made to put on masques, and play the fool. The men of whom we speak, after losing the heart's fresh gaiety, imagined a wild philosophy of pleasure, and came hither to act out their latest day-dream. They gathered followers from all that giddy tribe, whose whole life is like the festal days of soberer men. In their train were minstrels, not unknown in London streets; wandering players, whose theatres had been the halls of noblemen; mummers, rope-dancers, and mountebanks, who would long be missed at wakes, church-ales, and fairs; in a word, mirth-makers of every sort, such as abounded in that age, but now began to be discountenanced by the rapid growth of Puritanism. Light had their footsteps been on land, and as lightly they came across the sea. Many had been maddened by their previous troubles into a gay despair; others were as madly gay in the flush of youth, like the May Lord and his Lady; but whatever might be the quality of their mirth, old and young were gay at Merry Mount. The young deemed themselves happy. The elder spirits, if they knew that mirth was but the counterfeit of happiness, yet followed the false shadow wilfully, because at least her garments glittered brightest. Sworn triflers of a lifetime, they would not venture among the sober truths of life, not even to be truly blest.

All the hereditary pastimes of Old England were transplanted hither. The King of Christmas was duly crowned, and the Lord of Misrule bore potent sway. On the Eve of St. John, they felled whole acres of the forest to make bon-fires, and danced by the blaze all night, crowned with garlands, and throwing flowers into the flame. At harvest time, though their crop was of the smallest, they made an image with the sheaves of Indian corn, and wreathed it with autumnal garlands, and bore it home triumphantly. But what chiefly charac-terized the colonists of Merry Mount, was their veneration for the May-Pole. It has made their true history a poet's tale. Spring decked the hallowed emblem with young blossoms and fresh green boughs; Summer brought roses of the deepest blush, and the perfected foliage of the forest; Autumn enriched it with that red and yellow gorgeousness, which converts each wild-wood leaf into a painted flower; and Winter silvered it with sleet, and hung it round with icicles, till it flashed in the cold sunshine, itself a frozen sunbeam. Thus each alternate season did homage to the May-Pole, and paid it a tribute of its own richest splendor. Its votaries danced round it, once, at least, in every month; sometimes they called it their religion, or their altar; but always, it was the banner-staff of Merry Mount.

Unfortunately, there were men in the new world, of a sterner faith than these May-Pole worshippers. Not far from Merry Mount was a settlement of Puritans, most dismal wretches, who said their prayers before daylight, and then wrought in the forest or the cornfield, till evening made it prayer time again. Their weapons were always at hand, to shoot down the straggling savage. When they met in conclave, it was never to keep up the old English mirth, but to hear sermons three hours long, or to proclaim bounties on the heads of wolves and the scalps of Indians. Their festivals were fast-days, and their chief pastime the singing of psalms. Woe to the youth or maiden, who did but dream of a dance! The selectman nodded to the constable; and there sat the light-heeled reprobate in the stocks; or if he danced, it was round the whipping-post, which might be termed the Puritan May-Pole.

A party of these grim Puritans, toiling through the difficult woods, each with a horse-load of iron armor to burthen his footsteps, would sometimes draw near the sunny precincts of Merry Mount. There were the silken colonists, sporting round their May-Pole; perhaps teaching a bear to dance, or striving to communicate their mirth to the grave Indian; or masquerading in the skins of deer and wolves, which they had hunted for that especial purpose. Often, the whole colony were playing at blindman's bluff, magistrates and all with their eyes bandaged, except a single scape-goat, whom the blinded sinners pursued by the tinkling of the bells at his garments. Once, it is said, they were seen following a flower-decked corpse, with merriment and festive music, to his grave. But did the dead man laugh? In their quietest times, they sang ballads and told tales, for the edification of their pious visitors; or perplexed them with juggling tricks; or grinned at them through horse-collars; and when sport itself grew wearisome, they made game of their own stupidity, and began a yawning match. At the very least of these enormities, the men of iron shook their heads and frowned so darkly, that the revelers looked up, imagining that a momentary cloud had overcast the sunshine, which was to be perpetual there. On the other hand, the Puritans affirmed, that, when a psalm was pealing from their place of worship, the echo, which the forest sent them back, seemed often like the chorus of a jolly catch, closing with a roar of laughter. Who but the fiend, and his bond-slaves, the crew of Merry Mount, had thus disturbed them! In due time, a feud arose, stern and bitter on one side, and as serious on the other as any thing could be, among such light spirits as had sworn allegiance to the May-Pole. The future complexion of New

England was involved in this important quarrel. Should the grisly saints establish their jurisdiction over the gay sinners, then would their spirits darken all the clime, and make it a land of clouded visages, of hard toil, of sermon and psalm, forever. But should the banner-staff of Merry Mount be fortunate, sunshine would break upon the hills, and flowers would beautify the forest, and late posterity do homage to the May-Pole!

After these authentic passages from history, we return to the nuptials of the Lord and Lady of the May. Alas! we have delayed too long, and must darken our tale too suddenly. As we glance again at the May-Pole, a solitary sunbeam is fading from the summit, and leaves only a faint golden tinge, blended with the hues of the rainbow banner. Even that dim light is now withdrawn, relinquishing the whole domain of Merry Mount to the evening gloom, which has rushed so instantaneously from the black surrounding woods. But some of these black shadows have rushed forth in human shape.

Yes: with the setting sun, the last day of mirth had passed from Merry Mount. The ring of gay masquers was disordered and broken; the stag lowered his antlers in dismay; the wolf grew weaker than a lamb; the bells of the morrice-dancers tinkled with tremulous affright. The Puritans had played a characteristic part in the May-Pole mummeries. Their darksome figures were intermixed with the wild shapes of their foes, and made the scene a picture of the moment, when waking thoughts start up amid the scattered fantasies of a dream. The leader of the hostile party stood in the centre of the circle, while the rout of monsters cowered around him, like evil spirits in the presence of a dread magician. No fantastic foolery could look him in the face. So stern was the energy of his aspect, that the whole man, visage, frame, and soul, seemed wrought of iron, gifted with life and thought, yet all of one substance with his head-piece and breast-plate. It was the Puritan of Puritans; it was Endicott himself!

"Stand off, priest of Baal!" said he, with a grim frown, and laying no reverent hand upon the surplice. "I know thee, Blackstone!* Thou art the man, who couldst not abide the rule even of thine own corrupted church, and hast come hither to preach iniquity, and to give example of it in thy life. But now shall it be seen that the Lord hath sanctified this wilderness for his peculiar people. Woe unto them that would defile it! And first for this flower-decked abomination, the altar of thy worship!"

And with his keen sword, Endicott assaulted the hallowed May-Pole. Nor long did it resist his arm. It groaned with a dismal sound; it showered leaves,

* Did Governor Endicott speak less positively, we should suspect a mistake here. The Rev. Mr. Blackstone, though an eccentric, is not known to have been an immoral man. We rather doubt his identity with the priest of Merry Mount.

and rose-buds upon the remorseless enthusiast; and finally, with all its green boughs, and ribbons, and flowers, symbolic of departed pleasures, down fell the banner-staff of Merry Mount. As it sank, tradition says, the evening sky grew darker, and the woods threw forth a more sombre shadow.

"There," cried Endicott, looking triumphantly on his work, "there lies the only May-Pole in New England! The thought is strong within me, that, by its fall, is shadowed forth the fate of light and idle mirth-makers, amongst us and our posterity. Amen, saith John Endicott!"

"Amen!" echoed his followers.

But the votaries of the May-Pole gave one groan for their idol. At the sound, the Puritan leader glanced at the crew of Comus, each a figure of broad mirth, yet, at this moment, strangely expressive of sorrow and dismay.

"Valiant captain," quoth Peter Palfrey, the Ancient of the band, "what order shall be taken with the prisoners?"

"I thought not to repent me of cutting down a May-Pole," replied Endicott, "yet now I could find in my heart to plant it again, and give each of these bestial pagans one other dance round their idol. It would have served rarely for a whipping-post!"

"But there are pine trees enow," suggested the lieutenant.

"True, good Ancient," said the leader. "Wherefore, bind the heathen crew, and bestow on them a small matter of stripes apiece, as earnest of our future justice. Set some of the rogues in the stocks to rest themselves, so soon as Providence shall bring us to one of our own well-ordered settlements, where such accommodations may be found. Further penalties, such as branding and cropping of ears, shall be thought of hereafter."

"How many stripes for the priest?" inquired Ancient Palfrey.

"None as yet," answered Endicott, bending his iron frown upon the culprit. "It must be for the Great and General Court to determine, whether stripes and long imprisonment, and other grievous penalty, may atone for his transgressions. Let him look to himself! For such as violate our civil order, it may be permitted us to show mercy. But woe to the wretch that troubleth our religion!"

"And this dancing bear," resumed the officer. "Must he share the stripes of his fellows?"

"Shoot him through the head!" said the energetic Puritan. "I suspect witchcraft in the beast."

"Here be a couple of shining ones," continued Peter Palfrey, pointing his weapon at the Lord and Lady of the May. "They seem to be of high station among these mis-doers. Methinks their dignity will not be fitted with less than a double share of stripes."

Endicott rested on his sword, and closely surveyed the dress and aspect of the hapless pair. There they stood, pale, downcast, and apprehensive. Yet there was an air of mutual support, and of pure affection, seeking aid and giving it, that showed them to be man and wife, with the sanction of a priest upon their love. The youth, in the peril of the moment, had dropped his gilded staff, and thrown his arm about the Lady of the May, who leaned against his breast, too lightly to burthen him, but with weight enough to express that their destinies were linked together, for good or evil. They looked first at each other, and then into the grim captain's face. There they stood, in the first hour of wedlock, while the idle pleasures, of which their companions were the emblems, had given place to the sternest cares of life, personified by the dark Puritans. But never had their youthful beauty seemed so pure and high, as when its glow was chastened by adversity.

"Youth," said Endicott, "ye stand in an evil case, thou and thy maiden wife. Make ready presently; for I am minded that ye shall both have a token to remember your wedding-day!"

"Stern man," exclaimed the May Lord, "how can I move thee? Were the means at hand, I would resist to the death. Being powerless, I entreat! Do with me as thou wilt; but let Edith go untouched!"

"Not so," replied the immitigable zealot. "We are not wont to show an idle courtesy to that sex, which requireth the stricter discipline. What sayest thou, maid? Shall thy silken bridegroom suffer thy share of the penalty, besides his own?"

"Be it death," said Edith, "and lay it all on me!"

Truly, as Endicott had said, the poor lovers stood in a woeful case. Their foes were triumphant, their friends captive and abased, their home desolate, the benighted wilderness around them, and a rigorous destiny, in the shape of the Puritan leader, their only guide. Yet the deepening twilight could not altogether conceal, that the iron man was softened; he smiled, at the fair spectacle of early love; he almost sighed, for the inevitable blight of early hopes.

"The troubles of life have come hastily on this young couple," observed Endicott. "We will see how they comport themselves under their present trials, ere we burthen them with greater. If, among the spoil, there be any garments of a more decent fashion, let them be put upon this May Lord and his Lady, instead of their glistening vanities. Look to it, some of you."

"And shall not the youth's hair be cut?" asked Peter Palfrey, looking with abhorrence at the love-lock and long glossy curls of the young man.

"Crop it forthwith, and that in the true pumpkin-shell fashion," answered the captain. "Then bring them along with us, but more gently than their fellows. There be qualities in the youth, which may make him valiant to fight, and sober to toil, and pious to pray; and in the maiden, that may fit her to become a mother in our Israel, bringing up babes in better nurture than her own hath been. Nor think ye, young ones, that they are the happiest, even in our lifetime of a moment, who misspend it in dancing round a May-Pole!"

And Endicott, the severest Puritan of all who laid the rock-foundation of New England, lifted the wreath of roses from the ruin of the May-Pole, and threw it, with his own gauntleted hand, over the heads of the Lord and Lady of the May. It was a deed of prophecy. As the moral gloom of the world overpowers all systematic gaiety, even so was their home of wild mirth made desolate amid the sad forest. They returned to it no more. But, as their flowery garland was wreathed of the brightest roses that had grown there, so, in the tie that united them, were intertwined all the purest and best of their early joys. They went heavenward, supporting each other along the difficult path which it was their lot to tread, and never wasted one regretful thought on the vanities of Merry Mount.

Defender of the Faith

Philip Roth

The American Republic has among its primary purposes the protection of the rights of individuals, free and equal. It also defends the rights of individuals to practice their several religions. But the simultaneous exaltation of the happiness-seeking and rights-bearing individual and the protection of distinct religious and ethnic groupings pose a challenge to our national self-identification as (unhyphenated) Americans. This story (1959) by Philip Roth (born 1933) about religious tolerance, and especially its abuse, explores these tensions as they emerge in the one institution whose mission is defined in service to the nation as a whole: the military.

What happens when obligations to the whole are in tension with one's religious (or ethnic) commitments? How tolerant can we afford to be of "mixed identities," especially when ethnic and religious identities are exploited by self-seeking individuals to disguise and justify their own pursuit of advantage and happiness? Who in the story is the "defender of the faith"? Which faith(s)?

In May of 1945, only a few weeks after the fighting had ended in Europe, I was rotated back to the States, where I spent the remainder of the war with a training company at Camp Crowder, Missouri. We had been racing across Germany so swiftly during the late winter and spring that when I boarded the plane that drizzly morning in Berlin, I couldn't believe our destination lay to the west. My mind might inform me otherwise, but there was an inertia of the spirit that told me we were flying to a new front where we would disembark and continue our push eastward—eastward until we'd circled the globe, marching through villages along whose twisting, cobbled streets crowds of the enemy would watch us take possession of what up till then they'd considered their own. I had changed enough in two years not to mind the trembling of the old people, the crying of the very young, the uncertain fear in the eyes of the once-arrogant. After two years I had been fortunate enough to develop an infantry-man's heart, which, like his feet, at first aches and swells, but finally grows horny enough for him to travel the weirdest paths without feeling a thing.

Captain Paul Barrett was to be my C.O. at Camp Crowder. The day I reported for duty he came out of his office to shake my hand. He was short, gruff, and fiery, and indoors or out he wore his polished helmet liner down on his little eyes. In Europe he had received a battlefield commission and a serious chest wound, and had been returned to the States only a few months before. He spoke easily to me, but was, I thought, unnecessarily abusive towards the troops. At the evening formation, he introduced me.

"Gentlemen," he called. "Sergeant Thurston, as you know, is no longer with this Company. Your new First Sergeant is Sergeant Nathan Marx here. He is a veteran of the European theater and consequently will take no shit."

I sat up late in the orderly room that evening, trying halfheartedly to solve the riddle of duty rosters, personnel forms, and morning reports. The CQ slept with his mouth open on a mattress on the floor. A trainee stood reading the next day's duty roster, which was posted on the bulletin board directly inside the screen door. It was a warm evening and I could hear the men's radios play-ing dance music over in the barracks.

The trainee, who I knew had been staring at me whenever I looked grog-gily into the forms, finally took a step in my direction.

"Hey, Sarge—we having a G.I. party tomorrow night?" A G.I. party is a barracks-cleaning.

"You usually have them on Friday nights?"

"Yes," and then he added mysteriously, "that's the whole thing."

"Then you'll have a G.I. party."

He turned away and I heard him mumbling. His shoulders were moving and I wondered if he was crying.

"What's your name, soldier?" I asked.

He turned, not crying at all. Instead his green-speckled eyes, long and nar-row, flashed like fish in the sun. He walked over to me and sat on the edge of my desk.

He reached out a hand. "Sheldon," he said.

"Stand on your own two feet, Sheldon."

Climbing off the desk, he said, "Sheldon Grossbart." He smiled wider at the intimacy into which he'd led me.

"You against cleaning the barracks Friday night, Grossbart? Maybe we shouldn't have G.I. parties—maybe we should get a maid." My tone startled me: I felt like a Charlie McCarthy, with every top sergeant I had ever known as my Edgar Bergen.

"No, Sergeant." He grew serious, but with a seriousness that seemed only to be the stifling of a smile. "It's just G.I. parties on Friday night, of all nights . . ."

He slipped up to the corner of the desk again—not quite sitting, but not quite standing either. He looked at me with those speckled eyes flashing and then made a gesture with his hand. It was very slight, no more than a rotation back and forth of the wrist, and yet it managed to exclude from our affairs everything else in the orderly room, to make the two of us the center of the world. It seemed, in fact, to exclude everything about the two of us except our hearts. "Sergeant Thurston was one thing," he whispered, an eye flashing to the sleeping CQ "but we thought with you here, things might be a little different."

"We?"

"The Jewish personnel."

"Why?" I said, harshly.

He hesitated a moment, and then, uncontrollably, his hand went up to his mouth. "I mean . . ." he said.

"What's on your mind?" Whether I was still angry at the "Sheldon" business or something else, I hadn't a chance to tell—but clearly I was angry.

". . . we thought you . . . Marx, you know, like Karl Marx. The Marx brothers. Those guys are all . . . M-A-R-X, isn't that how you spell it, Sergeant?"

"M-A-R-X."

"Fishbein said—" He stopped. "What I mean to say, Sergeant—" His face and neck were red, and his mouth moved but no words came out. In a moment, he raised himself to attention, gazing down at me. It was as though he had suddenly decided he could expect no more sympathy from me than from Thurston, the reason being that I was of Thurston's faith and not his. The young man had managed to confuse himself as to what my faith really was, but I felt no desire to straighten him out. Very simply, I didn't like him.

When I did nothing but return his gaze, he spoke, in an altered tone. "You see, Sergeant," he explained to me, "Friday nights, Jews are supposed to go to services."

"Did Sergeant Thurston tell you you couldn't go to them when there was a G.I. party?"

"No."

"Did he say you had to stay and scrub the floors?"

"No, Sergeant."

"Did the Captain say you had to stay and scrub the floors?"

"That isn't it, Sergeant. It's the other guys in the barracks." He leaned toward me. "They think we're goofing off. But we're not. That's when Jews go to services, Friday night. We have to."

"Then go."

"But the other guys make accusations. They have no right."

"That's not the Army's problem, Grossbart. It's a personal problem you'll have to work out yourself."

"But it's un*fair*."

I got up to leave. "There's nothing I can do about it," I said.

Grossbart stiffened in front of me. "But this is a matter of *religion*, sir."

"Sergeant."

"I mean 'Sergeant,'" he said, almost snarling.

"Look, go see the chaplain. The I.G. You want to see Captain Barrett, I'll arrange an appointment."

"No, no. I don't want to make trouble, Sergeant. That's the first thing they throw up to you. I just want my rights!"

"Damn it, Grossbart, stop whining. You have your rights. You can stay and scrub floors or you can go to *shul*—"

The smile swam in again. Spittle gleamed at the corners of his mouth. "You mean church, Sergeant."

"I mean *shul*, Grossbart!" I walked past him and outside. Near me I heard the scrunching of a guard's boots on gravel. In the lighted windows of the barracks the young men in T-shirts and fatigue pants were sitting on their bunks, polishing their rifles. Suddenly there was a light rustling behind me. I turned and saw Grossbart's dark frame fleeing back to the barracks, racing to tell his Jewish friends that they were right—that like Karl and Harpo, I was one of them.

The next morning, while chatting with the Captain, I recounted the incident of the previous evening, as if to unburden myself of it. Somehow in the telling it seemed to the Captain that I was not so much explaining Grossbart's position as defending it.

"Marx, I'd fight side by side with a nigger if the fellow proved to me he was a man. I pride myself," the Captain said looking out the window, "that I've got an open mind. Consequently, Sergeant, nobody gets special treatment here, for the good *or* the bad. All a man's got to do is prove himself. A man fires well on the range, I give him a weekend pass. He scores high in PT, he gets a weekend pass. He *earns* it." He turned from the window and pointed a finger at me. "You're a Jewish fellow, am I right, Marx?"

"Yes, sir."

"And I admire you. I admire you because of the ribbons on your chest, not because you had a hem stitched on your dick before you were old enough to even know you had one. I judge a man by what he shows me on the field of battle, Sergeant. It's what he's got *here*," he said, and then, though I expected he would point to his heart, he jerked a thumb towards the buttons straining to hold his blouse across his belly. "Guts," he said.

"Okay, sir, I only wanted to pass on to you how the men felt."

"Mr. Marx, you're going to be old before your time if you worry about how the men feel. Leave that stuff to the Chaplain—pussy, the clap, church picnics with the little girls from Joplin, that's all his business, not yours. Let's us train these fellas to shoot straight. If the Jewish personnel feels the other men are accusing them of goldbricking . . . well, I just don't know. Seems awful funny how suddenly the Lord is calling so loud in Private Grossman's ear he's just got to run to church."

"Synagogue," I said.

"Synagogue is right, Sergeant. I'll write that down for handy reference. Thank you for stopping by."

That evening, a few minutes before the company gathered outside the orderly room for the chow formation, I called the CQ, Corporal Robert LaHill, in to see me. LaHill was a dark burly fellow whose hair curled out of his clothes wherever it could. He carried a glaze in his eyes that made one think of caves and dinosaurs. "LaHill," I said, "when you take the formation, remind the men that they're free to attend church services *whenever* they are held, provided they report to the orderly room before they leave the area."

LaHill didn't flicker; he scratched his wrist, but gave no indication that he'd heard or understood.

"LaHill," I said, "*church*. You remember? Church, priest, Mass, confession . . ."

He curled one lip into a ghastly smile; I took it for a signal that for a second he had flickered back up into the human race.

"Jewish personnel who want to attend services this evening are to fall out in front of the orderly room at 1900." And then I added, "By order of Captain Barrett."

A little while later, as a twilight softer than any I had seen that year dropped over Camp Crowder, I heard LaHill's thick, inflectionless voice outside my window: "Give me your ears, troopers. Toppie says for me to tell you that at 1900 hours all Jewish personnel is to fall out in front here if they wants to attend the Jewish Mass."

At seven o'clock, I looked out of the orderly-room window and saw three soldiers in starched khakis standing alone on the dusty quadrangle. They looked at their watches and fidgeted while they whispered back and forth. It was getting darker, and alone on the deserted field they looked tiny. When I walked to the door I heard the noises of the G.I. party coming from the surrounding barracks—bunks being pushed to the wall, faucets pounding water into buckets, brooms whisking at the wooden floors. In the windows big puffs of cloth moved round and round, cleaning the dirt away for Saturday's inspection. I walked outside and the moment my foot hit the ground I thought I heard Grossbart, who was now in the center, call to the other two, "Ten-*hut*!" Or maybe when they all three jumped to attention, I imagined I heard the command.

At my approach, Grossbart stepped forward. "Thank you, sir," he said.

"Sergeant, Grossbart," I reminded him. "You call officers 'Sir.' I'm not an officer. You've been in the Army three weeks—you know that."

He turned his palms out at his sides to indicate that, in truth, he and I lived beyond convention. "Thank you, anyway," he said.

"Yes," the tall boy behind him said. "Thanks a lot."

And the third whispered, "Thank you," but his mouth barely fluttered so that he did not alter by more than a lip's movement, the posture of attention.

"For what?" I said.

Grossbart snorted, happily. "For the announcement before. The Corporal's announcement. It helped. It made it . . ."

"Fancier." It was the tall boy finishing Grossbart's sentence.

Grossbart smiled. "He means formal, sir. Public," he said to me. "Now it won't seem as though we're just taking off, goldbricking, because the work has begun."

"It was by order of Captain Barrett," I said.

"Ahh, but you pull a little weight . . ." Grossbart said. "So we thank you." Then he turned to his companions. "Sergeant Marx, I want you to meet Larry Fishbein."

The tall boy stepped forward and extended his hand. I shook it. "You from New York?" he asked.

"Yes."

"Me too." He had a cadaverous face that collapsed inward from his cheekbone to his jaw, and when he smiled—as he did at the news of our communal attachment—revealed a mouthful of bad teeth. He blinked his eyes a good deal, as though he were fighting back tears. "What borough?" he asked.

I turned to Grossbart. "It's five after seven. What time are services?"

"*Shul*," he smiled, "is in ten minutes. I want you to meet Mickey Halpern. This is Nathan Marx, our Sergeant."

The third boy hopped forward. "Private Michael Halpern." He saluted.

"Salute officers, Halpern." The boy dropped his hand, and in his nervousness checked to see if his shirt pockets were buttoned on the way down.

"Shall I march them over, sir?" Grossbart asked, "or are you coming along?"

From behind Grossbart, Fishbein piped up. "Afterwards they're having refreshments. A Ladies' Auxiliary from St. Louis, the rabbi told us last week."

"The chaplain," whispered Halpern.

"You're welcome to come along," Grossbart said.

To avoid his plea, I looked away, and saw, in the windows of the barracks, a cloud of faces staring out at the four of us.

"Look, hurry out of here, Grossbart."

"Okay, then," he said. He turned to the others. "Double time, *march*!" and they started off, but ten feet away Grossbart spun about, and running backwards he called to me, "Good *shabus*, sir." And then the three were swallowed into the Missouri dusk.

Even after they'd disappeared over the parade grounds, whose green was now a deep twilight blue, I could hear Grossbart singing the double-time cadence, and as it grew dimmer and dimmer it suddenly touched some deep memory—as did the slant of light—and I was remembering the shrill sounds of a Bronx playground, where years ago, beside the Grand Concourse, I had played on long spring evenings such as this. Those thin fading sounds . . . It was a pleasant memory for a young man so far from peace and home, and it brought so very many recollections with it that I began to grow exceedingly tender about myself. In fact, I indulged myself to a reverie so strong that I felt within as though a hand had opened and was reaching down inside. It had to reach so very far to touch me. It had to reach past those days in the forests of Belgium and the dying I'd refused to weep over; past the nights in those German farmhouses whose books we'd burned to warm us, and which I couldn't bother to mourn; past those endless stretches when I'd shut off all softness I might feel for my fellows, and managed even to deny myself the posture of a conqueror—the swagger that I, as a Jew, might well have worn as my boots whacked against the rubble of Münster, Braunschweig, and finally Berlin.

But now one night noise, one rumor of home and time past, and memory plunged down through all I had anesthetized and came to what I suddenly remembered to be myself. So it was not altogether curious that in search of more of me I found myself following Grossbart's tracks to Chapel No. 3 where the Jewish services were being held.

I took a seat in the last row, which was empty. Two rows in front sat Grossbart, Fishbein, and Halpern, each holding a little white dixie cup. Fishbein was pouring the contents of his cup into Grossbart's, and Grossbart looked mirthful as the liquid drew a purple arc between his hand and Fishbein's. In the glary yellow light, I saw the chaplain on the pulpit chanting the first line of the responsive reading. Grossbart's prayerbook remained closed on his lap; he swished the cup around. Only Halpern responded in prayer. The fingers of his right hand were spread wide across the cover of the book, and his cap was pulled down low onto his brow so that it was round like a *yarmulke* rather than long and pointed. From time to time, Grossbart wet his lips at the cup's edge; Fishbein, his long yellow face, a dying light bulb, looked from here to there, leaning forward at the neck to catch sight of the faces down the row, in front—then behind. He saw me and his eyelids beat a tattoo. His elbow slid into Grossbart's side, his neck inclined towards his friend, and then, when the congregation responded, Grossbart's voice was among them. Fishbein looked into his book now too; his lips, however, didn't move.

Finally it was time to drink the wine. The chaplain smiled down at them as Grossbart swigged in one long gulp, Halpern sipped, meditating, and Fishbein faked devotion with an empty cup.

At last the chaplain spoke: "As I look down amongst the congregation—" he grinned at the word, "this night, I see many new faces, and I want to welcome you to Friday night services here at Camp Crowder. I am Major Leo Ben Ezra, your chaplain . . ." Though an American, the chaplain spoke English very deliberately, syllabically almost, as though to communicate, above all, to the lip-readers in the audience. "I have only a few words to say before we adjourn to the refreshment room where the kind ladies of the Temple Sinai, St. Louis, Missouri, have a nice setting for you."

Applause and whistling broke out. After a momentary grin, the chaplain raised his palms to the congregation, his eyes flicking upward a moment, as if to remind the troops where they were and Who Else might be in attendance. In the sudden silence that followed, I thought I heard Grossbart's cackle—"Let the goyim clean the floors!" Were those the words? I wasn't sure, but Fishbein, grinning, nudged Halpern. Halpern looked dumbly at him, then went back to his prayerbook, which had been occupying him all through the rabbi's talk. One hand tugged at the black kinky hair that stuck out under his cap. His lips moved.

The rabbi continued. "It is about the food that I want to speak to you for a moment. I know, I know, I know," he intoned, wearily, "how in the mouths of most of you the *trafe* food tastes like ashes. I know how you gag, some of you, and how your parents suffer to think of their children eating foods unclean and offensive to the palate. What can I tell you? I can only say close your eyes and swallow as best you can. Eat what you must to live and throw away the rest. I wish I could help more. For those of you who find this impossible, may I ask that you try and try, but then come to see me in private where, if your revulsion is such, we will have to seek aid from those higher up."

A round of chatter rose and subsided; then everyone sang "Ain Keloha-noh"; after all those years I discovered I still knew the words.

Suddenly, the service over, Grossbart was upon me. "Higher up? He means the General?"

"Hey, Shelly," Fishbein interrupted, "he means God." He smacked his face and looked at Halpern. "How high can you go!"

"Shhh!" Grossbart said. "What do you think, Sergeant?"

"I don't know. You better ask the chaplain."

"I'm going to. I'm making an appointment to see him in private. So is Mickey."

Halpern shook his head. "No, no, Sheldon . . ."

"You have rights, Mickey. They can't push us around."

"It's okay. It bothers my mother, not me . . ."

Grossbart looked at me. "Yesterday he threw up. From the hash. It was all ham and God knows what else."

"I have a cold—that was why," Halpern said. He pushed his *yamalkah* back into a cap.

"What about you, Fishbein?" I asked. "You kosher too?"

He flushed, which made the yellow more gray than pink. "A little. But I'll let it ride. I have a very strong stomach. And I don't eat a lot anyway . . ." I continued to look at him, and he held up his wrist to re-enforce what he'd just said. His watch was tightened to the last hole and he pointed that out to me. "So I don't mind."

"But services are important to you?" I asked him.

He looked at Grossbart. "Sure, sir."

"Sergeant."

"Not so much at home," said Grossbart, coming between us, "but away from home it gives one a sense of his Jewishness."

"We have to stick together," Fishbein said.

I started to walk towards the door; Halpern stepped back to make way for me.

"That's what happened in Germany," Grossbart was saying, loud enough for me to hear. "They didn't stick together. They let themselves get pushed around."

I turned. "Look, Grossbart, this is the Army, not summer camp."

He smiled. "So?" Halpern tried to sneak off, but Grossbart held his arm. "So?" he said again.

"Grossbart," I asked, "how old are you?"

"Nineteen."

"And you?" I said to Fishbein.

"The same. The same month even."

"And what about him?" I pointed to Halpern, who'd finally made it safely to the door.

"Eighteen," Grossbart whispered. "But he's like he can't tie his shoes or brush his teeth himself. I feel sorry for him."

"I feel sorry for all of us, Grossbart, but just act like a man. Just don't overdo it."

"Overdo what, sir?"

"The sir business. Don't overdo that," I said, and I left him standing there. I passed by Halpern but he did not look up. Then I was outside, black surrounded me—but behind I heard Grossbart call, "Hey, Mickey, *liebschen*, come on back. Refreshments!"

Liebschen! My grandmother's word for me!

One morning, a week later, while I was working at my desk, Captain Barrett shouted for me to come into his office. When I entered, he had his helmet liner squashed down so that I couldn't even see his eyes. He was on the phone, and when he spoke to me, he cupped one hand over the mouthpiece.

"Who the fuck is Grossbart?"

"Third platoon, Captain," I said. "A trainee."

"What's all this stink about food? His mother called a goddam congressman about the food . . ." He uncovered the mouthpiece and slid his helmet up so I could see the curl of his bottom eyelash. "Yes, sir," he said into the phone. "Yes, sir. I'm still here, sir. I'm asking Marx here right now . . ."

He covered the mouthpiece again and looked back to me. "Lightfoot Harry's on the phone," he said, between his teeth. "This congressman calls General Lyman who calls Colonel Sousa who calls the Major who calls me. They're just dying to stick this thing on me. What's a matter," he shook the phone at me, "I don't feed the troops? What the hell is this?"

"Sir, Grossbart is strange . . ." Barrett greeted that with a mockingly indulgent smile. I altered my approach. "Captain, he's a very orthodox Jew and so he's only allowed to eat certain foods."

"He throws up, the congressman said. Every time he eats something his mother says he throws up!"

"He's accustomed to observing the dietary laws, Captain."

"So why's his old lady have to call the White House!"

"Jewish parents, sir, they're apt to be more protective than you expect. I mean Jews have a very close family life. A boy goes away from home, sometimes the mother is liable to get very upset. Probably the boy *mentioned* something in a letter and his mother misinterpreted."

"I'd like to punch him one right in the mouth. There's a goddam war on and he wants a silver platter!"

"I don't think the boy's to blame, sir. I'm sure we can straighten it out by just asking him. Jewish parents worry—"

"*All* parents worry, for Christ sake. But they don't get on their high horse and start pulling strings—"

I interrupted, my voice higher, tighter than before. "The home life, Captain, is so very important . . . but you're right, it may sometimes get out of hand. It's a very wonderful thing, Captain, but because it's so close, this kind of thing—"

He didn't listen any longer to my attempt to present both myself and Light-foot Harry with an explanation for the letter. He turned back to the phone. "Sir?" he said. "Sir, Marx here tells me Jews have a tendency to be pushy. He says he thinks he can settle it right here in the Company . . . Yes, sir . . . I *will* call back, sir, soon as I can . . ." He hung up. "Where are the men, Sergeant?"

"On the range."

With a whack on the top, he crushed his helmet over his eyes, and charged out of his chair. "We're going for a ride."

The Captain drove and I sat beside him. It was a hot spring day and under my newly starched fatigues it felt as though my armpits were melting down onto my sides and chest. The roads were dry and by the time we reached the firing range, my teeth felt gritty with dust though my mouth had been shut the whole trip. The Captain slammed the brakes on and told me to get the hell out and find Grossbart.

I found him on his belly, firing wildly at the 500 feet target. Waiting their turns behind him were Halpern and Fishbein. Fishbein, wearing a pair of rimless G.I. glasses I hadn't seen on him before, gave the appearance of an old peddler who would gladly have sold you the rifle and cartridges that were slung all over him. I stood back by the ammo boxes, waiting for Grossbart to finish spraying the distant targets. Fishbein straggled back to stand near me.

"Hello, Sergeant Marx."

"How are you?" I mumbled.

"Fine, thank you. Sheldon's really a good shot."

"I didn't notice."

"I'm not so good, but I think I'm getting the hang of it now . . . Sergeant, I don't mean to, you know, ask what I shouldn't . . ." The boy stopped. He was trying to speak intimately but the noise of the shooting necessitated that he shout at me.

"What is it?" I asked. Down the range I saw Captain Barrett standing up in the jeep, scanning the line for me and Grossbart.

"My parents keep asking and asking where we're going. Everybody says the Pacific. I don't care, but my parents . . . If I could relieve their minds I think I could concentrate more on my shooting."

"I don't know where, Fishbein. Try to concentrate anyway."

"Sheldon says you might be able to find out—"

"I don't know a thing, Fishbein. You just take it easy, and don't let Sheldon—"

"*I'm* taking it easy, Sergeant. It's at home—"

Grossbart had just finished on the line and was dusting his fatigues with one hand. I left Fishbein's sentence in the middle.

"Grossbart, the Captain wants to see you."

He came toward us. His eyes blazed and twinkled. "Hi!"

"Don't point that goddam rifle!"

"I wouldn't shoot you, Sarge." He gave me a smile wide as a pumpkin as he turned the barrel aside.

"Damn you, Grossbart—this is no joke! Follow me."

I walked ahead of him and had the awful suspicion that behind me Grossbart was *marching*, his rifle on his shoulder, as though he were a one-man detachment.

At the jeep he gave the Captain a rifle salute. "Private Sheldon Grossbart, sir."

"At ease, Grossman." The captain slid over to the empty front seat, and crooking a finger, invited Grossbart closer.

"Bart, sir. Sheldon Gross*bart*. It's a common error." Grossbart nodded to me—*I* understand, he indicated. I looked away, just as the mess truck pulled up to the range, disgorging a half dozen K.P.'s with rolled-up sleeves. The mess sergeant screamed at them while they set up the chow line equipment.

"Grossbart, your mama wrote some congressman that we don't feed you right. Do you know that?" the Captain said.

"It was my father, sir. He wrote to Representative Franconi that my religion forbids me to eat certain foods."

"What religion is that, Grossbart?"

"Jewish."

"Jewish, *sir*," I said to Grossbart.

"Excuse me, sir. 'Jewish, sir.'"

"What have you been living on?" the Captain asked. "You've been in the Army a month already. You don't look to me like you're falling to pieces."

"I eat because I have to, sir. But Sergeant Marx will testify to the fact that I don't eat one mouthful more than I need to in order to survive."

"Marx," Barrett asked, "is that so?"

"I've never seen Grossbart eat, sir," I said.

"But you heard the rabbi," Grossbart said. "He told us what to do, and I listened."

The Captain looked at me. "Well, Marx?"

"I still don't know what he eats and doesn't eat, sir."

Grossbart raised his rifle, as though to offer it to me. "But, Sergeant—"

"Look, Grossbart, just answer the Captain's questions!" I said sharply.

Barrett smiled at me and I resented it. "All right, Grossbart," he said, "What is it you want? The little piece of paper? You want out?"

"No, sir. Only to be allowed to live as a Jew. And for the others, too."

"What others?"

"Fishbein, sir, and Halpern."

"They don't like the way we serve either?"

"Halpern throws up, sir. I've seen it."

"I thought *you* throw up."

"Just once, sir. I didn't know the sausage was sausage."

"We'll give menus, Grossbart. We'll show training films about the food, so you can identify when we're trying to poison you."

Grossbart did not answer. Out before me, the men had been organized into two long chow lines. At the tail end of one I spotted Fishbein—or rather, his glasses spotted me. They winked sunlight back at me like a friend. Halpern stood next to him, patting inside his collar with a khaki handkerchief. They moved with the line as it began to edge up towards the food. The mess sergeant was still screaming at the K.P.'s, who stood ready to ladle out the food, bewildered. For a moment I was actually terrorized by the thought that somehow the mess sergeant was going to get involved in Grossbart's problem.

"Come over here, Marx," the Captain said to me. "Marx, you're a Jewish fella, am I right?"

I played straight man. "Yes, sir."

"How long you been in the Army? Tell this boy."

"Three years and two months."

"A year in combat, Grossbart. Twelve goddam months in combat all through Europe. I admire this man," the Captain said, snapping a wrist against my chest. "But do you hear him peeping about the food? Do you? I want an answer, Grossbart. Yes or no."

"No, sir."

"And why not? He's a Jewish fella."

"Some things are more important to some Jews than other things to other Jews."

Barrett blew up. "Look, Grossbart, Marx here is a good man, a goddam *hero*. When you were sitting on your sweet ass in high school, Sergeant Marx was killing Germans. Who does more for the Jews, you by throwing up over a lousy piece of sausage, a piece of firstcut meat—or Marx by killing those Nazi bastards? If I was a Jew, Grossbart, I'd kiss this man's feet. He's a goddam hero, you know that? And *he* eats what we give him. Why do you have to cause trouble is what I want to know! What is it you're buckin' for, a discharge?"

"No, sir."

"I'm talking to a *wall*! Sergeant, get him out of my way." Barrett pounced over to the driver's seat. "I'm going to see the chaplain!" The engine roared, the jeep spun around, and then, raising a whirl of dust, the Captain was headed back to camp.

For a moment, Grossbart and I stood side by side, watching the jeep. Then he looked at me and said, "I don't want to start trouble. That's the first thing they toss up to us."

When he spoke I saw that his teeth were white and straight, and the sight of them suddenly made me understand that Grossbart actually did have parents: that once upon a time someone had taken little Sheldon to the dentist. He was someone's son. Despite all the talk about his parents, it was hard to believe in Grossbart as a child, an heir—as related by blood to anyone, mother, father, or, above all, to me. This realization led me to another.

"What does your father do, Grossbart?" I asked, as we started to walk back towards the chow line.

"He's a tailor."

"An American?"

"Now, yes. A son in the Army," he said, jokingly.

"And your mother?" I asked.

He winked. "A *ballabusta*—she practically sleeps with a dustcloth in her hand."

"She's also an immigrant?"

"All she talks is Yiddish, still."

"And your father too?"

"A little English. 'Clean,' 'Press,' 'Take the pants in . . .' That's the extent of it. But they're good to me . . ."

"Then, Grossbart—" I reached out and stopped him. He turned towards me and when our eyes met his seemed to jump back, shiver in their sockets. He looked afraid. "Grossbart, then you were the one who wrote that letter, weren't you?"

It took only a second or two for his eyes to flash happy again. "Yes." He walked on, and I kept pace. "It's what my father *would* have written if he had known how. It was his name, though. *He* signed it. He even mailed it. I sent it home. For the New York postmark."

I was astonished, and he saw it. With complete seriousness, he thrust his right arm in front of me. "Blood is blood, Sergeant," he said, pinching the blue vein in his wrist.

"What the hell *are* you trying to do, Grossbart? I've seen you eat. Do you know that? I told the Captain I don't know what you eat, but I've seen you eat like a hound at chow."

"We work hard, Sergeant. We're in training. For a furnace to work, you've got to feed it coal."

"If you wrote the letter, Grossbart, then why did you say you threw up all the time?"

"I was really talking about Mickey there. But he would never write, Sergeant, though I pleaded with him. He'll waste away to nothing if I don't help. Sergeant, I used my name, my father's name, but it's Mickey and Fishbein too I'm watching out for."

"You're a regular Messiah, aren't you?"

We were at the chow line now.

"That's a good one, Sergeant." He smiled. "But who knows? Who can tell? Maybe you're the Messiah . . . a little bit. What Mickey says is the Messiah is a collective idea. He went to Yeshiva, Mickey, for a while. He says *together* we're the Messiah. Me a little bit, you a little bit . . . You should hear that kid talk, Sergeant, when he gets going."

"Me a little bit, you a little bit. You'd like to believe that, wouldn't you, Grossbart? That makes everything so clean for you."

"It doesn't seem too bad a thing to believe, Sergeant. It only means we should all give a little, is all . . ."

I walked off to eat my rations with the other noncoms.

Two days later a letter addressed to Captain Barrett passed over my desk. It had come through the chain of command—from the office of Congressman Franconi, where it had been received, to General Lyman, to Colonel Sousa, to Major Lamont, to Captain Barrett. I read it over twice while the Captain was at the officers' mess. It was dated May 14th, the day Barrett had spoken with Grossbart on the rifle range.

> Dear Congressman:
>
> First let me thank you for your interest in behalf of my son, Private Sheldon Grossbart. Fortunately, I was able to speak with Sheldon on the phone the other night, and I think I've been able to solve our problem. He is, as I mentioned in my last letter, a very religious boy, and it was only with the greatest difficulty that I could persuade him that the religious thing to do—what God Himself would want Sheldon to do—would be to suffer the pangs of religious remorse for the good of his country and all mankind. It took some doing, Congressman, but finally he saw the light. In fact, what he said (and I wrote down the words on a scratch pad so as never to forget), what he said was, "I guess you're right, Dad. So many millions of my fel-

low Jews gave up their lives to the enemy, the least I can do is live for a while minus a bit of my heritage so as to help end this struggle and regain for all the children of God dignity and humanity." That, Congressman, would make any father proud.

By the way, Sheldon wanted me to know—and to pass on to you—the name of a soldier who helped him reach this decision: SERGEANT NATHAN MARX. Sergeant Marx is a combat veteran who is Sheldon's First Sergeant. This man has helped Sheldon over some of the first hurdles he's had to face in the Army, and is in part responsible for Sheldon's changing his mind about the dietary laws. I know Sheldon would appreciate any recognition Marx could receive.

Thank you and good luck. I look forward to seeing your name on the next election ballot.

Respectfully,
Samuel E. Grossbart

Attached to the Grossbart communiqué was a communiqué addressed to General Marshall Lyman, the post commander, and signed by Representative Charles E. Franconi of the House of Representatives. The communiqué informed General Lyman that Sergeant Nathan Marx was a credit to the U.S. Army and the Jewish people.

What was Grossbart's motive in recanting? Did he feel he'd gone too far? Was the letter a strategic retreat—a crafty attempt to strengthen what he considered our alliance? Or had he actually changed his mind, via an imaginary dialogue between Grossbart *père* and *fils*? I was puzzled, but only for a few days—that is, only until I realized that whatever his reasons, he had actually decided to disappear from my life: he was going to allow himself to become just another trainee. I saw him at inspection but he never winked; at chow formations but he never flashed me a sign; on Sundays, with the other trainees, he would sit around watching the noncoms' softball team, for whom I pitched, but not once did he speak an unnecessary or unusual word to me. Fishbein and Halpern retreated from sight too, at Grossbart's command I was sure. Apparently he'd seen that wisdom lay in turning back before he plunged us over into the ugliness of privilege undeserved. Our separation allowed me to forgive him our past encounters, and, finally, to admire him for his good sense.

Meanwhile, free of Grossbart, I grew used to my job and my administrative tasks. I stepped on a scale one day and discovered I had truly become a noncombatant: I had gained seven pounds. I found patience to get past the first three pages of a book. I thought about the future more and more, and wrote

letters to girls I'd known before the war—I even got a few answers. I sent away
to Columbia for a Law School catalogue. I continued to follow the war in the
Pacific, but it was not my war and I read of bombings and battles like a civilian. I thought I could see the end in sight and sometimes at night I dreamed
that I was walking on streets of Manhattan—Broadway, Third Avenue, and
116th Street, where I had lived those three years I'd attended Columbia College. I curled myself around these dreams and I began to be happy.

And then one Saturday when everyone was away and I was alone in the
orderly room reading a month-old copy of *The Sporting News*, Grossbart
reappeared.

"You a baseball fan, Sergeant?"

I looked up. "How are you?"

"Fine," Grossbart said. "They're making a soldier out of me."

"How are Fishbein and Halpern?"

"Coming along," he said. "We've got no training this afternoon. They're
at the movies."

"How come you're not with them?"

"I wanted to come over and say hello."

He smiled—a shy, regular-guy smile, as though he and I well knew that
our friendship drew its sustenance from unexpected visits, remembered birth-
days, and borrowed lawnmowers. At first it offended me, and then the feeling
was swallowed by the general uneasiness I felt at the thought that everyone on
the post was locked away in a dark movie theater and I was here alone with
Grossbart. I folded my paper.

"Sergeant," he said, "I'd like to ask a favor. It is a favor and I'm making no
bones about it."

He stopped, allowing me to refuse him a hearing—which, of course, forced
me into a courtesy I did not intend. "Go ahead."

"Well, actually it's two favors."

I said nothing.

"The first one's about these rumors. Everybody says we're going to the
Pacific."

"As I told your friend Fishbein, I don't know. You'll just have to wait to find
out. Like everybody else."

"You think there's a chance of any of us going East?"

"Germany," I said, "maybe."

"I meant New York."

"I don't think so, Grossbart. Offhand"

"Thanks for the information, Sergeant," he said.

"It's not information, Grossbart. Just what I surmise."

"It certainly would be good to be near home. My parents . . . you know."
He took a step towards the door and then turned back. "Oh the other thing.
May I ask the other?"

"What is it?"

"The other thing is—I've got relatives in St. Louis and they say they'll give
me a whole Passover dinner if I can get down there. God, Sergeant, that'd
mean an awful lot to me."

I stood up. "No passes during basic, Grossbart."

"But we're off from now till Monday morning, Sergeant. I could leave the
post and no one would even know"

"I'd know. You'd know."

"But that's all. Just the two of us. Last night I called my aunt and you
should have heard her. 'Come, come,' she said. 'I got gefilte fish, *chrain*, the
works!' Just a day Sergeant, I'd take the blame if anything happened."

"The captain isn't here to sign a pass."

"You could sign."

"Look, Grossbart—"

"Sergeant, for two months practically I've been eating *trafe* till I want to
die."

"I thought you'd made up your mind to live with it. To be minus a little
bit of heritage."

He pointed a finger at me. "You!" he said. "That wasn't for you to read!"

"I read it. So what."

"That letter was addressed to a congressman."

"Grossbart, don't feed me any crap. You *wanted* me to read it."

"Why are you persecuting me, Sergeant?"

"Are you kidding!"

"I've run into this before," he said, "but never from my own!"

"Get out of here, Grossbart! Get the hell out of my sight!"

He did not move. "Ashamed, that's what you are. So you take it out on the
rest of us. They say Hitler himself was half a Jew. Seeing this, I wouldn't doubt it!"

"What are you trying to do with me, Grossbart? What are you after? You
want me to give you special privileges, to change the food, to find out about
your orders, to give you weekend passes."

"You even talk like a goy!" Grossbart shook his fist. "Is this a weekend pass
I'm asking for? Is a Seder sacred or not?"

Seder! It suddenly occurred to me that Passover had been celebrated weeks
before. I confronted Grossbart with the fact.

"That's right," he said. "Who says no? A month ago, and *I* was in the field
eating hash! And now all I ask is a simple favor—a Jewish boy I thought would

understand. My aunt's willing to go out of her way—to make a Seder a month later—" He turned to go, mumbling.

"Come back here!" I called. He stopped and looked at me. "Grossbart, why can't you be like the rest? Why do you have to stick out like a sore thumb? Why do you beg for special treatment?"

"Because I'm a Jew, Sergeant. I *am* different. Better, maybe not. But different."

"This is a war, Grossbart. For the time being *be* the same."

"I refuse."

"What?"

"I refuse. I can't stop being me, that's all there is to it." Tears came to his eyes. "It's a hard thing to be a Jew. But now I see what Mickey says—it's a harder thing to stay one." He raised a hand sadly toward me. "Look at you."

"Stop crying!"

"Stop this, stop that, stop the other thing! You stop, Sergeant. Stop closing your heart to your own!" And wiping his face with his sleeve, he ran out the door. "The least we can do for one another . . . the least . . ."

An hour later I saw Grossbart headed across the field. He wore a pair of starched khakis and carried only a little leather ditty bag. I went to the door and from the outside felt the heat of the day. It was quiet—not a soul in sight except over by the mess hall four K.P.'s sitting round a pan, sloped forward from the waists, gabbing and peeling potatoes in the sun.

"Grossbart!" I called.

He looked toward me and continued walking.

"Grossbart, get over here!"

He turned and stepped into his long shadow. Finally he stood before me.

"Where are you going?" I said.

"St. Louis. I don't care."

"You'll get caught without a pass."

"So I'll get caught without a pass."

"You'll go to the stockade."

"I'm in the stockade." He made an about-face and headed off.

I let him go only a step: "Come back here," I said, and he followed me into the office, where I typed out a pass and signed the Captain's name and my own initials after it.

He took the pass from me and then, a moment later, he reached out and grabbed my hand. "Sergeant, you don't know how much this means to me."

"Okay. Don't get in any trouble."

"I wish I could show you how much this means to me."

"Don't do me any favors. Don't write any more congressmen for citations."

Amazingly, he smiled. "You're right. I won't. But let me do something."

"Bring me a piece of that gefilte fish. Just get out of here."

"I will! With a slice of carrot and a little horseradish. I won't forget."

"All right. Just show your pass at the gate. And don't tell *anybody*."

"I won't. It's a month late, but a good Yom Tov to you."

"Good Yom Tov, Grossbart," I said.

"You're a good Jew, Sergeant. You like to think you have a hard heart, but underneath you're a fine decent man. I mean that."

Those last three words touched me more than any words from Grossbart's mouth had the right to. "All right, Grossbart. Now call me 'sir' and get the hell out of here."

He ran out the door and was gone. I felt very pleased with myself—it was a great relief to stop fighting Grossbart. And it had cost me nothing. Barrett would never find out, and if he did, I could manage to invent some excuse. For a while I sat at my desk, comfortable in my decision. Then the screen door flew back and Grossbart burst in again. "Sergeant!" he said. Behind him I saw Fishbein and Halpern, both in starched khakis, both carrying ditty bags exactly like Grossbart's.

"Sergeant, I caught Mickey and Larry coming out of the movies. I almost missed them."

"Grossbart, did I say tell no one?"

"But my aunt said I could bring friends. That I should, in fact."

"I'm the Sergeant, Grossbart—not your aunt!"

Grossbart looked at me in disbelief; he pulled Halpern up by his sleeve. "Mickey, tell the Sergeant what this would mean to you."

"Grossbart, for God's sake, spare us—"

"Tell him what you told me, Mickey. How much it would mean."

Halpern looked at me and, shrugging his shoulders, made his admission. "A lot."

Fishbein stepped forward without prompting. "This would mean a great deal to me and my parents, Sergeant Marx."

"No!" I shouted.

Grossbart was shaking his head. "Sergeant, I could see you denying me, but how you can deny Mickey a Yeshivah boy, that's beyond me."

"I'm not denying Mickey anything. You just pushed a little too hard, Grossbart. *You* denied him."

"I'll give him my pass, then," Grossbart said. "I'll give him my aunt's address and a little note. At least let him go."

In a second he had crammed the pass into Halpern's pants' pocket. Halpern looked at me, Fishbein too. Grossbart was at the door, pushing it open. "Mickey, bring me a piece of gefilte fish at least." And then he was outside again.

The three of us looked at one another and then I said, "Halpern, hand that pass over."

He took it from his pocket and gave it to me. Fishbein had now moved to the doorway, where he lingered. He stood there with his mouth slightly open and then pointed to himself. "And me?" he asked.

His utter ridiculousness exhausted me. I slumped down in my seat and felt pulses knocking at the back of my eyes. "Fishbein," I said, "you understand I'm not trying to deny you anything, don't you? If it was my Army I'd serve gefilte fish in the mess hall. I'd sell kugel in the PX, honest to God."

Halpern smiled.

"You understand, don't you, Halpern?"

"Yes, Sergeant."

"And you, Fishbein? I don't want enemies. I'm just like you—I want to serve my time and go home. I miss the same things you miss."

"Then, Sergeant," Fishbein interrupted, "Why don't you come too?"

"Where?"

"To St. Louis. To Shelley's aunt. We'll have a regular Seder. Play hide-the-matzah." He gave a broad, black-toothed smile.

I saw Grossbart in the doorway again, on the other side of the screen.

"Pssst!" He waved a piece of paper. "Mickey, here's the address. Tell her I couldn't get away."

Halpern did not move. He looked at me and I saw the shrug moving up his arms into his shoulders again. I took the cover off my typewriter and made out passes for him and Fishbein. "Go," I said, "the three of you."

I thought Halpern was going to kiss my hand.

That afternoon, in a bar in Joplin, I drank beer and listened with half an ear to the Cardinal game. I tried to look squarely at what I'd become involved in, and began to wonder if perhaps the struggle with Grossbart wasn't as much my fault as his. What was I that I had to *muster* generous feelings? Who was I to have been feeling so grudging, so tight-hearted? After all, I wasn't being asked to move the world. Had I a right, then, or a reason, to clamp down on Grossbart, when that meant clamping down on Halpern, too? And Fishbein, that ugly agreeable soul wouldn't he suffer in the bargain also? Out of the many recollections that had tumbled over me these past few days, I heard from some childhood moment my grandmother's voice: "What are you making a *tsimas*?" It was what she would ask my mother when, say, I had cut myself with a knife and her daughter was busy bawling me out. I would need a hug and a kiss and my mother would moralize! But my grandmother knew—mercy overrides justice. I should have known it, too. Who was Nathan Marx to be such a pennypincher with kindness?

Surely, I thought, the Messiah himself—if he should ever come—won't niggle over nickels and dimes. God willing, he'll hug and kiss.

The next day, while we were playing softball over on the Parade Grounds, I decided to ask Bob Wright, who was noncom in charge over at Classification and Assignment, where he thought our trainees would be sent when their cycle ended in two weeks. I asked casually, between innings, and he said, "They're pushing them all into the Pacific. Shulman cut the orders on your boys the other day."

The news shocked me, as though I were father to Halpern, Fishbein, and Grossbart.

That night I was just sliding into sleep when someone tapped on the door. "What is it?"

"Sheldon."

He opened the door and came in. For a moment I felt his presence without being able to see him. "How was it?" I asked, as though to the darkness.

He popped into sight before me. "Great, Sergeant." I felt my springs sag; Grossbart was sitting on the edge of the bed. I sat up.

"How about you?" he asked. "Have a nice weekend?"

"Yes."

He took a deep paternal breath. "The others went to sleep . . ." We sat silently for a while, as a homey feeling invaded my ugly little cubicle: the door was locked, the cat out, the children safely in bed.

"Sergeant, can I tell you something? Personal?"

I did not answer and he seemed to know why. "Not about me. About Mickey. Sergeant, I never felt for anybody like I feel for him. Last night I heard Mickey in the bed next to me. He was crying so, it could have broken your heart. Real sobs."

"I'm sorry to hear that."

"I had to talk to him to stop him. He held my hand, Sergeant—he wouldn't let it go. He was almost hysterical. He kept saying if he only knew where we were going. Even if he knew it *was* the Pacific, that would be better than noth-ing. Just to know."

Long ago, someone had taught Grossbart the sad law that only lies can get the truth. Not that I couldn't believe in Halpern's crying—his eyes *always* seemed red-rimmed. But, fact or not, it became a lie when Grossbart uttered it. He was entirely strategic. But then—it came with the force of indictment—so was I! There are strategies of aggression, but there are strategies of retreat, as well. And so, recognizing that I, myself, had not been without craft and guile, I told him what I knew. "It is the Pacific."

He let out a small gasp, which was not a lie. "I'll tell him. I wish it was otherwise."

"So do I."

He jumped on my words. "You mean you think you could do something? A change maybe?"

"No, I couldn't do a thing."

"Don't you know anybody over at C & A?"

"Grossbart, there's nothing I can do. If your orders are for the Pacific then it's the Pacific."

"But Mickey."

"Mickey, you, me—everybody, Grossbart. There's nothing to be done. Maybe the war'll end before you go. Pray for a miracle."

"But—"

"Good night, Grossbart." I settled back, and was relieved to feel the springs upbend again as Grossbart rose to leave. I could see him clearly now; his jaw had dropped and he looked like a dazed prizefighter. I noticed for the first time a little paper bag in his hand.

"Grossbart"—I smiled—"my gift?"

"Oh, yes, Sergeant. Here, from all of us." He handed me the bag. "It's egg roll."

"Egg roll?" I accepted the bag and felt a damp grease spot on the bottom. I opened it, sure that Grossbart was joking.

"We thought you'd probably like it. You know, Chinese egg roll. We thought you'd probably have a taste for—"

"Your aunt served egg roll?"

"She wasn't home."

"Grossbart, she invited you. You told me she invited you and your friends."

"I know. I just reread the letter. *Next* week."

I got out of bed and walked to the window. It was black as far off as I could see. "Grossbart," I said. But I was not calling him.

"What?"

"What are you, Grossbart? Honest to God, what are you?"

I think it was the first time I'd asked him a question for which he didn't have an immediate answer.

"How can you do this to people?" I asked.

"Sergeant, the day away did us all a world of good. Fishbein, you should see him, he *loves* Chinese food."

"But the Seder," I said.

"We took second best, Sergeant."

Rage came charging at me. I didn't sidestep—I grabbed it, pulled it in, hugged it to my chest.

"Grossbart, you're a liar! You're a schemer and a crook! You've got no respect for anything! Nothing at all! Not for me, for the truth, not even for poor Halpern! You use us all—"

"Sergeant, Sergeant, I feel for Mickey, honest to God, I do. I *love* Mickey. I try—"

"You try! You feel!" I lurched towards him and grabbed his shirt front. I shook him furiously. "Grossbart, get out. Get out and stay the hell away from me! Because if I see you, I'll make your life miserable. *You understand that?*"

"Yes."

I let him free, and when he walked from the room I wanted to spit on the floor where he had stood. I couldn't stop the fury from rising in my heart. It engulfed me, owned me, till it seemed I could only rid myself of it with tears or an act of violence. I snatched from the bed the bag Grossbart had given me and with all my strength threw it out the window. And the next morning, as the men policed the area around the barracks, I heard a great cry go up from one of the trainees who'd been anticipating only this morning handful of cigarette butts and candy wrappers. "Egg roll!" he shouted. "Holy Christ, Chinese goddam egg roll!"

A week later when I read the orders that had come down from C & A I couldn't believe my eyes. Every single trainee was to be shipped to Camp Stoneham, California, and from there to the Pacific. Every trainee but one: Private Sheldon Grossbart was to be sent to Fort Monmouth, New Jersey. I read the mimeographed sheet several times. Dee, Farrell, Fishbein, Fuselli, Fylypowycz, Glinicki, Gromke, Gucwa, Halpern, Hardy, Helebrandt . . . right down to Anton Zygadlo, all were to be headed West before the month was out. All except Grossbart. He had pulled a string and I wasn't it.

I lifted the phone and called C & A.

The voice on the other end said smartly, "Corporal Shulman, sir."

"Let me speak to Sergeant Wright."

"Who is this calling, sir?"

"Sergeant Marx."

And to my surprise, the voice said, "*Oh.*" Then: "Just a minute, Sergeant."

Shulman's *oh* stayed with me while I waited for Wright to come to phone. Why *oh*? Who was Shulman? And then, so simply, I knew I'd discovered the string Grossbart had pulled. In fact, I could hear Grossbart the day he'd discovered Shulman, in the PX, or the bowling alley, or maybe even at services. "Glad to meet you. Where you from? Bronx? Me too. Do you know so-and-so? And so-and-so? Me too! You work at C & A? Really? Hey, how's chances of getting East? Could you do something? Change something? Swindle, cheat, lie? We gotta help each other, you know . . . if the Jews in Germany . . ."

At the other end Bob Wright answered. "How are you, Nate? How's the pitching arm?"

"Good. Bob, I wonder if you could do me a favor." I heard clearly my own words and they so reminded me of Grossbart that I dropped more easily than I could have imagined into what I had planned. "This may sound crazy, Bob, but I got a kid here on orders to Monmouth who wants them changed. He had a brother killed in Europe and he's hot to go to the Pacific. Says he'd feel like a coward if he wound up stateside. I don't know, Bob, can anything be done? Put somebody else in the Monmouth slot?"

"Who?" he asked cagily.

"Anybody. First guy on the alphabet. I don't care. The kid just asked if something could be done."

"What's his name?"

"Grossbart, Sheldon."

Wright didn't answer.

"Yeah," I said, "he's a Jewish kid, so he thought I could help him out. You know."

"I guess I can do something," he finally said. "The Major hasn't been around here for weeks—TDY to the golf course. I'll try, Nate, that's all I can say."

"I'd appreciate it, Bob. See you Sunday," and I hung up, perspiring.

And the following day the corrected orders appeared: Fishbein, Fuselli, Fylypowycz, Glinicki, Gromke, Grossbart, Gucwa, Halpern, Hardy . . . Lucky Private Harley Alton was to go to Fort Monmouth, New Jersey, where for some reason or other, they wanted an enlisted man with infantry training.

After chow that night I stopped back at the orderly room to straighten out the guard duty roster. Grossbart was waiting for me. He spoke first.

"You son of a bitch!"

I sat down at my desk and while he glared down at me I began to make the necessary alterations in the duty roster.

"What do you have against me?" he cried. "Against my family? Would it kill you for me to be near my father, God knows how many months he has left to him."

"Why?"

"His heart," Grossbart said. "He hasn't had enough troubles in a lifetime, you've got to add to them. I curse the day I ever met you, Marx! Shulman told me what happened over there. There's no limit to your anti-Semitism, is there! The damage you've done here isn't enough. You have to make a special phone call! You really want me dead!"

I made the last few notations in the duty roster and got up to leave. "Good night, Grossbart."

"You owe me an explanation!" He stood in my path.

"Sheldon, you're the one who owes explanations."

He scowled. "To *you*?"

"To me, I think so, yes. Mostly to Fishbein and Halpern."

"That's right, twist things around. I owe nobody nothing, I've done all I could do for them. Now I think I've got the right to watch out for myself."

"For each other we have to learn to watch out, Sheldon. You told me yourself."

"You call this watching out for me, what you did?"

"No. For all of us."

I pushed him aside and started for the door. I heard his furious breathing behind me, and it sounded like steam rushing from the engine of his terrible strength.

"You'll be all right," I said from the door. And, I thought, so would Fishbein and Halpern be all right, even in the Pacific, if only Grossbart could continue to see in the obsequiousness of the one, the soft spirituality of the other, some profit for himself.

I stood outside the orderly room, and I heard Grossbart weeping behind me. Over in the barracks, in the lighted windows, I could see the boys in their T-shirts sitting on their bunks talking about their orders, as they'd been doing for the past two days. With a kind of quiet nervousness, they polished shoes, shined belt buckles, squared away underwear, trying as best they could to accept their fate. Behind me, Grossbart swallowed hard, accepting his. And then, resisting with all my will an impulse to turn and seek pardon for my vindictiveness, I accepted my own.

4

Toward a More
Robust Citizenry:
The Virtues of Civic Life

Self-Command and Self-Respect

Project for Moral Perfection

from The Autobiography

Benjamin Franklin

Arguably more than other American Founders, Benjamin Franklin (1706–1790) gave serious attention to the education and character needed for citizens of the newly founded Republic. Keenly aware of the importance of self-command for both individual flourishing and effective social activity, Franklin understood why the turbulent human soul must first be tamed if we are to become reasonable, free, and responsible social beings and citizens. Many of his writings, from the Dogood Papers *(1722) to his* Autobiography *(from which this selection, written in 1784, is taken), sought to promote these goals. The centerpiece of the Autobiography is his "bold and arduous Project" to reconstitute himself by arriving at moral perfection. By this device, Franklin depicts a middle-class citizen of an individualistic, democratic, and commercial society, which places health, wealth, self-esteem, and public reputation within reach of any American who would imitate Franklin's cultivation of useful self-command. For Franklin, the principle of American democracy is freedom—freedom from inherited modes and orders, freedom for felicity and engagement in public life—and moral virtue is its critical means.*

When you read the list of enumerated virtues, along with their explanations and commentary, ask yourself what a person who embodied these virtues would be like. Would these virtues produce both a good human being and a good citizen? How does Franklin's conception of the virtues compare to more traditional religious conceptions? What virtues are essential for citizens of a modern, commercial republic? What virtues would you add to, or subtract from, Franklin's list? Should we each undertake something like Franklin's project of moral self-improvement?

It was about this time [circa 1728] that I conceiv'd the bold and arduous Project of arriving at moral Perfection. I wish'd to live without committing any Fault at any time; I would conquer all that either Natural Inclination, Custom, or Company might lead me into. As I knew, or thought I knew, what was right and wrong, I did not see why I might not *always* do the one and avoid the other. But I soon found I had undertaken a Task of more Difficulty than I had imagined: While my Care was employ'd in guarding against one Fault, I was often surpriz'd by another. Habit took the Advantage of Inattention. Inclination was sometimes too strong for Reason. I concluded at length, that the mere speculative Conviction that it was our Interest to be compleatly virtuous, was not sufficient to prevent our Slipping, and that the contrary Habits must be broken and good Ones acquired and established, before we can have any Dependance on a steady uniform Rectitude of Conduct. For this purpose I therefore contriv'd the following Method.—

In the various Enumerations of the moral Virtues I had met with in my Reading, I found the Catalogue more or less numerous, as different Writers included more or fewer Ideas under the same Name. Temperance, for Example, was by some confin'd to Eating & Drinking, while by others it was extended to mean the moderating every other Pleasure, Appetite, Inclination or Passion, bodily or mental, even to our Avarice & Ambition. I propos'd to myself, for the sake of Clearness, to use rather more Names with fewer Ideas annex'd to each, than a few Names with more Ideas; and I included under Thirteen Names of Virtues all that at that time occurr'd to me as necessary or desirable, and annex'd to each a short Precept, which fully express'd the Extent I gave to its Meaning.—

These Names of Virtues with their Precepts were

    1. TEMPERANCE.

Eat not to Dulness.

Drink not to Elevation.

    2. SILENCE.

Speak not but what may benefit others or yourself. Avoid trifling Conversation.

    3. ORDER.

Let all your Things have their Places. Let each Part of your Business have its Time.

    4. RESOLUTION.

Resolve to perform what you ought. Perform without fail what you resolve.

    5. FRUGALITY.

Make no Expence but to do good to others or yourself: i.e. Waste nothing.

6. INDUSTRY.

Lose no Time.—Be always employ'd in something useful.—Cut off all unnecessary Actions.—

7. SINCERITY.

Use no hurtful Deceit.

Think innocently and justly; and, if you speak, speak accordingly.

8. JUSTICE.

Wrong none, by doing Injuries or omitting the Benefits that are your Duty.

9. MODERATION.

Avoid Extreams. Forbear resenting Injuries so much as you think they deserve.

10. CLEANLINESS.

Tolerate no Uncleanness in Body, Cloaths or Habitation.—

11. TRANQUILITY.

Be not disturbed at Trifles, or at Accidents common or unavoidable.

12. CHASTITY.

Rarely use Venery but for Health or Offspring; Never to Dulness, Weakness, or the Injury of your own or another's Peace or Reputation.—

13. HUMILITY.

Imitate Jesus and Socrates.—

My Intention being to acquire the *Habitude* of all these Virtues, I judg'd it would be well not to distract my Attention by attempting the whole at once, but to fix it on one of them at a time, and when I should be Master of that, then to proceed to another, and so on till I should have gone thro' the thirteen. And as the previous Acquisition of some might facilitate the Acquisition of certain others, I arrang'd them with that View as they stand above. *Temperance* first, as it tends to procure that Coolness & Clearness of Head, which is so necessary where constant Vigilance was to be kept up, and Guard maintained, against the unremitting Attraction of ancient Habits, and the Force of perpetual Temptations. This being acquir'd & establish'd, *Silence* would be more easy, and my Desire being to gain Knowledge at the same time that I improv'd in Virtue, and considering that in Conversation it was obtain'd rather by the Use of the Ears than of the Tongue, & therefore wishing to break a Habit I was getting into of Prattling, Punning & Joking, which only made me acceptable to trifling Company, I gave *Silence* the second Place. This, and the next, *Order,* I expected would allow me more Time for attending to my Project and my Studies; *Resolution,* once become habitual, would keep me firm in my Endeavours to obtain all the subsequent Virtues; *Frugality* & *Industry,* by freeing me from my remaining Debt, & producing Affluence & Independance, would make more easy the

Practice of *Sincerity* and *Justice*, &c. &c. Conceiving then that agreeable to the Advice of Pythagoras in his Golden Verses, daily Examination would be necessary, I contriv'd the following Method for conducting that Examination.

I made a little Book in which I allotted a Page for each of the Virtues. I rul'd each Page with red Ink so as to have seven Columns, one for each Day of the Week, marking each Column with a Letter for the Day. I cross'd these Columns with thirteen red Lines, marking the Beginning of each Line with the first Letter of one of the Virtues, on which Line & in its proper Column I might mark by a little black Spot every Fault I found upon Examination, to have been committed respecting that Virtue upon that Day.

Form of the Pages

	TEMPERANCE.						
	Eat not to Dulness. *Drink not to Elevation.*						
	S	M	T	W	T	F	S
T							
S	• •	•		•		•	
O	•	•	•		•	•	•
R			•			•	
F		•	•				
I			•				
S							
J							
M							
Cl							
T							
Ch							
H							

I determined to give a Week's strict Attention to each of the Virtues successively. Thus in the first Week my great Guard was to avoid every the least Offence against Temperance, leaving the other Virtues to their ordinary Chance, only marking every Evening the Faults of the Day. Thus if in the first Week I could keep my first Line marked T clear of Spots, I suppos'd the Habit of that Virtue so much strengthen'd and its opposite weaken'd, that I might venture extending my Attention to include the next, and for the following

Week keep both Lines clear of Spots. Proceeding thus to the last, I could go thro' a Course compleat in Thirteen Weeks, and four Courses in a Year.—And like him who having a Garden to weed, does not attempt to eradicate all the bad Herbs at once, which would exceed his Reach and his Strength, but works on one of the Beds at a time, & having accomplish'd the first proceeds to a second; so I should have, (I hoped) the encouraging Pleasure of seeing on my Pages the Progress I made in Virtue, by clearing successively my Lines of their Spots, till in the End by a Number of Courses, I should be happy in viewing a clean Book after a thirteen Weeks daily Examination. . . .

The Precept of *Order* requiring that *every Part of my Business should have its allotted Time*, one Page in my little Book contain'd the following Scheme of Employment for the Twenty-four Hours of a natural Day,

The Morning Quest-ion, What Good shall I do this Day?	5	Rise, wash and address Powerful Good-ness; contrive Day's Business and take the Resolution of the Day; prosecute the present Study: and breakfast?—
	6	
	7	
	8	
	9	Work.
	10	
	11	
	12	Read, or overlook my Accounts, and dine.
	1	
	2	
	3	Work.
	4	
	5	
	6	
	7	Put Things in their Places, Supper, Musick, or Diversion, or Con-versation, Examination of the Day.
Evening Question, What Good have I done to day?	8	
	9	
	10	
	11	
	12	
	1	Sleep.—
	2	
	3	
	4	

I enter'd upon the Execution of this Plan for Self Examination, and continu'd it with occasional Intermissions for some time. I was surpriz'd to find myself so much fuller of Faults than I had imagined, but I had the Satisfaction of seeing them diminish. To avoid the Trouble of renewing now & then my little Book, which by scraping out the Marks on the Paper of old Faults to make room for new Ones in a new Course, became full of Holes: I transferr'd my Tables & Precepts to the Ivory Leaves of a Memorandum Book, on which the Lines were drawn with red Ink that made a durable Stain, and on those Lines I mark'd my Faults with a black Lead Pencil, which Marks I could easily wipe out with a wet Sponge. After a while I went thro' one Course only in a Year, and afterwards only one in several Years; till at length I omitted them entirely, being employ'd in Voyages & Business abroad with a Multiplicity of Affairs, that interfered. But I always carried my little Book with me. My Scheme of ORDER, gave me the most Trouble, and I found, that tho' it might be practicable where a Man's Business was such as to leave him the Disposition of his Time, that of a Journey-man Printer for instance, it was not possible to be exactly observ'd by a Master, who must mix with the World, and often receive People of Business at their own Hours.—*Order* too, with regard to Places for Things, Papers, &c. I found extreamly difficult to acquire. I had not been early accustomed to it, & having an exceeding good Memory, I was not so sensible of the Inconvenience attending Want of Method. This Article therefore cost me so much painful Attention & my Faults in it vex'd me so much, and I made so little Progress in Amendment, & had such frequent Relapses, that I was almost ready to give up the Attempt, and content my self with a faulty Character in that respect. Like the Man who in buying an Ax of a Smith my neighbour, desired to have the whole of its Surface as bright as the Edge; the Smith consented to grind it bright for him if he would turn the Wheel. He turn'd while the Smith press'd the broad Face of the Ax hard & heavily on the Stone, which made the Turning of it very fatiguing. The Man came every now & then from the Wheel to see how the Work went on; and at length would take his Ax as it was without farther Grinding. No, says the Smith, Turn on, turn on; we shall have it bright by and by; as yet 'tis only speckled. Yes, says the Man; but—*I think I like a speckled Ax best.*—And I believe this may have been the Case with many who having for want of some such Means as I employ'd found the Difficulty of obtaining good, & breaking bad Habits, in other Points of Vice & Virtue, have given up the Struggle, & concluded that *a speckled Ax was best.* For something that pretended to be Reason was every now and then suggesting to me, that such extream Nicety as I exacted of my self might be a kind of Foppery in Morals, which if it were known would make me ridiculous; that a perfect Character might be attended with the Inconvenience of being envied and hated; and that a benevolent Man should allow a few Faults in himself, to keep his Friends in Countenance. In Truth I found myself incorrigible with respect to *Order*; and now I am grown old, and my Memory bad, I feel very sensibly the want of it. But on the whole, tho' I never arrived at the Perfection I had been so ambitious of obtaining, but fell far short of it, yet I was by the Endeavour a better and happier Man than I otherwise should have been, if I had not attempted it; As those who aim at perfect Writing by imitating the engraved Copies, tho' they never reach the wish'd for Excellence of those Copies, their Hand is mended by the Endeavour, and is tolerable while it continues fair & legible.—

And it may be well my Posterity should be informed, that to this little Artifice, with the Blessing of God, their Ancestor ow'd the constant Felicity of his Life down to his 79th Year in which this is written. What Reverses may attend the Remainder is in the Hand of Providence: But if they arrive the Reflection on past Happiness enjoy'd ought to help his bearing them with more Resignation. To *Temperance* he ascribes his long-continu'd Health, & what is still left to him of a good Constitution. To *Industry* and *Frugality* the early Easiness of his Circumstances, & Acquisition of his Fortune, with all that Knowledge which enabled him to be an useful Citizen, and obtain'd for him some Degree of Reputation among the Learned. To *Sincerity* & *Justice* the Confidence of his Country, and the honourable Employs it conferr'd upon him. And to the joint Influence of the whole Mass of the Virtues, even in the imperfect State he was able to acquire them, all that Evenness of Temper, & that Chearfulness in Conversation which makes his Company still sought for, & agreable even to his younger Acquaintance. I hope therefore that some of my Descendants may follow the Example & reap the Benefit.— . . .

My List of Virtues contain'd at first but twelve: But a Quaker Friend having kindly inform'd me that I was generally thought proud; that my Pride show'd itself frequently in Conversation; that I was not content with being in the right when discussing any Point, but was overbearing & rather insolent; of which he convinc'd me by mentioning several Instances;—I determined endeavouring to cure myself if I could of this Vice or Folly among the rest, and I added *Humility* to my List, giving an extensive Meaning to the Word.—I cannot boast of much Success in acquiring the *Reality* of this Virtue; but I had a good deal with regard to the *Appearance* of it.—I made it a Rule to forbear all direct Contradiction to the Sentiments of others, and all positive Assertion of my own. I even forbid myself agreable to the old Laws of our Junto, the Use of every Word or Expression in the Language that imported a fix'd Opinion; such as *certainly, undoubtedly,* &c. and I adopted instead of them, *I conceive, I apprehend,* or *I imagine* a thing to be so or so, or it so appears to me at present.—When another asserted something that I thought an Error, I deny'd my self the Pleasure of contradicting him abruptly, and of showing immediately some Absurdity in his Proposition; and in answering I began by observing that in certain Cases or Circumstances his Opinion would be right, but that in the present case there *appear'd* or *seem'd* to me some Difference, &c. I soon found the Advantage of this change in my Manners. The Conversations I engag'd in went on more pleasantly. The modest way in which I propos'd my Opinions, procur'd them a readier Reception and less Contradiction; I had less Mortification when I was found to be in the wrong, and I more easily prevail'd with others to give up their Mistakes & join with me when I happen'd to be in the right. And this mode, which I at first put on, with some violence to natural Inclination, became at length so easy & so habitual to me, that perhaps for these Fifty Years past no one has ever heard a dogmatical Expression escape me. And to this Habit (after my Character of Integrity) I think it principally owing, that I had early so much Weight with my Fellow Citizens, when I proposed new Institutions, or Alterations in the old; and so much Influence in public Councils when I became a Member. For I was but a bad Speaker, never eloquent, subject to much Hesitation in my choice of Words, hardly correct in Language, and yet I generally carried my Points.—

In reality there is perhaps no one of our natural Passions so hard to subdue as *Pride*. Disguise it, struggle with it, beat it down, stifle it, mortify it as much as one pleases, it is still alive, and will every now and then peep out and show itself. You will see it perhaps often in this History. For even if I could conceive that I had compleatly overcome it, I should probably be proud of my Humility.—

Pandora

Henry James

Benjamin Franklin provides advice to the would-be self-made American man, fit to function and thrive in a free and democratic society. While the virtues and self-command he champions appear to be gender-neutral, historically they would have been of far less civic value to America's women, whose activities were long limited largely to the domestic sphere and whose role in civic life was confined mainly to voluntary, local charitable activity. Yet in a society informed by the American creed, eventually a new type would come into its own: the self-made American girl, whose subtle portrait is brilliantly painted in this story, "Pandora," written in 1884 by Henry James (1843–1916). Part I, aboard a ship traveling from Bremen to New York, recounts the American initiation of a young German patriot, Count Otto Vogelstein, obtained through the social guidance of Mrs. Dangerfield; his evident attraction to the young American woman Pandora Day; and his equally evident repulsion from the rest of Pandora's family, the "silent senseless burghers." Part II begins eighteen months later at an exclusive Washington, D.C., salon at which Count Vogelstein encounters Pandora as she is exacting a promise from none other than the president of the United States. Throughout, the story illuminates what it means to be an American—as opposed to a European—and, especially, an American woman.

In her ability to rise, personally and socially, Pandora is a worthy counterpart of Benjamin Franklin, America's iconic self-made man. She, too, embraces careful self-discipline in order to free herself to pursue her worthy ambitions. But there are differences: Franklin's goal was public service; what is the goal for Pandora? In the story, Pandora demonstrates her considerable strengths and virtues; how do they compare with Franklin's? To what extent does self-command for the self-made woman differ from the self-command of the self-made man? Finally, consider her name: Pandora Day—the "lovely Day"—displays the open brightness evoked by her last name. But her first name recalls Pandora—"all gifts" or "all giving"—of Greek mythology, who from her jar unleashed myriad pains, hardships, and diseases upon human-kind while locking hope safely within. Are the gifts of the new Pandora, the self-made girl, equally ambiguous? Do the promises, possibilities, and hopes bred of free choice and equality also bring novel difficulties for American women, for marriage, and for family life?

I

It has long been the custom of the North German Lloyd steamers, which convey passengers from Bremen to New York, to anchor for several hours in the pleasant port of Southampton, where their human cargo receives many additions. An intelligent young German, Count Otto Vogelstein, hardly knew, a few years ago, whether to condemn this custom or approve it. He leaned over the bulwarks of the *Donau* as the American passengers crossed the plank—the travelers who embark at Southampton are mainly of that nationality—and curiously, indifferently, vaguely, through the smoke of his cigar, saw them absorbed in the huge capacity of the ship, where he had the agreeable consciousness that his own nest was comfortably made. To watch from a point of vantage the struggles of late comers—of the uninformed, the unprovided, the bewildered—is an occupation not devoid of sweetness, and there was nothing to mitigate the complacency with which our young friend gave himself up to it; nothing, that is, save a natural benevolence which had not yet been extinguished by the consciousness of official greatness. For Count Vogelstein was official, as I think you would have seen from the straightness of his back, the lustre of his light, elegant spectacles, and something discreet and diplomatic in the curve of his moustache, which looked as if it might well contribute to the principal function, as cynics say, of the lips—the concealment of thought. He had been appointed to the secretaryship of the German legation at Washington and in these first days of the autumn he was going to take possession of his post. He was a model character for such a purpose—serious, civil, ceremonious, stiff, inquisitive, stuffed with knowledge, and convinced that at present the German Empire is the country in the world most highly evolved. He was quite aware, however, of the claims of the United States, and that this portion of the globe offered a vast field for study. The process of inquiry had already begun, in spite of his having as yet spoken to none of his fellow-passengers; for Vogelstein inquired not only with his tongue—he inquired with his eyes (that is with his spectacles), with his ears, with his nose, with his palate, with all his senses and organs.

He was an excellent young man, and his only fault was that he had not a high sense of humour. He had enough, however, to suspect this deficiency, and he was aware that he was about to visit a highly humorous people. This suspicion gave him a certain mistrust of what might be said of him; and if circumspection is the essence of diplomacy, our young aspirant promised well. His mind contained several millions of facts, packed too closely together for the light breeze of the imagination to draw through the mass. He was impatient to report himself to his superior in Washington, and the loss of time in an English port could only incommode him, inasmuch as the study of English institutions was no part of his mission. But, on the other hand, the day was charming; the blue sea, in Southampton Water, pricked all over with light, had no movement but that of its infinite shimmer. And he was by no means sure that he should be happy in the United States, where doubtless he should find himself soon enough disembarked. He knew that this was not an important question and that happiness was an unscientific term, which he was ashamed to use even in the silence of his thoughts. But lost in the inconsiderate crowd, and feeling himself neither in his own country nor in that to which he was in a manner accredited, he was reduced to his mere personality; so that, for the moment, to fill himself out, he tried to have an opinion on the subject of this delay to which the German steamer was subjected in English waters. It appeared to him that it might be proved to be considerably greater than the occasion demanded.

Count Vogelstein was still young enough in diplomacy to think it necessary to have opinions. He had a good many, indeed, which had been formed without difficulty; they had been received ready-made from a line of ancestors who knew what they liked. This was, of course—and under pressure, being candid, he would have admitted it—an unscientific way of furnishing one's mind. Our young man was a stiff conservative, a Junker of Junkers; he thought modern democracy a temporary phase, and expected to find many arguments against it in the United States. In regard to these things, it was a pleasure to him to feel that, with his complete training, he had been taught thoroughly to appreciate the nature of evidence. The ship was heavily laden with German emigrants, whose mission in the United States differed considerably from Count Otto's. They hung over the bulwarks, densely grouped; they leaned forward on their elbows for hours, their shoulders kept on a level with their ears; the men in furred caps, smoking long-bowled pipes, the women with babies hidden in their shawls. Some were yellow Germans and some were black, and all of them looked greasy and matted with the sea-damp. They were destined to swell the current of western democracy; and Count Vogelstein doubtless said to himself that they would not improve its quality. Their numbers, however, were striking, and I know not what he thought of the nature of this evidence.

The passengers who came on board at Southampton were not of the greasy class; they were for the most part American families who had been spending the summer, or a longer period, in Europe. They had a great deal of luggage, innumerable bags and rugs and hampers and sea-chairs, and were composed largely of ladies of various ages, a little pale with anticipation, wrapped in striped shawls and crowned with very high hats and feathers. They darted to and fro across the gangway, looking for each other and for their scattered parcels; they separated and reunited, they exclaimed and declared, they eyed with dismay the occupants of the steerage, who seemed numerous enough to sink the vessel, and their voices sounded faint and far as they rose to Vogelstein's ear over the tarred sides of the ship. He observed that in the new contingent there were many young girls, and he remembered what a lady in Dresden had once said to him—that America was a country of girls. He wondered whether he should like that, and reflected that it would be a question to study, like everything else. He had known in Dresden an American family, in which there were three daughters who used to skate with the officers; and some of the ladies now coming on board seemed to him of that same habit, except that in the Dresden days feathers were not worn quite so high. . . .

It still wanted two hours of dinner, and, by the time Vogelstein's long legs had measured three or four miles on the deck, he was ready to settle himself in his sea-chair and draw from his pocket a Tauchnitz novel by an American author whose pages, he had been assured, would help to prepare him. On the back of his chair his name was painted in rather large letters, this being a precaution taken at the recommendation of a friend who had told him that on the American steamers the passengers—especially the ladies—thought nothing of pilfering one's little comforts. His friend had even said that in his place he would have his coronet painted. This cynical adviser had added that the Americans are greatly impressed by a coronet. I know not whether it was scepticism or modesty, but Count Vogelstein had omitted this ensign of his rank; the precious piece of furniture which on the Atlantic voyage, is depended upon to remain steady among general concussions, was emblazoned simply with his title and name. It happened, however, that the blazonry was huge; the back of the chair was covered with enormous German characters. This time there can be no doubt; it was modesty that caused the secretary of the legation, in placing himself, to turn this portion of his seat outward, away from the eyes of his companions—to present it to the balustrade of the deck. . . .

His glance was arrested by the figure of a young lady who had just ascended to the deck, and who paused at the mouth of the companion-way. In itself this was not an extraordinary phenomenon; but what attracted Vogelstein's attention was the fact that the young person appeared to have fixed her eyes on him. She was slim, brightly dressed, and rather pretty; Vogelstein remembered in a moment that he had noticed her among the people on the wharf at Southampton. She very soon saw that he was looking at her; whereupon she began to move along the deck with a step which seemed to indicate that she was coming straight towards him. Vogelstein had time to wonder whether she could be one of the girls he had known at Dresden; but he presently reflected that they would now be much older than this. It was true they came straight towards one, like that. This young lady, however, was no longer looking at him, and though she passed near him it was now tolerably clear that she had come upstairs simply to take a general survey. She was a quick, handsome, competent girl, and she wished to see what one could think of the ship, of the weather, of the appearance of England from such a position as that; possibly even of one's fellow-passengers. She satisfied herself promptly on these points, and then she looked about, while she walked, as if she were in search of a missing object; so that Vogelstein presently saw this was what she really had come up for. She passed near him again, and this time almost stopped, with her eyes bent upon him attentively. He thought her conduct remarkable, even after he had perceived that it was not at his face, with its yellow moustache, she was looking, but at the chair on which he was seated. Then those words of his friend came back to him,—the speech about the people, especially of the ladies, on the American steamers taking to themselves one's little belongings. Especially the ladies, he might well say; for here was one who apparently wished to pull from under him the very chair he was sitting on. He was afraid she would ask him for it, so he pretended to read, without meeting her eye. He was conscious that she hovered near him, and he was curious to see what she would do. It seemed to him strange that such a nice-looking girl (for her appearance was really charming) should endeavour by acts so flagrant to attract the attention of a secretary of legation. At last it became evident to him that she was trying to look round a corner, as it were, trying to see what was written on the back of his chair. "She wants to find out my name; she wants to see who I am!" This reflection passed through his mind, and caused him to raise his eyes. They rested on her own—which for an appreciable moment she did not withdraw. The latter were brilliant and expressive, and surmounted a delicate aquiline nose, which, though pretty, was perhaps just a trifle too hawk-like. It was the oddest coincidence in the world; the story Vogelstein had taken up treated of a flighty, forward little American girl, who plants herself in front of a young man in the garden of an hotel. Was not the conduct of this young lady a testimony to the truthfulness of the tale, and was not Vogelstein himself in the position of the young man in the garden? That young man ended by speaking to his invader (as she might be called), and after a short hesitation Vogelstein followed his example. "If she wants to know who I am, she's welcome," he said to himself; and he got out of the chair, seized it by the back, and, turning it round, exhibited the superscription to the girl. She coloured slightly, but she smiled and read his name, while Vogelstein raised his hat.

"I am much obliged to you. That's all right," she remarked, as if the discovery had made her very happy.

It seemed to him indeed all right that he should be Count Otto Vogelstein; this appeared even a rather flippant mode of disposing of the fact. By way of rejoinder, he asked her if she desired his seat.

"I am much obliged to you; of course not. I thought you had one of our chairs, and I didn't like to ask you. It looks exactly like one of ours; not so much now as when you sit in it. Please sit down again. I don't want to trouble you. We have lost one of ours, and I have been looking for it everywhere. They look so much alike; you can't tell till you see the back. Of course I see there will be no mistake about yours," the young lady went on, with a frank smile. "But we have such a small name—you can scarcely see it," she added, with the same friendly intention. "Our name is Day. If you see that on anything, I should be obliged if you would tell me. It isn't for myself, it's for my mother; she is so dependent on her chair, and that one I'm looking for pulls out so beautifully. Now that you sit down again and hide the lower part, it does look just like ours. Well, it must be somewhere. You must excuse me; I am much obliged to you."

This was a long and even confidential speech for a young woman, presumably unmarried, to make to a perfect stranger; but Miss Day acquitted herself of it with perfect simplicity and self-possession. She held up her head and stepped away, and Vogelstein could see that the foot she pressed upon the clean, smooth deck was slender and shapely. He watched her disappear through the trap by which she had ascended, and he felt more than ever like the young man in his American tale. The girl in the present case was older and not so pretty, as he could easily judge, for the image of her smiling eyes and speaking lips still hovered before him. He went back to his book with the feeling that it would give him some information about her. This was rather illogical, but it indicated a certain amount of curiosity on the part of Count Vogelstein. The girl in the book had a mother, it appeared, and so had this young lady; the former had also a brother, and he now remembered that he had noticed a young man on the wharf—a young man in a high hat and a white overcoat—who seemed united to Miss Day by this natural tie. And there was some one else too, as he gradually recollected, an older man, also in a high hat, but in a black overcoat—in black altogether—who completed the group, and who was presumably the head of the family. These reflections would indicate that Count Vogelstein read his volume of Tauchnitz rather interruptedly. Moreover, they represented a considerable waste of time; for was he not to be afloat, in an oblong box, for ten days, with such people, and could it be doubted he should see a great deal of them?

It may as well be said without delay that he did see a great deal of them. I have depicted with some precision the circumstances under which he made the acquaintance of Miss Day, because the event had a certain importance for this candid Teuton; but I must pass briefly over the incidents that immediately followed it. He wondered what it was open to him, after such an introduction, to do with regard to her, and he determined he would push through his American tale and discover what the hero did. But in a very short time he perceived that Miss Day had nothing in common with the heroine of that work, save a certain local quality and the fact that the male sex was not terrible to her. Her local quality, indeed, he took rather on trust than apprehended for himself. She was a native of a small town in the interior of the American continent; and a lady from New York, who was on the ship, and with whom he had a good deal of conversation, assured him Miss Day was exceedingly provincial. How this lady ascertained the fact did not appear, for Vogelstein observed that she held no communication with the girl. It is true that she threw some light on her processes by remarking to him that certain Americans could tell immediately who other Americans were, leaving him to judge whether or not she herself belonged to the discriminating class. She was a Mrs. Dangerfield, a handsome confidential, insinuating woman, and Vogelstein's talk with her took a turn that was almost philosophic. She convinced him, rather effectually, that even in a great democracy there are human differences, and that American life was full of social distinctions, of delicate shades, which foreigners are often too stupid to perceive. Did he suppose that every one knew every one else in the biggest country in the world, and that one was not as free to choose one's company there as in the most monarchical communities? She laughed these ideas to scorn, as Vogelstein tucked her beautiful furred coverlet (they reclined together a great deal in their elongated chairs) well over her feet. How free an American lady was to choose her company she abundantly proved by not knowing any one on the steamer but Count Otto.

He could see for himself that Mr. and Mrs. Day had not her peculiar stamp. They were fat, plain, serious people, who sat side by side on the deck for hours, looking straight before them. Mrs. Day had a white face, large cheeks, and small eyes; her forehead was surrounded with a multitude of little tight black curls, and her lips and cheeks moved as if she had always a lozenge in her mouth. She wore entwined about her head an article which Mrs. Danger-field spoke of as a "nuby"—a knitted pink scarf which covered her coiffure and encircled her neck, leaving among its convolutions a hole for her per-fectly expressionless face. Her hands were folded on her stomach, and in her still, swathed figure her little bead-like eyes, which occasionally changed their direction, alone represented life. Her husband had a stiff grey beard on his chin, and a bare, spacious upper lip, to which constant shaving had imparted a kind of hard glaze. His eyebrows were thick and his nostrils wide, and when he was uncovered, in the saloon, it was visible that his grizzled hair was dense and perpendicular. He might have looked rather grim and truculent, had it not been for the mild, familiar, accommodating gaze with which his large, light-coloured pupils—the leisurely eyes of a silent man—appeared to consider surrounding objects. He was evidently more friendly than fierce, but he was more diffident than friendly. He liked to look at you, but he would not have pretended to understand you much nor to classify you, and would have been sorry that it should put you under an obligation. He and his wife spoke some-times, but they seldom talked, and there was something passive and patient about them, as if they were victims of a spell. The spell, however, was evidently pleasant; it was the fascination of prosperity, the confidence of security, which sometimes makes people arrogant, but which had had such a different effect upon this simple satisfied pair, in which further development of every kind appeared to have been arrested.

Mrs. Dangerfield told Count Vogelstein that every morning, after break-fast, the hour at which he wrote his journal in his cabin, the old couple were guided upstairs and installed in their customary corner by Pandora. This she had learned to be the name of their elder daughter, and she was immensely amused by her discovery. "Pandora"—that was in the highest degree typical; it placed them in the social scale, if other evidence had been wanting; you could tell that a girl was from the interior, the mysterious interior about which Vogelstein's imagination was now quite excited, when she had such a name as that. This young lady managed the whole family, even a little the small beflounced sister, who, with bold, pretty, innocent eyes, a torrent of fair, silky hair, a crimson fez, such as is worn by male Turks, very much askew on top of it, and a way of galloping and straddling about the ship in any company she could pick up (she had long, thin legs, very short skirts, and stockings of every tint), was going home, in elaborate French clothes, to resume an interrupted education. Pandora overlooked and directed her relatives; Vogelstein could see that for himself, could see that she was very active and decided, that she had in a high degree the sentiment of responsibility, and settled most of the questions that could come up for a family from the interior. The voyage was remarkably fine, and day after day it was possible to sit there under the salt sky and feel one's self rounding the great curves of the globe. The long deck made a white spot in the sharp black circle of the ocean and in the intense sea-light, while the shadow of the smoke-streamers trembled on the familiar floor, the shoes of fellow-passengers, distinctive now, and in some cases irritating, passed and repassed, accompanied, in the air so tremendously "open," that rendered all voices weak and most remarks rather flat, by fragments of opinion on the run of the ship. Vogelstein by this time had finished his little American story, and now definitely judged that Pandora Day was not at all like the heroine. She was of quite another type; much more serious and preoccupied, and not at all keen, as he had supposed, about making the acquaintance of gentlemen. Her speaking to him that first afternoon had been, he was bound to believe, an incident without importance for herself, in spite of her having followed it up the next day by the remark, thrown at him as she passed, with a smile that was almost familiar, "It's all right, sir. I have found that old chair!" After this she had not spoken to him again, and had scarcely looked at him. She read a great deal, and almost always French books, in fresh yellow paper; not the lighter forms of that literature, but a volume of Sainte-Beuve, of Renan, or at the most, in the way of dissipation, of Alfred de Musset. She took frequent exercise, and almost always walked alone, not, apparently, having made many friends on the ship, and being without the resource of her parents, who, as has been related, never budged out of the cosy corner in which she planted them for the day. . . .

The days were long, but the voyage was short, and it had almost come to an end before Count Vogelstein yielded to an attraction peculiar in its nature and finally irresistible, and, in spite of Mrs. Dangerfield's warning, sought occasion for a little continuous talk with Miss Pandora Day. To mention this sentiment without mentioning sundry other impressions of his voyage, with which it had nothing to do, is perhaps to violate proportion and give a false idea; but to pass it by would be still more unjust. The Germans, as we know, are a transcendental people, and there was at last a vague fascination for Vogelstein in this quick, bright, silent girl, who could smile and turn vocal in an instant, who imparted a sort of originality to the filial character, and whose profile was delicate as she bent it over a volume which she cut as she read, or presented it, in absentminded attitudes, at the side of the ship, to the horizon they had left behind. But he felt it to be a pity, as regards a possible acquaintance with her, that her parents should be heavy little burghers, that her brother should not correspond to Vogelstein's conception of a young man of the upper class, and that her sister should be a Daisy Miller *en herbe*. Repeatedly warned by Mrs. Dangerfield, the young diplomatist was doubly careful as to the relations he might form at the beginning of his sojourn in the United States. Mrs. Dangerfield reminded him, and he had made the observation himself in other capitals, that the first year, and even the second, is the time for prudence. One is ignorant of proportions and values; one is exposed, lonely, thankful for attention; and one may give one's self away to people who afterwards prove a great encumbrance. Mrs. Dangerfield struck a note which resounded in Vogelstein's imagination. She assured him that if he didn't "look out" he would be falling in love with some American girl with an impossible family. In America, when one fell in love with a girl, there was nothing to do but marry her, and what should he say, for instance, to finding himself a near relation of Mr. and Mrs. P. W. Day? (These were the initials inscribed on the back of the two chairs of that couple.) Vogelstein felt the peril, for he could immediately think of a dozen men he knew who had married American girls. There appeared now to be a constant danger of marrying the American girl; it was something one had to reckon with, like the railway, the telegraph, the discovery of dynamite, the Chassepôt rifle, the socialistic spirit; it was one of the complications of modern life. . . .

Vogelstein had come up to walk, and as the girl brushed past him he distinguished Pandora's face (with Mrs. Dangerfield he always spoke of her as Pandora) under the veil that seemed intended to protect it from the sea-damp. He stopped, turned, hurried after her, threw away his cigar, and asked her if she would do him the honour to accept his arm. She declined his arm, but accepted his company, and he walked with her for an hour. They had a great deal of talk, and he remembered afterwards some of the things she said. There was now a certainty of the ship getting into dock the next morning but one, and this prospect afforded an obvious topic. Some of Miss Day's expressions struck him as singular; but, of course, as he knew, his knowledge of English was not nice enough to give him a perfect measure.

"I am not in a hurry to arrive; I am very happy here," she said. "I'm afraid I shall have such a time putting my people through."

"Putting them through?"

"Through the custom-house. We have made so many purchases. Well, I have written to a friend to come down, and perhaps he can help us. He's very well acquainted with the head. Once I'm chalked, I don't care. I feel like a kind of black-board by this time, any way. We found them awful in Germany."

Vogelstein wondered whether the friend she had written to was her lover, and if she were betrothed to him, especially when she alluded to him again as "that gentleman that is coming down." He asked her about her travels, her impressions, whether she had been long in Europe, and what she liked best; and she told him that they had gone abroad, she and her family, for a little fresh experience. Though he found her very intelligent he suspected she gave this as a reason because he was a German and she had heard that Germans were fond of culture. He wondered what form of culture Mr. and Mrs. Day had brought back from Italy, Greece, and Palestine (they had travelled for two years and been everywhere), especially when their daughter said, "I wanted father and mother to see the best things. I kept them three hours on the Acropolis. I guess they won't forget that!" Perhaps it was of Phidias and Pericles they were thinking, Vogelstein reflected, as they sat ruminating in their rugs. Pandora remarked also that she wanted to show her little sister everything while she was young; remarkable sights made so much more impression when the mind was fresh; she had read something of that sort in Goethe, somewhere. She had wanted to come herself when she was her sister's age; but her father was in business then, and they couldn't leave Utica. Vogelstein thought of the little sister frisking over the Parthenon and the Mount of Olives, and sharing for two years, the years of the schoolroom, this extraordinary odyssey of her parents, and wondered whether Goethe's dictum had been justified in this case. He asked Pandora if Utica were the seat of her family; if it were a pleasant place; if it would be an interesting city for him, as a stranger, to see. His companion replied frankly that it was horrid, but added that all the same she would ask him to "come and visit us at our home," if it weren't that they should probably soon leave it.

"Ah! You are going to live elsewhere?"

"Well, I'm working for New York. I flatter myself I have loosened them while we have been away. They won't find Utica the same; that was my idea. I want a big place, and, of course, Utica——" And the girl broke off, with a little sigh.

"I suppose Utica is small?" Vogelstein suggested.

"Well, no, it's middle-sized. I hate anything middling," said Pandora Day. She gave a light, dry laugh, tossing back her head a little as she made this declaration. And looking at her askance, in the dusk, as she trod the deck that vaguely swayed, he thought there was something in her air and port that carried out such a spirit.

"What is her social position?" he inquired of Mrs. Dangerfield the next day. "I can't make it out at all, it's so contradictory. She strikes me as having so much cultivation and so much spirit. Her appearance, too, is very neat. Yet her parents are little burghers. That is easily seen."

"Oh, social position!" Mrs. Dangerfield exclaimed, nodding two or three times, rather portentously. "What big expressions you use! Do you think everybody in the world has a social position? That is reserved for an infinitely small minority of mankind. You can't have a social position at Utica, any more than you can have an opera-box. Pandora hasn't got any; where should she have found it? Poor girl, it isn't fair of you to ask such questions as that."

"Well," said Vogelstein, "if she is of the lower class, that seems to me very—very—" And he paused a moment, as he often paused in speaking English, looking for his word.

"Very what, Count Vogelstein?"

"Very significant, very representative."

"Oh, dear, she isn't of the lower class," Mrs. Dangerfield murmured, helplessly.

"What is she, then?"

"Well, I'm bound to admit that since I was at home last she is a novelty. A girl like that, with such people—it's a new type."

"I like novelties," said Count Vogelstein, smiling, with an air of considerable resolution. He could not, however, be satisfied with an explanation that only begged the question; and when they disembarked in New York, he felt, even amid the confusion of the wharf and the heaps of disembowelled baggage, a certain acuteness of regret at the idea that Pandora and her family were about to vanish into the unknown. . . .

II

Vogelstein went wherever he was asked, on principle, partly to study American society, and partly because, in Washington, pastimes seemed to him not so numerous that one could afford to neglect occasions. Of course, at the end of two winters he had a good many of various kinds, and his study of American society had yielded considerable fruit. When, however, in April, during the second year of his residence, he presented himself at a large party given by Mrs. Bonnycastle, and of which it was believed that it would be the last serious affair of the season, his being there (and still more his looking very fresh and talkative) was not the consequence of a rule of conduct. He went to Mrs. Bonnycastle's simply because he liked the lady, whose receptions were the pleasantest in Washington, and because if he didn't go there he didn't know what he should do. . . .

Count Otto, that evening, knew every one, or almost every one. There were often inquiring strangers, expecting great things, from New York and Boston, and to them, in the friendly Washington way, the young German was promptly introduced. It was a society in which familiarity reigned, and in which people were liable to meet three times a day, so that their ultimate essence really became a matter of importance.

"I have got three new girls," Mrs. Bonnycastle said. "You must talk to them all."

"All at once?" Vogelstein asked, reversing in imagination a position which was not unknown to him. He had often, in Washington, been discoursed to at the same moment by several virginal voices.

"Oh no; you must have something different for each; you can't get off that way. Haven't you discovered that the American girl expects something especially adapted to herself? It's very well in Europe to have a few phrases that will do for any girl. The American girl isn't any girl; she's a remarkable individual in a remarkable genus. But you must keep the best this evening for Miss Day."

"For Miss Day!" Vogelstein exclaimed, staring. "Do you mean for Pandora?"

Mrs. Bonnycastle stared a moment, in return; then laughed very hard. "One would think you had been looking for her over the globe! So you know her already, and you call her by her pet name?"

"Oh no, I don't know her; that is, I haven't seen her, nor thought of her, from that day to this. We came to America in the same ship."

"Isn't she an American, then?"

"Oh yes; she lives at Utica, in the interior."

"In the interior of Utica? You can't mean my young woman then, who lives in New York, where she is a great beauty and a great success, and has been immensely admired this winter."

"After all," said Vogelstein, reflecting and a little disappointed, "the name is not so uncommon; it is perhaps another. But has she rather strange eyes, a little yellow, but very pretty, and a nose a little arched?"

"I can't tell you all that; I haven't seen her. She is staying with Mrs. Steuben. She only came a day or two ago, and Mrs. Steuben is to bring her. When she wrote to me to ask leave, she told me what I tell you. They haven't come yet."

Vogelstein felt a quick hope that the subject of this correspondence might indeed be the young lady he had parted from on the dock at New York, but the indications seemed to point the other way, and he had no wish to cherish an illusion. It did not seem to him probable that the energetic girl who had introduced him to Mr. Lansing would have the entree of the best house in Washington; besides, Mrs. Bonnycastle's guest was described as a beauty and as belonging to the brilliant city. . . .

At last he heard it mentioned that the President had arrived, had been some half-an-hour in the house, and he went in search of the illustrious guest, whose whereabouts at Washington parties was not indicated by a cluster of courtiers. He made it a point, whenever he found himself in company with the President, to pay him his respects; and he had not been discouraged by the fact that there was no association of ideas in the eye of the great man as he put out his hand, presidentially, and said, "Happy to see you, sir." Vogelstein felt himself taken for a mere constituent, possibly for an office-seeker; and he used to reflect at such moments that the monarchical form had its merits: it provided a line of heredity for the faculty of quick recognition. He had now some difficulty in finding the chief magistrate, and ended by learning that he was in the tea-room, a small apartment devoted to light refection, near the entrance of the house. Here Vogelstein presently perceived him, seated on a sofa, in conversation with a lady. There were a number of people about the table, eating, drinking, talking; and the couple on the sofa, which was not near it, but against the wall, in a kind of recess, looked a little withdrawn, as if they had sought seclusion and were disposed to profit by the diverted attention of the others. The President leaned back; his gloved hands, resting on either knee, made large white spots. He looked eminent, but he looked relaxed, and the lady beside him was making him laugh. Vogelstein caught her voice as he approached—he heard her say, "Well, now, remember; I consider it a promise." She was very prettily dressed, in rose-colour; her hands were clasped in her lap, and her eyes were attached to the presidential profile.

"Well, madam, in that case it's about the fiftieth promise I have given to-day."

It was just as he heard these words, uttered by her companion in reply, that Vogelstein checked himself, turned away, and pretended to be looking for a cup of tea. It was not customary to disturb the President, even simply to shake hands, when he was sitting on a sofa with a lady, and Vogelstein felt it in this case less possible than ever to break the rule, for the lady on the sofa was none other than Pandora Day. He had recognised her without her appearing to see him, and even in his momentary look he had perceived that she was now a person to be reckoned with. She had an air of elation, of success; she looked brilliant in her rose-coloured dress; she was extracting promises from the ruler of fifty millions of people. What an odd place to meet her, Vogelstein thought, and how little one could tell, after all, in America, who people were! He didn't want to speak to her yet; he wanted to wait a little and learn more; but, meanwhile, there was something attractive in the fact that she was just behind him, a few yards off, that if he should turn he might see her again. It was she whom Mrs. Bonnycastle had meant; it was she who was so much admired in New York. Her face was the same, yet Vogelstein had seen in a moment that she was vaguely prettier; he had recognised the arch of her nose, which suggested ambition. He took two ices, which he did not want, in order not to go away. He remembered her *entourage* on the steamer: her father and mother, the silent burghers, so little "of the world," her infant sister, so much of it, her humorous brother, with his tall hat and his influence in the smoking-room. He remembered Mrs. Dangerfield's warnings—yet her perplexities too, and the letter from Mr. Bellamy, and the introduction to Mr. Lansing, and the way Pandora had stooped down on the dirty dock, laughing and talking, mistress of the situation, to open her trunk for the customs. He was pretty sure that she had paid no duties that day; that had been the purpose, of course, of Mr. Bellamy's letter. Was she still in correspondence with this gentleman, and had he recovered from his sickness?* All this passed through Vogelstein's mind, and he saw that it was quite in Pandora's line to be mistress of the situation, for there was nothing, evidently, on the present occasion that could call itself her master. He drank his tea, and as he put down his cup he heard the President, behind him, say, "Well, I guess my wife will wonder why I don't come home."

"Why didn't you bring her with you?" Pandora asked.

"Well, she doesn't go out much. Then she has got her sister staying with her—Mrs. Runkle, from Natchez. She's a good deal of an invalid, and my wife doesn't like to leave her."

"She must be a very kind woman," Pandora remarked, sympathetically.

"Well, I guess she isn't spoiled yet."

"I should like very much to come and see her," said Pandora.

"Do come round. Couldn't you come some night?" the President responded.

"Well, I'll come some time. And I shall remind you of your promise."

"All right. There's nothing like keeping it up. Well," said the President, "I must bid good-bye to these kind folks."

Vogelstein heard him rise from the sofa, with his companion, and he gave the pair time to pass out of the room before him, which they did with a certain impressive deliberation, people making way for the ruler of fifty millions and looking with a certain curiosity at the striking pink person at his side. When, after a few moments, Vogelstein followed them across the hall, into one of the other rooms, he saw the hostess accompany the President to the door, and two foreign ministers and a judge of the Supreme Court address themselves to Pandora Day. He resisted the impulse to join this circle; if he spoke to her

---

* *In material excised from the end of Part I, Vogelstein and Pandora meet again on the dock as they prepare for customs inspection. Pandora's friend Mr. Bellamy was unable to meet her, owing to illness. But he had sent her a letter of introduction to his friend Mr. Lansing, a customs officer, who eases Pandora and her family through. As she departs, she bids the German adieu: "Good-bye, Count Vogelstein. I hope you'll judge us correctly!"*

at all he wished to speak to her alone. She continued, nevertheless, to occupy him, and when Mrs. Bonnycastle came back from the hall he immediately approached her with an appeal. "I wish you would tell me something more about that girl—that one, opposite, in pink?"

"The lovely Day—that is what they call her, I believe? I wanted you to talk with her."

"I find she is the one I have met. But she seems to be so different here. I can't make it out."

There was something in his expression which provoked Mrs. Bonnycastle to mirth. "How we do puzzle you Europeans; you look quite bewildered."

"I am sorry I look so; I try to hide it. But, of course, we are very simple. Let me ask, then, a simple question. Are her parents also in society?"

"Parents in society! D'où tombez-vous? Did you ever hear of a girl—in rose-colour—whose parents were in society?"

"Is she, then, all alone?" Count Vogelstein inquired, with a strain of melancholy in his voice.

Mrs. Bonnycastle stared at him a moment, with her laughter in her face. "You are too pathetic. Don't you know what she is? I supposed, of course, you knew."

"It's exactly what I am asking you."

"Why, she's the new type. It has only come up lately. They have had articles about it in the papers. That's the reason I told Mrs. Steuben to bring her."

"The new type? What new type, Mrs. Bonnycastle?" said Vogelstein, pleadingly, and conscious that all types in America were new.

Her laughter checked her reply for a moment, and by the time she had recovered herself the young lady from Boston, with whom Vogelstein had been talking, stood there to take leave. This, for an American type, was an old one, he was sure; and the process of parting between the guest and her hostess had an ancient elaboration. Vogelstein waited a little; then he turned away and walked up to Pandora Day, whose group of interlocutors had now been reinforced by a gentleman that had held an important place in the cabinet of the late occupant of the presidential chair. Vogelstein had asked Mrs. Bonnycastle if she were "all alone;" but there was nothing in her present situation that suggested isolation. She was not sufficiently alone for Vogelstein's taste; but he was impatient, and he hoped she would give him a few words to himself. She recognised him without a moment's hesitation, and with the sweetest smile, a smile that matched the tone in which she said, "I was watching you; I wondered if you were not going to speak to me."

"Miss Day was watching him," one of the foreign ministers exclaimed, "and we flattered ourselves that her attention was all with us!"

"I mean before," said the girl, "while I was talking with the President."

At this the gentlemen began to laugh, and one of them remarked that that was the way the absent were sacrificed, even the great; while another said that he hoped Vogelstein was duly flattered.

"Oh, I was watching the President too," said Pandora. "I have got to watch *him*. He has promised me something."

"It must be the mission to England," the judge of the Supreme Court suggested. "A good position for a lady; they have got a lady at the head, over there."

"I wish they would send you to my country," one of the foreign ministers suggested. "I would immediately get recalled."

"Why, perhaps in your country I wouldn't speak to you! It's only because you are here," the girl returned, with a gay familiarity which with her was evidently but one of the arts of defence. "You'll see what mission it is when it comes out. But I will speak to Count Vogelstein anywhere," she went on. "He's an older friend than any one here. I have known him in difficult days."

"Oh yes, on the ocean," said the young man, smiling. "On the watery waste, in the tempest!"

"Oh, I don't mean that so much; we had a beautiful voyage, and there wasn't any tempest. I mean when I was living in Utica. That's a watery waste, if you like, and a tempest there would have been a pleasant variety."

"Your parents seemed to me so peaceful!" Vogelstein exclaimed, with a vague wish to say something sympathetic.

"Oh, you haven't seen them on shore. At Utica they were very lively. But that is no longer our home. Don't you remember I told you I was working for New York? Well, I worked—I had to work hard. But we have moved."

"And I hope they're happy," said Vogelstein.

"My father and mother? Oh, they will be, in time. I must give them time. They are very young yet; they have years before them. And you have been always in Washington?" Pandora continued. "I suppose you have found out everything about everything."

"Oh no; there are some things I can't find out."

"Come and see me, and perhaps I can help you. I am very different from what I was on the ship. I have advanced a great deal since then."

"Oh, how was Miss Day on the ship?" asked the cabinet minister of the last administration.

"She was delightful, of course," said Vogelstein.

"He is very flattering; I didn't open my mouth!" Pandora cried. "Here comes Mrs. Steuben to take me to some other place. I believe it's a literary party, near the Capitol. Everything seems so separate in Washington. Mrs. Steuben is going to read a poem. I wish she would read it here; wouldn't it do as well?"

This lady, arriving, signified to Pandora the necessity of their moving on. But Miss Day's companions had various things to say to her before giving her up. She had an answer for each of them, and it was brought home to Vogelstein, as he listened, that, as she said, she has advanced a great deal. Daughter of small burghers as she was, she was really brilliant. . . .

Pandora gave her hand to Count Vogelstein, and asked him if he thought they should meet again. He answered that in Washington people were always meeting, and that at any rate he should not fail to come and see her. Hereupon, just as the two ladies were detaching themselves, Mrs. Steuben remarked that if Count Vogelstein and Miss Day wished to meet again the picnic would be a good chance—the picnic that she was getting up for the following Thursday. It was to consist of about twenty bright people, and they would go down the Potomac to Mount Vernon. Vogelstein answered that, if Mrs. Steuben thought him bright enough, he should be delighted to join the party; and he was told the hour for which the tryst was taken.

He remained at Mrs. Bonnycastle's after every one had gone, and then he informed this lady of his reason for waiting. Would she have mercy on him and let him know, in a single word, before he went to rest—for without it rest would be impossible—what was this famous type to which Pandora Day belonged?

"Gracious, you don't mean to say you have not found out that type yet!" Mrs. Bonnycastle exclaimed, with a return of her hilarity. "What have you been doing all the evening? You Germans may be thorough, but you certainly are not quick!"

It was Alfred Bonnycastle who at last took pity on him. "My dear Vogelstein, she is the latest, freshest fruit of our great American evolution. She is the self-made girl!" . . .

"Sit down, and we'll tell you all about it," Mrs. Bonnycastle said. "I like talking this way after a party's over. You can smoke, if you like, and Alfred will open another window. Well, to begin with, the self-made girl is a new feature. That, however, you know. In the second place, she isn't self-made at all. We all help to make her, we take such an interest in her."

"That's only after she's made!" Alfred Bonnycastle broke in. "But it's Vogelstein that takes an interest. What on earth has started you up so on the subject of Miss Day?"

Vogelstein explained, as well as he could, that it was merely the accident of his having crossed the ocean in the steamer with her; but he felt the inadequacy of this account of the matter, felt it more than his hosts, who could know neither how little actual contact he had had with her on the ship, how much he had been affected by Mrs. Dangerfield's warnings, nor how much observation at the same time he had lavished on her. He sat there half an hour, and the warm, dead stillness of the Washington night—nowhere are the nights so silent—came in at the open windows, mingled with a soft, sweet, earthy smell, the smell of growing things. Before he went away he had heard all about the self-made girl, and there was something in the picture that almost inspired him. She was possible, doubtless, only in America; American life had smoothed the way for her. She was not fast nor emancipated nor crude nor loud, and there was not in her, of necessity at least, a grain of the stuff of which the adventuress is made. She was simply very successful, and her success was entirely personal. She had not been born with the silver spoon of social opportunity; she had grasped it by honest exertion. You knew her by many different signs, but chiefly, infallibly, by the appearance of her parents. It was her parents that told the story; you always saw that her parents could never have made her. Her attitude with regard to them might vary, in innumerable ways; the great fact on her own side was that she had lifted herself from a lower social plane, done it all herself, and done it by the simple lever of her personality. In this view, of course, it was to be expected that she should leave the authors of her being in the shade. Sometimes she had them in her wake, lost in the bubbles and the foam that showed where she had passed; sometimes, as Alfred Bonnycastle said, she let them slide; sometimes she kept them in close confinement; sometimes she exhibited them to the public in discreet glimpses, in prearranged attitudes. But the general characteristic of the self-made girl was that, though it was frequently understood that she was privately devoted to her kindred, she never attempted to impose them on society, and it was striking that she was much better than they. They were almost always solemn and portentous, and they were for the most part of a deathly respectability. She was not necessarily snobbish, unless it was snobbish to want the best. She didn't cringe, she didn't make herself smaller than she was; on the contrary, she took a stand of her own, and attracted things to herself. Naturally, she was possible only in America, only in a country where certain competitions were absent. The natural history of this interesting creature was at last completely exhibited to Vogelstein, who, as he sat there in the animated stillness, with the fragrant breath of the western world in his nostrils, was convinced of what he had already suspected, that conversation in the United States is much more psychological than elsewhere. Another thing, as he learned, that you knew the self-made girl by was her culture, which was perhaps a little too obvious. She had usually got into society more or less by reading, and her conversation was apt to be garnished with literary allusions, even with sudden quotations. Vogelstein had not had time to observe this element as a developed form in Pandora Day; but Alfred Bonnycastle said that he wouldn't trust her to keep it under in a *tête-à-tête*. It was needless to say that these young persons had always been to Europe; that was usually the first thing they did. By this means they sometimes got into society in foreign lands before they did so at home; it was to be added, on the other hand, that this resource was less and less valuable; for Europe, in the United States, had less and less prestige, and people in the latter country now kept a watch on that roundabout road. All this applied perfectly to Pandora Day—the journey to Europe, the culture (as exemplified in the books she read on the ship), the effacement of the family. The only thing that was exceptional was the rapidity with which she had advanced; for the jump she had taken since he left her in the hands of Mr. Lansing struck Vogelstein, even after he had made all allowance for the abnormal homogeneity of American society, as really considerable. It took all her cleverness to account for it. When she moved her family from Utica, the battle appeared virtually to have been gained. . . .

Vogelstein's curiosity about Pandora Day had been much more quickened than checked by the revelations made to him in Mrs. Bonnycastle's drawing-room. It was a relief to see the young lady classified; but he had a desire, of which he had not been conscious before, to judge really to the end how well a girl could make herself. . . .

Mrs. Steuben's picnic was still three days distant. He called on Pandora a second time, and he met her each evening in the Washington world. It took very little of this to remind him that he was forgetting both Mrs. Dangerfield's warnings and the admonitions—long familiar to him—of his own conscience. Was he in peril of love? Was he to be sacrificed on the altar of the American girl—an altar at which those other poor fellows had poured out some of the bluest blood in Germany, and at which he had declared himself that he would never seriously worship? He decided that he was not in real danger; that he had taken his precautions too well. It was true that a young person who had succeeded so well for herself might be a great help to her husband; but Vogelstein, on the whole, preferred that his success should be his own; it would not be agreeable to him to have the air of being pushed by his wife. Such a wife as that would wish to push him; and he could hardly admit to himself that this was what fate had in reserve for him—to be propelled in his career by a young lady who would perhaps attempt to talk to the Kaiser as he had heard her the other night talk to the President. Would she consent to relinquish relations with her family, or would she wish still to borrow plastic relief from that domestic background? That her family was so impossible was to a certain extent an advantage; for if they had been a little better the question of a rupture would have been less easy. Vogelstein turned over these ideas in spite of his security, or perhaps, indeed, because of it. The security made them speculative and disinterested. They haunted him during the excursion to Mount Vernon, which took place according to traditions long established.

Mrs. Steuben's picnickers assembled on the steamer, and were set afloat on the big brown stream which had already seemed to Vogelstein to have too much bosom and too little bank. Here and there, however, he became conscious of a shore where there was something to look at, even though he was conscious at the same time that he had of old lost great opportunities of idyllic talk in not sitting beside Pandora Day on the deck of the North German Lloyd. The two turned round together to contemplate Alexandria, which for Pandora, as she declared, was a revelation of old Virginia. She told Vogelstein that she was always hearing about it during the civil war, years before. Little girl as she had been at the time, she remembered all the names that were on people's lips during those years of reiteration. This historic spot had a certain picturesqueness of decay, a reference to older things, to a dramatic past. The past of Alexandria appeared in the vista of three or four short streets, sloping up a hill and bordered with old brick warehouses, erected for merchandise that had ceased to come or go. It looked hot and blank and sleepy, down to the shabby waterside where tattered darkies dangled their bare feet from the edge of rotting wharves. Pandora was even more interested in Mount Vernon (when at last its wooded bluff began to command the river) than she had been in the Capitol; and after they had disembarked and ascended to the celebrated mansion she insisted on going into every room it contained. She declared that it had the finest situation in the world, and that it was a shame they didn't give it to the President for his villeggiatura. Most of her companions had seen the house often, and were now coupling themselves, in the grounds, according to their sympathies, so that it was easy for Vogelstein to offer the benefit of his own experience to the most inquisitive member of the party. They were not to lunch for another hour, and in the interval Vogelstein wandered about with Pandora. The breath of the Potomac, on the boat, had been a little harsh, but on the softly-curving lawn, beneath the clustered trees, with the river relegated to a mere shining presence far below and in the distance, the day gave out nothing but its mildness, the whole scene became noble and genial.

Vogelstein could joke a little on great occasions, and the present one was worthy of his humour. He maintained to his companion that the shallow, painted mansion looked like a false house, a "fly," a structure of daubed canvas, on the stage; but she answered him so well with certain economical palaces she had seen in Germany, where, as she said, there was nothing but china stoves and stuffed birds, that he was obliged to allow the home of Washington to be after all really *gemüthlich*. What he found so, in fact, was the soft texture of the day, his personal situation, the sweetness of his suspense. For suspense had decidedly become his portion; he was under a charm which made him feel he was watching his own life and that his susceptibilities were beyond his control. It hung over him that things might take a turn, from one hour to the other, which would make them very different from what they had been yet; and his heart certainly beat a little faster as he wondered what that turn might be. Why did he come to picnics on fragrant April days with American girls who might lead him too far? Would not such girls be glad to marry a Pomeranian count? And would they, after all, talk that way to the Kaiser? If he were to marry one of them he should have to give her some lessons. In their little tour of the house Vogelstein and his companion had had a great many fellow-visitors, who had also arrived by the steamer and who had hitherto not left them an ideal privacy. But the others gradually dispersed; they circled about a kind of showman, who was the authorised guide, a big, slow, genial, familiar man, with a large beard, and a humorous, edifying, patronising tone, which had immense success when he stopped here and there to make his points, to pass his eyes over his listening flock, then fix them quite above it with a meditative look, and bring out some ancient pleasantry as if it were a sudden inspiration. He made a cheerful thing even of a visit to the tomb of the *pater patriae*. It is enshrined in a kind of grotto in the grounds, and Vogelstein remarked to Pandora that he was a good man for the place, but that he was too familiar.

"Oh, he would have been familiar with Washington," said the girl, with the bright dryness with which she often uttered amusing things.

Vogelstein looked at her a moment, and it came over him, as he smiled, that she herself probably would not have been abashed even by the hero with whom history has taken fewest liberties. "You look as if you could hardly believe that," Pandora went on. "You Germans are always in such awe of great people." And it occurred to Vogelstein that perhaps, after all, Washington would have liked her manner, which was wonderfully fresh and natural. The man with the beard was an ideal cicerone for American shrines; he played upon the curiosity of his little band with the touch of a master, and drew them away to see the classic ice-house where the old lady had been found weeping in the belief it was Washington's grave. While this monument was under inspection Vogelstein and Pandora had the house to themselves, and they spent some time on a pretty terrace, upon which certain windows of the second floor opened—a little roofless verandah, which overhung in a manner, obliquely, all the magnificence of the view—the immense sweep of the river, the artistic plantations, the last-century garden, with its big box-hedges and remains of old espaliers. They lingered here for nearly half an hour, and it was in this spot that Vogelstein enjoyed the only approach to intimate conversation that fate had in store for him with a young woman in whom he had been unable to persuade himself that he was not interested. It is not necessary, and it is not possible, that I should reproduce this colloquy; but I may mention that it began—as they leaned against the parapet of the terrace and heard the fraternising voice of the showman wafted up to them from a distance—with his saying to her, rather abruptly, that he couldn't make out why they hadn't had more talk together when they crossed the ocean.

"Well, I can, if you can't," said Pandora. "I would have talked if you had spoken to me. I spoke to you first."

"Yes, I remember that," Vogelstein replied, rather awkwardly.

"You listened too much to Mrs. Dangerfield."

"To Mrs. Dangerfield?"

"That woman you were always sitting with; she told you not to speak to me. I have seen her in New York; she speaks to me now herself. She recommended you to have nothing to do with me."

"Oh, how can you say such dreadful things?" the young man murmured, blushing very red.

"You know you can't deny it. You were not attracted by my family. They are charming people when you know them. I don't have a better time anywhere than I have at home," the girl went on, loyally. "But what does it matter? My family are very happy. They are getting quite used to New York. Mrs. Dangerfield is a vulgar wretch; next winter she will call on me."

"You are unlike any girl I have ever seen; I don't understand you," said poor Vogelstein, with the colour still in his face.

"Well, you never will understand me, probably; but what difference does it make?"

Vogelstein attempted to tell her what difference it made, but I have not space to follow him here. It is known that when the German mind attempts to explain things it does not always reduce them to simplicity, and Pandora was first mystified, then amused, by some of her companion's revelations. At last I think she was a little frightened, for she remarked irrelevantly, with some decision, that lunch would be ready and they ought to join Mrs. Steuben. He walked slowly, on purpose, as they left the house together, for he had a vague feeling that he was losing her.

"And shall you be in Washington many days yet?" he asked her as they went.

"It will all depend. I am expecting some news. What I shall do will be influenced by that."

The way she talked about expecting news made him feel, somehow, that she had a career, that she was active and independent, so that he could scarcely hope to stop her as she passed. It was certainly true that he had never seen any girl like her. It would have occurred to him that the news she was expecting might have reference to the favour she had asked of the President, if he had not already made up his mind, in the calm of meditation, after that talk with the Bonnycastles, that this favour must be a pleasantry. What she had said to him had a discouraging, a somewhat chilling, effect; nevertheless it was not without a certain ardour that he asked of her whether, so long as she stayed in Washington, he might not come and see her.

"You may come as often as you like," she answered, "but you won't care for it long."

"You try to torment me," said Vogelstein.

She hesitated a moment. "I mean that I may have some of my family."

"I shall be delighted to see them once more."

She hesitated again. "There are some you have never seen."

In the afternoon, returning to Washington on the steamer, Count Vogelstein received a warning. It came from Mrs. Bonnycastle, and constituted, oddly enough, the second occasion on which an officious female friend had, on the deck of a vessel, advised him on the subject of Pandora Day.

"There is one thing we forgot to tell you, the other night, about the self-made girl," Mrs. Bonnycastle said. "It is never safe to fix your affections upon her, because she has almost always got an impediment somewhere in the background."

Vogelstein looked at her askance, but he smiled and said, "I should understand your information—for which I am so much obliged—a little better if I knew what you mean by an impediment."

"Oh, I mean she is always engaged to some young man who belongs to her earlier phase."

"Her earlier phase?"

"The time before she had made herself—when she lived at home. A young man from Utica, say. They usually have to wait; he is probably in a store. It's a long engagement."

"Do you mean a betrothal—to be married?"

"I don't mean anything German and transcendental. I mean that peculiarly American institution, a precocious engagement; to be married, of course."

Vogelstein very properly reflected that it was no use his having entered the diplomatic career if he were not able to bear himself as if this interesting generalisation had no particular message for him. He did Mrs. Bonnycastle, moreover, the justice to believe that she would not have taken up the subject so casually if she had suspected that she should make him wince. The whole thing was one of her jokes, and the notification, moreover, was really friendly. "I see, I see," he said in a moment. "The self-made girl has, of course, always had a past. Yes, and the young man in the store—from Utica—is part of her past."

"You express it perfectly," said Mrs. Bonnycastle. "I couldn't say it better myself."

"But, with her present, with her future, I suppose it's all over. How do you say it in America? She lets him slide."

"We don't say it at all!" Mrs. Bonnycastle cried. "She does nothing of the sort; for what do you take her? She sticks to him; that, at least, is what we expect her to do," Mrs. Bonnycastle added, more thoughtfully. "As I tell you, the type is new. We haven't yet had time for complete observations."

"Oh, of course, I hope she sticks to him," Vogelstein declared simply, and with his German accent more apparent, as it always was when he was slightly agitated.

For the rest of the trip he was rather restless. He wandered about the boat, talking little with the returning revellers. Towards the last, as they drew near Washington, and the white dome of the Capitol hung aloft before them, looking as simple as a suspended snowball, he found himself, on the deck, in proximity to Mrs. Steuben. He reproached himself with having rather neglected her during an entertainment for which he was indebted to her bounty, and he sought to repair his omission by a little friendly talk. But the only thing he could think of to say to her was to ask her by chance whether Miss Day were, to her knowledge, engaged.

Mrs. Steuben turned her Southern eyes upon him with a look of almost romantic compassion. "To my knowledge? Why, of course I would know! I should think you would know too. Didn't you know she was engaged? Why, she has been engaged since she was sixteen."

Vogelstein stared at the dome of the Capitol. "To a gentleman from Utica?"

"Yes, a native of her place. She is expecting him soon."

"Oh, I am so glad to hear it," said Vogelstein, who decidedly, for his career, had promise. "And is she going to marry him?"

"Why, what do people get engaged for? I presume they will marry before long."

"But why have they never done so, in so many years?"

"Well, at first she was too young, and then she thought her family ought to see Europe—of course they could see it better with her—and they spent some time there. And then Mr. Bellamy had some business difficulties which made him feel as if he didn't want to marry just then. But he has given up business, and I presume he feels more free. Of course it's rather long, but all the while they have been engaged. It's a true, true love," said Mrs. Steuben, who had a little flute-like way of sounding the adjective.

"Is his name Mr. Bellamy?" Vogelstein asked, with his haunting reminiscence. "D. F. Bellamy, eh? And has he been in a store?"

"I don't know what kind of business it was; it was some kind of business in Utica. I think he had a branch in New York. He is one of the leading gentlemen of Utica, and very highly educated. He's a good deal older than Miss Day. He is a very fine man. He stands very high in Utica. I don't know why you look as if you doubted it."

Vogelstein assured Mrs. Steuben that he doubted nothing, and indeed what she told him struck him as all the more credible, as it seemed to him eminently strange. Bellamy had been the name of the gentleman who, a year and a half before, was to have met Pandora on the arrival of the German steamer; it was in Bellamy's name that she had addressed herself with such effusion to Bellamy's friend, the man in the straw hat, who was to fumble in her mother's old clothes. This was a fact which seemed to Vogelstein to finish the picture of her contradictions; it wanted at present no touch to be complete. Yet even as it hung there before him it continued to fascinate him, and he stared at it, detached from surrounding things and feeling a little as if he had been pitched out of an overturned vehicle, till the boat bumped against one of the outstanding piles of the wharf at which Mrs. Steuben's party was to disembark. There was some delay in getting the steamer adjusted to the dock, during which the passengers stood watching the process, over the side and extracting what entertainment they might from the appearance of the various persons collected to receive it. There were darkies and loafers and hackmen, and also individuals with tufts on their chins, toothpicks in their mouths, their hands in their pockets, rumination in their jaws, and diamond-pins in their shirt-fronts, who looked as if they had sauntered over from Pennsylvania Avenue to while away half an hour, forsaking for that interval their various postures of inclination in the porticoes of the hotels and the doorways of the saloons.

"Oh, I am so glad! How sweet of you to come down!" It was a voice close to Vogelstein's shoulder that spoke these words, and the young secretary of legation had no need to turn to see from whom it proceeded. It had been in his ears the greater part of the day, though, as he now perceived, without the fullest richness of expression of which it was capable. Still less was he obliged to turn to discover to whom it was addressed, for the few simple words I have quoted had been flung across the narrowing interval of water, and a gentleman who had stepped to the edge of the dock without Vogelstein's observing him tossed back an immediate reply.

"I got here by the three o'clock train. They told me in K Street where you were, and I thought I would come down and meet you."

"Charming attention!" said Pandora Day, with her friendly laugh; and for some moments she and her interlocutor appeared to continue the conversation only with their eyes. Meanwhile Vogelstein's, also, were not idle. He looked at Pandora's visitor from head to foot, and he was aware that she was quite unconscious of his own nearness. The gentleman before him was tall, good-looking, well-dressed; evidently he would stand well not only at Utica, but, judging from the way he had planted himself on the dock, in any position which circumstances might compel him to take up. He was about forty years old; he had a black moustache and a business-like eye. He waved a gloved hand at Pandora, as if, when she exclaimed, "Gracious, ain't they long!" to urge her to be patient. She was patient for a minute, and then she asked him if he had any news. He looked at her an instant in silence, smiling, after which he drew from his pocket a large letter with an official seal, and shook it jocosely above his head. This was discreetly, covertly done. No one appeared to observe the little interview but Vogelstein. The boat was now touching the wharf, and the space between the pair was inconsiderable.

"Department of State?" Pandora asked, dropping her voice.

"That's what they call it."

"Well, what country?"

"What's your opinion of the Dutch?" the gentleman asked, for an answer.

"Oh, gracious!" cried Pandora.

"Well, are you going to wait for the return trip?" said the gentleman.

Vogelstein turned away, and presently Mrs. Steuben and her companions disembarked together. When this lady entered a carriage with Pandora, the gentleman who had spoken to the girl followed them; the others scattered, and Vogelstein, declining with thanks a "lift" from Mrs. Bonnycastle, walked home alone, in some intensity of meditation. Two days later he saw in a newspaper an announcement that the President had offered the post of Minister to Holland to D. F. Bellamy, of Utica; and in the course of a month he heard from Mrs. Steuben that Pandora's long engagement had terminated at the nuptial altar. He communicated this news to Mrs. Bonnycastle, who had not heard it, with the remark that there was now ground for a new induction as to the self-made girl.

Twenty-Two Days on a Chain Gang

BAYARD RUSTIN

As Benjamin Franklin's personal account makes clear, attaining self-command and self-respect is no easy matter under the best of circumstances. But self-command and self-respect are exceedingly hard to come by under conditions of oppression, degradation, and dehumanization. Such is the setting of this memoir by civil rights activist Bayard Rustin (1912–1987) about his twenty-two days on a chain gang in North Carolina, to which he was sentenced in 1949 for violating the Jim Crow (segregated) seating on a public bus. Rustin finds himself in the company of real criminals, including compulsive thieves and sex offenders, men with little self-control and less self-respect. But most degrading are the dehumanizing conditions and the abusiveness of the guards. Most remarkable, then, is Rustin's description of how he maintained both self-command and self-respect, avoiding the common alternatives of servility and seething rebellion.

What effect does Rustin's behavior—treating himself as equal to everyone else, including those with authority over him, and choosing the pathway of respect rather than defiance—have on his fellow prisoners and on his keepers? How does it contribute to the attainment of self-command and self-respect, even among the members of this marginal community? Rustin, concerned with the rehabilitation and reform of broken men, sees punishment as an impediment to self-improvement. Is he right? What enables Rustin to act as he does? Does the establishment of self-control always reside solely with the self? Rustin seems to point to two other possible sources: he says, "I could not help trying to act on the basis of my own Christian ideals about people," and in referring to the sex offender and the kleptomaniac, he emphasizes the role of psychiatrists and medicine in restoring the possibility of self-control. Is self-control within our control?

Late in the afternoon of Monday, March 21, 1949, I surrendered to the Orange County court at Hillsboro, North Carolina, to begin serving a thirty-day sentence imposed two years before for sitting in a bus seat out of the Jim Crow section. As afternoon waned into evening, I waited alone in a small cell of the county jail across the street. I had not eaten since morning, but no supper was forthcoming, and eventually I lay down on the mattressless iron bed and tried to sleep. Next morning I learned that only two meals were served daily—breakfast at seven A.M. and lunch at noon.

That morning I spent reading one of the books I had brought with me and wondering where I would be sent to do my time. At about two P.M. I was ordered to prepare to leave for a prison camp. Along with two other men I got into the "dog car"—a small, brown enclosed truck with a locked screen in the rear—and began to travel through the rain. An hour later we stopped at the state prison camp at Roxboro, and through the screen I could see the long, low building, circled by barbed wire, where I was to spend the next twenty-two days.

The camp was very unattractive, to put it mildly. There were no trees, grass only near the entrance and to one side. There was not one picture on the walls and no drawer, box, or container supplied for storing the few items one owned. While an effort was made to keep the place clean, there was always mud caked on the floor as soon as the men got in from work, since there was no change of shoes. Roaches were everywhere, though I never saw a bedbug. Once a week the mattresses were aired.

In the receiving room, under close supervision, I went through the routine of the new inmate: receiving a book of rules and a change of clothing, finger-printing, and—"You'll have to have all your hair cut off."

An inmate barber gleefully shaved my head and, with an expression of mock sadness, surveyed me from various angles. Finally he brought a small mirror and ceremoniously held it up for me. The final touch was his solemn pretense of brushing some hairs from my shirt. Then he told me to go out to the corridor, where an officer would show me to my bed. As I left, the three inmates who were in the room doubled up with laughter. Apparently they had discovered the reason for my schoolboy nickname, "Pinhead"!

Wordlessly the officer outside unlocked the dormitory door and motioned for me to go through.

Inside I found myself in one of two rooms into which a hundred men were crowded. Double-decker beds stood so close together that one had to turn sidewise to pass between them. Lights bright enough to read by remained on all night. The rule book states: "No inmate may get out of bed after lights are dimmed without asking permission of the guard," and so all night long men were crying out to a guard many yards away: "Gettin' up, Cap'n," "Closing the window, Cap'n," "Goin' to the toilet, Cap'n." I did not sleep soundly one night during my whole stay at Roxboro, though I went to bed tireder than I had ever been before.

The camp schedule at Roxboro began with the rising bell at five-thirty. By seven beds had been made, faces washed, breakfast served, and lines formed for leaving the camp for the ten-hour-day's work. We worked from seven until noon, had a half-hour for lunch, resumed work at twelve-thirty, and worked until five-thirty. Then we were counted in and left immediately for supper, without so much as a chance to wash hands and face. From six o'clock we were locked in the dormitory until lights were dimmed at eight-thirty. From then until five-thirty A.M. we were expected to sleep.

On the morning of March 23, my second day at camp, I shaved hurriedly. When I had finished, Easy Life, an inmate who had a nearby bed, apologetically asked if he might borrow my razor. He had a week's growth of hair on his face.

"Most of us ain't got no razors and can't buy none," he said. "But don't they give you a razor if you can't afford one?" I asked.

He looked at me and smiled. "We don't get nothing but the clothes we got on and a towel and soap—no comb, no brush, no toothbrush, no razor, no blades, no stamps, no writing paper, no pencils, nothing." Then he looked up and said thoughtfully, "They say, 'Another day, another dollar,' but all we gets for our week's work is one bag of stud."

I suppose my deep concern must have been reflected in my face, for he added, "Don't look so sad. T'ain't nothin! The boys say 'So round, so firm, so fully packed,' when you roll your own."

The guard swung open the doors for breakfast, and as Easy Life rushed to the front of the line he yelled back, "But the damn stuff sure does burn your tongue—that's why I like my tailor-mades," meaning factory-made cigarettes. He winked, laughed heartily, and was gone. I picked up my toothbrush and razor, and slowly walked to my bed to put them away.

A week later I was to remember the conversation. The one towel I had been given was already turning a reddish gray (like the earth of Persons County) despite the fact that I washed it every day. That towel was never changed as long as I stayed at Roxboro. Some of the men washed their towels but once a week, just after they bathed on Saturday.

Each week we were given one suit of underclothing, one pair of pants, a shirt, and a pair of socks. Even though we worked in the mud and rain, this was the only clothing we would get until the next week. By Tuesday, the stench in the dormitory from sweating feet and encrusted underclothing was thick enough to cut. As one fellow said, "Don't do no good to wash and put this sweat-soaked stuff on again."

Two weeks later I saw Easy Life borrowing my toothbrush. "My old lady's coming to visit today and I gotta shine my pearls somehow," he apologized.

I offered him thirty-five cents for a toothbrush. He accepted the money, thanked me, and said, "But if you don't mind I'll buy stamps with it. I can write my old lady ten letters with this. I can borrow Snake's toothbrush if I wanna, but he ain't never got no stamps, and I ain't never got no money."

I started from the camp for my first day's work on the road with anything but an easy mind. Our crew of fifteen men was met at the back gate by the walking boss, who directed the day's work, and by a guard who carried both a revolver and a shotgun. We were herded into the rear of a truck where we were under constant scrutiny by the armed guard, who rode behind in a small, glass-enclosed trailer. In that way we rode each day to whatever part of Persons County we were to work in. We would leave the truck when we were ordered to. At all times we had to be within sight of the guard, but at no time closer than thirty feet to him.

On this first day I got down from the truck with the rest of the crew. After several moments of complete silence, which seemed to leave everyone uneasy, the walking boss, whom I shall call Captain Jones, looked directly at me.

"Hey, you, tall boy! How much time you got?"

"Thirty days," I said politely.

"Thirty days, Sir."

"Thirty days, Sir," I said.

He took a newsclipping from his pocket and waved it up and down.

"You're the one who thinks he's smart. Ain't got no respect. Tries to be uppity. Well, we'll learn you. You'll learn you got to respect us down here. You ain't in Yankeeland now. We don't like no Yankee ways." He was getting angrier by the moment, his face flushed and his breath short.

"I would as lief step on the head of a damyankee as I would on the head of a rattlesnake," he barked. "Now you git this here thing straight," and he walked closer to me, his face quivering. "You do what you're told. You respect us, or . . ." He raised his hand threateningly but, instead of striking me, brought the back of his hand down across the mouth of the man on my left. Then he thrust a pick at me and ordered me to get to work.

I had never handled a pick in my life, but I tried. Captain Jones watched me sardonically for a few minutes. Then he grabbed the pick from me, raised it over his head, and sank it deep into the earth several times.

"There, now," he shouted. "Let's see you do it."

I took the pick and for about ten minutes succeeded in breaking the ground. Then my arms and back began to give out. Just as I was beginning to feel faint, a chain-ganger called Purple walked over and said quietly, "O.K. Let me use dat pick for a while. You take the shovel and, no matter what they say or do, keep workin', keep tryin', and keep yo' mouth shut."

I took the shovel and began to throw the loose dirt into the truck. My arms pained so badly that I thought each shovelful would be the last. Then gradually my strength seemed to return.

As Purple began to pick again, he whispered to me, "Now you're learnin'. Sometimes you'll give out, but you can't never give up—dat's chain-gangin'!" An hour later we moved to another job. As I sat in the truck I racked my mind for some way to convince Captain Jones that I was not "uppity," and at the same time to maintain self-respect. I hit upon two ideas. I would try to work more willingly and harder than anyone in the crew, and I would be as polite and considerate as possible.

When the truck stopped and we were ordered out, I made an effort to carry through my resolution by beginning work immediately. In my haste I came within twenty feet of the guard.

"Stop, you bastard!" he screamed, and pointed his revolver at my head. "Git back, git back. Don't rush me or I'll shoot the goddamned life out of you."

With heart pounding I moved across the road. Purple walked up to me, put a shovel in my hand, and said, "Follow me and do what I do."

We worked together spading heavy clay mud and throwing it into the truck. An hour later, when the walking boss went down the road for a Coca Cola, I complained to Purple about my aching arms. Purple smiled, patted me on the back, and said as he continued to work, "Man born of black woman is born to see black days."

But my first black day was not yet over. Just after lunch we had begun to do what the chain-gangers call "jumpin' shoulders," which means cutting the top from the shoulders of the road when they have grown too high. Usually the crew works with two trucks. There is scarcely a moment of delay and the work is extremely hard. Captain Jones was displeased with the rate of our work, and violently urged us to greater effort. In an attempt to obey, one of the chain-gangers struck another with his shovel. The victim complained, instantly and profanely. The words were hardly out of his mouth before the Captain strode across the road and struck the cursing chain-ganger in the face with his fist again and again. Then Captain Jones informed the crew, using the most violent profanity, that cursing would not be tolerated. "Not for one goddamned moment," he repeated over and over.

No one spoke; every man tried to work harder yet remain inconspicuous. The silence seemed to infuriate the Captain. He glared angrily at the toiling men, then yelled to the armed guard.

"Shoot hell out of the next one you find cursin'. Shoot straight for his feet. Cripple 'em up. That will learn 'em."

The guard lifted his rifle and aimed it at the chest of the man nearest him.

"Hell, no!" he drawled. "I ain't aimin' fer no feet. I like hearts and livers. That's what really learns 'em."

Everyone spaded faster. . . .

A few days later, I told several of the boys that I had decided to talk to the Captain to try to improve relations on the job, since I was sure the guards were taking it out on the men because of me. They urged me to keep still. "Quiet does it," they said. "No need to make things worse," they admonished. "He'll kick you square in the ass," Purple warned.

Nevertheless I stopped the Captain that morning and asked to speak with him. He seemed startled. I told him that I knew there were great differences in our attitudes on many questions but that I felt we could be friends. I said that on the first morning, when I had failed to address him as "Sir," I had meant no disrespect to him and if he felt I had been disrespectful I was willing to apologize. I suggested that perhaps I was really the one who deserved to be beaten in the face, if anyone did. I was willing to work as hard as I could, and if I failed again at my work I hoped he would speak to me about it and I would try to improve. Finally I said I could not help trying to act on the basis of my own Christian ideals about people but that I did try to respect and understand those who differed with me.

He stared at me without a word. Then after several moments he turned to the gun guard and said in an embarrassed tone, "Well, I'll be goddamned." Then he shouted, "O.K., if you can work, get to it! Talk ain't gonna git that there dirt on the truck. Fill her up." (Later I learned that the Captain had said to one of the chain-gangers that he would rather I call him a "dirty-son-of-a-bitch" than to look him in the face "and say nothin'.")

That evening he called us together.

"This Yankee boy ain't so bad," he said. "They just ruined him up there 'cause they don't know how to train you-all. But I think he'll be all right and if you-all will help him I think we can learn him. He's got a strong back and seems to be willing."

The chain-gangers glanced at one another. As we piled into the truck one of them turned to me and said, "When he says he'll learn you, this is what he means:

"When you're white you're right,
When you're yellow you're mellow,
When you're brown you're down,
When you're black, my God, stay back!"

The chain-gangers laughed. We pulled the canvas over our heads to protect us from the rain that had begun to pour down, and headed back to camp to eat supper. . . .

The morning after my conversation with Captain Jones we were instructed to go to the cement mixer, where we were to make cement pipe used in draining the roads and building bridges. We had been working twenty minutes when the Captain came to me carrying a new cap. He played with the cap on the end of his finger for a while and stared at my shaved head.

"You're gonna catch your death of cold," he said, "so I brought you a cap. You tip it like all the other boys whenever you speak to the Captain and the guards, or whenever they speak to you."

I had noticed the way the men bowed obsequiously and lifted their hats off their heads and held them in the air whenever they spoke to the guard. I had decided I would rather be cold than behave in this servile way. I thanked the Captain, put the cap on my head, and wore it until lunchtime. After lunch I put it in my pocket, never to wear it again in the presence of the Captain or the guards. . . .

One day the chain-gangers were on fire with the news that an old prisoner had returned. Bill was slender, tall, good-looking and sang very well. Some three years before he had raped his own three-year-old daughter and been put in jail for a year. This time he was "up" for having raped his eight-year-old niece.

It was difficult to believe all the tales the men told about Bill. One evening he came to me and asked me if I had time to talk with him. We talked for almost two hours. He was quite different from the description I had heard. He had provided well for his family, he had gone to church, but, as he pathetically admitted, he had "made some terrible mistakes." It was apparent that he wanted to wipe the slate clean, but in Roxboro jail he could never discover the reason for his unhappiness and troubles.

As I lay awake that night I wondered how ten hours a day of arduous physical labor could help this young man to become a constructive citizen. The tragedy of his being in the prison camp was highlighted by the extraordinary success that good psychiatrists and doctors are having today with men far more mixed up than Bill. I thought of the honesty with which he had discussed himself, of the light in his eyes when he had heard for the first time of the miracles modern doctors perform—and I knew that Bill deserved the best that society could offer him: a real chance to be cured, to return to his wife and children with the "devils cast out."

Then there was a young boy who had been arrested for stealing. It was obvious from his behavior that he was a kleptomaniac. I would see him spend half an hour going from one section of the dormitory to another, waiting, plotting, planning, and conniving to steal many small and useless items. Although he did not smoke, I saw him spend twenty minutes getting into a position to steal a box of matches, which he later threw away.

One day, after I had written a long letter for him, he began to tell me that he had stolen even as a child but that now he wanted to stop. As tears came to his eyes, he explained that he had been able to stop stealing valuable things but that he could not stop stealing entirely. I asked him if he really wanted to change. He said he thought so. But he added: "It's such a thrill. Just before I get my hands on what I'm gonna take, I feel so excited."

After that, as I watched him evening after evening, I wondered how many men throughout the world were languishing in jails—burdens to society— who might be cured if only they were in hospitals where they belonged. One thing was clear. Neither this boy, who reluctantly stole by compulsion, nor Bill could be helped by life on the chain gang. Nor could society be protected, for in a short time these men and thousands like them return to society not only uncured but with heightened resentment and a desire for revenge.

Early one morning Easy Life was talking with one of his friends, who had done time for stealing and was to be released that day. . . .

The hour was getting near for Easy Life's companion to depart. They brought in the pillowcase in which his clothes had been stored three months earlier. As he dumped his clothes onto the bed, they made one shapeless lump. He opened out his pants and began to get into them. They had a thousand creases. Then he put on the dirty shirt he had worn when he came in, and dressed in this way he left to begin a new life. He had no comb or toothbrush or razor, nor a penny in his pocket. The "dog cart" would come to pick him up and drop him somewhere near the railroad station in Durham.

I looked at him, his face aglow, happy that he would once again be "free," and wondered how he could be so happy without a cent, with no job, and with no prospects. I wondered what he would go through to get his first meal, since he had no home. I wondered where he would sleep. He said he knew a prostitute who might put him up. Prostitutes and fairies, he had said, "will always give a guy a break." I wondered where he would find a decent shirt or a pair of pants. Would he beg or borrow or steal?

I wondered if he would return. One day on the job the Captain had offered to bet ten to one that the man would be back before the week was up. As I saw him start forth, so ill prepared to face life in the city, I too felt that he would return. I asked Easy Life what he thought his friend would do when he got to town. Easy Life said, "He'll steal for sure if they don't get him first." I asked him what he meant. He said, "If the bulls don't get him for vagrancy 'fore sundown, he'll probably snatch something for to eat and some clothes to cover his ass with for the night."

"For vagrancy?" I asked.

"For vagrancy! Sure enough for vagrancy," Easy underlined. He then told me the story of a friend from South Carolina who had been on the chain gang. He, like all the others, was released without a penny in his pocket. While thumbing his way home, he was arrested for vagrancy soon after he crossed into South Carolina, and was back in jail for ninety days, less than two days after being released.

Between supper and "lights out" was our time for recreation. But for most of the men it was not a creative period. The rules permitted "harmless games," but there was not one set of checkers or chess or dominoes available, no material for the development of hobbies, and no books, only an occasional comic book. One newspaper came into the place, and few men had access to it. There were no organized sports, no library, no entertainment other than one motion picture a month.

Under these circumstances, recreation was limited to six forms, five of them definitely destructive. The first of these was "*dirty dozens*," a game played by one or two persons before an audience. Its object was to outdo one's opponent in grossly offensive descriptions of the opponent's female relatives—mother, sister, wife, or aunt. If a "player" succeeded in making a clever combination of obscene and profane words, the audience burst into laughter, and then quieted down to await the retaliation of the opponent. He in turn tried to paint a still more degrading picture of the relatives of his partner. No recreation attracted larger crowds or created more antagonism, for often men would be sucked into the game who actually did not want to play and became angered in the course of it.

Another form of recreation was the *telling of exaggerated stories about one's sex life.* These included tales of sexual relations with members of the same sex, with animals, with children and close relatives, and with each other. It was generally recognized that 70 percent of these tales were untrue, but the practice led to lying, to experimentation in abnormal sex relations, and to a general lowering of the moral standards of younger inmates, who continually were forced into the position of advocating strange practices as a means of maintaining status with the group.

Stealing "for the thrill of it" was yet another way in which numbers of men entertained themselves. One of the best friends I had in the camp had stolen stamps from me, returned them, and then described to me how he had done it. He had sent a friend to talk with me and had given the man who slept in the bed next to mine an old comic book to reduce the possibility of being detected. I asked him why he went to all that trouble, only to return my stamps. He explained that he had stamps, but, having nothing else to do, he wanted to "keep my hands warm."

Gambling was perhaps the chief form of recreation for those who had anything to gamble with. Men gambled for an extra sock stolen on the day of clothing exchange, or a sandwich smuggled from the kitchen, or a box of matches. The three games most widely used for gambling were Tonk and Skin, games played with an ordinary deck of cards, and throwing dice. Cheating was simple and common and led to constant arguments.

There was little or no effort to control the gambling, though it was against the rules. When a new night guard came on duty and complained to an old hand that the boys were playing dice in the rear of the dormitory, the older guard was overheard to say, "What da hell do I care! They gotta do sumpin, and dice keep 'em quiet."

Gossip and talking about one's sentence also consumed a great deal of time. Over and over again men related the story of their trial and told one another how they were "framed on bum raps." The gossip session was the stool pigeon's chief means of getting information to carry "up front." Even though men feared talking about one another, they did so because they felt that the gossip-mongers had to have something to tell the superintendent. As one of the chain-gangers expressed it, "That stool pigeon has got to sing sumpin, so it's better for me to give him sumpin good [i.e., helpful information for the authorities] to carry about somebody else, before somebody gives him sumpin bad to carry about me." This created an atmosphere of universal mistrust.

The most creative form of recreation was *rhyming and singing.* There were several quartets and trios and much informal singing, both on the job and in the dormitory. The poetry was almost always a description of life in the camp or of the desire for women or of the "fear of time." . . .

One of the most stifling elements of life on the road gang is the authoritarianism. The prisoner's life is completely regulated. He is informed that obedience will be rewarded and disobedience punished. . . .

Such unquestioning obedience may appear to be good and logical in theory, but in experience authoritarianism destroys the inner resourcefulness, creativity, and responsibility of the prisoner and creates, in wardens and prisoners alike, an attitude that life is cheap. The following illustrations indicate the degree to which respect for personality is violated. . . .

—The walking boss was heard commenting on one of his ace workers who had come back for the third time. "Now ain't that a shame—and he only got a year. I sure wish he had ten or more."

—Every day after lunch the walking bosses and armed guards would send the food remaining in their lunch kits to the chain-gangers. After the kits had been emptied, I noticed that the water boy always filled one of them with the corn pone from the prisoners' meal. One day I asked the water boy why he did this. He explained that the Captain fed that "stinkin' pone to his pigs." For a moment no one spoke. Then Softshoe said, "Pigs and convicts."

—Visiting days were the first and third Sundays of the month; visiting hours, from one to four. The visiting took place in the prison yard. There were two wire fences about five feet apart. The convicts stood in front of one, the visitors behind another. There in the yard, in summer, winter, rain, snow, sleet, they talked—if they could be heard. Visiting day was an event both longed for and dreaded because, as one of the chain-gangers so aptly put it, "We gotta meet the home folks like animals in the zoo." . . .

We must bear in mind that one result of the authoritarian system is to develop in the prisoners many of the same attitudes they themselves decry in the officials. The majority of the prisoners accept the idea that punishment can be just. In fact they share this basic premise with most of the judges whom they eternally criticize. Many prisoners would be more severe than judges in making the punishment fit the crime. In discussing a young man who had raped two children I heard Easy Life say, "The no-good bastard should have got ninety-nine years and one dark day." When a young man came into the camp who reportedly had stolen eight hundred dollars, his mother's life savings, a prisoner suggested, "They should have built a jail on top of him." To which another replied, "That's too damn good for the bastard. They should have gassed him, but quick."

The prisoners, like the judges, hold the superstition that two wrongs can make a right. A chain-ganger claims that his incarceration clears him; hence the deprivations of prison life are equal to his crime. He feels he is doubly absolved when he gets the worst of the bargain. But any punishment that affects his body or causes him to fear while in prison, he looks upon as unjustified. Consequently he feels, often while in prison and certainly upon release, that he is entitled to avenge this injustice by becoming an enemy of society. Thus the theory that two wrongs make a right becomes a vicious circle, destructive to wardens, prisoners, and society.

Let us see what the punishments are on the chain-gang. Section 5 of the rules book states:

> *For Minor Offenses*—[The superintendent will be permitted to] handcuff [the prisoner] and require [him] to remain in standing or sitting position for a reasonable period of time.

This form of punishment produces swollen feet and wrists, muscular cramps, and physical fatigue. During the period, if the prisoner is standing up, he does not eat but is taken down for fifteen or twenty minutes every few hours to urinate, defecate, and relax.

> *For Major Offenses*—Corporal punishment, with the approval of the Chairman of the State Highway and Public Works Commission, administered with a leather strap of *the approved type* and by some prison officer other than the person in immediate charge of said prisoner and only after physical examination by a competent physician, and such punishment must be administered either in the presence of a prison physician or a prison chaplain.

Another section of the rules book dealing with punishment and discipline states that the superintendent may place a prisoner on "restricted diet and solitary confinement, the period of punishment to be approved by the disciplinarian."

One chain-ganger whom I got to know very well had recently finished a period of such confinement in "the hole." For fourteen days James had been without any food except three soda crackers a day. "The bastards gave me all the water I could drink, and I'll be damned if I wasn't fool enough to drink a lot of it. Soon I began to get thinner, but my gut got bigger and bigger till I got scared and drank less and less till I ended by drinking only three glasses a day."

Although he was very weak, he was forced to go to work immediately. He was expected to work as hard as the others and be respectful to the same captain he felt was responsible for his hardship.

James had been sentenced to sixty days for larceny, which good behavior would have reduced to forty-four days. Because of one surly remark he not only had to spend fourteen days in that unlighted hole, on crackers and water, but also lost the sixteen days of good time. Actually James had begun to hate himself as much as he hated the Captain. "A man," he said, "who tips his hat to a son-of-a-bitch he hates the way I hate him ain't no man at all. If I'd-a been a man, I'd-a split his head wide open the minute I got half a chance."

Some punishments were administered that were not listed in the rules book, as when officers kicked, punched, or clubbed the inmates. . . .

One chain-ganger, a man named Joe, aged about fifty-two, was at the camp for thirty days—his fifth or sixth time to receive that same sentence for drunkenness. He said he was tired all the time, that he had pains in his back. Some of the chain-gangers said he was "damn lazy." For two days the Captain urged him to work harder. "Get some earth on that spade. I'm getting tired of you, Joe. You'd better give me some work." All the second day the Captain kept his eye on Joe. In mid-afternoon he walked over to Joe and said, "You're not going to do no work till I knock hell out you." He calmly struck Joe several times vigorously in the face. "Now maybe that will learn you," the Captain said as he walked away. Joe took off his cap, bowed obsequiously, and said, "Yessa, yessa, that sure will learn me." When the Captain had walked away Joe spat on the ground and said, "He's a dirty son-of-a-bitch and I hope he rots in hell."

The first thing a man did when he awoke in the morning was to look out the window. "How's the weather?" was always the first question. A heavy rain meant a day without work, and the fellows prayed for "sweet rain." It was not just because the work was hard but also for four other reasons, all having to do with working conditions:

1. The work was never done.
2. Thought and creativity in any form were not permitted.
3. Staying "under the gun" made for crowded, tense conditions.
4. The men felt like "things" rather than people on the job.

I believe they most disliked the feeling that no matter how hard they toiled, "the work on the highway ain't never done." When one job was finished there was always another. "Let's ride," the Captain would say, and off we would go. One fellow complained, "If we only knew that we had so much to do in a day, then I wouldn't mind the aches so much 'cause I could look to some rest at the end."

I had never before realized the importance, even to men doing the most monotonous manual labor, of knowing clearly the reasons for doing a job, and the dejection of spirit that subconsciously creeps in when men cannot see a job completed. One day when we dug out patches in the road which another crew would fill in, Purple expressed this feeling: "I reckon these holes will be filled by some fool 'rrested in Durham tonight, and he'll wonder where the hell they come from."

On the job the men were not permitted to use the kind of imagination that they put into their rhymes. Over and over again the walking boss would say, "Don't try to think. Do what I tell ya to do." Once when a resourceful chain-ganger offered a suggestion that might have improved or simplified the task, the walking boss said, "I'm paid to think; you're here to work." Softshoe used to say,

"When you're wrong, you're wrong,
But when you're right, you're wrong anyhow."

On two or three occasions when the Captain was away, the assistant walking boss was in charge of the crew. He was quite inexperienced as compared with one of the chain-gangers, James, who knew almost as much about the job as the Captain. One day in the Captain's absence James suggested to the assistant that a ditch should be cut a certain way. The assistant captain ordered otherwise. So fifteen men spent three and a half hours in water and mud digging a ditch forty feet long, four feet wide, and in places five feet deep. The next day the Captain told us that the work would have to be redone. The men looked knowingly at one another and started digging.

There was a regulation that each prisoner, except the trusties, must at all times be within eyeshot and gun range of the armed guard. The prisoners called this "under the gun." Another regulation was that at no time could a chain-ganger be seen to rest during his ten-hour day except during the two fifteen-minute smoking periods. These regulations made for continuous tension.

When digging or clearing ditches, our crew of fourteen to sixteen men was usually divided, half of them assigned to each side of the road. Since the amount of work on each side was seldom equal, the logical thing would have been for the crew that finished first to move on down the road. They could not do so because then they would not have been "under the gun." Or the crew that finished first could have rested for a few minutes and then moved on with the group. But the regulation that "all must be busy at all times" precluded such a step. The solution accepted was to put all fourteen men on one side, where we were jammed in so tightly on one another that work was dangerous, slow, and inefficient. We got on one another's nerves and often struck each other with tools.

Certain men in the crew, to avoid hardship and to give the impression they were working harder than the others, indulged in hiding other men's tools, pushing, or criticizing one another's work in loud voices in order to place themselves in more favored working positions or to get in a good light with the Captain for informing. Whenever we worked on ditches, tension in the evenings in the dormitory often ran high.

To me the most degrading condition of the job was the feeling that "I am not a person; I am a thing to be used." The men who worked us had the same attitude toward us as toward the tools we used. At times the walking bosses would stand around for hours while we worked, seeming to do nothing—just watching, often moving from foot to foot or walking from one side of the road to the other. It was under these conditions that they would select a "play-thing." One boy, Oscar, was often "it." Once the bored gun guard ordered Oscar to take off his cap and dance. With a broad smile on his face, he warned Oscar, "I'll shoot your heart out if you don't." As the guard trained his rifle on Oscar's chest, Oscar took off his cap, grinned, and danced vigorously. The guard and the walking boss screamed with laughter. Later most of the crew told Oscar that they hated him for pretending he had enjoyed the experience. But almost any of them would have reacted the same way.

To return to the story of my relations with Captain Jones. He had learned of my case and knew I was from the North. Several chain-gangers agreed that the newsclipping he waved about on the day he first lectured me was the Durham *Sun*'s article on my surrender. At any rate I am sure he felt that I was going to shirk and be difficult—that I would try to show off and challenge his authority.

My aims were really far different. I wanted to work hard so I would not be a burden to other chain-gangers. I wanted to accept the imprisonment in a quiet, unobtrusive manner. Only in this way, I believed, could the officials and guards be led to consider sympathetically the principle on which I was convicted. I did not expect them to agree with me, but I did want them to believe I cared enough about the ideals I was supposed to stand for so I could accept my punishment with a sense of humor, fairness, and constructive good will.

It would have been easy to be either servile or recalcitrant. The difficulty was to be constructive, to remove tension, and yet to maintain my balance and self-respect, at the same time giving ample evidence of respect for the Captain's personality.

I found him to be a very fine craftsman, who knew well the skills of his trade. I noted, too, that when it began to rain hard he was much more careful to leave immediately for the dormitory than were most of the other captains. Soon after our first unfortunate encounter, I mentioned these facts to him.

One morning when he came toward me with what I considered a hostile expression on his face (I was unskillfully making cement pipe), I decided to take the initiative. Before he could teach me I called over to him, "Captain Jones, I seem to need help. Would you have the time to show . . . ?" I could not finish my sentence.

"Damn well you need help," he said, but already I could notice a difference in his expression. He showed me how to scrape the steel forms and how to oil them. Thanking him politely, I told him that if he saw me doing poorly I hoped he would speak to me because I wanted to use the rest of my sentence to pick up as much knowledge as possible. He said, "Well, I can learn you," and walked away.

An hour later he returned, looked over my work, found it satisfactory, and said, "Well, Rusty, you're learnin'." That was the first time he had not called me "tall boy" or "hey-you-there."

For three days our relations improved, but on the fourth day when I reported for work he seemed very agitated. It turned out that an informer among the prisoners had told him I was urging the men not to wear caps so as not to have to tip them. Actually I did look upon the tipping of caps as degrading, for most of the men did it as a gesture of respect while inwardly they not only cursed the captains but also lost self-respect. When asked, I had told the men about my attitude but also had made it clear that my first concern was what the tipping did to them inside.

That same day I had another talk with the Captain. He seemed very impatient, but he did listen as I explained my position on wearing caps. Although he said nothing more to me, I later heard that he informed several men who had recently begun to go bareheaded that they should wear caps the year round or not at all. One of the prisoners said, "There is goin' to be some coldheaded spooks 'round here next January!" After that there was no further discussion of the caps and no effort to get men to wear them.

The next morning the Captain offered us cigarettes during smoking period. Since I did not smoke, I felt I should not take any and attempted to return them. "Rusty," he said, "they're for you whether you smoke or not." I accepted the cigarettes and gave them to another chain-ganger. This seemed to me a logical way to behave, but the Captain attached real significance to my having offered to return the cigarettes. That afternoon he told one of the men that I was filled with a lot of bad ideas but at least I was polite. Later he said to the armed guard, in the presence of Easy Life, that it was probably not my fault that I was "mixed up about so many things." He concluded, "Everything those damyankees touch the bastards spoil."

The Captain and I continued to disagree on many points, but as time went on, I felt, we came to recognize that despite our different attitudes we could work together and learn from each other.

One day toward the end of my sentence, the Captain stopped me.

"Well, how are you getting along, Rusty?" he said.

"Quite all right, Captain," I answered, "but I feel that some of the fellows need things. I hope to send in some toothbrushes, combs, and razors when I get home."

"Well, you got a surprise, didn't ya?" he asked.

"A surprise?" I said.

"Yes, indeed. You thought we was going to mistreat ya—but bad, didn't ya?"

"I didn't know what to expect," I said, "but I have learned a good deal here."

"Well, we can all learn something," he said, and walked away. That afternoon he treated the crew to a bottle of Royal Crown Cola.

Before I left, I decided to write the Captain a letter. The prisoners were astounded. "You can't write the Captain." "What do you think you're doin'?" "They ain't goin' to do nothin' but throw it in the shit pot."

I explained to the men that I was sure they could write anyone connected with the camp or the Prison Bureau. But even the more enlightened were skeptical. "I bet the Captain don't never get it," Purple said.

At any rate, I sat down and wrote the following letter to Captain Jones.

> Camp #508
> Roxboro, North Carolina
> Sunday, April 10, 1949
>
> Dear Captain Jones:
>
> If all goes well, I understand that I may be released this coming Wednesday morning. But before I go I want to say that I am pleased to have been placed in your work crew.
>
> Never having done similar work before, I am afraid I was not very apt, so all the more I want to thank you for all the help you gave me on the job. I feel that I learned a great deal.
>
> I want to thank you and Captain Duncan for the treats to cigarettes and soft drinks. As you probably know better than I do, life has not always been easy for most of the men who come to this camp. And such kindnesses mean more to us than words can express.
>
> I trust that your cold will have cleared up soon.
>
> > Sincerely,
> > Bayard Rustin

The Captain's reaction to the letter was very interesting. He was seen passing it around to the other captains and to several guards. He never mentioned it to me, but he did seem to have an honest, friendly feeling toward me during my last days at the camp.

Now most of the inmates were pleased that I had written the letter. On my last night in camp one of the chain-gangers asked me if I would help him compose a letter to an official.

"Your letter sure done some good," he said. "Guess it won't hurt me none to try."

This one successful attempt to modify the authoritarian setup should not, however, carry undue weight. There was much working in my favor. Many persons wrote and visited me; people outside sent packages to the community kit; I had a short sentence; and I got on well with the other chain-gangers. All this made it easier for me to approach the Captain and to do so with some degree of confidence. On the other hand, this experience does indicate that even in trying circumstances (for both the Captain and me) it was possible to reach a working solution without losing one's self-respect or submitting completely to outside authority.

There are three methods of dealing with offenders against society once they are apprehended: retribution, deterrence, and rehabilitation. Prison officials and men generally lay claim more or less to advocating all three. At present the public thinks that offenders should be punished. There are many different reasons why this is so, among them the belief that the average criminal responds to nothing but fear and penalties. Yet there is some real evidence that only through the very opposite of fear and punishment—intelligent good will—can men be reached and challenged and changes brought about.

Three experiences during my stay at Roxboro exemplify Auden's statement, "What can be loved can be cured," and suggest that we can expect true rehabilitation only when we have rejected punishment, which is revenge, and have begun to utilize the terrific healing and therapeutic power of forgiveness and nonviolence.

On the final Saturday of my stay, the Captain was away and his assistant directed the work. While the assistant was not so skillful as the Captain, he was more gentle, more considerate, and willing on occasion to consult the crew on procedure. Before we began work he explained clearly what was to be done. For five hours that morning, in the presence of a director who was not tense, who did not curse, and who permitted the men to help plan the work, many constructive things occurred. The men were cooperative, they worked cheerfully, tension was reduced, and the time passed more quickly than usual. When we returned to the dormitory, Purple, who had a way with turning phrases, referred to the morning's work as a "halfday of heaven."

Stealing was the chief problem in the dormitory. The night I arrived, my fountain pen, stamps, razor, and twenty blades were stolen. The next morning my writing paper disappeared. All these things had been locked away in a box, so I decided to follow the policy of not locking up my belongings. I announced that in the future all my stamps, money, food, writing paper, etc., were for the use of the community, but that in order to divide things according to need, I hoped that before anyone took anything he would consult me. As small boxes of food and other things were sent to me, they were added to the community kit. Gradually the following things occurred:

1. After a week, except for four candy bars, there was no stealing from the community kit.
2. Other men made contributions to the community kit.
3. Inmates began to unlock their unsafe strongboxes and bring things to the open community kit for safekeeping. As one of the fellows said, "If anyone is caught snatching from that box, the boys won't think much of him."
4. Two packages of cigarettes were stolen from a chain-ganger. Then it was announced that unless they turned up, money would be taken from the community kit to pay for them. The cigarettes were found on the floor the next morning.

Finally there is the example of our party. Near the end of my second week in camp several boxes of candy, cookies, cakes, dates, peanuts, and fruit juice were sent in to be added to the community kit. It was suggested that we have a party, but practically all the inmates were against it. They said, "The fellows will behave like pigs." It would be impossible to keep order, they added, and a few husky people would get all the food.

The decision was that I should select the committee to put on the party. I purposely chose the three men known to be the biggest thieves in the camp, and they accepted. The others were disheartened. "Now we know the party is wrecked. Those guys will eat half the stuff themselves before it even starts!" they groaned.

Nevertheless the boxes were turned over to them to be kept for two days until the party. Except for the disappearance of the four candy bars already mentioned, all the food was kept intact, and six candy bars were donated to replace the four stolen ones. The party itself was well organized and orderly, and the left-over food was returned to the community kit. Perhaps more significant was the fact that one man, noted for stealing, became known as one of the most capable men in the camp. He was so thorough that he appointed a sergeant-at-arms for the party, whose business was to patrol the floor to watch for stealing or disorder. Fortunately the sergeant-at-arms had no business at all and gave up his job before the party was half over.

I certainly do not want to imply that we had in any real sense dealt with the problem of stealing in the camp. However, the stimuli of expectancy, trust, and responsibility had, for the moment at least, brought about positive responses—faithfulness to duty, imagination, and sharing. Would more such gentle stimuli over longer periods of time, accompanied by proper diet, medical care, music education, good quarters, and respectful treatment, be more effective finally than retribution and punishment? If the law of cause and effect still operates in human relations, the answer seems clear.

The Last Flogging

from My Bondage and My Freedom

Frederick Douglass

Unlike Bayard Rustin, whose degrading experience on the chain gang was of short duration and was provoked by his activism against segregation, Frederick Douglass (circa 1818–1895) was born into slavery and suffered its cruelties at the hands of an especially malicious overseer, Edward Covey. This selection is excerpted from his 1855 memoir, My Bondage and My Freedom, *which recounts Douglass's early life as a slave, his daring escape to freedom, and his distinguished career as an abolitionist orator and political activist. Douglass's rise to self-respect was achieved through self-assertion and open defiance, self-consciously undertaken at the risk of his life.*

Commenting on his battle with Covey, Douglass reports: "I was a changed being after that fight. I was nothing before; I WAS A MAN NOW. . . . A man, without force, is without the essential dignity of humanity." Is Douglass right? To what should we attribute his ability to stand up for himself? How important is "fighting back" to self-respect? Under what circumstances might it show self-command rather than its absence? Which is more admirable, and under which circumstances, in confronting your oppressor: defiant self-assertion through force or turning the other cheek and loving your enemy? Whose way of dealing with those who seek to degrade you seems better to you, and why: Bayard Rustin's or Frederick Douglass's?

Sleep itself does not always come to the relief of the weary in body, and the broken in spirit; especially when past troubles only foreshadow coming disasters. The last hope had been extinguished. My master, who I did not venture to hope would protect me as *a man*, had even now refused to protect me as *his property*; and had cast me back, covered with reproaches and bruises, into the hands of a stranger to that mercy which was the soul of the religion he professed. May the reader never spend such a night as that allotted to me, previous to the morning which was to herald my return to the den of horrors from which I had made a temporary escape.

I remained all night—sleep I did not—at St. Michael's; and in the morning (Saturday) I started off, according to the order of Master Thomas, feeling that I had no friend on earth, and doubting if I had one in heaven. I reached Covey's about nine o'clock; and just as I stepped into the field, before I had reached the house, Covey, true to his snakish habits, darted out at me from a fence corner, in which he had secreted himself, for the purpose of securing me. He was amply provided with a cowskin and a rope; and he evidently intended to *tie me up*, and to wreak his vengeance on me to the fullest extent. I should have been an easy prey, had he succeeded in getting his hands upon me, for I had taken no refreshment since noon on Friday; and this, together with the pelting, excitement, and the loss of blood, had reduced my strength. I, however, darted back into the woods, before the ferocious hound could get hold of me, and buried myself in a thicket, where he lost sight of me. The corn-field afforded me cover, in getting to the woods. But for the tall corn, Covey would have overtaken me, and made me his captive. He seemed very much chagrined that he did not catch me, and gave up the chase, very reluctantly; for I could see his angry movements, toward the house from which he had sallied, on his foray.

Well, now I am clear of Covey, and of his wrathful lash, for the present. I am in the wood, buried in its somber gloom, and hushed in its solemn silence; hid from all human eyes; shut in with nature and nature's God, and absent from all human contrivances. Here was a good place to pray; to pray for help for deliverance—a prayer I had often made before. But how could I pray? Covey could pray—Capt. Auld could pray—I would fain pray; but doubts (arising partly from my own neglect of the means of grace, and partly from the sham religion which everywhere prevailed, cast in my mind a doubt upon all religion, and led me to the conviction that prayers were unavailing and delusive) prevented my embracing the opportunity, as a religious one. Life, in itself, had almost become burdensome to me. All my outward relations were against me; I must stay here and starve, (I was already hungry,) or go home to Covey's, and have my flesh torn to pieces, and my spirit humbled under the cruel lash of Covey. This was the painful alternative presented to me. The day was long and irksome. My physical condition was deplorable. I was weak, from the toils of the previous day, and from the want of food and rest; and had been so little concerned about my appearance, that I had not yet washed the blood from my garments. I was an object of horror, even to myself. Life, in Baltimore, when most oppressive, was a paradise to this. What had I done, what had my parents done, that such a life as this should be mine? That day, in the woods, I would have exchanged my manhood for the brutehood of an ox.

Night came. I was still in the woods, unresolved what to do. Hunger had not yet pinched me to the point of going home, and I laid myself down in the leaves to rest; for I had been watching for hunters all day, but not being molested during the day, I expected no disturbance during the night. I had come to the conclusion that Covey relied upon hunger to drive me home; and in this I was quite correct—the facts showed that he had made no effort to catch me, since morning.

During the night, I heard the step of a man in the woods. He was coming toward the place where I lay. A person lying still has the advantage over one walking in the woods, in the daytime, and this advantage is much greater at night. I was not able to engage in a physical struggle, and I had recourse to the common resort of the weak. I hid myself in the leaves to prevent discovery. But, as the night rambler in the woods drew nearer, I found him to be a *friend*, not an enemy; it was a slave of Mr. William Groomes, of Easton, a kind hearted fellow, named "Sandy." Sandy lived with Mr. Kemp that year, about four miles from St. Michael's. He, like myself, had been hired out by the year; but, unlike myself, had not been hired out to be broken. Sandy was the husband of a free woman, who lived in the lower part of "*Pot-pie Neck*," and he was now on his way through the woods, to see her, and to spend the Sabbath with her.

As soon as I had ascertained that the disturber of my solitude was not an enemy, but the good-hearted Sandy—a man as famous among the slaves of the neighborhood for his good nature, as for his good sense—I came out from my hiding place, and made myself known to him. I explained the circumstances of the past two days, which had driven me to the woods, and he deeply compassionated my distress. It was a bold thing for him to shelter me, and I could not ask him to do so; for, had I been found in his hut, he would have suffered the penalty of thirty-nine lashes on his bare back, if not something worse. But, Sandy was too generous to permit the fear of punishment to prevent his relieving a brother bondman from hunger and exposure; and, therefore, on his own motion, I accompanied him to his home, or rather to the home of his wife—for the house and lot were hers. His wife was called up—for it was now about midnight—a fire was made, some Indian meal was soon mixed with salt and water, and an ash cake was baked in a hurry to relieve my hunger. Sandy's wife was not behind him in kindness—both seemed to esteem it a privilege to succor me; for, although I was hated by Covey and by my master, I was loved by the colored people, because *they* thought I was hated for my knowledge, and persecuted because I was feared. I was the *only* slave *now* in that region who could read and write. There had been one other man, belonging to Mr. Hugh

Hamilton, who could read, (his name was "Jim,") but he, poor fellow, had, shortly after my coming into the neighborhood, been sold off to the far south. I saw Jim ironed, in the cart, to be carried to Easton for sale,—pinioned like a yearling for the slaughter. My knowledge was now the pride of my brother slaves; and, no doubt, Sandy felt something of the general interest in me on that account. The supper was soon ready, and though I have feasted since, with honorables, lord mayors and aldermen, over the sea, my supper on ash cake and cold water, with Sandy, was the meal, of all my life, most sweet to my taste, and now most vivid in my memory.

Supper over, Sandy and I went into a discussion of what was *possible* for me, under the perils and hardships which now overshadowed my path. The question was, must I go back to Covey, or must I now attempt to run away? Upon a careful survey, the latter was found to be impossible; for I was on a narrow neck of land, every avenue from which would bring me in sight of pursuers. There was the Chesapeake bay to the right, and "Pot-pie" river to the left, and St. Michael's and its neighborhood occupying the only space through which there was any retreat.

I found Sandy an old advisor. He was not only a religious man, but he professed to believe in a system for which I have no name. He was a genuine African, and had inherited some of the so called magical powers, said to be possessed by African and eastern nations. He told me that he could help me; that, in those very woods, there was an herb, which in the morning might be found, possessing all the powers required for my protection, (I put his thoughts in my own language;) and that, if I would take his advice, he would procure me the root of the herb of which he spoke. He told me further, that if I would take that root and wear it on my right side, it would be impossible for Covey to strike me a blow; that with this root about my person, no white man could whip me. He said he had carried it for years, and that he had fully tested its virtues. He had never received a blow from a slaveholder since he carried it; and he never expected to receive one, for he always meant to carry that root as a protection. He knew Covey well, for Mrs. Covey was the daughter of Mr. Kemp; and he (Sandy) had heard of the barbarous treatment to which I was subjected, and he wanted to do something for me.

Now all this talk about the root, was, to me, very absurd and ridiculous, if not positively sinful. I at first rejected the idea that the simple carrying a root on my right side, (a root, by the way, over which I walked every time I went into the woods,) could possess any such magic power as he ascribed to it, and I was, therefore, not disposed to cumber my pocket with it. I had a positive aversion to all pretenders to "*divination*." It was beneath one of my intelligence to countenance such dealings with the devil, as this power implied. But, with all my learning—it was really precious little—Sandy was more than a match for me. "My book learning," he said, "had not kept Covey off me," (a powerful argument just then,) and he entreated me, with flashing eyes, to try this. If it did me no good, it could do me no harm, and it would cost me nothing, any way. Sandy was so earnest, and so confident of the good qualities of this weed, that, to please him, rather than from any conviction of its excellence, I was induced to take it. He had been to me the good Samaritan, and had, almost providentially, found me, and helped me when I could not help myself; how did I know but that the hand of the Lord was in it? With thoughts of this sort, I took the roots from Sandy, and put them in my right hand pocket.

This was, of course, Sunday morning. Sandy now urged me to go home, with all speed, and to walk up bravely to the house, as though nothing had happened. I saw in Sandy too deep an insight into human nature, with all his superstition, not to have some respect for his advice; and perhaps, too, a slight gleam or shadow of his superstition had fallen upon me. At any rate, I started off toward Covey's, as directed by Sandy. Having, the previous night, poured my griefs into Sandy's ears, and got him enlisted in my behalf, having made his wife a sharer in my sorrows, and having, also, become well refreshed by sleep and food, I moved off, quite courageously, toward the much dreaded Covey's. Singularly enough, just as I entered his yard gate, I met him and his wife, dressed in their Sunday best—looking as smiling as angels—on their way to church. The manner of Covey astonished me. There was something really benignant in his countenance. He spoke to me as never before; told me that the pigs had got into the lot, and he wished me to drive them out; inquired how I was, and seemed an altered man. This extraordinary conduct of Covey, really made me begin to think that Sandy's herb had more virtue in it than I, in my pride, had been willing to allow; and, had the day been other than Sunday, I should have attributed Covey's altered manner solely to the magic power of the root. I suspected, however, that the *Sabbath*, and not the *root*, was the real explanation of Covey's manner. His religion hindered him from breaking the Sabbath, but not from breaking my skin. He had more respect for the *day* than for the *man*, for whom the day was mercifully given; for while he would cut and slash my body during the week, he would not hesitate, on Sunday, to teach me the value of my soul, or the way of life and salvation by Jesus Christ.

All went well with me till Monday morning; and then, whether the root had lost its virtue, or whether my tormentor had gone deeper into the black art than myself, (as was sometimes said of him,) or whether he had obtained a special indulgence, for his faithful Sabbath day's worship, it is not necessary for me to know, or to inform the reader; but, this much I *may* say,—the pious and benignant smile which graced Covey's face on *Sunday*, wholly disappeared on *Monday*. Long before daylight, I was called up to go and feed, rub, and curry the horses. I obeyed the call, and I would have so obeyed it, had it been made at an earlier hour, for I had brought my mind to a firm resolve, during that Sunday's reflection, viz: to obey every order, however unreasonable, if it were possible, and, if Mr. Covey should then undertake to beat me, to defend and protect myself to the best of my ability. My religious views on the subject of resisting my master, had suffered a serious shock, by the savage persecution to which I had been subjected, and my hands were no longer tied by my religion. Master Thomas's indifference had severed the last link. I had now to this extent "backslidden" from this point in the slave's religious creed; and I soon had occasion to make my fallen state known to my Sunday-pious brother, Covey.

Whilst I was obeying his order to feed and get the horses ready for the field, and when in the act of going up the stable loft for the purpose of throwing down some blades, Covey sneaked into the stable, in his peculiar snake-like way, and seizing me suddenly by the leg, he brought me to the stable floor, giving my newly mended body a fearful jar. I now forgot my *roots*, and remembered my pledge to *stand up in my own defense*. The brute was endeavoring skillfully to get a slip-knot on my legs, before I could draw up my feet. As soon as I found what he was up to, I gave a sudden spring, (my two day's rest had been of much service to me,) and by that means, no doubt, he was able to bring me to the floor so heavily. He was defeated in his plan of tying me. While down, he seemed to think he had me very securely in his power. He little thought he was—as the rowdies say—"in" for a "rough and tumble" fight; but such was the fact. Whence came the daring spirit necessary to grapple with a man who, eight-and-forty hours before, could, with his slightest word have made me tremble like a leaf in a storm, I do not know; at any rate, *I was resolved to fight*, and, what was better still, I was actually hard at it. The fighting madness had come upon me, and I found my strong fingers firmly attached to the throat of my cowardly tormentor; as heedless of consequences, at the moment, as though we stood as equals before the law. The very color of the man was forgotten. I felt as supple as a cat, and was ready for the snakish creature at every turn. Every blow of his was parried, though I dealt no blows in turn. I was strictly on the *defensive*, preventing him from injuring me, rather than trying to injure him. I flung him on the ground several times, when he meant to have hurled me there. I held him so firmly by the throat, that his blood followed my nails. He held me, and I held him.

All was fair, thus far, and the contest was about equal. My resistance was entirely unexpected, and Covey was taken all aback by it, for he trembled in every limb. "*Are you going to resist*, you scoundrel?" said he. To which, I returned a polite *"yes, sir,"* steadily gazing my interrogator in the eye, to meet the first approach or dawning of the blow, which I expected my answer would call forth. But, the conflict did not long remain thus equal. Covey soon cried out lustily for help; not that I was obtaining any marked advantage over him, or was injuring him, but because he was gaining none over me, and was not able, single handed, to conquer me. He called for his cousin Hughes, to come to his assistance, and now the scene was changed. I was compelled to give blows, as well as to parry them; and, since I was, in any case, to suffer for resistance, I felt (as the musty proverb goes) that "I might as well be hanged for an old sheep as a lamb." I was still *defensive* toward Covey, but *aggressive* toward Hughes; and, at the first approach of the latter, I dealt a blow, in my desperation, which fairly sickened my youthful assailant. He went off, bending over with pain, and manifesting no disposition to come within my reach again. The poor fellow was in the act of trying to catch and tie my right hand, and while flattering himself with success, I gave him the kick which sent him staggering away in pain, at the same time that I held Covey with a firm hand.

Taken completely by surprise, Covey seemed to have lost his usual strength and coolness. He was frightened, and stood puffing and blowing, seemingly unable to command words or blows. When he saw that poor Hughes was standing half bent with pain—his courage quite gone—the cowardly tyrant asked if I "meant to persist in my resistance." I told him "I *did mean to resist, come what might;*" that I had been by him treated like a *brute*, during the last six months; and that I should stand it *no longer.* With that, he gave me a shake, and attempted to drag me toward a stick of wood, that was lying just outside the stable door. He meant to knock me down with it; but, just as he leaned over to get the stick, I seized him with both hands by the collar, and, with a vigorous and sudden snatch, I brought my assailant harmlessly, his full length, on the *not over* clean ground—for we were now in the cow yard. He had selected the place for the fight, and it was but right that he should have all the advantages of his own selection.

By this time, Bill, the hired man, came home. He had been to Mr. Hemsley's, to spend the Sunday with his nominal wife, and was coming home on Monday morning, to go to work. Covey and I had been skirmishing from before daybreak, till now, that the sun was almost shooting his beams over the eastern woods, and we were still at it. I could not see where the matter was to terminate. He evidently was afraid to let me go, lest I should again make off to the woods; otherwise, he would probably have obtained arms from the house, to frighten me. Holding me, Covey called upon Bill for assistance. The scene here, had something comic about it. "Bill," who knew *precisely* what Covey wished him to do, affected ignorance, and pretended he did not know what to do. "What shall I do, Mr. Covey," said Bill. "Take hold of him—take hold of him!" said Covey. With a toss of his head, peculiar to Bill, he said, "indeed, Mr. Covey, I want to go to work." "*This is* your work," said Covey; "take hold of him." Bill replied, with spirit, "My master hired me here, to work, and *not* to help you whip Frederick." It was now my turn to speak. "Bill" said I, "don't put your hands on me." To which he replied, "MY GOD! Frederick, I ain't goin' to tech ye," and Bill walked off, leaving Covey and myself to settle our matters as best we might.

But, my present advantage was threatened when I saw Caroline (the slave-woman of Covey) coming to the cow yard to milk, for she was a powerful woman, and could have mastered me very easily, exhausted as I now was. As soon as she came into the yard, Covey attempted to rally her to his aid. Strangely—and, I may add, fortunately—Caroline was in no humor to take a hand in any such sport. We were all in open rebellion, that morning. Caroline answered the command of her master to "*take hold of me*," precisely as Bill had answered, but in *her*, it was at greater peril so to answer; she was the slave of Covey, and he could do what he pleased with her. It was *not* so with Bill, and Bill knew it. Samuel Harris, to whom Bill belonged, did not allow his slaves to be beaten, unless they were guilty of some crime which the law would punish. But, poor Caroline, like myself, was at the mercy of the merciless Covey; nor did she escape the dire effects of her refusal. He gave her several sharp blows.

Covey at length (two hours had elapsed) gave up the contest. Letting me go, he said,—puffing and blowing at a great rate—"now, you scoundrel, go to your work; I would not have whipped you half so much as I have had you not resisted." The fact was, *he had not whipped me at all*. He had not, in all the scuffle, drawn a single drop of blood from me. I had drawn blood from him; and, even without this satisfaction, I should have been victorious, because my aim had not been to injure him, but to prevent his injuring me.

During the whole six months that I lived with Covey, after this transaction, he never laid on me the weight of his finger in anger. He would, occasionally, say he did not want to have to get hold of me again—a declaration which I had no difficulty in believing; and I had a secret feeling, which answered, "you need not wish to get hold of me again, for you will be likely to come off worse in a second fight than you did in the first."

Well, my dear reader, this battle with Mr. Covey,—undignified as it was, and as I fear my narration of it is—was the turning point in my "*life as a slave*." It rekindled in my breast the smouldering embers of liberty; it brought up my Baltimore dreams, and revived a sense of my own manhood. I was a changed being after that fight. I was *nothing* before; I WAS A MAN NOW. It recalled to life my crushed self-respect and my self-confidence, and inspired me with a renewed determination to be A FREEMAN. A man, without force, is without the essential dignity of humanity. Human nature is so constituted, that it cannot *honor* a helpless man, although it can *pity* him; and even this it cannot do long, if the signs of power do not arise.

He can only understand the effect of this combat on my spirit, who has himself incurred something, hazarded something, in repelling the unjust and cruel aggressions of a tyrant. Covey was a tyrant, and a cowardly one, withal. After resisting him, I felt as I had never felt before. It was a resurrection from the dark and pestiferous tomb of slavery, to the heaven of comparative freedom. I was no longer a servile coward, trembling under the frown of a brother worm of the dust, but, my long-cowed spirit was roused to an attitude of manly independence. I had reached the point, at which I was *not afraid to die*. This spirit made me a freeman in *fact*, while I remained a slave in *form*. When a slave cannot be flogged he is more than half free. He has a domain as broad as his own manly heart to defend, and he is really "*a power on earth*." While slaves prefer their lives, with flogging, to instant death, they will always find christians enough, like unto Covey, to accommodate that preference. From this time, until that of my escape from slavery, I was never fairly whipped. Several attempts were made to whip me, but they were always unsuccessful. Bruises I did get, as I shall hereafter inform the reader; but the case I have been describing, was the end of the brutification to which slavery had subjected me.

The reader will be glad to know why, after I had so grievously offended Mr. Covey, he did not have me taken in hand by the authorities; indeed, why the law of Maryland, which assigns hanging to the slave who resists his master, was not put in force against me; at any rate, why I was not taken up, as is usual in such cases, and publicly whipped, for an example to other slaves, and as a means of deterring me from committing the same offense again. I confess, that the easy manner in which I got off, was, for a long time, a surprise to me, and I cannot, even now, fully explain the cause.

The only explanation I can venture to suggest, is the fact, that Covey was, probably, ashamed to have it known and confessed that he had been mastered by a boy of sixteen. Mr. Covey enjoyed the unbounded and very valuable reputation, of being a first rate overseer and *negro breaker*. By means of this reputation, he was able to procure his hands for *very trifling* compensation, and with very great ease. His interest and his pride mutually suggested the wisdom of passing the matter by, in silence. The story that he had undertaken to whip a lad, and had been resisted, was, of itself, sufficient to damage him; for his bearing should, in the estimation of slaveholders, be of that imperial order that should make such an occurrence *impossible*. I judge from these circumstances, that Covey deemed it best to give me the go-by. It is, perhaps, not altogether creditable to my natural temper, that, after this conflict with Mr. Covey, I did, at times, purposely aim to provoke him to an attack, by refusing to keep with the other hands in the field, but I could never bully him to another battle. I had made up my mind to do him serious damage, if he ever again attempted to lay violent hands on me.

> "Hereditary bondmen, know ye not
> Who would be free, themselves must strike the blow?"

Law-Abidingness and Justice:
Toward Public Order

The Perpetuation of Our Political Institutions (Address to the Young Men's Lyceum of Springfield, Illinois)

ABRAHAM LINCOLN

According to its Preamble, the United States Constitution has as one of its aims to "establish justice." Understanding law as the path to justice, "We the people of the United States" bound ourselves to a fundamental law that would organize our polity and guide the statutory laws. Half a century later, on January 27, 1838, an aspiring young politician named Abraham Lincoln gave a speech on "the perpetuation of our political institutions," in which he worried that Americans were increasingly inclined to take the law into their own hands. In the grip of strong passions, they were substituting vigilante justice for the justice of law.*

After tracing the dangerous effects of this slide into lawlessness and mob rule, Lincoln proposes a solution: "Let every American, every lover of liberty, every well wisher to his posterity, swear by the blood of the Revolution, never to violate in the least particular, the laws of the country; and never to toler-ate their violation by others. . . . Let reverence for the laws . . . become the political religion *of the nation." Well aware of the dilemma posed by unjust laws, Lincoln nonetheless insists on law-abidingness: "bad laws, if they exist, should be repealed as soon as possible, still while they continue in force, for the sake of example, they should be religiously observed." Such "reverence for the constitution and laws," Lincoln argues, is one of the new pillars of the temple of liberty, indispensable for preserving our political institutions and retaining the attachment of the citizens, now that the founding generation had gone to rest.*

---

* *Lincoln referred to recent lynchings of gamblers and murderers (suspected gamblers and murder-ers, that is), but was reticent about the incident uppermost in the minds of his listeners: the shooting of the abolitionist Elijah P. Lovejoy at Alton, Illinois, on November 7, 1837.*

What is "reverence for the laws"? Does it differ from fear of punishment? Is reverence always part of law-abidingness, or does it add something new—and if so, what? Is reverence (or political religion) necessary to the preservation of our political institutions? Is it sufficient for binding citizens to the Republic? If not, what else is needed? Is Lincoln right that disobedience always undermines respect for law? In a democracy (where laws are arrived at by majority rule), must we obey bad laws in order not to undercut good laws or law itself? Would the case for disobedience be stronger under other, nondemocratic forms of government? What is the relation between "political religion" (reverence for the laws) and religion as most citizens know it (reverence for God)? What happens if the two conflict?

As a subject for the remarks of the evening, *the perpetuation of our political institutions*, is selected.

In the great journal of things happening under the sun, we, the American People, find our account running, under date of the nineteenth century of the Christian era. We find ourselves in the peaceful possession, of the fairest portion of the earth, as regards extent of territory, fertility of soil, and salubrity of climate. We find ourselves under the government of a system of political institutions, conducing more essentially to the ends of civil and religious liberty, than any of which the history of former times tells us. We, when mounting the stage of existence, found ourselves the legal inheritors of these fundamental blessings. We toiled not in the acquirement or establishment of them—they are a legacy bequeathed us, by a *once* hardy, brave, and patriotic, but *now* lamented and departed race of ancestors. Their's was the task (and nobly they performed it) to possess themselves, and through themselves, us, of this goodly land; and to uprear upon its hills and its valleys, a political edifice of liberty and equal rights; 'tis ours only, to transmit these, the former, unprofaned by the foot of an invader; the latter, undecayed by the lapse of time, and untorn by usurpation—to the latest generation that fate shall permit the world to know. This task of gratitude to our fathers, justice to ourselves, duty to posterity, and love for our species in general, all imperatively require us faithfully to perform.

How, then, shall we perform it? At what point shall we expect the approach of danger? By what means shall we fortify against it? Shall we expect some transatlantic military giant, to step the Ocean, and crush us at a blow? Never! All the armies of Europe, Asia and Africa combined, with all the treasure of the earth (our own excepted) in their military chest; with a Buonaparte for a commander, could not by force, take a drink from the Ohio, or make a track on the Blue Ridge, in a trial of a thousand years.

At what point then is the approach of danger to be expected? I answer, if it ever reach us, it must spring up amongst us. It cannot come from abroad. If destruction be our lot, we must ourselves be its author and finisher. As a nation of freemen, we must live through all time, or die by suicide.

I hope I am over wary; but if I am not, there is, even now, something of ill-omen amongst us. I mean the increasing disregard for law which pervades the country; the growing disposition to substitute the wild and furious passions, in lieu of the sober judgement of Courts; and the worse than savage mobs, for the executive ministers of justice. This disposition is awfully fearful in any community; and that it now exists in ours, though grating to our feelings to admit, it would be a violation of truth, and an insult to our intelligence, to deny. Accounts of outrages committed by mobs, form the every-day news of the times. They have pervaded the country, from New England to Louisiana;—they are neither peculiar to the eternal snows of the former, nor the burning suns of the latter;—they are not the creature of climate—neither are they confined to the slaveholding, or the non-slaveholding States. Alike, they spring up among the pleasure hunting masters of Southern slaves, and the order loving citizens of the land of steady habits. Whatever, then, their cause may be, it is common to the whole country.

It would be tedious, as well as useless, to recount the horrors of all of them. Those happening in the State of Mississippi, and at St. Louis, are, perhaps, the most dangerous in example, and revolting to humanity. In the Mississippi case, they first commenced by hanging the regular gamblers: a set of men, certainly not following for a livelihood, a very useful, or very honest occupation; but one which, so far from being forbidden by the laws, was actually licensed by an act of the Legislature, passed but a single year before. Next, negroes, suspected of conspiring to raise an insurrection, were caught up and hanged in all parts of the State: then, white men, supposed to be leagued with the negroes; and finally, strangers, from neighboring States, going thither on business, were, in many instances, subjected to the same fate. Thus went on this process of hanging, from gamblers to negroes, from negroes to white citizens, and from these to strangers; till, dead men were seen literally dangling from the boughs of trees upon every road side; and in numbers almost sufficient, to rival the native Spanish moss of the country, as a drapery of the forest.

Turn, then, to that horror-striking scene at St. Louis. A single victim was only sacrificed there. His story is very short; and is, perhaps, the most highly tragic, of anything of its length, that has ever been witnessed in real life. A mulatto man, by the name of McIntosh, was seized in the street, dragged to the suburbs of the city, chained to a tree, and actually burned to death; and all within a single hour from the time he had been a freeman, attending to his own business, and at peace with the world.

Such are the effects of mob law; and such are the scenes, becoming more and more frequent in this land so lately famed for love of law and order; and the stories of which, have even now grown too familiar, to attract any thing more, than an idle remark.

But you are, perhaps, ready to ask, "What has this to do with the perpetuation of our political institutions?" I answer, it has much to do with it. Its direct consequences are, comparatively speaking, but a small evil; and much of its danger consists, in the proneness of our minds, to regard its direct, as its only consequences. Abstractly considered, the hanging of the gamblers at Vicksburg, was of but little consequence. They constitute a portion of population, that is worse than useless in any community; and their death, if no pernicious example be set by it, is never matter of reasonable regret with any one. If they were annually swept, from the stage of existence, by the plague or small pox, honest men would, perhaps, be much profited, by the operation. Similar too, is the correct reasoning, in regard to the burning of the negro at St. Louis. He had forfeited his life, by the perpetration of an outrageous murder, upon one of the most worthy and respectable citizens of the city; and had he not died as he did, he must have died by the sentence of the law, in a very short time afterwards. As to him alone, it was as well the way it was, as it could otherwise have been. But the example in either case, was fearful. When men take it in their heads to day, to hang gamblers, or burn murderers, they should recollect, that, in the confusion usually attending such transactions, they will be as likely to hang or burn some one, who is neither a gambler nor a murderer as one who is; and that, acting upon the example they set, the mob of to-morrow, may, and probably will, hang or burn some of them, by the very same mistake. And not only so; the innocent, those who have ever set their faces against violations of law in every shape, alike with the guilty, fall victims to the ravages of mob law; and thus it goes on, step by step, till all the walls erected for the defense of the persons and property of individuals, are trodden down, and disregarded. But all this even, is not the full extent of the evil. By such examples, by instances of the perpetrators of such acts going unpunished, the lawless in spirit, are encouraged to become lawless in practice; and having been used to no restraint, but dread of punishment, they thus become, absolutely unrestrained. Having ever regarded Government as their deadliest bane, they make a jubilee of the suspension of its operations; and pray for nothing so much, as its total annihilation. While, on the other hand, good men, men who love tranquility, who desire to abide by the laws, and enjoy their benefits, who would gladly spill their blood in the defense of their country; seeing their property destroyed; their families insulted, and their lives endangered; their persons injured; and seeing nothing in prospect that forebodes a change for the better; become tired of, and disgusted with, a Government that offers them no protection; and are not much averse to a change in which they imagine they have nothing to lose. Thus, then, by the operation of this mobocratic spirit, which all must admit, is now abroad in the land, the strongest bulwark of any Government, and particularly of those constituted like ours, may effectually be broken down and destroyed—I mean the *attachment* of the People. Whenever this effect shall be produced among us; whenever the vicious portion of population shall be permitted to gather in bands of hundreds and thousands, and burn churches, ravage and rob provision stores, throw printing presses into rivers, shoot editors, and hang and burn obnoxious persons at pleasure, and with impunity; depend on it, this Government cannot last. By such things, the feelings of the best citizens will become more or less alienated from it; and thus it will be left without friends, or with too few, and those few too weak, to make their friendship effectual. At such a time and under such circumstances, men of sufficient talent and ambition will not be wanting to seize the opportunity, strike the blow, and overturn that fair fabric, which for the last half century, has been the fondest hope, of the lovers of freedom, throughout the world.

I know the American People are *much* attached to their Government;—I know they would suffer *much* for its sake;—I know they would endure evils long and patiently, before they would ever think of exchanging it for another. Yet, notwithstanding all this, if the laws be continually despised and disregarded, if their rights to be secure in their persons and property, are held by no better tenure than the caprice of a mob, the alienation of their affections from the Government is the natural consequence; and to that, sooner or later, it must come.

Here then, is one point at which danger may be expected.

The question recurs "how shall we fortify against it?" The answer is simple. Let every American, every lover of liberty, every well wisher to his posterity, swear by the blood of the Revolution, never to violate in the least particular, the laws of the country; and never to tolerate their violation by others. As the patriots of seventy-six did to the support of the Declaration of Independence, so to the support of the Constitution and Laws, let every American pledge his life, his property, and his sacred honor;—let every man remember that to violate the law, is to trample on the blood of his father, and to tear the character of his own, and his children's liberty. Let reverence for the laws, be breathed by every American mother, to the lisping babe, that prattles on her lap—let it be taught in schools, in seminaries, and in colleges;—let it be written in Primmers, spelling books, and in Almanacs;—let it be preached from the pulpit, proclaimed in legislative halls, and enforced in courts of justice. And, in short, let it become the *political religion* of the nation; and let the old and the young, the rich and the poor, the grave and the gay, of all sexes and tongues, and colors and conditions, sacrifice unceasingly upon its altars.

While ever a state of feeling, such as this, shall universally, or even, very generally prevail throughout the nation, vain will be every effort, and fruitless every attempt, to subvert our national freedom.

When I so pressingly urge a strict observance of all the laws, let me not be understood as saying there are no bad laws, nor that grievances may not arise, for the redress of which, no legal provisions have been made. I mean to say no such thing. But I do mean to say, that, although bad laws, if they exist, should be repealed as soon as possible, still while they continue in force, for the sake of example, they should be religiously observed. So also in unprovided cases. If such arise, let proper legal provisions be made for them with the least possible delay; but, till then, let them if not too intolerable, be borne with.

There is no grievance that is a fit object of redress by mob law. In any case that arises, as for instance, the promulgation of abolitionism, one of two positions is necessarily true; that is, the thing is right within itself, and therefore deserves the protection of all law and all good citizens; or, it is wrong, and therefore proper to be prohibited by legal enactments; and in neither case, is the interposition of mob law, either necessary, justifiable, or excusable.

But, it may be asked, why suppose danger to our political institutions? Have we not preserved them for more than fifty years? And why may we not for fifty times as long?

We hope there is no *sufficient* reason. We hope all dangers may be overcome; but to conclude that no danger may ever arise, would itself be extremely dangerous. There are now, and will hereafter be, many causes, dangerous in their tendency, which have not existed heretofore; and which are not too insignificant to merit attention. That our government should have been maintained in its original form from its establishment until now, is not much to be wondered at. It had many props to support it through that period, which now are decayed, and crumbled away. Through that period, it was felt by all, to be an undecided experiment; now, it is understood to be a successful one. Then, all that sought celebrity and fame, and distinction, expected to find them in the success of that experiment. Their *all* was staked upon it:—their destiny was *inseparably* linked with it. Their ambition aspired to display before an admiring world, a practical demonstration of the truth of a proposition, which had hitherto been considered, at best no better, than problematical; namely, *the capability of a people to govern themselves*. If they succeeded, they were to be immortalized; their names were to be transferred to counties and cities, and rivers and mountains; and to be revered and sung, and toasted through all time. If they failed, they were to be called knaves and fools, and fanatics for a fleeting hour; then to sink and be forgotten. They succeeded. The experiment is successful; and thousands have won their deathless names in making it so. But the game is caught; and I believe it is true, that with the catching, end the pleasures of the chase. This field of glory is harvested, and the crop is already appropriated. But new reapers will arise, and *they*, too, will seek a field. It is to deny, what the history of the world tells us is true, to suppose that men of ambition and talents will not continue to spring up amongst us. And, when they do, they will as naturally seek the gratification of their ruling passion, as others have *so* done before them. The question then, is, can that gratification be found in supporting and maintaining an edifice that has been erected by others? Most certainly it cannot. Many great and good men sufficiently qualified for any task they should undertake, may ever be found, whose ambition would inspire to nothing beyond a seat in Congress, a gubernatorial or a presidential chair; *but such belong not to the family of the lion, or the tribe of the eagle.* What! think you these places would satisfy an Alexander, a Caesar, or a Napoleon? Never! Towering genius disdains a beaten path. It seeks regions hitherto unexplored. It sees *no distinction* in adding story to story, upon the monuments of fame, erected to the memory of others. It *denies* that it is glory enough to serve under any chief. It *scorns* to tread in the footsteps of *any* predecessor, however illustrious. It thirsts and burns for distinction; and, if possible, it will have it, whether at the expense of emancipating slaves, or enslaving freemen. Is it unreasonable then to expect, that some man possessed of the loftiest genius, coupled with ambition sufficient to push it to its utmost stretch, will at some time, spring up among us? And when such a one does, it will require the people to be united with each other, attached to the government and laws, and generally intelligent, to successfully frustrate his designs.

Distinction will be his paramount object; and although he would as willingly, perhaps more so, acquire it by doing good as harm; yet, that opportunity being past, and nothing left to be done in the way of building up, he would set boldly to the task of pulling down.

Here then, is a probable case, highly dangerous, and such a one as could not have well existed heretofore.

Another reason which *once was;* but which, to the same extent, is *now no more*, has done much in maintaining our institutions thus far. I mean the powerful influence which the interesting scenes of the revolution had upon the *passions* of the people as distinguished from their judgment. By this influence, the jealousy, envy, and avarice, incident to our nature, and so common to a state of peace, prosperity, and conscious strength, were, for the time, in a great measure smothered and rendered inactive; while the deep rooted principles of *hate*, and the powerful motive of *revenge*, instead of being turned against each other, were directed exclusively against the British nation. And thus, from the force of circumstances, the basest principles of our nature, were either made to lie dormant, or to become the active agents in the advancement of the noblest cause—that of establishing and maintaining civil and religious liberty.

But this state of feeling *must fade, is fading, has faded*, with the circumstances that produced it.

I do not mean to say, that the scenes of the revolution *are now* or *ever will be* entirely forgotten; but that like every thing else, they must fade upon the memory of the world, and grow more and more dim by the lapse of time. In history, we hope, they will be read of, and recounted, so long as the bible shall be read;—but even granting that they will, their influence *cannot be* what it heretofore has been. Even then, they *cannot be* so universally known, nor so vividly felt, as they were by the generation just gone to rest. At the close of that struggle, nearly every adult male had been a participator in some of its scenes. The consequence was, that of those scenes, in the form of a husband, a father, a son or a brother, a *living history was* to be found in every family— a history bearing the indubitable testimonies of its own authenticity, in the limbs mangled, in the scars of wounds received, in the midst of the very scenes related—a history, too, that could be read and understood alike by all, the wise and the ignorant, the learned and the unlearned. But *those* histories are gone. They *can* be read no more forever. They *were* a fortress of strength; but, what invading foeman could *never do*, the silent artillery of time *has done*; the leveling of its walls. They are gone. They *were* a forest of giant oaks; but the all resistless hurricane has swept over them, and left only, here and there, a lonely trunk, despoiled of its verdure, shorn of its foliage; unshading and unshaded, to murmur in a few more gentle breezes, and to combat with its mutilated limbs, a few more ruder storms, then to sink, and be no more.

They *were* the pillars of the temple of liberty; and now, that they have crumbled away, that temple must fall, unless we, their descendants, supply their places with other pillars, hewn from the solid quarry of sober reason. Passion has helped us; but can do so no more. It will in future be our enemy. Reason, cold, calculating, unimpassioned reason, must furnish all the materials for our future support and defence. Let those materials be moulded into *general intelligence, sound morality* and, in particular, *a reverence for the constitution and laws*; and, that we improved to the last; that we remained free to the last; that we revered his name to the last; that, during his long sleep, we permitted no hostile foot to pass over or desecrate his resting place; shall be that which to learn the last trump shall awaken our WASHINGTON.

Upon these let the proud fabric of freedom rest, as the rock of its basis; and as truly as has been said of the only greater institution, *the gates of hell shall not prevail against it.*"

Letter from Birmingham Jail

Martin Luther King Jr.

Since what is legal is not identical to what is just, what to think when the two diverge? What can we—what should we—do about unjust laws? Our own Declaration of Independence asserts that we have a right to alter or abolish any government that is destructive of our rights. This right of revolution is, however, a last resort. What options do we have against less systemic evils—for instance, a particular unjust law or a set of laws (like racial segregation) within an otherwise decent regime? Of course, in a democracy, one always has the methods of voting, lobbying, and persuading fellow citizens through the exercise of free speech, free press, assembly, and petition. But what if such means prove unavailing, or if second-class citizenship has foreclosed their exercise? What if the majority persists in injustice, even in the face of consti-tutional obligations? Is there some option between obedience and revolution? Must it be the ballot or the bullet?

The distinguished clergyman and civil-rights leader Martin Luther King Jr. (1929–1968), following Thoreau and Gandhi, sought to find some middle ground between law-abidingness and lawlessness. King's famous justifica-tion of civil disobedience—the present selection—appeared in a letter to a group of Alabama clergymen who had issued a public statement criticizing his methods. The open letter was published on April 16, 1963, while he was still serving a jail sentence for his involvement in civil-rights demonstrations in Birmingham.

Lincoln and King are two of America's (and the world's) moral lights. Yet they disagree on this fundamental issue of the relationship of law and justice. Is King right that disobedience can be "civil"? Do you agree with him that lawbreaking done right ("openly," "lovingly," and "with a willingness to accept the penalty") expresses "the highest respect for law"? Or is Lincoln right that lawbreaking is always uncivil and destructive of civil government? Is there an eternal law—King's "the moral law or the law of God"—that serves as a standard by which to judge humanly made law? How can one know with certainty the content of that law? King's case for open civil disobedience appears to presuppose the basic decency and moral persuadability of the American people. If so, is civil disobedience really necessary? Is civil disobedience obsolete—a once-fitting tactic to address the unique problem of second-class citizenship, but no longer suitable as a universal principle? Or are there situations where it could or should be used today?

April 16, 1963[*]

My Dear Fellow Clergymen:

While confined here in the Birmingham city jail, I came across your recent statement calling my present activities "unwise and untimely." Seldom do I pause to answer criticism of my work and ideas. If I sought to answer all the criticisms that cross my desk, my secretaries would have little time for anything other than such correspondence in the course of the day, and I would have no time for constructive work. But since I feel that you are men of genuine good will and that your criticisms are sincerely set forth, I want to try to answer your statement in what I hope will be patient and reasonable terms.

I think I should indicate why I am here in Birmingham, since you have been influenced by the view which argues against "outsiders coming in." I have the honor of serving as president of the Southern Christian Leadership Conference, an organization operating in every southern state, with headquarters in Atlanta, Georgia. We have some eighty-five affiliated organizations across the South, and one of them is the Alabama Christian Movement for Human Rights. Frequently we share staff, educational and financial resources with our affiliates. Several months ago the affiliate here in Birmingham asked us to be on call to engage in a nonviolent direct-action program if such were deemed necessary. We readily consented, and when the hour came we lived up to our promise. So I, along with several members of my staff, am here because I was invited here. I am here because I have organizational ties here.

---

[*] Author's note: This response to a published statement by eight fellow clergymen from Alabama . . . was composed under somewhat constricting circumstances. Begun on the margins of the newspaper in which the statement appeared while I was in jail, the letter was continued on scraps of writing paper supplied by a friendly Negro trusty, and concluded on a pad my attorneys were eventually permitted to leave me. Although the text remains in substance unaltered, I have indulged in the author's prerogative of polishing it for publication.

But more basically, I am in Birmingham because injustice is here. Just as the prophets of the eighth century B.C. left their villages and carried their "thus saith the Lord" far beyond the boundaries of their home towns, and just as the Apostle Paul left his village of Tarsus and carried the gospel of Jesus Christ to the far corners of the Greco-Roman world, so am I compelled to carry the gospel of freedom beyond my own home town. Like Paul, I must constantly respond to the Macedonian call for aid.

Moreover, I am cognizant of the interrelatedness of all communities and states. I cannot sit idly by in Atlanta and not be concerned about what happens in Birmingham. Injustice anywhere is a threat to justice everywhere. We are caught in an inescapable network of mutuality, tied in a single garment of destiny. Whatever affects one directly, affects all indirectly. Never again can we afford to live with the narrow, provincial "outside agitator" idea. Anyone who lives inside the United States can never be considered an outsider anywhere within its bounds.

You deplore the demonstrations taking place in Birmingham. But your statement, I am sorry to say, fails to express a similar concern for the conditions that brought about the demonstrations. I am sure that none of you would want to rest content with the superficial kind of social analysis that deals merely with effects and does not grapple with underlying causes. It is unfortunate that demonstrations are taking place in Birmingham, but it is even more unfortunate that the city's white power structure left the Negro community with no alternative.

In any nonviolent campaign there are four basic steps: collection of the facts to determine whether injustices exist; negotiation; self-purification; and direct action. We have gone through all these steps in Birmingham. There can be no gainsaying the fact that racial injustice engulfs this community. Birmingham is probably the most thoroughly segregated city in the United States. Its ugly record of brutality is widely known. Negroes have experienced grossly unjust treatment in the courts. There have been more unsolved bombings of Negro homes and churches in Birmingham than in any other city in the nation. These are the hard, brutal facts of the case. On the basis of these conditions, Negro leaders sought to negotiate with the city fathers. But the latter consistently refused to engage in good-faith negotiation.

Then, last September, came the opportunity to talk with leaders of Birmingham's economic community. In the course of the negotiations, certain promises were made by the merchants—for example, to remove the stores' humiliating racial signs. On the basis of these promises, the Reverend Fred Shuttlesworth and the leaders of the Alabama Christian Movement for Human Rights agreed to a moratorium on all demonstrations. As the weeks and months went by, we realized that we were the victims of a broken promise. A few signs, briefly removed, returned; the others remained.

As in so many past experiences, our hopes had been blasted, and the shadow of deep disappointment settled upon us. We had no alternative except to prepare for direct action, whereby we would present our very bodies as a means of laying our case before the conscience of the local and the national community. Mindful of the difficulties involved, we decided to undertake a process of self-purification. We began a series of workshops on nonviolence, and we repeatedly asked ourselves: "Are you able to accept blows without retaliating?" "Are you able to endure the ordeal of jail?" We decided to schedule our direct-action program for the Easter season, realizing that except for Christmas, this is the main shopping period of the year. Knowing that a strong economic-withdrawal program would be the by-product of direct action, we felt that this would be the best time to bring pressure to bear on the merchants for the needed change.

Then it occurred to us that Birmingham's mayoralty election was coming up in March, and we speedily decided to postpone action until after election day. When we discovered that the Commissioner of Public Safety, Eugene "Bull" Connor, had piled up enough votes to be in the run-off, we decided again to postpone action until the day after the run-off so that the demonstrations could not be used to cloud the issues. Like many others, we waited to see Mr. Connor defeated, and to this end we endured postponement after postponement. Having aided in this community need, we felt that our direct-action program could be delayed no longer.

You may well ask: "Why direct action? Why sit-ins, marches and so forth? Isn't negotiation a better path?" You are quite right in calling for negotiation. Indeed, this is the very purpose of direct action. Nonviolent direct action seeks to create such a crisis and foster such a tension that a community which has constantly refused to negotiate is forced to confront the issue. It seeks so to dramatize the issue that it can no longer be ignored. My citing the creation of tension as part of the work of the nonviolent-resister may sound rather shocking. But I must confess that I am not afraid of the word "tension." I have earnestly opposed violent tension, but there is a type of constructive, nonviolent tension which is necessary for growth. Just as Socrates felt that it was necessary to create a tension in the mind so that individuals could rise from the bondage of myths and half-truths to the unfettered realm of creative analysis and objective appraisal, so must we see the need for nonviolent gad-flies to create the kind of tension in society that will help men rise from the dark depths of prejudice and racism to the majestic heights of understanding and brotherhood.

The purpose of our direct-action program is to create a situation so crisis-packed that it will inevitably open the door to negotiation. I therefore concur with you in your call for negotiation. Too long has our beloved Southland been bogged down in a tragic effort to live in monologue rather than dialogue.

One of the basic points in your statement is that the action that I and my associates have taken in Birmingham is untimely. Some have asked: "Why didn't you give the new city administration time to act?" The only answer that I can give to this query is that the new Birmingham administration must be prodded about as much as the outgoing one, before it will act. We are sadly mistaken if we feel that the election of Albert Boutwell as mayor will bring the millennium to Birmingham. While Mr. Boutwell is a much more gentle person than Mr. Connor, they are both segregationists, dedicated to maintenance of the status quo. I have hope that Mr. Boutwell will be reasonable enough to see the futility of massive resistance to desegregation. But he will not see this without pressure from devotees of civil rights. My friends, I must say to you that we have not made a single gain in civil rights without determined legal and nonviolent pressure. Lamentably, it is an historical fact that privileged groups seldom give up their privileges voluntarily. Individuals may see the moral light and voluntarily give up their unjust posture; but, as Reinhold Niebuhr has reminded us, groups tend to be more immoral than individuals.

We know through painful experience that freedom is never voluntarily given by the oppressor; it must be demanded by the oppressed. Frankly, I have yet to engage in a direct-action campaign that was "well timed" in the view of those who have not suffered unduly from the disease of segregation. For years now I have heard the word "Wait!" It rings in the ear of every Negro with piercing familiarity. This "Wait" has almost always meant "Never." We must come to see, with one of our distinguished jurists, that "justice too long delayed is justice denied."

We have waited for more than 340 years for our constitutional and God-given rights. The nations of Asia and Africa are moving with jetlike speed toward gaining political independence, but we still creep at horse-and-buggy pace toward gaining a cup of coffee at a lunch counter. Perhaps it is easy for those who have never felt the stinging darts of segregation to say, "Wait." But when you have seen vicious mobs lynch your mothers and fathers at will and drown your sisters and brothers at whim; when you have seen hate-filled policemen curse, kick and even kill your black brothers and sisters; when you see the vast majority of your twenty million Negro brothers smothering in an airtight cage of poverty in the midst of an affluent society; when you suddenly find your tongue twisted and your speech stammering as you seek to explain to your six-year-old daughter why she can't go to the public amusement park that has just been advertised on television, and see tears welling up in her eyes when she is told that Funtown is closed to colored children, and see ominous clouds of inferiority beginning to form in her little mental sky, and see her beginning to distort her personality by developing an unconscious bitterness toward white people; when you have to concoct an answer for a five-year-old son who is asking: "Daddy, why do white people treat colored people so mean?"; when you take a cross-county drive and find it necessary to sleep night after night in the uncomfortable corners of your automobile because no motel will accept you; when you are humiliated day in and day out by nagging signs reading "white" and "colored"; when your first name becomes "nigger," your middle name becomes "boy" (however old you are) and your last name becomes "John," and your wife and mother are never given the respected title "Mrs."; when you are harried by day and haunted by night by the fact that you are a Negro, living constantly at tiptoe stance, never quite knowing what to expect next, and are plagued with inner fears and outer resentments; when you are forever fighting a degenerating sense of "nobodiness"—then you will understand why we find it difficult to wait. There comes a time when the cup of endurance runs over, and men are no longer willing to be plunged into the abyss of despair. I hope, sirs, you can understand our legitimate and unavoidable impatience.

You express a great deal of anxiety over our willingness to break laws. This is certainly a legitimate concern. Since we so diligently urge people to obey the Supreme Court's decision of 1954 outlawing segregation in the public schools, at first glance it may seem rather paradoxical for us consciously to break laws. One may well ask: "How can you advocate breaking some laws and obeying others?" The answer lies in the fact that there are two types of laws: just and unjust. I would be the first to advocate obeying just laws. One has not only a legal but a moral responsibility to obey just laws. Conversely, one has a moral responsibility to disobey unjust laws. I would agree with St. Augustine that "an unjust law is no law at all."

Now, what is the difference between the two? How does one determine whether a law is just or unjust? A just law is a man-made code that squares with the moral law or the law of God. An unjust law is a code that is out of harmony with the moral law. To put it in the terms of St. Thomas Aquinas: An unjust law is a human law that is not rooted in eternal law and natural law. Any law that uplifts human personality is just. Any law that degrades human personality is unjust. All segregation statutes are unjust because segregation distorts the soul and damages the personality. It gives the segregator a false sense of superiority and the segregated a false sense of inferiority. Segregation, to use the terminology of the Jewish philosopher Martin Buber, substitutes an

"I–it" relationship for an "I–thou" relationship and ends up relegating persons to the status of things. Hence segregation is not only politically, economically and sociologically unsound, it is morally wrong and sinful. Paul Tillich has said that sin is separation. Is not segregation an existential expression of man's tragic separation, his awful estrangement, his terrible sinfulness? Thus it is that I can urge men to obey the 1954 decision of the Supreme Court, for it is morally right; and I can urge them to disobey segregation ordinances, for they are morally wrong.

Let us consider a more concrete example of just and unjust laws. An unjust law is a code that a numerical or power majority group compels a minority group to obey but does not make binding on itself. This is *difference* made legal. By the same token, a just law is a code that a majority compels a minority to follow and that it is willing to follow itself. This is *sameness* made legal.

Let me give another explanation. A law is unjust if it is inflicted on a minority that, as a result of being denied the right to vote, had no part in enacting or devising the law. Who can say that the legislature of Alabama which set up that state's segregation laws was democratically elected? Throughout Alabama all sorts of devious methods are used to prevent Negroes from becoming registered voters, and there are some counties in which, even though Negroes constitute a majority of the population, not a single Negro is registered. Can any law enacted under such circumstances be considered democratically structured?

Sometimes a law is just on its face and unjust in its application. For instance, I have been arrested on a charge of parading without a permit. Now, there is nothing wrong in having an ordinance which requires a permit for a parade. But such an ordinance becomes unjust when it is used to maintain segregation and to deny citizens the First-Amendment privilege of peaceful assembly and protest.

I hope you are able to see the distinction I am trying to point out. In no sense do I advocate evading or defying the law, as would the rabid segregationist. That would lead to anarchy. One who breaks an unjust law must do so openly, lovingly, and with a willingness to accept the penalty. I submit that an individual who breaks a law that conscience tells him is unjust, and who willingly accepts the penalty of imprisonment in order to arouse the conscience of the community over its injustice, is in reality expressing the highest respect for law.

Of course, there is nothing new about this kind of civil disobedience. It was evidenced sublimely in the refusal of Shadrach, Meshach and Abednego to obey the laws of Nebuchadnezzar, on the ground that a higher moral law was at stake. It was practiced superbly by the early Christians, who were willing to face hungry lions and the excruciating pain of chopping blocks rather than submit to certain unjust laws of the Roman Empire. To a degree, academic freedom is a reality today because Socrates practiced civil disobedience. In our own nation, the Boston Tea Party represented a massive act of civil disobedience.

We should never forget that everything Adolf Hitler did in Germany was "legal" and everything the Hungarian freedom fighters did in Hungary was "illegal." It was "illegal" to aid and comfort a Jew in Hitler's Germany. Even so, I am sure that, had I lived in Germany at the time, I would have aided and comforted my Jewish brothers. If today I lived in a Communist country where certain principles dear to the Christian faith are suppressed, I would openly advocate disobeying that country's antireligious laws.

I must make two honest confessions to you, my Christian and Jewish brothers. First, I must confess that over the past few years I have been gravely disappointed with the white moderate. I have almost reached the regrettable conclusion that the Negro's great stumbling block in his stride toward freedom is not the White Citizen's Counciler or the Ku Klux Klanner, but the white moderate, who is more devoted to "order" than to justice; who prefers a negative peace which is the absence of tension to a positive peace which is the presence of justice; who constantly says: "I agree with you in the goal you seek, but I cannot agree with your methods of direct action"; who paternalistically believes he can set the timetable for another man's freedom; who lives by a mythical concept of time and who constantly advises the Negro to wait for a "more convenient season." Shallow understanding from people of good will is more frustrating than absolute misunderstanding from people of ill will. Lukewarm acceptance is much more bewildering than outright rejection.

I had hoped that the white moderate would understand that law and order exist for the purpose of establishing justice and that when they fail in this purpose they become the dangerously structured dams that block the flow of social progress. I had hoped that the white moderate would understand that the present tension in the South is a necessary phase of the transition from an obnoxious negative peace, in which the Negro passively accepted his unjust plight, to a substantive and positive peace, in which all men will respect the dignity and worth of human personality. Actually, we who engage in nonviolent direct action are not the creators of tension. We merely bring to the surface the hidden tension that is already alive. We bring it out in the open, where it can be seen and dealt with. Like a boil that can never be cured so long as it is covered up but must be opened with all its ugliness to the natural medicines of air and light, injustice must be exposed, with all the tension its exposure creates, to the light of human conscience and the air of national opinion before it can be cured.

In your statement you assert that our actions, even though peaceful, must be condemned because they precipitate violence. But is this a logical assertion?

Isn't this like condemning a robbed man because his possession of money pre-cipitated the evil act of robbery? Isn't this like condemning Socrates because his unswerving commitment to truth and his philosophical inquiries precipitated the act by the misguided populace in which they made him drink hemlock? Isn't this like condemning Jesus because his unique God-consciousness and never-ceasing devotion to God's will precipitated the evil act of crucifixion? We must come to see that, as the federal courts have consistently affirmed, it is wrong to urge an individual to cease his efforts to gain his basic constitutional rights because the quest may precipitate violence. Society must protect the robbed and punish the robber.

I had also hoped that the white moderate would reject the myth concerning time in relation to the struggle for freedom. I have just received a letter from a white brother in Texas. He writes: "All Christians know that the colored people will receive equal rights eventually, but it is possible that you are in too great a religious hurry. It has taken Christianity almost two thousand years to accom-plish what it has. The teachings of Christ take time to come to earth." Such an attitude stems from a tragic misconception of time, from the strangely irratio-nal notion that there is something in the very flow of time that will inevitably cure all ills. Actually, time itself is neutral; it can be used either destructively or constructively. More and more I feel that the people of ill will have used time much more effectively than have the people of good will. We will have to repent in this generation not merely for the hateful words and actions of the bad people but for the appalling silence of the good people. Human progress never rolls in on wheels of inevitability; it comes through the tireless efforts of men willing to be co-workers with God, and without this hard work, time itself becomes an ally of the forces of social stagnation. We must use time creatively, in the knowledge that the time is always ripe to do right. Now is the time to make real the promise of democracy and transform our pending national elegy into a creative psalm of brotherhood. Now is the time to lift our national policy from the quicksand of racial injustice to the solid rock of human dignity.

You speak of our activity in Birmingham as extreme. At first I was rather disappointed that fellow clergymen would see my nonviolent efforts as those of an extremist. I began thinking about the fact that I stand in the middle of two opposing forces in the Negro community. One is a force of complacency, made up in part of Negroes who, as a result of long years of oppression, are so drained of self-respect and a sense of "somebodiness" that they have adjusted to segregation; and in part of a few middle-class Negroes who, because of a degree of academic and economic security and because in some ways they profit by segregation, have become insensitive to the problems of the masses. The other force is one of bitterness and hatred, and it comes perilously close to advocating violence. It is expressed in the various black nationalist groups that are springing up across the nation, the largest and best-known being Elijah Muhammad's Muslim movement. Nourished by the Negro's frustration over the continued existence of racial discrimination, this movement is made up of people who have lost faith in America, who have absolutely repudiated Christianity, and who have concluded that the white man is an incorrigible "devil."

I have tried to stand between these two forces, saying that we need emulate neither the "do nothingism" of the complacent nor the hatred and despair of the black nationalist. For there is the more excellent way of love and nonviolent protest. I am grateful to God that, through the influence of the Negro church, the way of nonviolence became an integral part of our struggle.

If this philosophy had not emerged, by now many streets of the South would, I am convinced, be flowing with blood. And I am further convinced that if our white brothers dismiss as "rabble-rousers" and "outside agitators" those of us who employ nonviolent direct action, and if they refuse to support our nonviolent efforts, millions of Negroes will, out of frustration and despair, seek solace and security in black-nationalist ideologies—a development that would inevitably lead to a frightening racial nightmare.

Oppressed people cannot remain oppressed forever. The yearning for freedom eventually manifests itself, and that is what has happened to the American Negro. Something within has reminded him of his birthright of freedom, and something without has reminded him that it can be gained. Consciously or unconsciously, he has been caught up by the *Zeitgeist*, and with his black brothers of Africa and his brown and yellow brothers of Asia, South America and the Caribbean, the United States Negro is moving with a sense of great urgency toward the promised land of racial justice. If one recognizes this vital urge that has engulfed the Negro community, one should readily understand why public demonstrations are taking place. The Negro has many pent-up resentments and latent frustrations, and he must release them. So let him march; let him make prayer pilgrimages to the city hall; let him go on freedom rides—and try to understand why he must do so. If his repressed emotions are not released in nonviolent ways, they will seek expression through violence; this is not a threat but a fact of history. So I have not said to my people: "Get rid of your discontent." Rather, I have tried to say that this normal and healthy discontent can be channeled into the creative outlet of nonviolent direct action. And now this approach is being termed extremist.

But though I was initially disappointed at being categorized as an extremist, as I continued to think about the matter I gradually gained a measure of satisfaction from the label. Was not Jesus an extremist for love: "Love your enemies, bless them that curse you, do good to them that hate you, and pray for them which despitefully use you, and persecute you." Was not Amos an extremist for justice: "Let justice roll down like waters and righteousness like an ever-flowing stream." Was not Paul an extremist for the Christian gospel: "I bear in my body the marks of the Lord Jesus." Was not Martin Luther an extremist: "Here I stand; I cannot do otherwise, so help me God." And John Bunyan: "I will stay in jail to the end of my days before I make a butchery of my conscience." And Abraham Lincoln: "This nation cannot survive half slave and half free." And Thomas Jefferson: "We hold these truths to be self-evident, that all men are created equal . . ." So the question is not whether we will be extremists, but what kind of extremists we will be. Will we be extremists for hate or for love? Will we be extremists for the preservation of injustice or for the extension of justice? In that dramatic scene on Calvary's hill three men were crucified. We must never forget that all three were crucified for the same crime—the crime of extremism. Two were extremists for immorality, and thus fell below their environment. The other, Jesus Christ, was an extremist for love, truth and goodness, and thereby rose above his environment. Perhaps the South, the nation and the world are in dire need of creative extremists.

I had hoped that the white moderate would see this need. Perhaps I was too optimistic; perhaps I expected too much. I suppose I should have realized that few members of the oppressor race can understand the deep groans and passionate yearnings of the oppressed race, and still fewer have the vision to see that injustice must be rooted out by strong, persistent and determined action. I am thankful, however, that some of our white brothers in the South have grasped the meaning of this social revolution and committed themselves to it. They are still all too few in quantity, but they are big in quality. Some—such as Ralph McGill, Lillian Smith, Harry Golden, James McBride Dabbs, Ann Braden and Sarah Patton Boyle—have written about our struggle in eloquent and prophetic terms. Others have marched with us down nameless streets of the South. They have languished in filthy, roach-infested jails, suffering the abuse and brutality of policemen who view them as "dirty nigger-lovers." Unlike so many of their moderate brothers and sisters, they have recognized the urgency of the moment and sensed the need for powerful "action" antidotes to combat the disease of segregation.

Let me take note of my other major disappointment. I have been so greatly disappointed with the white church and its leadership. Of course, there are some notable exceptions. I am not unmindful of the fact that each of you has taken some significant stands on this issue. I commend you, Reverend Stallings, for your Christian stand on this past Sunday, in welcoming Negroes to your worship service on a nonsegregated basis. I commend the Catholic leaders of this state for integrating Spring Hill College several years ago.

But despite these notable exceptions, I must honestly reiterate that I have been disappointed with the church. I do not say this as one of those negative critics who can always find something wrong with the church. I say this as a minister of the gospel, who loves the church; who was nurtured in its bosom; who has been sustained by its spiritual blessings and who will remain true to it as long as the cord of life shall lengthen.

When I was suddenly catapulted into the leadership of the bus protest in Montgomery, Alabama, a few years ago, I felt we would be supported by the white church. I felt that the white ministers, priests and rabbis of the South would be among our strongest allies. Instead, some have been outright opponents, refusing to understand the freedom movement and misrepresenting its leaders; all too many others have been more cautious than courageous and have remained silent behind the anesthetizing security of stained-glass windows.

In spite of my shattered dreams, I came to Birmingham with the hope that the white religious leadership of this community would see the justice of our cause and, with deep moral concern, would serve as the channel through which our just grievances could reach the power structure. I had hoped that each of you would understand. But again I have been disappointed.

I have heard numerous southern religious leaders admonish their worshipers to comply with a desegregation decision because it is the law, but I have longed to hear white ministers declare: "Follow this decree because integration is morally right and because the Negro is your brother." In the midst of blatant injustices inflicted upon the Negro, I have watched white churchmen stand on the sideline and mouth pious irrelevancies and sanctimonious trivialities. In the midst of a mighty struggle to rid our nation of racial and economic injustice, I have heard many ministers say: "Those are social issues, with which the gospel has no real concern." And I have watched many churches commit themselves to a completely other-worldly religion which makes a strange, un-Biblical distinction between body and soul, between the sacred and the secular.

I have traveled the length and breadth of Alabama, Mississippi and all the other southern states. On sweltering summer days and crisp autumn mornings I have looked at the South's beautiful churches with their lofty spires pointing heavenward. I have beheld the impressive outlines of her massive religious-education buildings. Over and over I have found myself asking: "What kind of people worship here? Who is their God? Where were their voices when the lips of Governor Barnett dripped with words of interposition and nullification? Where were they when Governor Wallace gave a clarion call for defiance and hatred? Where were their voices of support when bruised and weary Negro men and women decided to rise from the dark dungeons of complacency to the bright hills of creative protest?"

Yes, these questions are still in my mind. In deep disappointment I have wept over the laxity of the church. But be assured that my tears have been tears of love. There can be no deep disappointment where there is not deep love. Yes, I love the church. How could I do otherwise? I am in the rather unique position of being the son, the grandson and the great-grandson of preachers. Yes, I see the church as the body of Christ. But, oh! How we have blemished and scarred that body through social neglect and through fear of being nonconformists.

There was a time when the church was very powerful—in the time when the early Christians rejoiced at being deemed worthy to suffer for what they believed. In those days the church was not merely a thermometer that recorded the ideas and principles of popular opinion; it was a thermostat that transformed the mores of society. Whenever the early Christians entered a town, the people in power became disturbed and immediately sought to convict the Christians for being "disturbers of the peace" and "outside agitators." But the Christians pressed on, in the conviction that they were "a colony of heaven," called to obey God rather than man. Small in number, they were big in commitment. They were too God-intoxicated to be "astronomically intimidated." By their effort and example they brought an end to such ancient evils as infanticide and gladiatorial contests.

Things are different now. So often the contemporary church is a weak, ineffectual voice with an uncertain sound. So often it is an archdefender of the status quo. Far from being disturbed by the presence of the church, the power structure of the average community is consoled by the church's silent—and often even vocal—sanction of things as they are.

But the judgment of God is upon the church as never before. If today's church does not recapture the sacrificial spirit of the early church, it will lose its authenticity, forfeit the loyalty of millions, and be dismissed as an irrelevant social club with no meaning for the twentieth century. Every day I meet young people whose disappointment with the church has turned into outright disgust.

Perhaps I have once again been too optimistic. Is organized religion too inextricably bound to the status quo to save our nation and the world? Perhaps I must turn my faith to the inner spiritual church, the church within the church, as the true *ekklesia* and the hope of the world. But again I am thankful to God that some noble souls from the ranks of organized religion have broken loose from the paralyzing chains of conformity and joined us as active partners in the struggle for freedom. They have left their secure congregations and walked the streets of Albany, Georgia, with us. They have gone down the highways of the South on tortuous rides for freedom. Yes, they have gone to jail with us. Some have been dismissed from their churches, have lost the support of their bishops and fellow ministers. But they have acted in the faith that right defeated is stronger than evil triumphant. Their witness has been the spiritual salt that has preserved the true meaning of the gospel in these troubled times. They have carved a tunnel of hope through the dark mountain of disappointment.

I hope the church as a whole will meet the challenge of this decisive hour. But even if the church does not come to the aid of justice, I have no despair about the future. I have no fear about the outcome of our struggle in Birmingham, even if our motives are at present misunderstood. We will reach the goal of freedom in Birmingham and all over the nation, because the goal of America is freedom. Abused and scorned though we may be, our destiny is tied up with America's destiny. Before the pilgrims landed at Plymouth, we were here. Before the pen of Jefferson etched the majestic words of the Declaration of Independence across the pages of history, we were here. For more than two centuries our forebears labored in this country without wages; they made cotton king; they built the homes of their masters while suffering gross injustice and shameful humiliation—and yet out of a bottomless vitality they continued to thrive and develop. If the inexpressible cruelties of slavery could not stop us, the opposition we now face will surely fail. We will win our freedom because the sacred heritage of our nation and the eternal will of God are embodied in our echoing demands.

Before closing I feel impelled to mention one other point in your statement that has troubled me profoundly. You warmly commended the Birmingham police force for keeping "order" and "preventing violence." I doubt that you would have so warmly commended the police force if you had seen its dogs sinking their teeth into unarmed, nonviolent Negroes. I doubt that you would so quickly commend the policemen if you were to observe their ugly and inhumane treatment of Negroes here in the city jail; if you were to watch them push and curse old Negro women and young Negro girls; if you were to see them slap and kick old Negro men and young boys; if you were to observe them, as they did on two occasions, refuse to give us food because we wanted to sing our grace together. I cannot join you in your praise of the Birmingham police department.

It is true that the police have exercised a degree of discipline in handling the demonstrators. In this sense they have conducted themselves rather "nonviolently" in public. But for what purpose? To preserve the evil system of segregation. Over the past few years I have consistently preached that nonviolence demands that the means we use must be as pure as the ends we seek. I have tried to make clear that it is wrong to use immoral means to attain moral ends. But now I must affirm that it is just as wrong, or perhaps even more so, to use moral means to preserve immoral ends. Perhaps Mr. Connor and his policemen have been rather nonviolent in public, as was Chief Pritchett in Albany, Georgia, but they have used the moral means of nonviolence to maintain the immoral end of racial injustice. As T. S. Eliot has said: "The last temptation is the greatest treason: To do the right deed for the wrong reason."

I wish you had commended the Negro sit-inners and demonstrators of Birmingham for their sublime courage, their willingness to suffer and their amazing discipline in the midst of great provocation. One day the South will recognize its real heroes. They will be the James Merediths, with the noble sense of purpose that enables them to face jeering and hostile mobs, and with the agonizing loneliness that characterizes the life of the pioneer. They will be old, oppressed, battered Negro women, symbolized in a seventy-two-year-old woman in Montgomery, Alabama, who rose up with a sense of dignity and with her people decided not to ride segregated buses, and who responded with ungrammatical profundity to one who inquired about her weariness: "My feets is tired, but my soul is at rest." They will be the young high school and college students, the young ministers of the gospel and a host of their elders, courageously and nonviolently sitting in at lunch counters and willingly going to jail for conscience' sake. One day the South will know that when these disinherited children of God sat down at lunch counters, they were in reality standing up for what is best in the American dream and for the most sacred values in our Judaeo-Christian heritage, thereby bringing our nation back to those great wells of democracy which were dug deep by the founding fathers in their formulation of the Constitution and the Declaration of Independence.

Never before have I written so long a letter. I'm afraid it is much too long to take your precious time. I can assure you that it would have been much shorter if I had been writing from a comfortable desk, but what else can one do when he is alone in a narrow jail cell, other than write long letters, think long thoughts and pray long prayers?

If I have said anything in this letter that overstates the truth and indicates an unreasonable impatience, I beg you to forgive me. If I have said anything that understates the truth and indicates my having a patience that allows me to settle for anything less than brotherhood, I beg God to forgive me.

I hope this letter finds you strong in the faith. I also hope that circumstances will soon make it possible for me to meet each of you, not as an integrationist or a civil-rights leader but as a fellow clergyman and a Christian brother. Let us all hope that the dark clouds of racial prejudice will soon pass away and the deep fog of misunderstanding will be lifted from our fear-drenched communities, and in some not too distant tomorrow the radiant stars of love and brotherhood will shine over our great nation with all their scintillating beauty.

Yours for the cause of Peace and Brotherhood,
Martin Luther King Jr.

A Jury of Her Peers

SUSAN GLASPELL

This story by Susan Glaspell (1876–1948), playwright, actress, and writer, raises questions not about the justice of the law but about its proper enforcement, not about the obligation to obey it but about how to judge those who allegedly have violated it. The story (1917), inspired by an actual case in Iowa a few years earlier, is set in the rural Midwest. Law enforcement officials and a key witness, joined by the wives of the sheriff and the witness, search the domestic scene of the crime, seeking clues to why the woman of the house might have murdered her husband.

To what extent do or should a suspect's circumstances and motives excuse the commission of a crime? What are the limits of sympathy and understanding when it comes to enforcing the law? Is it really true that to understand is to forgive? When, if ever, may one be excused for taking the law into one's own hands? When, if ever, is it permissible to withhold evidence? What are the obligations of sworn jurors—or any other citizen—to the enforcement of the law? The men and the women in the story have decidedly different outlooks, sympathies, and insights. With which group do you most sympathize and why? Were you Mrs. Hale or Mrs. Peters, would you have done as they did? Would you wish their reasons to govern the juries of your peers? Who is a "peer," fit to judge?

When Martha Hale opened the storm-door and got a cut of the north wind, she ran back for her big woolen scarf. As she hurriedly wound that round her head her eye made a scandalized sweep of her kitchen. It was no ordinary thing that called her away—it was probably farther from ordinary than anything that had ever happened in Dickson County. But what her eye took in was that her kitchen was in no shape for leaving: her bread all ready for mixing, half the flour sifted and half unsifted.

She hated to see things half done; but she had been at that when the team from town stopped to get Mr. Hale, and then the sheriff came running in to say his wife wished Mrs. Hale would come too—adding, with a grin, that he guessed she was getting scarey and wanted another woman along. So she had dropped everything right where it was.

"Martha!" now came her husband's impatient voice. "Don't keep folks waiting out here in the cold."

She again opened the storm-door, and this time joined the three men and the one woman waiting for her in the big two-seated buggy.

After she had the robes tucked around her she took another look at the woman who sat beside her on the back seat. She had met Mrs. Peters the year before at the county fair, and the thing she remembered about her was that she didn't seem like a sheriff's wife. She was small and thin and didn't have a strong voice. Mrs. Gorman, sheriff's wife before Gorman went out and Peters came in, had a voice that somehow seemed to be backing up the law with every word. But if Mrs. Peters didn't look like a sheriff's wife, Peters made it up in looking like a sheriff. He was to a dot the kind of man who could get himself elected sheriff—a heavy man with a big voice, who was particularly genial with the law-abiding, as if to make it plain that he knew the difference between criminals and non-criminals. And right there it came into Mrs. Hale's mind, with a stab, that this man who was so pleasant and lively with all of them was going to the Wrights' now as a sheriff.

"The country's not very pleasant this time of year," Mrs. Peters at last ventured, as if she felt they ought to be talking as well as the men.

Mrs. Hale scarcely finished her reply, for they had gone up a little hill and could see the Wright place now, and seeing it did not make her feel like talking. It looked very lonesome this cold March morning. It had always been a lonesome-looking place. It was down in a hollow, and the poplar trees around it were lonesome-looking trees. The men were looking at it and talking about what had happened. The county attorney was bending to one side of the buggy, and kept looking steadily at the place as they drew up to it.

"I'm glad you came with me," Mrs. Peters said nervously, as the two women were about to follow the men in through the kitchen door.

Even after she had her foot on the door-step, her hand on the knob, Martha Hale had a moment of feeling she could not cross that threshold. And the reason it seemed she couldn't cross it now was simply because she hadn't crossed it before. Time and time again it had been in her mind, "I ought to go over and see Minnie Foster"—she still thought of her as Minnie Foster, though for twenty years she had been Mrs. Wright. And then there was always something to do and Minnie Foster would go from her mind. But *now* she could come.

The men went over to the stove. The women stood close together by the door. Young Henderson, the county attorney, turned around and said, "Come up to the fire, ladies."

Mrs. Peters took a step forward, then stopped. "I'm not—cold," she said.

And so the two women stood by the door, at first not even so much as looking around the kitchen.

The men talked for a minute about what a good thing it was the sheriff had sent his deputy out that morning to make a fire for them, and then Sheriff Peters stepped back from the stove, unbuttoned his outer coat, and leaned his hands on the kitchen table in a way that seemed to mark the beginning of official business. "Now, Mr. Hale," he said in a sort of semi-official voice, "before we move things about, you tell Mr. Henderson just what it was you saw when you came here yesterday morning."

The county attorney was looking around the kitchen.

"By the way," he said, "has anything been moved?" He turned to the sheriff. "Are things just as you left them yesterday?"

Peters looked from cupboard to sink; from that to a small worn rocker a little to one side of the kitchen table.

"It's just the same."

"Somebody should have been left here yesterday," said the county attorney.

"Oh—yesterday," returned the sheriff, with a little gesture as of yesterday having been more than he could bear to think of. "When I had to send Frank to Morris Center for that man who went crazy—let me tell you. I had my hands full *yesterday*. I knew you could get back from Omaha by to-day, George, and as long as I went over everything here myself—"

"Well, Mr. Hale," said the county attorney, in a way of letting what was past and gone go, "tell just what happened when you came here yesterday morning."

Mrs. Hale, still leaning against the door, had that sinking feeling of the mother whose child is about to speak a piece. Lewis often wandered along and got things mixed up in a story. She hoped he would tell this straight and plain, and not say unnecessary things that would just make things harder for Minnie Foster. He didn't begin at once, and she noticed that he looked queer—as if standing in that kitchen and having to tell what he had seen there yesterday made him almost sick.

"Yes, Mr. Hale?" the county attorney reminded.

"Harry and I had started to town with a load of potatoes," Mrs. Hale's husband began.

Harry was Mrs. Hale's oldest boy. He wasn't with them now, for the very good reason that those potatoes never got to town yesterday and he was taking them this morning, so he hadn't been home when the sheriff stopped to say he wanted Mr. Hale to come over to the Wright place and tell the county attorney his story there, where he could point it all out. With all Mrs. Hale's other emotions came the fear now that maybe Harry wasn't dressed warm enough—they hadn't any of them realized how that north wind did bite.

"We come along this road," Hale was going on, with a motion of his hand to the road over which they had just come, "and as we got in sight of the house I says to Harry, 'I'm goin' to see if I can't get John Wright to take a telephone.' You see," he explained to Henderson, "unless I can get somebody to go in with me they won't come out this branch road except for a price *I* can't pay. I'd spoke to Wright about it once before; but he put me off, saying folks talked too much anyway, and all he asked was peace and quiet—guess you know about how much he talked himself. But I thought maybe if I went to the house and talked about it before his wife, and said all the women-folks liked the telephones, and that in this lonesome stretch of road it would be a good thing—well, I said to Harry that that was what I was going to say—though I said at the same time that I didn't know as what his wife wanted made much difference to John—"

Now, there he was!—saying things he didn't need to say. Mrs. Hale tried to catch her husband's eye, but fortunately the county attorney interrupted with:

"Let's talk about that a little later, Mr. Hale. I do want to talk about that, but I'm anxious now to get along to just what happened when you got here."

When he began this time, it was very deliberately and carefully:

"I didn't see or hear anything. I knocked at the door. And still it was all quiet inside. I knew they must be up—it was past eight o'clock. So I knocked again, louder, and I thought I heard somebody say, 'Come in.' I wasn't sure—I'm not sure yet. But I opened the door—this door," jerking a hand toward the door by which the two women stood. "And there, in that rocker"—pointing to it—"sat Mrs. Wright."

Everyone in the kitchen looked at the rocker. It came into Mrs. Hale's mind that that rocker didn't look in the least like Minnie Foster—the Minnie Foster of twenty years before. It was a dingy red, with wooden rungs up the back, and the middle rung was gone, and the chair sagged to one side.

"How did she—look?" the county attorney was inquiring.

"Well," said Hale, "she looked—queer."

"How do you mean—queer?"

As he asked it he took out a note-book and pencil. Mrs. Hale did not like the sight of that pencil. She kept her eye fixed on her husband, as if to keep him from saying unnecessary things that would go into that note-book and make trouble.

Hale did speak guardedly, as if the pencil had affected him too.

"Well, as if she didn't know what she was going to do next. And kind of—done up."

"How did she seem to feel about your coming?"

"Why, I don't think she minded—one way or other. She didn't pay much attention. I said, 'Ho' do, Mrs. Wright? It's cold, ain't it?' And she said. 'Is it?'—and went on pleatin' at her apron.

"Well, I was surprised. She didn't ask me to come up to the stove, or to sit down, but just set there, not even lookin' at me. And so I said: 'I want to see John.'

"And then she—laughed. I guess you would call it a laugh.

"I thought of Harry and the team outside, so I said, a little sharp, 'Can I see John?' 'No,' says she—kind of dull like. 'Ain't he home?' says I. Then she looked at me. 'Yes,' says she, 'he's home.' 'Then why can't I see him?' I asked her, out of patience with her now. ''Cause he's dead' says she, just as quiet and dull—and fell to pleatin' her apron. 'Dead?' says I, like you do when you can't take in what you've heard.

"She just nodded her head, not getting a bit excited, but rockin' back and forth.

"'Why—where is he?' says I, not knowing *what* to say.

"She just pointed upstairs—like this"—pointing to the room above.

"I got up, with the idea of going up there myself. By this time I—didn't know what to do. I walked from there to here; then I says: 'Why, what did he die of?'

"'He died of a rope around his neck,' says she; and just went on pleatin' at her apron."

Hale stopped speaking, and stood staring at the rocker, as if he were still seeing the woman who had sat there the morning before. Nobody spoke; it was as if every one were seeing the woman who had sat there the morning before.

"And what did you do then?" the county attorney at last broke the silence.

"I went out and called Harry. I thought I might—need help. I got Harry in, and we went upstairs." His voice fell almost to a whisper. "There he was—lying over the—"

"I think I'd rather have you go into that upstairs," the county attorney interrupted, "where you can point it all out. Just go on now with the rest of the story."

"Well, my first thought was to get that rope off. It looked—"

He stopped, his face twitching.

"But Harry, he went up to him, and he said, 'No, he's dead all right, and we'd better not touch anything.' So we went downstairs.

"She was still sitting that same way. 'Has anybody been notified?' I asked. 'No,' says she, unconcerned.

"'Who did this, Mrs. Wright?' said Harry. He said it businesslike, and she stopped pleatin' at her apron. 'I don't know,' she says. 'You don't *know*?' says Harry. 'Weren't you sleepin' in the bed with him?' 'Yes,' says she, 'but I was on the inside.' 'Somebody slipped a rope round his neck and strangled him, and you didn't wake up?' says Harry. 'I didn't wake up,' she said after him.

"We may have looked as if we didn't see how that could be, for after a minute she said, 'I sleep sound.'

"Harry was going to ask her more questions, but I said maybe that weren't our business; maybe we ought to let her tell her story first to the coroner or the sheriff. So Harry went fast as he could over to High Road—the Rivers' place, where there's a telephone."

"And what did she do when she knew you had gone for the coroner?" The attorney got his pencil in his hand all ready for writing.

"She moved from that chair to this one over here"—Hale pointed to a small chair in the corner—"and just sat there with her hands held together and looking down. I got a feeling that I ought to make some conversation, so I said I had come in to see if John wanted to put in a telephone; and at that she started to laugh, and then she stopped and looked at me—scared."

At the sound of a moving pencil the man who was telling the story looked up.

"I dunno—maybe it wasn't scared," he hastened; "I wouldn't like to say it was. Soon Harry got back, and then Dr. Lloyd came, and you, Mr. Peters, and so I guess that's all I know that you don't."

He said that last with relief, and moved a little, as if relaxing. Everyone moved a little. The county attorney walked toward the stair door.

"I guess we'll go upstairs first—then out to the barn and around there."

He paused and looked around the kitchen.

"You're convinced there was nothing important here?" he asked the sheriff. "Nothing that would—point to any motive?"

The sheriff too looked all around, as if to re-convince himself.

"Nothing here but kitchen things," he said, with a little laugh for the insignificance of kitchen things.

The county attorney was looking at the cupboard—a peculiar, ungainly structure, half closet and half cupboard, the upper part of it being built in the wall, and the lower part just the old-fashioned kitchen cupboard. As if its queerness attracted him, he got a chair and opened the upper part and looked in. After a moment he drew his hand away sticky.

"Here's a nice mess," he said resentfully.

The two women had drawn nearer, and now the sheriff's wife spoke.

"Oh—her fruit," she said, looking to Mrs. Hale for sympathetic understanding.

She turned back to the county attorney and explained: "She worried about that when it turned so cold last night. She said the fire would go out and her jars might burst."

Mrs. Peters' husband broke into a laugh.

"Well, can you beat the woman! Held for murder, and worrying about her preserves!"

The young attorney set his lips.

"I guess before we're through with her she may have something more serious than preserves to worry about."

"Oh, well," said Mrs. Hale's husband, with good-natured superiority, "women are used to worrying over trifles."

The two women moved a little closer together. Neither of them spoke. The county attorney seemed suddenly to remember his manners—and think of his future.

"And yet," said he, with the gallantry of a young politician, "for all their worries, what would we do without the ladies?"

The women did not speak, did not unbend. He went to the sink and began washing his hands. He turned to wipe them on the roller towel—whirled it for a cleaner place.

"Dirty towels! Not much of a housekeeper, would you say, ladies?"

He kicked his foot against some dirty pans under the sink.

"There's a great deal of work to be done on a farm," said Mrs. Hale stiffly.

"To be sure. And yet"—with a little bow to her—"I know there are some Dickson County farm-houses that do not have such roller towels." He gave it a pull to expose its full length again.

"Those towels get dirty awful quick. Men's hands aren't always as clean as they might be."

"Ah, loyal to your sex, I see," he laughed. He stopped and gave her a keen look. "But you and Mrs. Wright were neighbors. I suppose you were friends, too."

Martha Hale shook her head.

"I've seen little enough of her of late years. I've not been in this house—it's more than a year."

"And why was that? You didn't like her?"

"I liked her well enough," she replied with spirit. "Farmers' wives have their hands full, Mr. Henderson. And then—" She looked around the kitchen.

"Yes?" he encouraged.

"It never seemed a very cheerful place," said she, more to herself than to him.

"No," he agreed; "I don't think anyone would call it cheerful. I shouldn't say she had the home-making instinct."

"Well, I don't know as Wright had, either," she muttered.

"You mean they didn't get on very well?" he was quick to ask.

"No; I don't mean anything," she answered, with decision. As she turned a little away from him, she added: "But I don't think a place would be any the cheerfuller for John Wright's bein' in it."

"I'd like to talk to you about that a little later, Mrs. Hale," he said. "I'm anxious to get the lay of things upstairs now."

He moved toward the stair door, followed by the two men.

"I suppose anything Mrs. Peters does'll be all right?" the sheriff inquired. "She was to take in some clothes for her, you know—and a few little things. We left in such a hurry yesterday."

The county attorney looked at the two women whom they were leaving alone there among the kitchen things.

"Yes—Mrs. Peters," he said, his glance resting on the woman who was not Mrs. Peters, the big farmer woman who stood behind the sheriff's wife. "Of course Mrs. Peters is one of us," he said, in a manner of entrusting responsibility. "And keep your eye out, Mrs. Peters, for anything that might be of use. No telling; you women might come upon a clue to the motive—and that's the thing we need."

Mr. Hale rubbed his face after the fashion of a showman getting ready for a pleasantry.

"But would the women know a clue if they did come upon it?" he said; and, having delivered himself of this, he followed the others through the stair door.

The women stood motionless and silent, listening to the footsteps, first upon the stairs, then in the room above them.

Then, as if releasing herself from something strange, Mrs. Hale began to arrange the dirty pans under the sink, which the county attorney's disdainful push of the foot had deranged.

"I'd hate to have men comin' into my kitchen," she said testily—"snoopin' round and criticizin'."

"Of course it's no more than their duty," said the sheriff's wife, in her manner of timid acquiescence.

"Duty's all right," replied Mrs. Hale bluffly; "but I guess that deputy sheriff that come out to make the fire might have got a little of this on." She gave the roller towel a pull. "Wish I'd thought of that sooner! Seems mean to talk about her for not having things slicked up, when she had to come away in such a hurry."

She looked around the kitchen. Certainly it was not "slicked up." Her eye was held by a bucket of sugar on a low shelf. The cover was off the wooden bucket, and beside it was a paper bag—half full.

Mrs. Hale moved toward it.

"She was putting this in there," she said to herself—slowly.

She thought of the flour in her kitchen at home—half sifted, half not sifted. She had been interrupted, and had left things half done. What had interrupted Minnie Foster? Why had that work been left half done? She made a move as if to finish it,—unfinished things always bothered her,—and then she glanced around and saw that Mrs. Peters was watching her—and she didn't want Mrs. Peters to get that feeling she had got of work begun and then—for some reason—not finished.

"It's a shame about her fruit," she said, and walked toward the cupboard that the county attorney had opened, and got on the chair, murmuring: "I wonder if it's all gone."

It was a sorry enough looking sight, but "Here's one that's all right," she said at last. She held it toward the light. "This is cherries, too." She looked again. "I declare I believe that's the only one."

With a sigh, she got down from the chair, went to the sink, and wiped off the bottle.

"She'll feel awful bad, after all her hard work in the hot weather. I remember the afternoon I put up my cherries last summer."

She set the bottle on the table, and, with another sigh, started to sit down in the rocker. But she did not sit down. Something kept her from sitting down in that chair. She straightened—stepped back, and, half turned away, stood looking at it; seeing the woman who had sat there "pleatin' at her apron."

The thin voice of the sheriff's wife broke in upon her: "I must be getting those things from the front room closet." She opened the door into the other room, started in, stepped back. "You coming with me, Mrs. Hale?" she asked nervously. "You—you could help me get them."

They were soon back—the stark coldness of that shut-up room was not a thing to linger in.

"My!" said Mrs. Peters, dropping the things on the table and hurrying to the stove.

Mrs. Hale stood examining the clothes the woman who was being detained in town had said she wanted.

"Wright was close!" she exclaimed, holding up a shabby black shirt that bore the marks of much making over. "I think maybe that's why she kept so much to herself. I s'pose she felt she couldn't do her part; and then, you don't enjoy things when you feel shabby. She used to wear pretty clothes and be lively—when she was Minnie Foster, one of the town girls, singing in the choir. But that—oh, that was twenty years ago."

With a carefulness in which there was something tender, she folded the shabby clothes and piled them at one corner of the table. She looked up at Mrs. Peters, and there was something in the other woman's look that irritated her.

"She don't care," she said to herself. "Much difference it makes to her whether Minnie Foster had pretty clothes when she was a girl."

Then she looked again, and she wasn't so sure; in fact, she hadn't at any time been perfectly sure about Mrs. Peters. She had that shrinking manner, and yet her eyes looked as if they could see a long way into things.

"This all you was to take in?" asked Mrs. Hale.

"No," said the sheriff's wife; "she said she wanted an apron. Funny thing to want," she ventured in her nervous little way, "for there's not much to get you dirty in jail, goodness knows. But I suppose just to make her feel more natural. If you're used to wearing an apron—. She said they were in the bottom drawer of this cupboard. Yes—here they are. And then her little shawl that always hung on the stair door."

She took the small gray shawl from behind the door leading upstairs, and stood a minute looking at it.

Suddenly Mrs. Hale took a quick step toward the other woman.

"Mrs. Peters!"

"Yes, Mrs. Hale?"

"Do you think she—did it?"

A frightened look blurred the other thing in Mrs. Peters' eyes.

"Oh, I don't know," she said, in a voice that seemed to shrink away from the subject.

"Well, I don't think she did," affirmed Mrs. Hale stoutly. "Asking for an apron, and her little shawl. Worryin' about her fruit."

"Mr. Peters says—." Footsteps were heard in the room above; she stopped, looked up, then went on in a lowered voice: "Mr. Peters says—it looks bad for her. Mr. Henderson is awful sarcastic in a speech, and he's going to make fun of her saying she didn't—wake up."

For a moment Mrs. Hale had no answer. Then, "Well, I guess John Wright didn't wake up—when they was slippin' that rope under his neck," she muttered.

"No, it's *strange*," breathed Mrs. Peters. "They think it was such a—funny way to kill a man."

She began to laugh; at sound of the laugh, abruptly stopped.

"That's just what Mr. Hale said," said Mrs. Hale, in a resolutely natural voice. "There was a gun in the house. He says that's what he can't understand."

"Mr. Henderson said, coming out, that what was needed for the case was a motive. Something to show anger—or sudden feeling."

"Well, I don't see any signs of anger around here," said Mrs. Hale. "I don't—"

She stopped. It was as if her mind tripped on something. Her eye was caught by a dish-towel in the middle of the kitchen table. Slowly she moved toward the table. One half of it was wiped clean, the other half messy. Her eyes made a slow, almost unwilling turn to the bucket of sugar and the half empty bag beside it. Things begun—and not finished.

After a moment she stepped back, and said, in that manner of releasing herself:

"Wonder how they're finding things upstairs? I hope she had it a little more red up there. You know,"—she paused, and feeling gathered,—"it seems kind of *sneaking*: locking her up in town and coming out here to get her own house to turn against her!"

"But, Mrs. Hale," said the sheriff's wife, "the law is the law."

"I s'pose 'tis," answered Mrs. Hale shortly.

She turned to the stove, saying something about that fire not being much to brag of. She worked with it a minute, and when she straightened up she said aggressively:

"The law is the law—and a bad stove is a bad stove. How'd you like to cook on this?"—pointing with the poker to the broken lining. She opened the oven door and started to express her opinion of the oven; but she was swept into her own thoughts, thinking of what it would mean, year after year, to have that stove to wrestle with. The thought of Minnie Foster trying to bake in that oven—and the thought of her never going over to see Minnie Foster—.

She was startled by hearing Mrs. Peters say: "A person gets discouraged—and loses heart."

The sheriff's wife had looked from the stove to the sink—to the pail of water which had been carried in from outside. The two women stood there silent, above them the footsteps of the men who were looking for evidence against the woman who had worked in that kitchen. That look of seeing into things, of seeing through a thing to something else, was in the eyes of the sheriff's wife now. When Mrs. Hale next spoke to her, it was gently:

"Better loosen up your things, Mrs. Peters. We'll not feel them when we go out."

Mrs. Peters went to the back of the room to hang up the fur tippet she was wearing. A moment later she exclaimed, "Why, she was piecing a quilt," and held up a large sewing basket piled high with quilt pieces.

Mrs. Hale spread some of the blocks on the table.

"It's log-cabin pattern," she said, putting several of them together, "Pretty, isn't it?"

They were so engaged with the quilt that they did not hear the footsteps on the stairs. Just as the stair door opened Mrs. Hale was saying:

"Do you suppose she was going to quilt it or just knot it?"

The sheriff threw up his hands.

"They wonder whether she was going to quilt it or just knot it!"

There was a laugh for the ways of women, a warming of hands over the stove, and then the county attorney said briskly:

"Well, let's go right out to the barn and get that cleared up."

"I don't see as there's anything so strange," Mrs. Hale said resentfully, after the outside door had closed on the three men—"our taking up our time with little things while we're waiting for them to get the evidence. I don't see as it's anything to laugh about."

"Of course they've got awful important things on their minds," said the sheriff's wife apologetically.

They returned to an inspection of the block for the quilt. Mrs. Hale was looking at the fine, even sewing, and preoccupied with thoughts of the woman who had done that sewing, when she heard the sheriff's wife say, in a queer tone:

"Why, look at this one."

She turned to take the block held out to her.

"The sewing," said Mrs. Peters, in a troubled way. "All the rest of them have been so nice and even—but—this one. Why, it looks as if she didn't know what she was about!"

Their eyes met—something flashed to life, passed between them; then, as if with an effort, they seemed to pull away from each other. A moment Mrs. Hale sat there, her hands folded over that sewing which was so unlike all the rest of the sewing. Then she had pulled a knot and drawn the threads.

"Oh, what are you doing, Mrs. Hale?" asked the sheriff's wife, startled.

"Just pulling out a stitch or two that's not sewed very good," said Mrs. Hale mildly.

"I don't think we ought to touch things," Mrs. Peters said, a little helplessly.

"I'll just finish up this end," answered Mrs. Hale, still in that mild, matter-of-fact fashion.

She threaded a needle and started to replace bad sewing with good. For a little while she sewed in silence. Then, in that thin, timid voice, she heard:

"Mrs. Hale!"

"Yes, Mrs. Peters?"

"What do you suppose she was so—nervous about?"

"Oh, *I* don't know," said Mrs. Hale, as if dismissing a thing not important enough to spend much time on. "I don't know as she was—nervous. I sew awful queer sometimes when I'm just tired."

She cut a thread, and out of the corner of her eye looked up at Mrs. Peters. The small, lean face of the sheriff's wife seemed to have tightened up. Her eyes had that look of peering into something. But next moment she moved, and said in her thin, indecisive way:

"Well, I must get those clothes wrapped. They may be through sooner than we think. I wonder where I could find a piece of paper—and string."

"In that cupboard, maybe," suggested Mrs. Hale, after a glance around.

One piece of the crazy sewing remained unripped. Mrs. Peters' back turned, Martha Hale now scrutinized that piece, compared it with the dainty, accurate sewing of the other blocks. The difference was startling. Holding this block made her feel queer, as if the distracted thoughts of the woman who had perhaps turned to it to try and quiet herself were communicating themselves to her.

Mrs. Peters' voice roused her.

"Here's a bird-cage," she said. "Did she have a bird, Mrs. Hale?"

"Why, I don't know whether she did or not." She turned to look at the cage Mrs. Peters was holding up. "I've not been here in so long." She sighed. "There was a man round last year selling canaries cheap—but I don't know as she took one. Maybe she did. She used to sing real pretty herself."

Mrs. Peters looked around the kitchen.

"Seems kind of funny to think of a bird here." She half laughed—an attempt to put up a barrier. "But she must have had one—or why would she have a cage? I wonder what happened to it."

"I suppose maybe the cat got it," suggested Mrs. Hale, resuming her sewing.

"No; she didn't have a cat. She's got that feeling some people have about cats—being afraid of them. When they brought her to our house yesterday, my cat got in the room, and she was real upset and asked me to take it out."

"My sister Bessie was like that," laughed Mrs. Hale.

The sheriff's wife did not reply. The silence made Mrs. Hale turn round. Mrs. Peters was examining the bird-cage.

"Look at this door," she said slowly. "It's broke. One hinge has been pulled apart."

Mrs. Hale came nearer.

"Looks as if someone must have been—rough with it."

Again their eyes met—startled, questioning, apprehensive. For a moment neither spoke nor stirred. Then Mrs. Hale, turning away, said brusquely:

"If they're going to find any evidence, I wish they'd be about it. I don't like this place."

"But I'm awful glad you came with me, Mrs. Hale." Mrs. Peters put the bird-cage on the table and sat down. "It would be lonesome for me—sitting here alone."

"Yes, it would, wouldn't it?" agreed Mrs. Hale, a certain determined naturalness in her voice. She had picked up the sewing, but now it dropped in her lap, and she murmured in a different voice: "But I tell you what I *do* wish, Mrs. Peters. I wish I had come over sometimes when she was here. I wish—I had."

"But of course you were awful busy, Mrs. Hale. Your house—and your children."

"I could've come," retorted Mrs. Hale shortly. "I stayed away because it weren't cheerful—and that's why I ought to have come. I"—she looked around—"I've never liked this place. Maybe because it's down in a hollow and you don't see the road. I don't know what it is, but it's a lonesome place, and always was. I wish I had come over to see Minnie Foster sometimes. I can see now—" She did not put it into words.

"Well, you mustn't reproach yourself," counseled Mrs. Peters. "Somehow, we just don't see how it is with other folks till—something comes up."

"Not having children makes less work," mused Mrs. Hale, after a silence, "but it makes a quiet house—and Wright out to work all day—and no company when he did come in. Did you know John Wright, Mrs. Peters?"

"Not to know him. I've seen him in town. They say he was a good man."

"Yes—good," conceded John Wright's neighbor grimly. "He didn't drink, and kept his word as well as most, I guess, and paid his debts. But he was a hard man, Mrs. Peters. Just to pass the time of day with him—." She stopped, shivered a little. "Like a raw wind that gets to the bone." Her eye fell upon the cage on the table before her, and she added, almost bitterly: "I should think she would've wanted a bird!"

Suddenly she leaned forward, looking intently at the cage. "But what do you s'pose went wrong with it?"

"I don't know," returned Mrs. Peters; "unless it got sick and died."

But after she said it she reached over and swung the broken door. Both women watched it as if somehow held by it.

"You didn't know—her?" Mrs. Hale asked, a gentler note in her voice.

"Not till they brought her yesterday," said the sheriff's wife.

"She—come to think of it, she was kind of like a bird herself. Real sweet and pretty, but kind of timid and—fluttery. How—she—did—change."

That held her for a long time. Finally, as if struck with a happy thought and relieved to get back to everyday things, she exclaimed:

"Tell you what, Mrs. Peters, why don't you take the quilt in with you? It might take up her mind."

"Why, I think that's a real nice idea, Mrs. Hale," agreed the sheriff's wife, as if she too were glad to come into the atmosphere of a simple kindness. "There couldn't possibly be any objection to that, could there? Now, just what will I take? I wonder if her patches are in here—and her things?"

They turned to the sewing basket.

"Here's some red," said Mrs. Hale, bringing out a roll of cloth. Underneath that was a box. "Here, maybe her scissors are in here—and her things." She held it up. "What a pretty box! I'll warrant that was something she had a long time ago—when she was a girl."

She held it in her hand a moment; then, with a little sigh, opened it.

Instantly her hand went to her nose.

"Why—!"

Mrs. Peters drew nearer—then turned away.

"There's something wrapped up in this piece of silk," faltered Mrs. Hale.

"This isn't her scissors," said Mrs. Peters, in a shrinking voice.

Her hand not steady, Mrs. Hale raised the piece of silk. "Oh, Mrs. Peters!" she cried. "It's—"

Mrs. Peters bent closer.

"It's the bird," she whispered.

"But, Mrs. Peters!" cried Mrs. Hale. "*Look* at it! Its *neck*—look at its neck! It's all—other side *to*."

She held the box away from her.

The sheriff's wife again bent closer.

"Somebody wrung its neck," said she, in a voice that was slow and deep.

And then again the eyes of the two women met—this time clung together in a look of dawning comprehension, of growing horror. Mrs. Peters looked from the dead bird to the broken door of the cage. Again their eyes met. And just then there was a sound at the outside door. Mrs. Hale slipped the box under the quilt pieces in the basket, and sank into the chair before it. Mrs. Peters stood holding to the table. The county attorney and the sheriff came in from outside.

"Well, ladies," said the county attorney, as one turning from serious things to little pleasantries, "have you decided whether she was going to quilt it or knot it?"

"We think," began the sheriff's wife in a flurried voice, "that she was going to—knot it."

He was too preoccupied to notice the change that came in her voice on that last.

"Well, that's very interesting, I'm sure," he said tolerantly. He caught sight of the bird-cage. "Has the bird flown?"

"We think the cat got it," said Mrs. Hale in a voice curiously even.

He was walking up and down, as if thinking something out.

"Is there a cat?" he asked absently.

Mrs. Hale shot a look up at the sheriff's wife.

"Well, not *now*," said Mrs. Peters. "They're superstitious, you know; they leave."

She sank into her chair.

The county attorney did not heed her. "No sign at all of anyone having come in from the outside," he said to Peters, in the manner of continuing an interrupted conversation. "Their own rope. Now let's go upstairs again and go over it, piece by piece. It would have to have been someone who knew just the—"

The stair door closed behind them and their voices were lost.

The two women sat motionless, not looking at each other, but as if peering into something and at the same time holding back. When they spoke now it was as if they were afraid of what they were saying, but as if they could not help saying it.

"She liked the bird," said Martha Hale, low and slowly. "She was going to bury it in that pretty box."

"When I was a girl," said Mrs. Peters, under her breath, "my kitten—there was a boy took a hatchet, and before my eyes—before I could get there—" She covered her face an instant. "If they hadn't held me back I would have"— she caught herself, looked upstairs where footsteps were heard, and finished weakly—"hurt him."

Then they sat without speaking or moving.

"I wonder how it would seem," Mrs. Hale at last began, as if feeling her way over strange ground—"never to have had any children around?" Her eyes made a slow sweep of the kitchen, as if seeing what that kitchen had meant through all the years. "No, Wright wouldn't like the bird," she said after that— "a thing that sang. She used to sing. He killed that too." Her voice tightened.

Mrs. Peters moved uneasily.

"Of course we don't know who killed the bird."

"I knew John Wright," was Mrs. Hale's answer.

"It was an awful thing was done in this house that night, Mrs. Hale," said the sheriff's wife. "Killing a man while he slept—slipping a thing round his neck that choked the life out of him."

Mrs. Hale's hand went out to the bird-cage.

"His neck. Choked the life out of him."

"We don't *know* who killed him," whispered Mrs. Peters wildly. "We don't *know*."

Mrs. Hale had not moved. "If there had been years and years of—nothing, then a bird to sing to you, it would be awful—still—after the bird was still."

It was as if something within her not herself had spoken, and it found in Mrs. Peters something she did not know as herself.

"I know what stillness is," she said, in a queer, monotonous voice. "When we homesteaded in Dakota, and my first baby died—after he was two years old—and me with no other then—"

Mrs. Hale stirred.

"How soon do you suppose they'll be through looking for the evidence?"

"I know what stillness is," repeated Mrs. Peters, in just that same way. Then she too pulled back. "The law has got to punish crime, Mrs. Hale," she said in her tight little way.

"I wish you'd seen Minnie Foster," was the answer, "when she wore a white dress with blue ribbons, and stood up there in the choir and sang."

The picture of that girl, the fact that she had lived neighbor to that girl for twenty years, and had let her die for lack of life, was suddenly more than she could bear.

"Oh, I *wish* I'd come over here once in a while!" she cried. "That was a crime! That was a crime! Who's going to punish that?"

"We mustn't take on," said Mrs. Peters, with a frightened look toward the stairs.

"I might 'a' *known* she needed help! I tell you, it's *queer*, Mrs. Peters. We live close together, and we live far apart. We all go through the same things—it's all just a different kind of the same thing! If it weren't—why do you and I *understand*? Why do we *know*—what we know this minute?"

She dashed her hand across her eyes. Then, seeing the jar of fruit on the table, she reached for it and choked out:

"If I was you I wouldn't *tell* her her fruit was gone! Tell her it *ain't*. Tell her it's all right—all of it. Here—take this in to prove it to her! She—she may never know whether it was broke or not."

She turned away.

Mrs. Peters reached out for the bottle of fruit as if she were glad to take it—as if touching a familiar thing, having something to do, could keep her from something else. She got up, looked about for something to wrap the fruit in, took a petticoat from the pile of clothes she had brought from the front room, and nervously started winding that round the bottle.

"My!" she began, in a high, false voice, "it's a good thing the men couldn't hear us! Getting all stirred up over a little thing like a—dead canary." She hurried over that. "As if that could have anything to do with—with—My, wouldn't they *laugh*?"

Footsteps were heard on the stairs.

"Maybe they would," muttered Mrs. Hale—"maybe they wouldn't."

"No, Peters," said the county attorney incisively; "it's all perfectly clear, except the reason for doing it. But you know juries when it comes to women. If there was some definite thing—something to show. Something to make a story about. A thing that would connect up with this clumsy way of doing it."

In a covert way Mrs. Hale looked at Mrs. Peters. Mrs. Peters was looking at her. Quickly they looked away from each other. The outer door opened and Mr. Hale came in.

"I've got the team round now," he said. "Pretty cold out there."

"I'm going to stay here awhile by myself," the county attorney suddenly announced. "You can send Frank out for me, can't you?" he asked the sheriff. "I want to go over everything. I'm not satisfied we can't do better."

Again, for one brief moment, the two women's eyes found one another.

The sheriff came up to the table.

"Did you want to see what Mrs. Peters was going to take in?"

The county attorney picked up the apron. He laughed.

"Oh, I guess they're not very dangerous things the ladies have picked out."

Mrs. Hale's hand was on the sewing basket in which the box was concealed. She felt that she ought to take her hand off the basket. She did not seem able to. He picked up one of the quilt blocks which she had piled on to cover the box. Her eyes felt like fire. She had a feeling that if he took up the basket she would snatch it from him.

But he did not take it up. With another little laugh, he turned away, saying:

"No; Mrs. Peters doesn't need supervising. For that matter, a sheriff's wife is married to the law. Ever think of it that way, Mrs. Peters?"

Mrs. Peters was standing beside the table. Mrs. Hale shot a look up at her; but she could not see her face. Mrs. Peters had turned away. When she spoke, her voice was muffled.

"Not—just that way," she said.

"Married to the law!" chuckled Mrs. Peters' husband. He moved toward the door into the front room, and said to the county attorney:

"I just want you to come in here a minute, George. We ought to take a look at these windows."

"Oh—windows," said the county attorney scoffingly.

"We'll be right out, Mr. Hale," said the sheriff to the farmer, who was still waiting by the door.

Hale went to look after the horses. The sheriff followed the county attorney into the other room. Again—for one final moment—the two women were alone in that kitchen.

Martha Hale sprang up, her hands tight together, looking at that other woman, with whom it rested. At first she could not see her eyes, for the sheriff's wife had not turned back since she turned away at that suggestion of being married to the law. But now Mrs. Hale made her turn back. Her eyes made her turn back. Slowly, unwillingly, Mrs. Peters turned her head until her eyes met the eyes of the other woman. There was a moment when they held each other in a steady, burning look in which there was no evasion or flinching. Then Martha Hale's eyes pointed the way to the basket in which was hidden the thing that would make certain the conviction of the other woman—that woman who was not there and yet who had been there with them all through that hour.

For a moment Mrs. Peters did not move. And then she did it. With a rush forward, she threw back the quilt pieces, got the box, tried to put it in her handbag. It was too big. Desperately she opened it, started to take the bird out. But there she broke—she could not touch the bird. She stood there helpless, foolish.

There was the sound of a knob turning in the inner door. Martha Hale snatched the box from the sheriff's wife, and got it in the pocket of her big coat just as the sheriff and the county attorney came back into the kitchen.

"Well, Henry," said the county attorney facetiously, "at least we found out that she was not going to quilt it. She was going to—what is it you call it, ladies?"

Mrs. Hale's hand was against the pocket of her coat.

"We call it—knot it, Mr. Henderson."

Courage and Self-Sacrifice:
Toward Country and Its Ideals

On Roy Benavidez

from Why Courage Matters

JOHN MCCAIN (WITH MARK SALTER)

A well-ordered community under the rule of law sometimes finds itself under threat from external enemies or confronts dangers to its vital interests abroad. Under these circumstances, the virtues of peacetime are not enough. What is needed is the willingness to risk life and limb for the sake of the community, its interests, and its ideals. What is required, in a word, is courage. In the actual circumstances of battle, however, the display of courage does not clearly fit this abstract account of why people do brave things. The present selection, excerpted from a collection of profiles in courage by Senator John McCain (born 1936), offers the remarkable example of Roy Benavidez (aka Raul Perez Benavidez, 1935–1998), partly to illuminate his heroism, partly to display the mystery of what made it possible. How do you understand his heroism? How might it be related to the rest of his life, before and after? McCain claims that Benavidez's heroism and courage can offer instruction for our own lives. Do you agree? If so, why and how?

"A kind of madness" is how a friend of mine, a Marine Corps veteran of the Vietnam War, described the courage displayed by men whose battlefield heroics had earned them the Medal of Honor. "It's impossible to comprehend, really, even if you witness it. . . . It's one mad moment. You never think anyone you know is really capable of it. Not even the toughest, bravest, best men in the company. They're as surprised as anyone to see it. And if someone does do it, and lives, they probably never do it again. You might think the guy who's always running around in a fight, exposing himself to enemy fire, yelling a lot, might do it. But that's not what happens. They just get killed usually."

Select at random a dozen Medal of Honor recipients and read the citations that accompany their decorations. Some will describe a single lonely act of heroism, one man's self-sacrifice that saved the lives of his comrades, who will remember the act for the rest of their lives with feelings of gratitude and lasting obligation mixed with something that feels much like shame—shame that one's life, no matter how good and useful, no matter how honorable, might not deserve to have been ransomed at such a cost. All the citations will record acts of great heroism, of course. But some might seem plausible, if just barely so. The reader might even fantasize himself capable of such heroism, under extreme circumstances, without feeling too ashamed of the presumption. Maybe you are. At least one, however, will tell of such incredible daring, such epic courage, that no witness to it could imagine himself, or anyone he knows, capable of it. It might be the story of Roy Benavidez.

Special Forces master sergeant Roy Benavidez was the son of a Texas sharecropper. Orphaned at a young age, quiet and mistaken as slow, derided as a "dumb Mexican" by his classmates, he left school in the eighth grade to work in the cotton fields. He joined the army at nineteen. On his first tour in Vietnam, in 1964, he stepped on a land mine. Army doctors thought the wound would be permanently crippling. It wasn't. He recovered and became a Green Beret.

During his second combat tour, in the early morning of May 2, 1968, in Loc Ninh, Vietnam, Sergeant Benavidez monitored by radio a twelve-man reconnaissance patrol. Three Green Berets, friends of his, and nine Montagnard tribesmen had been dropped in the dense jungle west of Loc Ninh, just inside Cambodia. No man aboard the low-flying helicopters beating noisily toward the landing zone that morning could have been unaware of how dangerous the assignment was. Considered an enemy sanctuary, the area was known to be vigilantly patrolled by a sizable force of the North Vietnamese army intent on keeping it so. Once on the ground, the twelve men were almost immediately engaged by the enemy and soon surrounded by a force that grew to a battalion.

The mission had been a mistake, and three helicopters were ordered to evacuate the besieged patrol. Fierce small arms and antiaircraft fire, wounding several crew members, forced the helicopters to return to base. Listening on the radio, Benavidez heard one of his friends scream, "Get us out of here!" and, "So much shooting it sounded like a popcorn machine." He jumped into one of the returning helicopters, volunteering for a second evacuation attempt. When he arrived at the scene, he found that none of the patrol had made it to the landing zone. Four were already dead, including the team leader, and the other eight were wounded and unable to move. Carrying a knife and a medic bag, Benavidez made the sign of the cross, leapt from the helicopter hovering ten feet off the ground, and ran seventy yards to his injured comrades. Before he reached them, he was shot in the leg, face, and head. He got up and kept moving.

When he reached their position, he armed himself with an enemy rifle, began to treat the wounded, reposition them, distribute ammunition, and call in air strikes. He threw smoke grenades to indicate their location and ordered the helicopter pilot to come in close to pick up the wounded. He dragged four of the wounded aboard, and then, while under intense fire and returning fire with his captured weapon, he ran alongside the helicopter as it flew just a few feet off the ground toward the others. He got the rest of the wounded aboard, as well as the dead, except for the fallen team leader. As he raced to retrieve his body, and the classified documents the dead man had carried, he was shot in the stomach and grenade fragments cut into his back.

Before he could make his way back toward the helicopter, the pilot was fatally wounded and the aircraft crashed upside down. He helped the wounded escape the burning wreckage and organized them in a defensive perimeter. He called for air strikes and fire from circling gunships to suppress the ever increasing enemy fire enough to allow another evacuation attempt. Critically wounded, Benavidez moved constantly along the perimeter, bringing water and ammunition to the defenders, treating their wounds, encouraging them to hold on. He sustained several more gunshot wounds, but he continued to fight. For six hours.

When another extraction helicopter landed, he helped the wounded toward it, one and two at a time. On his second trip, an enemy soldier ran up behind him and struck him with his rifle butt. Sergeant Benavidez turned to close with the man and his bayonet and fought him, hand to hand, to the death. Wounded again, he recovered the rest of his comrades. As the last were lifted onto the helicopter, he exchanged more gunfire with the enemy, killing two more Vietnamese soldiers, and then ran back to collect the classified documents before at last climbing aboard and collapsing, apparently dead.

The army doctor back at Loc Ninh thought him dead anyway. Bleeding profusely, his intestines spilling from his stomach wounds, completely immobile, and unable to speak, Benavidez was placed into a body bag. As the doctor began to pull up the black shroud's zipper, Roy Benavidez spit in his face. They flew him to Saigon for surgery, where he began a year in hospitals recovering from seven serious gunshot wounds, twenty-eight shrapnel wounds, and bayonet wounds in both arms.

Hard to believe, isn't it, what this one man did? And why? Because his buddies called out to him? Because the training just took over? Because it was automatic, he was in the moment, aware of what was required of him but senseless to the probable futility of his efforts? These are the sort of explanations you usually hear from someone who has distinguished himself in battle. They really don't help us understand. They mean something, but as an explanation for that kind of heroism, they are as unenlightening to me as haiku poetry. What kind of training prepares you to do that? What kind of unit solidarity, how great the love and trust for the man to your right and your left, inspires you to the superhuman heroics of Roy Benavidez?

I'll be damned if I know. I was trained to be an aviator, not a Special Forces commando. But how does anyone—Green Beret, navy SEAL, whatever—learn to be that brave? How do you build that kind of courage in someone? It certainly appears to be superhuman and incomprehensible to those with a more human-size supply, brave and resourceful though they may be. I can't explain it. No one I know can.

We are taught to understand, correctly, that courage is not the absence of fear, but the capacity for action despite our fears. Does anyone have that great a store of courage that he would think himself capable of meaningful action with the eruption of fear that any one of us would have felt rise in our throats and burn our hearts were we to find ourselves in the hopeless situation of Roy Benavidez? I wouldn't. I don't know anyone who would, and I've known some very brave men. I doubt very much Roy Benavidez thought he would. I would challenge the sanity of any reader who imagines the possibility of possessing such mastery over fear. It's not to be expected in anyone. No courage could contend with such fear, and animate our limbs, and control our minds. Fear would have to be vanquished completely.

Roy Benavidez jumped off the helicopter, acutely aware of the situation, perhaps, of the enemy's strength, of their location, of the circumstances of his comrades, of what needed to be done, but somehow insensate to the hopelessness of it all, to the gravity of his wounds, to the futility of fighting on. What pushed him? A tsunami of adrenaline? What carried him through? A sublime fatalism, driven by love or sense of duty to resign himself completely to the situation, whatever its horrors, and make his last hour his greatest? We can't know. All we can know is that in one moment of madness, six hours long, Roy Benavidez became to the men he saved, and maybe to himself, an avenging angel of God, masterful, indomitable, and utterly fearless.

If we can't comprehend his heroism or imagine possessing his courage, can it offer our own lives any instruction? I believe it can. Roy's life won't teach us how to save eight men while sustaining several dozen wounds. An act of heroism, of extraordinary courage, the grandeur of it, won't easily inspire us to act in imitation, but it can inspire us to emulate its author. For that, we should learn what we can of the whole experience of the subject, the hero's life, as it was before and after, and believe that trying to emulate the character it reveals is one tried way to prepare for the tests that might await us and gain hope that our courage will not be wanting in the moment.

We must accept the fact that some heroes, whether their courage was momentary or constant, might have led less than admirable lives. I don't think, however extraordinary the courage, that it will attain the grandeur of the inspirational to a sound mind were it motivated by selfish or malevolent purposes, or exercised by someone whose life, on the whole, was contemptible. Unless, of course, an act of heroism was an anomaly in the life that preceded it and character changing thereafter. The stories cherished most by all sinners whose consciences are not permanently mute concern the life-redeeming act of courage. They're not, however, as abundant in real life as they are in fiction. Better to look to the lives of good men and women who in a crucible risked or sacrificed their own security for someone else.

What do we know of Roy Benavidez's life before and after that moment of madness? We know that he was a good man. The straitened circumstances of his youth did not embitter him or lead him astray. The constant, lifelong pain of his wounds didn't undo him. His valor was not properly recognized for thirteen years. In 1981, Ronald Reagan—who said of his heroism that were it a movie script "you wouldn't believe it"—replaced the Distinguished Service Cross that General William Westmoreland had given Roy in 1968 with the Medal of Honor. The delay didn't seem to bother Roy. "I don't like to be called a hero," he complained, and then, in the familiar refrain of veterans from all wars, he offered the observation, "The real heroes are the ones who gave their lives for their country." That kind of humility from surviving veterans who distinguished themselves in combat is so commonplace that we've come to expect it from them. We don't take it seriously. We even suspect that it's false. We don't see how remarkable it is. They mean it. Every word.

Roy stayed in the army until he retired in 1976. Then he lived on his pension and disability pay and spent his time speaking at schools and to youth groups, counseling troubled kids, encouraging them to stay in school and off drugs. In 1998, on his deathbed, with two pieces of shrapnel still in his heart, he proclaimed: "I'm proud to be an American."

The navy named a ship after him and the army a building. His hometown erected a statue. But Hollywood never made a movie about him. No one would have believed it.

Letter to Sarah

Sullivan Ballou

Examples of courage in the face of mortal danger and examples of willing self-sacrifice in the service of country are the subject of story, song, and legend. But rarely do we have a more moving and self-conscious account than the one presented in this letter by Major Sullivan Ballou (1829–1861) of the Second Rhode Island regiment of the Union army to his wife, Sarah, early in the Civil War.

How does Ballou understand and explain the choice he faces? Why does he choose as he does? Imagining yourself as the recipient of this letter, how would you receive and judge his choice?

July 14, 1861
Camp Clark, Washington

My very dear Sarah:

The indications are very strong that we shall move in a few days—perhaps tomorrow. Lest I should not be able to write again I feel impelled to write a few lines that may fall under your eye when I shall be no more. . . .

Our movement may be one of a few days duration and full of pleasure— and it may be one of severe conflict and death to me. "Not by my will, but Thine O God be done." If it is necessary that I should fall on the battlefield for my country, I am ready. I have no misgivings about, or lack of confidence in the cause in which I am engaged, and my courage does not halt or falter. I know how strongly American Civilization now leans on the triumph of the government, and how great a debt we owe to those who went before us through the blood and sufferings of the Revolution. And I am willing—perfectly willing—

to lay down all my joys in this life, to help maintain this Government, and to pay that debt. . . .

But, my dear wife, when I know that with my own joys I lay down nearly all of yours, and replace them in this life with cares and sorrows—when, after having eaten for long years the bitter fruit of orphanage myself, I must offer it as their only sustenance to my dear little children—is it weak or dishonorable, while the banner of my purpose floats calmly and proudly in the breeze that my unbounded love of you, my darling wife and children, should struggle in fierce, though useless, contest with my love of Country?

I cannot describe to you my feelings on this calm summer night, when two thousand men are sleeping around me, many of them enjoying the last, perhaps before that of death—and I, suspicious that Death is creeping behind me with his fatal dart, am communing with God, my Country, and thee.

I have sought most closely and diligently, and often in my breast, for a wrong motive in thus hazarding the happiness of those I loved and could not find one. A pure love of my Country and the principles I have often advocated before the people, and "the name of honor that I love more than I fear death" have called upon me, and I have obeyed.

Sarah, my love for you is deathless, it seems to bind me with mighty cables that nothing but Omnipotence could break; and yet my love of Country comes over me like a strong wind and bears me unresistably on with all these chains to the battle field.

The memories of the blissful moments I have spent with you come creeping over me, and I feel most gratified to God and to you that I have enjoyed them so long. And hard it is for me to give them up and burn to ashes the hopes of future years, when, God willing, we might still have lived and loved together, and seen our sons grown up to honorable manhood, around us. I have, I know, but few and small claims upon Divine Providence, but something whispers to me—perhaps it is the wafted prayer of my little Edgar—that I shall return to my loved ones unharmed. If I do not, my dear Sarah, never forget how much I love you, and when my last breath escapes me on the battlefield, it will whisper your name. Forgive my many faults, and the many pains I have caused you. How thoughtless and foolish I have often times been! How gladly would I wash out with my tears every little spot upon your happiness . . . and struggle with all the misfortunes of this world to shield you and my dear children from harm. But I cannot. I must watch you from the spirit land and hover near you, while you buffet the storms with your precious little freight, and wait with sad patience till we meet to part no more.

But, O Sarah! if the dead can come back to this earth and flit unseen around those they loved, I shall always be near you, in the gladdest days and in the darkest nights . . . always, always, and if there be a soft breeze upon your cheek, it shall be my breath, as the cool air fans your throbbing temple, it shall be my spirit passing by. Sarah, do not mourn me dead; think I am gone and wait for thee, for we shall meet again. . . .

As for my little boys, they will grow up as I have done, and never know a father's love and care. Little Willie is too young to remember me long, and my blue-eyed Edgar will keep my frolics with him among the dimmest memories of his childhood. Sarah, I have unlimited confidence in your maternal care and your development of their characters and feel that God will bless you in your holy work.

Tell my two mothers I call God's blessing upon them.

O Sarah, I wait for you there. Come to me, and lead thither my children.

Sullivan Ballou was killed a week later at the First Battle of Bull Run.

Chamberlain

from The Killer Angels

Michael Shaara

The two previous selections, one more recent, one older, offer historical pre-sentations of courage and the readiness to risk one's life for one's country. But courage is a virtue difficult to cultivate, especially among self-interested citi-zens oriented toward the pursuit of their own happiness. At the extreme, why shouldn't I prefer the preservation of myself to the preservation of my nation? If there is both a natural and cultural tendency to cowardice, how is cour-age to be cultivated? Although courage usually grows only through repeated acts in the face of fear and danger, inspiring speeches can rally groups of men on the eve of battle. The next two selections—the first excerpted from The Killer Angels *by Michael Shaara (1928–1988), an account of the Battle of Gettysburg during the Civil War, and the second from World War II— exemplify two such inspiriting speeches, in some ways similar, in some ways very different.*

Colonel Joshua Lawrence Chamberlain, before the war a professor of rhetoric at Bowdoin College, is faced with the unexpected burden of guard-ing 120 mutinous soldiers, eager to return home after two years in the Union army. Summoned to march toward battle and lacking men to guard these prisoners, Chamberlain appeals to them to join his regiment, succeeding beyond his wildest expectations. What are the various aspects of Chamber-lain's appeal? How and why do his words—and his deeds—succeed with these previously recalcitrant men? Imagine yourself among the mutineers: would you have been moved to join the fight, and why?

He dreamed of Maine and ice black water; he awoke to a murderous sun. A voice calling: "Colonel, darlin'." He squinted: the whiskery face of Buster Kilrain.

"Colonel, darlin', I hate to be a-wakin' ye, but there's a message here ye ought to be seein'."

Chamberlain had slept on the ground; he rolled to a sitting position. Light boiled in through the tent flap. Chamberlain closed his eyes.

"And how are ye feelin' this mornin', Colonel, me lad?"

Chamberlain ran his tongue around his mouth. He said briefly, dryly, "Ak."

"We're about to be havin' guests, sir, or I wouldn't be wakin' ye."

Chamberlain looked up through bleary eyes. He had walked eighty miles in four days through the hottest weather he had ever known and he had gone down with sunstroke. He felt eerie fragility, like a piece of thin glass in a high hot wind. He saw a wooden canteen, held in the big hand of Kilrain, cold drops of water on varnished sides. He drank. The world focused.

". . . one hundred and twenty men," Kilrain said.

Chamberlain peered at him.

"They should be arriving any moment," Kilrain said. He was squatting easily, comfortably, in the opening of the tent, the light flaming behind him.

"Who?" Chamberlain said.

"They are sending us some mutineers," Kilrain said with fatherly patience. "One hundred and twenty men from the old Second Maine, which has been disbanded."

"Mutineers?"

"Ay. What happened was that the enlistment of the old Second ran out and they were all sent home except one hundred and twenty, which had foolishly signed *three*-year papers, and so they all had one year to go, only *they* all thought they was signing to fight with the Second, and Second only, and so they mutinied. One hundred and twenty. Are you all right, Colonel?"

Chamberlain nodded vaguely.

"Well, these poor fellers did not want to fight no more, naturally, being Maine men of a certain intelligence, and refused, only nobody will send them home, and nobody knew what to do with them, until they thought of *us*, being as we are the other Maine regiment here in the army. There's a message here signed by Meade himself. That's the new General we got now, sir, if you can keep track as they go by. The message says they'll be sent here this morning and they are to fight, and if they don't fight you can feel free to shoot them."

"Shoot?"

"Ay."

"Let me see." Chamberlain read painfully. His head felt very strange indeed, but he was coming awake into the morning as from a long way away and he could begin to hear the bugles out across the fields. Late to get moving today. Thank God. Somebody gave us an extra hour. Bless him. He read:

. . . you are therefore authorized to shoot any man who refuses to do his duty. Shoot?

He said, "These are all *Maine* men?"

"Yes, sir. Fine big fellers. I've seen them. Loggin' men. You may remember there was a bit of a brawl some months back, during the mud march? These fellers were famous for their fists."

Chamberlain said, "One hundred and twenty."

"Yes, sir."

"Somebody's crazy."

"Yes, sir."

"How many men do we now have in this Regiment?"

"Ah, somewhat less than two hundred and fifty, sir, as of yesterday. Countin' the officers."

"How do I take care of a hundred and twenty mutinous men?"

"Yes, sir," Kilrain sympathized. "Well, you'll have to talk to them, sir."

Chamberlain sat for a long moment silently trying to function. He was thirty-four years old, and on this day one year ago he had been a professor of rhetoric at Bowdoin College. He had no idea what to do. But it was time to go out into the sun. He crawled forward through the tent flap and stood up, blinking, swaying, one hand against the bole of a tree. He was a tall man, somewhat picturesque. He wore stolen blue cavalry trousers and a three-foot sword, and the clothes he wore he had not taken off for a week. He had a grave, boyish dignity, that clean-eyed, scrubbed-brain, naïve look of the happy professor.

Kilrain, a white-haired man with the build of an ape, looked up at him with fatherly joy. "If ye'll ride the *horse* today, Colonel, which the Lord hath provided, instead of walkin' in the dust with the others fools, ye'll be all right—if ye wear the hat. It's the *walkin'*, do you see, that does the great harm."

"*You* walked," Chamberlain said grumpily, thinking: shoot them? *Maine* men? How can I shoot Maine men? I'll never be able to go home.

"Ah, but, Colonel, darlin', I've been in the infantry since before you was born. It's them first few thousand miles. After that, a man gets a limber to his feet."

"Hey, Lawrence. How you doin'?"

Younger brother, Tom Chamberlain, bright-faced, high-voiced, a new lieutenant, worshipful. The heat had not seemed to touch him. Chamberlain nodded. Tom said critically, "You lookin' kinda peaked. Why don't you ride the horse?"

Chamberlain gloomed. But the day was not as bright as it had seemed through the opening of the tent. He looked upward with relief toward a darkening sky. The troops were moving in the fields, but there had been no order to march.

The wagons were not yet loaded. He thought: God bless the delay. His mind was beginning to function. All down the road and all through the trees the troops were moving, cooking, the thousands of troops and thousands of wagons of the Fifth Corps, Army of the Potomac, of which Chamberlain's Twentieth Maine was a minor fragment. But far down the road there was motion.

Kilrain said, "There they come."

Chamberlain squinted. Then he saw troops on the road, a long way off.

The line of men came slowly up the road. There were guards with fixed bayonets. Chamberlain could see the men shuffling, strange pathetic spectacle, dusty, dirty, ragged men, heads down, faces down: it reminded him of a history-book picture of impressed seamen in the last war with England. But these men would have to march all day, in the heat. Chamberlain thought: not possible.

Tom was meditating. "Gosh, Lawrence. There's almost as many men there as we got in the whole regiment. How we going to guard them?"

Chamberlain said nothing. He was thinking: How do you force a man to fight—for freedom? The idiocy of it jarred him. Think on it later. Must do something now.

There was an officer, a captain, at the head of the column. The Captain turned them in off the road and herded them into an open space in the field near the Regimental flag. The men of the Regiment, busy with coffee, stood up to watch. The Captain had a loud voice and used obscene words. He assembled the men in two long ragged lines and called them to attention, but they ignored him. One slumped to the ground, more exhaustion than mutiny. A guard came forward and yelled and probed with a bayonet, but abruptly several more men sat down and then they all did, and the Captain began yelling, but the guards stood grinning confusedly, foolishly, having gone as far as they would go, unwilling to push further unless the men here showed some threat, and the men seemed beyond threat, merely enormously weary. Chamberlain took it all in as he moved toward the Captain. He put his hands behind his back and came forward slowly, studiously. The Captain pulled off dirty gloves and shook his head with contempt, glowering up at Chamberlain.

"Looking for the commanding officer, Twentieth Maine."

"You've found him," Chamberlain said.

"That's him all right." Tom's voice, behind him, very proud. Chamberlain suppressed a smile.

"You Chamberlain?" The Captain stared at him grimly, insolently, showing what he thought of Maine men.

Chamberlain did not answer for a long moment, looking into the man's eyes until the eyes suddenly blinked and dropped, and then Chamberlain said softly, "*Colonel* Chamberlain to you."

The Captain stood still for a moment, then slowly came to attention, slowly saluted. Chamberlain did not return it. He looked past the Captain at the men, most of whom had their heads down. But there were eyes on him. He looked back and forth down the line, looking for a familiar face. That would help. But there was no one he knew.

"Captain Brewer, sir. Ah. One-eighteen Pennsylvania." The Captain tugged in his coat front, produced a sheaf of papers. "If you're the commanding officer, sir, then I present you with these here prisoners." He handed the papers. Chamberlain took them, glanced down, handed them back to Tom. The Captain said, "You're welcome to 'em, God knows. Had to use the bayonet to get 'em moving. You got to sign for 'em, Colonel."

Chamberlain said over his shoulder, "Sign it, Tom." To the Captain he said, "You're relieved, Captain."

The Captain nodded, pulling on the dirty gloves. "You're authorized to use whatever force necessary, Colonel." He said that loudly, for effect. "If you have to shoot 'em, why, you go right ahead. Won't nobody say nothin'."

"You're relieved, Captain," Chamberlain said. He walked past the Captain, closer to the men, who did not move, who did not seem to notice him. One of the guards stiffened as Chamberlain approached, looked past him to his captain. Chamberlain said, "You men can leave now. We don't need any guards."

He stood in front of the men, ignoring the guards. They began to move off. Chamberlain stood for a moment looking down. Some of the faces turned up. There was hunger and exhaustion and occasional hatred. Chamberlain said, "My name is Chamberlain. I'm Colonel, Twentieth Maine."

Some of them did not even raise their heads. He waited another moment. Then he said, "When did you eat last?"

More heads came up. There was no answer. Then a man in the front row said huskily, in a whiskey voice, "We're hungry, Colonel."

Another man said, "They been tryin' to break us by not feedin' us." Chamberlain looked: a scarred man, hatless, hair plastered thinly on the scalp like strands of black seaweed. The man said, "We ain't broke yet."

Chamberlain nodded. A hard case. But we'll begin with food. He said, "They just told us you were coming a little while ago. I've told the cook to butcher a steer. Hope you like it near to raw; not much time to cook." Eyes opened wide. He could begin to see the hunger on the faces, like the yellow shine of sickness. He said, "We've got a ways to go today and you'll be coming with us, so you better eat hearty. We're all set for you back in the trees." He saw Glazier Estabrook standing huge-armed and peaceful in the shade of a nearby tree. "Glazier," Chamberlain said, "you show these men where to go. You fellas eat up and then I'll come over and hear what you have to say."

No man moved. Chamberlain turned away. He did not know what he would do if they did not choose to move. He heard a voice: "Colonel?"

He turned. The scarred man was standing.

"Colonel, we got grievances. The men elected me to talk for 'em."

"Right." Chamberlain nodded. "You come on with me and talk. The rest of you fellas go eat." He beckoned to the scarred man and waved to Glazier Estabrook. He turned again, not waiting for the men to move off, not sure they would go, began to walk purposefully toward the blessed dark, wondering again how big a guard detail it would take, thinking he might wind up with more men out of action than in, and also: what are you going to say? Good big boys they are. Seen their share of action.

"Gosh, Lawrence," Tom Chamberlain said.

"Smile," Chamberlain said cheerily, "and don't call me Lawrence. Are they moving?" He stopped and glanced pleasantly backward, saw with delight that the men were up and moving toward the trees, toward food. He grinned, plucked a book from his jacket, handed it to Tom.

"Here. This is Casey's *Manual of Infantry Tactics*. You study it, maybe someday you'll make a soldier." He smiled at the scarred man, extended a hand. "What's your name?"

The man stopped, looked at him for a long cold second. The hand seemed to come up against gravity, against his will. Automatic courtesy: Chamberlain was relying on it.

"I'm not usually that informal," Chamberlain said with the same light, calm, pleasant manner that he had developed when talking to particularly rebellious students who had come in with a grievance and who hadn't yet learned that the soft answer turneth away wrath. *Some* wrath. "But I suppose somebody ought to welcome you to the Regiment."

The man said, "I don't feel too kindly, Colonel."

Chamberlain nodded. He went on inside the tent, the scarred man following, and sat down on a camp stool, letting the man stand. He invited the man to have coffee, which the man declined, and then listened silently to the man's story.

The scarred man spoke calmly and coldly, looking straight into Chamberlain's eyes. A good stubborn man. There was a bit of the lawyer about him: he used chunky phrases about law and justice. But he had heavy hands with thick muscular fingers and black fingernails and there was a look of power to him, a coiled tight set to the way he stood, balanced, ugly, slightly contemptuous, but watchful, trying to gauge Chamberlain's strength.

Chamberlain said, "I see."

"I been in eleven different engagements, Colonel. How many you been in?"

"Not that many," Chamberlain said.

"I done my share. We all have. Most of us—" he gestured out the tent flap into the morning glare—"there's some of them no damn good but most of them been all the way there and back. Damn good men. Shouldn't ought to use them this way. Looky here." He pulled up a pants leg. Chamberlain saw a purple gash, white scar tissue. The man let the pants leg fall. Chamberlain said nothing. The man looked at his face, seemed suddenly embarrassed, realized he had gone too far. For the first time he was uncertain. But he repeated, "I done my share."

Chamberlain nodded. The man was relaxing slowly. It was warm in the tent; he opened his shirt. Chamberlain said, "What's your name?"

"Bucklin. Joseph Bucklin."

"Where you from?"

"Bangor."

"Don't know any Bucklins. Farmer?"

"Fishermen."

Former Sergeant Kilrain put his head in the tent. "Colonel, there's a courier comin'."

Chamberlain nodded. Bucklin said, "I'm tired, Colonel. You know what I mean? I'm tired. I've had all of this army and all of these officers, this damned Hooker and this goddamned idiot Meade, all of them, the whole bloody lousy rotten mess of sick-brained pot-bellied scabheads that ain't fit to lead a johnny detail, ain't fit to pour pee outen a boot with instructions on the heel. I'm tired. We are good men and we had our own good flag and these goddamned idiots use us like we was cows or dogs or even worse. We ain't gonna win this war. We can't win no how because of these lame-brained bastards from West Point, these goddamned gentlemen, these *officers*. Only one officer knew what he was doin: McClellan, and look what happened to *him*. I just as soon go home and let them damn Johnnies go home and the hell with it."

He let it go, out of breath. He had obviously been waiting to say that to some officer for a long time. Chamberlain said, "I get your point."

Kilrain announced, "Courier, sir."

Chamberlain rose, excused himself, stepped out into the sunlight. A bright-cheeked lieutenant, just dismounted, saluted him briskly.

"Colonel Chamberlain, sir, Colonel Vincent wishes to inform you that the corps is moving out at once and that you are instructed to take the advance. The Twentieth Maine has been assigned to the first position in line. You will send out flankers and advance guards."

"My compliments to the Colonel." Chamberlain saluted, turned to Kilrain and Ellis Spear, who had come up. "You heard him, boys. Get the Regiment up. Sound the *General*, strike the tents." Back inside the tent, he said cheerfully to Bucklin, "We're moving out. You better hurry up your eating. Tell your men I'll be over in a minute. I'll think on what you said."

Bucklin slipped by him, went away. Chamberlain thought: we're first in line.

"Kilrain."

The former sergeant was back.

"Sir."

"Where we headed?"

"West, sir. Pennsylvania somewhere. That's all I know."

"Listen, Buster. You're a private now and I'm not supposed to keep you at headquarters in that rank. If you want to go on back to the ranks, you just say so, because I feel obligated—well, you don't have to be here, but listen, I need you."

"Then I'll be stayin', Colonel, laddie." Kilrain grinned.

"But you know I can't promote you. Not after that episode with the bottle. Did you have to pick an officer?"

Kilrain grinned. "I was not aware of rank, sir, at the time. And he was the target which happened to present itself."

"Buster, you haven't got a bottle about?"

"Is the Colonel in need of a drink, sir?"

"I meant . . . forget it. All right, Buster, move 'em out."

Kilrain saluted, grinning, and withdrew. The only professional in the regiment. The drinking would kill him. Well. He would die happy. Now. What do I say to *them*?

Tom came in, saluted.

"The men from the Second Maine are being fed, sir."

"Don't call me sir."

"Well, Lawrence, Great God A-Mighty—"

"You just be careful of the name business in front of the men. Listen, we don't want anybody to think there's favoritism."

Tom put on the wounded look, face of the ruptured deer. "General Meade has his *son* as his adjutant."

"That's different. Generals can do anything. Nothing quite so much like God on earth as a general on a battlefield." The tent was coming down about his head; he stepped outside to avoid the collapse. The General and God was a nice parallel. They have your future in their hands and they have all power and know all. He grinned, thinking of Meade surrounded by his angelic staff: Dan Butterfield, wild Dan Sickles. But *what do I say?*

"Lawrence, what you goin' to do?"

Chamberlain shook his head. The regiment was up and moving.

"God, you can't shoot them. You do that, you'll never go back to Maine when the war's over."

"I know that." Chamberlain meditated. "Wonder if *they* do?"

He heard a flare of bugles, looked down the road toward Union Mills. The next regiment, the Eighty-Third Pennsylvania, was up and forming. He saw wagons and ambulances moving out into the road. He could feel again the yellow heat. Must remember to cover up. More susceptible to sunstroke now. Can't afford a foggy head. He began to walk slowly toward the grove of trees.

Kilrain says tell the truth.

Which is?

Fight. Or we'll shoot you.

Not true. I won't shoot anybody.

He walked slowly out into the sunlight. He thought: but the truth is much more than that. Truth is too personal. Don't know if I can express it. He paused in the heat. Strange thing. You would die for it without further question, but you had a hard time talking about it. He shook his head. I'll wave no more flags for home. No tears for Mother. Nobody ever died for apple pie.

He walked slowly toward the dark grove. He had a complicated brain and there were things going on back there from time to time that he only dimly understood, so he relied on his instincts, but he was learning all the time. The faith itself was simple: he believed in the dignity of man. His ancestors were Huguenots, refugees of a chained and bloody Europe. He had learned their stories in the cradle. He had grown up believing in America and the individual and it was a stronger faith than his faith in God. This was the land where no man had to bow. In this place at last a man could stand up free of the past, free of tradition and blood ties and the curse of royalty and become what he wished to become. This was the first place on earth where the man mattered more than the state. True freedom had begun here and it would spread eventually over all the earth. But it had begun *here*. The fact of slavery upon this incredibly beautiful new clean earth was appalling, but more even than that was the horror of old Europe, the curse of nobility, which the South was transplanting to new soil. They were forming a new aristocracy, a new breed of glittering men, and Chamberlain had come to crush it. But he was fighting for the dignity of man and in that way he was fighting for himself. If men were equal in America, all these former Poles and English and Czechs and blacks, then they were equal everywhere, and there was really no such thing as a foreigner; there were only free men and slaves. And so it was not even patriotism but a new faith. The Frenchman may fight for France, but the American fights for mankind, for freedom; for the people, not the land.

Yet the words had been used too often and the fragments that came to Chamberlain now were weak. A man who has been shot at is a new realist, and what do you say to a realist when the war is a war of ideals? He thought finally. Well, I owe them the truth at least. Might's well begin with that.

The Regiment had begun to form. Chamberlain thought: At least it'll be a short speech. He walked slowly toward the prisoners.

Glazier Estabrook was standing guard, leaning patiently on his rifle. He was a thick little man of about forty. Except for Kilrain he was the oldest man in the Regiment, the strongest man Chamberlain had ever seen. He waved happily as Chamberlain came up but went on leaning on the rifle. He pointed at one of the prisoners.

"Hey, Colonel, you know who this is? This here is Dan Burns from Orono. I know his daddy. Daddy's a preacher. You really ought to hear him. Best damn cusser I ever heard. Knows more fine swear words than any man in Maine, I bet. Hee."

Chamberlain smiled. But the Burns boy was looking at him with no expression. Chamberlain said, "You fellas gather round."

He stood in the shade, waited while they closed in silently, watchfully around him. In the background the tents were coming down, the wagons were hitching, but some of the men of the Regiment had come out to watch and listen. Some of the men here were still chewing. But they were quiet, attentive.

Chamberlain waited a moment longer. Now it was quiet in the grove and the clink of the wagons was sharp in the distance. Chamberlain said, "I've been talking with Bucklin. He's told me your problem."

Some of the men grumbled. Chamberlain heard no words clearly. He went on speaking softly so that they would have to quiet to hear him.

"I don't know what I can do about it. I'll do what I can. I'll look into it as soon as possible. But there's nothing I can do today. We're moving out in a few minutes and we'll be marching all day and we may be in a big fight before nightfall. But as soon as I can, I'll do what I can."

They were silent, watching him. Chamberlain began to relax. He had made many speeches and he had a gift for it. He did not know what it was, but when he spoke most men stopped to listen. Fanny said it was something in his voice. He hoped it was there now.

"I've been ordered to take you men with me. I've been told that if you don't come I can shoot you. Well, you know I won't do that. Not Maine men. I won't shoot any man who doesn't want this fight. Maybe someone else will, but I won't. So that's that."

He paused again. There was nothing on their faces to lead him.

"Here's the situation. I've been ordered to take you along, and that's what I'm going to do. Under guard if necessary. But you can have your rifles if you want them. The whole Reb army is up the road a ways waiting for us and this is no time for an argument like this. I tell you this: we sure can use you. We're down below half strength and we need you, no doubt of that. But whether you fight or not is up to you. Whether you come along, well, you're coming."

Tom had come up with Chamberlain's horse. Over the heads of the prisoners Chamberlain could see the Regiment falling into line out in the flaming road. He took a deep breath.

"Well, I don't want to preach to you. You know who we are and what we're doing here. But if you're going to fight alongside us there's a few things I want you to know."

He bowed his head, not looking at eyes. He folded his hands together.

"This Regiment was formed last fall, back in Maine. There were a thousand of us then. There's not three hundred of us now." He glanced up briefly. "But what is left is choice."

He was embarrassed. He spoke very slowly, staring at the ground.

"Some of us volunteered to fight for Union. Some came in mainly because we were bored at home and this looked like it might be fun. Some came because we were ashamed not to. Many of us came . . . because it was the right thing to do. All of us have seen men die. Most of us never saw a black man back home. We think on that, too. But freedom . . . is not just a word."

He looked up in to the sky, over silent faces.

"This is a different kind of army. If you look at history you'll see men fight for pay, or women, or some other kind of loot. They fight for land, or because a king makes them, or just because they like killing. But we're here for something new. I don't . . . this hasn't happened much in the history of the world. We're an army going out to set other men free."

He bent down, scratched the black dirt into his fingers. He was beginning to warm to it; the words were beginning to flow. No one in front of him was moving. He said, "This is free ground. All the way from here to the Pacific Ocean. No man has to bow. No man born to royalty. Here we judge you by what *you* do, not by what your father was. Here you can be *something*. Here's a place to build a home. It isn't the land—there's always more land. It's the idea that we all have value, you and me, we're worth something more than the dirt. I never saw dirt I'd die for, but I'm not asking you to come join us and fight for dirt. What we're all fighting for, in the end, is each other."

Once he started talking he broke right through the embarrassment and there was suddenly no longer a barrier there. The words came out of him in a clear river, and he felt himself silent and suspended in the grove listening to himself speak, carried outside himself and looking back down on the silent faces and himself speaking, and he felt the power in him, the power of his cause. For an instant he could see black castles in the air; he could create centuries of screaming, eons of torture. Then he was back in sunlit Pennsylvania. The bugles were blowing and he was done.

He had nothing else to say. No one moved. He felt the embarrassment return. He was suddenly enormously tired. The faces were staring up at him like white stones. Some heads were down. He said, "Didn't mean to preach. Sorry. But I thought . . . you should know who we are." He had forgotten how tiring it was just to speak. "Well, this is still the army, but you're as free as I can make you. Go ahead and talk for a while. If you want your rifles for this fight you'll have them back and nothing else will be said. If you won't join us you'll come along under guard. When this is over I'll do what I can to see that you get fair treatment. Now we have to move out." He stopped, looked at them. The faces showed nothing. He said slowly, "I think if we lose this fight the war will be over. So if you choose to come with us I'll be personally grateful. Well. We have to move out."

He turned, left silence behind him. Tom came up with the horse—a pale-gray lightfooted animal. Tom's face was shiny red.

"My Lawrence, you sure talk pretty."

Chamberlain grunted. He was really tired. Rest a moment. He paused with his hands on the saddle horn. There was a new vague doubt stirring in his brain. Something troubled him; he did not know why.

"You ride today, Lawrence. You look weary."

Chamberlain nodded. Ellis Spear was up. He was Chamberlain's ranking officer, an ex-teacher from Wiscasset who was impressed with Chamberlain's professorship. A shy man, formal, but very competent. He gestured toward the prisoners.

"Colonel, what do you suggest we do with them?"

"Give them a moment. Some of them may be willing to fight. Tom, you go back and see what they say. We'll have to march them under guard. Don't know what else to do. I'm not going to shoot them. We can't leave them here."

The Regiment had formed out in the road, the color bearers in front. Chamberlain mounted, put on the wide-brimmed hat with the emblem of the infantry, began walking his horse slowly across the field toward the road. The uneasiness still troubled him. He had missed something, he did not know what. Well, he was an instinctive man; the mind would tell him sooner or later. Perhaps it was only that when you try to put it into words you cannot express it truly, it never sounds as you dream it. But then . . . you were asking them to die.

Ellis Speer was saying, "How far are we from Pennsylvania, Colonel, you have any idea?"

"Better than twenty miles." Chamberlain squinted upward. "Going to be another hot day."

He moved to the head of the column. The troops were moving slowly, patiently, setting themselves for the long march. After a moment Tom came riding up. His face was delighted. Chamberlain said, "How many are going to join us?"

Tom grinned hugely. "Would you believe it? All but six."

"*How many?*"

"I counted, by actual count, one hundred and fourteen."

"Well." Chamberlain rubbed his nose, astounded.

Tom said, still grinning, "Brother, you did real good."

"They're all marching together?"

"Right. Glazier's got the six hardheads in tow."

"Well, get all the names and start assigning them to different companies. I don't want them bunched up, spread them out. See about their arms."

"Yes, sir, Colonel, sir."

Chamberlain reached the head of the column. The road ahead was long and straight, rising toward a ridge of trees. He turned in his saddle, looked back, saw the entire Fifth Corps forming behind him. He thought: 120 new men. Hardly noticeable in such a mass. And yet . . . he felt a moment of huge joy. He called for road guards and skirmishers and the Twentieth Maine began to move toward Gettysburg.

Speech to the Third Army

GEORGE S. PATTON JR.

This selection, taken from The Unknown Patton, *a biography by Charles M. Province, deals with the memorable speech by General George Patton (1885–1945) to the Third Army on June 5, 1944, the eve of the Allied invasion of Europe. The first part presents the background, the second the speech itself (as compiled by Province, drawing on many sources and presented as a third-person narrative). Famous for his rapport with his men, Patton was a charismatic leader and an inspirational speaker. According to Province, an Army veteran and the founder and president of the George S. Patton Jr. Historical Society, "Patton always knew exactly what he wanted to say to his soldiers and he never needed notes. . . . Instead of [using] empty, generalized rhetoric of no substance . . . Patton spoke to his men in simple, down to earth language that they understood. He told them truthful lessons he had learned that would keep them alive." He also had "a unique ability regarding profanity": when he wanted his men to remember something important, he gave it to them "double dirty." As Patton explained: "It may not sound nice to some bunch of little old ladies at an afternoon tea party, but it helps my soldiers to remember. You can't run an army without profanity; and it has to be eloquent profanity."*

The tone, manner, and content of Patton's speech are very different from that of Joshua Lawrence Chamberlain. Unlike Chamberlain, who addresses battle-weary veterans, Patton addresses men who are poised for their first battle; like Chamberlain, he knows that many of them will die in the ensuing combat. How does Patton seek to encourage the men? To what does he appeal? And how does he succeed? Imagining yourself in the audience, what would have been your reaction?

Somewhere in England
June 5th, 1944

The big camp buzzed with a tension. For hundreds of eager rookies, newly arrived from the states, it was a great day in their lives. This day marked their first taste of the "real thing." Now they were not merely puppets in brown uniforms. They were not going through the motions of soldiering with three thousand miles of ocean between them and English soil. They were actually in the heart of England itself. They were waiting for the arrival of that legendary figure, Lieutenant General George S. Patton Jr.—old "Blood and Guts" himself, about whom many a colorful chapter would be written for the schoolboys of tomorrow. Patton of the brisk, purposeful stride. Patton of the harsh, compelling voice, the lurid vocabulary, the grim and indomitable spirit that carried him and his Army to glory in Africa and Sicily. They called him "America's Fightingest General." He was no desk commando. He was the man who was sent for when the going got rough and a fighter was needed. He was the most hated and feared American of all on the part of the German Army.

Patton was coming and the stage was being set. He would address a move which might have a far reaching effect on the global war that, at the moment, was a TOP-SECRET in the files in Washington, D.C.

The men saw the camp turn out "en masse" for the first time and in full uniform, too. Today their marching was not lackadaisical. It was serious and the men felt the difference. From the lieutenants in charge of the companies on down in rank they felt the difference.

In long columns they marched down the hill from the barracks. They counted cadence while marching. They turned off to the left, up the rise and so on down into the roped off field where the General was to speak. Gold braid and stripes were everywhere. Soon, company by company, the hillside was a solid mass of brown. It was a beautiful fresh English morning. The tall trees lined the road and swayed gently in the breeze. Across the field, a British farmer calmly tilled his soil. High upon a nearby hill a group of British soldiers huddled together, waiting for the coming of the General. Military Police were everywhere wearing their white leggings, belts, and helmets. They were brisk and grim. The twittering of the birds in the trees could be heard above the dull murmur of the crowd and soft, white clouds floated lazily overhead as the men settled themselves and lit cigarettes.

On the special platform near the speakers stand, Colonels and Majors were a dime a dozen. Behind the platform stood General Patton's "Guard of Honor"; all specially chosen men. At their right was a band playing rousing marches while the crowd waited and on the platform a nervous sergeant repeatedly tested the loudspeaker. The moment grew near and the necks began to crane to view the tiny winding road that led to Stourport-on-Severn. A captain stepped to the microphone. "When the General arrives," he said sonorously, "the band will play the Generals March and you will all stand at attention."

By now the rumor had gotten around that Lieutenant General Simpson, Commanding General of the Fourth Army, was to be with General Patton. The men stirred expectantly. Two of the big boys in one day!

At last, the long black car, shining resplendently in the bright sun, roared up the road, preceded by a jeep full of Military Police. A dead hush fell over the hillside. There he was! Impeccably dressed. With knee high, brown, gleaming boots, shiny helmet, and his Colt .45 Peacemaker swinging in its holster on his right side.

Patton strode down the incline and then straight to the stiff backed "Guard of Honor." He looked them up and down. He peered intently into their faces and surveyed their backs. He moved through the ranks of the statuesque band like an avenging wraith and, apparently satisfied, mounted the platform with Lieutenant General Simpson and Major General Cook, the Corps Commander, at his side.

Major General Cook then introduced Lieutenant General Simpson, whose Army was still in America, preparing for their part in the war.

"We are here," said General Simpson, "to listen to the words of a great man. A man who will lead you all into whatever you may face with heroism, ability, and foresight. A man who has proven himself amid shot and shell. My greatest hope is that some day soon, I will have my own Army fighting with his, side by side."

General Patton arose and strode swiftly to the microphone. The men snapped to their feet and stood silently. Patton surveyed the sea of brown with a grim look. "Be seated," he said. The words were not a request, but a command. The General's voice rose high and clear.

"Men, this stuff that some sources sling around about America wanting out of this war, not wanting to fight, is a crock of bullshit. Americans love to fight, traditionally. All real Americans love the sting and clash of battle. You are here today for three reasons. First, because you are here to defend your homes and your loved ones. Second, you are here for your own self respect, because you would not want to be anywhere else. Third, you are here because you are real men and all real men like to fight. When you, here, everyone of you, were kids, you all admired the champion marble player, the fastest runner, the toughest boxer, the big league ball players, and the All-American football players. Americans love a winner. Americans will not tolerate a loser. Americans despise cowards. Americans play to win all of the time. I wouldn't give a hoot in hell for a man who lost and laughed. That's why Americans have never lost nor will ever lose a war; for the very idea of losing is hateful to an American."

The General paused and looked over the crowd. "You are not all going to die," he said slowly. "Only two percent of you right here today would die in a major battle. Death must not be feared. Death, in time, comes to all men. Yes, every man is scared in his first battle. If he says he's not, he's a liar. Some men are cowards but they fight the same as the brave men or they get the hell slammed out of them watching men fight who are just as scared as they are. The real hero is the man who fights even though he is scared. Some men get over their fright in a minute under fire. For some, it takes an hour. For some, it takes days. But a real man will never let his fear of death overpower his honor, his sense of duty to his country, and his innate manhood. Battle is the most magnificent competition in which a human being can indulge. It brings out all that is best and it removes all that is base. Americans pride themselves on being He Men and they ARE He Men. Remember that the enemy is just as frightened as you are, and probably more so. They are not supermen."

"All through your Army careers, you men have bitched about what you call 'chicken shit drilling.' That, like everything else in this Army, has a definite purpose. That purpose is alertness. Alertness must be bred into every soldier. I don't give a fuck for a man who's not always on his toes. You men are veterans or you wouldn't be here. You are ready for what's to come. A man must be alert at all times if he expects to stay alive. If you're not alert, sometime, a German son-of-an-asshole-bitch is going to sneak up behind you and beat you to death with a sockful of shit!" The men roared in agreement.

Patton's grim expression did not change. "There are four hundred neatly marked graves somewhere in Sicily," he roared into the microphone, "all because one man went to sleep on the job." He paused and the men grew silent. "But they are German graves, because we caught the bastard asleep before they did." The General clutched the microphone tightly, his jaw out-thrust, and he continued, "An Army is a team. It lives, sleeps, eats, and fights as a team. This individual heroic stuff is pure horse shit. The bilious bastards who write that kind of stuff for the *Saturday Evening Post* don't know any more about real fighting under fire than they know about fucking!"

The men slapped their legs and rolled in glee. This was Patton as the men had imagined him to be, and in rare form, too. He hadn't let them down. He was all that he was cracked up to be, and more. He had IT!

"We have the finest food, the finest equipment, the best spirit, and the best men in the world," Patton bellowed. He lowered his head and shook it pensively. Suddenly he snapped erect, faced the men belligerently and thundered, "Why, by God, I actually pity those poor sons-of-bitches we're going up against. By God, I do." The men clapped and howled delightedly. There would be many a barracks tale about the "Old Man's" choice phrases. They would become part and parcel of Third Army's history and they would become the bible of their slang.

"My men don't surrender," Patton continued, "I don't want to hear of any soldier under my command being captured unless he has been hit. Even if you are hit, you can still fight back. That's not just bull shit either. The kind of man that I want in my command is just like the lieutenant in Libya, who, with a Luger against his chest, jerked off his helmet, swept the gun aside with one hand, and busted the hell out of the Kraut with his helmet. Then he jumped on the gun and went out and killed another German before they knew what the hell was coming off. And, all of that time, this man had a bullet through a lung. There was a real man!"

Patton stopped and the crowd waited. He continued more quietly, "All of the real heroes are not storybook combat fighters, either. Every single man in this Army plays a vital role. Don't ever let up. Don't ever think that your job is unimportant. Every man has a job to do and he must do it. Every man is a vital link in the great chain. What if every truck driver suddenly decided that he didn't like the whine of those shells overhead, turned yellow, and jumped headlong into a ditch? The cowardly bastard could say, 'Hell, they won't miss me, just one man in thousands.' But, what if every man thought that way? Where in the hell would we be now? What would our country, our loved ones, our homes, even the world, be like? No, Goddamnit, Americans don't think like that. Every man does his job. Every man serves the whole. Every department, every unit, is important in the vast scheme of this war. The ordnance men are needed to supply the guns and machinery of war to keep us rolling. The Quartermaster is needed to bring up food and clothes because where we are going there isn't a hell of a lot to steal. Every last man on K.P. has a job to do, even the one who heats our water to keep us from getting the 'G.I. Shits.'"

Patton paused, took a deep breath, and continued, "Each man must not think only of himself, but also of his buddy fighting beside him. We don't want yellow cowards in this Army. They should be killed off like rats. If not, they will go home after this war and breed more cowards. The brave men will breed more brave men. Kill off the Goddamned cowards and we will have a nation of brave men. One of the bravest men that I ever saw was a fellow on top of a telegraph pole in the midst of a furious fire fight in Tunisia. I stopped and asked what the hell he was doing up there at a time like that. He answered, 'Fixing the wire, Sir.' I asked, 'Isn't that a little unhealthy right about now?' He answered, 'Yes, Sir, but the Goddamned wire has to be fixed.' I asked, 'Don't those planes strafing the road bother you?' And he answered, 'No, Sir, but you sure as hell do!' Now, there was a real man. A real soldier. There was a man who devoted all he had to his duty, no matter how seemingly insignificant his duty might appear at the time, no matter how great the odds. And you should have seen those trucks on the road to Tunisia. Those drivers were magnificent. All day and all night they rolled over those son-of-a-bitching roads, never stopping, never faltering from their course, with shells bursting all around them all of the time. We got through on good old American guts. Many of those men drove for over forty consecutive hours. These men weren't combat men, but they were soldiers with a job to do. They did it, and in one hell of a way they did it. They were part of a team. Without team effort, without them, the fight would have been lost. All of the links in the chain pulled together and the chain became unbreakable."

The General paused and stared challengingly over the silent ocean of men. One could have heard a pin drop anywhere on that vast hillside. The only sound was the stirring of the breeze in the leaves of the bordering trees and the busy chirping of the birds in the branches of the trees at the General's left.

"Don't forget," Patton barked, "you men don't know that I'm here. No mention of that fact is to be made in any letters. The world is not supposed to know what the hell happened to me. I'm not supposed to be commanding this Army. I'm not even supposed to be here in England. Let the first bastards to find out be the Goddamned Germans. Some day I want to see them raise up on their piss-soaked hind legs and howl, 'Jesus Christ, it's the Goddamned Third Army again and that son-of-a-fucking-bitch Patton.'"

"We want to get the hell over there," Patton continued, "the quicker we clean up this Goddamned mess, the quicker we can take a little jaunt against the purple pissing Japs and clean out their nest, too. Before the Goddamned Marines get all of the credit."

The men roared approval and cheered delightedly. This statement had real significance behind it. Much more than met the eye and the men instinctively sensed the fact. They knew that they themselves were going to play a very great part in the making of world history. They were being told as much right now. Deep sincerity and seriousness lay behind the General's colorful words. The men knew and understood it. They loved the way he put it, too, as only he could.

Patton continued quietly, "Sure, we want to go home. We want this war over with. The quickest way to get it over with is to go get the bastards who started it. The quicker they are whipped, the quicker we can go home. The shortest way home is through Berlin and Tokyo. And when we get to Berlin," he yelled, "I am personally going to shoot that paper hanging son-of-a-bitch Hitler. Just like I'd shoot a snake!"

"When a man is lying in a shell hole, if he just stays there all day, a German will get to him eventually. The hell with that idea. The hell with taking it. My men don't dig foxholes. I don't want them to. Foxholes only slow up an offensive. Keep moving. And don't give the enemy time to dig one either. We'll win this war, but we'll win it only by fighting and by showing the Germans that we've got more guts than they have; or ever will have. We're not going to just shoot the sons-of-bitches, we're going to rip out their living Goddamned guts and use them to grease the treads of our tanks. We're going to murder those lousy Hun cocksuckers by the bushel-fucking-basket. War is a bloody, killing business. You've got to spill their blood, or they will spill yours. Rip them up the belly. Shoot them in the guts. When shells are hitting all around you and you wipe the dirt off your face and realize that instead of dirt it's the blood and guts of what once was your best friend beside you, you'll know what to do!"

"I don't want to get any messages saying, 'I am holding my position.' We are not holding a Goddamned thing. Let the Germans do that. We are advancing constantly and we are not interested in holding onto anything, except the enemy's balls. We are going to twist his balls and kick the living shit out of him all of the time. Our basic plan of operation is to advance and to keep on advancing regardless of whether we have to go over, under, or through the enemy. We are going to go through him like crap through a goose; like shit through a tin horn!"

"From time to time there will be some complaints that we are pushing our people too hard. I don't give a good Goddamn about such complaints. I believe in the old and sound rule that an ounce of sweat will save a gallon of blood. The harder WE push, the more Germans we will kill. The more Germans we kill, the fewer of our men will be killed. Pushing means fewer casualties. I want you all to remember that."

The General paused. His eagle-like eyes swept over the hillside. He said with pride, "There is one great thing that you men will all be able to say after this war is over and you are home once again. You may be thankful that twenty years from now when you are sitting by the fireplace with your grandson on your knee and he asks you what you did in the great World War II, you WON'T have to cough, shift him to the other knee and say, 'Well, your Granddaddy shoveled shit in Louisiana.' No, Sir, you can look him straight in the eye and say, 'Son, your Granddaddy rode with the Great Third Army and a Son-of-a-Goddamned-Bitch named Georgie Patton!'"

The Veteran

STEPHEN CRANE

The field of battle is most famously the home of the brave. Yet ordinary life is not without its threats to life and limb, and facing the fears induced by these dangers seems also to require some form of courage. In "The Veteran," written in 1896, Stephen Crane (1871–1900) explicitly invites consideration of the relation between courage in war and courage at home, as well as the similarities and differences between facing enemy fire and facing the fire of flaming buildings. What is the connection between the old man's speeches in the grocery and to his grandson and his deeds when the barn is burning? Does the courage displayed in this story resemble that displayed in battle? Why is the story called "The Veteran"? How does civil society benefit from the presence of veterans?

Out of the low window could be seen three hickory trees placed irregularly in a meadow that was resplendent in spring-time green. Farther away, the old dismal belfry of the village church loomed over the pines. A horse meditating in the shade of one of the hickories lazily swished his tail. The warm sunshine made an oblong of vivid yellow on the floor of the grocery.

"Could you see the whites of their eyes?" said the man who was seated on a soap-box.

"Nothing of the kind," replied old Henry warmly. "Just a lot of flitting figures, and I let go at where they 'peared to be the thickest. Bang!"

"Mr. Fleming," said the grocer. His deferential voice expressed somehow the old man's exact social weight. "Mr. Fleming, you never was frightened much in them battles, was you?"

The veteran looked down and grinned. Observing his manner the entire group tittered. "Well, I guess I was," he answered finally. "Pretty well scared, sometimes. Why, in my first battle I thought the sky was falling down. I thought the world was coming to an end. You bet I was scared."

Every one laughed. Perhaps it seemed strange and rather wonderful to them that a man should admit the thing, and in the tone of their laughter there was probably more admiration than if old Fleming had declared that he had always been a lion. Moreover, they knew that he had ranked as an orderly sergeant, and so their opinion of his heroism was fixed. None, to be sure, knew how an orderly sergeant ranked, but then it was understood to be somewhere just shy of a major-general's stars. So when old Henry admitted that he had been frightened there was a laugh.

"The trouble was," said the old man, "I thought they were all shooting at me. Yes, sir. I thought every man in the other army was aiming at me in particular and only me. And it seemed so darned unreasonable, you know. I wanted to explain to 'em what an almighty good fellow I was, because I thought then they might quit all trying to hit me. But I couldn't explain, and they kept on being unreasonable—blim!—blam!—bang! So I run!"

Two little triangles of wrinkles appeared at the corners of his eyes. Evidently he appreciated some comedy in this recital. Down near his feet, however, little Jim, his grandson, was visibly horror-stricken. His hands were clasped nervously, and his eyes were wide with astonishment at this terrible scandal, his most magnificent grandfather telling such a thing.

"That was at Chancellorsville. Of course, afterward I got kind of used to it. A man does. Lots of men, though, seem to feel all right from the start. I did, as soon as I 'got on to it,' as they say now, but at first I was pretty flustered. Now, there was young Jim Conklin, old Si Conklin's son—that used to keep the tannery—you none of you recollect him—well, he went into it from the start just as if he was born to it. But with me it was different. I had to get used to it."

When little Jim walked with his grandfather he was in the habit of skipping along on the stone pavement in front of the three stores and the hotel of the town and betting that he could avoid the cracks. But upon this day he walked soberly, with his hand gripping two of his grandfather's fingers. Sometimes he kicked abstractedly at dandelions that curved over the walk. Any one could see that he was much troubled.

"There's Sickles's colt over in the medder, Jimmie," said the old man. "Don't you wish you owned one like him?"

"Um," said the boy, with a strange lack of interest. He continued his reflections. Then finally he ventured: "Grandpa—now—was that true what you was telling those men?"

"What?" asked the grandfather. "What was I telling them?"

"Oh, about your running."

"Why, yes, that was true enough, Jimmie. It was my first fight, and there was an awful lot of noise, you know."

Jimmie seemed dazed that this idol, of its own will, should so totter. His stout boyish idealism was injured.

Presently the grandfather said: "Sickles's colt is going for a drink. Don't you wish you owned Sickles's colt, Jimmie?"

The boy merely answered: "He ain't as nice as our'n." He lapsed then into another moody silence.

One of the hired men, a Swede, desired to drive to the county seat for purposes of his own. The old man loaned him a horse and an unwashed buggy. It appeared later that one of the purposes of the Swede was to get drunk.

After quelling some boisterous frolic of the farm-hands and boys in the garret, the old man had that night gone peacefully to sleep when he was aroused by clamoring at the kitchen door. He grabbed his trousers, and they waved out behind as he dashed forward. He could hear the voice of the Swede, screaming and blubbering. He pushed the wooden button, and, as the door flew open, the Swede, a maniac, stumbled inward, chattering, weeping, still screaming. "De barn fire! Fire! Fire! De barn fire! Fire! Fire! Fire!"

There was a swift and indescribable change in the old man. His face ceased instantly to be a face; it became a mask, a gray thing, with horror written about the mouth and eyes. He hoarsely shouted at the foot of the little rickety stairs, and immediately, it seemed, there came down an avalanche of men. No one knew that during this time the old lady had been standing in her night-clothes at the bed room door, yelling: "What's th' matter? What's th' matter? What's th' matter?"

When they dashed toward the barn it presented to their eyes its usual appearance, solemn, rather mystic in the black night. The Swede's lantern was overturned at a point some yards in front of the barn doors. It contained a wild little conflagration of its own, and even in their excitement some of those who ran felt a gentle secondary vibration of the thrifty part of their minds at sight of this overturned lantern. Under ordinary circumstances it would have been a calamity.

But the cattle in the barn were trampling, trampling, trampling, and above this noise could be heard a humming like the song of innumerable bees. The old man hurled aside the great doors, and a yellow flame leaped out at one corner and sped and wavered frantically up the old grey wall. It was glad, terrible, this single flame, like the wild banner of deadly and triumphant foes.

The motley crowd from the garret had come with all the pails of the farm. They flung themselves upon the well. It was a leisurely old machine, long dwelling in indolence. It was in the habit of giving out water with a sort of reluctance. The men stormed at it, cursed it, but it continued to allow the buckets to be filled only after the wheezy windlass had howled many protests at the mad-handed men.

With his opened knife in his hand old Fleming himself had gone head-long into the barn, where the stifling smoke swirled with the air-currents, and where could be heard in its fulness the terrible chorus of the flames, laden with tones of hate and death, a hymn of wonderful ferocity.

He flung a blanket over an old mare's head, cut the halter close to the manger, led the mare to the door, and fairly kicked her out to safety. He returned with the same blanket and rescued one of the work-horses. He took five horses out, and then came out himself with his clothes bravely on fire. He had no whiskers, and very little hair on his head. They soused five pailfuls of water on him. His eldest son made a clean miss with the sixth pailful because the old man had turned and was running down the decline and around to the basement of the barn where were the stanchions of the cows. Some one noticed at the time that he ran very lamely, as if one of the frenzied horses had smashed his hip.

The cows, with their heads held in the heavy stanchions, had thrown themselves, strangled themselves, tangled themselves: done everything which the ingenuity of their exuberant fear could suggest to them.

Here as at the well the same thing happened to every man save one. Their hands went mad. They became incapable of everything save the power to rush into dangerous situations.

The old man released the cow nearest the door, and she, blind drunk with terror, crashed into the Swede. The Swede had been running to and fro bab-bling. He carried an empty milk-pail, to which he clung with an unconscious fierce enthusiasm. He shrieked like one lost as he went under the cow's hoofs, and the milk-pail, rolling across the floor, made a flash of silver in the gloom.

Old Fleming took a fork, beat off the cow, and dragged the paralyzed Swede to the open air. When they had rescued all the cows save one, which had so fastened herself that she could not be moved an inch, they returned to the front of the barn and stood sadly, breathing like men who had reached the final point of human effort.

Many people had come running. Someone had even gone to the church, and now, from the distance, rang the tocsin note of the old bell. There was a long flare of crimson on the sky which made remote people speculate as to the whereabouts of the fire.

The long flames sang their drumming chorus in voices of the heaviest bass. The wind whirled clouds of smoke and cinders into the faces of the spectators. The form of the old barn was outlined in black amid these masses of orange-hued flames.

And then came this Swede again, crying as one who is the weapon of the sinister fates. "De colts! De colts! You have forgot de colts!"

Old Fleming staggered. It was true; they had forgotten the two colts in the box-stalls at the back of the barn. "Boys," he said, "I must try to get 'em out." They clamored about him then, afraid for him, afraid of what they should see. Then they talked wildly each to each. "Why, it's sure death!" "He would never get out!" "Why, it's suicide for a man to go in there!" Old Fleming stared absent-mindedly at the open doors. "The poor little things," he said. He rushed into the barn.

When the roof fell in, a great funnel of smoke swarmed toward the sky, as if the old man's mighty spirit, released from its body—a little bottle—had swelled like the genie of fable. The smoke was tinted rose-hue from the flames, and perhaps the unutterable midnights of the universe will have no power to daunt the color of this soul.

The Devil and Daniel Webster

STEPHEN VINCENT BENÉT

Courage and self-sacrifice are needed not only in response to physical danger. People are also called upon to make sacrifices for the sake of loved ones and neighbors, and to surrender personal prosperity and happiness to uphold their country's or their personal ideals. In "The Devil and Daniel Webster" (1937), Stephen Vincent Benét (1898–1943) gives examples of both sorts of sacrifice. Jabez Stone, a New Hampshire farmer despairingly down on his luck, sells his soul to the devil for all eternity in exchange for worldly prosperity and the ability to care for his family. Yet when the time comes for giving the devil his due, Stone wants to renege on his bargain. He turns for assistance to the great Daniel Webster. Moved by neighborly regard for a fellow New Hampshireman, Webster takes and eventually wins the case for Stone.

Whereas Stone was willing to trade his soul for worldly success, Webster hazards his own success and happiness on Stone's behalf. What moves him to do so? In the name of what does Webster appeal to the jury, comprising rogues and traitors, and how does he succeed? At a certain point, Webster, realizing that the jurors have come for him and not for Stone, ceases to litigate for just one person and pleads for something greater. What is the connection between Webster's concern for his neighbor, for the ideals of his country, and for "man as man"? Where is courage in this story? How does it compare to the courage displayed on the battlefield?

I

It's a story they tell in the border country, where Massachusetts joins Vermont and New Hampshire.

Yes, Dan'l Webster's dead—or, at least, they buried him. But every time there's a thunder storm around Marshfield, they say you can hear his rolling voice in the hollows of the sky. And they say that if you go to his grave and speak loud and clear, "Dan'l Webster—Dan'l Webster!" the ground'll begin to shiver and the trees begin to shake. And after a while you'll hear a deep voice saying, "Neighbor, how stands the Union?" Then you better answer the Union stands as she stood, rock-bottomed and copper sheathed, one and indivisible, or he's liable to rear right out of the ground. At least, that's what I was told when I was a youngster.

You see, for a while, he was the biggest man in the country. He never got to be President, but he was the biggest man. There were thousands that trusted in him right next to God Almighty, and they told stories about him and all the things that belonged to him that were like the stories of patriarchs and such. They said, when he stood up to speak, stars and stripes came right out in the sky, and once he spoke against a river and made it sink into the ground. They said, when he walked the woods with his fishing rod, Killall, the trout would jump out of the streams right into his pockets, for they knew it was no use putting up a fight against him; and, when he argued a case, he could turn on the harps of the blessed and the shaking of the earth underground. That was the kind of man he was, and his big farm up at Marshfield was suitable to him. The chickens he raised were all white meat down through the drumsticks, the cows were tended like children, and the big ram he called Goliath had horns with a curl like a morning-glory vine and could butt through an iron door. But Dan'l wasn't one of your gentlemen farmers; he knew all the ways of the land, and he'd be up by candlelight to see that the chores got done. A man with a mouth like a mastiff, a brow like a mountain and eyes like burning anthracite—that was Dan'l Webster in his prime. And the biggest case he argued never got written down in the books, for he argued it against the devil, nip and tuck and no holds barred. And this is the way I used to hear it told.

There was a man named Jabez Stone, lived at Cross Corners, New Hampshire. He wasn't a bad man to start with, but he was an unlucky man. If he planted corn, he got borers; if he planted potatoes, he got blight. He had good enough land, but it didn't prosper him; he had a decent wife and children, but the more children he had, the less there was to feed them. If stones cropped up in his neighbor's field, boulders boiled up in his; if he had a horse with the spavins, he'd trade it for one with the staggers and give something extra. There's some folks bound to be like that, apparently. But one day Jabez Stone got sick of the whole business.

He'd been plowing that morning and he'd just broke the plowshare on a rock that he could have sworn hadn't been there yesterday. And, as he stood looking at the plowshare, the off horse began to cough—that ropy kind of cough that means sickness and horse doctors. There were two children down with the measles, his wife was ailing, and he had a whitlow on his thumb. It was about the last straw for Jabez Stone. "I vow," he said, and he looked around him kind of desperate—"I vow it's enough to make a man want to sell his soul to the devil! And I would, too, for two cents!"

Then he felt a kind of queerness come over him at having said what he'd said; though, naturally, being a New Hampshireman, he wouldn't take it back. But, all the same, when it got to be evening and, as far as he could see, no notice had been taken, he felt relieved in his mind, for he was a religious man. But notice is always taken, sooner or later, just like the Good Book says. And, sure enough, next day, about supper time, a soft-spoken, dark-dressed stranger drove up in a handsome buggy and asked for Jabez Stone.

Well, Jabez told his family it was a lawyer, come to see him about a legacy. But he knew who it was. He didn't like the looks of the stranger, nor the way he smiled with his teeth.

They were white teeth, and plentiful—some say they were filed to a point, but I wouldn't vouch for that. And he didn't like it when the dog took one look at the stranger and ran away howling, with his tail between his legs. But having passed his word, more or less, he stuck to it, and they went out behind the barn and made their bargain. Jabez Stone had to prick his finger to sign, and the stranger lent him a silver pin. The wound healed clean, but it left a little white scar.

II

After that, all of a sudden, things began to pick up and prosper for Jabez Stone. His cows got fat and his horses sleek, his crops were the envy of the neighborhood, and lightning might strike all over the valley, but it wouldn't strike his barn. Pretty soon, he was one of the prosperous people of the county; they asked him to stand for selectman, and he stood for it; there began to be talk of running him for state senate. All in all, you might say the Stone family was as happy and contented as cats in a dairy. And so they were, except for Jabez Stone.

He'd been contented enough, the first few years. It's a great thing when bad luck turns; it drives most other things out of your head. True, every now and then, especially in rainy weather, the little white scar on his finger would give him a twinge. And once a year, punctual as clockwork, the stranger with the handsome buggy would come driving by. But the sixth year, the stranger lighted, and, after that, his peace was over for Jabez Stone.

The stranger came up through the lower field, switching his boots with a cane—they were handsome black boots, but Jabez Stone never liked the look of them, particularly the toes. And, after he'd passed the time of day, he said, "Well, Mr. Stone, you're a hummer! It's a very pretty property you've got here, Mr. Stone."

"Well, some might favor it and others might not," said Jabez Stone, for he was a New Hampshireman.

"Oh, no need to decry your industry!" said the stranger, very easy, showing his teeth in a smile. "After all, we know what's been done, and it's been according to contract and specifications. So when—ahem—the mortgage falls due next year, you shouldn't have any regrets."

"Speaking of that mortgage, mister," said Jabez Stone, and he looked around for help to the earth and the sky, "I'm beginning to have one or two doubts about it."

"Doubts?" said the stranger, not quite so pleasantly.

"Why, yes," said Jabez Stone. "This being the U.S.A. and me always having been a religious man." He cleared his throat and got bolder.

"Yes, sir," he said, "I'm beginning to have considerable doubts as to that mortgage holding in court."

"There's courts and courts," said the stranger, clicking his teeth. "Still, we might as well have a look at the original document." And he hauled out a big black pocketbook, full of papers. "Sherwin, Slater, Stevens, Stone," he muttered. "I, Jabez Stone, for a term of seven years—Oh, it's quite in order, I think."

But Jabez Stone wasn't listening, for he saw something else flutter out of the black pocketbook. It was something that looked like a moth, but it wasn't a moth. And as Jabez Stone stared at it, it seemed to speak to him in a small sort of piping voice, terrible small and thin, but terrible human.

"Neighbor Stone!" it squeaked. "Neighbor Stone! Help me! For God's sake, help me!"

But before Jabez Stone could stir hand or foot, the stranger whipped out a big bandanna handkerchief, caught the creature in it, just like a butterfly, and started tying up the ends of the bandanna.

"Sorry for the interruption," he said. "As I was saying—"

But Jabez Stone was shaking all over like a scared horse.

"That's Miser Stevens' voice!" he said, in a croak. "And you've got him in your handkerchief!"

The stranger looked a little embarrassed.

"Yes, I really should have transferred him to the collecting box," he said with a simper. "But there were some rather unusual specimens there and I didn't want them crowded. Well, well, these little contretemps will occur."

"I don't know what you mean by contertan," said Jabez Stone, "but that was Miser Stevens' voice! And he ain't dead! You can't tell me he is! He was just as spry and mean as a woodchuck, Tuesday!"

"In the midst of life—" said the stranger, kind of pious. "Listen!" Then a bell began to toll in the valley and Jabez Stone listened, with the sweat running down his face. For he knew it was tolled for Miser Stevens and that he was dead.

"These long-standing accounts," said the stranger with a sigh; "one really hates to close them. But business is business."

He still had the bandanna in his hand, and Jabez Stone felt sick as he saw the cloth struggle and flutter.

"Are they all as small as that?" he asked hoarsely.

"Small?" said the stranger. "Oh, I see what you mean. Why, they vary." He measured Jabez Stone with his eyes, and his teeth showed. "Don't worry, Mr. Stone," he said. "You'll go with a very good grade. I wouldn't trust you outside the collecting box. Now, a man like Dan'l Webster, of course—well, we'd have to build a special box for him, and even at that, I imagine the wing spread would astonish you. He'd certainly be a prize. I wish we could see our way clear to him. But, in your case, as I was saying—"

"Put that handkerchief away!" said Jabez Stone, and he began to beg and to pray. But the best he could get at the end was a three years' extension, with conditions.

But till you make a bargain like that, you've got no idea of how fast four years can run. By the last months of those years, Jabez Stone's known all over the state and there's talk of running him for governor—and it's dust and ashes in his mouth. For every day, when he gets up, he thinks, "There's one more night gone," and every night when he lies down, he thinks of the black pocketbook and the soul of Miser Stevens, and it makes him sick at heart. Till, finally, he can't bear it any longer, and, in the last days of the last year, he hitches his horse and drives off to seek Dan'l Webster. For Dan'l was born in New Hampshire, only a few miles from Cross Corners, and it's well known that he has a particular soft spot for old neighbors.

III

It was early in the morning when he got to Marshfield, but Dan'l was up already, talking Latin to the farm hands and wrestling with the ram, Goliath, and trying out a new trotter and working up speeches to make against John C. Calhoun. But when he heard a New Hampshireman had come to see him, he dropped every thing else he was doing, for that was Dan'l's way. He gave Jabez Stone a breakfast that five men couldn't eat, went into the living history of every man and woman in Cross Corners, and finally asked him how he could serve him.

Jabez Stone allowed that it was a kind of mortgage case.

"Well, I haven't pleaded a mortgage case in a long time, and I don't generally plead now, except before the Supreme Court," said Dan'l, "but if I can, I'll help you."

"Then I've got hope for the first time in ten years," said Jabez Stone, and told him the details.

Dan'l walked up and down as he listened, hands behind his back, now and then asking a question, now and then plunging his eyes at the floor, as if they'd bore through it like gimlets. When Jabez Stone had finished, Dan'l puffed out his cheeks and blew. Then he turned to Jabez Stone and a smile broke over his face like the sunrise over Monadnock.

"You've certainly given yourself the devil's own row to hoe, Neighbor Stone," he said, "but I'll take your case."

"You'll take it?" said Jabez Stone, hardly daring to believe.

"Yes," said Dan'l Webster. "I've got about seventy-five other things to do and the Missouri Compromise to straighten out, but I'll take your case. For if two New Hampshiremen aren't a match for the devil, we might as well give the country back to the Indians."

Then he shook Jabez Stone by the hand and said, "Did you come down here in a hurry?"

"Well, I admit I made time," said Jabez Stone.

"You'll go back faster," said Dan'l Webster, and he told 'em to hitch up Constitution and Constellation to the carriage. They were matched grays with one white forefoot, and they stepped like greased lightning.

Well, I won't describe how excited and pleased the whole Stone family was to have the great Dan'l Webster for a guest, when they finally got there. Jabez Stone had lost his hat on the way, blown off when they overtook a wind, but he didn't take much account of that. But after supper he sent the family off to bed, for he had most particular business with Mr. Webster. Mrs.

Stone wanted them to sit in the front parlor, but Dan'l Webster knew front parlors and said he preferred the kitchen. So it was there they sat, waiting for the stranger, with a jug on the table between them and a bright fire on the hearth—the stranger being scheduled to show up on the stroke of midnight, according to specification.

Well, most men wouldn't have asked for better company than Dan'l Webster and a jug. But with every tick of the clock Jabez Stone got sadder and sadder. His eyes roved round, and though he sampled the jug you could see he couldn't taste it. Finally, on the stroke of 11:30 he reached over and grabbed Dan'l Webster by the arm.

"Mr. Webster, Mr. Webster!" he said, and his voice was shaking with fear and a desperate courage. "For God's sake, Mr. Webster, harness your horses and get away from this place while you can!"

"You've brought me a long way, neighbor, to tell me you don't like my company," said Dan'l Webster, quite peaceable, pulling at the jug.

"Miserable wretch that I am!" groaned Jabez Stone. "I've brought you a devilish way, and now I see my folly. Let him take me if he wills. I don't hanker after it, I must say, but I can stand it. But you're the Union's stay and New Hampshire's pride! He mustn't get you, Mr. Webster! He mustn't get you!"

Dan'l Webster looked at the distracted man, all gray and shaking in the firelight, and laid a hand on his shoulder.

"I'm obliged to you, Neighbor Stone," he said gently. "It's kindly thought of. But there's a jug on the table and a case in hand. And I never left a jug or a case half finished in my life."

And just at that moment there was a sharp rap on the door.

"Ah," said Dan'l Webster, very coolly, "I thought your clock was a trifle slow, Neighbor Stone." He stepped to the door and opened it. "Come in!" he said.

The stranger came in—very dark and tall he looked in the firelight. He was carrying a box under his arm—a black, japanned box with little air holes in the lid. At the sight of the box, Jabez Stone gave a low cry and shrank into a corner of the room.

"Mr. Webster, I presume," said the stranger, very polite, but with his eyes glowing like a fox's deep in the woods.

"Attorney of record for Jabez Stone," said Dan'l Webster, but his eyes were glowing too. "Might I ask your name?"

"I've gone by a good many," said the stranger carelessly. "Perhaps Scratch will do for the evening. I'm often called that in these regions."

Then he sat down at the table and poured himself a drink from the jug. The liquor was cold in the jug, but it came steaming into the glass.

"And now," said the stranger, smiling and showing his teeth, "I shall call upon you, as a law-abiding citizen, to assist me in taking possession of my property."

Well, with that the argument began—and it went hot and heavy. At first, Jabez Stone had a flicker of hope, but when he saw Dan'l Webster being forced back at point after point, he just sat scrunched in his corner, with his eyes on that japanned box. For there wasn't any doubt as to the deed or the signature— that was the worst of it. Dan'l Webster twisted and turned and thumped his fist on the table, but he couldn't get away from that. He offered to compromise the case; the stranger wouldn't hear of it. He pointed out the property had increased in value, and state senators ought to be worth more; the stranger stuck to the letter of the law. He was a great lawyer, Dan'l Webster, but we know who's the King of Lawyers, as the Good Book tells us, and it seemed as if, for the first time, Dan'l Webster had met his match.

Finally, the stranger yawned a little. "Your spirited efforts on behalf of your client do you credit, Mr. Webster," he said, "but if you have no more arguments to adduce, I'm rather pressed for time—" and Jabez Stone shuddered.

Dan'l Webster's brow looked dark as a thundercloud. "Pressed or not, you shall not have this man!" he thundered. "Mr. Stone is an American citizen, and no American citizen may be forced into the service of a foreign prince. We fought England for that in '12 and we'll fight all hell for it again!"

"Foreign?" said the stranger. "And who calls me a foreigner?"

"Well, I never yet heard of the dev—of your claiming American citizenship," said Dan'l Webster with surprise.

"And who with better right?" said the stranger, with one of his terrible smiles. "When the first wrong was done to the first Indian, I was there. When the first slaver put out for the Congo, I stood on her deck. Am I not in your books and stories and beliefs, from the first settlements on? Am I not spoken of, still, in every church in New England? 'Tis true the North claims me for a Southerner, and the South for a Northerner, but I am neither. I am merely an honest American like yourself—and of the best descent—for, to tell the truth, Mr. Webster, though I don't like to boast of it, my name is older in this country than yours."

"Aha!" said Dan'l Webster, with the veins standing out in his forehead. "Then I stand on the Constitution! I demand a trial for my client!"

"The case is hardly one for an ordinary court," said the stranger, his eyes flickering. "And, indeed, the lateness of the hour—"

"Let it be any court you choose, so it is an American judge and an American jury!" said Dan'l Webster in his pride. "Let it be the quick or the dead; I'll abide the issue!"

"You have said it," said the stranger, and pointed his finger at the door. And with that, and all of a sudden, there was a rushing of wind outside and a noise of footsteps. They came, clear and distinct, through the night. And yet, they were not like the footsteps of living men.

"In God's name, who comes by so late?" cried Jabez Stone, in an ague of fear.

"The jury Mr. Webster demands," said the stranger, sipping at his boiling glass. "You must pardon the rough appearance of one or two; they will have come a long way."

IV

And with that the fire burned blue and the door blew open and twelve men entered, one by one.

If Jabez Stone had been sick with terror before, he was blind with terror now. For there was Walter Butler, the loyalist, who spread fire and horror through the Mohawk Valley in the times of the Revolution; and there was Simon Girty, the renegade, who saw white men burned at the stake and whooped with the Indians to see them burn. His eyes were green, like a catamount's, and the stains on his hunting shirt did not come from the blood of the deer. King Philip was there, wild and proud as he had been in life, with the great gash in his head that gave him his death wound, and cruel Governor Dale, who broke men on the wheel. There was Morton of Merry Mount, who so vexed the Plymouth Colony, with his flushed, loose, handsome face and his hate of the godly. There was Teach, the bloody pirate, with his black beard curling on his breast. The Reverend John Smeet, with his strangler's hands and his Geneva gown, walked as daintily as he had to the gallows. The red print of the rope was still around his neck, but he carried a perfumed handkerchief in one hand. One and all, they came into the room with the fires of hell still upon them, and the stranger named their names and their deeds as they came, till the tale of twelve was told. Yet the stranger had told the truth—they had all played a part in America.

"Are you satisfied with the jury, Mr. Webster?" said the stranger mockingly, when they had taken their places.

The sweat stood upon Dan'l Webster's brow, but his voice was clear.

"Quite satisfied," he said. "Though I miss General Arnold from the company."

"Benedict Arnold is engaged upon other business," said the stranger, with a glower. "Ah, you asked for a justice, I believe."

He pointed his finger once more, and a tall man, soberly clad in Puritan garb, with the burning gaze of the fanatic, stalked into the room and took his judge's place.

"Justice Hathorne is a jurist of experience," said the stranger. "He presided at certain witch trials once held in Salem. There were others who repented of the business later, but not he."

"Repent of such notable wonders and undertakings?" said the stern old justice. "Nay, hang them—hang them all!" And he muttered to himself in a way that struck ice into the soul of Jabez Stone.

Then the trial began, and, as you might expect, it didn't look anyways good for the defense. And Jabez Stone didn't make much of a witness in his own behalf. He took one look at Simon Girty and screeched, and they had to put him back in his corner in a kind of swoon.

It didn't halt the trial, though; the trial went on, as trials do. Dan'l Webster had faced some hard juries and hanging judges in his time, but this was the hardest he'd ever faced, and he knew it. They sat there with a kind of glitter in their eyes, and the stranger's smooth voice went on and on. Every time he'd raise an objection, it'd be "Objection sustained," but whenever Dan'l objected, it'd be "Objection denied." Well, you couldn't expect fair play from a fellow like this Mr. Scratch.

It got to Dan'l in the end, and he began to heat, like iron in the forge. When he got up to speak he was going to flay that stranger with every trick known to the law, and the judge and jury too. He didn't care if it was contempt of court or what would happen to him for it. He didn't care any more what happened to Jabez Stone. He just got madder and madder, thinking of what he'd say. And yet, curiously enough, the more he thought about it, the less he was able to arrange his speech in his mind. Till, finally, it was time for him to get up on his feet, and he did so, all ready to bust out with lightnings and denunciations. But before he started he looked over the judge and jury for a moment, such being his custom. And he noticed the glitter in their eyes was twice as strong as before, and they all leaned forward. Like hounds just before they get the fox, they looked, and the blue mist of evil in the room thickened as he watched them. Then he saw what he'd been about to do, and he wiped his forehead, as a man might who's just escaped falling into a pit in the dark.

For it was him they'd come for, not only Jabez Stone. He read it in the glitter of their eyes and in the way the stranger hid his mouth with one hand. And if he fought them with their own weapons, he'd fall into their power; he knew that, though he couldn't have told you how. It was his own anger and horror that burned in their eyes; and he'd have to wipe that out or the case was lost. He stood there for a moment, his black eyes burning like anthracite. And then he began to speak.

He started off in a low voice, though you could hear every word. They say he could call on the harps of the blessed when he chose. And this was just as simple and easy as a man could talk. But he didn't start out by condemning or reviling. He was talking about the things that make a country a country, and a man a man.

And he began with the simple things that everybody's known and felt— the freshness of a fine morning when you're young, and the taste of food when you're hungry, and the new day that's every day when you're a child. He took them up and he turned them in his hands. They were good things for any man. But without freedom, they sickened. And when he talked of those enslaved, and the sorrows of slavery, his voice got like a big bell. He talked of the early days of America and the men who had made those days. It wasn't a spread-eagle speech, but he made you see it. He admitted all the wrong that had ever been done. But he showed how, out of the wrong and the right, the suffering and the starvations, something new had come. And everybody had played a part in it, even the traitors.

Then he turned to Jabez Stone and showed him as he was—an ordinary man who'd had hard luck and wanted to change it. And, because he'd wanted to change it, now he was going to be punished for all eternity. And yet there was good in Jabez Stone, and he showed that good. He was hard and mean, in some ways, but he was a man. There was sadness in being a man, but it was a proud thing too. And he showed what the pride of it was till you couldn't help feeling it. Yes, even in hell, if a man was a man, you'd know it. And he wasn't pleading for any one person any more, though his voice rang like an organ. He was telling the story and the failures and the endless journey of mankind. They got tricked and trapped and bamboozled, but it was a great journey. And no demon that was ever foaled could know the inwardness of it—it took a man to do that.

V

The fire began to die on the hearth and the wind before morning to blow. The light was getting gray in the room when Dan'l Webster finished. And his words came back at the end to New Hampshire ground, and the one spot of land that each man loves and clings to. He painted a picture of that, and to each one of that jury he spoke of things long forgotten. For his voice could search the heart, and that was his gift and his strength. And to one, his voice was like the forest and its secrecy, and to another like the sea and the storms of the sea; and one heard the cry of his lost nation in it, and another saw a little harmless scene he hadn't remembered for years. But each saw something. And when Dan'l Webster finished he didn't know whether or not he'd saved Jabez Stone. But he knew he'd done a miracle. For the glitter was gone from the eyes of judge and jury, and, for the moment, they were men again, and knew they were men.

"The defense rests," said Dan'l Webster, and stood there like a mountain. His ears were still ringing with his speech, and he didn't hear any thing else till he heard Judge Hathorne say, "The jury will retire to consider its verdict."

Walter Butler rose in his place and his face had a dark, gay pride on it. "The jury has considered its verdict," he said, and looked the stranger full in the eye. "We find for the defendant, Jabez Stone."

With that, the smile left the stranger's face, but Walter Butler did not flinch.

"Perhaps 'tis not strictly in accordance with the evidence," he said, "but even the damned may salute the eloquence of Mr. Webster."

With that, the long crow of a rooster split the gray morning sky, and judge and jury were gone from the room like a puff of smoke and as if they had never been there. The stranger turned to Dan'l Webster, smiling wryly. "Major Butler was always a bold man," he said. "I had not thought him quite so bold. Nevertheless, my congratulations, as between two gentlemen."

"I'll have that paper first, if you please," said Dan'l Webster, and he took it and tore it into four pieces. It was queerly warm to the touch. "And now," he said, "I'll have you!" and his hand came down like a bear trap on the stranger's arm. For he knew that once you bested anybody like Mr. Scratch in fair fight, his power on you was gone. And he could see that Mr. Scratch knew it too.

The stranger twisted and wriggled, but he couldn't get out of that grip. "Come, come, Mr. Webster," he said, smiling palely. "This sort of thing is ridic—ouch!—is ridiculous. If you're worried about the costs of the case, naturally, I'd be glad to pay—"

"And so you shall!" said Dan'l Webster, shaking him till his teeth rattled. "For you'll sit right down at that table and draw up a document, promising never to bother Jabez Stone nor his heirs or assigns nor any other New Hampshireman till doomsday! For any hades we want to raise in this state, we can raise ourselves, without assistance from strangers."

"Ouch!" said the stranger. "Ouch! Well, they never did run very big to the barrel, but—ouch!—I agree!"

So he sat down and drew up the document. But Dan'l Webster kept his hand on his coat collar all the time.

"And, now, may I go?" said the stranger, quite humble, when Dan'l'd seen the document was in proper and legal form.

"Go?" said Dan'l, giving him another shake. "I'm still trying to figure out what I'll do with you. For you've settled the costs of the case, but you haven't settled with me. I think I'll take you back to Marshfield," he said, kind of reflective. "I've got a ram there named Goliath that can butt through an iron door. I'd kind of like to turn you loose in his field and see what he'd do."

Well, with that the stranger began to beg and to plead. And he begged and he pled so humble that finally Dan'l, who was naturally kind-hearted, agreed to let him go. The stranger seemed terrible grateful for that and said, just to show they were friends, he'd tell Dan'l's fortune before leaving. So Dan'l agreed to that, though he didn't take much stock in fortune-tellers ordinarily.

But, naturally, the stranger was a little different. Well, he pried and he peered at the line in Dan'l's hands. And he told him one thing and another that was quite remarkable. But they were all in the past.

"Yes, all that's true, and it happened," said Dan'l Webster. "But what's to come in the future?"

The stranger grinned, kind of happily, and shook his head. "The future's not as you think it," he said. "It's dark. You have a great ambition, Mr. Webster."

"I have," said Dan'l firmly, for everybody knew he wanted to be President.

"It seems almost within your grasp," said the stranger, "but you will not attain it. Lesser men will be made President and you will be passed over."

"And, if I am, I'll still be Daniel Webster," said Dan'l. "Say on."

"You have two strong sons," said the stranger, shaking his head. "You look to found a line. But each will die in war and neither reach greatness."

"Live or die, they are still my sons," said Dan'l Webster. "Say on."

"You have made great speeches," said the stranger. "You will make more."

"Ah," said Dan'l Webster.

"But the last great speech you make will turn many of your own against you," said the stranger. "They will call you Ichabod; they will call you by other names. Even in New England some will say you have turned your coat and sold your country, and their voices will be loud against you till you die."

"So it is an honest speech, it does not matter what men say," said Dan'l Webster. Then he looked at the stranger and their glances locked. "One question," he said. "I have fought for the Union all my life. Will I see that fight won against those who would tear it apart?"

"Not while you live," said the stranger, grimly, "but it will be won. And after you are dead, there are thousands who will fight for your cause, because of words that you spoke."

"Why, then, you long-barreled, slab-sided, lantern-jawed, fortune-telling note shaver!" said Dan'l Webster, with a great roar of laughter, "be off with you to your own place before I put my mark on you! For, by the thirteen original colonies, I'd go to the Pit itself to save the Union!"

And with that he drew back his foot for a kick that would have stunned a horse. It was only the tip of his shoe that caught the stranger, but he went flying out of the door with his collecting box under his arm.

"And now," said Dan'l Webster, seeing Jabez Stone beginning to rouse from his swoon, "let's see what's left in the jug, for it's dry work talking all night. I hope there's pie for breakfast, Neighbor Stone."

But they say that whenever the devil comes near Marshfield, even now, he gives it a wide berth. And he hasn't been seen in the state of New Hampshire from that day to this. I'm not talking about Massachusetts or Vermont.

Civility, Tolerance, Compassion:
Toward Neighbors

Contract

RING LARDNER

After considering the virtues of self-command and self-respect, and the civic requirements of law, order, and national defense, we turn next to the virtues needed for living with one's neighbors in everyday life—civility in common intercourse, tolerance of different ways and outlooks, and concern for their troubles and well-being. Not by accident is civility a prime requirement for civil life. Less warm than genuine friendship, civility involves restrained ways of acting and especially speaking that facilitate living amicably with one another, a mode of keeping social peace by avoiding insult and wounded vanity.

In "Contract" (1929), sports columnist and storywriter Ring Lardner (1885–1933) shines a light on civility and its discontents. A young couple, climbing the social ladder with a move to the suburbs, engages their new neighbors in the seemingly innocuous and trivial pastime of playing contract bridge. But the encounters turn out to be anything but civil.

How do we judge the behavior of Mr. Shelton and his neighbors? How much honesty does civil speech permit? How much civility does honesty allow? If we consider the contract bridge table a microcosm of a larger society, resting upon a social contract, what can we learn from this story about civility and civil speech?

When the Sheltons were settled in their new home in the pretty little suburb of Linden, Mrs. Shelton was afraid nobody would call on them. Her husband was afraid somebody would. For ages Mrs. Shelton had bravely pretended to share her husband's aversion to a social life; he hated parties that numbered more than four people and she had convincingly, so she thought, played the rôle of indifference while declining invitations she would have given her right eye to accept. Shelton had not been fooled much, but his dislike of "crowds" was so great that he seldom sought to relieve her martyrdom by insisting that they "go" somewhere.

This was during the first six years of their connubial existence, while it was necessary to live, rather economically, in town. Recently, however, Shelton's magazine had advanced him to a position as associate editor and he was able, with the assistance of a benignant bond and mortgage company, to move into a house in Linden. Mrs. Shelton was sure suburbanites would be less tedious and unattractive than people they had known in the city and that it would not be fatal to her spouse to get acquainted and play around a little; anyway she could make friends with other wives, if they were willing, and perhaps enjoy afternoons of contract bridge, a game she had learned to love in three lessons. At the same time Shelton resolved to turn over a new leaf for his wife's sake and give her to understand that he was open for engagements, secretly hoping, as I have hinted, that Linden's denizens would treat them as if they were quarantined.

Mrs. Shelton's fears were banished, and Shelton's resolution put to a test, on an evening of their second week in the new house. They were dropped in on by Mr. and Mrs. Robert French who lived three blocks away. Mrs. French was pretty and Shelton felt inclined to like her until she remarked how fascinating it must be to edit a magazine and meet Michael Arlen. French had little to say, being occupied most of the while in a petting party with his mustache.

Mrs. Shelton showed Mrs. French her seven hooked rugs. Mrs. French said, "Perfectly darling!" seven times, inquired where each of the seven had been procured and did not listen to the answers. Shelton served highballs of eighty dollar Scotch he had bought from a Linden bootlegger. French commented favorably on the Scotch. Shelton thought it was terrible himself and that French was a poor judge, or was being polite, or was deceived by some flavor lurking in the mustache. Mrs. Shelton ran out of hooked rugs and Mrs. French asked whether they played contract. Mrs. Shelton hesitated from habit. Shelton swallowed hard and replied that they did, and liked it very much.

"That's wonderful!" said Mrs. French. "Because the Wilsons have moved to Chicago. They were crazy about contract and we used to have a party every Wednesday night; two tables—the Wilsons, ourselves, and the Dittmars and Camerons. It would be just grand if you two would take the Wilsons' place. We have dinner at somebody's house and next Wednesday is our turn. Could you come?"

Mrs. Shelton again hesitated and Shelton (to quote O. O. McIntyre) once more took the bull by the horns.

"It sounds fine!" he said. "We haven't anything else on for that night, have we, dear?"

His wife uttered an astonished no and the Frenches left.

"What in the world has happened to you?" demanded Mrs. Shelton.

"Nothing at all. They seem like nice people and we've got to make friends here. Besides, it won't be bad playing cards."

"I don't know about contract," said Mrs. Shelton doubtfully. "You've got good card sense, and the only time you played it, you were all right. But I'm afraid I'll make hideous mistakes."

"Why should you? And even if you do, what of it?"

"These people are probably whizzes."

"I don't care if they're Lenz's mother-in-law."

"But you'll care if they criticize you."

"Of course I will. People, and especially strangers, have no more right to criticize your bridge playing than your clothes or your complexion."

"You know that's silly. Bridge is a game."

"Tennis is a game, too. But how often do you hear one tennis player say to another, 'You played that like an old fool!'?"

"You're not partners in tennis."

"You are in doubles. However, criticism in bridge is not confined to partners. I've made bonehead plays in bridge (I'll admit it), and been laughed at and scolded for them by opponents who ought to have kissed me. It's a conviction of most bridge players, and some golf players, that God sent them into the world to teach. At that, what they tell you isn't intended for your edification and future good. It's just a way of announcing 'I'm smart and you're a lunkhead.' And to my mind it's a revelation of bad manners and bad sportsmanship. If I asked somebody what I did wrong, that's different. But when they volunteer—"

It was an old argument and Mrs. Shelton did not care to continue it. She knew she couldn't win and she was sleepy. Moreover, she was so glad they were "going out" on her husband's own insistence that she felt quite kindly toward him. She did hope, though, that their new acquaintances would suppress their educational complex if any.

On Wednesday night this hope was knocked for a double row of early June peas. Mrs. Shelton was elected to play with French, Mrs. Cameron and Mr. Dittmar. Mrs. Cameron was what is referred to as a statuesque blonde, but until you were used to her you could think of nothing but her nostrils, where she might easily have carried two after dinner mints. Mr. Dittmar appeared to be continuing to enjoy his meal long after it was over. And French had to deal one-handed to be sure his mustache remained loyal. These details distracted Mrs. Shelton's mind to such an extent that she made a few errors and was called for them. But she didn't mind that and her greatest distraction was caused by words and phrases that came from the other table, where her husband was engaged with Mr. Cameron, Mrs. Dittmar and the hostess.

The French cocktails had been poured from an eye-dropper and Shelton maintained perfect control of his temper and tongue. His polite reception of each criticism was taken as a confession of ignorance and a willingness to learn, and his three table-mates were quick to assume the rôle of faculty, with him as the entire student-body. He was stepped on even when he was dummy, his partner at the time, Mrs. Dittmar, attributing the loss of a trick to the manner in which he had laid out his cards, the light striking the nine of diamonds in such a way as to make her think it was an honor.

Mrs. Dittmar had married a man much younger than herself and was trying to disguise that fact by acting much younger than he. An eight-year-old child who is kind of backward hardly ever plays contract bridge; otherwise, if you didn't look at Mrs. Dittmar and judged only by her antics and manner of speech, you would have thought Dittmar had spent the final hours of his courtship waiting outside the sub-primary to take her home. Mrs. French, when she was not picking flaws in Shelton's play, sought to make him feel at home by asking intelligent questions about his work—"Do the people who draw the illustrations read the stories first?" "Does H. C. Witwer talk Negro dialect all the time?" And "How old is Peter B. Kinney?" Cameron, from whom Work, Lenz, Whitehead and Shepard had plagiarized the game, was frankly uninterested in anything not connected with it. The stake was half a cent a point and the pains he took to see that his side's score was correct or better proved all the rumors about the two Scotchmen.

Mrs. Shelton was well aware that her husband was the politest man in the world when sober; yet he truly amazed her that evening by his smiling acquiescence to all that was said. From the snatches she overheard, she knew he must be afire inside and it was really wonderful of him not to show it.

There was a time when Mrs. Dittmar passed and he passed and Cameron bid two spades. Mrs. French passed and Mrs. Dittmar bid three hearts, a denial of her partner's spades if Shelton ever heard one. Shelton passed and Cameron went four hearts, which stood. Shelton held four spades to the nine, four diamonds to the king, two small hearts and the eight, six and five of clubs. He led the trey of diamonds. I am not broadcasting the battle play by play, but when it was over, "Oh, partner! Any other opening and we could have set them," said Mrs. French.

"My! My! My! My! Leading away from a king!" gurgled the child-wife.

"That lead was all that saved us," said Cameron.

They waited for Shelton to apologize and explain, all prepared to scrunch him if he did either.

"I guess I made a mistake," he said.

"Haven't you played much bridge?" asked Mrs. French.

"Evidently not enough," he replied.

"It's a game you can't learn in a minute," said Cameron.

"Never you mind!" said Mrs. Dittmar. "I've played contract ever since it came out, and Daddy still scolds me terribly for some of the things I do."

Shelton presumed that Daddy was her husband. Her father must be dead or at least too feeble to scold.

There was a time when a hand was passed around.

"Oh! A goulash!" crowed Mrs. Dittmar.

"Do you play them, Mr. Shelton?" asked his hostess.

"Yes," said Shelton.

"Mrs. Shelton," called Mrs. Dittmar to the other table, "does your big man play goulashes?"

"Oh, yes," said Mrs. Shelton.

"You're sure you know what they are," said Cameron to Shelton.

"I've played them often," said the latter.

"A goulash," said the hostess, "is where the hand is passed and then we all put our hands together like this and cut them and the dealer deals five around twice and then three. It makes crazy hands, but it's thrilling."

"And the bidding is different," said Mrs. Dittmar, his partner at this stage. "Big mans mustn't get too wild."

Shelton, who had dealt, looked at his hand and saw no temptation to get wild; at least, not any wilder than he was. He had the king, queen and jack of spades, four silly hearts, four very young clubs and two diamonds of no standing. He passed. Cameron bid three clubs and Mrs. Dittmar four diamonds. That was enough to make game (they already had thirty), and when Mrs. French went by, Shelton unhesitatingly did the same. So did Cameron. It developed that Mrs. Dittmar had the ace, king, jack, ten and another diamond. Cameron had none and Mrs. French reeked with them. The bidder was set two. Her honors counted one hundred and the opponents' net profit was two hundred, Mrs. Dittmar being vulnerable, or "venerable," as Mrs. French laughingly, but not very tactfully, called it.

Cameron lighted into Mrs. French for not doubling Mrs. Dittmar and Mrs. French observed that she guessed she knew what she was doing. Shelton hoped this would develop into a brawl, but it was forgotten when Mrs. Dittmar asked him querulously why he had not shown her his spades, a suit of which she had held the ace, ten to five.

"We're lucky, partner," said Mrs. French to Cameron. "They could have made four spades like a breeze."

"I'd have lost only the ace of hearts and queen of diamonds," said Mrs. Dittmar, doubtless figuring that the maid would have disposed of her two losing clubs when she swept next morning.

"In this game, everything depends on the bidding," said Mrs. French to Shelton. "You *must* give your partner all the information you can."

"Don't coach him!" said Cameron with an exasperating laugh. "He's treating us pretty good."

"Maybe," said Mrs. French to Mrs. Dittmar, "he would have shown you his spades if you had bid three diamonds instead of four."

"But you see," said Mrs. Dittmar, "we needed four for game and I didn't know if he'd think of that."

And there was a time when Shelton bid a fair no trump and was raised to three by his partner, Cameron, who held king, queen, ten to five hearts and the ace of clubs for a re-entry. The outstanding hearts were bunched in Mrs. French's hand, Shelton himself having the lone ace. After he had taken a spade trick, led his ace of hearts and then a low club to make all of dummy's hearts good (which turned out to be impossible), he put over two deep sea finesses of the eight and nine of diamonds from the dummy hand, made four odd and heard Cameron murmur, "A fool for luck!"

"My! What a waste of good hearts!" said Mrs. Dittmar, ignoring the facts that they weren't good hearts, that if he had continued with them, Mrs. French would have taken the jack and led to her (Mrs. Dittmar's) four good spade tricks, and that with the ace of clubs gone, Shelton couldn't have got back in the dummy's hands with a pass from Judge Landis.

At the close of a perfect evening, the Sheltons were six dollars ahead and invited to the Dittmars' the following Wednesday. Mrs. Shelton expected an explosion on the way home, but was agreeably disappointed. Shelton seemed quite cheerful. He had a few jocose remarks to make about their new pals, but gave the impression that he had enjoyed himself. Knowing him as she did, she might have suspected that a plot was hatching in his mind. However, his behavior was disarming and she thought he had at last found a "crowd" he didn't object to, that they would now be neighborly and gregarious for the first time in their married life.

On the train from the city Friday afternoon, Shelton encountered Gale Bartlett, the writer, just returned from abroad. Bartlett was one of the star contributors to Shelton's magazine and it was he who had first suggested Linden when Shelton was considering a suburban home. He had a place there himself though most of his time was spent in Paris and he was back now for only a brief stay.

"How do you like it?" he asked.

"Fine," said Shelton.

"Whom have you met?"

"Three married couples, the Camerons, the Frenches and the Dittmars."

"God Lord!" said Bartlett. "I don't know the Dittmars but otherwise you're slumming. Cameron and French are new rich who probably made their money in a hotel washroom. I think they met their wives on an excursion to Far Rockaway. How did you happen to get acquainted?"

"The Frenches called on us, and Wednesday night we went to their house for dinner and bridge."

"Bridge!"

"Contract bridge at that."

"Well, maybe Dittmar's a contractor. But from what I've seen of the Frenches and Camerons, they couldn't even cut the cards without smearing them with shoe polish. You break loose from them before they forget themselves and hand you a towel."

"We're going to the Dittmars' next Wednesday night."

"Either call it off or keep it under your hat. I'll introduce you to people that are people! I happen to know them because my wife went to their sisters' boarding school. I'll see that you get the entree and then you can play bridge with bridge players."

Shelton brightened at the prospect. He knew his wife was too kind-hearted to wound the Camerons et al. by quitting them cold and it was part of his scheme, all of it in fact, to make them do the quitting. With the conviction that she would be more than compensated by the promised acquaintance of people they both could really like, he lost what few scruples he had against separating her from people who sooner or later would drive him to the electric chair. The thing must be done at the first opportunity, next Wednesday at the Dittmars'. It would be kind of fun, but unpleasant, too, the unpleasant part consisting in the mental anguish it would cause her and the subsequent days, not many he hoped, when she wouldn't be speaking to him at all.

Fate, in the form of one of Mrs. Shelton's two-day headaches, brought about the elimination of the unpleasant part. The ache began Wednesday afternoon and from past experience, she knew she would not be able to sit through a dinner or play cards that night. She telephoned her husband.

"Say we can't come," was his advice.

"But I hate to do that. They'll think we don't want to and they won't ask us again. I wish you'd go, and maybe they could ask somebody in to take my place. I don't suppose you'd consider that, would you?"

Shelton thought it over a moment and said yes, he would.

Before retiring to her darkened room and her bed, Mrs. Shelton called up Mrs. Dittmar. Mrs. Dittmar expressed her sympathy in baby talk and said it was all right for Mr. Shelton to come alone; it was more than all right, Mrs. Shelton gathered, because Mrs. Dittmar's brother was visiting her and they would be just eight.

Shelton, who had learned long ago that his wife did not want him around when her head was threatening to burst open, stayed in town until six o'clock, preparing himself for the evening's task with liberal doses of the business manager's week-old-rye. He was not going to be tortured by any drought such as he had endured at the Frenches'. He arrived at the party in grand shape and, to his surprise, was plied with cocktails potent enough to keep him on edge.

Mrs. Dittmar's brother (she called him her dreat, big B'udder) was an amateur jazz pianist. (Or rather, peeanist.) He was proving his amateur standing when Shelton got there and something in the way he treated "Rhapsody in Blue" made Shelton resolve to open fire at once. His eagerness was increased when, on the way to the dining room, Mrs. Dittmar observed that her b'udder had not played much contract "either" and she must be sure and not put them (Shelton and B'udder) at the same table, for they might draw each other as partners and that would hardly be fair.

Dinner began and so did Shelton.

"A week ago," he said, "you folks criticized my bridge playing."

The Camerons, Dittmars and Frenches looked queer.

"You didn't mind it, I hope," said Mrs. Dittmar. "We were just trying to teach you."

"I didn't mind it much," said Shelton. "But I was just wondering whether it was good manners for one person to point out another person's mistakes when the other person didn't ask to have them pointed out."

"Why," said Cameron, "when one person don't know as much about a thing as other people, it's their duty to correct him."

"You mean just in bridge," said Shelton.

"I mean in everything," said Cameron.

"And the person criticized or corrected has no right to resent it?" said Shelton.

"Certainly not!"

"Does everybody here agree with that?"

"Yes," "Of course," "Sure," came from the others.

"Well, then," said Shelton, "I think it's my duty to tell you, Mr. Cameron, that soup should be dipped away from you and not toward you."

There was a puzzled silence, then a laugh, to which Cameron contributed feebly.

"If that's right I'm glad to know it, and I certainly don't resent your telling me," he said.

"It looks like Mr. Shelton was out for revenge," said Mrs. Cameron.

"And I must inform you, Mrs. Cameron," said Shelton, "that 'like' is not a conjunction. 'It looks as if Mr. Shelton were out for revenge' would be the correct phrasing."

A smothered laugh at the expense of Mrs. Cameron, whose embarrassment showed itself in a terrifying distension of the nostrils. Shelton decided not to pick on her again.

"Let's change the subject," said Mrs. Dittmar. "Mr. Shelton's a mean, bad man and he'll make us cwy."

"That verb," said Shelton, "is cry, not cwy. It is spelled c-r-y."

"Tell a story, Bob," said Mrs. French to her husband.

"Well, let's see," said French. "I'll tell the one about the Scotchman and the Jew playing golf. Stop me if anybody's heard it."

"I have, for one," said Shelton.

"Maybe the others haven't," said French.

"They must have been unconscious for years," said Shelton. "But go ahead and tell it. I knew I couldn't stop you."

French went ahead and told it, and the others laughed as a rebuke to Shelton.

Cameron wanted things understood.

"You see," he said, "the reason we made a few little criticisms of your bridge game was because we judged you were a new beginner."

"I think 'beginner' is enough, without the 'new,'" said Shelton. "I don't know any old beginners excepting, perhaps, people old in years who are doing something or taking up something for the first time. But probably you judged I was a beginner at bridge because of mistakes I made, and you considered my apparent inexperience justified you in criticizing me."

"Yes," said Cameron.

"Well," said Shelton, "I judge from observing Mrs. French eat her fish that she is a new beginner at eating and I take the liberty of stating that the fork ought never to be conveyed to the mouth with the left hand, even by a left-handed eater. To be sure, these forks are salad forks, not fish forks, as Mrs. Dittmar may believe. But even salad forks, substituting for fish forks, must not be carried mouthward by the left hand."

A storm was gathering and Mrs. Cameron sought to ward it off. She asked Mrs. Dittmar what had become of Peterson, a butler.

"He just up and left me last week," said Mrs. Dittmar. "He was getting too impudent, though, and you can bet I didn't object to him going."

"'His going,'" said Shelton. "A participle used as a substantive is modified in the possessive."

Everyone pretended not to hear him.

"This new one is grand!" said Mrs. Dittmar. "I didn't get up till nearly eleven o'clock this morning—"

"Eleven!" exclaimed Mrs. French.

"Yes. Imagine!" said Mrs. Dittmar. "The itta girl just overslept herself, that's all."

"Mrs. Dittmar," said Shelton, "I have no idea who the itta girl is, but I am interested in your statement that she overslept herself. Would it be possible for her, or any other itta girl, to oversleep somebody else? If it were a sleeping contest, I should think 'outsleep' would be preferable, but even so I can't understand how a girl of any size outsleeps herself."

The storm broke. Dittmar sprang to his feet.

"That's enough, Shelton!" he bellowed. "We've had enough of this nonsense! More than enough!"

"I think," said Shelton, "that the use of the word 'enough' three times in one short speech is more than enough. It grates on me to hear or read a word reiterated like that. I suggest as synonyms 'plenty,' 'a sufficiency,' 'an abundance,' 'a plethora.'"

"Shut your smart aleck mouth and get out!"

"Carl! Carl! Musn't lose temper!" said Mrs. Dittmar. "Lose temper and can't digest food. Daddy mustn't lose temper and be sick all nighty night."

"Shelton just thinks he's funny," said Cameron.

"He's drunk and he'll leave my house at once!" said Dittmar.

"If that's the way you feel about it," said Shelton.

He stopped on the way out to bid Mrs. Dittmar's brother goodnight.

"Good-night, B'udder old boy," he said. "I'm glad to have met you, but sorry to learn you're deaf."

"Deaf! What makes you think I'm deaf?"

"I understood your sister to say you played the piano by ear."

Knowing his wife would have taken something to make her sleep, and therefore not afraid of disturbing her, Shelton went home, got out a bottle of Linden Scotch and put the finishing touches on his bender. In the morning Mrs. Shelton was a little better and came to the breakfast table where he was fighting an egg.

"Well, what kind of time did you have?"

"Glorious! Much more exciting than at the Frenches'. Mrs. Dittmar's brother is a piano playing fool."

"Oh, wasn't there any bridge then?"

"No. Just music and banter."

"Maybe the brother can't play contract and I spoiled the party by not going."

"Oh, no. *You* didn't spoil the party!"

"And do we go to the Camerons' next Wednesday?"

"I don't believe so. Nothing was said."

They did go next Wednesday night to the palatial home of E. M. Pardee, a friend of Gale Bartlett's and one of the real aristocrats of Linden. After dinner, Mrs. Pardee asked the Sheltons whether they played contract, and they said they did. The Pardees, not wishing to impoverish the young immigrants, refused to play "families." They insisted on cutting and Shelton cut Mrs. Pardee.

"Oh, Mr. Shevlin," she said at the end of the first hand, "why *didn't* you lead me a club? You *must* watch the discards!"

Author's Postscript: This story won't get me anything but the money I am paid for it. Even if it be read by those with whom I usually play—Mr. C., Mrs. W., Mr. T., Mrs. R., and the rest—they will think I mean two other fellows and tear into me like wolves next time I bid a slam and make one odd.

The Blue Hotel

STEPHEN CRANE

Civility, an essential virtue governing life among fellow citizens, may be insufficient for dealing with those "others" whose differences from us are more profound. National identity, patriotism, and citizenship unavoidably make distinctions between who is in and who is out. How then should citizens stand with respect to strangers, especially when their ways and beliefs appear to be at odds with our own? Such questions are powerfully raised by Stephen Crane (1871–1900) in "The Blue Hotel" (1899), set in the Great Plains, crossroads of nineteenth-century America, where people of all "creeds, classes, egotisms" pass through and where anything can happen. The uniquely colored blue hotel, situated on the outskirts of a barely civilized Fort Romper, Nebraska, stands out for its promise of shelter, hospitality, community, and camaraderie to any and all whom the railroad brings to town. The story presents the tragedy of one such visitor, "the Swede." Crane invites us to consider what is needed to protect the lives and well-being of strangers, especially those who might rub us the wrong way.

What do Crane's careful portraits of the hotelkeeper, his son, the cowboy, the Easterner, and the gambler—recognizable American types all—reveal about the obstacles to law-abidingness, tolerance, and civil peace? Because Crane's tale encourages readers to view the Swede as do the people of Fort Romper, he forces us to reflect on how we do—and how we should—act toward strangers. Which virtues, evident here only by their absence, does this story highlight? What would you have done regarding the Swede?

I

The Palace Hotel at Fort Romper was painted a light blue, a shade that is on the legs of a kind of heron, causing the bird to declare its position against any background. The Palace Hotel, then, was always screaming and howling in a way that made the dazzling winter landscape of Nebraska seem only a gray swampish hush. It stood alone on the prairie, and when the snow was falling the town two hundred yards away was not visible. But when the traveler alighted at the railway station he was obliged to pass the Palace Hotel before he could come upon the company of low clap-board houses which composed Fort Romper, and it was not to be thought that any traveler could pass the Palace Hotel without looking at it. Pat Scully, the proprietor, had proved himself a master of strategy when he chose his paints. It is true that on clear days, when the great trans-continental expresses, long lines of swaying Pullmans, swept through Fort Romper, passengers were overcome at the sight, and the cult that knows the brown-reds and the subdivisions of the dark greens of the East expressed shame, pity, horror, in a laugh. But to the citizens of this prairie town, and to the people who would naturally stop there, Pat Scully had performed a feat. With this opulence and splendor, these creeds, classes, egotisms, that streamed through Romper on the rails day after day, they had no color in common.

As if the displayed delights of such a blue hotel were not sufficiently enticing, it was Scully's habit to go every morning and evening to meet the leisurely trains that stopped at Romper and work his seductions upon any man that he might see wavering, gripsack in hand.

One morning, when a snow-crusted engine dragged its long string of freight cars and its one passenger coach to the station, Scully performed the marvel of catching three men. One was a shaky and quick-eyed Swede, with a great shining cheap valise; one was a tall bronzed cowboy, who was on his way to a ranch near the Dakota line; one was a little silent man from the East, who didn't look it, and didn't announce it. Scully practically made them prisoners. He was so nimble and merry and kindly that each probably felt it would be the height of brutality to try to escape. They trudged off over the creaking board sidewalks in the wake of the eager little Irishman. He wore a heavy fur cap squeezed tightly down on his head. It caused his two red ears to stick out stiffly, as if they were made of tin.

At last, Scully, elaborately, with boisterous hospitality, conducted them through the portals of the blue hotel. The room which they entered was small. It seemed to be merely a proper temple for an enormous stove, which, in the center, was humming with god-like violence. At various points on its surface the iron had become luminous and glowed yellow from the heat. Beside the stove Scully's son Johnnie was playing High-Five with an old farmer who had whiskers both gray and sandy. They were quarreling. Frequently the old farmer turned his face toward a box of sawdust—colored brown from tobacco juice—that was behind the stove, and spat with an air of great impatience and irritation. With a loud flourish of words Scully destroyed the game of cards, and bustled his son upstairs with part of the baggage of the new guests. He himself conducted them to three basins of the coldest water in the world. The cowboy and the Easterner burnished themselves fiery red with this water, until it seemed to be some kind of a metal polish. The Swede, however, merely dipped his fingers gingerly and with trepidation. It was notable that throughout this series of small ceremonies the three travelers were made to feel that Scully was very benevolent. He was conferring great favors upon them. He handed the towel from one to the other with an air of philanthropic impulse.

Afterward they went to the first room, and, sitting about the stove, listened to Scully's officious clamor at his daughters, who were preparing the midday meal. They reflected in the silence of experienced men who tread carefully amid new people. Nevertheless, the old farmer, stationary, invincible in his chair near the warmest part of the stove, turned his face from the sawdust box frequently and addressed a glowing commonplace to the strangers. Usually he was answered in short but adequate sentences by either the cowboy or the Easterner. The Swede said nothing. He seemed to be occupied in making furtive estimates of each man in the room. One might have thought that he had the sense of silly suspicion which comes to guilt. He resembled a badly frightened man.

Later, at dinner, he spoke a little, addressing his conversation entirely to Scully. He volunteered that he had come from New York, where for ten years he had worked as a tailor. These facts seemed to strike Scully as fascinating, and afterward he volunteered that he had lived at Romper for fourteen years. The Swede asked about the crops and the price of labor. He seemed barely to listen to Scully's extended replies. His eyes continued to rove from man to man.

Finally, with a laugh and a wink, he said that some of these Western communities were very dangerous; and after his statement he straightened his legs under the table, tilted his head, and laughed again, loudly. It was plain that the demonstration had no meaning to the others. They looked at him wondering and in silence.

II

As the men trooped heavily back into the front room, the two little windows presented views of a turmoiling sea of snow. The huge arms of the wind were making attempts—mighty, circular, futile—to embrace the flakes as they sped. A gate-post like a still man with a blanched face stood aghast amid this profligate fury. In a hearty voice Scully announced the presence of a blizzard. The guests of the blue hotel, lighting their pipes, assented with grunts of lazy masculine contentment. No island of the sea could be exempt in the degree of this little room with its humming stove. Johnnie, son of Scully, in a tone which defined his opinion of his ability as a card-player, challenged the old farmer of both gray and sandy whiskers to a game of High-Five. The farmer agreed with a contemptuous and bitter scoff. They sat close to the stove, and squared their knees under a wide board. The cowboy and the Easterner watched the game with interest. The Swede remained near the window, aloof, but with a countenance that showed signs of an inexplicable excitement.

The play of Johnnie and the gray-beard was suddenly ended by another quarrel. The old man arose while casting a look of heated scorn at his adversary. He slowly buttoned his coat, and then stalked with fabulous dignity from the room. In the discreet silence of all other men the Swede laughed. His laughter rang somehow childish. Men by this time had begun to look at him askance, as if they wished to inquire what ailed him.

A new game was formed jocosely. The cowboy volunteered to become the partner of Johnnie, and they all then turned to ask the Swede to throw in his lot with the little Easterner. He asked some questions about the game, and learning that it wore many names, and that he had played it when it was under an alias, he accepted the invitation. He strode toward the men nervously, as if he expected to be assaulted. Finally, seated, he gazed from face to face and laughed shrilly. This laugh was so strange that the Easterner looked up quickly, the cowboy sat intent and with his mouth open, and Johnnie paused, holding the cards with still fingers.

Afterward there was a short silence. Then Johnnie said: "Well, let's get at it. Come on now!" They pulled their chairs forward until their knees were bunched under the board. They began to play, and their interest in the game caused the others to forget the manner of the Swede.

The cowboy was a board-whacker. Each time that he held superior cards he whanged them, one by one, with exceeding force, down upon the improvised table, and took the tricks with a glowing air of prowess and pride that sent thrills of indignation into the hearts of his opponents. A game with a board-whacker in it is sure to become intense. The countenances of the Easterner and the Swede were miserable whenever the cowboy thundered down his aces and kings, while Johnnie, his eyes gleaming with joy, chuckled and chuckled.

Because of the absorbing play none considered the strange ways of the Swede. They paid strict heed to the game. Finally, during a lull caused by a new deal, the Swede suddenly addressed Johnnie: "I suppose there have been a good many men killed in this room." The jaws of the others dropped and they looked at him.

"What in hell are you talking about?" said Johnnie.

The Swede laughed again his blatant laugh, full of a kind of false courage and defiance. "Oh, you know what I mean all right," he answered.

"I'm a liar if I do!" Johnnie protested. The card was halted, and the men stared at the Swede. Johnnie evidently felt that as the son of the proprietor he should make a direct inquiry. "Now, what might you be drivin' at, mister?" he asked. The Swede winked at him. It was a wink full of cunning. His fingers shook on the edge of the board. "Oh, maybe you think I have been to nowheres. Maybe you think I'm a tenderfoot?"

"I don't know nothin' about you," answered Johnnie, "and I don't give a damn where you've been. All I got to say is that I don't know what you're driving at. There hain't never been nobody killed in this room."

The cowboy, who had been steadily gazing at the Swede, then spoke. "What's wrong with you, mister?"

Apparently it seemed to the Swede that he was formidably menaced. He shivered and turned white near the corners of his mouth. He sent an appealing glance in the direction of the little Easterner. During these moments he did not forget to wear his air of advanced pot-valor. "They say they don't know what I mean," he remarked mockingly to the Easterner.

The latter answered after prolonged and cautious reflection. "I don't understand you," he said, impassively.

The Swede made a movement then which announced that he thought he had encountered treachery from the only quarter where he had expected sympathy if not help. "Oh, I see you are all against me. I see—"

The cowboy was in a state of deep stupefaction. "Say," he cried, as he tumbled the deck violently down upon the board. "Say, what are you gittin' at, hey?"

The Swede sprang up with the celerity of a man escaping from a snake on the floor. "I don't want to fight!" he shouted. "I don't want to fight!"

The cowboy stretched his long legs indolently and deliberately. His hands were in his pockets. He spat into the sawdust box. "Well, who the hell thought you did?" he inquired.

The Swede backed rapidly toward a corner of the room. His hands were out protectingly in front of his chest, but he was making an obvious struggle to control his fright. "Gentlemen," he quavered, "I suppose I am going to be killed before I can leave this house! I suppose I am going to be killed before I can leave this house!" In his eyes was the dying swan look. Through the windows could be seen the snow turning blue in the shadow of dusk. The wind tore at the house and some loose thing beat regularly against the clap-boards like a spirit tapping.

A door opened, and Scully himself entered. He paused in surprise as he noted the tragic attitude of the Swede. Then he said: "What's the matter here?"

The Swede answered him swiftly and eagerly: "These men are going to kill me."

"Kill you!" ejaculated Scully. "Kill you! What are you talkin'?"

The Swede made the gesture of a martyr.

Scully wheeled sternly upon his son. "What is this, Johnnie?"

The lad had grown sullen. "Damned if I know," he answered. "I can't make no sense to it." He began to shuffle the cards, fluttering them together with an angry snap. "He says a good many men have been killed in this room, or something like that. And he says he's goin' to be killed here too. I don't know what ails him. He's crazy, I shouldn't wonder."

Scully then looked for explanation to the cowboy, but the cowboy simply shrugged his shoulders.

"Kill you?" said Scully again to the Swede. "Kill you? Man, you're off your nut."

"Oh, I know," burst out the Swede. "I know what will happen. Yes, I'm crazy—yes. Yes, of course, I'm crazy—yes. But I know one thing—" There was a sort of sweat of misery and terror upon his face. "I know I won't get out of here alive."

The cowboy drew a deep breath, as if his mind was passing into the last stages of dissolution. "Well, I'm dog-goned," he whispered to himself.

Scully wheeled suddenly and faced his son. "You've been troublin' this man!"

Johnnie's voice was loud with its burden of grievance. "Why, good Gawd, I ain't done nothin' to 'im."

The Swede broke in. "Gentlemen, do not disturb yourselves. I will leave this house. I will go 'way because—" He accused them dramatically with his glance. "Because I do not want to be killed."

Scully was furious with his son. "Will you tell me what is the matter, you young divil? What's the matter, anyhow? Speak out!"

"Blame it," cried Johnnie in despair, "don't I tell you I don't know. He—he says we want to kill him, and that's all I know. I can't tell what ails him."

The Swede continued to repeat: "Never mind, Mr. Scully, never mind. I will leave this house. I will go away, because I do not wish to be killed. Yes, of course, I am crazy—yes. But I know one thing! I will go away. I will leave this house. Never mind, Mr. Scully, never mind. I will go away."

"You will not go 'way," said Scully. "You will not go 'way until I hear the reason of this business. If anybody has troubled you I will take care of him. This is my house. You are under my roof, and I will not allow any peaceable man to be troubled here." He cast a terrible eye upon Johnnie, the cowboy, and the Easterner.

"Never mind, Mr. Scully, never mind. I will go 'way. I do not wish to be killed." The Swede moved toward the door, which opened upon the stairs. It was evidently his intention to go at once for his baggage.

"No, no," shouted Scully peremptorily; but the white-faced man slid by him and disappeared. "Now," said Scully severely, "what does this mane?"

Johnnie and the cowboy cried together: "Why, we didn't do nothin' to 'im!"

Scully's eyes were cold. "No," he said, "you didn't?"

Johnnie swore a deep oath. "Why, this is the wildest loon I ever see. We didn't do nothin' at all. We were jest sittin' here playin' cards and he—"

The father suddenly spoke to the Easterner. "Mr. Blanc," he asked, "what has these boys been doin'?"

The Easterner reflected again. "I didn't see anything wrong at all," he said at last slowly.

Scully began to howl. "But what does it mane?" He stared ferociously at his son. "I have a mind to lather you for this, me boy."

Johnnie was frantic. "Well, what have I done?" he bawled at his father.

III

"I think you are tongue-tied," said Scully finally to his son, the cowboy and the Easterner, and at the end of this scornful sentence he left the room.

Upstairs the Swede was swiftly fastening the straps of his great valise. Once his back happened to be half-turned toward the door, and hearing a noise there, he wheeled and sprang up, uttering a loud cry. Scully's wrinkled visage showed grimly in the light of the small lamp he carried. This yellow effulgence, streaming upward, colored only his prominent features, and left his eyes, for instance, in mysterious shadow. He resembled a murderer.

"Man, man!" he exclaimed, "have you gone daffy?"

"Oh, no! Oh, no!" rejoined the other. "There are people in this world who know pretty nearly as much as you do—understand?"

For a moment they stood gazing at each other. Upon the Swede's deathly pale cheeks were two spots brightly crimson and sharply edged, as if they had been carefully painted. Scully placed the light on the table and sat himself on the edge of the bed. He spoke ruminatively. "By cracky, I never heard of such a thing in my life. It's a complete muddle. I can't for the soul of me think how you ever got this idea into your head." Presently he lifted his eyes and asked: "And did you sure think they were going to kill you?"

The Swede scanned the old man as if he wished to see into his mind. "I did," he said at last. He obviously suspected that this answer might precipitate an outbreak. As he pulled on a strap his whole arm shook, the elbow wavering like a bit of paper.

Scully banged his hand impressively on the foot-board of the bed. "Why, man, we're goin' to have a line of ilictric street-cars in this town next spring."

"'A line of electric street-cars,'" repeated the Swede stupidly.

"And," said Scully, "there's a new railroad goin' to be built down from Broken Arm to here. Not to mintion the four churches and the smashin' big brick school-house. Then there's the big factory, too. Why, in two years Romper'll be a met-tro-*pol*-is."

Having finished the preparation of his baggage, the Swede straightened himself. "Mr. Scully," he said with sudden hardihood, "how much do I owe you?"

"You don't owe me anythin'," said the old man angrily.

"Yes, I do," retorted the Swede. He took seventy-five cents from his pocket and tendered it to Scully; but the latter snapped his fingers in disdainful refusal. However, it happened that they both stood gazing in a strange fashion at three silver pieces on the Swede's open palm.

"I'll not take your money," said Scully at last. "Not after what's been goin' on here." Then a plan seemed to strike him. "Here," he cried, picking up his lamp and moving toward the door. "Here! Come with me a minute."

"No," said the Swede in overwhelming alarm.

"Yes," urged the old man. "Come on! I want you to come and see a picter— just across the hall—in my room."

The Swede must have concluded that his hour was come. His jaw dropped and his teeth showed like a dead man's. He ultimately followed Scully across the corridor, but he had the step of one hung in chains.

Scully flashed the light high on the wall of his own chamber. There was revealed a ridiculous photograph of a little girl. She was leaning against a balustrade of gorgeous decoration, and the formidable bang to her hair was prominent. The figure was as graceful as an upright sled-stake, and, withal, it was of the hue of lead. "There," said Scully tenderly. "That's the picter of my little girl that died. Her name was Carrie. She had the purtiest hair you ever saw! I was that fond of her, she—"

Turning then he saw that the Swede was not contemplating the picture at all, but, instead, was keeping keen watch on the gloom in the rear.

"Look, man!" shouted Scully heartily. "That's the picter of my little gal that died. Her name was Carrie. And then here's the picter of my oldest boy, Michael. He's a lawyer in Lincoln an' doin' well. I gave that boy a grand eddycation, and I'm glad for it now. He's a fine boy. Look at 'im now. Ain't he bold as blazes, him there in Lincoln, an honored an' respicted gintleman. An honored an' respicted gintleman," concluded Scully with a flourish. And so saying, he smote the Swede jovially on the back.

The Swede faintly smiled.

"Now," said the old man, "there's only one more thing." He dropped suddenly to the floor and thrust his head beneath the bed. The Swede could hear his muffled voice. "I'd keep it under me piller if it wasn't for that boy Johnnie. Then there's the old woman—Where is it now? I never put it twice in the same place. Ah, now come out with you!"

Presently he backed clumsily from under the bed, dragging with him an old coat rolled into a bundle. "I've fetched him," he muttered. Kneeling on the floor he unrolled the coat and extracted from its heart a large yellow-brown whisky bottle.

His first maneuver was to hold the bottle up to the light. Reassured, apparently, that nobody had been tampering with it, he thrust it with a generous movement toward the Swede.

The weak-kneed Swede was about to eagerly clutch this element of strength, but he suddenly jerked his hand away and cast a look of horror upon Scully.

"Drink," said the old man affectionately. He had arisen to his feet, and now stood facing the Swede.

There was a silence. Then again Scully said: "Drink!"

The Swede laughed wildly. He grabbed the bottle, put it to his mouth, and as his lips curled absurdly around the opening and his throat worked, he kept his glance burning with hatred upon the old man's face.

IV

After the departure of Scully the three men, with the card-board still upon their knees, preserved for a long time an astounded silence. Then Johnnie said: "That's the dod-dangest Swede I ever see."

"He ain't no Swede," said the cowboy scornfully.

"Well, what is he then?" cried Johnnie. "What is he then?"

"It's my opinion," replied the cowboy deliberately, "he's some kind of a Dutchman." It was a venerable custom of the country to entitle as Swedes all light-haired men who spoke with a heavy tongue. In consequence the idea of the cowboy was not without its daring. "Yes, sir," he repeated. "It's my opinion this feller is some kind of a Dutchman."

"Well, he says he's a Swede, anyhow," muttered Johnnie sulkily. He turned to the Easterner: "What do you think, Mr. Blanc?"

"Oh, I don't know," replied the Easterner.

"Well, what do you think makes him act that way?" asked the cowboy.

"Why, he's frightened!" The Easterner knocked his pipe against a rim of the stove. "He's clear frightened out of his boots."

"What at?" cried Johnnie and cowboy together.

The Easterner reflected over his answer.

"What at?" cried the others again.

"Oh, I don't know, but it seems to me this man has been reading dime-novels, and he thinks he's right out in the middle of it—the shootin' and stab-bin' and all."

"But," said the cowboy, deeply scandalized, "this ain't Wyoming, ner none of them places. This is Nebrasker."

"Yes," added Johnnie, "an' why don't he wait till he gits *out West?*"

The traveled Easterner laughed. "It isn't different there even—not in these days. But he thinks he's right in the middle of hell."

Johnnie and the cowboy mused long.

"It's awful funny," remarked Johnnie at last.

"Yes," said the cowboy. "This is a queer game. I hope we don't git snowed in, because then we'd have to stand this here man bein' around with us all the time. That wouldn't be no good."

"I wish pop would throw him out," said Johnnie.

Presently they heard a loud stamping on the stairs, accompanied by ring-ing jokes in the voice of old Scully, and laughter, evidently from the Swede. The men around the stove stared vacantly at each other. "Gosh," said the cow-boy. The door flew open, and old Scully, flushed and anecdotal, came into the room. He was jabbering at the Swede, who followed him, laughing bravely. It was the entry of two roysterers from a banquet hall.

"Come now," said Scully sharply to the three seated men, "move up and give us a chance at the stove." The cowboy and the Easterner obediently sidled their chairs to make room for the newcomers. Johnnie, however, simply arranged himself in a more indolent attitude, and then remained motionless.

"Come! Git over, there," said Scully.

"Plenty of room on the other side of the stove," said Johnnie.

"Do you think we want to sit in the draught?" roared the father.

But the Swede here interposed with a grandeur of confidence. "No, no. Let the boy sit where he likes," he cried in a bullying voice to the father.

"All right! All right!" said Scully deferentially. The cowboy and the Easterner exchanged glances of wonder.

The five chairs were formed in a crescent about one side of the stove. The Swede began to talk; he talked arrogantly, profanely, angrily. Johnnie, the cowboy and the Easterner maintained a morose silence, while old Scully appeared to be receptive and eager, breaking in constantly with sympathetic ejaculations.

Finally the Swede announced that he was thirsty. He moved in his chair, and said that he would go for a drink of water.

"I'll git it for you," cried Scully at once.

"No," said the Swede contemptuously. "I'll get it for myself." He arose and stalked with the air of an owner off into the executive parts of the hotel.

As soon as the Swede was out of hearing Scully sprang to his feet and whispered intensely to the others. "Upstairs he thought I was tryin' to poison 'im."

"Say," said Johnnie, "this makes me sick. Why don't you throw 'im out in the snow?"

"Why, he's all right now," declared Scully. "It was only that he was from the East and he thought this was a tough place. That's all. He's all right now."

The cowboy looked with admiration upon the Easterner. "You were straight," he said. "You were on to that there Dutchman."

"Well," said Johnnie to his father, "he may be all right now, but I don't see it. Other time he was scared, and now he's too fresh."

Scully's speech was always a combination of Irish brogue and idiom, Western twang and idiom, and scraps of curiously formal diction taken from the story-books and newspapers. He now hurled a strange mass of language at the head of his son. "What do I keep? What do I keep? What do I keep?" he demanded in a voice of thunder. He slapped his knee impressively, to indicate that he himself was going to make reply, and that all should heed. "I keep a hotel," he shouted. "A hotel, do you mind? A guest under my roof has sacred privileges. He is to be intimidated by none. Not one word shall he hear that would prijudice him in favor of goin' away. I'll not have it. There's no place in this here town where they can say they iver took in a guest of mine because he was afraid to stay here." He wheeled suddenly upon the cowboy and the Easterner. "Am I right?"

"Yes, Mr. Scully," said the cowboy, "I think you're right."

"Yes, Mr. Scully," said the Easterner, "I think you're right."

V

At six-o'clock supper, the Swede fizzed like a fire-wheel. He sometimes seemed on the point of bursting into riotous song, and in all his madness he was encouraged by old Scully. The Easterner was incased in reserve; the cowboy sat in wide-mouthed amazement, forgetting to eat, while Johnnie wrathily demolished great plates of food. The daughters of the house when they were obliged to replenish the biscuits approached as warily as Indians, and, having succeeded in their purposes, fled with ill-concealed trepidation. The Swede domineered the whole feast, and he gave it the appearance of a cruel bacchanal. He seemed to have grown suddenly taller; he gazed, brutally disdainful, into every face. His voice rang through the room. Once when he jabbed out harpoon-fashion with his fork to pinion a biscuit the weapon nearly impaled the hand of the Easterner which had been stretched quietly out for the same biscuit.

After supper, as the men filed toward the other room, the Swede smote Scully ruthlessly on the shoulder. "Well, old boy, that was a good square meal." Johnnie looked hopefully at his father; he knew that shoulder was tender from an old fall; and indeed it appeared for a moment as if Scully was going to flame out over the matter, but in the end he smiled a sickly smile and remained silent. The others understood from his manner that he was admitting his responsibility for the Swede's new viewpoint.

Johnnie, however, addressed his parent in an aside. "Why don't you license somebody to kick you downstairs?" Scully scowled darkly by way of reply.

When they were gathered about the stove, the Swede insisted on another game of High-Five. Scully gently deprecated the plan at first, but the Swede turned a wolfish glare upon him. The old man subsided, and the Swede canvassed the others. In his tone there was always a great threat. The cowboy and the Easterner both remarked indifferently that they would play. Scully said that he would presently have to go to meet the 6.58 train, and so the Swede turned menacingly upon Johnnie. For a moment their glances crossed like blades, and then Johnnie smiled and said: "Yes, I'll play."

They formed a square with the little board on their knees. The Easterner and the Swede were again partners. As the play went on, it was noticeable that the cowboy was not board-whacking as usual. Meanwhile, Scully, near the lamp, had put on his spectacles and, with an appearance curiously like an old priest, was reading a newspaper. In time he went out to meet the 6.58 train, and, despite his precautions, a gust of polar wind whirled into the room as he opened the door. Besides scattering the cards, it chilled the players to the marrow. The Swede cursed frightfully. When Scully returned, his entrance disturbed a cozy and friendly scene. The Swede again cursed. But presently they were once more intent, their heads bent forward and their hands moving swiftly. The Swede had adopted the fashion of board-whacking.

Scully took up his paper and for a long time remained immersed in matters which were extraordinarily remote from him. The lamp burned badly, and once he stopped to adjust the wick. The newspaper as he turned from page to page rustled with a slow and comfortable sound. Then suddenly he heard three terrible words: "You are cheatin'!"

Such scenes often prove that there can be little of dramatic import in environment. Any room can present a tragic front; any room can be comic. This little den was now hideous as a torture-chamber. The new faces of the men themselves had changed it upon the instant. The Swede held a huge fist in front of Johnnie's face, while the latter looked steadily over it into the blazing orbs of his accuser. The Easterner had grown pallid; the cowboy's jaw had dropped in that expression of bovine amazement which was one of his important mannerisms. After the three words, the first sound in the room was made by Scully's paper as it floated forgotten to his feet. His spectacles had also fallen from his nose, but by a clutch he had saved them in air. His hand, grasping the spectacles, now remained poised awkwardly and near his shoulder. He stared at the card-players.

Probably the silence was while a second elapsed. Then, if the floor had been suddenly twitched out from under the men they could not have moved quicker. The five had projected themselves headlong toward a common point. It happened that Johnnie in rising to hurl himself upon the Swede had stumbled slightly because of his curiously instinctive care for the cards and the board. The loss of the moment allowed time for the arrival of Scully, and also allowed the cowboy time to give the Swede a great push which sent him staggering back. The men found tongue together, and hoarse shouts of rage, appeal or fear burst from every throat. The cowboy pushed and jostled feverishly at the Swede, and the Easterner and Scully clung wildly to Johnnie; but, through the smoky air, above the swaying bodies of the peace-compellers, the eyes of the two warriors ever sought each other in glances of challenge that were at once hot and steely.

Of course the board had been overturned, and now the whole company of cards was scattered over the floor, where the boots of the men trampled the fat and painted kings and queens as they gazed with their silly eyes at the war that was waging above them.

Scully's voice was dominating the yells. "Stop now! Stop, I say! Stop, now—"

Johnnie, as he struggled to burst through the rank formed by Scully and the Easterner, was crying: "Well, he says I cheated! He says I cheated! I won't allow no man to say I cheated! If he says I cheated, he's a——!"

The cowboy was telling the Swede: "Quit, now! Quit, d'ye hear—"

The screams of the Swede never ceased. "He did cheat! I saw him! I saw him—"

As for the Easterner, he was importuning in a voice that was not heeded. "Wait a moment, can't you? Oh, wait a moment. What's the good of a fight over a game of cards? Wait a moment—"

In this tumult no complete sentences were clear. "Cheat"—"Quit"—"He says"—These fragments pierced the uproar and rang out sharply. It was remarkable that whereas Scully undoubtedly made the most noise, he was the least heard of any of the riotous band.

Then suddenly there was a great cessation. It was as if each man had paused for breath, and although the room was still lighted with the anger of men, it could be seen that there was no danger of immediate conflict, and at once Johnnie, shouldering his way forward, almost succeeded in confronting the Swede. "What did you say I cheated for? What did you say I cheated for? I don't cheat and I won't let no man say I do!"

The Swede said: "I saw you! I saw you!"

"Well," cried Johnnie, "I'll fight any man what says I cheat!"

"No, you won't," said the cowboy. "Not here."

"Ah, be still, can't you?" said Scully, coming between them.

The quiet was sufficient to allow the Easterner's voice to be heard. He was repeating: "Oh, wait a moment, can't you? What's the good of a fight over a game of cards? Wait a moment."

Johnnie, his red face appearing above his father's shoulder, hailed the Swede again. "Did you say I cheated?"

The Swede showed his teeth. "Yes."

"Then," said Johnnie, "we must fight."

"Yes, fight," roared the Swede. He was like a demoniac. "Yes, fight! I'll show you what kind of a man I am! I'll show you who you want to fight! Maybe you think I can't fight! Maybe you think I can't! I'll show you, you skin, you card-sharp! Yes, you cheated! You cheated! You cheated!"

"Well, let's git at it, then, mister," said Johnnie coolly.

The cowboy's brow was beaded with sweat from his efforts in intercepting all sorts of raids. He turned in despair to Scully. "What are you goin' to do now?"

A change had come over the Celtic visage of the old man. He now seemed all eagerness; his eyes glowed.

"We'll let them fight," he answered stalwartly. "I can't put up with it any longer. I've stood this damned Swede till I'm sick. We'll let them fight."

VI

The men prepared to go out of doors. The Easterner was so nervous that he had great difficulty in getting his arms into the sleeves of his new leather-coat. As the cowboy drew his fur-cap down over his ears his hands trembled. In fact, Johnnie and old Scully were the only ones who displayed no agitation. These preliminaries were conducted without words.

Scully threw open the door. "Well, come on," he said. Instantly a terrific wind caused the flame of the lamp to struggle at its wick, while a puff of black smoke sprang from the chimney-top. The stove was in mid-current of the blast, and its voice swelled to equal the roar of the storm. Some of the scarred and bedabbled cards were caught up from the floor and dashed helplessly against the further wall. The men lowered their heads and plunged into the tempest as into a sea.

No snow was falling, but great whirls and clouds of flakes, swept up from the ground by the frantic winds, were streaming southward with the speed of bullets. The covered land was blue with the sheen of an unearthly satin, and there was no other hue save where at the low black railway station—which seemed incredibly distant—one light gleamed like a tiny jewel. As the men floundered into a thigh-deep drift, it was known that the Swede was bawling out something. Scully went to him, put a hand on his shoulder and projected an ear. "What's that you say?" he shouted.

"I say," bawled the Swede again, "I won't stand much show against this gang. I know you'll all pitch on me."

Scully smote him reproachfully on the arm. "Tut, man," he yelled. The wind tore the words from Scully's lips and scattered them far a-lee.

"You are all a gang of—" boomed the Swede, but the storm also seized the remainder of this sentence.

Immediately turning their backs upon the wind, the men had swung around a corner to the sheltered side of the hotel. It was the function of the little house to preserve here, amid this great devastation of snow, an irregular V-shape of heavily-incrusted grass, which crackled beneath the feet. One could imagine the great drifts piled against the windward side. When the party reached the comparative peace of this spot it was found that the Swede was still bellowing.

"Oh, I know what kind of a thing this is! I know you'll all pitch on me. I can't lick you all!"

Scully turned upon him panther-fashion. "You'll not have to whip all of us. You'll have to whip my son Johnnie. An' the man what troubles you durin' that time will have me to dale with."

The arrangements were swiftly made. The two men faced each other, obedient to the harsh commands of Scully, whose face, in the subtly luminous gloom, could be seen set in the austere impersonal lines that are pictured on the countenances of the Roman veterans. The Easterner's teeth were chattering, and he was hopping up and down like a mechanical toy. The cowboy stood rock-like.

The contestants had not stripped off any clothing. Each was in his ordinary attire. Their fists were up, and they eyed each other in a calm that had the elements of leonine cruelty in it.

During this pause, the Easterner's mind, like a film, took lasting impressions of three men—the iron-nerved master of the ceremony; the Swede, pale, motionless, terrible; and Johnnie, serene yet ferocious, brutish yet heroic. The entire prelude had in it a tragedy greater than the tragedy of action, and this aspect was accentuated by the long mellow cry of the blizzard, as it sped the tumbling and wailing flakes into the black abyss of the south.

"Now!" said Scully.

The two combatants leaped forward and crashed together like bullocks. There was heard the cushioned sound of blows, and of a curse squeezing out from between the tight teeth of one.

As for the spectators, the Easterner's pent-up breath exploded from him with a pop of relief, absolute relief from the tension of the preliminaries. The cowboy bounded into the air with a yowl. Scully was immovable as from supreme amazement and fear at the fury of the fight which he himself had permitted and arranged.

For a time the encounter in the darkness was such a perplexity of flying arms that it presented no more detail than would a swiftly-revolving wheel. Occasionally a face, as if illumined by a flash of light, would shine out, ghastly and marked with pink spots. A moment later, the men might have been known as shadows, if it were not for the involuntary utterance of oaths that came from them in whispers.

Suddenly a holocaust of warlike desire caught the cowboy, and he bolted forward with the speed of a broncho. "Go it, Johnnie; go it! Kill him! Kill him!"

Scully confronted him. "Kape back," he said; and by his glance the cowboy could tell that this man was Johnnie's father.

To the Easterner there was a monotony of unchangeable fighting that was an abomination. This confused mingling was eternal to his sense, which was concentrated in a longing for the end, the priceless end. Once the fighters lurched near him, and as he scrambled hastily backward, he heard them breathe like men on the rack.

"Kill him, Johnnie! Kill him! Kill him! Kill him!" The cowboy's face was contorted like one of those agony-masks in museums.

"Keep still," said Scully icily.

Then there was a sudden loud grunt, incomplete, cut-short, and Johnnie's body swung away from the Swede and fell with sickening heaviness to the grass. The cowboy was barely in time to prevent the mad Swede from flinging himself upon his prone adversary. "No, you don't," said the cowboy, interposing an arm. "Wait a second."

Scully was at his son's side. "Johnnie! Johnnie, me boy?" His voice had a quality of melancholy tenderness. "Johnnie? Can you go on with it?" He looked anxiously down into the bloody pulpy face of his son.

There was a moment of silence, and then Johnnie answered in his ordinary voice: "Yes, I—it—yes."

Assisted by his father he struggled to his feet. "Wait a bit now till you git your wind," said the old man.

A few paces away the cowboy was lecturing the Swede. "No, you don't! Wait a second!"

The Easterner was plucking at Scully's sleeve. "Oh, this is enough," he pleaded. "This is enough! Let it go as it stands. This is enough!"

"Bill," said Scully, "git out of the road." The cowboy stepped aside. "Now." The combatants were actuated by a new caution as they advanced toward collision. They glared at each other, and then the Swede aimed a lightning blow that carried with it his entire weight. Johnnie was evidently half-stupid from weakness, but he miraculously dodged, and his fist sent the over-balanced Swede sprawling.

The cowboy, Scully and the Easterner burst into a cheer that was like a chorus of triumphant soldiery, but before its conclusion the Swede had scuffled agilely to his feet and come in berserk abandon at his foe. There was another perplexity of flying arms, and Johnnie's body again swung away and fell, even as a bundle might fall from a roof. The Swede instantly staggered to a little wind-waved tree and leaned upon it, breathing like an engine, while his savage and flame-lit eyes roamed from face to face as the men bent over Johnnie. There was a splendor of isolation in his situation at this time which the Easterner felt once when, lifting his eyes from the man on the ground, he beheld that mysterious and lonely figure, waiting.

"Are you any good yet, Johnnie?" asked Scully in a broken voice.

The son gasped and opened his eyes languidly. After a moment he answered: "No—I ain't—any good—any—more." Then, from shame and bodily ill, he began to weep, the tears furrowing down through the blood-stains on his face. "He was too—too—too heavy for me."

Scully straightened and addressed the waiting figure. "Stranger," he said, evenly, "it's all up with our side." Then his voice changed into that vibrant huskiness which is commonly the tone of the most simple and deadly announcements. "Johnnie is whipped."

Without replying, the victor moved off on the route to the front door of the hotel.

The cowboy was formulating new and unspellable blasphemies. The Easterner was startled to find that they were out in a wind that seemed to come direct from the shadowed arctic floes. He heard again the wail of the snow as it was flung to its grave in the south. He knew now that all this time the cold had been sinking into him deeper and deeper, and he wondered that he had not perished. He felt indifferent to the condition of the vanquished man.

"Johnnie, can you walk?" asked Scully.

"Did I hurt—hurt him any?" asked the son.

"Can you walk, boy? Can you walk?"

Johnnie's voice was suddenly strong. There was a robust impatience in it. "I asked you whether I hurt him any!"

"Yes, yes, Johnnie," answered the cowboy consolingly; "he's hurt a good deal."

They raised him from the ground, and as soon as he was on his feet he went tottering off, rebuffing all attempts at assistance. When the party rounded the corner they were fairly blinded by the pelting of the snow. It burned their faces like fire. The cowboy carried Johnnie through the drift to the door. As they entered some cards again rose from the floor and beat against the wall.

The Easterner rushed to the stove. He was so profoundly chilled that he almost dared to embrace the glowing iron. The Swede was not in the room. Johnnie sank into a chair, and folding his arms on his knees, buried his face in them. Scully, warming one foot and then the other at a rim of the stove, muttered to himself with Celtic mournfulness. The cowboy had removed his fur-cap, and with a dazed and rueful air he was now running one hand through his tousled locks. From overhead they could hear the creaking of boards, as the Swede tramped here and there in his room.

The sad quiet was broken by the sudden flinging open of a door that led toward the kitchen. It was instantly followed by an inrush of women. They precipitated themselves upon Johnnie amid a chorus of lamentation. Before they carried their prey off to the kitchen, there to be bathed and harangued with that mixture of sympathy and abuse which is a feat of their sex, the mother straightened herself and fixed old Scully with an eye of stern reproach.

"Shame be upon you, Patrick Scully!" she cried. "Your own son, too. Shame be upon you!"

"There, now! Be quiet, now!" said the old man weakly.

"Shame be upon you, Patrick Scully!" The girls rallying to this slogan, sniffed disdainfully in the direction of those trembling accomplices, the cowboy and the Easterner. Presently they bore Johnnie away, and left the three men to dismal reflection.

VII

"I'd like to fight this here Dutchman myself," said the cowboy, breaking a long silence.

Scully wagged his head sadly. "No, that wouldn't do. It wouldn't be right. It wouldn't be right."

"Well, why wouldn't it?" argued the cowboy. "I don't see no harm in it."

"No," answered Scully with mournful heroism. "It wouldn't be right. It was Johnnie's fight, and now we mustn't whip the man just because he whipped Johnnie."

"Yes, that's true enough," said the cowboy; "but—he better not get fresh with me, because I couldn't stand no more of it."

"You'll not say a word to him," commanded Scully, and even then they heard the tread of the Swede on the stairs. His entrance was made theatric. He swept the door back with a bang and swaggered to the middle of the room. No one looked at him. "Well," he cried, insolently, at Scully, "I s'pose you'll tell me now how much I owe you?"

The old man remained stolid. "You don't owe me nothin'."

"Huh!" said the Swede, "huh! Don't owe 'im nothin'."

The cowboy addressed the Swede. "Stranger, I don't see how you come to be so gay around here."

Old Scully was instantly alert. "Stop!" he shouted, holding his hand forth, fingers upward. "Bill, you shut up!"

The cowboy spat carelessly into the sawdust box. "I didn't say a word, did I?" he asked.

"Mr. Scully," called the Swede, "how much do I owe you?" It was seen that he was attired for departure, and that he had his valise in his hand.

"You don't owe me nothin'," repeated Scully in his same imperturbable way.

"Huh!" said the Swede. "I guess you're right. I guess if it was any way at all, you'd owe me somethin'. That's what I guess." He turned to the cowboy.

"'Kill him! Kill him! Kill him!'" he mimicked, and then guffawed victoriously. "'Kill him!'" He was convulsed with ironical humor.

But he might have been jeering the dead. The three men were immovable and silent, staring with glassy eyes at the stove.

The Swede opened the door and passed into the storm, giving one derisive glance backward at the still group.

As soon as the door was closed, Scully and the cowboy leaped to their feet and began to curse. They trampled to and fro, waving their arms and smashing into the air with their fists. "Oh, but that was a hard minute!" wailed Scully. "That was a hard minute! Him there leerin' and scoffin'! One bang at his nose was worth forty dollars to me that minute! How did you stand it, Bill?"

"How did I stand it?" cried the cowboy in a quivering voice. "How did I stand it? Oh!"

The old man burst into sudden brogue. "I'd loike to take that Swade," he wailed, "and hould 'im down on a shtone flure and bate 'im to a jelly wid a shtick!"

The cowboy groaned in sympathy. "I'd like to git him by the neck and ha-ammer him"—he brought his hand down on a chair with a noise like a pistol-shot—"hammer that there Dutchman until he couldn't tell himself from a dead coyote!"

"I'd bate 'im until he—"

"I'd show *him* some things—"

And then together they raised a yearning fanatic cry. "Oh-o-oh! if we only could—"

"Yes!"

"Yes!"

"And then I'd—"

"O-o-oh!"

VIII

The Swede, tightly gripping his valise, tacked across the face of the storm as if he carried sails. He was following a line of little naked gasping trees, which he knew must mark the way of the road. His face, fresh from the pounding of Johnnie's fists, felt more pleasure than pain in the wind and the driving snow. A number of square shapes loomed upon him finally, and he knew them as the houses of the main body of the town. He found a street and made travel along it, leaning heavily upon the wind whenever, at a corner, a terrific blast caught him.

He might have been in a deserted village. We picture the world as thick with conquering and elate humanity, but here, with the bugles of the tempest pealing, it was hard to imagine a peopled earth. One viewed the existence of man then as a marvel, and conceded a glamour of wonder to these lice which were caused to cling to a whirling, fire-smote, ice-locked, disease-stricken, space-lost bulb. The conceit of man was explained by this storm to be the very engine of life. One was a coxcomb not to die in it. However, the Swede found a saloon.

In front of it an indomitable red light was burning, and the snow-flakes were made blood-color as they flew through the circumscribed territory of the lamp's shining. The Swede pushed open the door of the saloon and entered. A sanded expanse was before him, and at the end of it four men sat about a table drinking. Down one side of the room extended a radiant bar, and its guardian was leaning upon his elbows listening to the talk of the men at the table. The Swede dropped his valise upon the floor, and, smiling fraternally upon the barkeeper, said: "Gimme some whisky, will you?" The man placed a bottle, a whisky-glass, and glass of ice-thick water upon the bar. The Swede poured himself an abnormal portion of whisky and drank it in three gulps. "Pretty bad night," remarked the bartender indifferently. He was making the pretension of blindness, which is usually a distinction of his class; but it could have been seen that he was furtively studying the half-erased blood-stains on the face of the Swede. "Bad night," he said again.

"Oh, it's good enough for me," replied the Swede, hardily, as he poured himself some more whisky. The barkeeper took his coin and maneuvered it through its reception by the highly-nickeled cash-machine. A bell rang; a card labeled "20 cts." had appeared.

"No," continued the Swede, "this isn't too bad weather. It's good enough for me."

"So?" murmured the barkeeper languidly.

The copious drams made the Swede's eyes swim, and he breathed a trifle heavier. "Yes, I like this weather. I like it. It suits me." It was apparently his design to impart a deep significance to these words.

"So?" murmured the bartender again. He turned to gaze dreamily at the scroll-like birds and bird-like scrolls which had been drawn with soap upon the mirrors back of the bar.

"Well, I guess I'll take another drink," said the Swede presently. "Have something?"

"No, thanks; I'm not drinkin'," answered the bartender. Afterward he asked: "How did you hurt your face?"

The Swede immediately began to boast loudly. "Why, in a fight. I thumped the soul out of a man down here at Scully's hotel."

The interest of the four men at the table was at last aroused.

"Who was it?" said one.

"Johnnie Scully," blustered the Swede. "Son of the man what runs it. He will be pretty near dead for some weeks, I can tell you. I made a nice thing of him, I did. He couldn't get up. They carried him in the house. Have a drink?"

Instantly the men in some subtle way incased themselves in reserve. "No, thanks," said one. The group was of curious formation. Two were prominent local business men; one was the district-attorney; and one was a professional gambler of the kind known as "square." But a scrutiny of the group would not have enabled an observer to pick the gambler from the men of more reputable pursuits. He was, in fact, a man so delicate in manner, when among people of fair class, and so judicious in his choice of victims, that in the strictly masculine part of the town's life he had come to be explicitly trusted and admired. People called him a thoroughbred. The fear and contempt with which his craft was regarded was undoubtedly the reason that his quiet dignity shone conspicuous above the quiet dignity of men who might be merely hatters, billiard-markers or grocery clerks. Beyond an occasional unwary traveler, who came by rail, this gambler was supposed to prey solely upon reckless and senile farmers, who, when flush with good crops, drove into town in all the pride and confidence of an absolutely invulnerable stupidity. Hearing at times in circuitous fashion of the despoilment of such a farmer, the important men of Romper invariably laughed in contempt of the victim, and if they thought of the wolf at all, it was with a kind of pride at the knowledge that he would never dare think of attacking their wisdom and courage. Besides, it was popular that this gambler had a real wife and two real children in a neat cottage in a suburb, where he led an exemplary home life, and when any one even suggested a discrepancy in his character, the crowd immediately vociferated descriptions of this virtuous family circle. Then men who led exemplary home lives, and men who did not lead exemplary home lives, all subsided in a bunch, remarking that there was nothing more to be said.

However, when a restriction was placed upon him—as, for instance, when a strong clique of members of the new Pollywog Club refused to permit him, even as a spectator, to appear in the rooms of the organization—the candor and gentleness with which he accepted the judgment disarmed many of his foes and made his friends more desperately partisan. He invariably distinguished between himself and a respectable Romper man so quickly and frankly that his manner actually appeared to be a continual broadcast compliment.

And one must not forget to declare the fundamental fact of his entire position in Romper. It is irrefutable that in all affairs outside of his business, in all matters that occur eternally and commonly between man and man, this thieving card-player was so generous, so just, so moral, that, in a contest, he could have put to flight the consciences of nine-tenths of the citizens of Romper.

And so it happened that he was seated in this saloon with the two prominent local merchants and the district-attorney.

The Swede continued to drink raw whisky, meanwhile babbling at the barkeeper and trying to induce him to indulge in potations. "Come on. Have a drink. Come on. What—no? Well, have a little one then. By gawd, I've whipped a man to-night, and I want to celebrate. I whipped him good, too. Gentlemen," the Swede cried to the men at the table, "have a drink?"

"Ssh!" said the barkeeper.

The group at the table, although furtively attentive, had been pretending to be deep in talk, but now a man lifted his eyes toward the Swede and said shortly: "Thanks. We don't want any more."

At this reply the Swede ruffled out his chest like a rooster. "Well," he exploded, "it seems I can't get anybody to drink with me in this town. Seems so, don't it? Well!"

"Ssh!" said the barkeeper.

"Say," snarled the Swede, "don't you try to shut me up. I won't have it. I'm a gentleman, and I want people to drink with me. And I want 'em to drink with me now. *Now*—do you understand?" He rapped the bar with his knuckles.

Years of experience had calloused the bartender. He merely grew sulky. "I hear you," he answered.

"Well," cried the Swede, "listen hard then. See those men over there? Well, they're going to drink with me, and don't you forget it. Now you watch."

"Hi!" yelled the barkeeper, "this won't do!"

"Why won't it?" demanded the Swede. He stalked over to the table, and by chance laid his hand upon the shoulder of the gambler. "How about this?" he asked, wrathfully. "I asked you to drink with me."

The gambler simply twisted his head and spoke over his shoulder. "My friend, I don't know you."

"Oh, hell!" answered the Swede, "come and have a drink."

"Now, my boy," advised the gambler kindly, "take your hand off my shoulder and go 'way and mind your own business." He was a little slim man, and it seemed strange to hear him use this tone of heroic patronage to the burly Swede. The other men at the table said nothing.

"What? You won't drink with me, you little dude! I'll make you then! I'll make you!" The Swede had grasped the gambler frenziedly at the throat, and was dragging him from his chair. The other men sprang up. The barkeeper dashed around the corner of his bar. There was a great tumult, and then was seen a long blade in the hand of the gambler. It shot forward, and a human body, this citadel of virtue, wisdom, power, was pierced as easily as if it had been a melon. The Swede fell with a cry of supreme astonishment.

The prominent merchants and the district-attorney must have at once tumbled out of the place backward. The bartender found himself hanging limply to the arm of a chair and gazing into the eyes of a murderer.

"Henry," said the latter, as he wiped his knife on one of the towels that hung beneath the bar-rail, "you tell 'em where to find me. I'll be home, waiting for 'em." Then he vanished. A moment afterward the barkeeper was in the street dinning through the storm for help, and, moreover, companionship.

The corpse of the Swede, alone in the saloon, had its eyes fixed upon a dreadful legend that dwelt a-top of the cash-machine. "This registers the amount of your purchase."

IX

Months later, the cowboy was frying pork over the stove of a little ranch near the Dakota line, when there was a quick thud of hoofs outside, and, presently, the Easterner entered with the letters and the papers.

"Well," said the Easterner at once, "the chap that killed the Swede has got three years. Wasn't much, was it?"

"He has? Three years?" The cowboy poised his pan of pork, while he ruminated upon the news. "Three years. That ain't much."

"No. It was a light sentence," replied the Easterner as he unbuckled his spurs. "Seems there was a good deal of sympathy for him in Romper."

"If the bartender had been any good," observed the cowboy thoughtfully, "he would have gone in and cracked that there Dutchman on the head with a bottle in the beginnin' of it and stopped all this here murderin'."

"Yes, a thousand things might have happened," said the Easterner tartly.

The cowboy returned his pan of pork to the fire, but his philosophy continued. "It's funny, ain't it? If he hadn't said Johnnie was cheatin' he'd be alive this minute. He was an awful fool. Game played for fun, too. Not for money. I believe he was crazy."

"I feel sorry for that gambler," said the Easterner.

"Oh, so do I," said the cowboy. "He don't deserve none of it for killin' who he did."

"The Swede might not have been killed if everything had been square."

"Might not have been killed?" exclaimed the cowboy. "Everythin' square? Why, when he said that Johnnie was cheatin' and acted like such a jackass?

And then in the saloon he fairly walked up to git hurt?" With these arguments the cowboy browbeat the Easterner and reduced him to rage.

"You're a fool!" cried the Easterner viciously. "You're a bigger jackass than the Swede by a million majority. Now let me tell you one thing. Let me tell you something. Listen! Johnnie *was* cheating!"

"'Johnnie,'" said the cowboy blankly. There was a minute of silence, and then he said robustly: "Why, no. The game was only for fun."

"Fun or not," said the Easterner, "Johnnie was cheating. I saw him. I know it. I saw him. And I refused to stand up and be a man. I let the Swede fight it out alone. And you—you were simply puffing around the place and wanting to fight. And then old Scully himself! We are all in it! This poor gambler isn't even a noun. He is kind of an adverb. Every sin is the result of a collaboration. We, five of us, have collaborated in the murder of this Swede. Usually there are from a dozen to forty women really involved in every murder, but in this case it seems to be only five men—you, I, Johnnie, old Scully, and that fool of an unfortunate gambler came merely as a culmination, the apex of a human movement, and gets all the punishment."

The cowboy, injured and rebellious, cried out blindly into this fog of mysterious theory. "Well, I didn't do anythin', did I?"

The Traveler

Wallace Stegner

The American ideal of self-reliance and our confidence in science and technology to protect us from harm can cause us to forget a deep truth about human life: our vulnerability, neediness, and dependence on others. Beyond civility and tolerance, we often stand in need of sympathy, compassion, and kind assistance from others. How does a nation that encourages independent individualism also cultivate the requisite neighborly dispositions?

In "The Traveler" (1951), Wallace Stegner (1909–1993) invites and rewards attention to this question. An unnamed traveling salesman, with a car full of drugs promising cures for many diseases, is stranded on a freezing night in snow-covered rural Vermont when his automobile suddenly dies, miles away from the nearest farm. Abandoning his now useless devices, the traveler sets out, eerily alone amidst indifferent nature, in search of a haven against his frosty death. Arriving eventually at an isolated farmhouse, he discovers an old man at death's door, in the anxious care of his eleven-year-old grandson.

What light does this story shed on the meaning of compassion and on the relation between charity and one's own identity? What are the effects of this remarkable encounter on the boy and on the traveler? What does Stegner mean when he says about the traveler, "he had looked outward and for one unmistakable instant recognized himself"? What sorts of "medicines" heal the human wounds of our neighbors and ourselves?

He was rolling in the first early dark down a snowy road, his headlights pinched between dark walls of trees, when the engine coughed, recovered, coughed again, and died. Down a slight hill he coasted in compression, working the choke, but at the bottom he had to pull over against the three-foot wall of plowed snow. Snow creaked under the tires as the car eased to a stop. The heater fan unwound with a final tinny sigh.

Here in its middle age this hitherto dependable mechanism had betrayed him, but he refused to admit immediately that he was betrayed. Some speck of dirt or bubble of water in the gas line, some momentary short circuit, some splash of snow on distributor points or plug connections—something that would cure itself before long. But turning off the lights and pressing on the starter brought no result; he held the choke out for several seconds, and got only the hopeful stink of gasoline; he waited and let the flooded carburetor rest and tried again, and nothing. Eventually he opened the door and stepped out onto the packed snow of the road.

It was so cold that his first breath turned to iron in his throat, the hairs in his nostrils webbed into instant ice, his eyes stung and watered. In the faint starlight and the bluish luminescence of the snow everything beyond a few yards away swam deceptive and without depth, glimmering with things half seen or imagined. Beside the dead car he stood with his head bent, listening, and there was not a sound. Everything on the planet might have died in the cold.

Indecisively seeking help, he walked to the top of the next rise, but the faintly darker furrow of the road blurred and disappeared in the murk, the shadows pressed inward, there was no sign of a light. Back at the car he made the efforts that the morality of self-reliance demanded: trying to see by the backward diffusion of the headlamps, he groped over the motor, feeling for broken wires or loose connections, until he had satisfied himself that he was helpless. He had known all along that he was.

His hands were already stung with cold, and around his ankles between low shoes and trouser cuffs he felt the chill like leg irons. When he had last stopped, twenty miles back, it had been below zero. It could be ten or fifteen below now. So what did he do, stranded in mid-journey fifty miles or more from his destination? He could hardly go in for help, leaving the sample cases, because the right rear door didn't lock properly. A little jiggling swung it open. And all those drugs, some of them designed to cure anything—wonder drugs, sulfas, streptomycin, Aureomycin, penicillin, pills and anti-toxins and unguents—represented not only a value but a danger. They should not be left around loose. Someone might think they really *would* cure anything.

Not quite everything, he told the blue darkness. Not a fouled-up distributor or a cranky coil box. Absurdly, there came into his mind a fragment of an ancient hymn to mechanical transport:

> If she runs out of dope, just fill her up with soap
> And the little Ford will ramble right along.

He saw himself pouring a bottle of penicillin into the gas tank and driving off with the exhaust blowing happy smoke rings. A mock-heroic montage of scientific discovery unreeled itself—white-coated scientists peering into microscopes, adjusting gauges, pipetting precious liquids, weighing grains of powder on minuscule scales. Messenger boys sped with telegrams to the desks of busy executives. A group of observers stood beside an assembly line while the first tests were made. They broke a car's axle with sledges, gave it a drink of the wonder compound, and drove it off. They demolished the carburetor and cured it with one application. They yanked loose all the wires and watched the same magic set the motor purring.

But here he stood in light overcoat and thin leather gloves, without overshoes, and his car all but blocked the road, and the door could not be locked, and there was not a possibility that he could carry the heavy cases with him to the next farm or village. He switched on the headlights again and studied the roadside they revealed, and saw a rail fence, with cedars and spruces behind it. When more complex gadgets and more complex cures failed, there was always the lucifer match.

Ten minutes later he was sitting with the auto robe over his head and shoulders and his back against the plowed snowbank, digging the half-melted snow from inside his shoes and gloating over the growing light and warmth of the fire. He had a supply of fence rails good for an hour. In that time, someone would come along and he could get a push or two. In this country, in winter, no one ever passed up a stranded motorist.

In the stillness the flames went straight upward; the heat was wonderfully pleasant on icy hands and numb ankles and stiffened face. He looked across the road, stained by horses, broken by wheel and runner tracks, and saw how the roadside acquired definition and sharp angles and shadows in the firelight. He saw too how he would look to anyone coming along: like a calendar picture.

But no one came along. Fifteen minutes stretched into a half hour, he had only two broken pieces of rail left, the fire sizzled, half floating in the puddle of its melting. Restlessly he rose with the blanket around him and walked back up the road a hundred steps. Eastward, above jagged trees, he saw the sky where it lightened to moonrise, but here there was still only the blue glimmer of starlight on the snow. Something long buried and forgotten tugged in him, and a shiver not entirely from cold prickled his whole body with gooseflesh. There had been times in his childhood when he had walked home alone and been temporarily lost in nights like this. In many years he could not remember being out alone under such a sky. He felt spooked, his feet were chilled lumps, his nose leaked. Down the hill, car and snow swam deceptively together; the red wink of the fire seemed inexpressibly far off.

Abruptly he did not want to wait in that lonely snow-banked ditch any longer. The sample cases could look after themselves, any motorist who passed could take his own chances. He would walk ahead to the nearest help, and if he found himself getting too cold on the way, he could always build another fire. The thought of action cheered him; he admitted to himself that he was all but terrified at the silence and the iron cold.

Closing the car doors, he dropped his key case, and panic stopped his pulse as he bent and frantically, with bare hand, brushed away the snow until he found it. The powdery snow ached and burned at his fingertips. He held them a last moment to the fire, and then, bundled like a squaw, with the blanket held across nose and mouth to ease the harshness of the cold in his lungs, he started up the road that looked as smooth as a tablecloth, but was deceptively rough and broken. He thought of what he had had every right to expect for this evening. By now, eight o'clock or so, he should have had a smoking supper, the luxury of a hot bath, the pleasure of a brandy in a comradely bar. By now he should be in pajamas making out sales reports by the bedlight, in a room where steam knocked comfortingly in the radiators and the help of a hundred hands was available to him at a word into the telephone. For all of this to be torn away suddenly, for him to be stumbling up a deserted road in danger of freezing to death, just because some simple mechanical part that had functioned for thirty thousand miles refused to function any longer, this was outrage, and he hated it. He thought of garage men and service station attendants he could blame. Ignoring the evidence of the flooded carburetor, he brooded about watered gas that could make ice in the gas line. A man was dependent on too many people; he was at everybody's mercy.

And then, on top of the second long rise, he met the moon.

Instantly the character of the night changed. The uncertain starlight was replaced at a step by an even flood of blue-white radiance. He looked across a snow meadow and saw how a rail fence had every stake and rider doubled in solid shadow, and how the edge of woods beyond was blackest India ink. The road ahead was drawn with a ruler, one bank smoothed by the flood of light, the other deeply shadowed. As he looked into the eye of the moon he saw the air shiver and glint with falling particles of frost.

In this White Christmas night, this Good King Wenceslas night, he went warily, not to be caught in sentimentality, and to an invisible audience he deprecated it profanely as a night in which no one would believe. Yet here it was, and he in it. With the coming of the moon the night even seemed to warm; he found that he could drop the blanket from across his face and drink the still air.

Along the roadside as he passed the meadow and entered woods again the moon showed him things. In moonlit openings he saw the snow stitched with tiny perfect tracks, mouse or weasel or the three-toed crowding tracks of partridge. These too, an indigenous part of the night, came back to him as things once known and long forgotten. In his boyhood he had trapped and hunted the animals that made such tracks as these; it was as if his mind were a snowfield where the marks of their secret little feet had been printed long ago. With a queer tightening of the throat, with an odd pride, he read the trail of a fox that had wallowed through the soft snow from the woods, angling into the packed road and along it for a little way and out again, still angling, across the plowed bank, and then left a purposeful trail of cleanly punched tracks, the hind feet in line with the front, across the clean snow and into the opposite woods, from shadow across moonlight and into shadow again.

Turning with the road, he passed through the stretch of woods and came into the open to see the moon-white, shadow-black buildings of a farm, and the weak bloom of light in a window.

His feet whined on the snow, dry as metal powder, as he turned in the loop of drive the county plow had cleared. But as he approached the house doubt touched him. In spite of the light, the place looked unused, somehow. No dog welcomed him. The sound of his feet in the snow was alien, the hammer of his knuckles on the door an intrusion. Looking upward for some trace of telephone wires, he saw none, and he could not tell whether the quivering of the air that he thought he saw above the chimney was heat or smoke or the phantasmal falling frost.

"Hello?" he said, and knocked again. "Anybody home?" No sound answered him. He saw the moon glint on the great icicles along the eaves. His numb hand ached with the pain of knocking; he pounded with the soft edge of his fist.

Answer finally came, not from the door before which he stood, but from the barn, down at the end of a staggered string of attached sheds. A door creaked open against a snowbank and a figure with a lantern appeared, stood for a moment, and came running. The traveler wondered at the way it came, lurching and stumbling in the uneven snow, until it arrived at the porch and he saw that it was a boy of eleven or twelve. The boy set his lantern on the porch; between the upturned collar of his mackinaw and the down-pulled stocking cap his face was a pinched whiteness, his eyes enormous. He stared at the traveler until the traveler became aware of the blanket he still held over head and shoulders, and began to laugh.

"My car stopped on me, a mile or so up the road," he said. "I was just hunting a telephone or some place where I could get help."

The boy swallowed, wiped the back of his mitt across his nose. "Grandpa's sick!" he blurted, and opened the door. Warmth rushed in their faces, cold rushed in at their backs, warm and cold mingled in an eddy of air as the door closed. The traveler saw a cot bed pulled close to the kitchen range, and on the cot an old man covered with a quilt, who breathed heavily and whose closed eyes did not open when the two came near. The gray-whiskered cheeks were sunken, the mouth open to expose toothless gums in a parody look of ancient mischief.

"He must've had a shock," the boy said. "I came in from chores and he was on the floor." He stared at the mummy under the quilt, and he swallowed.

"Has he come to at all?"

"No."

"Only the two of you live here?"

"Yes."

"No telephone?"

"No."

"How long ago did you find him?"

"Chore time. About six."

"Why didn't you go for help?"

The boy looked down, ashamed. "It's near two miles. I was afraid he'd . . ."

"But you left him. You were out in the barn."

"I was hitching up to go," the boy said. "I'd made up my mind."

The traveler backed away from the stove, his face smarting with the heat, his fingers and feet beginning to ache. He looked at the old man and knew that here, as at the car, he was helpless. The boy's thin anxious face told him how thoroughly his own emergency had been swallowed up in this other one. He had been altered from a man in need of help to one who must give it. Salesman of wonder cures, he must now produce something to calm this over-worried boy, restore a dying man. Rebelliously, victimized by circumstances, he said, "Where were you going for help?"

"The Hill place. They've got a phone."

"How far are they from a town?"

"About five miles."

"Doctor there?"

"Yes."

"If I took your horse and—what is it, sleigh?—could someone at the Hills' bring them back, do you think?"

"Cutter. One of the Hill boys could, I should say."

"Or would you rather go, while I look after your grandpa?"

"He don't know you," the boy said directly. "If he should wake up he might . . . wonder . . . it might . . ."

The traveler grudgingly gave up the prospect of staying in the warm kitchen while the boy did the work. And he granted that it was extraordinarily sensitive of the boy to know how it might disturb a man to wake from sickness in his own house and stare into the face of an utter stranger. "Yes," he said. "Well, I could call the doctor from the Hills'. Two miles, did you say?"

"About." The boy had pulled the stocking cap off so that his hair stood on end above his white forehead. He had odd eyes, very large and dark and intelligent, with an expectancy in them.

The traveler, watching him with interest, said, "How long have you lived with your grandfather?"

"Two years."

"Parents living?"

"No, sir, that's why."

"Go to school?"

He got a queer sidling look. "Have to till you're sixteen."

"Is that the only reason you go?"

What he was trying to force out of the boy came out indirectly, with a shrugging of the shoulders. "Grandpa would take me out if he could."

"Would you be glad?"

"No, sir," the boy said, but would not look at him. "I like school."

The traveler consciously corked his flow of questions. Once he himself had been an orphan living with his grandparents on a back farm; he wondered if this boy went as he had gone, knocking in imagination at all of life's closed doors.

The old man's harsh breathing filled the overwarm room. "Well," the traveler said, "maybe you'd better go finish hitching up. It's been thirty years since I harnessed a horse. I'll keep an eye on your grandpa."

Pulling the stocking cap over his disheveled hair, the boy slid out of the door. The traveler unbuttoned his overcoat and sat down beside the old man, felt the spurting weak pulse, raised one eyelid with his thumb and looked without comprehension at the uprolled eye. He knew it was like feeling over a chilling motor for loose wires, and after two or three abortive motions he gave it up and sat contemplating the gray, sunken face, the unfamiliar face of an old man who would die, and thinking that the face was the only unfamiliar thing about the whole night. The kitchen smells, coffee and peanut butter and the moldy, barky smell of wood from the woodbox, and the smell of the hot range and of paint baking in the heat, those were as familiar as light or dark. The spectacular night outside, the snowfields and the moon and the mysterious woods, the tracks venturing out across the snow from the protective eaves of firs and skunk spruce, the speculative, imagining expression of the boy's eyes, were just as familiar. He sat bemused, touching some brink as a man will walk along a cutbank trying to knock loose the crumbling overhang with an outstretched foot. The ways a man fitted in with himself and with other human beings were curious and complex.

And when he heard the jingle and creak outside, and buttoned himself into the overcoat again and wrapped his shoulders in the blanket and stepped out into the yard, there was a moment when the boy passed him the lines and they stood facing each other in the broken snow.

It was a moment like farewell, like a poignant parting. Touched by his pressing sense of familiarity and by a sort of compassion, the traveler reached out and laid his hand on the boy's shoulder. "Don't worry," he said. "I'll have someone back here right away. Your grandfather will be all right. Just keep him warm and don't worry."

He climbed into the cutter and pulled over his lap the balding buffalo robe he found there; the scallop of its felt edges was like a key that fitted a door. The horses breathed jets of steam in the moonlight, restlessly moving, jingling their harness bells, as the moment lengthened itself. The traveler saw how the boy, now that his anxiety was somewhat quieted, now that he had been able to unload part of his burden, watched him with a thousand questions in his face, and he remembered how he himself, thirty years ago, had searched the faces of passing strangers for something he could not name, how he had listened to their steps and seen their shadows lengthen ahead of them down roads that led to unimaginable places, and how he had ached with the desire to know them, who they were. But none of them had looked back at him as he tried now to look at this boy.

He was glad that no names had been spoken and no personal histories exchanged to obscure this meeting, for sitting in the sleigh above the boy's white upturned serious face, he felt that some profound contact had unintentionally, almost casually, been made.

For half a breath he was utterly bewitched, frozen at the heart of some icy dream. Abruptly he slapped the reins across the backs of the horses; the cutter jerked and then slid smoothly out towards the road. The traveler looked back once, to fix forever the picture of himself standing silently watching himself go. As he slid into the road the horses broke into a trot. The icy flow of air locked his throat and made him let go the reins with one hand to pull the hairy, wool-smelling edge of the blanket all but shut across his face.

Along a road he had never driven he went swiftly towards an unknown farm and an unknown town, to distribute according to some wise law part of the burden of the boy's emergency and his own; but he bore in his mind, bright as moonlight over snow, a vivid wonder, almost an awe. For from the most chronic and incurable of ills, identity, he had looked outward and for one unmistakable instant recognized himself.

Bartleby, the Scrivener:
A Story of Wall-Street

Herman Melville

The summons to compassion and neighborliness is often most difficult to answer when the suffering we confront seems beyond our capacity to remedy. Poverty invites us to give money. Illness calls for medical care. But how do we respond to those maimed in soul and spirit—the homeless, helpless, and hopeless in our midst? No story presents this problem more powerfully than "Bartleby, the Scrivener" (1853) by Herman Melville (1819–1891). In this story, a nameless, middling lawyer—perhaps an American everyman—struggles to do right by Bartleby, an "incurably forlorn" man in his employ, who "prefers not" to make any effort on his own behalf or to accept the kind of help that is offered. Melville makes deft use of images of walls—the brick walls of Wall Street and the Tombs (the city jail), the partitions and doors in the office—to call attention to the imprisonment of the spirit and the barriers separating one soul from another.

*The mysterious Bartleby invites multiple interpretations: Is he, for example, a victim of corporate America or technological progress, a quiet rebel against American commercialism, a sufferer from mental illness ("luny"), or a suffering Christ-like figure "sent" to test the proud of heart? But our attention is drawn more to the lawyer-citizen: How do we assess his responses to Bartleby? What might he have done differently? What prevents him from adhering to the divine injunction that "ye love one another"? What do you make of the coda the lawyer-narrator adds at the end, especially his final words, "Ah Bartleby! Ah humanity!"? Are people like Bartleby best understood as human beings with problems to be solved ("*DO* something") or as fellow sufferers who most need our companionship ("*BE* there")? Is the problem-solving mentality to defeat disease, poverty, and misfortune compatible with the mentality to respond lovingly to our existential joys and sorrows?*

I am a rather elderly man. The nature of my avocations for the last thirty years has brought me into more than ordinary contact with what would seem an interesting and somewhat singular set of men, of whom as yet nothing that I know of has ever been written:—I mean the law-copyists or scriveners. I have known very many of them, professionally and privately, and if I pleased, could relate divers histories, at which good-natured gentlemen might smile, and sentimental souls might weep. But I waive the biographies of all other scriveners for a few passages in the life of Bartleby, who was a scrivener of the strangest I ever saw or heard of. While of other law-copyists I might write the complete life, of Bartleby nothing of that sort can be done. I believe that no materials exist for a full and satisfactory biography of this man. It is an irreparable loss to literature. Bartleby was one of those beings of whom nothing is ascertainable, except from the original sources, and in his case those are very small. What my own astonished eyes saw of Bartleby, *that* is all I know of him, except, indeed, one vague report which will appear in the sequel.

Ere introducing the scrivener, as he first appeared to me, it is fit I make some mention of myself, my *employés*, my business, my chambers, and general surroundings; because some such description is indispensable to an adequate understanding of the chief character about to be presented.

Imprimis: I am a man who, from his youth upwards, has been filled with a profound conviction that the easiest way of life is the best. Hence, though I belong to a profession proverbially energetic and nervous, even to turbulence, at times, yet nothing of that sort have I ever suffered to invade my peace. I am one of those unambitious lawyers who never addresses a jury, or in any way draws down public applause; but in the cool tranquillity of a snug retreat, do a snug business among rich men's bonds and mortgages and title-deeds. All who know me, consider me an eminently *safe* man. The late John Jacob Astor, a personage little given to poetic enthusiasm, had no hesitation in pronouncing my first grand point to be prudence; my next, method. I do not speak it in vanity, but simply record the fact, that I was not unemployed in my profession by the late John Jacob Astor; a name which, I admit, I love to repeat, for it hath a rounded and orbicular sound to it, and rings like unto bullion. I will freely add, that I was not insensible to the late John Jacob Astor's good opinion.

Some time prior to the period at which this little history begins, my avocations had been largely increased. The good old office, now extinct in the State of New-York, of a Master in Chancery, had been conferred upon me. It was not a very arduous office, but very pleasantly remunerative. I seldom lose my temper; much more seldom indulge in dangerous indignation at wrongs and outrages; but I must be permitted to be rash here and declare, that I consider the sudden and violent abrogation of the office of Master in Chancery, by the new Constitution, as a——premature act; inasmuch as I had counted upon a life-lease of the profits, whereas I only received those of a few short years. But this is by the way.

My chambers were up stairs at No.— Wall-street. At one end they looked upon the white wall of the interior of a spacious sky-light shaft, penetrating the building from top to bottom. This view might have been considered rather tame than otherwise, deficient in what landscape painters call "life." But if so, the view from the other end of my chambers offered, at least, a contrast, if nothing more. In that direction my windows commanded an unobstructed view of a lofty brick wall, black by age and everlasting shade; which wall required no spy-glass to bring out its lurking beauties, but for the benefit of all near-sighted spectators, was pushed up to within ten feet of my window panes. Owing to the great height of the surrounding buildings, and my chambers being on the second floor, the interval between this wall and mine not a little resembled a huge square cistern.

At the period just preceding the advent of Bartleby, I had two persons as copyists in my employment, and a promising lad as an office-boy. First, Turkey; second, Nippers; third, Ginger Nut. These may seem names, the like of which are not usually found in the Directory. In truth they were nicknames, mutually conferred upon each other by my three clerks, and were deemed expressive of their respective persons or characters. Turkey was a short, pursy Englishman of about my own age, that is, somewhere not far from sixty. In the morning, one might say, his face was of a fine florid hue, but after twelve o'clock, meridian—his dinner hour—it blazed like a grate full of Christmas coals; and continued blazing—but, as it were, with a gradual wane—till 6 o'clock, P.M. or thereabouts, after which I saw no more of the proprietor of the face, which gaining its meridian with the sun, seemed to set with it, to rise, culminate, and decline the following day, with the like regularity and undiminished glory. There are many singular coincidences I have known in the course of my life, not the least among which was the fact, that exactly when Turkey displayed his fullest beams from his red and radiant countenance, just then, too, at that critical moment, began the daily period when I considered his business capacities as seriously disturbed for the remainder of the twenty-four hours. Not that he was absolutely idle, or averse to business then; far from it. The difficulty was, he was apt to be altogether too energetic. There was a strange, inflamed, flurried, flighty recklessness of activity about him. He would be incautious in dipping his pen into his inkstand. All his blots upon my documents, were dropped there after twelve o'clock, meridian. Indeed, not only would he be reckless and sadly given to making blots in the afternoon, but some days he went further, and was rather noisy. At such times, too, his face flamed with augmented blazonry, as if cannel coal had been heaped on anthracite. He made an unpleasant racket with his chair; spilled his sand-box; in mending his pens, impatiently split them all to pieces, and threw them on the floor in a sudden passion; stood up and leaned over his table, boxing his papers about in a most indecorous manner, very sad to behold in an elderly man like him. Nevertheless, as he was in many ways a most valuable person to me, and all the time before twelve o'clock, meridian, was the quickest, steadiest creature too, accomplishing a great deal of work in a style not easy to be matched—for these reasons, I was willing to overlook his eccentricities, though indeed, occasionally, I remonstrated with him. I did this very gently, however, because, though the civilest, nay, the blandest and most reverential of men in the morning, yet in the afternoon he was disposed, upon provocation, to be slightly rash with his tongue, in fact, insolent. Now, valuing his morning services as I did, and resolved not to lose them; yet, at the same time made uncomfortable by his inflamed ways after twelve o'clock; and being a man of peace, unwilling by my admonitions to call forth unseemly retorts from him; I took upon me, one Saturday noon (he was always worse on Saturdays), to hint to him, very kindly, that perhaps now that he was growing old, it might be well to abridge his labors; in short, he need not come to my chambers after twelve o'clock, but, dinner over, had best go home to his lodgings and rest himself till tea-time. But no; he insisted upon his afternoon devotions. His countenance became intolerably fervid, as he oratorically assured me—gesticulating with a long ruler at the other end of the room—that if his services in the morning were useful, how indispensable, then, in the afternoon?

"With submission, sir," said Turkey on this occasion, "I consider myself your right-hand man. In the morning I but marshal and deploy my columns; but in the afternoon I put myself at their head, and gallantly charge the foe, thus!"—and he made a violent thrust with the ruler.

"But the blots, Turkey," intimated I.

"True,—but, with submission, sir, behold these hairs! I am getting old. Surely, sir, a blot or two of a warm afternoon is not to be severely urged against gray hairs. Old age—even if it blot the page—is honorable. With submission, sir, we *both* are getting old."

This appeal to my fellow-feeling was hardly to be resisted. At all events, I saw that go he would not. So I made up my mind to let him stay, resolving, nevertheless, to see to it, that during the afternoon he had to do with my less important papers.

Nippers, the second on my list, was a whiskered, sallow, and, upon the whole, rather piratical-looking young man of about five and twenty. I always deemed him the victim of two evil powers—ambition and indigestion. The ambition was evinced by a certain impatience of the duties of a mere copyist, an unwarrantable usurpation of strictly professional affairs, such as the original drawing up of legal documents. The indigestion seemed betokened in an occasional nervous testiness and grinning irritability, causing the teeth to audibly grind together over mistakes committed in copying; unnecessary maledictions, hissed, rather than spoken, in the heat of business; and especially by a continual discontent with the height of the table where he worked. Though of a very ingenious mechanical turn, Nippers could never get this table to suit him. He put chips under it, blocks of various sorts, bits of pasteboard, and at last went so far as to attempt an exquisite adjustment by final pieces of folded blotting-paper. But no invention would answer. If, for the sake of easing his back, he brought the table lid at a sharp angle well up towards his chin, and wrote there like a man using the steep roof of a Dutch house for his desk:—then he declared that it stopped the circulation in his arms. If now he lowered the table to his waistbands, and stooped over it in writing, then there was a sore aching in his back. In short, the truth of the matter was, Nippers knew not what he wanted. Or, if he wanted any thing, it was to be rid of a scrivener's table altogether. Among the manifestations of his diseased ambition was a fondness he had for receiving visits from certain ambiguous-looking fellows in seedy coats, whom he called his clients. Indeed I was aware that not only was he, at times, considerable of a ward-politician, but he occasionally did a little business at the Justices' courts, and was not unknown on the steps of the Tombs. I have good reason to believe, however, that one individual who called upon him at my chambers, and who, with a grand air, he insisted was his client, was no other than a dun, and the alleged title-deed, a bill. But with all his failings, and the annoyances he caused me, Nippers, like his compatriot Turkey, was a very useful man to me; wrote a neat, swift hand; and, when he chose, was not deficient in a gentlemanly sort of deportment. Added to this, he always dressed in a gentlemanly sort of way; and so, incidentally, reflected credit upon my chambers. Whereas with respect to Turkey, I had much ado to keep him from being a reproach to me. His clothes were apt to look oily and smell of eating-houses. He wore his pantaloons very loose and baggy in summer. His coats were execrable; his hat not to be handled. But while the hat was a thing of indifference to me, inasmuch as his natural civility and deference, as a dependent Englishman, always led him to doff it the moment he entered the room, yet his coat was another matter. Concerning his coats, I reasoned with him; but with no effect. The truth was, I suppose, that a man with so small an income, could not afford to sport such a lustrous face and a lustrous coat at one and the same time. As Nippers once observed, Turkey's money went chiefly for red ink. One winter day I presented Turkey with a highly-respectable looking coat of my own, a padded gray coat, of a most comfortable warmth, and which buttoned straight up from the knee to the neck. I thought Turkey would appreciate the favor, and abate his rashness and obstreperousness of afternoons. But no. I verily believe that buttoning himself up in so downy and blanket-like a coat had a pernicious effect upon him; upon the same principle that too much oats are bad for horses. In fact, precisely as a rash, restive horse is said to feel his oats, so Turkey felt his coat. It made him insolent. He was a man whom prosperity harmed.

Though concerning the self-indulgent habits of Turkey I had my own private surmises, yet touching Nippers I was well persuaded that whatever might be his faults in other respects, he was, at least, a temperate young man. But indeed, nature herself seemed to have been his vintner, and at his birth charged him so thoroughly with an irritable, brandy-like disposition, that all subsequent potations were needless. When I consider how, amid the stillness of my chambers, Nippers would sometimes impatiently rise from his seat, and stooping over his table, spread his arms wide apart, seize the whole desk, and move it, and jerk it, with a grim, grinding motion on the floor, as if the table were a perverse voluntary agent, intent on thwarting and vexing him; I plainly perceive that for Nippers, brandy and water were altogether superfluous.

It was fortunate for me that, owing to its peculiar cause—indigestion—the irritability and consequent nervousness of Nippers, were mainly observable in the morning, while in the afternoon he was comparatively mild. So that Turkey's paroxysms only coming on about twelve o'clock, I never had to do with their eccentricities at one time. Their fits relieved each other like guards. When Nippers' was on, Turkey's was off; and *vice versa*. This was a good natural arrangement under the circumstances.

Ginger Nut, the third on my list, was a lad some twelve years old. His father was a carman, ambitious of seeing his son on the bench instead of a cart, before he died. So he sent him to my office as student at law, errand boy, and cleaner and sweeper, at the rate of one dollar a week. He had a little desk to himself, but he did not use it much. Upon inspection, the drawer exhibited a great array of the shells of various sorts of nuts. Indeed, to this quick-witted youth the whole noble science of the law was contained in a nut-shell. Not the least among the employments of Ginger Nut, as well as one which he discharged with the most alacrity, was his duty as cake and apple purveyor for Turkey and Nippers. Copying law papers being proverbially a dry, husky sort of business, my two scriveners were fain to moisten their mouths very often with Spitzenbergs to be had at the numerous stalls nigh the Custom House and Post Office. Also, they sent Ginger Nut very frequently for that peculiar cake—small, flat, round, and very spicy—after which he had been named by them. Of a cold morning when business was but dull, Turkey would gobble up scores of these cakes, as if they were mere wafers—indeed they sell them at the rate of six or eight for a penny—the scrape of his pen blending with the crunching of the crisp particles in his mouth. Of all the fiery afternoon blunders and flurried rashnesses of Turkey, was his once moistening a ginger-cake between his lips, and clapping it on to a mortgage for a seal. I came within an ace of dismissing him then. But he mollified me by making an oriental bow, and saying—"With submission, sir, it was generous of me to find you in stationery on my own account."

Now my original business—that of a conveyancer and title hunter, and drawer-up of recondite documents of all sorts—was considerably increased by receiving the master's office. There was now great work for scriveners. Not only must I push the clerks already with me, but I must have additional help. In answer to my advertisement, a motionless young man one morning, stood upon my office threshold, the door being open, for it was summer. I can see that figure now—pallidly neat, pitiably respectable, incurably forlorn! It was Bartleby.

After a few words touching his qualifications, I engaged him, glad to have among my corps of copyists a man of so singularly sedate an aspect, which I thought might operate beneficially upon the flighty temper of Turkey, and the fiery one of Nippers.

I should have stated before that ground glass folding-doors divided my premises into two parts, one of which was occupied by my scriveners, the other by myself. According to my humor I threw open these doors, or closed them. I resolved to assign Bartleby a corner by the folding-doors, but on my side of them, so as to have this quiet man within easy call, in case any trifling thing was to be done. I placed his desk close up to a small side-window in that part of the room, a window which originally had afforded a lateral view of certain grimy back-yards and bricks, but which, owing to subsequent erections, commanded at present no view at all, though it gave some light. Within three feet of the panes was a wall, and the light came down from far above, between two lofty buildings, as from a very small opening in a dome. Still further to a satisfactory arrangement, I procured a high green folding screen, which might entirely isolate Bartleby from my sight, though not remove him from my voice. And thus, in a manner, privacy and society were conjoined.

At first Bartleby did an extraordinary quantity of writing. As if long famishing for something to copy, he seemed to gorge himself on my documents. There was no pause for digestion. He ran a day and night line, copying by sunlight and by candle-light. I should have been quite delighted with his application, had he been cheerfully industrious. But he wrote on silently, palely, mechanically.

It is, of course, an indispensable part of a scrivener's business to verify the accuracy of his copy, word by word. Where there are two or more scriveners in an office, they assist each other in this examination, one reading from the copy, the other holding the original. It is a very dull, wearisome, and lethargic affair. I can readily imagine that to some sanguine temperaments it would be altogether intolerable. For example, I cannot credit that the mettlesome poet Byron would have contentedly sat down with Bartleby to examine a law document of, say five hundred pages, closely written in a crimpy hand.

Now and then, in the haste of business, it had been my habit to assist in comparing some brief document myself, calling Turkey or Nippers for this purpose. One object I had in placing Bartleby so handy to me behind the screen, was to avail myself of his services on such trivial occasions. It was on the third day, I think, of his being with me, and before any necessity had arisen for having his own writing examined, that, being much hurried to complete a small affair I had in hand, I abruptly called to Bartleby. In my haste and natural expectancy of instant compliance, I sat with my head bent over the original on my desk, and my right hand sideways, and somewhat nervously extended with the copy, so that immediately upon emerging from his retreat, Bartleby might snatch it and proceed to business without the least delay.

In this very attitude did I sit when I called to him, rapidly stating what it was I wanted him to do—namely, to examine a small paper with me. Imagine my surprise, nay, my consternation, when without moving from his privacy, Bartleby in a singularly mild, firm voice, replied, "I would prefer not to."

I sat awhile in perfect silence, rallying my stunned faculties. Immediately it occurred to me that my ears had deceived me, or Bartleby had entirely misunderstood my meaning. I repeated my request in the clearest tone I could assume. But in quite as clear a one came the previous reply, "I would prefer not to."

"Prefer not to," echoed I, rising in high excitement, and crossing the room with a stride. "What do you mean? Are you moon-struck? I want you to help me compare this sheet here—take it," and I thrust it towards him.

"I would prefer not to," said he.

I looked at him steadfastly. His face was leanly composed; his gray eye dimly calm. Not a wrinkle of agitation rippled him. Had there been the least uneasiness, anger, impatience or impertinence in his manner; in other words, had there been any thing ordinarily human about him, doubtless I should have violently dismissed him from the premises. But as it was, I should have as soon thought of turning my pale plaster-of-paris bust of Cicero out of doors. I stood gazing at him awhile, as he went on with his own writing, and then reseated myself at my desk. This is very strange, thought I. What had one best do? But my business hurried me. I concluded to forget the matter for the present, reserving it for my future leisure. So calling Nippers from the other room, the paper was speedily examined.

A few days after this, Bartleby concluded four lengthy documents, being quadruplicates of a week's testimony taken before me in my High Court of Chancery. It became necessary to examine them. It was an important suit, and great accuracy was imperative. Having all things arranged I called Turkey, Nippers and Ginger Nut from the next room, meaning to place the four copies in the hands of my four clerks, while I should read from the original. Accordingly Turkey, Nippers and Ginger Nut had taken their seats in a row, each with his document in hand, when I called to Bartleby to join this interesting group.

"Bartleby! quick, I am waiting."

I heard a slow scrape of his chair legs on the uncarpeted floor, and soon he appeared standing at the entrance of his hermitage.

"What is wanted?" said he mildly.

"The copies, the copies," said I hurriedly. "We are going to examine them. There"—and I held towards him the fourth quadruplicate.

"I would prefer not to," he said, and gently disappeared behind the screen.

For a few moments I was turned into a pillar of salt, standing at the head of my seated column of clerks. Recovering myself, I advanced towards the screen, and demanded the reason for such extraordinary conduct.

"*Why* do you refuse?"

"I would prefer not to."

With any other man I should have flown outright into a dreadful passion, scorned all further words, and thrust him ignominiously from my presence. But there was something about Bartleby that not only strangely disarmed me, but in a wonderful manner touched and disconcerted me. I began to reason with him.

"These are your own copies we are about to examine. It is labor saving to you, because one examination will answer for your four papers. It is common usage. Every copyist is bound to help examine his copy. Is it not so? Will you not speak? Answer!"

"I prefer not to," he replied in a flute-like tone. It seemed to me that while I had been addressing him, he carefully revolved every statement that I made; fully comprehended the meaning; could not gainsay the irresistible conclusions; but, at the same time, some paramount consideration prevailed with him to reply as he did.

"You are decided, then, not to comply with my request—a request made according to common usage and common sense?"

He briefly gave me to understand that on that point my judgment was sound. Yes: his decision was irreversible.

It is not seldom the case that when a man is browbeaten in some unprecedented and violently unreasonable way, he begins to stagger in his own plainest faith. He begins, as it were, vaguely to surmise that, wonderful as it may be, all the justice and all the reason is on the other side. Accordingly, if any disinterested persons are present, he turns to them for some reinforcement for his own faltering mind.

"Turkey," said I, "what do you think of this? Am I not right?"

"With submission, sir," said Turkey, with his blandest tone, "I think that you are."

"Nippers," said I, "what do *you* think of it?"

"I think I should kick him out of the office."

(The reader of nice perceptions will here perceive that, it being morning, Turkey's answer is couched in polite and tranquil terms, but Nippers replies in ill-tempered ones. Or, to repeat a previous sentence, Nippers' ugly mood was on duty and Turkey's off.)

"Ginger Nut," said I, willing to enlist the smallest suffrage in my behalf, "what do *you* think of it?"

"I think, sir, he's a little *luny*," replied Ginger Nut with a grin.

"You hear what they say," said I, turning towards the screen, "come forth and do your duty."

But he vouchsafed no reply. I pondered a moment in sore perplexity. But once more business hurried me. I determined again to postpone the consideration of this dilemma to my future leisure. With a little trouble we made out to examine the papers without Bartleby, though at every page or two, Turkey deferentially dropped his opinion that this proceeding was quite out of the common; while Nippers, twitching in his chair with a dyspeptic nervousness, ground out between his set teeth occasional hissing maledictions against the stubborn oaf behind the screen. And for his (Nippers's) part, this was the first and the last time he would do another man's business without pay.

Meanwhile Bartleby sat in his hermitage, oblivious to every thing but his own peculiar business there.

Some days passed, the scrivener being employed upon another lengthy work. His late remarkable conduct led me to regard his ways narrowly. I observed that he never went to dinner; indeed that he never went any where. As yet I had never of my personal knowledge known him to be outside of my office. He was a perpetual sentry in the corner. At about eleven o'clock though, in the morning, I noticed that Ginger Nut would advance toward the opening in Bartleby's screen, as if silently beckoned thither by a gesture invisible to me where I sat. The boy would then leave the office jingling a few pence, and reappear with a handful of ginger-nuts which he delivered in the hermitage, receiving two of the cakes for his trouble.

He lives, then, on ginger-nuts, thought I; never eats a dinner, properly speaking; he must be a vegetarian then; but no; he never eats even vegetables, he eats nothing but ginger-nuts. My mind then ran on in reveries concerning the probable effects upon the human constitution of living entirely on ginger-nuts. Ginger-nuts are so called because they contain ginger as one of their peculiar constituents, and the final flavoring one. Now what was ginger? A hot, spicy thing. Was Bartleby hot and spicy? Not at all. Ginger, then, had no effect upon Bartleby. Probably he preferred it should have none.

Nothing so aggravates an earnest person as a passive resistance. If the individual so resisted be of a not inhumane temper, and the resisting one perfectly harmless in his passivity; then, in the better moods of the former, he will endeavor charitably to construe to his imagination what proves impossible to be solved by his judgment. Even so, for the most part, I regarded Bartleby and his ways. Poor fellow! thought I, he means no mischief; it is plain he intends no insolence; his aspect sufficiently evinces that his eccentricities are involuntary. He is useful to me. I can get along with him. If I turn him away, the chances are he will fall in with some less indulgent employer, and then he will be rudely treated, and perhaps driven forth miserably to starve. Yes. Here I can cheaply purchase a delicious self-approval. To befriend Bartleby; to humor him in his strange wilfulness, will cost me little or nothing, while I lay up in my soul what will eventually prove a sweet morsel for my conscience. But this mood was not invariable with me. The passiveness of Bartleby sometimes irritated me. I felt strangely goaded on to encounter him in new opposition, to elicit some angry spark from him answerable to my own. But indeed I might as well have essayed to strike fire with my knuckles against a bit of Windsor soap. But one afternoon the evil impulse in me mastered me, and the following little scene ensued:

"Bartleby," said I, "when those papers are all copied, I will compare them with you."

"I would prefer not to."

"How? Surely you do not mean to persist in that mulish vagary?"

No answer.

I threw open the folding-doors near by, and turning upon Turkey and Nippers, exclaimed:

"Bartleby a second time says, he won't examine his papers. What do you think of it, Turkey?"

It was afternoon, be it remembered. Turkey sat glowing like a brass boiler, his bald head steaming, his hands reeling among his blotted papers.

"Think of it?" roared Turkey; "I think I'll just step behind his screen, and black his eyes for him!"

So saying, Turkey rose to his feet and threw his arms into a pugilistic position. He was hurrying away to make good his promise, when I detained him, alarmed at the effect of incautiously rousing Turkey's combativeness after dinner.

"Sit down, Turkey," said I, "and hear what Nippers has to say. What do you think of it, Nippers? Would I not be justified in immediately dismissing Bartleby?"

"Excuse me, that is for you to decide, sir. I think his conduct quite unusual, and indeed unjust, as regards Turkey and myself. But it may only be a passing whim."

"Ah," exclaimed I, "you have strangely changed your mind then—you speak very gently of him now."

"All beer," cried Turkey; "gentleness is effects of beer—Nippers and I dined together to-day. You see how gentle *I* am, sir. Shall I go and black his eyes?"

"You refer to Bartleby, I suppose. No, not to-day, Turkey," I replied; "pray, put up your fists."

I closed the doors, and again advanced towards Bartleby. I felt additional incentives tempting me to my fate. I burned to be rebelled against again. I remembered that Bartleby never left the office.

"Bartleby," said I, "Ginger Nut is away; just step round to the Post Office, won't you? (it was but a three minutes walk,) and see if there is any thing for me."

"I would prefer not to."

"You *will* not?"

"I *prefer* not."

I staggered to my desk, and sat there in a deep study. My blind inveteracy returned. Was there any other thing in which I could procure myself to be ignominiously repulsed by this lean, penniless wight?—my hired clerk? What added thing is there, perfectly reasonable, that he will be sure to refuse to do?

"Bartleby!"

No answer.

"Bartleby," in a louder tone.

No answer.

"Bartleby," I roared.

Like a very ghost, agreeably to the laws of magical invocation, at the third summons, he appeared at the entrance of his hermitage.

"Go to the next room, and tell Nippers to come to me."

"I prefer not to," he respectfully and slowly said, and mildly disappeared.

"Very good, Bartleby," said I, in a quiet sort of serenely severe self-possessed tone, intimating the unalterable purpose of some terrible retribution very close at hand. At the moment I half intended something of the kind. But upon the whole, as it was drawing towards my dinner-hour, I thought it best to put on my hat and walk home for the day, suffering much from perplexity and distress of mind.

Shall I acknowledge it? The conclusion of this whole business was, that it soon became a fixed fact of my chambers, that a pale young scrivener, by the name of Bartleby, had a desk there; that he copied for me at the usual rate of four cents a folio (one hundred words); but he was permanently exempt from examining the work done by him, that duty being transferred to Turkey and Nippers, out of compliment doubtless to their superior acuteness; moreover, said Bartleby was never on any account to be dispatched on the most trivial errand of any sort; and that even if entreated to take upon him such a matter, it was generally understood that he would prefer not to—in other words, that he would refuse point-blank.

As days passed on, I became considerably reconciled to Bartleby. His steadiness, his freedom from all dissipation, his incessant industry (except when he chose to throw himself into a standing revery behind his screen), his great stillness, his unalterableness of demeanor under all circumstances, made him a valuable acquisition. One prime thing was this,—*he was always there;*—first in the morning, continually through the day, and the last at night. I had a singular confidence in his honesty. I felt my most precious papers perfectly safe in his hands. Sometimes to be sure I could not, for the very soul of me, avoid falling into sudden spasmodic passions with him. For it was exceeding difficult to bear in mind all the time those strange peculiarities, privileges, and unheard of exemptions, forming the tacit stipulations on Bartleby's part under which he remained in my office. Now and then, in the eagerness of dispatching pressing business, I would inadvertently summon Bartleby, in a short, rapid tone, to put his finger, say, on the incipient tie of a bit of red tape with which I was about compressing some papers. Of course, from behind the screen the usual answer, "I prefer not to," was sure to come; and then, how could a human creature with the common infirmities of our nature, refrain from bitterly exclaiming upon such perverseness—such unreasonableness. However, every added repulse of this sort which I received only tended to lessen the probability of my repeating the inadvertence.

Here it must be said, that according to the custom of most legal gentlemen occupying chambers in densely-populated law buildings, there were several keys to my door. One was kept by a woman residing in the attic, which person weekly scrubbed and daily swept and dusted my apartments. Another was kept by Turkey for convenience sake. The third I sometimes carried in my own pocket. The fourth I knew not who had.

Now, one Sunday morning I happened to go to Trinity Church, to hear a celebrated preacher, and finding myself rather early on the ground, I thought I would walk around to my chambers for a while. Luckily I had my key with me; but upon applying it to the lock, I found it resisted by something inserted from the inside. Quite surprised, I called out; when to my consternation a key was turned from within; and thrusting his lean visage at me, and holding the door ajar, the apparition of Bartleby appeared, in his shirt sleeves, and otherwise in a strangely tattered dishabille, saying quietly that he was sorry, but he was deeply engaged just then, and—preferred not admitting me at present. In a brief word or two, he moreover added, that perhaps I had better walk round the block two or three times, and by that time he would probably have concluded his affairs.

Now, the utterly unsurmised appearance of Bartleby, tenanting my law-chambers of a Sunday morning, with his cadaverously gentlemanly *nonchalance*, yet withal firm and self-possessed, had such a strange effect upon me, that incontinently I slunk away from my own door, and did as desired. But not without sundry twinges of impotent rebellion against the mild effrontery of this unaccountable scrivener. Indeed, it was his wonderful mildness chiefly, which not only disarmed me, but unmanned me, as it were. For I consider that one, for the time, is a sort of unmanned when he tranquilly permits his hired clerk to dictate to him, and order him away from his own premises. Furthermore, I was full of uneasiness as to what Bartleby could possibly be doing in my office in his shirt sleeves, and in an otherwise dismantled condition of a Sunday morning. Was any thing amiss going on? Nay, that was out of the question. It was not to be thought of for a moment that Bartleby was an immoral person. But what could he be doing there?—copying? Nay again, whatever might be his eccentricities, Bartleby was an eminently decorous person. He would be the last man to sit down to his desk in any state approaching to nudity. Besides, it was Sunday; and there was something about Bartleby that forbade the supposition that he would by any secular occupation violate the proprieties of the day.

Nevertheless, my mind was not pacified; and full of a restless curiosity, at last I returned to the door. Without hindrance I inserted my key, opened it, and entered. Bartleby was not to be seen. I looked round anxiously, peeped behind his screen; but it was very plain that he was gone. Upon more closely examining the place, I surmised that for an indefinite period Bartleby must have ate, dressed, and slept in my office, and that too without plate, mirror, or bed. The cushioned seat of a ricketty old sofa in one corner bore the faint impress of a lean, reclining form. Rolled away under his desk, I found a blanket; under the empty grate, a blacking box and brush; on a chair, a tin basin, with soap and a ragged towel; in a newspaper a few crumbs of ginger-nuts and a morsel of cheese. Yes, thought I, it is evident enough that Bartleby has been making his home here, keeping bachelor's hall all by himself. Immediately then the thought came sweeping across me, What miserable friendlessness and loneliness are here revealed! His poverty is great; but his solitude, how horrible! Think of it. Of a Sunday, Wall-street is deserted as Petra; and every night of every day it is an emptiness. This building too, which of week-days hums with industry and life, at nightfall echoes with sheer vacancy, and all through Sunday is forlorn. And here Bartleby makes his home; sole spectator of a solitude which he has seen all populous—a sort of innocent and transformed Marius brooding among the ruins of Carthage!

For the first time in my life a feeling of overpowering stinging melancholy seized me. Before, I had never experienced aught but a not-unpleasing sadness. The bond of a common humanity now drew me irresistibly to gloom. A fraternal melancholy! For both I and Bartleby were sons of Adam. I remembered the bright silks and sparkling faces I had seen that day, in gala trim, swan-like sailing down the Mississippi of Broadway; and I contrasted them with the pallid copyist, and thought to myself, Ah, happiness courts the light, so we deem the world is gay; but misery hides aloof, so we deem that misery there is none. These sad fancyings—chimeras, doubtless, of a sick and silly brain—led on to other and more special thoughts, concerning the eccentricities of Bartleby. Presentiments of strange discoveries hovered round me. The scrivener's pale form appeared to me laid out, among uncaring strangers, in its shivering winding sheet.

Suddenly I was attracted by Bartleby's closed desk, the key in open sight left in the lock.

I mean no mischief, seek the gratification of no heartless curiosity, thought I; besides, the desk is mine, and its contents too, so I will make bold to look within. Every thing was methodically arranged, the papers smoothly placed. The pigeon holes were deep, and removing the files of documents, I groped into their recesses. Presently I felt something there, and dragged it out. It was an old bandanna handkerchief, heavy and knotted. I opened it, and saw it was a savings' bank.

I now recalled all the quiet mysteries which I had noted in the man. I remembered that he never spoke but to answer; that though at intervals he had considerable time to himself, yet I had never seen him reading—no, not even a newspaper; that for long periods he would stand looking out, at his pale window behind the screen, upon the dead brick wall; I was quite sure he never visited any refectory or eating house; while his pale face clearly indicated that he never drank beer like Turkey, or tea and coffee even, like other men; that he never went any where in particular that I could learn; never went out for a walk, unless indeed that was the case at present; that he had declined telling who he was, or whence he came, or whether he had any relatives in the world; that though so thin and pale, he never complained of ill health. And more than all, I remembered a certain unconscious air of pallid—how shall I call it?—of pallid haughtiness, say, or rather an austere reserve about him, which had positively awed me into my tame compliance with his eccentricities, when I had feared to ask him to do the slightest incidental thing for me, even though I might know, from his long-continued motionlessness, that behind his screen he must be standing in one of those dead-wall reveries of his.

Revolving all these things, and coupling them with the recently discovered fact that he made my office his constant abiding place and home, and not forgetful of his morbid moodiness; revolving all these things, a prudential feeling began to steal over me. My first emotions had been those of pure melancholy and sincerest pity; but just in proportion as the forlornness of Bartleby grew and grew to my imagination, did that same melancholy merge into fear, that pity into repulsion. So true it is, and so terrible too, that up to a certain point the thought or sight of misery enlists our best affections; but, in certain special cases, beyond that point it does not. They err who would assert that invariably this is owing to the inherent selfishness of the human heart. It rather proceeds from a certain hopelessness of remedying excessive and organic ill. To a sensitive being, pity is not seldom pain. And when at last it is perceived that such pity cannot lead to effectual succor, common sense bids the soul be rid of it. What I saw that morning persuaded me that the scrivener was the victim of innate and incurable disorder. I might give alms to his body; but his body did not pain him; it was his soul that suffered, and his soul I could not reach.

I did not accomplish the purpose of going to Trinity Church that morning. Somehow, the things I had seen disqualified me for the time from church-going. I walked homeward, thinking what I would do with Bartleby. Finally, I resolved upon this;—I would put certain calm questions to him the next morning, touching his history, &c., and if he declined to answer them openly and unreservedly (and I supposed he would prefer not), then to give him a twenty dollar bill over and above whatever I might owe him, and tell him his services were no longer required; but that if in any other way I could assist him, I would be happy to do so, especially if he desired to return to his native place, wherever that might be, I would willingly help to defray the expenses. Moreover, if, after reaching home, he found himself at any time in want of aid, a letter from him would be sure of a reply.

The next morning came.

"Bartleby," said I, gently calling to him behind his screen.

No reply.

"Bartleby," said I, in a still gentler tone, "come here; I am not going to ask you to do any thing you would prefer not to do—I simply wish to speak to you."

Upon this he noiselessly slid into view.

"Will you tell me, Bartleby, where you were born?"

"I would prefer not to."

"Will you tell me *any thing* about yourself?"

"I would prefer not to."

"But what reasonable objection can you have to speak to me? I feel friendly towards you."

He did not look at me while I spoke, but kept his glance fixed upon my bust of Cicero, which as I then sat, was directly behind me, some six inches above my head.

"What is your answer, Bartleby?" said I, after waiting a considerable time for a reply, during which his countenance remained immovable, only there was the faintest conceivable tremor of the white attenuated mouth.

"At present I prefer to give no answer," he said, and retired into his hermitage.

It was rather weak in me I confess, but his manner on this occasion nettled me. Not only did there seem to lurk in it a certain calm disdain, but his perverseness seemed ungrateful, considering the undeniable good usage and indulgence he had received from me.

Again I sat ruminating what I should do. Mortified as I was at his behavior, and resolved as I had been to dismiss him when I entered my office, nevertheless I strangely felt something superstitious knocking at my heart, and forbidding me to carry out my purpose, and denouncing me for a villain if I dared to breathe one bitter word against this forlornest of mankind. At last, familiarly drawing my chair behind his screen, I sat down and said: "Bartleby, never mind then about revealing your history; but let me entreat you, as a friend, to comply as far as may be with the usages of this office. Say now you will help to examine papers to-morrow or next day: in short, say now that in a day or two you will begin to be a little reasonable:—say so, Bartleby."

"At present I would prefer not to be a little reasonable," was his mildly cadaverous reply.

Just then the folding-doors opened, and Nippers approached. He seemed suffering from an unusually bad night's rest, induced by severer indigestion than common. He overheard those final words of Bartleby.

"*Prefer not*, eh?" gritted Nippers—"I'd *prefer* him, if I were you, sir," addressing me—"I'd *prefer* him; I'd give him preferences, the stubborn mule! What is it, sir, pray, that he *prefers* not to do now?"

Bartleby moved not a limb.

"Mr. Nippers," said I, "I'd prefer that you would withdraw for the present."

Somehow, of late I had got into the way of involuntarily using this word "prefer" upon all sorts of not exactly suitable occasions. And I trembled to think that my contact with the scrivener had already and seriously affected me in a mental way. And what further and deeper aberration might it not yet produce? This apprehension had not been without efficacy in determining me to summary measures.

As Nippers, looking very sour and sulky, was departing, Turkey blandly and deferentially approached.

"With submission, sir," said he, "yesterday I was thinking about Bartleby here, and I think that if he would but prefer to take a quart of good ale every day, it would do much towards mending him, and enabling him to assist in examining his papers."

"So you have got the word too," said I, slightly excited.

"With submission, what word, sir," asked Turkey, respectfully crowding himself into the contracted space behind the screen, and by so doing, making me jostle the scrivener. "What word, sir?"

"I would prefer to be left alone here," said Bartleby, as if offended at being mobbed in his privacy.

"*That's* the word, Turkey," said I—"*that's* it."

"Oh, *prefer*? oh yes—queer word. I never use it myself. But, sir, as I was saying, if he would but prefer—"

"Turkey," interrupted I, "you will please withdraw."

"Oh certainly, sir, if you prefer that I should."

As he opened the folding-door to retire, Nippers at his desk caught a glimpse of me, and asked whether I would prefer to have a certain paper copied on blue paper or white. He did not in the least roguishly accent the word prefer. It was plain that it involuntarily rolled from his tongue. I thought to myself, surely I must get rid of a demented man, who already has in some degree turned the tongues, if not the heads of myself and clerks. But I thought it prudent not to break the dismission at once.

The next day I noticed that Bartleby did nothing but stand at his window in his dead-wall revery. Upon asking him why he did not write, he said that he had decided upon doing no more writing.

"Why, how now? what next?" exclaimed I, "do no more writing?"

"No more."

"And what is the reason?"

"Do you not see the reason for yourself," he indifferently replied.

I looked steadfastly at him, and perceived that his eyes looked dull and glazed. Instantly it occurred to me, that his unexampled diligence in copying by his dim window for the first few weeks of his stay with me might have temporarily impaired his vision.

I was touched. I said something in condolence with him. I hinted that of course he did wisely in abstaining from writing for a while; and urged him to embrace that opportunity of taking wholesome exercise in the open air. This, however, he did not do. A few days after this, my other clerks being absent, and being in a great hurry to dispatch certain letters by the mail, I thought that, having nothing else earthly to do, Bartleby would surely be less inflexible than usual, and carry these letters to the post-office. But he blankly declined. So, much to my inconvenience, I went myself.

Still added days went by. Whether Bartleby's eyes improved or not, I could not say. To all appearance, I thought they did. But when I asked him if they did, he vouchsafed no answer. At all events, he would do no copying. At last, in reply to my urgings, he informed me that he had permanently given up copying.

"What!" exclaimed I; "suppose your eyes should get entirely well—better than ever before—would you not copy then?"

"I have given up copying," he answered, and slid aside.

He remained as ever, a fixture in my chamber. Nay—if that were possible—he became still more of a fixture than before. What was to be done? He would do nothing in the office: why should he stay there? In plain fact, he had now become a millstone to me, not only useless as a necklace, but afflictive to bear. Yet I was sorry for him. I speak less than truth when I say that, on his own account, he occasioned me uneasiness. If he would but have named a single relative or friend, I would instantly have written, and urged their taking the poor fellow away to some convenient retreat. But he seemed alone, absolutely alone in the universe. A bit of wreck in the mid Atlantic. At length, necessities connected with my business tyrannized over all other considerations. Decently as I could, I told Bartleby that in six days' time he must unconditionally leave the office. I warned him to take measures, in the interval, for procuring some other abode. I offered to assist him in this endeavor, if he himself would but take the first step towards a removal. "And when you finally quit me, Bartleby," added I, "I shall see that you go not away entirely unprovided. Six days from this hour, remember."

At the expiration of that period, I peeped behind the screen, and lo! Bartleby was there.

I buttoned up my coat, balanced myself, advanced slowly towards him, touched his shoulder, and said, "The time has come; you must quit this place; I am sorry for you; here is money; but you must go."

"I would prefer not," he replied, with his back still towards me.

"You *must*."

He remained silent.

Now I had an unbounded confidence in this man's common honesty. He had frequently restored to me sixpences and shillings carelessly dropped upon the floor, for I am apt to be very reckless in such shirt-button affairs. The proceeding then which followed will not be deemed extraordinary.

"Bartleby," said I, "I owe you twelve dollars on account; here are thirty-two; the odd twenty are yours.—Will you take it?" and I handed the bills towards him.

But he made no motion.

"I will leave them here then," putting them under a weight on the table. Then taking my hat and cane and going to the door I tranquilly turned and added—"After you have removed your things from these offices, Bartleby, you will of course lock the door—since every one is now gone for the day but you—and if you please, slip your key underneath the mat, so that I may have it in the morning. I shall not see you again; so good-bye to you. If hereafter in your new place of abode I can be of any service to you, do not fail to advise me by letter. Good-bye, Bartleby, and fare you well."

But he answered not a word; like the last column of some ruined temple, he remained standing mute and solitary in the middle of the otherwise deserted room.

As I walked home in a pensive mood, my vanity got the better of my pity. I could not but highly plume myself on my masterly management in getting rid of Bartleby. Masterly I call it, and such it must appear to any dispassionate thinker. The beauty of my procedure seemed to consist in its perfect quietness. There was no vulgar bullying, no bravado of any sort, no choleric hectoring, and striding to and fro across the apartment, jerking out vehement commands for Bartleby to bundle himself off with his beggarly traps. Nothing of the kind. Without loudly bidding Bartleby depart—as an inferior genius might have done—I *assumed* the ground that depart he must; and upon that assumption built all I had to say. The more I thought over my procedure, the more I was charmed with it. Nevertheless, next morning, upon awakening, I had my doubts,—I had somehow slept off the fumes of vanity. One of the coolest and wisest hours a man has, is just after he awakes in the morning. My procedure seemed as sagacious as ever,—but only in theory. How it would prove in practice—there was the rub. It was truly a beautiful thought to have assumed Bartleby's departure; but, after all, that assumption was simply my own, and none of Bartleby's. The great point was, not whether I had assumed that he would quit me, but whether he would prefer so to do. He was more a man of preferences than assumptions.

After breakfast, I walked down town, arguing the probabilities *pro* and *con.* One moment I thought it would prove a miserable failure, and Bartleby would be found all alive at my office as usual; the next moment it seemed certain that I should find his chair empty. And so I kept veering about. At the corner of Broadway and Canal-street, I saw quite an excited group of people standing in earnest conversation.

"I'll take odds he doesn't," said a voice as I passed.

"Doesn't go?—done!" said I, "put up your money."

I was instinctively putting my hand in my pocket to produce my own, when I remembered that this was an election day. The words I had overheard bore no reference to Bartleby, but to the success or non-success of some candidate for the mayoralty. In my intent frame of mind, I had, as it were, imagined that all Broadway shared in my excitement, and were debating the same question with me. I passed on, very thankful that the uproar of the street screened my momentary absent-mindedness.

As I had intended, I was earlier than usual at my office door. I stood listening for a moment. All was still. He must be gone. I tried the knob. The door was locked. Yes, my procedure had worked to a charm; he indeed must be vanished. Yet a certain melancholy mixed with this: I was almost sorry for my brilliant success. I was fumbling under the door mat for the key, which Bartleby was to have left there for me, when accidentally my knee knocked against a panel, producing a summoning sound, and in response a voice came to me from within—"Not yet; I am occupied."

It was Bartleby.

I was thunderstruck. For an instant I stood like the man who, pipe in mouth, was killed one cloudless afternoon long ago in Virginia, by summer lightning; at his own warm open window he was killed, and remained leaning out there upon the dreamy afternoon, till some one touched him, when he fell.

"Not gone!" I murmured at last. But again obeying that wondrous ascendancy which the inscrutable scrivener had over me, and from which ascendancy, for all my chafing, I could not completely escape, I slowly went down stairs and out into the street, and while walking round the block, considered what I should next do in this unheard-of perplexity. Turn the man out by an actual thrusting I could not; to drive him away by calling him hard names would not do; calling in the police was an unpleasant idea; and yet, permit him to enjoy his cadaverous triumph over me,—this too I could not think of. What was to be done? or, if nothing could be done, was there any thing further that I could *assume* in the matter? Yes, as before I had prospectively assumed that Bartleby would depart, so now I might retrospectively assume that departed he was. In the legitimate carrying out of this assumption, I might enter my office in a great hurry, and pretending not to see Bartleby at all, walk straight against him as if he were air. Such a proceeding would in a singular degree have the appearance of a home-thrust. It was hardly possible that Bartleby could withstand such an application of the doctrine of assumptions. But upon second thoughts the success of the plan seemed rather dubious. I resolved to argue the matter over with him again.

"Bartleby," said I, entering the office, with a quietly severe expression, "I am seriously displeased. I am pained, Bartleby. I had thought better of you. I had imagined you of such a gentlemanly organization, that in any delicate dilemma a slight hint would suffice—in short, an assumption. But it appears I am deceived. Why," I added, unaffectedly starting, "you have not even touched that money yet," pointing to it, just where I had left it the evening previous.

He answered nothing.

"Will you, or will you not, quit me?" I now demanded in a sudden passion, advancing close to him.

"I would prefer *not* to quit you," he replied, gently emphasizing the *not*.

"What earthly right have you to stay here? Do you pay any rent? Do you pay my taxes? Or is this property yours?"

He answered nothing.

"Are you ready to go on and write now? Are your eyes recovered? Could you copy a small paper for me this morning? or help examine a few lines? or step round to the post-office? In a word, will you do any thing at all, to give a coloring to your refusal to depart the premises?"

He silently retired into his hermitage.

I was now in such a state of nervous resentment that I thought it but prudent to check myself at present from further demonstrations. Bartleby and I were alone. I remembered the tragedy of the unfortunate Adams and the still more unfortunate Colt in the solitary office of the latter; and how poor Colt, being dreadfully incensed by Adams, and imprudently permitting himself to get wildly excited, was at unawares hurried into his fatal act—an act which certainly no man could possibly deplore more than the actor himself. Often it had occurred to me in my ponderings upon the subject, that had that altercation taken place in the public street, or at a private residence, it would not have terminated as it did. It was the circumstance of being alone in a solitary office, up stairs, of a building entirely unhallowed by humanizing domestic associations—an uncarpeted office, doubtless, of a dusty, haggard sort of appearance;—this it must have been, which greatly helped to enhance the irritable desperation of the hapless Colt.

But when this old Adam of resentment rose in me and tempted me concerning Bartleby, I grappled him and threw him. How? Why, simply by recalling the divine injunction: "A new commandment give I unto you, that ye love one another." Yes, this it was that saved me. Aside from higher considerations, charity often operates as a vastly wise and prudent principle—a great safe-guard to its possessor. Men have committed murder for jealousy's sake, and anger's sake, and hatred's sake, and selfishness' sake, and spiritual pride's sake; but no man that ever I heard of, ever committed a diabolical murder for sweet charity's sake. Mere self-interest, then, if no better motive can be enlisted, should, especially with high-tempered men, prompt all beings to charity and philanthropy. At any rate, upon the occasion in question, I strove to drown my exasperated feelings towards the scrivener by benevolently construing his conduct. Poor fellow, poor fellow! thought I, he don't mean any thing; and besides, he has seen hard times, and ought to be indulged.

I endeavored also immediately to occupy myself, and at the same time to comfort my despondency. I tried to fancy that in the course of the morning, at such time as might prove agreeable to him, Bartleby, of his own free accord, would emerge from his hermitage, and take up some decided line of march in the direction of the door. But no. Half-past twelve o'clock came; Turkey began to glow in the face, overturn his inkstand, and become generally obstreper-ous; Nippers abated down into quietude and courtesy; Ginger Nut munched his noon apple; and Bartleby remained standing at his window in one of his profoundest dead-wall reveries. Will it be credited? Ought I to acknowledge it? That afternoon I left the office without saying one further word to him.

Some days now passed, during which, at leisure intervals I looked a lit-tle into "Edwards on the Will," and "Priestley on Necessity." Under the cir-cumstances, those books induced a salutary feeling. Gradually I slid into the persuasion that these troubles of mine touching the scrivener, had been all predestinated from eternity, and Bartleby was billeted upon me for some mys-terious purpose of an all-wise Providence, which it was not for a mere mortal like me to fathom. Yes, Bartleby, stay there behind your screen, thought I; I shall persecute you no more; you are harmless and noiseless as any of these old chairs; in short, I never feel so private as when I know you are here. At last I see it, I feel it; I penetrate to the predestinated purpose of my life. I am content. Others may have loftier parts to enact; but my mission in this world, Bartleby, is to furnish you with office-room for such period as you may see fit to remain.

I believe that this wise and blessed frame of mind would have contin-ued with me, had it not been for the unsolicited and uncharitable remarks obtruded upon me by my professional friends who visited the rooms. But thus it often is, that the constant friction of illiberal minds wears out at last the best resolves of the more generous. Though to be sure, when I reflected upon it, it was not strange that people entering my office should be struck by the peculiar aspect of the unaccountable Bartleby, and so be tempted to throw out some sinister observations concerning him. Sometimes an attorney having business with me, and calling at my office, and finding no one but the scrivener there, would undertake to obtain some sort of precise information from him touching my whereabouts; but without heeding his idle talk, Bartleby would remain standing immovable in the middle of the room. So after contemplating him in that position for a time, the attorney would depart, no wiser than he came.

Also, when a Reference was going on, and the room full of lawyers and witnesses and business was driving fast; some deeply occupied legal gentleman present, seeing Bartleby wholly unemployed, would request him to run round to his (the legal gentleman's) office and fetch some papers for him. Thereupon, Bartleby would tranquilly decline, and yet remain idle as before. Then the lawyer would give a great stare, and turn to me. And what could I say? At last I was made aware that all through the circle of my professional acquaintance, a whisper of wonder was running round, having reference to the strange creature I kept at my office. This worried me very much. And as the idea came upon me of his possibly turning out a long-lived man, and keep occupying my chambers, and denying my authority; and perplexing my visitors; and scandalizing my professional reputation; and casting a general gloom over the premises; keeping soul and body together to the last upon his savings (for doubtless he spent but half a dime a day), and in the end perhaps outlive me, and claim possession of my office by right of his perpetual occupancy: as all these dark anticipations crowded upon me more and more, and my friends continually intruded their relentless remarks upon the apparition in my room; a great change was wrought in me. I resolved to gather all my faculties together, and for ever rid me of this intolerable incubus.

Ere revolving any complicated project, however, adapted to this end, I first simply suggested to Bartleby the propriety of his permanent departure. In a calm and serious tone, I commended the idea to his careful and mature consideration. But having taken three days to meditate upon it, he apprised me that his original determination remained the same; in short, that he still preferred to abide with me.

What shall I do? I now said to myself, buttoning up my coat to the last button. What shall I do? what ought I to do? what does conscience say I *should* do with this man, or rather ghost. Rid myself of him, I must; go, he shall. But how? You will not thrust him, the poor, pale, passive mortal,—you will not thrust such a helpless creature out of your door? you will not dishonor yourself by such cruelty? No, I will not, I cannot do that. Rather would I let him live and die here, and then mason up his remains in the wall. What then will you do? For all your coaxing, he will not budge. Bribes he leaves under your own paper-weight on your table; in short, it is quite plain that he prefers to cling to you.

Then something severe, something unusual must be done. What! surely you will not have him collared by a constable, and commit his innocent pallor to the common jail? And upon what ground could you procure such a thing to be done?—a vagrant, is he? What! he a vagrant, a wanderer, who refuses to budge? It is because he will *not* be a vagrant, then, that you seek to count him *as* a vagrant. That is too absurd. No visible means of support: there I have him. Wrong again: for indubitably he *does* support himself, and that is the only unanswerable proof that any man can show of his possessing the means so to do. No more then. Since he will not quit me, I must quit him. I will change my offices; I will move elsewhere; and give him fair notice, that if I find him on my new premises I will then proceed against him as a common trespasser.

Acting accordingly, next day I thus addressed him: "I find these chambers too far from the City Hall; the air is unwholesome. In a word, I propose to remove my offices next week, and shall no longer require your services. I tell you this now, in order that you may seek another place."

He made no reply, and nothing more was said.

On the appointed day I engaged carts and men, proceeded to my chambers, and having but little furniture, every thing was removed in a few hours. Throughout, the scrivener remained standing behind the screen, which I directed to be removed the last thing. It was withdrawn; and being folded up like a huge folio, left him the motionless occupant of a naked room. I stood in the entry watching him a moment, while something from within me upbraided me.

I re-entered, with my hand in my pocket—and—and my heart in my mouth.

"Good-bye, Bartleby; I am going—good-bye, and God some way bless you; and take that," slipping something in his hand. But it dropped upon the floor, and then,—strange to say—I tore myself from him whom I had so longed to be rid of.

Established in my new quarters, for a day or two I kept the door locked, and started at every footfall in the passages. When I returned to my rooms after any little absence, I would pause at the threshold for an instant, and attentively listen, ere applying my key. But these fears were needless. Bartleby never came nigh me.

I thought all was going well, when a perturbed looking stranger visited me, inquiring whether I was the person who had recently occupied rooms at No.— Wall-street.

Full of forebodings, I replied that I was.

"Then sir," said the stranger, who proved a lawyer, "you are responsible for the man you left there. He refuses to do any copying; he refuses to do any thing; he says he prefers not to; and he refuses to quit the premises."

"I am very sorry, sir," said I, with assumed tranquillity, but an inward tremor, "but, really, the man you allude to is nothing to me—he is no relation or apprentice of mine, that you should hold me responsible for him."

"In mercy's name, who is he?"

"I certainly cannot inform you. I know nothing about him. Formerly I employed him as a copyist; but he has done nothing for me now for some time past."

"I shall settle him then,—good morning, sir."

Several days passed, and I heard nothing more; and though I often felt a charitable prompting to call at the place and see poor Bartleby, yet a certain squeamishness of I know not what withheld me.

All is over with him, by this time, thought I at last, when through another week no further intelligence reached me. But coming to my room the day after, I found several persons waiting at my door in a high state of nervous excitement.

"That's the man—here he comes," cried the foremost one, whom I recognized as the lawyer who had previously called upon me alone.

"You must take him away, sir, at once," cried a portly person among them, advancing upon me, and whom I knew to be the landlord of No.— Wallstreet. "These gentlemen, my tenants, cannot stand it any longer; Mr. B——" pointing to the lawyer, "has turned him out of his room, and he now persists in haunting the building generally, sitting upon the banisters of the stairs by day, and sleeping in the entry by night. Every body is concerned; clients are leaving the offices; some fears are entertained of a mob; something you must do, and that without delay."

Aghast at this torrent, I fell back before it, and would fain have locked myself in my new quarters. In vain I persisted that Bartleby was nothing to me—no more than to any one else. In vain:—I was the last person known to have any thing to do with him, and they held me to the terrible account. Fearful then of being exposed in the papers (as one person present obscurely threatened) I considered the matter, and at length said, that if the lawyer would give me a confidential interview with the scrivener, in his (the lawyer's) own room, I would that afternoon strive my best to rid them of the nuisance they complained of.

Going up stairs to my old haunt, there was Bartleby silently sitting upon the banister at the landing.

"What are you doing here, Bartleby?" said I.

"Sitting upon the banister," he mildly replied.

I motioned him into the lawyer's room, who then left us.

"Bartleby," said I, "are you aware that you are the cause of great tribulation to me, by persisting in occupying the entry after being dismissed from the office?"

No answer.

"Now one of two things must take place. Either you must do something, or something must be done to you. Now what sort of business would you like to engage in? Would you like to re-engage in copying for some one?"

"No; I would prefer not to make any change."

"Would you like a clerkship in a dry-goods store?"

"There is too much confinement about that. No, I would not like a clerkship; but I am not particular."

"Too much confinement," I cried, "why you keep yourself confined all the time!"

"I would prefer not to take a clerkship," he rejoined, as if to settle that little item at once.

"How would a bar-tender's business suit you? There is no trying of the eyesight in that."

"I would not like it at all; though, as I said before, I am not particular."

His unwonted wordiness inspirited me. I returned to the charge.

"Well then, would you like to travel through the country collecting bills for the merchants? That would improve your health."

"No, I would prefer to be doing something else."

"How then would going as a companion to Europe, to entertain some young gentleman with your conversation,—how would that suit you?"

"Not at all. It does not strike me that there is any thing definite about that. I like to be stationary. But I am not particular."

"Stationary you shall be then," I cried, now losing all patience, and for the first time in all my exasperating connection with him fairly flying into a passion. "If you do not go away from these premises before night, I shall feel bound—indeed I *am* bound—to—to—to quit the premises myself!" I rather absurdly concluded, knowing not with what possible threat to try to frighten his immobility into compliance. Despairing of all further efforts, I was precipitately leaving him, when a final thought occurred to me—one which had not been wholly unindulged before.

"Bartleby," said I, in the kindest tone I could assume under such exciting circumstances, "will you go home with me now—not to my office, but my dwelling—and remain there till we can conclude upon some convenient arrangement for you at our leisure? Come, let us start now, right away."

"No: at present I would prefer not to make any change at all."

I answered nothing; but effectually dodging every one by the suddenness and rapidity of my flight, rushed from the building, ran up Wall-street towards Broadway, and jumping into the first omnibus was soon removed from pursuit. As soon as tranquillity returned I distinctly perceived that I had now done all that I possibly could, both in respect to the demands of the landlord and his tenants, and with regard to my own desire and sense of duty, to benefit Bartleby, and shield him from rude persecution. I now strove to be entirely care-free and quiescent; and my conscience justified me in the attempt; though indeed it was not so successful as I could have wished. So fearful was I of being again hunted out by the incensed landlord and his exasperated tenants, that, surrendering my business to Nippers, for a few days I drove about the upper part of the town and through the suburbs, in my rockaway; crossed over to Jersey City and Hoboken, and paid fugitive visits to Manhattanville and Astoria. In fact I almost lived in my rockaway for the time.

When again I entered my office, lo, a note from the landlord lay upon the desk. I opened it with trembling hands. It informed me that the writer had sent to the police, and had Bartleby removed to the Tombs as a vagrant. Moreover, since I knew more about him than any one else, he wished me to appear at that place, and make a suitable statement of the facts. These tidings had a conflicting effect upon me. At first I was indignant; but at last almost approved. The landlord's energetic, summary disposition had led him to adopt a procedure which I do not think I would have decided upon myself; and yet as a last resort, under such peculiar circumstances, it seemed the only plan.

As I afterwards learned, the poor scrivener, when told that he must be conducted to the Tombs, offered not the slightest obstacle, but in his pale unmoving way, silently acquiesced.

Some of the compassionate and curious bystanders joined the party; and headed by one of the constables arm in arm with Bartleby, the silent procession filed its way through all the noise, and heat, and joy of the roaring thoroughfares at noon.

The same day I received the note I went to the Tombs, or to speak more properly, the Halls of Justice. Seeking the right officer, I stated the purpose of my call, and was informed that the individual I described was indeed within. I then assured the functionary that Bartleby was a perfectly honest man, and greatly to be compassionated, however unaccountably eccentric. I narrated all I knew, and closed by suggesting the idea of letting him remain in as indulgent confinement as possible till something less harsh might be done—though indeed I hardly knew what. At all events, if nothing else could be decided upon, the alms-house must receive him. I then begged to have an interview.

Being under no disgraceful charge, and quite serene and harmless in all his ways, they had permitted him freely to wander about the prison, and especially in the inclosed grass-platted yard thereof. And so I found him there, standing all alone in the quietest of the yards, his face towards a high wall, while all around, from the narrow slits of the jail windows, I thought I saw peering out upon him the eyes of murderers and thieves.

"Bartleby!"

"I know you," he said, without looking round,—"and I want nothing to say to you."

"It was not I that brought you here, Bartleby," said I, keenly pained at his implied suspicion. "And to you, this should not be so vile a place. Nothing reproachful attaches to you by being here. And see, it is not so sad a place as one might think. Look, there is the sky, and here is the grass."

"I know where I am," he replied, but would say nothing more, and so I left him.

As I entered the corridor again, a broad meat-like man, in an apron, accosted me, and jerking his thumb over his shoulder said—"Is that your friend?"

"Yes."

"Does he want to starve? If he does, let him live on the prison fare, that's all."

"Who are you?" asked I, not knowing what to make of such an unofficially speaking person in such a place.

"I am the grub-man. Such gentlemen as have friends here, hire me to provide them with something good to eat."

"Is this so?" said I, turning to the turnkey.

He said it was.

"Well then," said I, slipping some silver into the grub-man's hands (for so they called him). "I want you to give particular attention to my friend there; let him have the best dinner you can get. And you must be as polite to him as possible."

"Introduce me, will you?" said the grub-man, looking at me with an expression which seemed to say he was all impatience for an opportunity to give a specimen of his breeding.

Thinking it would prove of benefit to the scrivener, I acquiesced; and asking the grub-man his name, went up with him to Bartleby.

"Bartleby, this is Mr. Cutlets; you will find him very useful to you."

"Your sarvant, sir, your sarvant," said the grub-man, making a low salutation behind his apron. "Hope you find it pleasant here, sir; nice grounds—cool apartments, sir—hope you'll stay with us some time—try to make it agreeable. May Mrs. Cutlets and I have the pleasure of your company to dinner, sir, in Mrs. Cutlets' private room?"

"I prefer not to dine to-day," said Bartleby, turning away. "It would disagree with me; I am unused to dinners." So saying he slowly moved to the other side of the inclosure, and took up a position fronting the dead-wall.

"How's this?" said the grub-man, addressing me with a stare of astonishment. "He's odd, aint he?"

"I think he is a little deranged," said I, sadly.

"Deranged? deranged is it? Well now, upon my word, I thought that friend of yourn was a gentleman forger; they are always pale and genteel-like, them forgers. I can't help pity 'em—can't help it, sir. Did you know Monroe Edwards?" he added touchingly, and paused. Then, laying his hand pityingly on my shoulder, sighed, "he died of consumption at Sing-Sing. So you weren't acquainted with Monroe?" .

"No, I was never socially acquainted with any forgers. But I cannot stop longer. Look to my friend yonder. You will not lose by it. I will see you again."

Some few days after this, I again obtained admission to the Tombs, and went through the corridors in quest of Bartleby; but without finding him.

"I saw him coming from his cell not long ago," said a turnkey, "may be he's gone to loiter in the yards."

So I went in that direction.

"Are you looking for the silent man?" said another turnkey passing me. "Yonder he lies—sleeping in the yard there. 'Tis not twenty minutes since I saw him lie down."

The yard was entirely quiet. It was not accessible to the common prisoners. The surrounding walls, of amazing thickness, kept off all sounds behind them. The Egyptian character of the masonry weighed upon me with its gloom. But a soft imprisoned turf grew under foot. The heart of the eternal pyramids, it seemed, wherein, by some strange magic, through the clefts, grass-seed, dropped by birds, had sprung.

Strangely huddled at the base of the wall, his knees drawn up, and lying on his side, his head touching the cold stones, I saw the wasted Bartleby. But nothing stirred. I paused; then went close up to him; stooped over, and saw that his dim eyes were open; otherwise he seemed profoundly sleeping. Something prompted me to touch him. I felt his hand, when a tingling shiver ran up my arm and down my spine to my feet.

The round face of the grub-man peered upon me now. "His dinner is ready. Won't he dine to-day, either? Or does he live without dining?"

"Lives without dining," said I, and closed the eyes.

"Eh!—He's asleep, aint he?"

"With kings and counsellors," murmured I.

There would seem little need for proceeding further in this history. Imagination will readily supply the meager recital of poor Bartleby's interment. But ere parting with the reader, let me say, that if this little narrative has sufficiently interested him, to awaken curiosity as to who Bartleby was, and what manner of life he led prior to the present narrator's making his acquaintance, I can only reply, that in such curiosity I fully share, but am wholly unable to gratify it. Yet here I hardly know whether I should divulge one little item of rumor, which came to my ear a few months after the scrivener's decease. Upon what basis it rested, I could never ascertain; and hence, how true it is I cannot now tell. But inasmuch as this vague report has not been without a certain strange suggestive interest to me, however sad, it may prove the same with some others; and so I will briefly mention it. The report was this: that Bartleby had been a subordinate clerk in the Dead Letter Office at Washington, from which he had been suddenly removed by a change in the administration. When I think over this rumor, hardly can I express the emotions which seize me. Dead letters! does it not sound like dead men? Conceive a man by nature and misfortune prone to a pallid hopelessness, can any business seem more fitted to heighten it than that of continually handling these dead letters, and assorting them for the flames? For by the cart-load they are annually burned. Sometimes from out the folded paper the pale clerk takes a ring:—the finger it was meant for, perhaps, moulders in the grave; a bank-note sent in swiftest charity:—he whom it would relieve, nor eats nor hungers any more; pardon for those who died despairing; hope for those who died unhoping; good tidings for those who died stifled by unrelieved calamities. On errands of life, these letters speed to death.

Ah Bartleby! Ah humanity!

Public-Spiritedness, Charity,
Reverence: Toward the Public Goods

The Open Boat

STEPHEN CRANE

In a polity founded to secure individual rights and the pursuit of personal happiness, cultivating public-spirited citizens can be a challenge. What are the spurs to collective action? What are the virtues and attitudes needed to secure the general welfare? How are they nurtured? Stephen Crane (1871–1900) explores these questions in "The Open Boat" (1897), a fictionalized account of the author's experience surviving a shipwreck when he was sent as a correspondent to cover the Cuban Revolution in 1896. In the story, four men—a newspaper correspondent, the ship's captain, the cook, and an oiler—try to row to safety in a ten-foot lifeboat. The little dinghy, precariously afloat off the coast of Florida, carries a small human society, each of whose members is concerned mainly with survival.

Although thrown together and living hard against an indifferent and deadly "state of nature," the four men in the open boat pull together for the good of the whole and the survival of each. What enables them to do so? Are the attitudes and virtues displayed here—and one should not neglect the importance of hope and trust—needed only in lifeboat circumstances? How does life aboard the dinghy differ from life on shore (as witnessed from the dinghy)? If the open boat is a microcosm of human society, are there lessons we may learn about the need for solidarity in everyday life?

A tale intended to be after the fact. Being the experience of four men from the sunk steamer *Commodore*

I

None of them knew the color of the sky. Their eyes glanced level, and were fastened upon the waves that swept toward them. These waves were of the hue of slate, save for the tops, which were of foaming white, and all of the men knew the colors of the sea. The horizon narrowed and widened, and dipped and rose, and at all times its edge was jagged with waves that seemed thrust up in points like rocks.

Many a man ought to have a bath-tub larger than the boat which here rode upon the sea. These waves were most wrongfully and barbarously abrupt and tall, and each froth-top was a problem in small boat navigation.

The cook squatted in the bottom and looked with both eyes at the six inches of gunwale which separated him from the ocean. His sleeves were rolled over his fat forearms, and the two flaps of his unbuttoned vest dangled as he bent to bail out the boat. Often he said: "Gawd! That was a narrow clip." As he remarked it he invariably gazed eastward over the broken sea.

The oiler, steering with one of the two oars in the boat, sometimes raised himself suddenly to keep clear of water that swirled in over the stern. It was a thin little oar and it seemed often ready to snap.

The correspondent, pulling at the other oar, watched the waves and wondered why he was there.

The injured captain, lying in the bow, was at this time buried in that profound dejection and indifference which comes, temporarily at least, to even the bravest and most enduring when, willy nilly, the firm fails, the army loses, the ship goes down. The mind of the master of a vessel is rooted deep in the timbers of her, though he command for a day or a decade, and this captain had on him the stern impression of a scene in the grays of dawn of seven turned faces, and later a stump of a top-mast with a white ball on it that slashed to and fro at the waves, went low and lower, and down. Thereafter there was something strange in his voice. Although steady, it was deep with mourning, and of a quality beyond oration or tears.

"Keep'er a little more south, Billie," said he.

"'A little more south,' sir," said the oiler in the stern.

A seat in this boat was not unlike a seat upon a bucking broncho, and, by the same token, a broncho is not much smaller. The craft pranced and reared, and plunged like an animal. As each wave came, and she rose for it, she seemed like a horse making at a fence outrageously high. The manner of her scramble over these walls of water is a mystic thing, and, moreover, at the top of them were ordinarily these problems in white water, the foam racing down from the summit of each wave, requiring a new leap, and a leap from the air. Then, after scornfully bumping a crest, she would slide, and race, and splash down a long incline and arrive bobbing and nodding in front of the next menace.

A singular disadvantage of the sea lies in the fact that after successfully surmounting one wave you discover that there is another behind it just as important and just as nervously anxious to do something effective in the way of swamping boats. In a ten-foot dinghy one can get an idea of the resources of the sea in the line of waves that is not probable to the average experience, which is never at sea in a dinghy. As each slaty wall of water approached, it shut all else from the view of the men in the boat, and it was not difficult to imagine that this particular wave was the final outburst of the ocean, the last effort of the grim water. There was a terrible grace in the move of the waves, and they came in silence, save for the snarling of the crests.

In the wan light, the faces of the men must have been gray. Their eyes must have glinted in strange ways as they gazed steadily astern. Viewed from a balcony, the whole thing would doubtlessly have been weirdly picturesque. But the men in the boat had no time to see it, and if they had had leisure there were other things to occupy their minds. The sun swung steadily up the sky, and they knew it was broad day because the color of the sea changed from slate to emerald-green, streaked with amber lights, and the foam was like tumbling snow. The process of the breaking day was unknown to them. They were aware only of this effect upon the color of the waves that rolled toward them.

In disjointed sentences the cook and the correspondent argued as to the difference between a life-saving station and a house of refuge. The cook had said: "There's a house of refuge just north of the Mosquito Inlet Light, and as soon as they see us, they'll come off in their boat and pick us up."

"As soon as who see us?" said the correspondent.

"The crew," said the cook.

"Houses of refuge don't have crews," said the correspondent. "As I understand them, they are only places where clothes and grub are stored for the benefit of shipwrecked people. They don't carry crews."

"Oh, yes, they do," said the cook.

"No, they don't," said the correspondent.

"Well, we're not there yet, anyhow," said the oiler, in the stern.

"Well," said the cook, "perhaps it's not a house of refuge that I'm thinking of as being near Mosquito Inlet Light. Perhaps it's a life-saving station."

"We're not there yet," said the oiler, in the stern.

II

As the boat bounced from the top of each wave, the wind tore through the hair of the hatless men, and as the craft plopped her stern down again the spray slashed past them. The crest of each of these waves was a hill, from the top of which the men surveyed, for a moment, a broad tumultuous expanse, shining and wind-riven. It was probably splendid. It was probably glorious, this play of the free sea, wild with lights of emerald and white and amber.

"Bully good thing it's an on-shore wind," said the cook. "If not, where would we be? Wouldn't have a show."

"That's right," said the correspondent.

The busy oiler nodded his assent.

Then the captain, in the bow, chuckled in a way that expressed humor, contempt, tragedy, all in one. "Do you think we've got much of a show, now, boys?" said he.

Whereupon the three were silent, save for a trifle of hemming and hawing. To express any particular optimism at this time they felt to be childish and stupid, but they all doubtless possessed this sense of the situation in their mind. A young man thinks doggedly at such times. On the other hand, the ethics of their condition was decidedly against any open suggestion of hopelessness. So they were silent.

"Oh, well," said the captain, soothing his children, "we'll get ashore all right."

But there was that in his tone which made them think, so the oiler quoth: "Yes! If this wind holds!"

The cook was bailing. "Yes! If we don't catch hell in the surf."

Canton flannel gulls flew near and far. Sometimes they sat down on the sea, near patches of brown sea-weed that rolled over the waves with a movement like carpets on line in a gale. The birds sat comfortably in groups, and they were envied by some in the dinghy, for the wrath of the sea was no more to them than it was to a covey of prairie chickens a thousand miles inland. Often they came very close and stared at the men with black bead-like eyes. At these times they were uncanny and sinister in their unblinking scrutiny, and the men hooted angrily at them, telling them to be gone. One came, and evidently decided to alight on the top of the captain's head. The bird flew parallel to the boat and did not circle, but made short sidelong jumps in the air in chicken-fashion. His black eyes were wistfully fixed upon the captain's head. "Ugly brute," said the oiler to the bird. "You look as if you were made with a jack-knife." The cook and the correspondent swore darkly at the creature. The captain naturally wished to knock it away with the end of the heavy painter, but he did not dare do it, because anything resembling an emphatic gesture would have capsized this freighted boat, and so with his open hand, the captain gently and carefully waved the gull away. After it had been discouraged from the pursuit the captain breathed easier on account of his hair, and others breathed easier because the bird struck their minds at this time as being somehow grewsome and ominous.

In the meantime the oiler and the correspondent rowed. And also they rowed.

They sat together in the same seat, and each rowed an oar. Then the oiler took both oars; then the correspondent took both oars; then the oiler; then the correspondent. They rowed and they rowed. The very ticklish part of the business was when the time came for the reclining one in the stern to take his turn at the oars. By the very last star of truth, it is easier to steal eggs from under a hen than it was to change seats in the dinghy. First the man in the stern slid his hand along the thwart and moved with care, as if he were of Sèvres. Then the man in the rowing seat slid his hand along the other thwart. It was all done with the most extraordinary care. As the two sidled past each other, the whole party kept watchful eyes on the coming wave, and the captain cried: "Look out now! Steady there!"

The brown mats of sea-weed that appeared from time to time were like islands, bits of earth. They were travelling, apparently, neither one way nor the other. They were, to all intents stationary. They informed the men in the boat that it was making progress slowly toward the land.

The captain, rearing cautiously in the bow, after the dinghy soared on a great swell, said that he had seen the lighthouse at Mosquito Inlet. Presently the cook remarked that he had seen it. The correspondent was at the oars, then, and for some reason he too wished to look at the light-house, but his back was toward the far shore and the waves were important, and for some time he could not seize an opportunity to turn his head. But at last there came a wave more gentle than the others, and when at the crest of it he swiftly scoured the western horizon.

"See it?" said the captain.

"No," said the correspondent, slowly, "I didn't see anything."

"Look again," said the captain. He pointed. "It's exactly in that direction."

At the top of another wave, the correspondent did as he was bid, and this time his eyes chanced on a small still thing on the edge of the swaying horizon. It was precisely like the point of a pin. It took an anxious eye to find a lighthouse so tiny.

"Think we'll make it, Captain?"

"If this wind holds and the boat don't swamp, we can't do much else," said the captain.

The little boat, lifted by each towering sea, and splashed viciously by the crests, made progress that in the absence of sea-weed was not apparent to those in her. She seemed just a wee thing wallowing, miraculously, top-up, at the mercy of five oceans. Occasionally, a great spread of water, like white flames, swarmed into her.

"Bail her, cook," said the captain, serenely.

"All right, Captain," said the cheerful cook.

III

It would be difficult to describe the subtle brotherhood of men that was here established on the seas. No one said that it was so. No one mentioned it. But it dwelt in the boat, and each man felt it warm him. They were a captain, an oiler, a cook, and a correspondent, and they were friends, friends in a more curiously iron-bound degree than may be common. The hurt captain, lying against the water-jar in the bow, spoke always in a low voice and calmly, but he could never command a more ready and swiftly obedient crew than the motley three of the dinghy. It was more than a mere recognition of what was best for the common safety. There was surely in it a quality that was personal and heartfelt. And after this devotion to the commander of the boat there was this comradeship that the correspondent, for instance, who had been taught to be cynical of men, knew even at the time was the best experience of his life. But no one said that it was so. No one mentioned it.

"I wish we had a sail," remarked the captain. "We might try my overcoat on the end of an oar and give you two boys a chance to rest." So the cook and the correspondent held the mast and spread wide the overcoat. The oiler steered, and the little boat made good way with her new rig. Sometimes the oiler had to scull sharply to keep a sea from breaking into the boat, but other-wise sailing was a success.

Meanwhile the light-house had been growing slowly larger. It had now almost assumed color, and appeared like a little gray shadow on the sky. The man at the oars could not be prevented from turning his head rather often to try for a glimpse of this little gray shadow.

At last, from the top of each wave the men in the tossing boat could see land. Even as the light-house was an upright shadow on the sky, this land seemed but a long black shadow on the sea. It certainly was thinner than paper. "We must be about opposite New Smyrna," said the cook, who had coasted this shore often in schooners. "Captain, by the way, I believe they abandoned that life-saving station there about a year ago."

"Did they?" said the captain.

The wind slowly died away. The cook and the correspondent were not now obliged to slave in order to hold high the oar. But the waves continued their old impetuous swooping at the dinghy, and the little craft, no longer under way, struggled woundily over them. The oiler or the correspondent took the oars again.

Shipwrecks are *apropos* of nothing. If men could only train for them and have them occur when the men had reached pink condition, there would be less drowning at sea. Of the four in the dinghy none had slept any time worth mentioning for two days and two nights previous to embarking in the dinghy, and in the excitement of clambering about the deck of a foundering ship they had also forgotten to eat heartily.

For these reasons, and for others, neither the oiler nor the correspondent was fond of rowing at this time. The correspondent wondered ingenuously how in the name of all that was sane could there be people who thought it amusing to row a boat. It was not an amusement; it was a diabolical punishment, and even a genius of mental aberrations could never conclude that it was anything but a horror to the muscles and a crime against the back. He mentioned to the boat in general how the amusement of rowing struck him, and the weary-faced oiler smiled in full sympathy. Previously to the foundering, by the way, the oiler had worked double-watch in the engine-room of the ship.

"Take her easy, now, boys," said the captain. "Don't spend yourselves. If we have to run a surf you'll need all your strength, because we'll sure have to swim for it. Take your time."

Slowly the land arose from the sea. From a black line it became a line of black and a line of white—trees and sand. Finally, the captain said that he could make out a house on the shore. "That's the house of refuge, sure," said the cook. "They'll see us before long, and come out after us."

The distant light-house reared high. "The keeper ought to be able to make us out now, if he's looking through a glass," said the captain. "He'll notify the life-saving people."

"None of those other boats could have got ashore to give word of the wreck," said the oiler, in a low voice. "Else the life-boat would be out hunting us."

Slowly and beautifully the land loomed out of the sea. The wind came again. It had veered from the northeast to the southeast. Finally, a new sound struck the ears of the men in the boat. It was the low thunder of the surf on the shore. "We'll never be able to make the light-house now," said the captain. "Swing her head a little more north, Billie."

"'A little more north,' sir," said the oiler.

Whereupon the little boat turned her nose once more down the wind, and all but the oarsman watched the shore grow. Under the influence of this expansion doubt and direful apprehension was leaving the minds of the men. The management of the boat was still most absorbing, but it could not prevent a quiet cheerfulness. In an hour, perhaps, they would be ashore.

Their back-bones had become thoroughly used to balancing in the boat and they now rode this wild colt of a dinghy like circus men. The correspondent thought that he had been drenched to the skin, but happening to feel in the top pocket of his coat, he found therein eight cigars. Four of them were soaked with seawater; four were perfectly scatheless. After a search, somebody produced three dry matches, and thereupon the four waifs rode impudently in their little boat, and with an assurance of an impending rescue shining in their eyes, puffed at the big cigars and judged well and ill of all men. Everybody took a drink of water.

IV

"Cook," remarked the captain, "there don't seem to be any signs of life about your house of refuge."

"No," replied the cook. "Funny they don't see us!"

A broad stretch of lowly coast lay before the eyes of the men. It was of dunes topped with dark vegetation. The roar of the surf was plain, and sometimes they could see the white lip of a wave as it spun up the beach. A tiny house was blocked out black upon the sky. Southward, the slim light-house lifted its little gray length.

Tide, wind, and waves were swinging the dinghy northward. "Funny they don't see us," said the men.

The surf's roar was here dulled, but its tone was, nevertheless, thunderous and mighty. As the boat swam over the great rollers, the men sat listening to this roar. "We'll swamp sure," said everybody.

It is fair to say here that there was not a life-saving station within twenty miles in either direction, but the men did not know this fact and in consequence they made dark and opprobrious remarks concerning the eyesight of the nation's life-savers. Four scowling men sat in the dinghy and surpassed records in the invention of epithets.

"Funny they don't see us."

The light-heartedness of a former time had completely faded. To their sharpened minds it was easy to conjure pictures of all kinds of incompetency and blindness and, indeed, cowardice. There was the shore of the populous land, and it was bitter and bitter to them that from it came no sign.

"Well," said the captain, ultimately, "I suppose we'll have to make a try for ourselves. If we stay out here too long, we'll none of us have strength left to swim after the boat swamps."

And so the oiler, who was at the oars, turned the boat straight for the shore. There was a sudden tightening of muscles. There was some thinking.

"If we don't all get ashore—" said the captain. "If we don't all get ashore, I suppose you fellows know where to send news of my finish?"

They then briefly exchanged some addresses and admonitions. As for the reflections of the men, there was a great deal of rage in them. Perchance they might be formulated thus: "If I am going to be drowned—if I am going to be drowned—if I am going to be drowned, why, in the name of the seven mad gods who rule the sea, was I allowed to come thus far and contemplate sand and trees? Was I brought here merely to have my nose dragged away as I was about to nibble the sacred cheese of life? It is preposterous. If this old ninny-woman, Fate, cannot do better than this, she should be deprived of the management of men's fortunes. She is an old hen who knows not her intention. If she has decided to drown me, why did she not do it in the beginning and save me all this trouble. The whole affair is absurd. . . . But, no, she cannot mean to drown me. She dare not drown me. She cannot drown me. Not after all this work." Afterward the man might have had an impulse to shake his fist at the clouds. "Just you drown me, now, and then hear what I call you!"

The billows that came at this time were more formidable. They seemed always just about to break and roll over the little boat in a turmoil of foam. There was a preparatory and long growl in the speech of them. No mind unused to the sea would have concluded that the dinghy could ascend these sheer heights in time. The shore was still afar. The oiler was a wily surfman. "Boys," he said, swiftly, "she won't live three minutes more and we're too far out to swim. Shall I take her to sea again, Captain?"

"Yes! Go ahead!" said the captain.

This oiler, by a series of quick miracles, and fast and steady oarsmanship, turned the boat in the middle of the surf and took her safely to sea again.

There was a considerable silence as the boat bumped over the furrowed sea to deeper water. Then somebody in gloom spoke. "Well, anyhow, they must have seen us from the shore by now."

The gulls went in slanting flight up the wind toward the gray desolate east. A squall, marked by dingy clouds, and clouds brick-red, like smoke from a burning building, appeared from the southeast.

"What do you think of those life-saving people? Ain't they peaches?"

"Funny they haven't seen us."

"Maybe they think we're out here for sport! Maybe they think we're fishin'. Maybe they think we're damned fools."

It was a long afternoon. A changed tide tried to force them southward, but wind and wave said northward. Far ahead, where coast-line, sea, and sky formed their mighty angle, there were little dots which seemed to indicate a city on the shore.

"St. Augustine?"

The captain shook his head. "Too near Mosquito Inlet."

And the oiler rowed, and then the correspondent rowed. Then the oiler rowed. It was a weary business. The human back can become the seat of more aches and pains than are registered in books for the composite anatomy of a regiment. It is a limited area, but it can become the theatre of innumerable muscular conflicts, tangles, wrenches, knots, and other comforts.

"Did you ever like to row, Billie?" asked the correspondent.

"No," said the oiler. "Hang it."

When one exchanged the rowing-seat for a place in the bottom of the boat, he suffered a bodily depression that caused him to be careless of everything save an obligation to wiggle one finger. There was cold sea-water swashing to and fro in the boat, and he lay in it. His head, pillowed on a thwart, was within an inch of the swirl of a wave crest, and sometimes a particularly obstreperous sea came in-board and drenched him once more. But these matters did not annoy him. It is almost certain that if the boat had capsized he would have tumbled comfortably out upon the ocean as if he felt sure it was a great soft mattress.

"Look! There's a man on the shore!"

"Where?"

"There! See 'im? See 'im?"

"Yes, sure! He's walking along."

"Now he's stopped. Look! He's facing us!"

"He's waving at us!"

"So he is! By thunder!"

"Ah, now, we're all right! Now we're all right! There'll be a boat out here for us in half an hour."

"He's going on. He's running. He's going up to that house there."

The remote beach seemed lower than the sea, and it required a searching glance to discern the little black figure. The captain saw a floating stick and they rowed to it. A bath-towel was by some weird chance in the boat, and, tying this on the stick, the captain waved it. The oarsman did not dare turn his head, so he was obliged to ask questions.

"What's he doing now?"

"He's standing still again. He's looking, I think. . . . There he goes again. Toward the house. . . . Now he's stopped again."

"Is he waving at us?"

"No, not now! he was, though."

"Look! There comes another man!"

"He's running."

"Look at him go, would you."

"Why, he's on a bicycle. Now he's met the other man. They're both waving at us. Look!"

"There comes something up the beach."

"What the devil is that thing?"

"Why, it looks like a boat."

"Why, certainly it's a boat."

"No, it's on wheels."

"Yes, so it is. Well, that must be the life-boat. They drag them along shore on a wagon."

"That's the life-boat, sure."

"No, by ——, it's—it's an omnibus."

"I tell you it's a life-boat."

"It is not! It's an omnibus. I can see it plain. See? One of those big hotel omnibuses."

"By thunder, you're right. It's an omnibus, sure as fate. What do you suppose they are doing with an omnibus? Maybe they are going around collecting the life-crew, hey?"

"That's it, likely. Look! There's a fellow waving a little black flag. He's standing on the steps of the omnibus. There come those other two fellows. Now they're all talking together. Look at the fellow with the flag. Maybe he ain't waving it!"

"That ain't a flag, is it? That's his coat. Why, certainly, that's his coat."

"So it is. It's his coat. He's taken it off and is waving it around his head. But would you look at him swing it!"

"Oh, say, there isn't any life-saving station there. That's just a winter resort hotel omnibus that has brought over some of the boarders to see us drown."

"What's that idiot with the coat mean? What's he signaling, anyhow?"

"It looks as if he were trying to tell us to go north. There must be a life-saving station up there."

"No! He thinks we're fishing. Just giving us a merry hand. See? Ah, there, Willie."

"Well, I wish I could make something out of those signals. What do you suppose he means?"

"He don't mean anything. He's just playing."

"Well, if he'd just signal us to try the surf again, or to go to sea and wait, or go north, or go south, or go to hell—there would be some reason in it. But look at him. He just stands there and keeps his coat revolving like a wheel. The ass!"

"There come more people."

"Now there's quite a mob. Look! Isn't that a boat?"

"Where? Oh, I see where you mean. No, that's no boat."

"That fellow is still waving his coat."

"He must think we like to see him do that. Why don't he quit it. It don't mean anything."

"I don't know. I think he is trying to make us go north. It must be that there's a life-saving station there somewhere."

"Say, he ain't tired yet. Look at 'im wave."

"Wonder how long he can keep that up. He's been revolving his coat ever since he caught sight of us. He's an idiot. Why aren't they getting men to bring a boat out. A fishing boat—one of those big yawls—could come out here all right. Why don't he do something?"

"Oh, it's all right, now."

"They'll have a boat out here for us in less than no time, now that they've seen us."

A faint yellow tone came into the sky over the low land. The shadows on the sea slowly deepened. The wind bore coldness with it, and the men began to shiver.

"Holy smoke!" said one, allowing his voice to express his impious mood, "if we keep on monkeying out here! If we've got to flounder out here all night!"

"Oh, we'll never have to stay here all night! Don't you worry. They've seen us now, and it won't be long before they'll come chasing out after us."

The shore grew dusky. The man waving a coat blended gradually into this gloom, and it swallowed in the same manner the omnibus and the group of people. The spray, when it dashed uproariously over the side, made the voyagers shrink and swear like men who were being branded.

"I'd like to catch the chump who waved the coat. I feel like soaking him one, just for luck."

"Why? What did he do?"

"Oh, nothing, but then he seemed so damned cheerful."

In the meantime the oiler rowed, and then the correspondent rowed, and then the oiler rowed. Gray-faced and bowed forward, they mechanically, turn by turn, plied the leaden oars. The form of the light-house had vanished from the southern horizon, but finally a pale star appeared, just lifting from the sea. The streaked saffron in the west passed before the all-merging darkness, and the sea to the east was black. The land had vanished, and was expressed only by the low and drear thunder of the surf.

"If I am going to be drowned—if I am going to be drowned—if I am going to be drowned, why, in the name of the seven mad gods who rule the sea, was I allowed to come thus far and contemplate sand and trees? Was I brought here merely to have my nose dragged away as I was about to nibble the sacred cheese of life?"

The patient captain, drooped over the water-jar, was sometimes obliged to speak to the oarsman.

"Keep her head up! Keep her head up!"

"'Keep her head up,' sir." The voices were weary and low.

This was surely a quiet evening. All save the oarsman lay heavily and listlessly in the boat's bottom. As for him, his eyes were just capable of noting the tall black waves that swept forward in a most sinister silence, save for an occasional subdued growl of a crest.

The cook's head was on a thwart, and he looked without interest at the water under his nose. He was deep in other scenes. Finally he spoke. "Billie," he murmured, dreamfully, "what kind of pie do you like best?"

V

"Pie," said the oiler and the correspondent, agitatedly. "Don't talk about those things, blast you!"

"Well," said the cook, "I was just thinking about ham sandwiches, and—"

A night on the sea in an open boat is a long night. As darkness settled finally, the shine of the light, lifting from the sea in the south, changed to full gold. On the northern horizon a new light appeared, a small bluish gleam on the edge of the waters. These two lights were the furniture of the world. Otherwise there was nothing but waves.

Two men huddled in the stern, and distances were so magnificent in the dinghy that the rower was enabled to keep his feet partly warmed by thrusting them under his companions. Their legs indeed extended far under the rowing-seat until they touched the feet of the captain forward. Sometimes, despite the efforts of the tired oarsman, a wave came piling into the boat, an icy wave of the night, and the chilling water soaked them anew. They would twist their bodies for a moment and groan, and sleep the dead sleep once more, while the water in the boat gurgled about them as the craft rocked.

The plan of the oiler and the correspondent was for one to row until he lost the ability, and then arouse the other from his sea-water couch in the bottom of the boat.

The oiler plied the oars until his head drooped forward, and the overpowering sleep blinded him. And he rowed yet afterward. Then he touched a man in the bottom of the boat, and called his name. "Will you spell me for a little while?" he said, meekly.

"Sure, Billie," said the correspondent, awakening and dragging himself to a sitting position. They exchanged places carefully, and the oiler, cuddling down in the sea-water at the cook's side, seemed to go to sleep instantly.

The particular violence of the sea had ceased. The waves came without snarling. The obligation of the man at the oars was to keep the boat headed so that the tilt of the rollers would not capsize her, and to preserve her from filling when the crests rushed past. The black waves were silent and hard to be seen in the darkness. Often one was almost upon the boat before the oarsman was aware.

In a low voice the correspondent addressed the captain. He was not sure that the captain was awake, although this iron man seemed to be always awake. "Captain, shall I keep her making for that light north, sir?"

The same steady voice answered him. "Yes. Keep it about two points off the port bow."

The cook had tied a life-belt around himself in order to get even the warmth which this clumsy cork contrivance could donate, and he seemed almost stove-like when a rower, whose teeth invariably chattered wildly as soon as he ceased his labor, dropped down to sleep.

The correspondent, as he rowed, looked down at the two men sleeping under foot. The cook's arm was around the oiler's shoulders, and, with their fragmentary clothing and haggard faces, they were the babes of the sea, a grotesque rendering of the old babes in the wood.

Later he must have grown stupid at his work, for suddenly there was a growling of water, and a crest came with a roar and a swash into the boat, and it was a wonder that it did not set the cook afloat in his life-belt. The cook continued to sleep, but the oiler sat up, blinking his eyes and shaking with the new cold.

"Oh, I'm awful sorry, Billie," said the correspondent, contritely.

"That's all right, old boy," said the oiler, and lay down again and was asleep.

Presently it seemed that even the captain dozed, and the correspondent thought that he was the one man afloat on all the oceans. The wind had a voice as it came over the waves, and it was sadder than the end.

There was a long, loud swishing astern of the boat, and a gleaming trail of phosphorescence, like blue flame, was furrowed on the black waters. It might have been made by a monstrous knife.

Then there came a stillness, while the correspondent breathed with the open mouth and looked at the sea.

Suddenly there was another swish and another long flash of bluish light, and this time it was alongside the boat, and might almost have been reached with an oar. The correspondent saw an enormous fin speed like a shadow through the water, hurling the crystalline spray and leaving the long glowing trail.

The correspondent looked over his shoulder at the captain. His face was hidden, and he seemed to be asleep. He looked at the babes of the sea. They certainly were asleep. So, being bereft of sympathy, he leaned a little way to one side and swore softly into the sea.

But the thing did not then leave the vicinity of the boat. Ahead or astern, on one side or the other, at intervals long or short, fled the long sparkling streak, and there was to be heard the whiroo of the dark fin. The speed and power of the thing was greatly to be admired. It cut the water like a gigantic and keen projectile.

The presence of this biding thing did not affect the man with the same horror that it would if he had been a picnicker. He simply looked at the sea dully and swore in an undertone.

Nevertheless, it is true that he did not wish to be alone with the thing. He wished one of his companions to awaken by chance and keep him company with it. But the captain hung motionless over the water-jar and the oiler and the cook in the bottom of the boat were plunged in slumber.

VI

"If I am going to be drowned—if I am going to be drowned—if I am going to be drowned, why, in the name of the seven mad gods who rule the sea, was I allowed to come thus far and contemplate sand and trees?"

During this dismal night, it may be remarked that a man would conclude that it was really the intention of the seven mad gods to drown him, despite the abominable injustice of it. For it was certainly an abominable injustice to drown a man who had worked so hard, so hard. The man felt it would be a crime most unnatural. Other people had drowned at sea since galleys swarmed with painted sails, but still—

When it occurs to a man that nature does not regard him as important, and that she feels she would not maim the universe by disposing of him, he at first wishes to throw bricks at the temple, and he hates deeply the fact that there are no bricks and no temples. Any visible expression of nature would surely be pelleted with his jeers.

Then, if there be no tangible thing to hoot he feels, perhaps, the desire to confront a personification and indulge in pleas, bowed to one knee, and with hands supplicant, saying: "Yes, but I love myself."

A high cold star on a winter's night is the word he feels that she says to him. Thereafter he knows the pathos of his situation.

The men in the dinghy had not discussed these matters, but each had, no doubt, reflected upon them in silence and according to his mind. There was seldom any expression upon their faces save the general one of complete weariness. Speech was devoted to the business of the boat.

To chime the notes of his emotion, a verse mysteriously entered the correspondent's head. He had even forgotten that he had forgotten this verse, but it suddenly was in his mind.

> A soldier of the Legion lay dying in Algiers,
> There was lack of woman's nursing, there was dearth of woman's tears;
> But a comrade stood beside him, and he took that comrade's hand,
> And he said: "I never more shall see my own, my native land."

In his childhood, the correspondent had been made acquainted with the fact that a soldier of the Legion lay dying in Algiers, but he had never regarded it as important. Myriads of his school-fellows had informed him of the soldier's plight, but the dinning had naturally ended by making him perfectly indifferent. He had never considered it his affair that a soldier of the Legion lay dying in Algiers, nor had it appeared to him as a matter for sorrow. It was less to him than breaking of a pencil's point.

Now, however, it quaintly came to him as a human, living thing. It was no longer merely a picture of a few throes in the breast of a poet, meanwhile drinking tea and warming his feet at the grate; it was an actuality—stern, mournful, and fine.

The correspondent plainly saw the soldier. He lay on the sand with his feet out straight and still. While his pale left hand was upon his chest in an attempt to thwart the going of his life, the blood came between his fingers. In the far Algerian distance, a city of low square forms was set against a sky that was faint with the last sunset hues. The correspondent, plying the oars and dreaming of the slow and slower movements of the lips of the soldier, was moved by a profound and perfectly impersonal comprehension. He was sorry for the soldier of the Legion who lay dying in Algiers.

The thing which had followed the boat and waited had evidently grown bored at the delay. There was no longer to be heard the slash of the cut-water, and there was no longer the flame of the long trail. The light in the north still glimmered, but it was apparently no nearer to the boat. Sometimes the boom of the surf rang in the correspondent's ears, and he turned the craft seaward then and rowed harder. Southward, someone had evidently built a watch-fire on the beach. It was too low and too far to be seen, but it made a shimmering, rose-ate reflection upon the bluff back of it, and this could be discerned from the boat. The wind came stronger, and sometimes a wave suddenly raged out like a mountain-cat, and there was to be seen the sheen and sparkle of a broken crest.

The captain, in the bow, moved on his water-jar and sat erect. "Pretty long night," he observed to the correspondent. He looked at the shore. "Those life-saving people take their time."

"Did you see that shark playing around?"

"Yes, I saw him. He was a big fellow, all right."

"Wish I had known you were awake."

Later the correspondent spoke into the bottom of the boat.

"Billie!" There was a slow and gradual disentanglement. "Billie, will you spell me?"

"Sure," said the oiler.

As soon as the correspondent touched the cold comfortable sea-water in the bottom of the boat, and had huddled close to the cook's life-belt he was deep in sleep, despite the fact that his teeth played all the popular airs. This sleep was so good to him that it was but a moment before he heard a voice call his name in a tone that demonstrated the last stages of exhaustion. "Will you spell me?"

"Sure, Billie."

The light in the north had mysteriously vanished, but the correspondent took his course from the wide-awake captain.

Later in the night they took the boat farther out to sea, and the captain directed the cook to take one oar at the stern and keep the boat facing the seas. He was to call out if he should hear the thunder of the surf. This plan enabled the oiler and the correspondent to get respite together. "We'll give those boys a chance to get into shape again," said the captain. They curled down and, after a few preliminary chatterings and trembles, slept once more the dead sleep. Neither knew they had bequeathed to the cook the company of another shark, or perhaps the same shark.

As the boat caroused on the waves, spray occasionally bumped over the side and gave them a fresh soaking, but this had no power to break their repose. The ominous slash of the wind and the water affected them as it would have affected mummies.

"Boys," said the cook, with the notes of every reluctance in his voice, "she's drifted in pretty close. I guess one of you had better take her to sea again." The correspondent, aroused, heard the crash of the toppled crests.

As he was rowing, the captain gave him some whiskey and water, and this steadied the chills out of him. "If I ever get ashore and anybody shows me even a photograph of an oar—"

At last there was a short conversation.

"Billie. . . . Billie, will you spell me?"

"Sure," said the oiler.

VII

When the correspondent again opened his eyes, the sea and the sky were each of the gray hue of the dawning. Later, carmine and gold was painted upon the waters. The morning appeared finally, in its splendor, with a sky of pure blue, and the sunlight flamed on the tips of the waves.

On the distant dunes were set many little black cottages, and a tall white wind-mill reared above them. No man, nor dog, nor bicycle appeared on the beach. The cottages might have formed a deserted village.

The voyagers scanned the shore. A conference was held in the boat. "Well," said the captain, "if no help is coming, we might better try a run through the surf right away. If we stay out here much longer we will be too weak to do anything for ourselves at all." The others silently acquiesced in this reasoning. The boat was headed for the beach. The correspondent wondered if none ever ascended the tall wind-tower, and if then they never looked seaward. This tower was a giant, standing with its back to the plight of the ants. It represented in a degree, to the correspondent, the serenity of nature amid the struggles of the individual—nature in the wind, and nature in the vision of men. She did not seem cruel to him then, nor beneficent, nor treacherous, nor wise. But she was indifferent, flatly indifferent. It is, perhaps, plausible that a man in this situation, impressed with the unconcern of the universe, should see the innumerable flaws of his life and have them taste wickedly in his mind and wish for another chance. A distinction between right and wrong seems absurdly clear to him, then, in this new ignorance of the grave-edge, and he understands that if he were given another opportunity he would mend his conduct and his words, and be better and brighter during an introduction, or at a tea.

"Now, boys," said the captain, "she is going to swamp sure. All we can do is to work her in as far as possible, and then when she swamps, pile out and scramble for the beach. Keep cool now, and don't jump until she swamps sure."

The oiler took the oars. Over his shoulders he scanned the surf. "Captain," he said, "I think I'd better bring her about, and keep her head-on to the seas and back her in."

"All right, Billie," said the captain. "Back her in." The oiler swung the boat then and, seated in the stern, the cook and the correspondent were obliged to look over their shoulders to contemplate the lonely and indifferent shore.

The monstrous inshore rollers heaved the boat high until the men were again enabled to see the white sheets of water scudding up the slanted beach. "We won't get in very close," said the captain. Each time a man could wrest his attention from the rollers, he turned his glance toward the shore, and in the expression of the eyes during this contemplation there was a singular quality. The correspondent, observing the others, knew that they were not afraid, but the full meaning of their glances was shrouded.

As for himself, he was too tired to grapple fundamentally with the fact. He tried to coerce his mind into thinking of it, but the mind was dominated at this time by the muscles, and the muscles said they did not care. It merely occurred to him that if he should drown it would be a shame.

There were no hurried words, no pallor, no plain agitation. The men simply looked at the shore. "Now, remember to get well clear of the boat when you jump," said the captain.

Seaward the crest of a roller suddenly fell with a thunderous crash, and the long white comber came roaring down upon the boat.

"Steady now," said the captain. The men were silent. They turned their eyes from the shore to the comber and waited. The boat slid up the incline, leaped at the furious top, bounced over it, and swung down the long back of the wave. Some water had been shipped and the cook bailed it out.

But the next crest crashed also. The tumbling boiling flood of white water caught the boat and whirled it almost perpendicular. Water swarmed in from all sides. The correspondent had his hands on the gunwale at this time, and when the water entered at that place he swiftly withdrew his fingers, as if he objected to wetting them.

The little boat, drunken with this weight of water, reeled and snuggled deeper into the sea.

"Bail her out, cook! Bail her out," said the captain.

"All right, Captain," said the cook.

"Now, boys, the next one will do for us, sure," said the oiler. "Mind to jump clear of the boat."

The third wave moved forward, huge, furious, implacable. It fairly swallowed the dinghy, and almost simultaneously the men tumbled into the sea. A piece of life-belt had lain in the bottom of the boat, and as the correspondent went overboard he held this to his chest with his left hand.

The January water was icy, and he reflected immediately that it was colder than he had expected to find it off the coast of Florida. This appeared to his dazed mind as a fact important enough to be noted at the time. The coldness of the water was sad; it was tragic. This fact was somehow so mixed and confused with his opinion of his own situation that it seemed almost a proper reason for tears. The water was cold.

When he came to the surface he was conscious of little but the noisy water. Afterward he saw his companions in the sea. The oiler was ahead in the race. He was swimming strongly and rapidly. Off to the correspondent's left, the cook's great white and corked back bulged out of the water, and in the rear the captain was hanging with his one good hand to the keel of the overturned dinghy.

There is a certain immovable quality to a shore, and the correspondent wondered at it amid the confusion of the sea.

It seemed also very attractive, but the correspondent knew that it was a long journey, and he paddled leisurely. The piece of life-preserver lay under him, and sometimes he whirled down the incline of a wave as if he were on a hand-sled.

But finally he arrived at a place in the sea where travel was beset with difficulty. He did not pause swimming to inquire what manner of current had caught him, but there his progress ceased. The shore was set before him like a bit of scenery on a stage, and he looked at it and understood with his eyes each detail of it.

As the cook passed, much farther to the left, the captain was calling to him, "Turn over on your back, cook! Turn over on your back and use the oar."

"All right, sir!" The cook turned on his back, and, paddling with an oar, went ahead as if he were a canoe.

Presently the boat also passed to the left of the correspondent with the captain clinging with one hand to the keel. He would have appeared like a man raising himself to look over a board fence, if it were not for the extraordinary gymnastics of the boat. The correspondent marvelled that the captain could still hold to it.

They passed on, nearer to shore—the oiler, the cook, the captain—and following them went the water-jar, bouncing gayly over the seas.

The correspondent remained in the grip of this strange new enemy—a current. The shore, with its white slope of sand and its green bluff, topped with little silent cottages, was spread like a picture before him. It was very near to him then, but he was impressed as one who in a gallery looks at a scene from Brittany or Holland.

He thought: "I am going to drown? Can it be possible? Can it be possible? Can it be possible?" Perhaps an individual must consider his own death to be the final phenomenon of nature.

But later a wave perhaps whirled him out of this small deadly current, for he found suddenly that he could again make progress toward the shore. Later still, he was aware that the captain, clinging with one hand to the keel of the dinghy, had his face turned away from the shore and toward him, and was calling his name. "Come to the boat! Come to the boat!"

In his struggle to reach the captain and the boat, he reflected that when one gets properly wearied, drowning must really be a comfortable arrangement, a cessation of hostilities accompanied by a large degree of relief, and he was glad of it, for the main thing in his mind for some moments had been horror of the temporary agony. He did not wish to be hurt.

Presently he saw a man running along the shore. He was undressing with most remarkable speed. Coat, trousers, shirt, everything flew magically off him.

"Come to the boat," called the captain.

"All right, Captain." As the correspondent paddled, he saw the captain let himself down to bottom and leave the boat. Then the correspondent performed his one little marvel of the voyage. A large wave caught him and flung him with ease and supreme speed completely over the boat and far beyond it. It struck him even then as an event in gymnastics, and a true miracle of the sea. An overturned boat in the surf is not a plaything to a swimming man.

The correspondent arrived in water that reached only to his waist, but his condition did not enable him to stand for more than a moment. Each wave knocked him into a heap, and the under-tow pulled at him.

Then he saw the man who had been running and undressing, and undressing and running, come bounding into the water. He dragged ashore the cook, and then waded toward the captain, but the captain waved him away, and sent him to the correspondent. He was naked, naked as a tree in winter, but a halo was about his head, and he shone like a saint. He gave a strong pull, and a long drag, and a bully heave at the correspondent's hand. The correspondent, schooled in the minor formulae, said: "Thanks, old man." But suddenly the man cried: "What's that?" He pointed a swift finger. The correspondent said: "Go."

In the shallows, face downward, lay the oiler. His forehead touched sand that was periodically, between each wave, clear of the sea.

The correspondent did not know all that transpired afterward. When he achieved safe ground he fell, striking the sand with each particular part of his body. It was as if he had dropped from a roof, but the thud was grateful to him.

It seems that instantly the beach was populated with men with blankets, clothes, and flasks, and women with coffee-pots and all the remedies sacred to their minds. The welcome of the land to the men from the sea was warm and generous, but a still and dripping shape was carried slowly up the beach, and the land's welcome for it could only be the different and sinister hospitality of the grave.

When it came night, the white waves paced to and fro in the moonlight, and the wind brought the sound of the great sea's voice to the men on shore, and they felt that they could then be interpreters.

Veterans Day Speech to the Semper Fi Society of St. Louis

John F. Kelly

Many American citizens are public-spirited at one time or another, but a remarkable minority of our fellow citizens—our police, firefighters, and military men and women—have made devotion to public safety and well-being their way of life, one that often bears a heavy price. In this (excerpted) speech delivered on November 13, 2010, to the Semper Fi Society of St. Louis—an organization supporting U.S. Marines and their families—Lieutenant General John F. Kelly, U.S. Marine Corps (born 1950), commander of the Multinational Force-West in Iraq from 2008 to 2009, pays moving tribute to the heroism of these supreme public servants. He also makes clear the debt that the rest of us owe these dedicated men and women, whose sacrifices make it possible for us to enjoy peace, freedom, and the pursuit of private happiness. He concludes with an account of a most remarkable display of self-sacrifice on the part of two Marines. (Four days before this speech was given, General Kelly's own son Robert was killed in action on a mission in Afghanistan, during his third tour of duty; another son remained in combat with the Marines.)

Where does such public-spiritedness come from, and how can it be cultivated? What is—what should be—the relation between the warriors and the larger community, especially when only a tiny minority of the population serves? Some might say that this speech is tragic, showing that superior men and women sacrifice and die for people less worthy, people whose patriotism amounts to little more than "a plastic flag in their car window." Do you agree with this judgment? Why or why not? What can the rest of us learn from these heroic examples? What is the best way to honor their service and sacrifice?

Nine years ago, four commercial aircraft took off from Boston, Newark, and Washington. Took off fully loaded with men, women, and children—all innocent, and all soon to die. These aircraft were targeted at the World Trade Towers in New York, the Pentagon, and likely the Capitol in Washington, D.C. Three found their mark. No American alive old enough to remember will ever forget exactly where they were, exactly what they were doing, and exactly who they were with at the moment they watched the aircraft dive into the World Trade Towers on what was, until then, a beautiful morning in New York City. Within the hour three thousand blameless human beings would be vaporized, incinerated, or crushed in the most agonizing ways imaginable. The most wretched among them—over two hundred—driven mad by heat, hopelessness, and utter desperation, leapt to their deaths from a thousand feet above lower Manhattan. We soon learned hundreds more were murdered at the Pentagon, and in a Pennsylvania farmer's field.

Once the buildings had collapsed and the immensity of the attack began to register, most of us had no idea of what to do, or where to turn. As a nation, we were scared like we had not been scared for generations. Parents hugged their children to gain as much as to give comfort. Strangers embraced in the streets, stunned and crying on one another's shoulders, seeking solace, as much as to give it. . . .

There was, however, a small segment of America that made very different choices that day—actions the rest of America stood in awe of on 9/11 and every day since. The first were our firefighters and police, their ranks decimated that day as they ran towards—not away from—danger and certain death. They were doing what they'd sworn to do—"protect and serve"—and went to their graves having fulfilled their sacred oath. Then there was you armed forces, and I know I am a little biased in my opinion here, but the best of them are Marines. Most wearing the Eagle, Globe, and Anchor today joined the unbroken ranks of American heroes after that fateful day not for money, or promises of bonuses or travel to exotic liberty ports, but for one reason and one reason alone: because of the terrible assault on our way of life by men they knew must be killed and extremist ideology that must be destroyed. A plastic flag in their car window was not their response to the murderous assault on our country. No, their response was a commitment to protect the nation, swearing an oath to their God to do so, to their deaths. When future generations ask why America is still free and the heyday of al-Qaeda and their terrorist allies was counted in days rather than in centuries as the extremists themselves predicted, our hometown heroes—soldiers, sailors, airmen, Coast Guardsmen, and Marines—can say, "Because of me and people like me who risked all to protect millions who will never know my name." . . .

America's civilian and military protectors both here at home and overseas have for nearly nine years fought this enemy to a standstill and have never for a second "wondered why." They know, and are not afraid. Their struggle is your struggle. . . . If anyone thinks you can somehow thank them for their service, and not support the cause for which they fight—America's survival—then they are lying to themselves and rationalizing away something in their lives, but, more importantly, they are slighting our warriors and mocking their commitment to the nation. . . .

It is a fact that our country today is in a life-and-death struggle against an evil enemy, but America as a whole is certainly not at war. Not as a country. Not as a people. Today, only a tiny fraction—less than a percent—shoulders the burden of fear and sacrifice, and they shoulder it for the rest of us. Their sons and daughters who serve are men and women of character who continue to believe in this country enough to put life and limb on the line without qualification, and without thought of personal gain, and they serve so that the sons and daughters of the other 99 percent don't have to. No big deal, though, as Marines have always been "the first to fight," paying in full the bill that comes with being free—for everyone else.

The comforting news for every American is that our men and women in uniform, and every Marine, is as good today as any in our history. . . . They have the same steel in their backs and have made their own mark, etching forever places like Ramadi, Fallujah, and Baghdad, Iraq, and Helmand and Sagin, Afghanistan, that are now part of the legend and stand just as proudly alongside Belleau Wood, Iwo Jima, Inchon, Hue City, Khe Sanh, and Ashau Valley, Vietnam. None of them has ever asked what their country could do for them, but always and with their lives asked what they could do for America. . . .

We can also take comfort in the fact that these young Americans are not born killers, but are good and decent young men and women who for going on ten years have performed remarkable acts of bravery and selflessness to a cause they have decided is bigger and more important than themselves. Only a few months ago they were delivering your paper, stocking shelves in the local grocery store, worshiping in church on Sunday, or playing hockey on local ice. Like my own two sons who are Marines and have fought in Iraq, and today in Sagin, Afghanistan, they are also the same kids that drove their cars too fast for your liking, and played the God-awful music of their generation too loud, but have no doubt they are the finest of their generation. Like those who went before them in uniform, we owe them everything. We owe them our safety. We owe them our prosperity. We owe them our freedom. We owe them our lives. Any one of them could have done something more self-serving with their lives as the vast majority of their age group elected to do after high school and college, but no, they chose to serve knowing full well a brutal war was in their future. They did not avoid the basic and cherished responsibility of a citizen—the defense of country—they welcomed it. They are the very best this country produces, and have put every one of us ahead of themselves. All are heroes for simply stepping forward, and we as a people owe a debt we can never fully pay. . . .

Over five thousand have died thus far in this war—eight thousand if you include the innocents murdered on 9/11. They are overwhelmingly working-class kids, the children of cops and firefighters, city and factory workers, schoolteachers and small business owners. With some exceptions they are from families short on stock portfolios and futures, but long on love of country and service to the nation. Just yesterday, too many were lost and a knock on the door late last night brought their families to their knees in a grief that will never, ever go away. Thousands more have suffered wounds since it all started, but like anyone who loses life or limb while serving others—including our firefighters and law enforcement personnel who on 9/11 were the first casualties of this war—they are not victims, as they knew what they were about, and were doing what they wanted to do. . . . Those with less of a sense of service to the nation never understand it when men and women of character step forward to look danger and adversity straight in the eye, refusing to blink, or give ground, even to their own deaths. The protected can't begin to understand the price paid so they and their families can sleep safe and free at night. No, they are not victims, but are warriors, your warriors, and warriors are never victims, regardless of how and where they fall. Death, or fear of death, has no power over them. Their paths are paved by sacrifice, sacrifices they gladly make—for you. . . .

Two years ago . . . [on] the 22nd of April 2008, two Marine infantry battalions . . . were switching out in Ramadi. . . . Two Marines, Corporal Jonathan Yale and Lance Corporal Jordan Haerter, twenty-two and twenty years old, respectively, one from each battalion, were assuming the watch together at the entrance gate of an outpost that contained a makeshift barracks housing fifty Marines. The same broken-down ramshackle building was also home to one hundred Iraqi police, also my men and our allies in the fight against the terrorists in Ramadi, a city until recently the most dangerous city on earth and owned by al-Qaeda. Yale was a dirt-poor mixed-race kid from Virginia with a wife and daughter, and a mother and sister who lived with him and he supported as well. He did this on a yearly salary of less than $23,000. Haerter, on the other hand, was a middle-class white kid from Long Island. They were from two completely different worlds. . . . But they were Marines, combat Marines, forged in the same crucible of Marine training, and because of this bond they were brothers as close, or closer, than if they were born of the same woman.

The mission orders they received from the sergeant squad leader I am sure went something like: "Okay, you two clowns, stand this post and let no unauthorized personnel or vehicles pass. You clear?" I am also sure Yale and Haerter then rolled their eyes and said in unison something like: "Yes, Sergeant," with just enough attitude that made the point without saying the words, "No kidding, sweetheart, we know what we're doing." They then relieved two other Marines on watch and took up their post at the entry control point of Joint Security Station Nasser, in the Sophia section of Ramadi, al Anbar, Iraq.

A few minutes later a large blue truck turned down the alleyway—perhaps sixty to seventy yards in length—and sped its way through the serpentine of concrete jersey walls. The truck stopped just short of where the two were posted and detonated, killing them both catastrophically. Twenty-four brick masonry houses were damaged or destroyed. A mosque one hundred yards away collapsed. The truck's engine came to rest two hundred yards away, knocking most of a house down before it stopped. Our explosive experts reckoned the blast was made of two thousand pounds of explosives. Two died, and because these two young infantrymen didn't have it in their DNA to run from danger, they saved 150 of their Iraqi and American brothers-in-arms. . . .

I traveled to Ramadi the next day and spoke individually to a half-dozen Iraqi police [who witnessed the event], all of whom told the same story. The blue truck turned down into the alley and immediately sped up as it made its way through the serpentine. They all said, "We knew immediately what was going on as soon as the two Marines began firing." The Iraqi police then related that some of them also fired, and then, to a man, ran for safety just prior to the explosion. All survived. Many were injured, some seriously. One of the Iraqis elaborated and with tears welling up said, "They'd run like any normal man would to save his life." "What he didn't know until then," he said, "and what he learned that very instant, was that Marines are not normal." Choking past the emotion, he said, "Sir, in the name of God no sane man would have stood there and done what they did." "No sane man." "They saved us all."

What we didn't know at the time, and only learned a couple of days later after I wrote a summary and submitted both Yale and Haerter for posthumous Navy Crosses, was that one of our security cameras, damaged initially in the blast, recorded some of the suicide attack. It happened exactly as the Iraqis had described it. It took exactly six seconds from when the truck entered the alley until it detonated.

You can watch the last six seconds of their young lives. Putting myself in their heads, I supposed it took about a second for the two Marines to separately come to the same conclusion about what was going on once the truck came into their view at the far end of the alley. Exactly no time to talk it over, or call the sergeant to ask what they should do. Only enough time to take half an instant and think about what the sergeant told them to do only a few minutes before: ". . . let no unauthorized personnel or vehicles pass." The two Marines had about five seconds left to live.

It took maybe another two seconds for them to present their weapons, take aim, and open up. By this time the truck was halfway through the barriers and gaining speed the whole time. Here, the recording shows a number of Iraqi police, some of whom had fired their AKs, now scattering like the normal and rational men they were—some running right past the Marines. They had three seconds left to live.

For about two seconds more, the recording shows the Marines' weapons firing nonstop, the truck's windshield exploding into shards of glass as their rounds take it apart and tore in to the body of the son of a bitch who is trying to get past them to kill their brothers—American and Iraqi—bedded down in the barracks totally unaware of the fact that their lives at that moment depended entirely on two Marines standing their ground. If they had been aware, they would have known they were safe—because two Marines stood between them and a crazed suicide bomber. The recording shows the truck careening to a stop immediately in front of the two Marines. In all of the instantaneous violence, Yale and Haerter never hesitated. By all reports and by the recording, they never stepped back. They never even started to step aside. They never even shifted their weight. With their feet spread shoulder-width apart, they leaned into the danger, firing as fast as they could work their weapons. They had only one second left to live.

The truck explodes. The camera goes blank. Two young men go to their God. Six seconds. Not enough time to think about their families, their country, their flag, or about their lives or their deaths, but more than enough time for two very brave young men to do their duty—into eternity. That is the kind of people who are on watch all over the world tonight—for you. . . .

Second Inaugural Address

ABRAHAM LINCOLN

Public-spiritedness can often be found when, as in "The Open Boat," every-one shares a common goal (in that case, survival) and pulls his oars in the same direction, or when, like the heroic Marines General Kelly described, a group of soldiers comes under enemy attack. But public life and democratic politics are highly, sometimes fiercely contested, owing to the clash of rival interests and competing visions of the common good. Once in our nation's history the conflict escalated into bloody civil war, threatening a perma-nent dissolution of the Union. Abraham Lincoln (1809–1865), who presided over the successful prosecution of the Civil War, also gave deep thought to what would be required to heal the nation after the war. In the Gettysburg Address, Lincoln summoned Americans to rededicate themselves to the cause of freedom and equality. Here, in his Second Inaugural Address (March 4, 1865), invoking theological speculation and quoting Scripture, Lincoln offers an interpretation of the meaning of the war, which enables him to summon all Americans to a new and more difficult public purpose.

How does Lincoln invite us to understand the Civil War? In what sense does he regard both North and South as guilty of the offense of American slavery? In the Gettysburg Address, Lincoln claims that the war is a test of whether our nation, or any nation conceived in liberty and dedicated to equality, can long endure. Here, with the end of the war in sight, he suggests that the test of our nation will henceforth be its capacity for charity, "firm-ness in the right," and the pursuit of a just and lasting peace. What does Lincoln mean by charity? What do we owe the newly freed slaves? What do we owe our defeated, but perhaps unreconciled, Southern brethren? What do we owe our soldiers, their widows and their orphans? How important is the religious appeal to Lincoln's summons for a new national purpose?

What lessons might Lincoln's summons offer us in dealing with our domestic political adversaries in the partisan battles of public life today?

Fellow Countrymen:

At this second appearing to take the oath of the presidential office, there is less occasion for an extended address than there was at the first. Then a statement, somewhat in detail, of a course to be pursued, seemed fitting and proper. Now, at the expiration of four years, during which public declarations have been constantly called forth on every point and phase of the great contest which still absorbs the attention, and engrosses the energies of the nation, little that is new could be presented. The progress of our arms, upon which all else chiefly depends, is as well known to the public as to myself; and it is, I trust, reasonably satisfactory and encouraging to all. With high hope for the future, no prediction in regard to it is ventured.

On the occasion corresponding to this four years ago, all thoughts were anxiously directed to an impending civil-war. All dreaded it—all sought to avert it. While the inaugural address was being delivered from this place, devoted altogether to *saving* the Union without war, insurgent agents were in the city seeking to *destroy* it without war—seeking to dissolve the Union, and divide effects, by negotiation. Both parties deprecated war; but one of them would *make* war rather than let the nation survive; and the other would *accept* war rather than let it perish. And the war came.

One-eighth of the whole population were colored slaves, not distributed generally over the Union, but localized in the Southern part of it. These slaves constituted a peculiar and powerful interest. All knew that this interest was, somehow, the cause of the war. To strengthen, perpetuate, and extend this interest was the object for which the insurgents would rend the Union, even by war; while the government claimed no right to do more than to restrict the territorial enlargement of it. Neither party expected for the war, the magnitude, or the duration, which it has already attained. Neither anticipated that the *cause* of the conflict might cease with, or even before, the conflict itself should cease. Each looked for an easier triumph, and a result less fundamental and astounding. Both read the same Bible, and pray to the same God; and each invokes His aid against the other. It may seem strange that any men should dare to ask a just God's assistance in wringing their bread from the sweat of other men's faces; but let us judge not that we be not judged. The prayers of both could not be answered; that of neither has been answered fully. The Almighty has His own purposes. "Woe unto the world because of offences! for it must needs be that offences come; but woe to that man by whom the offence cometh!" If we shall suppose that American Slavery is one of those offences which, in the providence of God, must needs come, but which, having continued through His appointed time, He now wills to remove, and that He gives to both North and South, this terrible war, as the woe due to those by whom the offence came, shall we discern therein any departure from those divine attributes which the believers in a Living God always ascribe to Him? Fondly do we hope—fervently do we pray—that this mighty scourge of war may speedily pass away. Yet, if God wills that it continue, until all the wealth piled by the bond-man's two hundred and fifty years of unrequited toil shall be sunk, and until every drop of blood drawn with the lash, shall be paid by another drawn with the sword, as was said three thousand years ago, so still it must be said "the judgments of the Lord, are true and righteous altogether."

With malice toward none; with charity for all; with firmness in the right, as God gives us to see the right, let us strive on to finish the work we are in; to bind up the nation's wounds; to care for him who shall have borne the battle, and for his widow, and his orphan—to do all which may achieve and cherish a just, and a lasting peace, among ourselves, and with all nations.

The Deacon

JOHN UPDIKE

Lincoln's Second Inaugural explicitly deploys reverence for the Almighty to inspire humility and invite Americans to charitable attitudes and righteous public purposes. Yet the relation between our religious life and our civic life has long been a complicated question. On one hand, we insist on the separation of church and state; on the other hand, we encourage free exercise of religious worship and religious toleration. On one hand, we worry (as did Publius in Federalist No. 10*) about religious zealotry and faction; on the other hand, we appreciate (as did George Washington in all three selections in this volume) the support organized religion provides for morality, community, and good-neighborliness. In this story (1970), John Updike (1932–2009) explores the persistence of religious affiliation in an increasingly secular and materialistic world.*

Why has Miles, an electrical engineer who frequently changes employers and locations, always been a dedicated deacon in a local church? After moving to New England, Miles initially elects, for the first time in his life, not to join a church, but he soon finds himself back at his post as deacon. What draws him to church, and what keeps him there? What is his attitude toward the past and its institutional and architectural legacies? What does Miles look up to or revere? How does his religious experience relate to his sense of civic and communal obligation? Do you admire him? How, if at all, is this deacon's life a model for us to imitate?

He passes the plate, and counts the money afterward—a large dogged-looking man, wearing metal-framed glasses that seem tight across his face and that bite into the flesh around his eyes. He wears for Sunday morning a clean white shirt, but a glance downward, as you lay on your thin envelope and pass the golden plate back to him, discovers fallen socks and scuffed shoes. And as he with his fellow-deacons strides forward toward the altar, his suit is revealed as the pants of one suit (gray) and the coat of another (brown). He is too much at home here. During the sermon, he stares toward a corner of the nave ceiling, which needs repair, and slowly, reverently, yet unmistakably chews gum. He lingers in the vestibule, with his barking, possessive laugh, when the rest of the congregation has passed into the sunshine and the dry-mouthed minister is fidgeting to be out of his cassock and home to lunch. The deacon's car, a dusty Dodge, is parked outside the parish hall most evenings. He himself wonders why he is there so often, how he slipped into this ceaseless round of men's suppers, of Christian Education Committee meetings, choir rehearsals, emergency sessions of the Board of Finance where hours churn by in irrelevant argument and prayerful silences that produce nothing. "Noth-ing," he says to his wife on returning, waking her. "The old fool refuses to amortize the debt." He means the treasurer. "His Eminence tells us foreign missions can't be applied to the oil bill even if we make it up in the summer at five per cent interest." He means the minister. "It was on the tip of my tongue to ask whence he derives all his business expertise."

"Why don't you resign?" she asks. "Let the young people get involved before they drop away."

"One more peace in Vietnam sermon, they'll drop away anyway." He falls heavily into bed, smelling of chewing gum. As with men who spend nights away from home drinking in bars, he feels guilty, but the motion, the bright-ness and excitement of the place where he has been continues in him: the var-nished old tables, the yellowing Sunday-school charts, the folding chairs and pocked linoleum, the cork bulletin board, the giggles of the children's choir leaving, the strange constant sense of dark sacred space surrounding their lit meeting room like the void upholding a bright planet. "One more blessing on the damn Vietcong," he mumbles, and the young minister's face, white and worriedly sucking a pipestem, skids like a vision of the Devil across his plagued mind. He has a headache. The sides of his nose, the tops of his cheeks, the space above his ears—wherever the frames of his glasses dig—dully hurt. His wife snores, neglected. In less than seven hours, the alarm clock will ring. This must stop. He must turn over a new leaf.

His name is Miles. He is over fifty, an electrical engineer. Every seven years or so, he changes employers and locations. He has been a member of the board of deacons of a prosperous Methodist church in Iowa, a complex of dashing blond brick-and-glass buildings set in acres of parking lot carved from a corn-field; then of a Presbyterian church in San Francisco, gold-rush Gothic clinging to the back of Nob Hill, attended on Sundays by a handful of Chinese businessmen and prostitutes in sunglasses and whiskery, dazed drop-out youths looking for a warm place in which to wind up their Saturday-night trips; then of another Presbyterian church in New York State, a dour granite chapel in a suburb of Schenectady; and most recently, in southeastern Pennsylvania, of a cryptlike Reformed church sunk among clouds of foliage so dense that the lights are kept burning in midday and the cobwebbed balconies swarm all summer with wasps. Though Miles has travelled far, he has never broken out of the loose net of Calvinist denominations that places almost every American within sight of a spire. He wonders why. He was raised in Ohio, in a village that had lost the tang of the frontier but kept its bleak narrowness, and was confirmed in the same colorless, bean-eating creed that millions in his generation have dismissed forever. He was not, as he understood the term, religious. Ceremony bored him. Closing his eyes to pray made him dizzy. He distinctly heard in the devotional service the overamplified tone of voice that in business matters would signal either ignorance or dishonesty. His profession prepared him to believe that our minds, with their crackle of self-importance, are merely collections of electrical circuits. He saw nothing about his body worth resurrecting. God, concretely considered, had a way of merging with that corner of the church ceiling that showed signs of water leakage. That men should be good, he did not doubt, or that social order demands personal sacrifice; but the Heavenly hypothesis, as it had fallen upon his ears these forty years of Sundays, crushes us all to the same level of unworthiness, and redeems us all indiscriminately, elevating especially, these days, the irresponsible—the unemployable, the riotous, the outrageous, the one in one hundred that strays. Neither God nor His ministers displayed love for deacons—indeed, Pharisees were the first objects of their wrath. Why persist, then, in work so thoroughly thankless, begging for pledges, pinching and scraping to save degenerate old buildings, facing rings of Sunday-school faces baked to adamant cynicism by hours of television-watching, attending fruitless meetings where the senile and the frustrated dominate, arguing, yawning, missing sleep, the company of his wife, the small, certain joys of home. Why? He had wanted to offer his children the Christian option, to begin them as citizens as he had begun; but all have left home now, are in college or married, and, as far as he can tactfully gather, are unchurched. So be it. He has done his part.

A new job offer arrives, irresistible, inviting him to New England. In Pennsylvania the Fellowship Society gives him a farewell dinner; his squad of Sunday-school teachers presents him with a pen set; he hands in his laborious financial records, his neat minutes of vague proceedings. He bows his head for the last time in that dark sanctuary smelling of moldering plaster and buzzing with captive wasps. He is free. Their new house is smaller, their new town is white. He does not join a church; he stays home reading the Sunday paper. Wincing, he flicks past religious news. He drives his wife north to admire the turning foliage. His evenings are immense. He reads through Winston Churchill's history of the Second World War; he installs elaborate electrical gadgets around the house, which now and then give his wife a shock. They go to drive-in movies, and sit islanded in a sea of fornication. They go bowling and square dancing, and feel ridiculous, too ponderous and slow. His wife, these years of evenings alone, has developed a time-passing pattern—television shows spaced with spells of sewing and dozing—into which he fits awkwardly. She listens to him grunt and sigh and grope for words. But Sunday mornings are the worst—blighted times haunted by the giddy swish and roar of churchward traffic on the road outside. He stands by the window; the sight of three little girls, in white beribboned hats, bluebird coats, and dresses of starched organdie, scampering home from Sunday school gives him a pang unholy in its keenness.

Behind him his wife says, "Why don't you go to church?"

"No, I think I'll wash the Dodge."

"You washed it last Sunday."

"Maybe I should take up golf."

"You want to go to church. Go. It's no sin."

"Not the Methodists. Those bastards in Iowa nearly worked me to death."

"What's the pretty white one in the middle of town? Congregational. We've never been Congregationalists; they'd let you alone."

"Are you sure you wouldn't like to take a drive?"

"I get carsick with all that starting and stopping. To tell the truth, it would be a relief to have you out of the house."

Already he is pulling off his sweater, to make way for a clean shirt. He puts on a coat that doesn't match his pants.

"I'll go," he says, "but I'll be damned if I'll join."

He arrives late, and sits staring at the ceiling. It is a wooden church, and the beams and ceiling boards in drying out have pulled apart. Above every clear-glass window he sees the dried-apple-colored stains of leakage. At the door, the minister, a very young pale man with a round moon face and a know-it-all pucker to his lips, clasps Miles's hand as if never to let it go. "We've been looking for you, Miles. We received a splendid letter about you from your Reformed pastor in Pennsylvania. As you know, since the U.C.C. merger you don't even need to be reconfirmed. There's a men's supper this Thursday. We'll hope to see you there." Some minister's hands, Miles has noticed, grow fatty under the pressure of being so often shaken, and others dwindle to the bones; this one's, for all his fat face, is mostly bones.

The church as a whole is threadbare and scrawny; it makes no resistance to his helpless infiltration of the Men's Club, the Board of Finance, the Debt Liquidation and Building Maintenance Committee. He and a few shaggy Pilgrim Youth paint the Sunday-school chairs Chinese red. He and one grimy codger and three bottles of beer clean the furnace room of forgotten furniture and pageant props, of warped hymnals and unused programs still tied in the printer's bundles, of the gilded remnants of a dozen abandoned projects. Once he attends a committee meeting to which no one else comes. It is a gusty winter night, a night of cold rain from the sea, freezing on the roads. The minister has been up all night with the family of a suicide and cannot himself attend; he has dropped off the church keys with Miles.

The front door key, no bigger than a car key, seems magically small for so large a building. Is it the only one? Miles makes a mental note: have duplicates made. He turns on a light and waits for the other committee members—a retired banker and two maiden ladies. The furnace is running gamely, but with an audible limp in its stride. It is a coal burner converted to oil twenty years ago. The old cast-iron clinker grates are still heaped in a corner, too heavy to throw out. Should be sold for scrap. Every penny counts. Pinching and scraping. Miles thinks, as upon a mystery, upon the prodigality of heating a huge vacant barn like this with such an inefficient burner. Hot air rises direct from the basement to the ceiling, drying and spreading the wood. Fuel needle half gummed up. Waste. Nothing but waste, salvage and waste. And weariness.

Miles removes his glasses and rubs the chafed spots at the bridge of his nose. He replaces them to look at his watch. His watch has stopped, its small face wet from the storm like an excited child's. The electric clock in the minister's study has been unplugged. Bogus thrift. There are books: concordances, daily helps, through the year verse by verse, great sermons, best sermons, sermon hints, all second-hand, no, third-hand, worse, hundredth-hand, thousandth-hand, a coin rubbed blank. The books are leaning on their sides and half the shelves are empty. Empty. The desk is clean. No business conducted on it. He tests the minister's fountain pen and it is dry. Dry as an old snakeskin, dry as a locust husk that still clings to a tree.

In search of the time, Miles goes into the sanctuary. The 1880 pendulum clock on the choir balustrade still ticks. He can hear it in the dark, overhead. He switches on the nave lights. A moment passes before they come on. Some shaky connection in the toggle, the wiring doubtless rotten throughout the walls, a wonder it hasn't burnt down. Miles has never belonged to a wooden church before. Around and above him, like a stiff white forest, the hewn frame creaks and groans in conversation with the wind. The high black windows, lashed as if by handfuls of sand, seem to flinch, yet do not break, and Miles feels the timbers of this ark, with its ballast of tattered pews, give and sway with the fierce weather, yet hold; and this is why he has come, to share the pride of this ancient thing that will not quite die, to have it all to himself. Warm air from a grilled duct breathes on his ankles. Miles can see upward past the clock and the organ to the corner of the unused gallery where souvenirs of the church's past—Puritan pew doors, tin footwarmers, velvet collection bags, Victorian commemorative albums, cracking portraits of wigged pastors, oval photographs of deceased deacons, and inexplicable unlabelled ferrotypes of chubby cross children and picnics past—repose in dusty glass cases that are in themselves antiques. All this anonymous treasure Miles possesses by being here, like a Pharaoh hidden with his life's rich furniture, while the rain like a robber rattles to get in.

Yes, the deacon sees, it is indeed a preparation for death—an emptiness where many others have been, which is what death will be. It is good to be at home here. Nothing now exists but himself, this shell, and the storm. The windows clatter; the sand has turned to gravel, the rain has turned to sleet. The storm seizes the church by its steeple and shakes, but the walls were built with love, and withstand. The others are very late, they will not be coming; he is not displeased, he is serene. He turns out the lights. He locks the door.

The Artificial Nigger

Flannery O'Connor

The virtue of public-spiritedness and the willingness to care about the well-being of the community depend largely on our ability to recognize the equal humanity and dignity of our fellow citizens. In America, the greatest obstacle to such an attitude has historically been—and to a lesser extent remains so today—group prejudice and enmity: racial, ethnic, and religious. The causes and possible remedies for deep-seated prejudice were a preoccupation of Flannery O'Connor (1925–1964), who wrote profoundly about what she called "the tragedy of the South." She regarded the present story (1955) as "one of the best I've written, and this because there is a good deal more in it than I understand myself." Despite her editor's pleadings to change the title, she stuck with it; as she said, "There is nothing that screams out the tragedy of the South like what my uncle calls 'nigger statuary.'"

In the story, Mr. Head, who lives in a backwoods shack in rural Georgia, takes his grandson Nelson to Atlanta in order to show the superiority of his own ideas and ways. Can we understand what moves Mr. Head? What, according to the story, is the origin of racial prejudice? What happens to Mr. Head and Nelson in their encounter with the broken statue, the "artificial nigger"? What do they learn, and what in their prior experience made it possible for them to do so? To what extent does mutual respect require mutual suffering? Can you explain what happens to them, or might the experience be best understood as an "action of mercy"? What feelings and insights does this story inspire in you, especially regarding your own pride and prejudices? Are the virtues and attitudes needed for civic life in our own power to provide?

Mr. Head awakened to discover that the room was full of moonlight. He sat up and stared at the floor boards—the color of silver—and then at the ticking on his pillow, which might have been brocade, and after a second, he saw half of the moon five feet away in his shaving mirror, paused as if it were waiting for his permission to enter. It rolled forward and cast a dignifying light on everything. The straight chair against the wall looked stiff and attentive as if it were awaiting an order and Mr. Head's trousers, hanging to the back of it, had an almost noble air, like the garment some great man had just flung to his servant; but the face on the moon was a grave one. It gazed across the room and out the window where it floated over the horse stall and appeared to contemplate itself with the look of a young man who sees his old age before him.

Mr. Head could have said to it that age was a choice blessing and that only with years does a man enter into that calm understanding of life that makes him a suitable guide for the young. This, at least, had been his own experience.

He sat up and grasped the iron posts at the foot of his bed and raised himself until he could see the face on the alarm clock which sat on an overturned bucket beside the chair. The hour was two in the morning. The alarm on the clock did not work but he was not dependent on any mechanical means to awaken him. Sixty years had not dulled his responses; his physical reactions, like his moral ones, were guided by his will and strong character, and these could be seen plainly in his features. He had a long tube-like face with a long rounded open jaw and a long depressed nose. His eyes were alert but quiet, and in the miraculous moonlight they had a look of composure and of ancient wisdom as if they belonged to one of the great guides of men. He might have been Vergil summoned in the middle of the night to go to Dante, or better, Raphael, awakened by a blast of God's light to fly to the side of Tobias. The only dark spot in the room was Nelson's pallet, underneath the shadow of the window.

Nelson was hunched over on his side, his knees under his chin and his heels under his bottom. His new suit and hat were in the boxes that they had been sent in and these were on the floor at the foot of the pallet where he could get his hands on them as soon as he woke up. The slop jar, out of the shadow and made snow-white in the moonlight, appeared to stand guard over him like a small personal angel. Mr. Head lay back down, feeling entirely confident that he could carry out the moral mission of the coming day. He meant to be up before Nelson and to have the breakfast cooking by the time he awakened. The boy was always irked when Mr. Head was the first up. They would have to leave the house at four to get to the railroad junction by five-thirty. The train was to stop for them at five forty-five and they had to be there on time for this train was stopping merely to accommodate them.

This would be the boy's first trip to the city though he claimed it would be his second because he had been born there. Mr. Head had tried to point out to him that when he was born he didn't have the intelligence to determine his whereabouts but this had made no impression on the child at all and he continued to insist that this was to be his second trip. It would be Mr. Head's third trip. Nelson had said, "I will've already been there twict and I ain't but ten."

Mr. Head had contradicted him.

"If you ain't been there in fifteen years, how you know you'll be able to find your way about?" Nelson had asked. "How you know it hasn't changed some?"

"Have you ever," Mr. Head had asked, "seen me lost?"

Nelson certainly had not but he was a child who was never satisfied until he had given an impudent answer and he replied, "It's nowhere around here to get lost at."

"The day is going to come," Mr. Head prophesied, "when you'll find you ain't as smart as you think you are." He had been thinking about this trip for several months but it was for the most part in moral terms that he conceived it. It was to be a lesson that the boy would never forget. He was to find out from it that he had no cause for pride merely because he had been born in a city. He was to find out that the city is not a great place. Mr. Head meant him to see everything there is to see in a city so that he would be content to stay at home for the rest of his life. He fell asleep thinking how the boy would at last find out that he was not as smart as he thought he was.

He was awakened at three-thirty by the smell of fatback frying and he leaped off his cot. The pallet was empty and the clothes boxes had been thrown open. He put on his trousers and ran into the other room. The boy had a corn pone on cooking and had fried the meat. He was sitting in the half-dark at the table, drinking cold coffee out of a can. He had on his new suit and his new gray hat pulled low over his eyes. It was too big for him but they had ordered it a size large because they expected his head to grow. He didn't say anything but his entire figure suggested satisfaction at having arisen before Mr. Head.

Mr. Head went to the stove and brought the meat to the table in the skillet. "It's no hurry," he said. "You'll get there soon enough and it's no guarantee you'll like it when you do neither," and he sat down across from the boy whose hat teetered back slowly to reveal a fiercely expressionless face, very much the same shape as the old man's. They were grandfather and grandson but they looked enough alike to be brothers and brothers not too far apart in age, for Mr. Head had a youthful expression by daylight, while the boy's look was ancient, as if he knew everything already and would be pleased to forget it.

Mr. Head had once had a wife and daughter and when the wife died, the daughter ran away and returned after an interval with Nelson. Then one morning, without getting out of bed, she died and left Mr. Head with sole care of the year-old child. He had made the mistake of telling Nelson that he had been born in Atlanta. If he hadn't told him that, Nelson couldn't have insisted that this was going to be his second trip.

"You may not like it a bit," Mr. Head continued. "It'll be full of niggers."

The boy made a face as if he could handle a nigger.

"All right," Mr. Head said. "You ain't ever seen a nigger."

"You wasn't up very early," Nelson said.

"You ain't ever seen a nigger," Mr. Head repeated. "There hasn't been a nigger in this county since we run that one out twelve years ago and that was before you were born." He looked at the boy as if he were daring him to say he had ever seen a Negro.

"How you know I never saw a nigger when I lived there before?" Nelson asked. "I probably saw a lot of niggers."

"If you seen one you didn't know what he was," Mr. Head said, completely exasperated. "A six-month-old child don't know a nigger from anybody else."

"I reckon I'll know a nigger if I see one," the boy said and got up and straightened his slick sharply creased gray hat and went outside to the privy.

They reached the junction some time before the train was due to arrive and stood about two feet from the first set of tracks. Mr. Head carried a paper sack with some biscuits and a can of sardines in it for their lunch. A coarse-looking orange-colored sun coming up behind the east range of mountains was making the sky a dull red behind them, but in front of them it was still gray and they faced a gray transparent moon, hardly stronger than a thumbprint and completely without light. A small tin switch box and a black fuel tank were all there was to mark the place as a junction; the tracks were double and did not converge again until they were hidden behind the bends at either end of the clearing. Trains passing appeared to emerge from a tunnel of trees and, hit for a second by the cold sky, vanish terrified into the woods again. Mr. Head had had to make special arrangements with the ticket agent to have this train stop and he was secretly afraid it would not, in which case, he knew Nelson would say, "I never thought no train was going to stop for you." Under the useless morning moon the tracks looked white and fragile. Both the old man and the child stared ahead as if they were awaiting an apparition.

Then suddenly, before Mr. Head could make up his mind to turn back, there was a deep warning bleat and the train appeared, gliding very slowly, almost silently around the bend of trees about two hundred yards down the track, with one yellow front light shining. Mr. Head was still not certain it would stop and he felt it would make an even bigger idiot of him if it went by slowly. Both he and Nelson, however, were prepared to ignore the train if it passed them.

The engine charged by, filling their noses with the smell of hot metal and then the second coach came to a stop exactly where they were standing. A conductor with the face of an ancient bloated bulldog was on the step as if he expected them, though he did not look as if it mattered one way or the other to him if they got on or not. "To the right," he said.

Their entry took only a fraction of a second and the train was already speeding on as they entered the quiet car. Most of the travelers were still sleeping, some with their heads hanging off the chair arms, some stretched across two seats, and some sprawled out with their feet in the aisle. Mr. Head saw two unoccupied seats and pushed Nelson toward them. "Get in there by the winder," he said in his normal voice which was very loud at this hour of the morning. "Nobody cares if you sit there because it's nobody in it. Sit right there."

"I heard you," the boy muttered. "It's no use in you yelling," and he sat down and turned his head to the glass. There he saw a pale ghost-like face scowling at him beneath the brim of a pale ghost-like hat. His grandfather, looking quickly too, saw a different ghost, pale but grinning, under a black hat.

Mr. Head sat down and settled himself and took out his ticket and started reading aloud everything that was printed on it. People began to stir. Several woke up and stared at him. "Take off your hat," he said to Nelson and took off his own and put it on his knee. He had a small amount of white hair that had turned tobacco-colored over the years and this lay flat across the back of his head. The front of his head was bald and creased. Nelson took off his hat and put it on his knee and they waited for the conductor to come ask for their tickets.

The man across the aisle from them was spread out over two seats, his feet propped on the window and his head jutting into the aisle. He had on a light blue suit and a yellow shirt unbuttoned at the neck. His eyes had just opened and Mr. Head was ready to introduce himself when the conductor came up from behind and growled, "Tickets."

When the conductor had gone, Mr. Head gave Nelson the return half of his ticket and said, "Now put that in your pocket and don't lose it or you'll have to stay in the city."

"Maybe I will," Nelson said as if this were a reasonable suggestion.

Mr. Head ignored him. "First time this boy has ever been on a train," he explained to the man across the aisle, who was sitting up now on the edge of his seat with both feet on the floor.

Nelson jerked his hat on again and turned angrily to the window.

"He's never seen anything before," Mr. Head continued. "Ignorant as the day he was born, but I mean for him to get his fill once and for all."

The boy leaned forward, across his grandfather and toward the stranger. "I was born in the city," he said. "I was born there. This is my second trip." He said it in a high positive voice but the man across the aisle didn't look as if he understood. There were heavy purple circles under his eyes.

Mr. Head reached across the aisle and tapped him on the arm. "The thing to do with a boy," he said sagely, "is to show him all it is to show. Don't hold nothing back."

"Yeah," the man said. He gazed down at his swollen feet and lifted the left one about ten inches from the floor. After a minute he put it down and lifted the other. All through the car people began to get up and move about and yawn and stretch. Separate voices could be heard here and there and then a general hum. Suddenly Mr. Head's serene expression changed. His mouth almost closed and a light, fierce and cautious both, came into his eyes. He was looking down the length of the car. Without turning, he caught Nelson by the arm and pulled him forward. "Look," he said.

A huge coffee-colored man was coming slowly forward. He had on a light suit and a yellow satin tie with a ruby pin in it. One of his hands rested on his stomach which rode majestically under his buttoned coat, and in the other he held the head of a black walking stick that he picked up and set down with a deliberate outward motion each time he took a step. He was proceeding very slowly, his large brown eyes gazing over the heads of the passengers. He had a small white mustache and white crinkly hair. Behind him there were two young women, both coffee-colored, one in a yellow dress and one in a green. Their progress was kept at the rate of his and they chatted in low throaty voices as they followed him.

Mr. Head's grip was tightening insistently on Nelson's arm. As the procession passed them, the light from a sapphire ring on the brown hand that picked up the cane reflected in Mr. Head's eye, but he did not look up nor did the tremendous man look at him. The group proceeded up the rest of the aisle and out of the car. Mr. Head's grip on Nelson's arm loosened. "What was that?" he asked.

"A man," the boy said and gave him an indignant look as if he were tired of having his intelligence insulted.

"What kind of a man?" Mr. Head persisted, his voice expressionless.

"A fat man," Nelson said. He was beginning to feel that he had better be cautious.

"You don't know what kind?" Mr. Head said in a final tone.

"An old man," the boy said and had a sudden foreboding that he was not going to enjoy the day.

"That was a nigger," Mr. Head said and sat back.

Nelson jumped up on the seat and stood looking backward to the end of the car but the Negro had gone.

"I'd of thought you'd know a nigger since you seen so many when you was in the city on your first visit," Mr. Head continued. "That's his first nigger," he said to the man across the aisle.

The boy slid down into the seat. "You said they were black," he said in an angry voice. "You never said they were tan. How do you expect me to know anything when you don't tell me right?"

"You're just ignorant is all," Mr. Head said and he got up and moved over in the vacant seat by the man across the aisle.

Nelson turned backward again and looked where the Negro had disappeared. He felt that the Negro had deliberately walked down the aisle in order to make a fool of him and he hated him with a fierce raw fresh hate; and also, he understood now why his grandfather disliked them. He looked toward the window and the face there seemed to suggest that he might be inadequate to the day's exactions. He wondered if he would even recognize the city when they came to it.

After he had told several stories, Mr. Head realized that the man he was talking to was asleep and he got up and suggested to Nelson that they walk over the train and see the parts of it. He particularly wanted the boy to see the toilet so they went first to the men's room and examined the plumbing. Mr. Head demonstrated the ice-water cooler as if he had invented it and showed Nelson the bowl with the single spigot where the travelers brushed their teeth. They went through several cars and came to the diner.

This was the most elegant car in the train. It was painted a rich egg-yellow and had a wine-colored carpet on the floor. There were wide windows over the tables and great spaces of the rolling view were caught in miniature in the sides of the coffee pots and in the glasses. Three very black Negroes in white suits and aprons were running up and down the aisle, swinging trays and bowing and bending over the travelers eating breakfast. One of them rushed up to Mr. Head and Nelson and said, holding up two fingers, "Space for two!" but Mr. Head replied in a loud voice, "We eaten before we left!"

The waiter wore large brown spectacles that increased the size of his eye whites. "Stan' aside then please," he said with an airy wave of the arm as if he were brushing aside flies.

Neither Nelson nor Mr. Head moved a fraction of an inch. "Look," Mr. Head said.

The near corner of the diner, containing two tables, was set off from the rest by a saffron-colored curtain. One table was set but empty but at the other, facing them, his back to the drape, sat the tremendous Negro. He was speaking in a soft voice to the two women while he buttered a muffin. He had a heavy sad face and his neck bulged over his white collar on either side. "They rope them off," Mr. Head explained. Then he said, "Let's go see the kitchen," and they walked the length of the diner but the black waiter was coming fast behind them.

"Passengers are not allowed in the kitchen!" he said in a haughty voice. "Passengers are NOT allowed in the kitchen!"

Mr. Head stopped where he was and turned. "And there's good reason for that," he shouted into the Negro's chest, "because the cockroaches would run the passengers out!"

All the travelers laughed and Mr. Head and Nelson walked out, grinning. Mr. Head was known at home for his quick wit and Nelson felt a sudden keen pride in him. He realized the old man would be his only support in the strange place they were approaching. He would be entirely alone in the world if he were ever lost from his grandfather. A terrible excitement shook him and he wanted to take hold of Mr. Head's coat and hold on like a child.

As they went back to their seats they could see through the passing windows that the countryside was becoming speckled with small houses and shacks and that a highway ran alongside the train. Cars sped by on it, very small and fast. Nelson felt that there was less breath in the air than there had been thirty minutes ago. The man across the aisle had left and there was no one near for Mr. Head to hold a conversation with so he looked out the window, through his own reflection, and read aloud the names of the buildings they were passing. "The Dixie Chemical Corp!" he announced. "Southern Maid Flour! Dixie Doors! Southern Belle Cotton Products! Patty's Peanut Butter! Southern Mammy Cane Syrup!"

"Hush up!" Nelson hissed.

All over the car people were beginning to get up and take their luggage off the overhead racks. Women were putting on their coats and hats. The conductor stuck his head in the car and snarled, "Firstoppppmry," and Nelson lunged out of his sitting position, trembling. Mr. Head pushed him down by the shoulder.

"Keep your seat," he said in dignified tones. "The first stop is on the edge of town. The second stop is at the main railroad station." He had come by this knowledge on his first trip when he had got off at the first stop and had had to pay a man fifteen cents to take him into the heart of town. Nelson sat back down, very pale. For the first time in his life, he understood that his grandfather was indispensable to him.

The train stopped and let off a few passengers and glided on as if it had never ceased moving. Outside, behind rows of brown rickety houses, a line of blue buildings stood up, and beyond them a pale rose-gray sky faded away to nothing. The train moved into the railroad yard. Looking down, Nelson saw lines and lines of silver tracks multiplying and criss-crossing. Then before he could start counting them, the face in the window stared out at him, gray but distinct, and he looked the other way. The train was in the station. Both he and Mr. Head jumped up and ran to the door. Neither noticed that they had left the paper sack with the lunch in it on the seat.

They walked stiffly through the small station and came out of a heavy door into the squall of traffic. Crowds were hurrying to work. Nelson didn't know where to look. Mr. Head leaned against the side of the building and glared in front of him.

Finally Nelson said, "Well, how do you see what all it is to see?"

Mr. Head didn't answer. Then as if the sight of people passing had given him the clue, he said, "You walk," and started off down the street. Nelson followed, steadying his hat. So many sights and sounds were flooding in on him that for the first block he hardly knew what he was seeing. At the second corner, Mr. Head turned and looked behind him at the station they had left, a putty-colored terminal with a concrete dome on top. He thought that if he could keep the dome always in sight, he would be able to get back in the afternoon to catch the train again.

As they walked along, Nelson began to distinguish details and take note of the store windows, jammed with every kind of equipment—hardware, dry-goods, chicken feed, liquor. They passed one that Mr. Head called his particular attention to where you walked in and sat on a chair with your feet upon two rests and let a Negro polish your shoes. They walked slowly and stopped and stood at the entrances so he could see what went on in each place but they did not go into any of them. Mr. Head was determined not to go into any city store because on his first trip here, he had got lost in a large one and had found his way out only after many people had insulted him.

They came in the middle of the next block to a store that had a weighing machine in front of it and they both in turn stepped up on it and put in a penny and received a ticket. Mr. Head's ticket said, "You weigh 120 pounds. You are upright and brave and all your friends admire you." He put the ticket in his pocket, surprised that the machine should have got his character correct but his weight wrong, for he had weighed on a gram scale not long before and knew he weighed 110. Nelson's ticket said, "You weigh 98 pounds. You have a great destiny ahead of you but beware of dark women." Nelson did not know any women and he weighed only 68 pounds but Mr. Head pointed out that the machine had probably printed the number upside down, meaning the 9 for a 6.

They walked on and at the end of five blocks the dome of the terminal sank out of sight and Mr. Head turned to the left. Nelson could have stood in front of every store window for an hour if there had not been another more interesting one next to it. Suddenly he said, "I was born here!" Mr. Head turned and looked at him with horror. There was a sweaty brightness about his face. "This is where I come from!" he said.

Mr. Head was appalled. He saw the moment had come for drastic action. "Lemme show you one thing you ain't seen yet," he said and took him to the corner where there was a sewer entrance. "Squat down," he said, "and stick your head in there, and he held the back of the boy's coat while he got down and put his head in the sewer. He drew it back quickly, hearing a gurgling in the depths under the sidewalk. Then Mr. Head explained the sewer system, how the entire city was underlined with it, how it contained all the drainage and was full of rats and how a man could slide into it and be sucked along down endless pitchblack tunnels. At any minute any man in the city might be sucked into the sewer and never heard from again. He described it so well that Nelson was for some seconds shaken. He connected the sewer passages with the entrance to hell and understood for the first time how the world was put together in its lower parts. He drew away from the curb.

Then he said, "Yes, but you can stay away from the holes," and his face took on that stubborn look that was so exasperating to his grandfather. "This is where I come from!" he said.

Mr. Head was dismayed but he only muttered, "You'll get your fill," and they walked on. At the end of two more blocks he turned to the left, feeling that he was circling the dome; and he was correct for in a half-hour they passed in front of the railroad station again. At first Nelson did not notice that he was seeing the same stores twice but when they passed the one where you put your feet on the rests while the Negro polished your shoes, he perceived that they were walking in a circle.

"We done been here!" he shouted. "I don't believe you know where you're at!"

"The direction just slipped my mind for a minute," Mr. Head said and they turned down a different street. He still did not intend to let the dome get too far away and after two blocks in their new direction, he turned to the left. This street contained two- and three-story wooden dwellings. Anyone passing on the sidewalk could see into the rooms and Mr. Head, glancing through one window, saw a woman lying on an iron bed, looking out, with a sheet pulled over her. Her knowing expression shook him. A fierce-looking boy on a bicycle came driving down out of nowhere and he had to jump to the side to keep from being hit. "It's nothing to them if they knock you down," he said. "You better keep closer to me."

They walked on for some time on streets like this before he remembered to turn again. The houses they were passing now were all unpainted and the wood in them looked rotten; the street between was narrower. Nelson saw a colored man. Then another. Then another. "Niggers live in these houses," he observed.

"Well come on and we'll go somewheres else," Mr. Head said. "We didn't come to look at niggers," and they turned down another street but they continued to see Negroes everywhere. Nelson's skin began to prickle and they stepped along at a faster pace in order to leave the neighborhood as soon as possible. There were colored men in their undershirts standing in the doors and colored women rocking on the sagging porches. Colored children played in the gutters and stopped what they were doing to look at them. Before long they began to pass rows of stores with colored customers in them but they didn't pause at the entrances of these. Black eyes in black faces were watching them from every direction. "Yes," Mr. Head said, "this is where you were born—right here with all these niggers."

Nelson scowled. "I think you done got us lost," he said.

Mr. Head swung around sharply and looked for the dome. It was nowhere in sight. "I ain't got us lost either," he said. "You're just tired of walking."

"I ain't tired, I'm hungry," Nelson said. "Give me a biscuit."

They discovered then that they had lost the lunch.

"You were the one holding the sack," Nelson said. "I would have kepaholt of it."

"If you want to direct this trip, I'll go on by myself and leave you right here," Mr. Head said and was pleased to see the boy turn white. However, he realized they were lost and drifting farther every minute from the station. He was hungry himself and beginning to be thirsty and since they had been in the colored neighborhood, they had both begun to sweat. Nelson had on his shoes and he was unaccustomed to them. The concrete sidewalks were very hard. They both wanted to find a place to sit down but this was impossible and they kept on walking, the boy muttering under his breath, "First you lost the sack and then you lost the way," and Mr. Head growling from time to time, "Anybody wants to be from this nigger heaven can be from it!"

By now the sun was well forward in the sky. The odor of dinners cooking drifted out to them. The Negroes were all at their doors to see them pass. "Whyn't you ast one of these niggers the way?" Nelson said. "You got us lost."

"This is where you were born," Mr. Head said. "You can ast one yourself if you want to."

Nelson was afraid of the colored men and he didn't want to be laughed at by the colored children. Up ahead he saw a large colored woman leaning in a doorway that opened onto the sidewalk. Her hair stood straight out from her head for about four inches all around and she was resting on bare brown feet that turned pink at the sides. She had on a pink dress that showed her exact shape. As they came abreast of her, she lazily lifted one hand to her head and her fingers disappeared into her hair.

Nelson stopped. He felt his breath drawn up by the woman's dark eyes. "How do you get back to town?" he said in a voice that did not sound like his own.

After a minute she said, "You in town now," in a rich low tone that made Nelson feel as if a cool spray had been turned on him.

"How do you get back to the train?" he said in the same reed-like voice.

"You can catch you a car," she said.

He understood she was making fun of him but he was too paralyzed even to scowl. He stood drinking in every detail of her. His eyes traveled up from her great knees to her forehead and then made a triangular path from the glistening sweat on her neck down and across her tremendous bosom and over her bare arm back to where her fingers lay hidden in her hair. He suddenly wanted her to reach down and pick him up and draw him against her and then he wanted to feel her breath on his face. He wanted to look down and down into her eyes while she held him tighter and tighter. He had never had such a feeling before. He felt as if he were reeling down through a pitchblack tunnel.

"You can go a block down yonder and catch you a car take you to the railroad station, Sugarpie," she said.

Nelson would have collapsed at her feet if Mr. Head had not pulled him roughly away. "You act like you don't have any sense!" the old man growled.

They hurried down the street and Nelson did not look back at the woman. He pushed his hat sharply forward over his face which was already burning with shame. The sneering ghost he had seen in the train window and all the foreboding feelings he had on the way returned to him and he remembered that his ticket from the scale had said to beware of dark women and that his grandfather's had said he was upright and brave. He took hold of the old man's hand, a sign of dependence that he seldom showed.

They headed down the street toward the car tracks where a long yellow rattling trolley was coming. Mr. Head had never boarded a streetcar and he let that one pass. Nelson was silent. From time to time his mouth trembled slightly but his grandfather, occupied with his own problems, paid him no attention. They stood on the corner and neither looked at the Negroes who were passing, going about their business just as if they had been white, except that most of them stopped and eyed Mr. Head and Nelson. It occurred to Mr. Head that since the streetcar ran on tracks, they could simply follow the tracks. He gave Nelson a slight push and explained that they would follow the tracks on into the railroad station, walking, and they set off.

Presently to their great relief they began to see white people again and Nelson sat down on the sidewalk against the wall of a building. "I got to rest myself some," he said. "You lost the sack and the direction. You can just wait on me to rest myself."

"There's the tracks in front of us," Mr. Head said. "All we got to do is keep them in sight and you could have remembered the sack as good as me. This is where you were born. This is your old home town. This is your second trip. You ought to know how to do," and he squatted down and continued in this vein but the boy, easing his burning feet out of his shoes, did not answer.

"And standing there grinning like a chim-pan-zee while a nigger woman gives you directions. Great Gawd!" Mr. Head said.

"I never said I was nothing but born here," the boy said in a shaky voice. "I never said I would or wouldn't like it. I never said I wanted to come. I only said I was born here and I never had nothing to do with that. I want to go home. I never wanted to come in the first place. It was all your big idea. How you know you ain't following the tracks in the wrong direction?"

This last had occurred to Mr. Head too. "All these people are white," he said.

"We ain't passed here before," Nelson said. This was a neighborhood of brick buildings that might have been lived in or might not. A few empty automobiles were parked along the curb and there was an occasional passerby. The heat of the pavement came up through Nelson's thin suit. His eyelids began to droop, and after a few minutes his head tilted forward. His shoulders twitched once or twice and then he fell over on his side and lay sprawled in an exhausted fit of sleep.

Mr. Head watched him silently. He was very tired himself but they could not both sleep at the same time and he could not have slept anyway because he did not know where he was. In a few minutes Nelson would wake up, refreshed by his sleep and very cocky, and would begin complaining that he had lost the sack and the way. You'd have a mighty sorry time if I wasn't here, Mr. Head thought; and then another idea occurred to him. He looked at the sprawled figure for several minutes; presently he stood up. He justified what he was going to do on the grounds that it is sometimes necessary to teach a child a lesson he won't forget, particularly when the child is always reasserting his position with some new impudence. He walked without a sound to the corner about twenty feet away and sat down on a covered garbage can in the alley where he could look out and watch Nelson wake up alone.

The boy was dozing fitfully, half conscious of vague noises and black forms moving up from some dark part of him into the light. His face worked in his sleep and he had pulled his knees up under his chin. The sun shed a dull dry light on the narrow street; everything looked like exactly what it was. After a while Mr. Head, hunched like an old monkey on the garbage can lid, decided that if Nelson didn't wake up soon, he would make a loud noise by bamming his foot against the can. He looked at his watch and discovered that it was two o'clock. Their train left at six and the possibility of missing it was too awful for him to think of. He kicked his foot backwards on the can and a hollow boom reverberated in the alley.

Nelson shot up onto his feet with a shout. He looked where his grandfather should have been and stared. He seemed to whirl several times and then, picking up his feet and throwing his head back, he dashed down the street like a wild maddened pony. Mr. Head jumped off the can and galloped after but the child was almost out of sight. He saw a streak of gray disappearing diagonally a block ahead. He ran as fast as he could, looking both ways down every intersection, but without sight of him again. Then as he passed the third intersection, completely winded, he saw about half a block down the street a scene that stopped him altogether. He crouched behind a trash box to watch and get his bearings.

Nelson was sitting with both legs spread out and by his side lay an elderly woman, screaming. Groceries were scattered about the sidewalk. A crowd of women had already gathered to see justice done and Mr. Head distinctly heard the old woman on the pavement shout, "You've broken my ankle and your daddy'll pay for it! Every nickel! Police! Police!" Several of the women were plucking at Nelson's shoulder but the boy seemed too dazed to get up.

Something forced Mr. Head from behind the trash box and forward, but only at a creeping pace. He had never in his life been accosted by a policeman. The women were milling around Nelson as if they might suddenly all dive on him at once and tear him to pieces, and the old woman continued to scream that her ankle was broken and to call for an officer. Mr. Head came on so slowly that he could have been taking a backward step after each forward one, but when he was about ten feet away, Nelson saw him and sprang. The child caught him around the hips and clung panting against him.

The women all turned on Mr. Head. The injured one sat up and shouted, "You sir! You'll pay every penny of my doctor's bill that your boy has caused. He's a juve-nile delinquent! Where is an officer? Somebody take this man's name and address!"

Mr. Head was trying to detach Nelson's fingers from the flesh in the back of his legs. The old man's head had lowered itself into his collar like a turtle's; his eyes were glazed with fear and caution.

"Your boy has broken my ankle!" the old woman shouted. "Police!"

Mr. Head sensed the approach of the policeman from behind. He stared straight ahead at the women who were massed in their fury like a solid wall to block his escape. "This is not my boy," he said. "I never seen him before."

He felt Nelson's fingers fall out of his flesh.

The women dropped back, staring at him with horror, as if they were so repulsed by a man who would deny his own image and likeness that they could not bear to lay hands on him. Mr. Head walked on, through a space they silently cleared, and left Nelson behind. Ahead of him he saw nothing but a hollow tunnel that had once been the street.

The boy remained standing where he was, his neck craned forward and his hands hanging by his sides. His hat was jammed on his head so that there were no longer any creases in it. The injured woman got up and shook her fist at him and the others gave him pitying looks, but he didn't notice any of them. There was no policeman in sight.

In a minute he began to move mechanically, making no effort to catch up with his grandfather but merely following at about twenty paces. They walked on for five blocks in this way. Mr. Head's shoulders were sagging and his neck hung forward at such an angle that it was not visible from behind. He was afraid to turn his head. Finally he cut a short hopeful glance over his shoulder. Twenty feet behind him, he saw two small eyes piercing into his back like pitchfork prongs.

The boy was not of a forgiving nature but this was the first time he had ever had anything to forgive. Mr. Head had never disgraced himself before. After two more blocks, he turned and called over his shoulder in a high desperately gay voice, "Let's us go get us a Co' Cola somewheres!"

Nelson, with a dignity he had never shown before, turned and stood with his back to his grandfather.

Mr. Head began to feel the depth of his denial. His face as they walked on became all hollows and bare ridges. He saw nothing they were passing but he perceived that they had lost the car tracks. There was no dome to be seen anywhere and the afternoon was advancing. He knew that if dark overtook them in the city, they would be beaten and robbed. The speed of God's justice was only what he expected for himself, but he could not stand to think that his sins would be visited upon Nelson and that even now, he was leading the boy to his doom.

They continued to walk on block after block through an endless section of small brick houses until Mr. Head almost fell over a water spigot sticking up about six inches off the edge of a grass plot. He had not had a drink of water since early morning but he felt he did not deserve it now. Then he thought that Nelson would be thirsty and they would both drink and be brought together. He squatted down and put his mouth to the nozzle and turned a cold stream of water into his throat. Then he called out in the high desperate voice, "Come on and getcher some water!"

This time the child stared through him for nearly sixty seconds. Mr. Head got up and walked on as if he had drunk poison. Nelson, though he had not had water since some he had drunk out of a paper cup on the train, passed by the spigot, disdaining to drink where his grandfather had. When Mr. Head realized this, he lost all hope. His face in the waning afternoon light looked ravaged and abandoned. He could feel the boy's steady hate, traveling at an even pace behind him and he knew that (if by some miracle they escaped being murdered in the city) it would continue just that way for the rest of his life. He knew that now he was wandering into a black strange place where nothing was like it had ever been before, a long old age without respect and an end that would be welcome because it would be the end.

As for Nelson, his mind had frozen around his grandfather's treachery as if he were trying to preserve it intact to present at the final judgment. He walked without looking to one side or the other, but every now and then his mouth would twitch and this was when he felt, from some remote place inside himself, a black mysterious form reach up as if it would melt his frozen vision in one hot grasp.

The sun dropped down behind a row of houses and hardly noticing, they passed into an elegant suburban section where mansions were set back from the road by lawns with birdbaths on them. Here everything was entirely deserted. For blocks they didn't pass even a dog. The big white houses were like partially submerged icebergs in the distance. There were no sidewalks, only drives, and these wound around and around in endless ridiculous circles. Nelson made no move to come nearer to Mr. Head. The old man felt that if he saw a sewer entrance he would drop down into it and let himself be carried away; and he could imagine the boy standing by, watching with only a slight interest, while he disappeared.

A loud bark jarred him to attention and he looked up to see a fat man approaching with two bulldogs. He waved both arms like someone shipwrecked on a desert island. "I'm lost!" he called. "I'm lost and can't find my way and me and this boy have got to catch this train and I can't find the station. Oh Gawd I'm lost! Oh hep me Gawd I'm lost!"

The man, who was bald-headed and had on golf knickers, asked him what train he was trying to catch and Mr. Head began to get out his tickets, trembling so violently he could hardly hold them. Nelson had come up to within fifteen feet and stood watching.

"Well," the fat man said, giving him back the tickets, "you won't have time to get back to town to make this but you can catch it at the suburb stop. That's three blocks from here," and he began explaining how to get there.

Mr. Head stared as if he were slowly returning from the dead and when the man had finished and gone off with the dogs jumping at his heels, he turned to Nelson and said breathlessly, "We're going to get home!"

The child was standing about ten feet away, his face bloodless under the gray hat. His eyes were triumphantly cold. There was no light in them, no feeling, no interest. He was merely there, a small figure, waiting. Home was nothing to him.

Mr. Head turned slowly. He felt he knew now what time would be like without seasons and what heat would be like without light and what man would be like without salvation. He didn't care if he never made the train and if it had not been for what suddenly caught his attention, like a cry out of the gathering dusk, he might have forgotten there was a station to go to.

He had not walked five hundred yards down the road when he saw, within reach of him, the plaster figure of a Negro sitting bent over on a low yellow brick fence that curved around a wide lawn. The Negro was about Nelson's size and he was pitched forward at an unsteady angle because the putty that held him to the wall had cracked. One of his eyes was entirely white and he held a piece of brown watermelon.

Mr. Head stood looking at him silently until Nelson stopped at a little distance. Then as the two of them stood there, Mr. Head breathed, "An artificial nigger!"

It was not possible to tell if the artificial Negro were meant to be young or old; he looked too miserable to be either. He was meant to look happy because his mouth was stretched up at the corners but the chipped eye and the angle he was cocked at gave him a wild look of misery instead.

"An artificial nigger!" Nelson repeated in Mr. Head's exact tone.

The two of them stood there with their necks forward at almost the same angle and their shoulders curved in almost exactly the same way and their hands trembling identically in their pockets. Mr. Head looked like an ancient child and Nelson like a miniature old man. They stood gazing at the artificial Negro as if they were faced with some great mystery, some monument to another's victory that brought them together in their common defeat. They could both feel it dissolving their differences like an action of mercy. Mr. Head had never known before what mercy felt like because he had been too good to deserve any, but he felt he knew now. He looked at Nelson and understood that he must say something to the child to show that he was still wise and in the look the boy returned he saw a hungry need for that assurance. Nelson's eyes seemed to implore him to explain once and for all the mystery of existence.

Mr. Head opened his lips to make a lofty statement and heard himself say, "They ain't got enough real ones here. They got to have an artificial one."

After a second, the boy nodded with a strange shivering about his mouth, and said, "Let's go home before we get ourselves lost again."

Their train glided into the suburb stop just as they reached the station and they boarded it together, and ten minutes before it was due to arrive at the junction, they went to the door and stood ready to jump off if it did not stop; but it did, just as the moon, restored to its full splendor, sprang from a cloud and flooded the clearing with light. As they stepped off, the sage grass was shivering gently in shades of silver and the clinkers under their feet glittered with a fresh black light. The treetops, fencing the junction like the protecting walls of a garden, were darker than the sky which was hung with gigantic white clouds illuminated like lanterns.

Mr. Head stood very still and felt the action of mercy touch him again but this time he knew that there were no words in the world that could name it. He understood that it grew out of agony, which is not denied to any man and which is given in strange ways to children. He understood it was all a man could carry into death to give his Maker and he suddenly burned with shame that he had so little of it to take with him. He stood appalled, judging himself with the thoroughness of God, while the action of mercy covered his pride like a flame and consumed it. He had never thought himself a great sinner before but he saw now that his true depravity had been hidden from him lest it cause him despair. He realized that he was forgiven for sins from the beginning of time, when he had conceived in his own heart the sin of Adam, until the present, when he had denied poor Nelson. He saw that no sin was too monstrous for him to claim as his own, and since God loved in proportion as He forgave, he felt ready at that instant to enter Paradise.

Nelson, composing his expression under the shadow of his hat brim, watched him with a mixture of fatigue and suspicion, but as the train glided past them and disappeared like a frightened serpent into the woods, even his face lightened and he muttered, "I'm glad I've went once, but I'll never go back again!"

Dosie, of Killakeet Island

Homer Hickam

In contrast to O'Connor's story about fear, denial, and sin, in which redemption comes in a surprising form, Homer Hickam (born 1943) tells a story (2006) about the well-functioning fellowship of Christian believers. The residents of a small fishing village unite to rescue a young woman from the likelihood of grief-induced suicide. The islanders have embraced this woman as one of their own even though she is not native to the island and remains aloof from its main activities (fishing and raising the young). Hickam presents the action of the story as an illustration of John 15:12–13: "This is my commandment, that you love one another as I have loved you. Greater love hath no man than this, that a man lay down his life for his friends." Although the members of this community are rather taciturn, this is a love-drenched story. We see the love that neighbors and friends can have for one another; we see the love that human beings can have for nature and animals; we see the love of country during time of war; we see the erotic love of man and woman; and overarching all, we are reminded of God's love.

Can love really serve as the bond of community? Perhaps the oddest feature of the story is Purdy, the winking and smiling pelican that many of the islanders regard as God's messenger.* What role does Purdy play in this story? When the preacher recommends prayer to Queenie, it seems to be Purdy who answers that prayer—and in the direction of self-giving action rather than fatalistic acceptance. Purdy reappears at the end of the story to guide Herman in his bold self-giving action as well. What is the place of self-reliance and self-sacrifice in the religion of the Killakeeters?

---

* *Because pelicans were believed to feed their young with their own blood in times of famine, the pelican has long been a symbol of Christ's Passion and of the Eucharist.*

A mile down the beach from the great spire of the Killakeet lighthouse, a cottage sat amongst the sand dunes and sea oats, surrounded by a picket fence entwined with roses. It had a full-front porch (or "pizer," as it was called in those parts), a cedar-shake roof, and dormer windows in the island style. A sign on the cottage's front gate read *Dosie's Delight*, and on the pizer, shaded by an ancient fig tree, were several inviting rocking chairs. It was a peaceful little house, and very quiet except for the cries of gulls, and the rumble of the ocean, and the whisper of sand blown by a ceaseless breeze. In 1943, which was a time of war, a young woman named Theodosia "Dosie" Crossan lived here alone, not counting her beloved mare Genie who occupied the stable behind.

In those days, the people of Killakeet Island mostly cared about two things: fishing and raising their children (although they also clammed in season). Since Dosie didn't fish and was childless, there was a great deal of difference between her and all the other island ladies. Only a few Killakeeter women had ever traveled much farther than the mainland of North Carolina, which was a ferry boat ride across Pamlico Sound, but Dosie had been raised a rich man's coddled daughter and lived in many grand places, even Baltimore and New York City, and had traveled extensively in Europe. During her childhood, her wealthy parents kept a summer home on the island and the Crossans were the richest people Killakeeters had ever seen. Then change came, as it always will, and Dosie's father went bust in the great stock crash of 1929. The Crossan cottage was shut up for the next dozen years without a single member of the family returning.

One soft blue day in the Autumn of 1941, a woman arrived on the ferry, leading to the jingle of tack and the creak of saddle leather a big, brown quarter-horse down the plank onto Killakeet sand. At first, people didn't recognize this woman in jodhpurs, riding boots, and leather jacket, and were a bit astonished when she introduced herself as Dosie Crossan. But when they looked a bit closer, there was no doubt that this was indeed little Dosie, "all growed up." Gradually, it came out that Dosie had led quite the life since she had last trod on a Killakeet beach. She had discovered what it meant to be hungry and cold, she had loved a few men too many, including musicians, and she had not been loved back enough in return. In short, Dosie Crossan had left Killakeet a pretty girl of hopes and dreams, and returned to it a world-weary, though still quite lovely, woman of experience.

Dosie moved into her family's summer cottage (which, it turned out, her father had given her as a birthday present).When asked why she'd returned, she told people it was to find herself, which seemed a bit curious since she was standing right there in front of them. But Dosie knew what she needed, which was most of all to think and also rid herself of several phantoms, one of which was a trumpet player. While she was busy thinking and exorcising musicians, she also discovered, to her surprise, that she enjoyed creating art with the shells and beach glass and shark's teeth she found on her walks up and down the spindrift beaches. Before long, her fame as an artisan spread and she had herself quite the lucrative little business, her island-inspired jewelry coveted by the fine moneyed ladies along the coast even as far inland as Raleigh. As she hoped it might, the island had healed her. To her astonishment, one day Dosie realized she was content. That was when she made her sign, *Dosie's Delight*, and hung it from her gate.

Contentment, however, is a condition on this Earth that is not allowed to remain for long. Philosophers make much of this but the reason is simple: contentment and tedium are fellow travelers. So Dosie began to keep company with Ensign Josh Thurlow, the eldest son of the Killakeet lighthouse keeper, and a bit of a rough customer. Dosie and Josh had known each other as children but then Dosie had gone off to accomplish her years of wandering through the Depression while Josh joined the Coast Guard and shipped off on the Bering Sea Patrol. A few months before Dosie's return, Josh coincidentally had returned to Killakeet to skipper the 83-foot patrol boat *Maudie Jane*. Josh was a big bull of a man, and a widower with a reputation for being unreliable with women. Dosie, though blessed with a face and figure that tended to take a man's breath away, was cautious around men, and her tongue could be tart. From the start, their romance was like a Gulf Stream waterspout, dangerous and filled with spitting wind and tumult, but ultimately glorious and wildly beautiful. Appropriately, it was after an argument that they fell in love high on the parapet of the Killakeet lighthouse.

But then the war came, and Josh was sent off to the South Pacific, and Dosie became one of those women who also serve, by waiting. Faithfully, she wrote him a letter every week. Josh wrote back, occasionally.

It was in December of 1943 that the master of the ferry that made the crossing from Morehead City to Killakeet on Mondays, Wednesdays, and Fridays came with a telegram addressed to Keeper Jack, Josh's father. Naturally, just in case it was bad news, the master had opened the telegram and read it, then tucked it inside his brass-buttoned coat where it hung as heavy as a lead brick. That was because the telegram was bad news indeed, an announcement from the Department of the Navy (which in those days included the Coast Guard) that Josh had gone missing and was presumed dead. "Poor Josh!" the master erupted, startling the mate who was at the wheel. Then, since he knew her well, the master added, "Poor Dosie!" In fact, so upset was the master that the mate had to steer the rest of the way, even making the landing, which was less than well-done, the bow crunching hard onto the beach. The master absently cuffed the mate alongside the ear but otherwise scarcely noticed. He thumped down the plank into the sand, chanting to himself, "Poor Josh, poor Dosie, and poor Keeper Jack too!"

The master took the cut across Killakeet that led to the lighthouse, meeting along the way Queenie O'Neal, the proprietress of the Hammerhead Hotel in the little settlement known as Whalebone City. He sadly apprised Queenie of the contents of the telegram, which, he knew, was tantamount to telling everyone on the island. By the time the master knocked on Keeper Jack's door and handed the telegram over, a mob was already charging down the beach toward the keeper's house.

With a cat curling around his legs, Keeper Jack stood on his pizer beneath the shadow of the great lighthouse and read the telegram with practically the whole of the island's population gathered in his yard. To discover that Josh had been killed on some Godless Pacific island or drowned in a patch of tropical sea was more than most folks thought the old man could stand. But stand he did, straight and proud. He read the telegram again, this time aloud so all could hear, then invited the folks in for coffee and sweet potato biscuits, and many took him up on it. After a biscuit well slathered with fresh butter from the keeper's cow, Queenie pierced the parlor with a great sigh, stopping all conversation. "Who's going to break this to Dosie?" was all she wanted to know.

"It's my place to do it," Keeper Jack answered quietly, and no one saw fit to argue with him.

"Poor Dosie," the master lamented, tears dribbling into his whiskers, and no one argued with him, either.

Later it was, some two hours later after his last guest had gone, that the keeper rode old Thunder down the beach to Dosie's cottage, finding her in her riding clothes leaning against a pizer post, a mug of fresh-brewed coffee in her hand, her big blue eyes placidly studying the white-crested sea. Wind chimes tinkled in the gentle breeze. A calico cat slept on the banister, its tail covering its eyes. As if occupied by ghosts, the rockers on the pizer moved in the gentle breeze. Dosie smiled at the sight of the keeper who looked so much like Josh, but when he climbed off Thunder, the expression on his face caused her smile to vanish.

"Is he dead?" she asked, straight away.

"Gone missing and thought dead," Keeper Jack answered, his hand on her gate.

"Did they say where?"

"The South Pacific is all they wrote."

Dosie gave that some thought. "Lots of islands out there," she concluded. "And Josh is an island boy."

The keeper took off his service cap and turned it in his hands. "Dosie, honey, men don't go missing in those waters and turn up too often."

"Our Josh isn't just any man, Keeper," Dosie replied, though the last words came out a bit choked. A tear trickled down her cheek. Defiantly, she wiped it away with the rim of her mug, then drank her coffee down in a single gulp. She nodded to the keeper and went inside, closing the door gently but firmly behind her.

Keeper Jack, knowing the kind of woman Dosie was, that consoling hugs and platitudes weren't her style, turned around and wearily climbed back on Thunder.

Just then, he saw Herman Guthrie, Dosie's "fetch and carry boy," walking barefoot along the sand dunes with a string of fish over his shoulder. He waited until Herman came alongside and told him what had happened. "You need to watch out extra special for your Missus," the keeper added. "At least for a little while."

"Oh, sir, I'm sorry to hear about Captain Josh, but don't you worry about my Missus," Herman replied, though he was trembling and tears curved through his freckles. Embarrassed, he used his white sailor's cap to wipe his nose. "I'll cook her up a pan of these sea trout for supper and fix some sassafras tea before bedtime so's she can sleep."

"You're a blessing to her, Herman," the keeper answered, then rode back to the lighthouse. The sun was sinking fast behind the land and it was nearly past time for him to light the light, to warn the ships at sea of the deadly shoals of the Outer Banks. Keeping the ships safe was what the Thurlows had always done. "But, Lord, who keeps the Thurlows safe?" Keeper Jack asked aloud as he climbed the two hundred and sixty-six steps of the black iron staircase that spiraled like a Nautilus's chamber within the inner wall of the high tower. He stopped on the third landing to read the brass plaque his father had placed there, inscribed as it was with the words from the old hymn "Let the Lower Lights Be Burning":

> Brightly beams our Father's mercy
> From his lighthouse evermore;
> But to us He gives the keeping
> Of the lights along the shore.

"Amen," Keeper Jack said and felt strengthened. Near the top of the lighthouse, the stairs led to the watch room and the keeper went inside and poured kerosene into the holding tank, then pumped it tight with air. A dozen more steps higher took him to the lantern room where the great lens sat like a massive glass beehive. He lit the kerosene-soaked mantle, then released a clock-work mechanism. Ponderously, the heavy glass structure began to turn on chariot wheels along a circular track, sending shafts of light flashing across the sea like spokes on a fiery wheel. Ships passing by would be safe as long as they heeded the warning, and as long as the keeper kept the light no matter what else might be happening in his life, including the death of a son.

Keeper Jack walked out on the parapet and looked down the beach toward Dosie's cottage. There was a lamp in the window, a single lamp, and that was all. "Poor Dosie," he said into the wind, which impishly snatched his words away, flinging them into the night across the pounding sea.

A day passed, then another and another. No more telegrams arrived. The government had stated the situation and what else, after all, was there to be said? Josh Thurlow was missing, thought to be dead, and there was a war to be fought and that was an end to it.

Dosie was a member of the auxiliary Coast Guard Beach Patrol, which meant she and Genie routinely rode up and down the beach, looking for German U-boats and saboteurs. Often alongside was Bosun Rex Stewart and his horse, Jubal Early.

One day, a pleasant sunlit day, nothing had been seen during the entire patrol except the grumbling ocean and an occasional seagull. At the beginning of the war, the Germans had been busy along the Outer Banks, but lately, all had been quiet. Rex was nearly asleep in the saddle when Dosie abruptly announced, "I can't go on."

Startled, Rex jerked erect. "You're turning around? But we got another mile to go."

Dosie replied with a sigh. "Oh Rex, it isn't the patrol I'm talking about. It's me. I can't go on like this."

"Like what?" Rex asked, completely mystified.

"This. Living, you might say," Dosie answered, and her tone was miserable. "I came to this island to find myself and start a new life, and I guess I did. But now with Josh gone . . ." She shook her head, unable to finish the thought.

"So what are you going to do?" Rex fretted.

"I don't know. I just know I can't go on like this much longer." And then she would say no more.

Rex worried over her words for a night, then carried the gist of the conversation to Queenie O'Neal, whom he found in her kitchen, cooking breakfast for the fishermen down from Hatteras and Ocracoke and up from Beaufort who had arrived to take advantage of the recent run of menhaden off Killakeet's shores.

After Rex told her what Dosie had said, Queenie threw her hands to her mouth, then spoke between her fingers. "That don't sound good, Rex, not good at all." Then she lowered her hands and wiped them nervously on her apron while frowning in thought.

"What are we going to do?" Rex asked.

Queenie reached a conclusion. "I'll talk to the women," she said.

Rex looked relieved, and was. In fact, as far as he was concerned, the matter was resolved. A few hours later, Queenie gathered the women in her parlor and, over yaupon tea and corn bread, they all put their heads together. Most favored sending someone, such as a fisherman's widow of which there were more than a few, to give Dosie a good talking-to, but then Herman showed up with more disturbing news. "That's what came out of her mouth, all you ma'ams," Herman said, finishing up. "She said she was going to get her affairs in order. And she asked me if I would like Genie for my very own, that is if I thought I could care for her."

Queenie and the ladies of Killakeet were shocked at this development. "I believe I'd best have a word with the preacher," Queenie announced, and all agreed it was for the best.

Preacher Hemphill was a tall, spindly young man with bad knees and a humped back, a little nervous with his hands, and from way out west somewhere, maybe Alabama. He stood bowed over in the sand outside his church while Mrs. O'Neal related Dosie's situation. Preacher Hemphill searched his mind for a suitable piece of scripture but failed to find one. Stumped, he asked, "Has anyone ever killed hisself on Killakeet, Mrs. O'Neal?"

"Not so we'd know, Preacher," Queenie answered after some thought. "There's so many good ways to get yourself killed here, what with the weather and the sea and leaky boats and all, people just kind of let it happen when it happens. But Dosie's a bit different. She ain't a Killakeeter by birth, you know, and she's only lived here full-time for a couple of years. There's still a bit of the landsman in her, and you know the strange ideas folks from over there tend to get, no disrespect meant in your direction, of course."

"Well, I could go talk to her, and get her to pray with me some and such," Preacher Hemphill suggested. "But I'm not sure what I'd say except suicide is a sin."

"She surely knows it's a sin, Preacher," Queenie replied, as tartly as she dared to a man of God. "Only maybe she's come to a point where she don't care. Romance is a powerful thing and it can cloud judgment."

Preacher Hemphill nodded gravely. "Then you should pray, Mrs. O'Neal, pray for poor Dosie and pray for guidance. That's all that can be done."

Taking the preacher's advice, Queenie walked to the dunes just east of the Coast Guard station. It was a lonely spot, with nothing there but sand and the sea and the everlasting breeze. Queenie bowed her head and said a few words, then sensed someone had joined her. When she opened her eyes, she saw standing in the sea oats a pelican. Queenie recognized him at once. It was the ancient and legendary pelican everybody called Purdy. Queenie's grandfather had told tales about Purdy, and so had his father and his father's father. For as long as anyone could remember, Purdy had showed up on the island when and where he wanted to, seemed to impart some silent wisdom, then disappeared. It was easy to imagine why some people said God sent messages through him.

"So, Purdy," Queenie said, pondering the snowy white bird who regarded her with quizzical eyes, "what do you think about poor Dosie?"

Purdy turned away, then hunkered down on the soft sand, made pink by the sun struggling through the clouds, and Queenie thought surely he'd gone to sleep until he suddenly shook his feathers and raised his wings. Then he looked at her and closed one eye, giving Queenie the wink, and that was when she knew what had to be done. "Thank you, old thing," she said but it was to empty air since Purdy had vanished as quickly and quietly as he had come. "I wish you'd stop doing that," Queenie muttered, then went on to do what needed to be done.

When Queenie got home, she woke up her husband who was taking a snooze on the parlor couch. "Pump, we're going to throw Dosie a party!" she yelled into his thin and unconscious face. Pump was so startled by the news he tripped over his boat-sized feet getting up and sprawled headfirst into a bronze umbrella stand. Queenie took no note of her husband's subsequent moaning. She was already off to give the women the glorious news.

For the next few days, Dosie's party was the prime topic of conversation and activity on Killakeet. It was going to be the grandest party the island had ever known and it was for the best cause ever, to keep poor Dosie from doing herself in. But then the ferry master came to consult with Queenie. He had carried Dosie into Morehead City, he related, and then followed her to a lawyer's office. Taped to the lawyer's window, written on cardboard, was his specialty: *Last Wills and Testaments cheerfully drawn.* After that, a number of ominous events occurred. The weather turned gray and stormy, not particularly unusual, but there it was. A dolphin stranded itself near the lighthouse. A gull on the church steeple started to moan, then flung itself into the bell and died. Then the menhaden disappeared, just vanished as if a giant hand had scooped them all up. Although the dolphin was pushed back into the sea with no injury done, everybody agreed these omens meant time was running out for Dosie.

The party was held on a Thursday eve and to celebrate it, the weather cleared and no more gulls moaned and died on the church steeple, and the dolphins stayed out in the ocean where they belonged. The menhaden, however, remained truculently absent so there was some trepidation that all was not resolved. As the sun set and the light began to flash at the tip of the light-house, the people gathered in front of *Dosie's Delight* and began to sing the old hymn Killakeeters had sung for ages:

> Abide with me! Fast falls the eventide;
> The darkness deepens; Lord with me abide.
> When other helpers fail and comforts flee,
> Help of the helpless, oh, abide with me!

Dosie, dressed in a pale blue frock, an embroidered shawl, and white pumps—her Sunday clothes—came out on her pizer, listened to the singing with her head tilted and her eyes closed, then invited them in, everyone. Of course, Killakeet being a very small island, she had divined for days that a party was being planned in her honor, although she didn't know its purpose. In any case, she was prepared with a huge load of food on her table and after the other ladies added their own, it was groaning beneath the weight.

The preacher said the grace and everybody took up plates and began to eat. After the roast merganser, fried mullet, clams, and oysters with sides of biscuits and corn bread and messes of greens and navy beans had been eaten, there was celebratory fiddle-playing and rigorous dancing. Dosie happily swung arms with old Doc Folsom, the island's physician. She waltzed with Keeper Jack, sharing a silence.

She did the Charleston with Pump O'Neal and clog-danced with Rex Stewart. Then, finally, after exhaustion had set well in, it was time for the speeches and the prayers and the praises to God, all made with heartfelt sincerity, all to tell Dosie how much she was beloved and not to be sad and all she should do was take her lumps as best she could like everybody else.

Dosie seemed attentive and everybody was certain they had accomplished their mission. A few wandered off home but most settled down where they were, in the parlor or in the rockers on the pizer or out on the sand to take themselves a contented nap.

It was morning when the people of Killakeet first got an inkling that their work was for naught. Dosie had made up her mind and nothing, including any number of speeches, prayers, and praises, was going to change her course. Herman woke and saw his missus come out of the kitchen and start up the stairs. For a reason he couldn't discern, he felt anxious. "Where are you going, Missus?" he asked, politely.

"Upstairs, Herman," she said, which was fairly obvious.

"What for?" Herman demanded because he didn't like the look in her eye.

"Among my other intentions, I am going to get my pistol," she answered and went on.

Herman found Queenie O'Neal sitting on the beach with her arm around Pump, who had his head on her shoulder, both admiring the ocean, remarkable in itself since they'd lived alongside that very same ocean for more than fifty years. Beside them sat the ferry master who'd recently showed up, wondering where everybody was. "Missus O'Neal" Herman cried. "Dosie's gone upstairs to get her pistol and I reckon to put on her funerary clothes too!"

Queenie yelled and jumped to her feet, leaving Pump to fall over. She charged into the parlor and let loose with a screech that got everybody awake. *"Dosie's gone upstairs and she's got a gun!"*

There was a surge to the stairs, stopped by Dosie herself, who appeared at the top of it. She was wearing khaki breeches and riding boots and a blue denim shirt and her brown leather jacket. A canvas knapsack was slung over her shoulder. She was also carrying a big pistol, her father's somebody would later say. She stopped and looked at the crowd, then tucked the pistol in her belt.

"I hoped to go quietly," she said, "but I should have known I couldn't get away with anything on this island."

"Don't do it, Missus!" Herman cried out. "I'd miss you something fierce if you did!"

Dosie gave him an affectionate smile that made Herman's heart thump in his chest so hard he thought it would leap out. "And I'll miss you, too, Herman, but this is something I just have to do."

"No, Dosie," Preacher Hemphill intoned. "You mustn't. I looked it up in scriptures. *You are not your own. You are bought with a price.* It means you got to stay alive, don't matter how much you hurt."

"Pretty words, Preacher," Dosie answered, after a moment's frowning, "but they don't much apply to me."

"Well, they do, honey," Keeper Jack said, "if you're going to fly off to heaven because of Josh." He just couldn't say the word *suicide*.

"Is that what you all think I'm going to do?" She laughed, and shook her head. "I don't plan on going to heaven any time soon."

"Then what are you going to do, dear?" Queenie asked.

Dosie came down the rest of the stairs and went out on her pizer, the throng following. "I'm going to find Josh and bring him home," she said, simply and emphatically.

There was a stunned silence for a long second. Finally, Keeper Jack said, "But Dosie, dear, he's on the other side of the world."

"That's why he needs finding, Keeper," Dosie replied. "Now, everybody on Killakeet has things they have to do. Keeper, you have to light the light, and

Pump, you have to run the Hammerhead Hotel, and Queenie, you have to keep everybody apprised of what's happening on the island. Doc, you got to sew folks up, and Rex, you got to patrol, and Preacher Hemphill, you got to preach. All the rest of you have to catch your fish and raise your children. But me? All I've got to do is make my beach glass and shells and shark's teeth into art and I've got the rest of my life to get that done. Right now, I'm going to take the time to find my man. Herman, saddle Genie for me. I'd like a last ride. Ferry Master, I'd appreciate a ride across Pamlico Sound. That's the first part of my journey."

Keeper Jack's jaw had fallen open during Dosie's little speech. He managed to sputter, "But what then, Dosie? Where will you go? You'll have to cross the breadth of the country and then the Pacific Ocean. And there's a war on out there. It ain't like you can just catch a boat and go where you want to go."

"First thing to do is to get to Morehead City," Dosie answered. "Then I'll see what's next. That's the way I'll do the entire thing. Every place, I'll figure out how to get to the next place and so on. Herman, didn't I ask you to saddle Genie?"

Herman ran to the stable and soon had Genie standing by the gate. Dosie swung up in the saddle, then leaned over and softly spoke into the mare's ear, Genie answering with a low nicker. Straightening, Dosie said, "Well, Ferry Master, are me and the mate going to have to take your ferry across the Sound ourselves?"

The master thought not and off he went down the sand track at a fast pace. Dosie gave *Dosie's Delight* a last, fond look, then smiled down at the people of Killakeet. "You folks have been good to me, as good as anybody ever was, and I sure do appreciate your prayers and praise. I'll come back if I can." And with that, without so much as another glance over her shoulder, she clucked her tongue to Genie, and said, "Walk on, girl."

The people followed, silent, confused, but somehow hopeful. At the ferry, Dosie got off and handed over Genie's reins to Herman. "She's yours, Herman, if you still want her."

"Yes, Missus. Anyways, I'll keep her for you. And I'll look after the house, too."

"You'll find my will in the hutch," Dosie said. "You get the house if I don't come back."

"Oh no, Missus!" Herman cried. "I don't want your house!"

"Well, it's yours just the same," Dosie said, then gave Herman a quick hug and climbed aboard the ferry. The mate raised the plank and the master backed the little slab-sided vessel away. Dosie waved once and all the people on the beach waved back. Genie tossed her head and stamped her hooves. The men took off their hats and the women raised their aprons and dabbed at their eyes. For his part, Herman started to cry outright. Keeper Jack took Genie's reins from him and patted the big mare on her neck. "Good girl," he said, because she tended to be.

Herman was a snot-nosed mess. "Poor Missus," he sobbed. "And poor Josh."

"What do you mean, Herman?" the keeper asked. Then he said the strangest thing Herman thought he'd ever heard. "My boy Josh is the luckiest man I guess there is on Earth."

Herman couldn't believe his ears. "What's lucky about him?" he demanded.

Keeper Jack put his hand on Herman's shoulder. "Why, that he has a woman who loves him so much she'd go around the world to find him, even when nobody expects that she should."

All the men nodded agreement with wistful smiles. *Lucky Josh*, they all seemed to be saying although, them being men, no words were actually said out loud. Outraged, Herman threw off the keeper's hand and went to the women and told them the men's opinion. Queenie answered, "Herman, dear, you're right as rain. The men, as usual, have it all wrong. It ain't Josh what's lucky. It's that there girl on the ferry. Your Missus."

Herman was aghast. "But look here, Mrs. O'Neal, there she is all alone and she don't even know where she's going!"

"That's so true, Herman," Queenie answered with an odd little smile that all the women seemed to be wearing. "But it don't change that Dosie Crossan is as lucky as a woman can be. You see, she's fallen in love with a man she's willing to cross the world to find. Who'd of thunk it would have been the likes of Josh Thurlow, but there ain't no accounting for taste."

Lucky Dosie, the women sighed in unison.

Dizzy with confusion, Herman paced the sand, trying to find some sense in all that had transpired. He stopped and looked at the ferry, now nearly swallowed up in the pearly morning mists of the Sound. He looked at the people who'd raised him and they seemed like strangers. He kept trying to understand what they were getting at but he just couldn't. But then an answer of a sort began to form in Herman's mind. It was an answer he thought he'd heard in church. *Greater love hath no man than this, that a man lay down his life for his friends*. Herman said it out loud, almost without realizing it.

"And that goes for a woman, too, dear," Queenie advised.

"Well, I'll be blessed," Herman said, a glimmer of understanding settling into his soul. He was distracted by a ruffle of feathers and looked up to find Purdy perched on Genie's saddle. "I guess we're all blessed if somebody loves you and you love them back, ain't we, Purdy?" Herman asked. He got no answer, not directly, anyway, but it was the first time Herman realized a pelican could smile. And then something else settled into Herman's soul: a longing. He sought out his mama and told her what he had to do. The widow Guthrie looked hard at her son, then said, "Well, don't drown, and come back as soon as you can."

Herman hugged her, then sought out the keeper to ask him a question. "Will you look after Genie, sir?" he asked, and when the keeper said he would, Herman waded barefoot into Pamlico Sound. After a moment's hesitation, he tossed his cap into the air, threw himself forward, and swam as hard as he'd ever swum before.

5

The Goals of Civic Life

Lifting the Floor

The Ones Who Walk Away from Omelas

(Variation on a theme by William James)*

Ursula Le Guin

In a society that protects individual liberty and encourages the private pursuit of happiness, not all succeed in the chase. Some flourish; others get by; still others are miserable. The inevitable inequalities raise questions for a decent society about its obligations to those less well off, especially if they are miserable through no fault of their own. This story (1973) by science fiction writer Ursula Le Guin (born 1929)—she calls it a parable or "psychomyth"—troubles our complacent belief in the innocence of our own pursuit of happiness, and insists that we attend to the price paid by the least amongst us for the happiness of the majority. In the city of Omelas, misery is not an accidental side effect of progress that further progress might hope to alleviate; rather, the happiness of "all" depends on the city's conscious willingness to immiserate a single child. The young people of Omelas shed tears of anguish and disgust when they learn of this injustice, but they dry them "when they begin to perceive the terrible justice of reality, and to accept it." Yet a small number walk away from Omelas, each one alone, never to return.

What case can be made for those who stay in Omelas? What for those who leave? Are these the only two options? How much injustice to the miserable few is an acceptable price for the flourishing of the many? How much

---

* *Ursula Le Guin credits "meeting" William James, in his "Moral Philosopher and the Moral Life," with the idea for the story. The quote from James is: "Or if the hypothesis were offered us of a world in which Messrs. Fourier's and Bellamy's and Morris's utopias should all be outdone, and millions kept permanently happy on the one simple condition that a certain lost soul on the far-off edge of things should lead a life of lonely torture, what except a specific and independent sort of emotion can it be which would make us immediately feel, even though an impulse arose within us to clutch at the happiness so offered, how hideous a thing would be its enjoyment when deliberately accepted as the fruit of such a bargain?"*

sacrifice of personal and civic happiness is an acceptable price for lifting the
floor of the disadvantaged? Does this myth capture the truth about the rela-
tion between the advantaged and disadvantaged?

With a clamor of bells that set the swallows soaring, the Festival of Summer came to the city Omelas, bright-towered by the sea. The rigging of
the boats in harbor sparkled with flags. In the streets between houses with red
roofs and painted walls, between old moss-grown gardens and under avenues
of trees, past great parks and public buildings, processions moved. Some were
decorous: old people in long stiff robes of mauve and grey, grave master work-
men, quiet, merry women carrying their babies and chatting as they walked.
In other streets the music beat faster, a shimmering of gong and tambourine,
and the people went dancing, the procession was a dance. Children dodged
in and out, their high calls rising like the swallows' crossing flights over the
music and the singing. All the processions wound towards the north side of
the city, where on the great water-meadow called the Green Fields boys and
girls, naked in the bright air, with mud-stained feet and ankles and long, lithe
arms, exercised their restive horses before the race. The horses wore no gear
at all but a halter without bit. Their manes were braided with streamers of
silver, gold, and green. They flared their nostrils and pranced and boasted to
one another; they were vastly excited, the horse being the only animal who has
adopted our ceremonies as his own. Far off to the north and west the mountains stood up half encircling Omelas on her bay. The air of morning was so
clear that the snow still crowning the Eighteen Peaks burned with white-gold
fire across the miles of sunlit air, under the dark blue of the sky. There was just
enough wind to make the banners that marked the racecourse snap and flutter
now and then. In the silence of the broad green meadows one could hear the
music winding through the city streets, farther and nearer and ever approaching, a cheerful faint sweetness of the air that from time to time trembled and
gathered together and broke out into the great joyous clanging of the bells.

Joyous! How is one to tell about joy? How describe the citizens of Omelas?

They were not simple folk, you see, though they were happy. But we do
not say the words of cheer much any more. All smiles have become archaic.
Given a description such as this one tends to make certain assumptions.
Given a description such as this one tends to look next for the King, mounted
on a splendid stallion and surrounded by his noble knights, or perhaps in a
golden litter borne by great-muscled slaves. But there was no king. They did
not use swords, or keep slaves. They were not barbarians. I do not know the
rules and laws of their society, but I suspect that they were singularly few. As
they did without monarchy and slavery, so they also got on without the stock

exchange, the advertisement, the secret police, and the bomb. Yet I repeat that these were not simple folk, not dulcet shepherds, noble savages, bland utopians. They were not less complex than us. The trouble is that we have a bad habit, encouraged by pedants and sophisticates, of considering happiness as something rather stupid. Only pain is intellectual, only evil interesting. This is the treason of the artist: a refusal to admit the banality of evil and the terrible boredom of pain. If you can't lick 'em, join 'em. If it hurts, repeat it. But to praise despair is to condemn delight, to embrace violence is to lose hold of everything else. We have almost lost hold; we can no longer describe a happy man, nor make any celebration of joy. How can I tell you about the people of Omelas? They were not naive and happy children—though their children were, in fact, happy. They were mature, intelligent, passionate adults whose lives were not wretched. O miracle! but I wish I could describe it better. I wish I could convince you. Omelas sounds in my words like a city in a fairy tale, long ago and far away, once upon a time. Perhaps it would be best if you imagined it as your own fancy bids, assuming it will rise to the occasion, for certainly I cannot suit you all. For instance, how about technology? I think that there would be no cars or helicopters in and above the streets; this follows from the fact that the people of Omelas are happy people. Happiness is based on a just discrimination of what is necessary, what is neither necessary nor destructive, and what is destructive. In the middle category, however—that of the unnecessary but undestructive, that of comfort, luxury, exuberance, etc.—they could perfectly well have central heating, subway trains, washing machines, and all kinds of marvelous devices not yet invented here, floating light-sources, fuelless power, a cure for the common cold. Or they could have none of that; it doesn't matter. As you like it. I incline to think that people from towns up and down the coast have been coming in to Omelas during the last days before the Festival on very fast little trains and double-decked trams, and that the train station of Omelas is actually the handsomest building in town, though plainer than the magnificent Farmers' Market. But even granted trains, I fear that Omelas so far strikes some of you as goody-goody. Smiles, bells, parades, horses, bleh. If so, please add an orgy. If an orgy would help, don't hesitate. Let us not, however, have temples from which issue beautiful nude priests and priestesses already half in ecstasy and ready to copulate with any man or woman, lover or stranger, who desires union with the deep godhead of the blood, although that was my first idea. But really it would be better not to have any temples in Omelas—at least, not manned temples. Religion yes, clergy no. Surely the beautiful nudes can just wander about, offering themselves like divine souffles to the hunger of the needy and the rapture of the flesh. Let them join the processions. Let tambourines be struck above the copulations, and the glory of desire be proclaimed upon the gongs, and (a not unimportant point) let the offspring of these delightful rituals be beloved and looked after by all. One thing I know there is none of in Omelas is guilt. But what else should there be? I thought at first there were not drugs, but that is puritanical. For those who like it, the faint insistent sweetness of *drooz* may perfume the ways of the city, *drooz* which first brings a great lightness and brilliance to the mind and limbs, and then after some hours a dreamy languor, and wonderful visions at last of the very arcana and inmost secrets of the Universe, as well as exciting the pleasure of sex beyond belief; and it is not habit-forming. For more modest tastes I think there ought to be beer. What else, what else belongs in the joyous city? The sense of victory, surely, the celebration of courage. But as we did without clergy, let us do without soldiers. The joy built upon successful slaughter is not the right kind of joy; it will not do; it is fearful and it is trivial. A boundless and generous contentment, a magnanimous triumph felt not against some outer enemy but in communion with the finest and fairest in the souls of all men everywhere and the splendor of the world's summer: this is what swells the hearts of the people of Omelas, and the victory they celebrate is that of life. I really don't think many of them need to take *drooz*.

Most of the procession have reached the Green Fields by now. A marvelous smell of cooking goes forth from the red and blue tents of the provisioners. The faces of small children are amiably sticky; in the benign grey beard of a man a couple of crumbs of rich pastry are entangled. The youths and girls have mounted their horses and are beginning to group around the starting line of the course. An old woman, small, fat, and laughing, is passing out flowers from a basket, and tall young men wear her flowers in their shining hair. A child of nine or ten sits at the edge of the crowd, alone, playing on a wooden flute. People pause to listen, and they smile, but they do not speak to him, for he never ceases playing and never sees them, his dark eyes wholly rapt in the sweet, thin magic of the tune.

He finishes, and slowly lowers his hands holding the wooden flute.

As if that little private silence were the signal, all at once a trumpet sounds from the pavilion near the starting line: imperious, melancholy, piercing. The horses rear on their slender legs, and some of them neigh in answer. Soberfaced, the young riders stroke the horses' necks and soothe them, whispering, "Quiet, quiet, there my beauty, my hope...." They begin to form in rank along the starting line. The crowds along the racecourse are like a field of grass and flowers in the wind. The Festival of Summer has begun.

Do you believe? Do you accept the festival, the city, the joy? No? Then let me describe one more thing.

In a basement under one of the beautiful public buildings of Omelas, or perhaps in the cellar of one of its spacious private homes, there is a room. It has one locked door, and no window. A little light seeps in dustily between cracks in the boards, secondhand from a cobwebbed window somewhere across the cellar. In one corner of the little room a couple of mops, with stiff, clotted, foul-smelling heads stand near a rusty bucket. The floor is dirt, a little damp to the touch, as cellar dirt usually is. The room is about three paces long and two wide: a mere broom closet or disused tool room. In the room a child is sitting. It could be a boy or a girl. It looks about six, but actually is nearly ten. It is feeble-minded. Perhaps it was born defective, or perhaps it has become imbecile through fear, malnutrition, and neglect. It picks its nose and occasionally fumbles vaguely with its toes or genitals, as it sits hunched in the corner farthest from the bucket and the two mops. It is afraid of the mops. It finds them horrible. It shuts its eyes, but it knows the mops are still standing there; and the door is locked; and nobody will come. The door is always locked; and nobody ever comes, except that sometimes—the child has no understanding of time or interval—sometimes the door rattles terribly and opens, and a person, or several people, are there. One of them may come in and kick the child to make it stand up. The others never come close, but peer in at it with frightened, disgusted eyes. The food bowl and the water jug are hastily filled, the door is locked, the eyes disappear. The people at the door never say anything, but the child, who has not always lived in the tool room, and can remember sunlight and its mother's voice, sometimes speaks. "I will be good," it says. "Please let me out. I will be good!" They never answer. The child used to scream for help at night, and cry a good deal, but now it only makes a kind of whining, "eh-haa, eh-haa," and it speaks less and less often. It is so thin there are no calves to its legs; its belly protrudes; it lives on a half-bowl of corn meal and grease a day. It is naked. Its buttocks and thighs are a mass of festered sores, as it sits in its own excrement continually.

They all know it is there, all the people of Omelas. Some of them have ·come to see it, others are content merely to know it is there. They all know that it has to be there. Some of them understand why, and some do not, but they all understand that their happiness, the beauty of their city, the tenderness of their friendships, the health of their children, the wisdom of their scholars, the skill of their makers, even the abundance of their harvest and the kindly weathers of their skies, depend wholly on this child's abominable misery.

This is usually explained to children when they are between eight and twelve, whenever they seem capable of understanding; and most of those who come to see the child are young people, though often enough an adult comes, or comes back, to see the child. No matter how well the matter has been explained to them, these young spectators are always shocked and sickened at the sight. They feel disgust, which they had thought themselves superior to. They feel anger, outrage, impotence, despite all the explanations. They would like to do something for the child. But there is nothing they can do. If the child were brought up into the sunlight out of that vile place, if it were cleaned and fed and comforted, that would be a good thing indeed; but if it were done, in that day and hour all the prosperity and beauty and delight of Omelas would wither and be destroyed. Those are the terms. To exchange all the goodness and grace of every life in Omelas for that single, small improvement: to throw away the happiness of thousands for the chance of the happiness of one: that would be to let guilt within the walls indeed.

The terms are strict and absolute; there may not even be a kind word spoken to the child.

Often the young people go home in tears, or in a tearless rage, when they have seen the child and faced this terrible paradox. They may brood over it for weeks or years. But as time goes on they begin to realize that even if the child could be released, it would not get much good of its freedom: a little vague pleasure of warmth and food, no doubt, but little more. It is too degraded and imbecile to know any real joy. It has been afraid too long ever to be free of fear. Its habits are too uncouth for it to respond to humane treatment. Indeed, after so long it would probably be wretched without walls about it to protect it, and darkness for its eyes, and its own excrement to sit in. Their tears at the bitter injustice dry when they begin to perceive the terrible justice of reality, and to accept it. Yet it is their tears and anger, the trying of their generosity and the acceptance of their helplessness, which are perhaps the true source of the splendor of their lives. Theirs is no vapid, irresponsible happiness. They know that they, like the child, are not free. They know compassion. It is the existence of the child, and their knowledge of its existence, that makes possible the nobility of their architecture, the poignancy of their music, the profundity of their science. It is because of the child that they are so gentle with children. They know that if the wretched one were not there sniveling in the dark, the other one, the flute-player, could make no joyful music as the young riders line up in their beauty for the race in the sunlight of the first morning of summer.

Now do you believe in them? Are they not more credible? But there is one more thing to tell, and this is quite incredible.

At times one of the adolescent girls or boys who go to see the child does not go home to weep or rage, does not, in fact, go home at all. Sometimes also a man or woman much older falls silent for a day or two, and then leaves home. These people go out into the street, and walk down the street alone. They keep walking, and walk straight out of the city of Omelas, through the beautiful gates. They keep walking across the farmlands of Omelas. Each one goes alone, youth or girl, man or woman. Night falls; the traveler must pass down village streets, between the houses with yellow-lit windows, and on out into the darkness of the fields. Each alone, they go west or north, towards the mountains. They go on. They leave Omelas, they walk ahead into the darkness, and they do not come back. The place they go towards is a place even less imaginable to most of us than the city of happiness. I cannot describe it at all. It is possible that it does not exist. But they seem to know where they are going, the ones who walk away from Omelas.

Writings on Education

Thomas Jefferson

Unlike Ursula Le Guin's story, Thomas Jefferson's writings on education emphatically reject the view that the misery of some could be a workable foundation for the happiness of others. In the first excerpt here, from Notes on the State of Virginia *(1781), Jefferson recommends the education of all as the true floor of democracy. He calls for taxpayer-funded education for all children for three years, plus continuing taxpayer-funded education for poor children who demonstrate intellectual ability (those of "best genius"). The system accomplishes two related aims: basic education for all citizens and higher education for a select few who will become the nation's statesmen.* * *In the second selection, from the* Report of the Commissioners for the University of Virginia *(1818), Jefferson states that education should be both practical and political, beginning with what each citizen needs to know for "his own business" (contracts, accounts, and such) and then extending to his share in the public business. In the final selection, a letter defending the granting of patent rights to inventors (1813), Jefferson insists that by nature there is no such thing as intellectual property: ideas are shareable and communal in a way that real property is not. He highlights the global reach of ideas, suggesting that trade in ideas (including the spread of science and technology) contributes to equality. Mental emancipation is the precondition for material emancipation.*

Do you agree that the success of democracy depends on education? If so, is education properly a public rather than a private responsibility? What are

---

* *Jefferson hoped to find and elevate "natural aristocrats," possessed of virtues and talents, as opposed to "artificial aristocrats," who owed their position to birth and wealth. In keeping with his belief that democracy and meritocracy belong together, he later played a leading role in the founding of the University of Virginia.*

the aims of public schooling today? Why does Jefferson put such emphasis on the importance of history in the curriculum? Are democracy and meritocracy compatible, as Jefferson believes? Should our aim be equality of opportunity or equality of condition? How important is a free market in ideas? How would you try to educate future citizens and statesmen today?

Excerpt from Notes on the State of Virginia

Another object of the revisal is, to diffuse knowledge more generally through the mass of the people. This bill proposes to lay off every county into small districts of five or six miles square, called hundreds, and in each of them to establish a school for teaching reading, writing, and arithmetic. The tutor to be supported by the hundred, and every person in it entitled to send their children three years gratis, and as much longer as they please, paying for it. These schools to be under a visitor, who is annually to chuse the boy, of best genius in the school, of those whose parents are too poor to give them further education, and to send him forward to one of the grammar schools, of which twenty are proposed to be erected in different parts of the country, for teaching Greek, Latin, geography, and the higher branches of numerical arithmetic. Of the boys thus sent in any one year, trial is to be made at the grammar schools one or two years, and the best genius of the whole selected, and continued six years, and the residue dismissed. By this means twenty of the best geniuses will be raked from the rubbish annually, and be instructed, at the public expence, so far as the grammar schools go. At the end of six years instruction, one half are to be discontinued (from among whom the grammar schools will probably be supplied with future masters); and the other half, who are to be chosen for the superiority of their parts and disposition, are to be sent and continued three years in the study of such sciences as they shall chuse, at William and Mary college, the plan of which is proposed to be enlarged, as will be hereafter explained, and extended to all the useful sciences. The ultimate result of the whole scheme of education would be the teaching all the children of the state reading, writing, and common arithmetic: turning out ten annually of superior genius, well taught in Greek, Latin, geography, and the higher branches of arithmetic: turning out ten others annually, of still superior parts, who, to those branches of learning, shall have added such of the sciences as their genius shall have led them to: . . . —By that part of our plan which prescribes the selection of the youths of genius from among the classes of the poor, we hope to avail the state of those talents which nature has sown as liberally among the poor as the rich, but which perish without use, if not sought for and cultivated.—But of all the views of this law none is more important, none more legitimate, than that of rendering the people the safe, as they are the ultimate, guardians of their own liberty. For this purpose the reading in the first stage, where *they* will receive their whole education, is proposed, as has been said, to be chiefly historical. History by apprising them of the past will enable them to judge of the future; it will avail them of the experience of other times and other nations; it will qualify them as judges of the actions and designs of men; it will enable them to know ambition under every disguise it may assume; and knowing it, to defeat its views. In every government on earth is some trace of human weakness, some germ of corruption and degeneracy, which cunning will discover, and wickedness insensibly open, cultivate, and improve. Every government degenerates when trusted to the rulers of the people alone. The people themselves therefore are its only safe depositories. And to render even them safe their minds must be improved to a certain degree.

Excerpt from Report of the Commissioners for the University of Virginia

The objects of this primary education determine its character and limits. These objects would be,

To give to every citizen the information he needs for the transaction of his own business;

To enable him to calculate for himself, and to express and preserve his ideas, his contracts and accounts, in writing;

To improve, by reading, his morals and faculties;

To understand his duties to his neighbors and country, and to discharge with competence the functions confided to him by either;

To know his rights; to exercise with order and justice those he retains; to choose with discretion the fiduciary of those he delegates; and to notice their conduct with diligence, with candor, and judgment;

And, in general, to observe with intelligence and faithfulness all the social relations under which he shall be placed.

To instruct the mass of our citizens in these, their rights, interests and duties, as men and citizens, being then the objects of education in the primary schools, whether private or public, in them should be taught reading, writing and numerical arithmetic, the elements of mensuration, (useful in so many callings,) and the outlines of geography and history. And this brings us to the point at which are to commence the higher branches of education, of which the Legislature require the development; those, for example, which are,

To form the statesmen, legislators and judges, on whom public prosperity and individual happiness are so much to depend;

To expound the principles and structure of government, the laws which regulate the intercourse of nations, those formed municipally for our own government, and a sound spirit of legislation, which, banishing all arbitrary and unnecessary restraint on individual action, shall leave us free to do whatever does not violate the equal rights of another;

To harmonize and promote the interests of agriculture, manufactures and commerce, and by well informed views of political economy to give a free scope to the public industry;

To develop the reasoning faculties of our youth, enlarge their minds, cultivate their morals, and instill into them the precepts of virtue and order;

To enlighten them with mathematical and physical sciences, which advance the arts, and administer to the health, the subsistence, and comforts of human life;

And, generally, to form them to habits of reflection and correct action, rendering them examples of virtue to others, and of happiness within themselves.

Letter to Isaac McPherson, Monticello, August 13, 1813

It has been pretended by some, (and in England especially,) that inventors have a natural and exclusive right to their inventions, and not merely for their own lives, but inheritable to their heirs. But while it is a moot question whether the origin of any kind of property is derived from nature at all, it would be singular to admit a natural and even an hereditary right to inventors. It is agreed by those who have seriously considered the subject, that no individual has, of natural right, a separate property in an acre of land, for instance. By an universal law, indeed, whatever, whether fixed or movable, belongs to all men equally and in common, is the property for the moment of him who occupies it, but when he relinquishes the occupation, the property goes with it. Stable ownership is the gift of social law, and is given late in the progress of society. It would be curious then, if an idea, the fugitive fermentation of an individual brain, could, of natural right, be claimed in exclusive and stable property. If nature has made any one thing less susceptible than all others of exclusive property, it is the action of the thinking power called an idea, which an individual may exclusively possess as long as he keeps it to himself; but the moment it is divulged, it forces itself into the possession of every one, and the receiver cannot dispossess himself of it. Its peculiar character, too, is that no one possesses the less, because every other possesses the whole of it. He who receives an idea from me, receives instruction himself without lessening mine; as he who lights his taper at mine, receives light without darkening me. That ideas should freely spread from one to another over the globe, for the moral and mutual instruction of man, and improvement of his condition, seems to have been peculiarly and benevolently designed by nature, when she made them, like fire, expansible over all space, without lessening their density in any point, and like the air in which we breathe, move, and have our physical being, incapable of confinement or exclusive appropriation. Inventions then cannot, in nature, be a subject of property. Society may give an exclusive right to the profits arising from them, as an encouragement to men to pursue ideas which may produce utility, but this may or may not be done, according to the will and convenience of the society, without claim or complaint from anybody.

Why Should a Colored Man Enlist?

FREDERICK DOUGLASS

*How to lift people out of degradation and despair? Others may provide mate-
rial aid and encouragement, but a case can be made that full success requires
people to stand up for themselves. Few better understood this necessity than
Frederick Douglass (circa 1818–1895), who during the Civil War urged his
fellow black Americans to overcome the degradation of slavery. Shortly after
the Emancipation Proclamation (January 1863), Douglass published a stirring message—"Men of Color, To Arms!"—and worked tirelessly to recruit
soldiers for the black regiment being organized in Massachusetts. Resistance
to the idea that blacks should fight for the Union led him, in April 1863, to
write the article reprinted here. By war's end, there were upwards of 180,000
black troops.*

*Imagine yourself an African-American reader at the time: How would
you respond to Douglass's article? Which of the nine reasons for enlisting
would move you and why? Can these ideas be applied to contemporary problems of degradation and despair?*

This question has been repeatedly put to us while raising men for the 54th
Massachusetts regiment during the past five weeks, and perhaps we cannot at present do a better service to the cause of our people or to the cause
of the country than by giving a few of the many reasons why a colored man
should enlist.

First. You are a man, although a colored man. If you were only a horse or
an ox, incapable of deciding whether the rebels are right or wrong, you would
have no responsibility, and might like the horse or the ox go on eating your
corn or grass, in total indifference, as to which side is victorious or vanquished
in this conflict. You are however no horse, and no ox, but a man, and whatever

concerns man should interest you. He who looks upon a conflict between right and wrong, and does not help the right against the wrong, despises and insults his own nature, and invites the contempt of mankind. As between the North and South, the North is clearly in the right and the South is flagrantly in the wrong. You should therefore, simply as a matter of right and wrong, give your utmost aid to the North. In presence of such a contest there is no neutrality for any man. You are either for the Government or against the Government. Manhood requires you to take sides, and you are mean or noble according to how you choose between action and inaction.—If you are sound in body and mind, there is nothing in your *color* to excuse you from enlisting in the service of the republic against its enemies. If *color* should not be a criterion of rights, neither should it be a standard of duty. The whole duty of a man, belongs alike to white and black.

"A man's a man for a' that."

Second. You are however, not only a man, but an American citizen, so declared by the highest legal adviser of the Government, and you have hitherto expressed in various ways, not only your willingness but your earnest desire to fulfil any and every obligation which the relation of citizenship imposes. Indeed, you have hitherto felt wronged and slighted, because while white men of all other nations have been freely enrolled to serve the country, you a native born citizen have been coldly denied the honor of aiding in defense of the land of your birth. The injustice thus done you is now repented of by the Government and you are welcomed to a place in the army of the nation. Should you refuse to enlist *now*, you will justify the past contempt of the Government towards you and lead it to regret having honored you with a call to take up arms in its defense. You cannot but see that here is a good reason why you should promptly enlist.

Third. A third reason why a colored man should enlist is found in the fact that every Negro-hater and slavery-lover in the land regards the arming of Negroes as a calamity and is doing his best to prevent it. Even now all the weapons of malice, in the shape of slander and ridicule, are used to defeat the filling up of the 54th Massachusetts (colored) regiment. In nine cases out of ten, you will find it safe to do just what your enemy would gladly have you leave undone. What helps you hurts him. Find out what he does not want and give him a plenty of it.

Fourth. You should enlist to learn the use of arms, to become familiar with the means of securing, protecting and defending your own liberty. A day may come when men shall learn war no more, when justice shall be so clearly apprehended, so universally practiced, and humanity shall be so profoundly loved and respected, that war and bloodshed shall be confined only to beasts of prey. Manifestly however, that time has not yet come, and while all men should labor to hasten its coming, by the cultivation of all the elements conducive to peace, it is plain that for the present no race of men can depend wholly upon moral means for the maintenance of their rights. Men must either be governed by love or by fear. They must love to do right or fear to do wrong. The only way open to any race to make their rights respected is to learn how to defend them. When it is seen that black men no more than white men can be enslaved with impunity, men will be less inclined to enslave and oppress them. Enlist therefore, that you may learn the art and assert the ability to defend yourself and your race.

Fifth. You are a member of a long enslaved and despised race. Men have set down your submission to Slavery and insult, to a lack of manly courage. They point to this fact as demonstrating your fitness only to be a servile class. You should enlist and disprove the slander, and wipe out the reproach. When you shall be seen nobly defending the liberties of your own country against rebels and traitors—brass itself will blush to use such arguments imputing cowardice against you.

Sixth. Whether you are or are not, entitled to all the rights of citizenship in this country has long been a matter of dispute to your prejudice. By enlisting in the service of your country at this trial hour, and upholding the National Flag, you stop the mouths of traducers and win applause even from the iron lips of ingratitude. Enlist and you make this your country in common with all other men born in the country or out of it.

Seventh. Enlist for your own sake. Decried and derided as you have been and still are, you need an act of this kind by which to recover your own self-respect. You have to some extent rated your value by the estimate of your enemies and hence have counted yourself less than you are. You owe it to yourself and your race to rise from your social debasement and take your place among the soldiers of your country, a man among men. Depend upon it, the subjective effect of this one act of enlisting will be immense and highly beneficial. You will stand more erect, walk more assured, feel more at ease, and be less liable to insult than you ever were before. He who fights the battles of America may claim America as his country—and have that claim respected. Thus in defending your country now against rebels and traitors you are defending your own liberty, honor, manhood and self-respect.

Eighth. You should enlist because your doing so will be one of the most certain means of preventing the country from drifting back into the whirlpool of Pro-Slavery Compromise at the end of the war, which is now our greatest danger. He who shall witness another Compromise with Slavery in this country will see the free colored man of the North more than ever a victim of the pride, lust, scorn and violence of all classes of white men. The whole North will be but another Detroit, where every white fiend may with impunity revel in unrestrained beastliness towards people of color; they may burn their houses, insult their wives and daughters, and kill indiscriminately. If you mean to live in this country now is the time for you to do your full share in making it a country where you and your children after you can live in comparative safety. Prevent a compromise with the traitors, compel them to come back to the Union whipped and humbled into obedience and all will be well. But let them come back as masters and all their hate and hellish ingenuity will be exerted to stir up the ignorant masses of the North to hate, hinder and persecute the free colored people of the North. That most inhuman of all modern enactments, with its bribed judges, and summary process, the Fugitive Slave Law, with all its infernal train of canting divines, preaching the gospel of kidnapping, as twelve years ago, will be revived against the free colored people of the North. One or two black brigades will do much to prevent all this.

Ninth. You should enlist because the war for the Union, whether men so call it or not, is a war for Emancipation. The salvation of the country, by the inexorable relation of cause and effect, can be secured only by the complete abolition of Slavery. The President has already proclaimed emancipation to the Slaves in the rebel States which is tantamount to declaring Emancipation in all the States, for Slavery must exist everywhere in the South in order to exist anywhere in the South. Can you ask for a more inviting, ennobling and soul enlarging work, than that of making one of the glorious Band who shall carry Liberty to your enslaved people? Remember that identified with the Slave in color, you will have a power that white soldiers have not, to attract them to your lines and induce them to take up arms in a common cause. One black Brigade will, for this work, be worth more than two white ones. Enlist, therefore, enlist without delay, enlist now, and forever put an end to the human barter and butchery which have stained the whole South with the warm blood of your people, and loaded its air with their groans. Enlist, and deserve not only well of your country, and win for yourselves, a name and a place among men, but secure to yourself what is infinitely more precious, the fast dropping tears of gratitude of your kith and kin marked out for destruction, and who are but now ready to perish.

When time's ample curtain shall fall upon our national tragedy, and our hillsides and valleys shall neither redden with the blood nor whiten with the bones of kinsmen and countrymen who have fallen in the sanguinary and wicked strife; when grim visaged war has smoothed his wrinkled front and our country shall have regained its normal condition as a leader of nations in the occupation and blessings of peace—and history shall record the names of heroes and martyrs—who bravely answered the call of patriotism and Liberty—against traitors, thieves and assassins—let it not be said that in the long list of glory, composed of men of all nations—there appears the name of no colored man.

Democracy and Education

BOOKER T. WASHINGTON

Like Frederick Douglass, Booker T. Washington (1856–1915) was a former slave who became a celebrated orator and statesman concerned with overcoming the legacy of slavery. Like Thomas Jefferson, Washington stressed the indispensable importance of education. Highly respected by both blacks and whites, the Tuskegee Institute founder sought to heal the divide between the races and to promote robust and independent citizens, largely by emphasizing the elevating power of basic education. * *This selection, a speech Washington delivered to a white audience at the Brooklyn Institute of Arts and Sciences on September 30, 1896, makes a passionate appeal for education both to raise the floor for degraded Southern blacks—and whites—and to improve the capacity of all Americans for responsible citizenship.*

What kind of education does Washington advocate, and for whom? What are the goals of this education? What does he mean when he suggests that neglecting the fate of the least among us degrades especially those who are strong and prospering? Do you agree? How does Washington's emphasis on Christian brotherhood, self-forgetfulness, and duty compare to Jefferson's more direct focus on the defense of individual liberty? What does Washington mean by "the American standard" by which he thinks all races in America must measure themselves? What is the status of higher education in Washington's thought? Times have changed since the turn of the twentieth century, but America still appears to have a large "underclass," in which gen-

---

* *His critics would later condemn him for his lack of political militancy, as well as for his emphasis on practical (or vocational) and moral—rather than liberal—education. (See, in this connection, the next selection from W. E. B. DuBois.) But Washington held his ground, and never abandoned his vision.*

eration after generation remains badly educated. Is Washington's message still relevant to us today?

It is said that the strongest chain is no stronger than its weakest link. In the Southern part of our country there are twenty-two millions of your brethren who are bound to you by ties which you cannot tear asunder if you would. The most intelligent man in your community has his intelligence darkened by the ignorance of a fellow citizen in the Mississippi bottoms. The most wealthy in your city would be more wealthy but for the poverty of a fellow being in the Carolina rice swamps. The most moral and religious among you has his religion and morality modified by the degradation of the man in the South whose religion is a mere matter of form or emotionalism.

The vote in your state that is cast for the highest and purest form of government is largely neutralized by the vote of the man in Louisiana whose ballot is stolen or cast in ignorance. When the South is poor, you are poor; when the South commits crime, you commit crime. My friends, there is no mistake; you must help us to raise the character of our civilization or yours will be lowered. No member of your race in any part of our country can harm the weakest and meanest member of mine without the proudest and bluest blood in the city of Brooklyn being degraded. The central ideal which I wish you to help me consider is the reaching and lifting up of the lowest, most unfortunate, negative element that occupies so large a proportion of our territory and composes so large a percentage of our population. It seems to me that there never was a time in the history of our country when those interested in education should more earnestly consider to what extent the mere acquiring of a knowledge of literature and science makes producers, lovers of labor, independent, honest, unselfish, and, above all, supremely good. Call education by what name you please, and if it fails to bring about these results among the masses it falls short of its highest end. The science, the art, the literature that fails to reach down and bring the humblest up to the fullest enjoyment of the blessings of our government is weak, no matter how costly the buildings or apparatus used, or how modern the methods in instruction employed. The study of arithmetic that does not result in making someone more honest and self-reliant is defective. The study of history that does not result in making men conscientious in receiving and counting the ballots of their fellow men is most faulty. The study of art that does not result in making the strong less willing to oppress the weak means little. How I wish that from the most humble log cabin schoolhouse in Alabama we could burn it, as it were, into the hearts and heads of all, that usefulness, service to our brother, is the supreme end of education. Putting the thought more directly as it applies to conditions in the South: Can you make your intelligence affect us in the same ratio that our ignorance affects you? Let us put a not improbable case. A great national question is to be decided, one that involves peace or war, the honor or dishonor of our nation—yea, the very existence of the government. The North and West are divided. There are five million votes to be cast in the South, and of this number one half are ignorant. Not only are one half the voters ignorant, but, because of this ignorant vote, corruption, dishonesty in a dozen forms have crept into the exercise of the political franchise, to the extent that the conscience of the intelligent class is soured in its attempts to defeat the will of the ignorant voters. Here, then, on the one hand you have an ignorant vote, and on the other hand an intelligent vote minus a conscience. The time may not be far off when to this kind of jury we shall have to look for the verdict that is to decide the course of our democratic institutions. . . .

With this preliminary survey, let us examine with more care the work to be done in the South before all classes will be fit for the highest duties of citizenship. . . . There are a few things of which I feel certain that furnish a basis for thought and action. . . . I know that wherever our life touches yours we help or hinder; that wherever your life touches ours you make us stronger or weaker. Further I know that almost every other race that tried to look the white man in the face has disappeared. . . . I know that only a few centuries ago in this country we went into slavery pagans: we came out Christians; we went into slavery pieces of property: we came out American citizens; we went into slavery without a language: we came out speaking the proud Anglo-Saxon tongue; we went into slavery with the slave chains clanking about our wrists: we came out with the American ballot in our hands. My friends, I submit it to your sober and candid judgment, if a race that is capable of such a test, such a transformation, is not worth saving and making a part, in reality as well as in name, of our democratic government. It is with an ignorant race as it is with a child: it craves at first the superficial, the ornamental, the signs of progress rather than the reality. The ignorant race is tempted to jump, at one bound, to the position that it has required years of hard struggle for others to reach. It seems to me that the temptation in education and missionary work is to do for a people a thousand miles away without always making a careful study of the needs and conditions of the people whom we are trying to help. The temptation is to run all people through a certain educational mold regardless of the condition of the subject or the end to be accomplished. Unfortunately for us as a race, our education was begun, just after the war, too nearly where New England education ended. We seemed to overlook the fact that we were dealing with a race that has little love for labor in their native land and consequently brought little love for labor with them to America. Added to this was the fact that they had been forced for two hundred and fifty years to labor without compensation under circumstances that were calculated to do anything but teach them the dignity, beauty, and civilizing power of intelligent labor. We forgot the industrial education that was given the Pilgrim Fathers of New England in clearing and planting its cold, bleak, and snowy hills and valleys, in providing shelter, founding the small mills and factories, in supplying themselves with home-made products, thus laying the foundation of an industrial life that now keeps going a large part of the colleges and missionary effort of the world. May I be tempted one step further in showing how prone we are to make our education formal, technical, instead of making it meet the needs of conditions regardless of formality and technicality? At least eighty per cent of my pupils in the South are found in the rural districts, and they are dependent on agriculture in some form for their support. Notwithstanding in this instance we have a whole race depending upon agriculture, and notwithstanding thirty years have passed since our freedom, aside from what we have done at Hampton and Tuskegee and one or two other institutions, not a thing has been attempted by state or philanthropy in the way of educating the race in this industry on which their very existence depends. Boys have been taken from the farms and educated in law, theology, Hebrew, and Greek—educated in everything else but the very subject they should know the most about. . . . Some time ago when we decided to make tailoring a part of our training at the Tuskegee Institute, I was amazed to find that it was almost impossible to find in the whole country an educated colored man who could teach the making of clothing. I could find them by the score who could teach astronomy, theology, Greek, or Latin, but almost none who could instruct in the making of clothing, something that has to be used by every one of us every day in the year. How often has my heart been made to sink as I have gone through the South and into the homes of the people and found women who could converse intelligently on Grecian history, who had studied geometry, could analyze the most complex sentences, and yet could not analyze the poorly cooked and still more poorly served bread and fat meat that they and their families were eating three times a day. . . . A short time ago, in one of our Southern cities, a colored man died who had received training as a skilled mechanic during the days of slavery. By his skill and industry he had built up a great business as a house contractor and builder. In this same city there are thirty-five thousand colored people, among them young men who have been well educated in languages and literature, but not a single one could be found who had been trained in architectural and mechanical drawing that could carry on the business which this ex-slave had built up, and so it was soon scattered to the wind. Aside from the work done in the institutions that I have mentioned, you will find no colored men who have been trained in the principles of architecture, notwithstanding the vast majority of the race is without homes. Here, then, are the three prime conditions for growth, for civilization—food, clothing, shelter—yet we have been the slaves of form and custom to such an extent that we have failed in a large measure to look matters squarely in the face and meet actual needs. . . . Understand, I speak in no fault-finding spirit, but with a feeling of deep regret for what has been done; but the future must be an improvement on the past.

I have endeavored to speak plainly in regard to the past, because I fear that the wisest and most interested have not fully comprehended the task which American slavery has laid at the doors of the Republic. Few, I fear, realize what is to be done before the seven million of my people in the South can be made a safe, helpful, progressive part of our institutions. The South, in proportion to its ability, has done well, but this does not change facts. Let me illustrate what I mean by a single example. In spite of all that has been done, I was in a county in Alabama a few days ago where there are some thirty thousand colored people and about seven thousand whites; in this county not a single public school for Negroes has been open this year longer than three months, not a single colored teacher has been paid more than fifteen dollars a month for his teaching. Not one of these schools was taught in a building worthy of the name of schoolhouse. In this county the state or public authorities do not own a dollar's worth of school property—not a schoolhouse, a blackboard, or a piece of crayon. Each colored child had spent on him this year for his education about fifty cents, while one of your children had spent on him this year for education not far from twenty dollars. And yet each citizen of this county is expected to share the burdens and privileges of our democratic form of government just as intelligently and conscientiously as the citizens of your beloved Kings County. A vote in this county means as much to the nation as a vote in the city of Boston. . . .

I have referred to industrial education as a means of fitting the millions of my people in the South for the duties of citizenship. Until there is industrial independence it is hardly possible to have a pure ballot. In the country districts of the Gulf states it is safe to say that not more than one black man in twenty owns the land he cultivates. Where so large a proportion of the people are dependent, live in other people's houses, eat other people's food, and wear clothes they have not paid for, it is a pretty hard thing to tell how they are going to vote. My remarks thus far have referred mainly to my own race. But there is another side. The longer I live and the more I study the question, the more I am convinced that it is not so much a problem as to what you will do with the Negro as what the Negro will do with you and your civilization. In considering this side of the subject, I thank God that I have grown to the point where

I can sympathize with a white man as much as I can sympathize with a black man. I have grown to the point where I can sympathize with a Southern white man as much as I can sympathize with a Northern white man. To me "a man's a man for a' that and a' that." As bearing upon democracy and education, what of your white brethren in the South, those who suffered and are still suffering the consequences of American slavery for which both you and they are responsible? You of the great and prosperous North still owe to your unfortunate brethren of the Caucasian race in the South, not less than to yourselves, a serious and uncompleted duty. What was the task you asked them to perform? Returning to their destitute homes after years of war to face blasted hopes, devastation, a shattered industrial system, you asked them to add to their own burdens that of preparing in education, politics, and economics in a few short years, for citizenship, four millions of former slaves. That the South, staggering under the burden, made blunders, and that in a measure there has been disappointment, no one need be surprised.

The educators, the statesmen, the philanthropists have never comprehended their duty toward the millions of poor whites in the South who were buffeted for two hundred years between slavery and freedom, between civilization and degradation, who were disregarded by both master and slave. It needs no prophet to tell the character of our future civilization when the poor white boy in the country districts of the South receives one dollar's worth of education and your boy twenty dollars' worth, when one never enters a library or reading room and the other has libraries and reading rooms in every ward and town. When one hears lectures and sermons once in two months and the other can hear a lecture or sermon every day in the year. When you help the South you help yourselves. Mere abuse will not bring the remedy. The time has come, it seems to me, when in this matter we should rise above party or race or sectionalism into the region of duty of man to man, citizen to citizen, Christian to Christian, and if the Negro who has been oppressed and denied rights in a Christian land can help you North and South to rise, can be the medium of your rising into this atmosphere of generous Christian brotherhood and self-forgetfulness, he will see in it a recompense for all that he has suffered in the past. Not very long ago a white citizen of the South boastingly expressed himself in public to this effect: "I am now forty-six years of age, but have never polished my own boots, have never saddled my own horse, have never built a fire in my own room, have never hitched a horse." He was asked a short time since by a lame man to hitch his horse, but refused and told him to get a Negro to do it. . . . I pity from the bottom of my heart any of God's creatures whence such a statement can emanate. Evidently here is a man who, as far as mere book training is concerned, is educated . . . but, so far as the real purpose of education is concerned—the making of men useful, honest, and liberal—this man has never been touched. . . . My friends, can we make our education reach down far enough to touch and help this man? Can we so control science, art, and literature as to make them to such an extent a means rather than an end; that the lowest and most unfortunate of God's creatures shall be lifted up, ennobled and glorified; shall be a freeman instead of a slave of narrow sympathies and wrong customs? Some years ago a bright young man of my race succeeded in passing a competitive examination for a cadetship at the United States naval academy at Annapolis. Says the young man, Mr. Henry Baker, in describing his stay at this institution: "I was several times attacked with stones and was forced finally to appeal to the officers, when a marine was detailed to accompany me across the campus and from the mess hall at meal times. My books were mutilated, my clothes were cut and in some instances destroyed, and all the petty annoyances which ingenuity could devise were inflicted upon me daily, and during seamanship practice aboard the *Dale* attempts were often made to do me personal injury while I would be aloft in the rigging. No one ever addressed me by name. I was called the Moke usually, the Nigger for variety. I was shunned as if I were a veritable leper and received curses and blows as the only method my persecutors had of relieving the monotony." Not once during the two years, with one exception, did any one of the more than four hundred cadets enrolled ever come to him with a word of advice, counsel, sympathy, or information, and he never held conversation with any one of them for as much as five minutes during the whole course of his experience at the academy, except on occasions when he was defending himself against their assaults. The one exception where the departure from the rule was made was in the case of a Pennsylvania boy, who stealthily brought him a piece of his birthday cake at twelve o' clock one night. The act so surprised Baker that his suspicions were aroused, but these were dispelled by the donor, who read to him a letter which he had received from his mother, from whom the cake came, in which she requested that a slice be given to the colored cadet who was without friends. I recite this incident and not for the purpose merely of condemning the wrong done a member of my race; no, no, not that. I mention the case, not for the one cadet, but for the sake of the four hundred cadets, for the sake of the four hundred American families, the four hundred American communities whose civilization and Christianity these cadets represented. Here were four hundred and more picked young men representing the flower of our country, who had passed through our common schools and were preparing themselves at public expense to defend the honor of our country. And yet, with grammar, reading, and arithmetic in the public schools, and with lessons in the arts of war, the principles of physical courage at Annapolis, both systems seemed to have utterly failed to prepare a single one of these young men for real life, that he could be brave enough, Christian enough, American enough, to take this poor defenseless black boy by the hand in open daylight and let the world know that he was his friend. Education, whether of black man or white man, that gives one physical courage to stand in front of the cannon and fails to give him moral courage to stand up in defense of right and justice is a failure. With all that the Brooklyn Institute of Arts and Sciences stands for in its equipment, its endowment, its wealth and culture, its instructors, can it produce a mother that will produce a boy that will not be ashamed to have the world know that he is a friend to the most unfortunate of God's creatures? Not long ago a mother, a black mother, who lived in one of your Northern states, had heard it whispered around in her community for years that the Negro was lazy, shiftless, and would not work. So when her boy grew to sufficient size, at considerable expense and great self-sacrifice, she had her boy thoroughly taught the machinist's trade. A job was secured in a neighboring shop. With dinner bucket in hand and spurred on by the prayers of the now happy mother, the boy entered the shop to begin his first day's work. What happened? Had any one of the twenty white Americans been so educated that he gave this stranger a welcome into their midst? No, not this. Every one of the twenty white men threw down his tools and deliberately walked out, swearing that he would not give a black man an opportunity to earn an honest living. Another shop was tried, with the same result, and still another and the same. Today this promising and ambitious black man is a wreck—a confirmed drunkard, with no hope, no ambition. My friends, who blasted the life of this young man? On whose hands does his blood rest? Our system of education, or want of education, is responsible. Can our public schools and colleges turn out a set of men that will throw open the doors of industry to all men everywhere, regardless of color, so all shall have the same opportunity to earn a dollar that they now have to spend a dollar? I know a good many species of cowardice and prejudice, but I know none equal to this. I know not who is the worst, the ex-slaveholder who perforce compelled his slave to work without compensation, or the man who perforce compels the Negro to refrain from working for compensation. My friends, we are one in this country. The question of the highest citizenship and the complete education of all concerns nearly ten million of my own people and over sixty million of yours. We rise as you rise; when we fall you fall. When you are strong we are strong; when we are weak you are weak. There is no power that can separate our destiny. The Negro can afford to be wronged; the white man cannot afford to wrong him. Unjust laws or customs that exist in many places regarding the races injure the white man and inconvenience the Negro. No race can wrong another race simply because it has the power to do so without being permanently injured in morals. The Negro can endure the temporary inconvenience, but the injury to the white man is permanent. It is for the white man to save himself from his degradation that I plead. If a white man steals a Negro's ballot it is the white man who is permanently injured. Physical death comes to the one Negro lynched in a county, but death of the morals—death of the soul—comes to the thousands responsible for the lynching. We are a patient, humble people. We can afford to work and wait. There is plenty in this country for us to do. Away up in the atmosphere of goodness, forbearance, patience, long-suffering, and forgiveness the workers are not many or overcrowded. If others would be little we can be great. If others would be mean we can be good. If others would push us down we can help push them up. Character, not circumstances, makes the man. It is more important that we be prepared for voting than that we vote, more important that we be prepared to hold office than that we hold office, more important that we be prepared for the highest recognition than that we be recognized. Those who fought and died on the battlefield performed their duty heroically and well, but a duty remains for you and me. The mere fiat of law could not make an ignorant voter an intelligent voter; could not make one citizen respect another; these results come to the Negro, as to all races, by beginning at the bottom and working up to the highest civilization and accomplishment. In the economy of God, there can be but one standard by which an individual can succeed—there is but one for a race. This country demands that every race measure itself by the American standard. By it a race must rise or fall, succeed or fail, and in the last analysis mere sentiment counts but little. During the next half-century and more my race must continue passing through the severe American crucible.

We are to be tested in our patience, in our forbearance, our power to endure wrong, to withstand temptation, to succeed, to acquire and use skill, our ability to compete, to succeed in commerce; to disregard the superficial for the real, the appearance for the substance; to be great and yet the servant of all. This, this is the passport to all that is best in the life of our republic, and the Negro must possess it or be debarred. In working out our destiny, while the main burden and center of activity must be with us, we shall need in a large measure the help, the encouragement, the guidance that the strong can give the weak. Thus helped, we of both races in the South shall soon throw off the shackles of racial and sectional prejudice and rise above the clouds of ignorance, narrowness, and selfishness into that atmosphere, that pure sunshine, where it will be our highest ambition to serve man, our brother, regardless of race or past conditions.

The Talented Tenth

W. E. B. DuBois

In this essay (1903), W. E. B. DuBois (1868–1963), educator, author, and civil-rights activist, vigorously advocates higher education for the best and brightest. The select few whom Jefferson called "natural aristocrats" DuBois calls "the talented tenth." Whereas Booker T. Washington believes that culture begins in the soil with agriculture and laboriously works its way upward, DuBois posits an aristocratic foundation for culture: "It is, ever was, and ever will be from the top downward that culture filters. The Talented Tenth rises and pulls all that are worth the saving up to their vantage ground. This is the history of human progress."*

How does DuBois understand the relation between education and democracy? What is the aim of education? What does DuBois mean in saying that "the object of all true education is not to make men carpenters, it is to make carpenters men"? Would Washington disagree? What are the points of agreement and disagreement among Jefferson, Washington, and DuBois? Is DuBois right that higher education for a few must come first and that all lower levels of education depend on the higher levels? In our own day, when

---

* DuBois here justifies his focus on educating the talented tenth by stressing how they will elevate the masses, but in other writings he describes education as a good that transcends its political usefulness. He gives a beautiful account of the quest engaged in by a "sovereign human soul that seeks to know itself and the world about it," thereby recognizing the power of education not only to "lift the floor" but also to "elevate the ceiling" of human well-being:

> *I sit with Shakespeare and he winces not. Across the color-line I move arm in arm with Balzac and Dumas, where smiling men and welcoming women glide in gilded halls. From out the caves of evening that swing between the strong-limbed earth and the tracery of the stars, I summon Aristotle and Aurelius and what soul I will, and they come all graciously with no scorn nor condescension. So, wed with Truth, I dwell above the Veil.*

college education has become broadly available, is the notion of a "talented tenth" obsolete or offensive? Do we pay sufficient attention to the education of the talented tenth? How would we identify "the talented tenth"? What education can reliably generate "leaders of thought and missionaries of culture"? What role do teachers play?

The Negro race, like all races, is going to be saved by its exceptional men. The problem of education, then, among Negroes must first of all deal with the Talented Tenth; it is the problem of developing the Best of this race that they may guide the Mass away from the contamination and death of the Worst, in their own and other races. Now the training of men is a difficult and intricate task. Its technique is a matter for educational experts, but its object is for the vision of seers. If we make money the object of man-training, we shall develop money-makers but not necessarily men; if we make technical skill the object of education, we may possess artisans but not, in nature, men. Men we shall have only as we make manhood the object of the work of the schools— intelligence, broad sympathy, knowledge of the world that was and is, and of the relation of men to it—this is the curriculum of that Higher Education which must underlie true life. On this foundation we may build bread winning, skill of hand and quickness of brain, with never a fear lest the child and man mistake the means of living for the object of life.

If this be true—and who can deny it—three tasks lay before me; first to show from the past that the Talented Tenth as they have risen among American Negroes have been worthy of leadership; secondly, to show how these men may be educated and developed; and thirdly, to show their relation to the Negro problem.

You misjudge us because you do not know us. From the very first it has been the educated and intelligent of the Negro people that have led and elevated the mass, and the sole obstacles that nullified and retarded their efforts were slavery and race prejudice; for what is slavery but the legalized survival of the unfit and the nullification of the work of natural internal leadership? Negro leadership, therefore, sought from the first to rid the race of this awful incubus. . . . In colonial days came Phillis Wheatley and Paul Cuffe striving against the bars of prejudice; and Benjamin Banneker, the almanac maker, voiced their longings when he said to Thomas Jefferson, . . . "Suffer me to recall to your mind that time, in which the arms of the British crown were exerted with every powerful effort, in order to reduce you to a state of servitude. . . . This, sir, was a time when you clearly saw into the injustice of a state of Slavery, and in which you had just apprehensions of the horrors of its condition. It was then that your abhorrence thereof was so excited, that you publicly held forth this true and invaluable doctrine, which is worthy to be recorded and remembered in all succeeding ages: 'We hold these truths to be self evident, that all men are created equal; that they are endowed with certain inalienable rights, and that among these are life, liberty and the pursuit of happiness.'" . . .

These and others we may call the Revolutionary group of distinguished Negroes—they were persons of marked ability, leaders of a Talented Tenth, standing conspicuously among the best of their time. They strove by word and deed to save the color line from becoming the line between the bond and free, but all they could do was nullified by Eli Whitney and the Curse of Gold. So they passed into forgetfulness.

But their spirit did not wholly die; here and there in the early part of the century came other exceptional men. Some were natural sons of unnatural fathers and were given often a liberal training and thus a race of educated mulattoes sprang up to plead for black men's rights. There was Ira Aldridge, whom all Europe loved to honor; there was that Voice crying in the Wilderness, David Walker. . . .

This was the wild voice that first aroused Southern legislators in 1829 to the terrors of abolitionism. . . .

Too little notice has been taken of the work which the Talented Tenth among Negroes took in the great abolition crusade. From the very day that a Philadelphia colored man became the first subscriber to Garrison's "Liberator," to the day when Negro soldiers made the Emancipation Proclamation possible, black leaders worked shoulder to shoulder with white men in a movement, the success of which would have been impossible without them. There was Purvis and Remond, Pennington and Highland Garnett, Sojourner Truth and Alexander Crummell, and above all, Frederick Douglass—what would the abolition movement have been without them? They stood as living examples of the possibilities of the Negro race . . . —they were the men who made American slavery impossible. . . .

Where were these black abolitionists trained? Some, like Frederick Douglass, were self-trained, but yet trained liberally; others, like Alexander Crummell and McCune Smith, graduated from famous foreign universities. Most of them rose up through the colored schools of New York and Philadelphia and Boston, taught by college-bred men. . . .

After emancipation came a new group of educated and gifted leaders: Langston, Bruce and Elliot, Greener, Williams and Payne. Through political organization, historical and polemic writing and moral regeneration, these men strove to uplift their people. It is the fashion of to-day to sneer at them and to say that with freedom Negro leadership should have begun at the plow and not in the Senate—a foolish and mischievous lie; two hundred and fifty years that black serf toiled at the plow and yet that toiling was in vain till the Senate passed the war amendments; and two hundred and fifty years more the half-free serf of to-day may toil at his plow, but unless he have political rights and righteously guarded civic status, he will still remain the poverty-stricken and ignorant plaything of rascals, that he now is. This all sane men know even if they dare not say it.

And so we come to the present—a day of cowardice and vacillation, of strident wide-voiced wrong and faint hearted compromise; of double-faced dallying with Truth and Right. Who are to-day guiding the work of the Negro people? The "exceptions" of course. And yet so sure as this Talented Tenth is pointed out, the blind worshippers of the Average cry out in alarm: "These are exceptions, look here at death, disease and crime—these are the happy rule." Of course they are the rule, because a silly nation made them the rule: Because for three long centuries this people lynched Negroes who dared to be brave, raped black women who dared to be virtuous, crushed dark-hued youth who dared to be ambitious, and encouraged and made to flourish servility and lewdness and apathy. But not even this was able to crush all manhood and chastity and aspiration from black folk. A saving remnant continually survives and persists, continually aspires, continually shows itself in thrift and ability and character. Exceptional it is to be sure, but this is its chiefest promise; it shows the capability of Negro blood, the promise of black men. . . .

Can the masses of the Negro people be in any possible way more quickly raised than by the effort and example of this aristocracy of talent and character? Was there ever a nation on God's fair earth civilized from the bottom upward? Never; it is, ever was and ever will be from the top downward that culture filters. The Talented Tenth rises and pulls all that are worth the saving up to their vantage ground. This is the history of human progress; and the two historic mistakes which have hindered that progress were the thinking first that no more could ever rise save the few already risen; or second, that it would better the unrisen to pull the risen down.

How then shall the leaders of a struggling people be trained and the hands of the risen few strengthened? There can be but one answer: The best and most capable of their youth must be schooled in the colleges and universities of the land. . . . A university is a human invention for the transmission of knowledge and culture from generation to generation, through the training of quick minds and pure hearts, and for this work no other human invention will suffice, not even trade and industrial schools.

All men cannot go to college but some men must; every isolated group or nation must have its yeast, must have for the talented few centers of training where men are not so mystified and befuddled by the hard and necessary toil of earning a living, as to have no aims higher than their bellies, and no God greater than Gold. This is true training, and thus in the beginning were the favored sons of the freedmen trained. . . . Where ought they to have begun to build? At the bottom, of course, quibbles the mole with his eyes in the earth. Aye! truly at the bottom, at the very bottom; at the bottom of knowledge, down in the very depths of knowledge there where the roots of justice strike into the lowest soil of Truth. And so they did begin; they founded colleges, and up from the colleges shot normal schools, and out from the normal schools went teachers, and around the normal teachers clustered other teachers to teach the public schools; the college trained in Greek and Latin and mathematics, 2,000 men; and these men trained full 50,000 others in morals and manners, and they in turn taught thrift and the alphabet to nine millions of men, who to-day hold $300,000,000 of property. It was a miracle—the most wonderful peace-battle of the 19th century, and yet to-day men smile at it, and in fine superiority tell us that it was all a strange mistake; that a proper way to found a system of education is first to gather the children and buy them spelling books and hoes; afterward men may look about for teachers, if haply they may find them; or again they would teach men Work, but as for Life—why, what has Work to do with Life, they ask vacantly. . . .

It has, however, been in the furnishing of teachers that the Negro college has found its peculiar function. Few persons realize how vast a work, how mighty a revolution has been thus accomplished. To furnish five millions and more of ignorant people with teachers of their own race and blood, in one generation, was not only a very difficult undertaking, but a very important one, in that, it placed before the eyes of almost every Negro child an attainable ideal. It brought the masses of the blacks in contact with modern civilization, made black men the leaders of their communities and trainers of the new generation. In this work college-bred Negroes were first teachers, and then teachers of teachers. And here it is that the broad culture of college work has been of peculiar value. Knowledge of life and its wider meaning, has been the point of the Negro's deepest ignorance, and the sending out of teachers whose training has not been simply for bread winning, but also for human culture, has been of inestimable value in the training of these men. . . .

The problem of training the Negro is to-day immensely complicated by the fact that the whole question of the efficiency and appropriateness of our present systems of education, for any kind of child, is a matter of active debate, in which final settlement seems still afar off. Consequently it often happens that persons arguing for or against certain systems of education for Negroes, have these controversies in mind and miss the real question at issue. The main question, so far as the Southern Negro is concerned, is: What under the present circumstance, must a system of education do in order to raise the Negro as quickly as possible in the scale of civilization? The answer to this question seems to me clear: It must strengthen the Negro's character, increase his knowledge and teach him to earn a living. Now it goes without saying, that it is hard to do all these things simultaneously or suddenly, and that at the same time it will not do to give all the attention to one and neglect the others; we could give black boys trades, but that alone will not civilize a race of ex-slaves; we might simply increase their knowledge of the world, but this would not necessarily make them wish to use this knowledge honestly; we might seek to strengthen character and purpose, but to what end if this people have nothing to eat or to wear? A system of education is not one thing, nor does it have a single definite object, nor is it a mere matter of schools. Education is that whole system of human training within and without the school house walls, which molds and develops men. If then we start out to train an ignorant and unskilled people with a heritage of bad habits, our system of training must set before itself two great aims—the one dealing with knowledge and character, the other part seeking to give the child the technical knowledge necessary for him to earn a living under the present circumstances. These objects are accomplished in part by the opening of the common schools on the one, and of the industrial schools on the other. But only in part, for there must also be trained those who are to teach these schools—men and women of knowledge and culture and technical skill who understand modern civilization, and have the training and aptitude to impart it to the children under them. There must be teachers, and teachers of teachers, and to attempt to establish any sort of a system of common and industrial school training, without *first* (and I say *first* advisedly) without *first* providing for the higher training of the very best teachers, is simply throwing your money to the winds. School houses do not teach themselves—piles of brick and mortar and machinery do not send out *men*. It is the trained, living human soul, cultivated and strengthened by long study and thought, that breathes the real breath of life into boys and girls and makes them human, whether they be black or white, Greek, Russian or American. Nothing, in these latter days, has so dampened the faith of thinking Negroes in recent educational movements, as the fact that such movements have been accompanied by ridicule and denouncement and decrying of those very institutions of higher training which made the Negro public school possible, and make Negro industrial schools thinkable. It was Fisk, Atlanta, Howard and Straight, those colleges born of the faith and sacrifice of the abolitionists, that placed in the black schools of the South the 30,000 teachers and more, which some, who depreciate the work of these higher schools, are using to teach their own new experiments. If Hampton, Tuskegee and the hundred other industrial schools prove in the future to be as successful as they deserve to be, then their success in training black artisans for the South, will be due primarily to the white colleges of the North and the black colleges of the South, which trained the teachers who to-day conduct these institutions. . . .

I would not deny, or for a moment seem to deny, the paramount necessity of teaching the Negro to work, and to work steadily and skillfully; or seem to depreciate in the slightest degree the important part industrial schools must play in the accomplishment of these ends, but I *do* say, and insist upon it, that it is industrialism drunk with its vision of success, to imagine that its own work can be accomplished without providing for the training of broadly cultured men and women to teach its own teachers, and to teach the teachers of the public schools.

But I have already said that human education is not simply a matter of schools; it is much more a matter of family and group life—the training of one's home, of one's daily companions, of one's social class. Now the black boy of the South moves in a black world—a world with its own leaders, its own thoughts, its own ideals. In this world he gets by far the larger part of his life training, and through the eyes of this dark world he peers into the veiled world beyond. Who guides and determines the education which he receives in his world? His teachers here are the group-leaders of the Negro people— the physicians and clergymen, the trained fathers and mothers, the influential and forceful men about him of all kinds; here it is, if at all, that the culture of the surrounding world trickles through and is handed on by the graduates of the higher schools. Can such culture training of group leaders be neglected? Can we afford to ignore it? Do you think that if the leaders of thought among Negroes are not trained and educated thinkers, that they will have no leaders? On the contrary a hundred half-trained demagogues will still hold the places they so largely occupy now, and hundreds of vociferous busy-bodies will multiply. You have no choice; either you must help furnish this race from within its own ranks with thoughtful men of trained leadership, or you must suffer the evil consequences of a headless misguided rabble.

I am an earnest advocate of manual training and trade teaching for black boys, and for white boys, too. I believe that next to the founding of Negro colleges the most valuable addition to Negro education since the war, has been industrial training for black boys. Nevertheless, I insist that the object of all true education is not to make men carpenters, it is to make carpenters men; there are two means of making the carpenter a man, each equally important: the first is to give the group and community in which he works, liberally trained teachers and leaders to teach him and his family what life means; the second is to give him sufficient intelligence and technical skill to make him an efficient workman; the first object demands the Negro college and college-bred men—not a quantity of such colleges, but a few of excellent quality; not too many college-bred men, but enough to leaven the lump, to inspire the masses, to raise the Talented Tenth to leadership; the second object demands a good system of common schools, well-taught, conveniently located and properly equipped. . . .

Men of America, the problem is plain before you. Here is a race transplanted through the criminal foolishness of your fathers. Whether you like it or not the millions are here, and here they will remain. If you do not lift them up, they will pull you down. Education and work are the levers to uplift a people. Work alone will not do it unless inspired by the right ideals and guided by intelligence. Education must not simply teach work—it must teach Life. The Talented Tenth of the Negro race must be made leaders of thought and missionaries of culture among their people. No others can do this work and Negro colleges must train men for it. The Negro race, like all other races, is going to be saved by its exceptional men.

He Who Spits at the Sky

WALLACE STEGNER

Prominent among the goals of civic life, especially on the progressive agenda, is the elimination of racism, discrimination, and inequity. Public campaigns to address these evils often mobilize individuals to identify themselves as parts of disadvantaged groups and to use group solidarity to secure their rights. Yet such "identity politics" must contend with the differences among individuals and their desires for purely personal happiness. At the same time, reform efforts may suffer if groups celebrate only their sociocultural distinctiveness and tribal loyalties become too strong.

In this story (1958), Wallace Stegner (1909–1993) explores these complications to social reform. Three Mexican American teenagers, jailed for a murder they did not commit, are released owing to the efforts of a committee of white progressives. At a party celebrating their release, one of the boys contemplates a new life away from Los Angeles, but the committee organizer insists that he remain part of a political movement to "make sure no such atmosphere of prejudice and race hatred ever gets created again. . . . We've got to organize the Mexican community . . . and you three are our strongest cards. If you run out, you weaken our hand." The party and the political agenda unravel, however, as a result of drink, erotic jealousies, wounded pride, and gang solidarity.

What can we learn from this story about social reform efforts that treat people primarily as members of vulnerable groups, without regard to their personal differences or individual aspirations? In the face of persistent discrimination, can individuals realize their aspirations without the help of reform movements that depend on identity politics? What happens if a group's attachment to values of honor, loyalty, and the avenging of disrespect gets in the way of its assimilation into the society informed by the American creed? Can efforts to lift the floor for our fellow citizens succeed when many people seem to act against their own best interests? What does it mean to "spit at the sky"? Who are the spitters in this story?

I had some pictures to take of the opening of a neighborhood house down by Exposition Park, and it was nearly ten before I got back to Hollywood. I had never been to Mazur's house. The address Carol had given me was on a cross street just off Franklin. As I parked and walked in, away from the snarl and slash of traffic, the quiet of a dark pocketed neighborhood closed around me. The air was damp and soft, as if it should smell of flowers, but I had such a thick head cold I could hardly breathe, much less smell the scented evening air of the city of the angels. If you want to know how I was feeling, press your face down into a tub of modeling clay and inhale.

The Mazur house turned out to be a sort of Frank Lloyd Wright prairie-style bungalow with Bauhaus extras. The picture window in front, showing fluted drapes glowing from the light inside, was obviously part of a remodeling job. So was the dim glass room that reached out along the side and threw the shadows of big cut-leaf philodendrons onto the lawn. A spotlight burned from under the low eaves into a flaming eucalyptus tree.

I heard voices through the door—pretty loud voices—but if it occurred to me that it was bad tactics to bring the Red Car kids straight out of San Quentin into a binge, I would have thought it Mazur's lookout, or the committee's. I was a spectator; I only took the pictures. It was 1946; I was just out of the army; I was a photographer for the Russell Foundation only while I waited for something better to turn up. If I had already stayed longer than I had expected to, that was Carol's doing—don't get the idea that I was either dedicated or involved. Juvenile delinquents, Mexican or otherwise, never appealed to me that much as a way of life. I was a professional photographer, Mr. Cool from up the coulee, in perfect health except for an infected frontal sinus, and my principal feeling as I stood on the Mazur doorstep was a hope that things would break up early and let me get home to bed. I found the Benzedrine inhaler in my pocket and dragged at it four or five times, until on the last drag the top of my head chilled suddenly as air came through. Then I replaced the cap and pushed my thumb against the doorbell. Nothing happened. I pushed it again.

This time steps—high heels—the bump of somebody running into something, an exclamation, the smash of breaking glass. I waited. After quite a pause the door opened, and I looked down on the platinum head of Debbie Mazur. She had reached up to open the door while she squatted by the puddle of her spilled drink. Some of her hair had come loose across her forehead.

"Goddamn," she said, brooding over the starlike puddle on the hardwood. She dabbed at her dress, pulled herself up by the doorknob and leaned against the door's edge and laughed in a soft four-highball sort of way.

"Hi," she said. "I know you."

It was true, she did. She inspected me. "You're Charlie Prescott, and we've been waiting for you. In a pig's eye. Come in."

She did not get out of the way but leaned in the opening, looking at me. "Oh, *Carol!*" she called without turning around. Her blue eyes were wide and innocent and by no means so dumb as they sometimes tried to look. She giggled. "I'm the girl that licked all the envelopes," she said. "They're giving me a Carnegie medal. Oh, *Carol!*"

She moved perhaps four inches and opened the door perhaps six. Her eyes took in my camera bag. "What've you been doing? Working? This late? You look like a goddamn doctor come to deliver the twins." Disdainfully she kicked a fragment of glass across the hall. "Well, come in, come in, get a drink and shake the collective hand. This is a celebration. Virtue has triumphed, and sin is crushed to earth."

She still didn't move back, but I squeezed through and stepped across the puddle of glass and whiskey. It wasn't quite clear to me whether she was keeping the door half closed because of noise and the neighbors or because she wanted me to rub up against her. This last I couldn't help. I got a blast of bourbon and perfume, the glance of an amused blue eye, and a satisfactory glimpse of a plunging neckline where Mrs. Mazur's obvious talents surged up under a froth of lace. Down below somewhere she must have been propped up like an overburdened fruit tree.

"I see," I said (which was true).

Carol came out of the smoke and noise of the living room, and Debbie Mazur shut the door. Twiddling her fingers in farewell, intensely energetic, dressed for a calendar picture, she departed, saying, "Make yourself at home. I got to get a rag, I guess." I put the camera bag behind the door.

"Ah, Charlie," Carol said. "I ought to be kicked for letting you do that job alone. How's your poor cold?"

"Just like id souds." The inhaler had given me ninety secoñds of relief; I was as thick again as a sock full of sand.

She reached up and pecked my cheek with a kiss. "Look oudt!" I said. "You'll *get* it, for hell's sake."

Just at that moment Debbie Mazur appeared at the far end of the hall. "Ah, ah!" she said, and vanished again, flapping a tea towel.

"What was that?" I said. "Edvy?"

"Edvy," Carol said. "Cub od id."

Several partitions of the old bungalow must have been knocked out to make the big room we entered. From one side of it, steps went down into the glass solarium; at the far end, double doors opened into a booklined study. The lights were spots and floods mounted on the walls to throw melodramatic blobs and ovals of brightness against the ceiling. Everybody was in a circle like Boy Scouts at a camporee.

We swam upstream against the voices until they paused and Guy Mazur stood up to reach across chairs and heads to shake hands. You have seen his type often enough, but hardly ever so perfect. He had the tanned skin and light-metal hair of the gracefully middle-aged Southern California demigod. I could imagine him in his earlier years, taking perfect back dives at the Coral Casino, or (for a gag, without losing his dignity) doing handstands and human pyramids with the acrobats and weight lifters on Muscle Beach. Maybe he was that *mens sana in corpore sano* you hear about. Certainly the single word that most described him was "confidence"; he had the air of being utterly at ease while others watched. His voice was a bassoon that played the scales of conviction; it wooed and reconciled and persuaded and reassured. His handshake told you that he was your friend, truly your friend, and that he would always be there when you needed him, but would not push himself forward with a lot of insincere protestations. He was a lawyer associated, in some way I never quite understood, with one of the studios, but he must have given half his time to betterment committees. The campaign that freed the Red Car boys was his initiative from beginning to end; he was much in the papers; his name appeared on the letterheads of two dozen good causes.

"Charlie, my friend!" he said with crinkling eyes. "Glad you got here. This is a great day. We doed it, boy, we doed it."

"Thanks to you," I said.

"Thanks to a hell of a good committee. They can all take a deep, deep bow, no kidding. You know everybody?"

I didn't, but it was easier to pretend I did. I shook some hands, waved at some people. Some I recognized: Jean Gauss, a radio sob sister, homely, freckled like a thrush; Pete Welling, a scriptwriter from MGM; a lawyer named Nemerov; a couple of church do-gooders; a graduate student from UCLA; some old-time radicals who looked as if they had done time with Debs. There were about a dozen of them, densely circled and deeply talkative, with glasses in their hands, and among them, oil trying its best to mix with water, looking grateful and trapped, were the Red Car boys and their chicks. The girls were as expected—little still-faced *pachucas* in tight skirts and high pompadours, wearing adjustable smiles. But the boys were changed from the last time I had seen them. San Quentin had sent them home without their drapes and their ducktails, and they looked like anybody's teenagers, not the baby gangsters, tea pushers, and knife-wielding zoot-suiters that the newspapers used to foam about.

Guy Mazur let himself back into the sofa with a comradely hand on the shoulder of Dago Aguirre, while Dago, angel-faced and deer-eyed, saluted me with a raised can of beer. Then he half stood up and stretched a long way to shake hands. "*Ese,* Señor Pictures." I waved at Chuey Bernal, out of reach on the other side. Chuey snapped to his feet, bowed stiffly three times. "Greetings, sir," he said. "*Hórale, jefe, hórale.* Good evening. Hello." He collapsed. From his cousin Lupe I got a sidelong smile *provocativo*; she was one of the prettiest, one I had photographed a good deal on the theory that if you are photographing Mexican poverty and social disruption, you may as well photograph it in a shape you would like to take to the movies. Away across the circle, outside of it really, Pepe Garcia was hunched confidentially close to a *pachuca* in a fringed skirt. From him I had what was his closest approach to a greeting—a backward jerk of the head, a thin smile, a glitter as black and expressionless as light flaking off a pair of obsidian chips. He had a high Aztec nose, a bladed face, and he was built long and limber, with a flexed look, a whiplike tension. I have seen a few boxers like that, middleweights at six feet one, with long arms and fast hands.

"I don't think you know all the girls," Carol was saying. "With Dago, that's Luz Esposito. Lupe you know. And with Pepe, that's Angelina Flores." Nods, smiles, salutes. Luz gave me an open, friendly stare, and Lupe wrinkled her nose with laughter; we had a game going that she was my chick. And from Angelina I had exactly the opposite of Pepe's cold glitter—a glance so hot and challenging that my hair prickled. God help the foolish and feeble; this one was a fiery furnace.

I dislike coming to parties late. There is a period during which all that you doused by your entrance has to come to a boil again, and in this case I couldn't miss the perception that the committee and their rescued lambs were having difficulty finding grounds for conversation. Eventually I found myself behind the sofa where Dago and Luz sat, and they twisted around to talk to me.

"It's good to see you out, Dago," I said. "You ought to feel good. How's your mother?"

It came out "bother," but he was too polite to smile. He said that his mother was well and very happy, and his sisters also. I said that Carol and I had looked in now and then, when we could, and he shot me a look from under extravagantly long, curved eyelashes. He had eyes to melt girls down like candles in a heat wave. "You helped her live," he said. "Much thanks."

"It was Carol's idea. And anyway we didn't do much. Anybody would have done as much."

"Nobody did," Dago said. Beside him, Luz burst out that Miss Vaughn was terrific, terrific. She was one you could trust, she had this fairness and this big heart. Whenever she came into a room, something great happened, everything got happy like parades and flags. We looked across to where Carol was talking with Jean Gauss, and she worked her eyebrows at us questioningly. We all laughed. Luz said, looking sidelong, "You two go together, is that it?" I replied that I was working hard to get her to barry be, which set her off in screams. "Man," she said sympathetically, "you got a real cold there. I mean, you're really *plugged*."

"What do you do now?" I asked Dago. "Got a job?"

"I might go up to Idaho. One of my uncles runs a potato farm for a guy. Sort of a *mayordomo*. Where my father was working when he got killed. It's a year-round job. I could take my mother and sisters."

"Coyote," Luz said. "Me too!" I moved my hand to let Guy Mazur lean back in the sofa.

"You?" Dago said. "I guess you could be left behind all right."

She beat on his chest. "You take me, *cholo*, you hear? Left behind, hey? I want to see Idaho, too. *Surote*, I'll show you. I'll chase you up there on a white horse. I'll make you into a doll and stick you full of pins."

Dago cringed away and reached his can of beer from between his feet. From beyond him on the sofa Guy Mazur said, turning, "Did I hear you say you've got a job?"

"Idaho!" Luz said. "Potatoes! Without me, he says. *Jijole!*"

"We can get you a job here," Mazur said.

"Sure," Dago said. "I guess so. I don't know, though; this Idaho looks better for the mother and sisters." His shoulder lifted delicately, and he shadowboxed a moment with the air. "I kind of like to get out of here. You spend a year in that *quinta*, too many people know you, the law is always around digging up some old bone. My dad liked Idaho, till that potato digger ran over him."

Debbie Mazur came with a tray of highballs and wet cans of beer and bent her full armament two feet from Dago's deer eyes. They never flickered. He took a can of beer and thanked her with his even, white-toothed smile, and Guy Mazur, with his arms spread along the sofa back, watched his young wife. His face was smooth, agreeable, half smiling, fond, possibly a bit insistent. When she held the tray toward him, he shook his head. The tray wobbled, and the drinks slopped. Debbie leaned (*O shield her, shield sweet Christabel!*) and sipped some from each glass, watching Guy all the time. His eyes seemed to indulge her, as if he were saying, Well, all right, if you must. Then the momentary untranslatable passage of eyes was broken off and Mazur was saying, "It isn't entirely a matter of what any individual would like, right now. Maybe you could do more good staying."

"More good?"

Mazur laughed and bent forward to straighten his trouser cuff and came up again. "Did you think we got you sprung so you could spend your time on the beach? Boy, you're part of something now that's bigger than you are. You're going to help make the world safe for democracy."

While Dago took a polite and attentive sip of beer, Debbie lingered with her tray. She said, "I should think if they could all get away, it'd be—"

"Action," Mazur was saying to Dago. "Action, education, education, action. All the time. Never letting up." His voice rode over Debbie's and wiped it out, and if my eyes told me anything just then, they told me she could have slapped him. He never even noticed he had cut her off.

"We've got to learn to think of ourselves as part of something bigger. Sure it was important you should get out of jail. But it's even more important we should make sure no such atmosphere of prejudice and race hatred ever gets created again. This town will never learn until the Mexican-Americans stand up and take the rights they're entitled to, fight for 'em, put the bigots and the fascists down. We've got to organize the Mexican community and mold its weakness into strength, and you three are our strongest cards. If you run out, you weaken our hand."

"The Red Car Committee isn't disbanding, then?" I said, and got an incredulous look.

"Disband? Just when we've got them by the short hairs? When you've got them running, that's when you turn loose the cavalry on them."

He had the whole circle listening and nodding. In the middle of it, Debbie suddenly hoisted her tray up on one hand, and standing like the Statue of Liberty, she recited in a nasal, uninflected voice, "We are not disbanding until every racist is down his hole and every discriminatory ordinance is off the books and every sadist is fired from the police force. We are continuing our fight until every roller rink and swimming pool and movie house opens its doors to all alike. We shall not be content until school opportunities and job opportunities are as free to Mexican and colored and Japanese and Chinese and Filipino as to others. . . ."

Guy Mazur ironically applauded while the rest of us stared. It was like hearing a strip queen quote Spinoza. Words like those should come out of peaked immigrant faces, from throats encased in gray utility-weight sweaters. The words didn't match the neckline here, or for that matter the complexion, which I was now convinced was her own, and which was like a Dutch barmaid's. And neither the words nor the looks matched the tone, which was like the edge of a broken bottle.

Staring hotly at her husband, she said, "It seems to me these kids have had their share. If they want to drop it and go live a normal life somewhere, why not? You can't *stuff* them and trot them out as examples of police discrimination all their lives. They're *people*, for God's sake!"

With a little grimace she passed her free hand across the faces of Luz and Dago. "I didn't mean to talk about you behind your back."

Neckline, calendar-cutie dress, platinum hair, and all, she was one of the few there who knew how it might feel to be a zoot-suiter just released from San Quentin and stuck in a room with a bunch of strangers to whom you owed too much. If you demetaled the hair and changed the dress and took the props out from under the figure, you might have quite a woman there.

We were all still, waiting for something. Carol had come around to the end of the sofa near me. From the other end Guy said lightly, "Sweetheart, you were always a great one for the sentimental approach. I'll leave that to you, you do it so well, and you leave the strategy to me. These kids are too important to be private citizens."

Debbie dropped her head sideward in dubious thought, looking at him across the lowered tray of glasses and cans. Her reflection in a beer can diverted her attention; she squinted and dropped her jaw in amazement; she put out her tongue and crossed her eyes. "Is this the face that licked a thousand envelopes?" she cried tragically, and like a relay runner passing the baton, she slapped a drink into the hand of the nearest committee member and lunged away. A brief uneasy silence swirled where she had been.

"The point is," Guy said, "you *are* too important to duck out now. Of course, you can do what you like, but I hope you'll see it the way we do." His smooth gray head lifted, and he called, "Pepe, maybe you ought to hear this." From the outer fringe of the circle Pepe lounged over and sat on the floor. His chick stood behind him, and he rolled his head back against her thighs.

"Now look," Guy said. "We can't get at the Mexican community through the politicians until we get rid of old Coyote on Horseback and the others. They'd sell out their own people any day. We'll get them come election time. But first we have to work through the unions. We've got to break the logjam and organize the pickers, and we've got to work on every other union with any Mexican membership. We want every local in Greater Los Angeles to hear you kids talk. Here you are, guilty of nothing but being Mexican and wearing drapes and maybe having a rumble now and then with kids from some other neighborhood. A kid is found dead in the road one morning, and bang, because you'd been in a fight with his crowd, you're in San Quentin for life. If it weren't for this committee, you'd still be there. I'm not asking for gratitude. All I'm saying is that you owe something to your own people and this democracy we're all trying to create. Ask yourselves if it wouldn't be better to stick right here, take the jobs we'll find you, and tell your story at a lot of meetings."

The pale head lifted again; the smooth face was still, the eyes almost closed. He could have been a UCLA halfback praying in the huddle, a stern, handsome hero headed, after graduation, for a job in public relations or the movies, a hero whose head was full of muscle and the assurance that God was with him in everything, whether he was blocking for the fullback or making a better deal with his sponsor about his athletic scholarship. In some surprise I asked myself when I had started being so mistrustful of him. On the record, he was a dedicated spirit. I was as convinced as he was that the Red Car boys were innocent, had been railroaded on purely circumstantial evidence. And it was no crime, at fifty, to look as if you were still good for five sets of singles or to wear a jacket that some tailor had worked on with love.

"That's all we're asking," Guy said. "Also, in the jobs we find you, you won't have to worry about the record following you. If it does, so much the better. And don't think the committee will be sitting on its duff while you work. Just let me tell you a few things. We're putting out a little book, for instance—the whole history of this case from the dragnet arrests until the final reversal. People all over the country are going to read that Supreme Court decision in thirty-six-point capitals and know the kind of conspiracy that put you behind bars. Now! Jean here has scheduled another radio series on the Mexican-American community. She'll want all three of you one of these days for an interview. Next week? Next week. Then there's the big long-range study Carol and Charlie have been working on. That'll be terrif, simply terrif, and I hear it'll be ready for the press in another couple of months. That reminds me, Charlie, can we beg some photographs to illustrate our booklet? Pete'll see you about it. Finally—don't let this out yet because we haven't got it absolutely in the cage—I think I've got Len Fowler talked into doing a full-length documentary on the *pachucos*, and if he does it, you know how it'll be done. The most, absolutely the most." Cocking a humorous eye at Dago, he added, "How'd you like to star in a picture called *The Kid from Happy Valley?*"

That was a joke. Happy Valley was the barrio these kids from La Loma had always feuded with. They groaned. Chuey Bernal looked all around with an Emmett Kelly crying face, put his hands up in a fighting pose as if someone had pushed him, nodded, half convinced by inner voices, and then shook his head hard. You could almost hear it rattle. "Happy Valley! Those guys are from Gonesville."

"Well, it sounds better than *The Kid from Fifty-eighth Street* or *The Kid from Watts*. And there's a nice irony in Happy Valley. Happy Valley with dirt floors and typhoid wells."

Pepe Garcia, rubbing his head slowly against his girl's thighs, said in a soft voice, "Tell him to work in a beef and we'll go over there and clean the place out for the camera. A real fight scene, man."

Mazur was laughing. "The solidarity of the Mexican-American community," he said. "And you talk about disbanding." It was neatly done; he had got them to make his point for him.

"Listen," said Nemerov, slight, nervous, dark, hopelessly typecast for a conspirator, with a tic in his left eyelid. "Listen. Here's another idea. What if we got together all the great unjust trials—you know, Lawrence Strike and Sacco-Vanzetti and Joe Hill and the Scottsboro Boys and the rest. Red Car too, naturally. Get them all into one set of covers. What an indictment of capitalist justice, eh? What a book that would make. Wouldn't it? Pete, couldn't you take that on? There's bound to be transcripts of all those cases. What do you think, Guy?"

I caught Carol's eye, wordlessly asking her if we had to stick around all night while the cell plotted strategy. The circle had broken out in contributions from several sides. The Red Car boys and their chicks watched and listened. Then Debbie Mazur came in again from somewhere with a bottle of bourbon in her hand and started tipping it into glasses that would hold still. In the kitchen she may have had a quick one to cool her irritation; her eyes as well as her complexion showed it now. "What I think," she said rather loudly, "is that there's a time and place for everything. For God's sake, I gave the maid the night off so we could dance and make whoopee and have a good time. So let's adjourn the meeting and dance."

When she nudged me with the bottle, I turned away and covered my glass with my hand. "Don't you think we ought to dance?" she asked.

I said with a mucous leer, "You bead you ad be?"

"You and me," she said. "The others are all right, but you're the cutest." She flung her arms around my neck and fastened a suckerfish kiss on me. The bottle dangling from her hand banged me between the shoulder blades. I couldn't breathe, and besides that, I was a regular Typhoid Mary, a Great Dismal Swamp where germs throve. Struggling, I broke loose for air and found myself looking right into Guy Mazur's eyes. Something passed off his face like breath off a mirror—or I thought it did. On the other hand, he may have been looking all the time the way he looked when I had got my breath and could see: tolerantly amused.

Debbie's arms were still around my neck. Past her ear I saw the smile on Dago Aguirre's face and Luz's rolling eyes. "Mmmmmmmm-mmmmmmmm-mmm!" Debbie said, and plunged off on some other errand. Voices tentatively picked up the talk again, but if she had meant to break up the meeting and force Guy off his planned course, she had done it. We were no longer a captive audience.

Taking my arm, Carol walked me over to the top of the steps looking down into the greenish dusk of the solarium. "You watch it," she said.

I went for the inhaler. "I can't take my eyes off it."

"Don't be a slob, Charlie. I mean really—watch it."

"For God's sake!" I said.

From the study at the far end of the room we heard the scrape of a needle across a record, and then Kid Ory or somebody took off on "Muskrat Ramble."

Raising her voice over the music, Carol said, "I do mean really. Guy and Debbie have had a beef going all evening. If she starts using you to get even with him, you could get hurt. And don't think you could play it cool. She's got too many hormones, and she's too damned smart."

I said, "I'm touched that you should worry, but relax. Otorhinolaryngology is working on your side."

The band, whatever it was, had a real beat. I saw Dago and Luz rise and excuse themselves from among the feet along the sofa. Chuey was already up, snapping his fingers and jerking his head with a gone spastic look while he waited for Lupe to fix her belt. Then Pepe uncoiled from the floor, folded his chick in his arm, and moved her off with jerky, light movements. Angelina made even jitterbugging, which is about as personal as pole vaulting, look sexy. Her face was wiped clean of all expression; the fringes of her skirt snapped.

As cleanly as a good axman splits a straight-grained block, the music had split the party in two. A couple of the nameless do-gooders rose and said good-bye all around. The double doorway of the study was full of prancing, jerking, twirling shapes. "Muskrat Ramble" rambled itself out; Chuey Bernal yelped and clapped and staggered with exhaustion; the phonograph squawked a horrible amplified squawk as somebody scraped the needle again.

"Darling," Guy Mazur called from a deep conversation with Nemerov and Welling, "can you turn it down a little? We hardly want the neighbors protesting."

Debbie appeared promptly in the study door. "In the words of Papa Hemingway, obscenity the neighbors."

"Not a bad idea," Mazur called good-naturedly. "But the committee might like to hear themselves think."

"Obscenity the committee, too," Debbie said. She disappeared, and in a moment Louis Armstrong came on in "Gut Bucket Blues," loud and dirty.

I said to Carol, "What are we? Planners or jivers? Saviors or delinquents?"

"The delinquents seem to be having more fun."

So we danced across the living room and into the study. It was a good thing to do; they welcomed us. When the record ended, we were all in a big collapse of laughing and clapping.

"You dance too mean," Chuey told his cousin Lupe. "I can't stand it."

"Angelina, she's who dances mean," Lupe said. "*Jijole!* Pepe, you better watch out."

Pepe smiled. Angelina's expressionlessness took on a shading of disdain. Then Debbie, who was minding the phonograph, put on a new record, set down her drink, and slid her feet in an exaggerated stalk across the floor. "Whose idea was this? I get up a dance and everybody's dancing except me. This is ladies' tag night. Tag!" She slapped Dago's arm, and Luz moved away, giggling. The loudspeaker hidden among the bookshelves was hammering out "Lady Be Good." Chuey tagged Carol, and I leaned against the desk between Luz and Lupe and dragged on the inhaler.

"Poor Señor Pictures," Lupe said. "You're smooched, too." She touched my mouth with a paper napkin and it came off red.

"It's a privilege," I said.

"She's beautiful," Luz said.

"You think so?"

"Oh, yes. Like a movie star."

"Keep your eye on your boyfriend."

"Don't you worry."

"He's already limping. She's wearing him down."

"Oh, limping. That's not her; that's his ankle."

"What's the matter with his ankle?"

"He broke it boxing, up in that jail. In the first round. But he finished the last two rounds with it broken, and still won."

We watched Dago hand off Debbie and turn and pick her up smoothly. She wasn't as smooth as he was, but she was giving her all. They were like a couple of old silent stars restored in their prime, Valentino and La Marr, personal appearance tonight only. And I could imagine Dago in that ring with his broken ankle. Not to quit, not even to grimace: His whole morality and the morality of his kind would have been involved. And however limited that morality was, it was neither small nor weak. "Quite a boy, your Dago," I said.

She smiled at me sidelong with her Indian eyes half closed. "I believe it," she said.

"You want to go to Idaho?"

"What do you think?"

"You'd get to dance squaw dances on some reservation," Lupe said. "What's so good with Idaho?"

"I don't know," Luz said. "I just don't want Dago in no more trouble. He goes out with the guys and they do something, steal a car or beat somebody up, and he won't tell on them and then he's in it, too. Maybe in Idaho there isn't this trouble all the time."

"Maybe in Idaho there isn't anything," Lupe said. "I bet they have last year's movies once a week. John Wayne in *The Fighting Seabees. Que suave!*"

The dance ended, and Debbie planted an enthusiastic kiss on Dago. Lupe cheered; Luz groaned. From the living room the sob sister and the graduate student in need of a haircut came to replenish their drinks. The sob sister smiled upon us, an indulgent auntie. "I wish I could do that. It looks like fun." It was not clear whether she meant the jitterbugging or the smooching, and her companion did not offer to teach her either one. He said only, "Soda or water?" and after a minute they drifted back to join the planning commission.

Chuey put on a slow, sullen blues, returned Carol to me, and picked up Lupe. Luz with a finger rubbed at the lipstick smear on Dago's mouth, and Pepe, in his controlled slouch, stood with a little smile before Debbie. Angelina twitched her fringed skirt out of the way and leaned with her hands behind her against the bookcases. Her indifference was considerable: She read titles on books; she opened an atlas on the desk. I wondered if I should go over and ask her to dance, but then her eyes wandered back from following Pepe in his graceful, dangerous, foot-placing, foot-withdrawing, spinning-and-releasing, handing-off and taking-back movements with Debbie, and she caught me looking. She so obviously hated me for watching her watch them that I stayed where I was.

We danced for a half hour or so, and before long Debbie had us all smeared with lipstick. She was everybody's big loving sister. She told Dago to go on up to Idaho and not let himself get captured by Guy's medicine show. She leaned back to look into the living room and laugh at the shrunken group there. "The planners," she said. "The thinkers. My God, they think the first thing you do to have fun is elect a chairman pro tem." Touching glasses again with Dago, she gave him an impulsive smooch. The girls laughed, but not very hard.

"Tell you a secret," Debbie said. "Mazur thinks he made you all out of tin and wound you up. Tell you another secret. He thinks he made me out of tin and wound me up, too." Silent and gleeful, she shrank her shoulders together with mirth and at once stiffened and marched around in a marvelously precise imitation of a mechanical toy. When she stopped, she found Pepe Garcia in front of her, wanting to dance again. Chuey put on another record.

Poor Angelina. I have a friend who practices a science he calls kinesics, the language of the body. From Angelina he would have got a plain statement. She had only three kinetic expressions. She could switch her tail, she could be as stiff as a wooden image, and she could shrivel like a wronged vampire. She was at the wronged-vampire stage as she moved in on Dago and led him off in a dance, and if she had danced mean before, she was pure poison now.

Pepe did not notice. Dancing with Debbie, he was a graceful scorpion carrying his stinger ready over his back, and when at the end of the record Debbie as usual flung her arms around him for the kiss, he was ready for her. Their bodies tightened together; their mouths made one mouth. The laughter and the talk died away in the study. I noticed that the kissers were right in the double doors, in plain sight from the living-room plotters. The sudden quiet from the study would make them look up if anything would.

Carol took my hand and led me, walking loud on her heels, to the still-spinning record player. As she turned it off, she hissed at me, "This is getting out of hand!"

"Well, you can't expect them to push her away."

Voices had begun again behind us; apparently Carol's movement had broken up the big clutch in the doorway. "It's all wrong," Carol said. "The kids are getting the idea that anything goes."

"Apparently it does."

"I wish to hell people wouldn't involve other people in their squabbles," she said, and for a second she looked as mean as Angelina. "If anything happens, it's the kids who'll suffer. They're vulnerable."

"Think we should go?"

She did not answer. Somebody was calling for more music. She put something on without looking. "Muskrat Ramble" again. When we turned around, Angelina and Dago were dancing by. She was throwing her little tail around and wearing the smile that the Gorgon made fashionable. Pepe was still dancing with Debbie, who looked about ready to pop out of her cocoon.

"We'd better stay," Carol said. "Somebody's got to keep the peace."

"Shall I hide the liquor? Pull a wire on the record player?"

She shook her head irritably.

"Why don't you talk to her?"

"She's past talking to."

"What if I went around shooting some pictures? Would that help?"

"Ah, Charlie," she said. "You're an angel, you're a darling."

So I went around snapping flashbulbs in people's faces, but the principal effect was to bring on a clamor from Debbie that I shoot her and Pepe jiving. She said she would blow it up into a photomural and paper the wall with it. I did my best to disperse things by posting people in corners with reflectors, but I did not capture Angelina. She and Dago were jiving on their own, and by now she was pure provocation. While I focused, I was aware of her out of the corner of my eye, her feet in an intricate pattern of yield and go, her tail wagging, her fringes snapping, her arms and shoulders suggesting embracings and entwinings and her face like cold stone. A deadly one, what the kids called a *bruja*. I hardly paid attention to the immortalizing of Debbie and Pepe, I was so interested in the other two.

So was Luz interested. I heard her mutter to Carol, "That Angie is mean, man. *Qué relajo!* If she tries anything with Dago, I'll scratch her eyes out."

"Dago's all right," Carol said. He did seem to be, at that. He was not contributing much to Angelina's show but looked amused and a little high. Debbie and Pepe, once I was through shooting them, were back practicing steps. Debbie missed a move, cried out with laughter, threw her arms around Pepe, stepped back, tried it again. She looked blowsy and hypnotized, purple-cheeked, moist as the captain of a Danish ladies' gymnastic team.

"Maybe it's time we all went home," Carol said finally, brightly, to Luz. "You kids have to be careful. You realize that, don't you?"

"*Se siente aviador*," Luz said, still with her eyes on Angelina. "She's high as a pilot. What does she think she's doing?"

Chuey, exhausted, had fallen into a chair and pulled Lupe on top of him and was emitting wolf cries, and Carol was turning her head in anger and bafflement from Debbie to Angelina and back when three of the ancient anarchs paused in the door to say good night. That gave Carol an opening. She shut off the record player. "We've got to go, too. Debbie, can I see you a minute?"

The look Debbie gave her was brighter and bluer than it had any right to be if she was as tight as she had been acting. "*One* minute," she said. "I'm just getting the hang of this."

They went out and off down the hall. By inspiration, a leader much in hope that he had followers, I looked into the living room, saying, "I wonder what they've got settled in there?," and walked in. When I got there, I found that everybody was with me except Pepe and Angelina. Well, they could stay in the study and weave their hooded necks at one another. The others could be handled.

The planning commission, what was left of it, regarded us with tolerance and some curiosity. "Finally wear yourselves out?" Mazur said. After all the tensions I had been aware of, I was surprised by the big confident boom of his voice. So far as he was concerned, some of us had just been in dancing. And he went straight back to where he had been when Debbie led the kids away. "How would a warehouse job suit you?" he said.

Chuey and Dago looked doubtfully at each other. Both were smeared with Debbie's lipstick. Dago good-naturedly let his head roll as Luz, behind him, yanked at his hair. "Work?" Chuey said. "You get out of that old *calabozo*, you don't feel like diving right into some *job*."

"Out here they don't serve those nice free jailhouse meals," Mazur said.

Chuey fainted halfway to the floor. "Did you ever eat one of those nice free jailhouse meals?"

"Come on," Mazur said. "We can put one of you in a warehouse job at one ninety an hour. Who wants it?"

"Hey," Chuey said. "One ninety? That ain't birdseed."

"ILWU," Mazur said. "A strong union and a great hiring hall." He was looking steadily at Dago.

"I don't know," Dago said softly. "My mother's sort of thinking Idaho."

"You won't get pay like that in the potatoes."

Dago nodded and lifted his shoulders dubiously. Nemerov, looking irritated, put a cigarette between his lips and took out a matchbook and said, with the matchbook in his fingers and the cigarette wobbling from his lips, "You've got a responsibility in this fight, too. Don't you think the rest of us have got families to think about? What do you think we're out here on the barricades for, fun? Nobody's persecuting *us*, or sending *us* to San Quentin." The tic winked in his eyelid; he broke a match trying to light it and tore off another. When he had lighted his cigarette, he shook out the match and dropped it on the floor and looked at Dago hard through the smoke. "We can't have just a few working and the rest getting the benefits. Everybody's got to work."

Dago sat silent, smiling and thinking, with his head a little on one side. Welling broke in in his light, eager voice, running all his words together. He was one of the hardest people to understand I ever listened to. I gathered that Dago would feel pretty crummy if he let others carry the whole load.

"Hey," Chuey said, "if Dago don't want that buck ninety, how about me?"

"I thought you didn't want to work," Nemerov said, still staring at Dago.

"Well, jeez," Chuey said, "I thought the idea was we all had to."

Dago sat still, with the dubious, demurring half-smile on his face and Luz's hand still in his hair. Then all at once Guy Mazur reached his arms along the sofa back in a long stretch. He yawned, and laughed at his own uninhibited noise. "Let's let it ride for now," he said. "You kids are O.K. You'll be in there, I know you will. A few days' vacation won't hurt you any. Let's call the meeting adjourned. How about one for the road?"

His hand slapped Chuey's knee, and as he rose, slapped again on Dago's back. He went over and mended the drinks of Nemerov and Welling and himself.

"Well," I said to Dago, "you've got lots of opportunities for public service."

"Sure. I guess I ought to, when you think about it. It's just . . . I don't know. I kind of think Idaho could be better."

"But you feel grateful to Guy and the committee."

"Why not?" Dago said. "We'd still be in there if it hadn't been for them." He shrugged, a handsome, almost a beautiful boy, and a thoughtful one, with feelings. His laugh was troubled. "Who do you say no to?" he said, and, twisting toward Luz, said something in Spanish or *pachucana*.

"No secrets," I said.

"It's just a saying. *El que al cielo escupe a la cara le cae.*"

"You know I don't speak Spanish."

"You spit at the sky, you get it back in the face," Luz said.

I was very thick in the head, and dry from breathing through my mouth. Cautiously, feeling that I had missed something, I said, "Who's been spitting at the sky?"

"Who hasn't?" Dago said. "Who wouldn't be?" As he pinched out his cigarette and dropped it in his cuff, here came Pepe and Angelina. She was three steps ahead of his easy slouch. They did not look like reconciled lovers; they looked like fighters going to their corners at the bell.

The sight of them curdled me. It was one thing to talk to a pair of nice youngsters like Dago and Luz, and another to deal with that pair. I felt what a mating theirs would be, corrupt seedbed and poisoned seed and a hatch of snakes and dragons, and I was suddenly irritated at Dago and Luz for even associating with such obvious bad ones. I was struggling for air like an asthmatic, and in no mood for Spanish riddles. I didn't care whether Dago himself or Mazur or Pepe or Angelina or Debbie or the whole bunch of them had been spitting at the sky. It was possible even Carol had been. It was more than possible that she ought to change her profession. My head ached, I needed air, and I had already hit the inhaler so many times that I could expect not to sleep.

Debbie and Carol came in from the hall. Debbie had combed her hair and tucked herself in, but she looked sulky. She carried a tray of cheese and crackers; Carol had a percolator that she plugged into a floor plug by the coffee table.

"Well," I said sourly as we walked aside. "What cheer?"

"Tears," Carol said. "Furies. He treats her like a child or a plaything. She's a muff dog who wants to retrieve ducks or trail bears. Nothing new for her, it just blew up tonight. She says he won't let her be a person."

"Is being a person such a delight?"

"Poor Charlie. Do you feel awful?"

"Yes."

"Could you stand it just a few more minutes? I'd like to get some coffee into the kids before they take off. Wouldn't you like some?"

"My head's too stuffed."

"Just five minutes," she said. "How has it been in here?"

"All right. Pressure on Dago to take their warehouse job and be an exhibit."

"Is he going to?"

"I don't know."

"I hope not. Debbie's absolutely right about that part of it."

"They want him here," I said. "Obviously he's the one they could make the most use of. Chuey's a featherbrain, and Pepe is a bad one on sight."

Silent, lips pursed, she stood looking back at them all. It struck me how complex a roomful of people could get, some manipulating others, some feeling responsibility to others, or to causes, or programs, or ideas, or the gang, or the party line, or something else. It was like a ship's deck full of lines and rigging all entangling your feet, and I wanted out. I said, "You start everybody to laughing merrily, and bring the party to a climax, and get some coffee down your kids. I'm going outside for some oxygen."

The night air was marvelously cool and damp, and I opened my mouth and took it in by the lungful. On both sides, down toward Franklin and up toward Los Feliz, went the hum and hush and whisper of traffic. Searchlights scissored around overhead, racing across the belly of the overcast. It seemed very peaceful; nobody was mad at anybody, or using anybody, or getting even with anybody. But my nose was still impenetrably shut, and a sharp pain stabbed me between the eyes as I stepped down onto the lawn.

The spotlight glared into the eucalyptus tree, the only color or decoration in the yard. There were no flower beds. The brilliant tree was posed there in a sweep of grass, its bloodred blossoms bedded in leaves lighted almost white against black holes of shadow. A true, calculated Mazur effect. I walked toward the corner of the solarium, not lighted itself but glowing with diffused light from the living room and shadowy with the hothouse jungle inside. Dew showered up from my toes, and looking back, I saw my own dark tracks. Wet feet would be fine for my cold. But the air was so pleasant and the lawn so soft underfoot that I went on. I was near the corner of the solarium when I saw the movement inside.

I didn't think; I simply stepped into the angle between house and glass porch, where it was darkest. As if a tube had been pushed through my head, I got a sudden, merciful draft of air. In the same instant I recognized the shadows inside. They were dancing—no, wrestling. She was pushing and beating at him as he bent her backward. Their heads darted and feinted like the heads of snakes. He was trying to kiss her.

She twisted sideways and wrenched away from him. They were no more than ten feet from me, and through the glass I heard him laugh. "You jealous bitch," he said, and brought his face close again. Her fingers flew at his face, but he caught one wrist, then the other, and got them into one hand and held them behind her while he hunted down her mouth again. Flattened back against the wall, my cleared head now sour with smog, I felt ugly spying on them, but I did not dare move now and reveal myself. Through the glass I heard her grunt as she tried to free her hands. Then one hand flashed up, and he jerked his head aside with an exclamation. They wrestled again; again he captured her wrists. He forced his face down to hers. Beyond them I saw Dago Aguirre's silhouette move into the doorway from the living room, at the head of the steps, and pause, looking down, with a coffee cup half raised to its lips.

He couldn't have missed seeing what I saw. Pepe, still with Angelina's wrists locked in his left hand, straightened backward and sideward from his conquering kiss, and as he did so, he knocked the girl down with one quick hooking blow.

I ran tiptoe across the wet grass to the door. There I waited a few breaths, wiping my wet shoes up the backs of my trousers and listening. A frantic uproar was going on inside. With everyone's attention focused on that, I turned the knob and slipped in.

Carol ran past down the hall without even seeing me. From the solarium Angelina's screaming came in raw bursts as mindless as a fire siren. When I stepped into the living room, there was a confused, vehement cluster at the top of the solarium steps. Debbie and Welling each held one of Angelina's arms; without them she would have fallen on her face. The floor all around her was splashed with blood, there was blood on her clothes and on the clothes of those who held her. Borne on by Angelina's weight, Debbie slipped in blood and nearly went down. The girl was bleeding incredibly, as if her throat had been cut.

Then Carol came running with towels in her hands, and Mazur and Nemerov moved in to help hold Angelina while Carol and Debbie worked with towels on her face, blotting the steady screaming and letting it burst out again and then blotting it once more. When they straightened her under the light, trying to see where she was hurt, I had a glimpse of the foolish, disarranged pompadour, the artificial little *pachuca* face smeared with blood and tears, and the quick, welling gash. Pepe had split her lips from her nose to the point of her chin.

Debbie was crying, "Stand up, Angelina, we can't . . . Don't cry, honey, you'll make it worse. Guy, call a doctor, we can't stop it, it just keeps coming!"

They led Angelina to the couch and got her lying down. Debbie and Carol were kneeling with their towels at her head. Mazur stood back, gnawing his lip, thinking.

"Guy," Debbie screamed at him, "do something, for God's sake! Call Schwartz!"

"No," Mazur said. "No doctor. Not here. We'll take her to the clinic. But we've got another problem."

"Oh, how can you talk about other problems? She's *bleeding* to death!"

"Not from a cut lip," Mazur said. He looked around at the room, spattered with blood—blood on Debbie and Carol, blood on the couch, blood all over Angelina, and pressed his lips together. "What happened?" he said. "Who saw it?"

But nobody had anything to say. The Mexican kids, all but Pepe, were in a tight, still group. Pepe stood against the wall, a red scratch across his cheekbone, his hands behind him. For a couple of seconds he stood the weight of all the eyes on him; then he shrugged the faintest, iciest little shrug. "She fell down."

Angelina sat up, tearing at the towels pressed against her face. In an instant her chin was wet with blood, she spattered blood as she screamed, "He hit me! Pepe hit me!"

Carol and Debbie fought her back down and muffled her in towels. We were all still watching Pepe, who hung there still as a gun on a wall. One shoulder moved. *"Anda pedo,"* he said. "She's crazy drunk. She don't know what she's doing. She fell down and hit her face on the steps."

Carol said, bitterly for her, "It doesn't upset you much that your girl's hurt."

"I didn't make her fall down," Pepe said.

"But you saw her fall?" Mazur said.

"I didn't say that. I'm coming up the steps ahead of her, and I hear her stumble, and look back, and there she is on the steps."

Unexpectedly, not knowing I was going to get into it until the words were out of my mouth, I said, "What's that scratch on your cheek?"

His hand started up—his right—and then he switched and brought out the left. His fingers touched the scratch, and they knew exactly where to find it. He put his hand back behind him and shrugged.

"Let's see your right hand."

He made no move to show it. His eyes said that he would have killed me as casually as he would have wrung a chicken's neck.

"Are you scared to?"

"What are you getting at?" Mazur said. "What makes you think he's lying? It was dark, the girl was high. She could have tripped."

"Could have, but didn't. I still want to see his hand."

"What would that show you?"

"Maybe the marks of her teeth."

"You think he did hit her."

"I know damned well he hit her. I saw him."

Now I was the one they were all looking at. "How?" Guy said. "From where?"

"Through the window. I was outside."

Mazur thought that over, with all its implications, while Angelina sobbed and hiccuped and moaned and was blotted with towels. "We've got to think about this," Mazur said.

"You can't!" Debbie cried, across Angelina's bloody length. "We've got to get this girl to a doctor!"

"In a minute," Mazur said. To me he said, "Suppose you're right."

"Suppose Angelina and I are right."

"Yes. But it's still your word against his."

"Thanks for your confidence," I said. I went into the hall and dug the Rolleiflex out of the bag and without flash, without anything but the oval blobs of Mazur's theatrical houselights, I went bang, bang, bang: the still Mexican kids; Pepe with his back to the wall; the committee leaning and crouched over Angelina, portraits of complicity.

"Nah, nah, nah!" Nemerov was saying. The tic jumped like a trapped insect in his eyelid.

Mazur said, "What was that for, Charlie?"

"Evidence, maybe."

"You want to turn Pepe in?"

"I don't want him to get away with it."

"What good would it do?" Mazur said. "What evidence have you got? Your word and Angelina's against his. Maybe that's enough to put him back in jail. Then what? Then what happens to our program, and the cause of justice, and all the rest? What happens to those kids over there?"

Those kids over there had turned to stone. Innocent as they were, they could not have been picked out in a lineup, by the best psychologist in America, as the innocent ones. They wore the same expressionlessness as Pepe wore. I looked for some acknowledgment or help in Dago's face and found nothing. His eyes were as flat as dry stones.

"We haven't got a lot of time," Mazur said. "We've got to get Angie to the clinic. It wouldn't do to bring a doctor here; he'd look around and deduce a massacre; he'd *have* to report to the cops. Let's think long-range. We're trying to right social injustice. We're all instruments in a cause. Think what else you'll do if you try to put Pepe back in jail."

I looked at Carol, crouched by the sofa with bloody towels in her hands. I listened to Angelina's diminishing moans and sobs. I looked at Pepe, tight-wound and ready to spring from his nonchalance against the wall. I looked at Chuey, foolish and stony, and at Lupe, beautiful and stony, and at Luz, dark and Indian and stony, and at Dago, the best of this whole bunch, stony.

"What if there's other evidence?" I said. "When I was outside there, I saw someone else through the window, someone at the head of the stairs. He saw it as plain as I did."

"Who?" Mazur said.

"I couldn't quite tell."

He gave a harsh bark of justified skepticism.

"Let's give whoever it was a chance to say."

I looked straight at Dago, and he looked straight back at me. We had an extraordinary exchange that included his past and present and future, his commitments, his hopes, most of all his solidarity with whatever had always been his enemy.

"I was there," he said. "I saw it. She fell down."

For another instant our eyes held. I could imagine what Carol was seeing and thinking, for she was the one truly committed to these kids, but I could not look at her. I looked only at Dago, the deer-eyed one, the one with a mother and sisters, the one whose father had been run over by a potato digger, the one who except for the Red Car Committee might still be in San Quentin and who except for the Red Car Committee might still have a chance at Idaho and a life. I could read his future now without tarot cards: Sometime some of his crowd would stick up a truckload of cigarettes or rob a liquor store; he would be involved, or an accomplice, or innocent; everybody would go back to San Quentin; sometime—a year, two years, three—we would hear on the radio that a prisoner had knifed a guard or another prisoner, and we would hear the name, Pepe Garcia, and hear the name of Dago Aguirre, a friend of the accused, who refused to talk. He would be blotted out as Angelina was blotted out, but not by compassionate helpers.

"O.K., that settles it," I said. "Let's get Angie to the clinic. Let's clean up after ourselves."

I opened the Rollei and took out the exposed film and found a wastebasket for it. Carol's big, troubled eyes met mine briefly as she and Debbie eased Angelina up off the sofa. But what I was most interested in, what held me, was Dago's face, still in a tight protective group with his friends. He pursed his lips; his stoniness dissolved into an ironic, fatalistic, rueful half-smile. He tipped his head back and made a motion of spitting upward.

The Best Years

WILLA CATHER

Programs to improve the lives of the poor and the disadvantaged often focus on altering external circumstances—for example, improving schools, promoting employment, eliminating discrimination, or providing support services. But these activities, albeit important, overlook the importance of families, where individuals are primarily shaped. This story by Willa Cather (1873–1947), written in 1945, shows a loving nuclear family as a center of moral and civic-minded instruction, as well as a repository of meaning and memory. The Ferguesson family's only daughter, Lesley, becomes a teacher— at the ripe age of fourteen—in a one-room schoolhouse in rural Nebraska. The county superintendent of public instruction, the New England–born Miss Knightly, marvels at the young girl's influence not just on the intellect of her charges but also on their behavior. The reader soon glimpses the explanation when Miss Knightly meets Lesley's mother and adoring siblings. The story vividly illustrates how a good upbringing ripples out in expanding circles, touching all in its wake.*

By story's end, the mother looks back fondly on her childrearing days, which were also days of economic struggle, calling them "the best years." She seems out of sorts with modern progress—"all this running around." What does the story indicate about the tensions between the old world and the new? Can families remain centers of stability in the era of locomotives ("power, conquest, triumph") and the even more revolutionary automobile?

---

* *This story is also a testament to an American innovation: public schools as an extension of the home rather than a dramatic separation from it. Under the guidance of a schoolmarm, the coeducational American schoolhouse breathed a spirit very different from that of the all-male world of ancient or aristocratic schooling.*

Must we choose between a world in which people do not die of pneumonia and a world in which families and communities remain deeply rooted? Can the balance represented by this particular family hold today? What might we do to foster such families?

I

On a bright September morning in the year 1899 Miss Evangeline Knightly was driving through the beautiful Nebraska land which lies between the Platte River and the Kansas line. She drove slowly, for she loved the country, and she held the reins loosely in her gloved hand. She drove about a great deal and always wore leather gauntlets. Her hands were small, well shaped and very white, but they freckled in hot sunlight.

Miss Knightly was a charming person to meet—and an unusual type in a new country: oval face, small head delicately set (the oval chin tilting inward instead of the square chin thrust out), hazel eyes, a little blue, a little green, tiny dots of brown. . . . Somehow these splashes of colour made light—and warmth. When she laughed, her eyes positively glowed with humour, and in each oval cheek a roguish dimple came magically to the surface. Her laugh was delightful because it was intelligent, discriminating, not the physical spasm which seizes children when they are tickled, and growing boys and girls when they are embarrassed. When Miss Knightly laughed, it was apt to be because of some happy coincidence or droll mistake. The farmers along the road always felt flattered if they could make Miss Knightly laugh. Her voice had as many colours as her eyes—nearly always on the bright side, though it had a beautiful gravity for people who were in trouble.

It is only fair to say that in the community where she lived Miss Knightly was considered an intelligent young woman, but plain—distinctly plain. The standard of female beauty seems to be the same in all newly settled countries: Australia, New Zealand, the farming country along the Platte. It is, and was, the glowing, smiling calendar girl sent out to advertise agricultural implements. Colour was everything, modelling was nothing. A nose was a nose—any shape would do; a forehead was the place where the hair stopped, chin utterly negligible unless it happened to be more than two inches long.

Miss Knightly's old mare, Molly, took her time along the dusty, sunflower-bordered roads that morning, occasionally pausing long enough to snatch off a juicy, leafy sunflower top in her yellow teeth. This she munched as she ambled along. Although Molly had almost the slowest trot in the world, she really preferred walking. Sometimes she fell into a doze and stumbled. Miss

Knightly also, when she was abroad on these long drives, preferred the leisurely pace. She loved the beautiful autumn country; loved to look at it, to breathe it. She was not a "dreamy" person, but she was thoughtful and very observing. She relished the morning; the great blue of the sky, smiling, cloudless,—and the land that lay level as far as the eye could see. The horizon was like a perfect circle, a great embrace, and within it lay the cornfields, still green, and the yellow wheat stubble, miles and miles of it, and the pasture lands where the white-faced cattle led lives of utter content. All their movements were deliberate and dignified. They grazed through all the morning; approached their metal water tank and drank. If the windmill had run too long and the tank had overflowed, the cattle trampled the overflow into deep mud and cooled their feet. Then they drifted off to graze again. Grazing was not merely eating, it was also a pastime, a form of reflection, perhaps meditation.

Miss Knightly was thinking, as Molly jogged along, that the barbed-wire fences, though ugly in themselves, had their advantages. They did not cut the country up into patterns as did the rail fences and stone walls of her native New England. They were, broadly regarded, invisible—did not impose themselves upon the eye. She seemed to be driving through a fineless land. On her left the Hereford cattle apparently wandered at will: the tall sunflowers hid the wire that kept them off the road. Far away, on the horizon line, a troop of colts were galloping, all in the same direction—purely for exercise, one would say. Between her and the horizon the white wheels of windmills told her where the farmhouses sat.

Miss Knightly was abroad this morning with a special purpose—to visit country schools. She was the County Superintendent of Public Instruction. A grim title, that, to put upon a charming young woman. . . . Fortunately it was seldom used except on reports which she signed, and there it was usually printed. She was not even called "the Superintendent." A country school-teacher said to her pupils: "I think Miss Knightly will come to see us this week. She was at Walnut Creek yesterday."

After she had driven westward through the pasture lands for an hour or so, Miss Knightly turned her mare north and very soon came into a rich farming district, where the fields were too valuable to be used for much grazing. Big red barns, rows of yellow straw stacks, green orchards, trim white farmhouses, fenced gardens.

Looking at her watch, Miss Knightly found that it was already after eleven o'clock. She touched Molly delicately with the whip and roused her to a jog trot. Presently they stopped before a little one-storey schoolhouse. All the windows were open. At the hitch-bar in the yard five horses were tethered—their saddles and bridles piled in an empty buckboard. There was a yard, but no fence—though on one side of the playground was a woven-wire fence covered with the vines of sturdy rambler roses—very pretty in the spring. It enclosed a cemetery—very few graves, very much sun and waving yellow grass, open to the singing from the schoolroom and the shouts of the boys playing ball at noon. The cemetery never depressed the children, and surely the school cast no gloom over the cemetery.

When Miss Knightly stopped before the door, a boy ran out to hand her from the buggy and to take care of Molly. The little teacher stood on the doorstep, her face lost, as it were, in a wide smile of tremulous gladness.

Miss Knightly took her hand, held it for a moment and looked down into the child's face—she was scarcely more—and said in the very gentlest shade of her many-shaded voice, "Everything going well, Lesley?"

The teacher replied in happy little gasps, "Oh yes, Miss Knightly! It's all so much easier than it was last year. I have some such lovely children—and they're all *good*!"

Miss Knightly took her arm, and they went into the schoolroom. The pupils grinned a welcome to the visitor. The teacher asked the conventional question: What recitation would she like to hear?

Whatever came next in the usual order, Miss Knightly said.

The class in geography came next. The children were "bounding" the States. When the North Atlantic States had been disposed of with more or less accuracy, the little teacher said they would now jump to the Middle West, to bring the lesson nearer home.

"Suppose we begin with Illinois. That is your State, Edward, so I will call on you."

A pale boy rose and came front of the class; a little fellow aged ten, maybe, who was plainly a newcomer—wore knee pants and stockings, instead of long trousers or blue overalls like the other boys. His hands were clenched at his sides, and he was evidently much frightened. Looking appealingly at the little teacher, he began in a high treble: "The State of Illinois is bounded on the north by Lake Michigan, on the east by Lake Michigan . . ." He felt he had gone astray, and language utterly failed. A quick shudder ran over him from head to foot, and an accident happened. His dark blue stockings grew darker still, and his knickerbockers very dark. He stood there as if nailed to the floor. The teacher went up to him and took his hand and led him to his desk.

"You're too tired, Edward," she said. "We're all tired, and it's almost noon. So you can all run out and play, while I talk to Miss Knightly and tell her how naughty you all are."

The children laughed (all but poor Edward), laughed heartily, as if they were suddenly relieved from some strain. Still laughing and punching each other they ran out into the sunshine.

Miss Knightly and the teacher (her name, by the way, was Lesley Ferguesson) sat down on a bench in the corner.

"I'm so sorry that happened, Miss Knightly. I oughtn't to have called on him. He's so new here, and he's a nervous little boy. I thought he'd like to speak up for his State. He seems homesick."

"My dear, I'm glad you did call on him, and I'm glad the poor little fellow had an accident,—if he doesn't get too much misery out of it. The way those children behaved astonished me. Not a wink, or grin, or even a look. Not a wink from the Haymaker boy. I watched him. His mother has no such delicacy. They have just the best kind of good manners. How do you do it, Lesley?"

Lesley gave a happy giggle and flushed as red as a poppy. "Oh, I don't do anything! You see they really *are* nice children. You remember last year I did have a little trouble—till they got used to me."

"But they all passed their finals, and one girl, who was older than her teacher, got a school."

"Hush, hush, ma'am! I'm afraid for the walls to hear it! Nobody knows our secret but my mother."

"I'm very well satisfied with the results of our crime, Lesley."

The girl blushed again. She loved to hear Miss Knightly speak her name, because she always sounded the *s* like a *z*, which made it seem gentler and more intimate. Nearly every one else, even her mother, hissed the *s* as if it were spelled "Lessley." It was embarrassing to have such a queer name, but she respected it because her father had chosen it for her.

"Where are you going to stay all night, Miss Knightly?" she asked rather timidly.

"I think Mrs. Ericson expects me to stay with her."

"Mrs. Hunt, where I stay, would be awful glad to have you, but I know you'll be more comfortable at Mrs. Ericson's. She's a lovely housekeeper." Lesley resigned the faint hope that Miss Knightly would stay where she herself boarded, and broke out eagerly:

"Oh, Miss Knightly, have you seen any of our boys lately? Mother's too busy to write to me often."

"Hector looked in at my office last week. He came to the Court House with a telegram for the sheriff. He seemed well and happy."

"Did he? But Miss Knightly, I wish he hadn't taken that messenger job. I hate so for him to quit school."

"Now, I wouldn't worry about that, my dear. School isn't everything. He'll be getting good experience every day at the depot."

"Do you think so? I haven't seen him since he went to work."

"Why, how long has it been since you were home?"

"It's over a month now. Not since my school started. Father has been working all our horses on the farm. Maybe you can share my lunch with me?"

"I brought a lunch for the two of us, my dear. Call your favourite boy to go to my buggy and get my basket for us. After lunch I would like to hear the advanced arithmetic class."

While the pupils were doing their sums at the blackboard, Miss Knightly herself was doing a little figuring. This was Thursday. Tomorrow she would visit two schools, and she had planned to spend Friday night with a pleasant family on Farmers' Creek. But she could change her schedule and give this homesick child a visit with her family in the county seat. It would inconvenience her very little.

When the class in advanced arithmetic was dismissed, Miss Knightly made a joking little talk to the children and told them about a very bright little girl in Scotland who knew nearly a whole play of Shakespeare's by heart, but who wrote in her diary: "Nine times nine is the Devil"; which proved, she said, that there are two kinds of memory, and God is very good to anyone to whom he gives both kinds. Then she asked if the pupils might have a special recess of half an hour, as a present from her. They gave her a cheer and out they trooped, the boys to the ball ground, and the girls to the cemetery, to sit neatly on the headstones and discuss Miss Knightly.

During their recess the Superintendent disclosed her plan. "I've been wondering, Lesley, whether you wouldn't like to go back to town with me after school tomorrow. We could get into MacAlpin by seven o'clock, and you could have all of Saturday and Sunday at home. Then we would make an early start Monday morning, and I would drop you here at the schoolhouse at nine o'clock."

The little teacher caught her breath—she became quite pale for a moment. "Oh Miss Knightly, could you? Could you?"

"Of course I can. I'll stop for you here at four o'clock tomorrow afternoon."

II

The dark secret between Lesley and Miss Knightly was that only this September had the girl reached the legal age for teachers, yet she had been teaching all last year when she was still under age!

Last summer, when the applicants for teachers' certificates took written examinations in the County Superintendent's offices at the Court House in MacAlpin, Lesley Ferguesson had appeared with some twenty-six girls and nine boys. She wrote all morning and all afternoon for two days. Miss Knightly found her paper one of the best in the lot. A week later, when all the papers were filed, Miss Knightly told Lesley she could certainly give her a school. The morning after she had thus notified Lesley, she found the girl herself waiting on the sidewalk in front of the house where Miss Knightly boarded.

"Could I walk over to the Court House with you, Miss Knightly? I ought to tell you something," she blurted out at once. "On that paper I didn't put down my real age. I put down sixteen, and I won't be fifteen until this September."

"But I checked you with the high-school records, Lesley."

"I know. I put it down wrong there, too. I didn't want to be the class baby, and I hoped I could get a school soon, to help out at home."

The County Superintendent thought she would long remember that walk to the Court House. She could see that the child had spent a bad night; and she had walked up from her home down by the depot, quite a mile away, probably without breakfast.

"If your age is wrong on both records, why do you tell me about it now?"

"Oh, Miss Knightly, I got to thinking about it last night, how if you did give me a school it might all come out, and mean people would say you knew about it and broke the law."

Miss Knightly was thoughtless enough to chuckle. "But, my dear, don't you see that if I didn't know about it until this moment, I am completely innocent?"

The child who was walking beside her stopped short and burst into sobs. Miss Knightly put her arm around those thin, eager, forward-reaching shoulders.

"Don't cry, dear. I was only joking. There's nothing very dreadful about it. You didn't give your age under oath, you know." The sobs didn't stop. "Listen, let me tell you something. That big Hatch boy put his age down as nineteen, and I know he was teaching down in Nemaha County four years ago. I can't always be sure about the age applicants put down. I have to use my judgment."

The girl lifted her pale, troubled face and murmured, "Judgment?"

"Yes. Some girls are older at thirteen than others are at eighteen. Your paper was one of the best handed in this year, and I am going to give you a school. Not a big one, but a nice one, in a nice part of the county. Now let's go into Ernie's coffee shop and have some more breakfast. You have a long walk home."

Of course, fourteen was rather young for a teacher in an ungraded school, where she was likely to have pupils of sixteen and eighteen in her classes. But Miss Knightly's "judgment" was justified by the fact that in June the school directors of the Wild Rose district asked to have "Miss Ferguesson" back for the following year.

III

At four o'clock on Friday afternoon Miss Knightly stopped at the Wild Rose schoolhouse to find the teacher waiting by the roadside, and the pupils already scattering across the fields, their tin lunch pails flashing back the sun. Lesley was standing almost in the road itself, her grey "telescope" bag at her feet. The moment old Molly stopped, she stowed her bag in the back of the buggy and climbed in beside Miss Knightly. Her smile was so eager and happy that her friend chuckled softly. "You still get a little homesick, don't you, Lesley?"

She didn't deny it. She gave a guilty laugh and murmured, "I do miss the boys."

The afternoon sun was behind them, throwing over the pastures and the harvested, resting fields that wonderful light, so yellow that it is actually orange. The three hours and the fourteen miles seemed not overlong. As the buggy neared the town of MacAlpin, Miss Knightly thought she could feel Lesley's heart beat. The girl had been silent a long while when she exclaimed:

"Look, there's the standpipe!"

The object of this emotion was a red sheet-iron tube which thrust its naked ugliness some eighty feet into the air and held the water supply for the town of MacAlpin. As it stood on a hill, it was the first thing one saw on approaching the town from the west. Old Molly, too, seemed to have spied this heartening landmark, for she quickened her trot without encouragement from the whip. From that point on, Lesley said not a word. There were two more low hills (very low), and then Miss Knightly turned off the main road and drove by a short cut through the baseball ground, to the south appendix of the town proper, the "depot settlement" where the Ferguessons lived.

Their house stood on a steep hillside—a storey-and-a-half frame house with a basement on the downhill side, faced with brick up to the first-floor level. When the buggy stopped before the yard gate, two little boys came running out of the front door. Miss Knightly's passenger vanished from her side—she didn't know just when Lesley alighted. Her attention was distracted by the appearance of the mother, with a third boy, still in kilts, trotting behind her.

Mrs. Ferguesson was not a person who could be overlooked. All the merchants in MacAlpin admitted that she was a fine figure of a woman. As she came down the little yard and out of the gate, the evening breeze ruffled her wavy auburn hair. Her quick step and alert, upright carriage gave one the impression that she got things done. Coming up to the buggy, she took Miss Knightly's hand.

"Why, it's Miss Knightly! And she's brought our girl along to visit us. That was mighty clever of you, Miss, and these boys will surely be a happy family. They do miss their sister." She spoke clearly, distinctly, but with a slight Missouri turn of speech.

By this time Lesley and her brothers had become telepathically one. Miss Knightly couldn't tell what the boys said to her, or whether they said anything, but they had her old canvas bag out of the buggy and up on the porch in no time at all. Lesley ran toward the front door, hurried back to thank Miss Knightly, and then disappeared, holding fast to the little chap in skirts. She had forgotten to ask at what time Miss Knightly would call for her on Monday, but her mother attended to that. When Mrs. Ferguesson followed the children through the hall and the little back parlour into the dining-room, Lesley turned to her and asked breathlessly, almost sharply:

"Where's Hector?"

"He's often late on Friday night, dear. He telephoned me from the depot and said not to wait supper for him—he'd get a sandwich at the lunch counter. Now how *are* you, my girl?" Mrs. Ferguesson put her hands on Lesley's shoulders and looked into her glowing eyes.

"Just fine, Mother. I like my school so much! And the scholars are nicer even than they were last year. I just love some of them."

At this the little boy in kilts (the fashion of the times, though he was four years old) caught his sister's skirt in his two hands and jerked it to get her attention. "No, no!" he said mournfully, "you don't love anybody but us!"

His mother laughed, and Lesley stooped and gave him the right hug he wanted.

The family supper was over. Mrs. Ferguesson put on her apron. "Sit right down, Lesley, and talk to the children. No, I won't let you help me. You'll help me most by keeping them out of my way. I'll scramble you an egg and fry you some ham, so sit right down in your own place. I have some stewed plums for your dessert, and a beautiful angel cake I bought at the Methodist bake sale. Your father's gone to some political meeting, so we had supper early. You'll be a nice surprise for him when he gets home. He hadn't been gone half an hour when Miss Knightly drove up. Sit still, dear, it only bothers me if anybody tries to help me. I'll let you wash the dishes afterward, like we always do."

Lesley sat down at the half-cleared table; an oval-shaped table which could be extended by the insertion of "leaves" when Mrs. Ferguesson had company. The room was already dusky (twilights are short in a flat country), and one of the boys switched on the light which hung by a cord high above the table. A shallow china shade over the bulb threw a glaring white light down on the sister and the boys who stood about her chair. Lesley wrinkled up her brow, but it didn't occur to her that the light was too strong. She gave herself up to the feeling of being at home. It went all through her, that feeling, like getting into a warm bath when one is tired. She was safe from everything, was where she wanted to be, where she ought to be. A plant that has been washed out by a rain storm feels like that, when a kind gardener puts it gently back into its own earth with its own group.

The two older boys, Homer and Vincent, kept interrupting each other, trying to tell her things, but she didn't really listen to what they said. The little fellow stood close beside her chair, holding on to her skirt, fingering the glass buttons on her jacket. He was named Bryan, for his father's hero, but he didn't fit the name very well. He was a rather wistful and timid child.

Mrs. Ferguesson brought the ham and eggs and the warmed-up coffee. Then she sat down opposite her daughter to watch her enjoy her supper. "Now don't talk to her, boys. Let her eat in peace."

Vincent spoke up. "Can't I just tell her what happened to my lame pigeon?"

Mrs. Ferguesson merely shook her head. She had control in that household, sure enough!

Before Lesley had quite finished her supper she heard the front door open and shut. The boys started up, but the mother raised a warning finger. They understood; a surprise. They were still as mice, and listened: A pause in the hall . . . he was hanging up his cap. Then he came in—the flower of the family.

For a moment he stood speechless in the doorway, the "incandescent" glaring full on his curly yellow hair and his amazed blue eyes. He was surprised indeed!

"Lesley!" he breathed, as if he were talking in his sleep.

She couldn't sit still. Without knowing that she got up and took a step, she had her arms around her brother. "It's me, Hector! Ain't I lucky? Miss Knightly brought me in."

"What time did you get here? You might have telephoned me, Mother."

"Dear, she ain't been here much more than half an hour."

"And Miss Knightly brought you in with old Molly, did she?" Oh, the lovely voice he had, that Hector!—warm, deliberate . . . it made the most commonplace remark full of meaning. He had to say merely that—and it told his appreciation of Miss Knightly's kindness, even a playful gratitude to Molly, her clumsy, fat, road-pounding old mare. He was tall for his age, was Hector, and he had the fair pink-cheeked complexion which Lesley should have had and didn't.

Mrs. Ferguesson rose. "Now let's all go into the parlour and talk. We'll come back and clear up afterward." With this she opened the folding doors, and they followed her and found comfortable chairs—there was even a homemade hassock for Bryan. There were real books in the sectional bookcases (old Ferg's fault), and there was a real Brussels carpet in soft colours on the floor. That was Lesley's fault. Most of her savings from her first year's teaching had gone into that carpet. She had chosen it herself from the samples which Marshall Field's travelling man brought to MacAlpin. There were comfortable old-fashioned pictures on the walls—"Venice by Moonlight" and such. Lesley and Hector thought it a beautiful room.

Of course the room was pleasant because of the feeling the children had for one another, and because in Mrs. Ferguesson there was authority and organization. Here the family sat and talked until Father came home. He was always treated a little like company. His wife and his children had a deep respect for him and for experimental farming, and profound veneration for William Jennings Bryan. Even little Bryan knew he was named for a great man, and must some day stop being afraid of the dark.

James Grahame Ferguesson was a farmer. He spent most of his time on what he called an "experimental farm." (The neighbours had other names for it—some of them amusing.) He was a loosely built man; had drooping shoulders carried with a forward thrust. He was a ready speaker, and usually made the Fourth of July speech in MacAlpin—spoke from a platform in the Court House grove, and even the farmers who joked about Ferguesson came to hear him. Alf Delaney declared: "I like to see anything done well—even talking. If old Ferg could shuck corn as fast as he can rustle the dictionary, I'd hire him, even if he is a Pop."

Old Ferg was not at all old—just turned forty—but he was fussy about the spelling of his name. He wrote it James Ferguesson. The merchants, even the local newspaper, simply would not spell it that way. They left letters out, or they put letters in. He complained about this repeatedly, and the result was that he was simply called "Ferg" to his face, and "old Ferg" to his back. His neighbours, both in town and in the country where he farmed, liked him because he gave them so much to talk about. He couldn't keep a hired man long at any wages. His habits were too unconventional. He rose early, saw to the chores like any other man, and went into the field for the morning. His lunch was a cold spread from his wife's kitchen, reinforced by hot tea. (The hired man was expected to bring his own lunch—outrageous!) After lunch Mr. Ferguesson took off his boots and lay down on the blue gingham sheets of a wide bed, and remained there until what he called "the cool of the afternoon." When that refreshing season arrived, he fed and watered his work horses, put the young gelding to his buckboard, and drove four miles to MacAlpin for his wife's hot supper. Mrs. Ferguesson, though not at all a meek woman or a stupid one, unquestioningly believed him when he told her that he did his best thinking in the afternoon. He hinted to her that he was working out in his head something that would benefit the farmers of the county more than all the corn and wheat they could raise even in a good year.

Sometimes Ferguesson did things she regretted—not because they were wrong, but because other people had mean tongues. When a fashion came in for giving names to farms which had hitherto been designated by figures (range, section, quarter, etc.), and his neighbours came out with "Lone Tree Farm," "Cold Spring Farm," etc., Ferguesson tacked on a cottonwood tree by his gate a neatly painted board inscribed: WIDE AWAKE FARM.

His neighbours, who could never get used to his afternoon siesta, were not long in converting this prophetic christening into "Hush-a-bye Farm." Mrs. Ferguesson overheard some of this joking on a Saturday night (she was marketing late after a lodge meeting on top of a busy day), and she didn't like it. On Sunday morning when he was dressing for church, she asked her husband why he ever gave the farm such a foolish name. He explained to her that the important crop on that farm was an idea. His farm was like an observatory where one watched the signs of the times and saw the great change that was coming for the benefit of all mankind. He even quoted Tennyson about looking into the future "far as human eye could see." It had been a long time since he had quoted any poetry to her. She sighed and dropped the matter.

On the whole, Ferg did himself a good turn when he put up that piece of nomenclature. People drove out of their way for miles to see it. They felt more kindly toward old Ferg because he wrote himself down such an ass. In a hardworking farming community a good joke is worth something. Ferguesson himself felt a gradual warming toward him among his neighbours. He ascribed it to the power of his oratory. It was really because he had made himself so absurd, but this he never guessed. Idealists are seldom afraid of ridicule—if they recognize it.

The Ferguesson children believed that their father was misunderstood by people of inferior intelligence, and that conviction gave them a "cause" which bound them together. They must do better than other children; better in school, and better on the playground. They must turn in a quarter of a dollar to help their mother out whenever they could. Experimental farming wasn't immediately remunerative.

Fortunately there was never any rent to pay. They owned their house down by the depot. When Mrs. Ferguesson's father died down in Missouri, she bought that place with what he left her. She knew that was the safe thing to do, her husband being a thinker. Her children were bound to her, and to that house, by the deepest, the most solemn loyalty. They never spoke of that covenant to each other, never even formulated it in their own minds—never. It was a consciousness they shared, and it gave them a family complexion.

On this Saturday of Lesley's surprise visit home, Father was with the family for breakfast. That was always a pleasant way to begin the day—especially on Saturday, when no one was in a hurry. He had grave good manners toward his wife and his children. He talked to them as if they were grown-up reasonable beings—talked a trifle as if from a rostrum, perhaps,—and he never indulged in small-town gossip. He was much more likely to tell them what he had read in the *Omaha World-Herald* yesterday; news of the State capital and the national capital. Sometimes he told them what a grasping selfish country England was. Very often he explained to them how the gold standard had kept the poor man down. The family seldom bothered him about petty matters— such as that Homer needed new shoes, or that the iceman's bill for the whole summer had come in for the third time. Mother would take care of that.

On this particular Saturday morning Ferguesson gave especial attention to Lesley. He asked her about her school, and had her name her pupils. "I think you are fortunate to have the Wild Rose school, Lesley," he said as he rose from the table. "The farmers up there are open-minded and prosperous. I have sometimes wished that I had settled up there, though there are certain advantages in living at the county seat. The educational opportunities are better. Your friendship with Miss Knightly has been a broadening influence."

He went out to hitch up the buckboard to drive to the farm, while his wife put up the lunch he was to take along with him, and Lesley went upstairs to make the beds.

"Upstairs" was a story in itself, a secret romance. No caller or neighbour had ever been allowed to go up there. All the children loved it—it was their very own world where there were no older people poking about to spoil things. And it was unique—not at all like other people's upstairs chambers. In her stuffy little bedroom out in the country Lesley had more than once cried for it.

Lesley and the boys liked space, not tight cubbyholes. Their upstairs was a long attic which ran the whole length of the house, from the front door downstairs to the kitchen at the back. Its great charm was that it was unlined. No plaster, no beaver-board lining; just the roof shingles, supported by long unplaned, splintery rafters that sloped from the sharp roof-peak down to the floor of the attic. Bracing these long roof rafters were cross rafters on which one could hang things—a little personal washing, a curtain for tableaux, a rope swing for Bryan.

In this spacious, undivided loft were two brick chimneys, going up in neat little stair-steps from the plank floor to the shingle roof—and out of it to the stars! The chimneys were of red, unglazed brick, with lines of white mortar to hold them together.

Last year, after Lesley first got her school, Mrs. Ferguesson exerted her authority and partitioned off a little room over the kitchen end of the "upstairs" for her daughter. Before that, all the children slept in this delightful attic. The three older boys occupied two wide beds, their sister her little single bed. Bryan, subject to croup, still slumbered downstairs near his mother, but he looked forward to his ascension as to a state of pure beatitude.

There was certainly room enough up there for widely scattered quarters, but the three beds stood in a row, as in a hospital ward. The children liked to be close enough together to share experiences.

Experiences were many. Perhaps the most exciting was when the driving, sleety snowstorms came on winter nights. The roof shingles were old and had curled under hot summer suns. In a driving snowstorm the frozen flakes sifted in through all those little cracks, sprinkled the beds and the children, melted on their faces, in their hair! That was delightful. The rest of you was snug and warm under blankets and comforters, with a hot brick at one's feet. The wind howled outside; sometimes the white light from the snow and the half-strangled moon came in through the single end window. Each child had his own dream-adventure. They did not exchange confidences; every "fellow" had a right to his own. They never told their love.

If they turned in early, they had a good while to enjoy the outside weather; they never went to sleep until after ten o'clock, for then came the sweetest morsel of the night. At that hour Number Seventeen, the westbound passenger, whistled in. The station and the engine house were perhaps an eighth of a mile down the hill, and from far away across the meadows the children could hear that whistle. Then came the heavy pants of the locomotive in the frosty air. Then a hissing—then silence: she was taking water.

On Saturdays the children were allowed to go down to the depot to see Seventeen come in. It was a fine sight on winter nights. Sometimes the great locomotive used to sweep in armoured in ice and snow, breathing fire like a dragon, its great red eye shooting a blinding beam along the white roadbed and shining wet rails. When it stopped, it panted like a great beast. After it was watered by the big hose from the overhead tank, it seemed to draw long deep breaths, ready to charge afresh over the great Western land.

Yes, they were grand old warriors, those towering locomotives of other days. They seemed to mean power, conquest, triumph—Jim Hill's dream. They set children's hearts beating from Chicago to Los Angeles. They were the awakeners of many a dream.

As she made the boys' beds that Saturday morning and put on clean sheets, Lesley was thinking she would give a great deal to sleep out here as she used to. But when she got her school last year, her mother had said she must have a room of her own. So a carpenter brought sheathing and "lined" the end of the long loft—the end over the kitchen; and Mrs. Ferguesson bought a little yellow washstand and a bowl and pitcher, and said with satisfaction: "Now you see, Lesley, if you were sick, we would have some place to take the doctor." To be sure, the doctor would have to be admitted through the kitchen, and then come up a dark winding stairway with two turns. (Mr. Ferguesson termed it "the turnpike." His old Scotch grandmother, he said, had always thus called a winding stairway.) And Lesley's room, when you got there, was very like a snug wooden box. It was possible, of course, to leave her door open into the long loft, where the wood was brown and the chimneys red and the weather always so close to one. Out there things were still wild and rough—it wasn't a bedroom or a chamber—it was a hall, in the old baronial sense, reminded her of the lines in their *Grimm's Fairy Tales* book:

> Return, return, thou youthful bride,
> This is a robbers' hall inside.

IV

When her daughter had put the attic to rights, Mrs. Ferguesson went uptown to do her Saturday marketing. Lesley slipped out through the kitchen door and sat down on the back porch. The front porch was kept neat and fit to receive callers, but the back porch was given over to the boys. It was a messy-looking place, to be sure. From the wooden ceiling hung two trapezes. At one corner four boxing gloves were piled in a broken chair. In the trampled, grassless back yard, two-by-fours, planted upright, supported a length of lead pipe on which Homer practised bar exercises. Lesley sat down on the porch floor, her feet on the ground, and sank into idleness and safety and perfect love.

The boys were much the dearest things in the world to her. To love them so much was just . . . happiness. To think about them was the most perfect form of happiness. Had they been actually present, swinging on the two trapezes, turning on the bar, she would have been too much excited, too actively happy to be perfectly happy. But sitting in the warm sun, with her feet on the good ground, even her mother away, she almost ceased to exist. The feeling of being at home was complete, absolute: it made her sleepy. And that feeling was not so much the sense of being protected by her father and mother as of being with, and being one with, her brothers. It was the clan feeling, which meant life or death for the blood, not for the individual. For some reason, or for no reason, back in the beginning, creatures wanted the blood to continue.

After the noonday dinner Mrs. Ferguesson thoughtfully confided to her daughter while they were washing the dishes:

"Lesley, I'm divided in my mind. I would so appreciate a quiet afternoon with you, but I've a sort of engagement with the P.E.O. A lady from Canada is to be there to talk to us, and I've promised to introduce her. And just when I want to have a quiet time with you."

Lesley gave a sigh of relief and thought how fortunate it is that circumstances do sometimes make up our mind for us. In that battered canvas bag upstairs there was a roll of arithmetic papers and "essays" which hung over her like a threat. Now she would have a still hour in their beautiful parlour to correct them; the shades drawn down, just enough light to read by, her father's unabridged at hand, and the boys playing bat and pitch in the back yard.

Lesley and her brothers were proud of their mother's good looks, and that she never allowed herself to become a household drudge, as so many of her neighbours did. She "managed," and the boys helped her to manage. For one thing, there were never any dreary tubs full of washing standing about, and there was no ironing day to make a hole in the week. They sent all the washing, even the sheets, to the town steam laundry. Hector, with his weekly wages as messenger boy, and Homer and Vincent with their stable jobs, paid for it. That simple expedient did away with the worst blight of the working man's home.

Mrs. Ferguesson was "public-spirited," and she was the friend of all good causes. The business men of the town agreed that she had a great deal of influence, and that her name added strength to any committee. She was generally spoken of as a very *practical* woman, with an emphasis which implied several things. She was a "joiner," too! She was a Royal Neighbor, and a Neighborly Neighbor, and a P.E.O., and an Eastern Star. She had even joined the Methodist Win-a-Couple, though she warned them that she could not attend their meetings, as she liked to spend some of her evenings at home.

Promptly at six thirty Monday morning Miss Knightly's old mare stopped in front of the Ferguessons' house. The four boys were all on the front porch. James himself carried Lesley's bag down and put it into the buggy. He thanked the Superintendent very courteously for her kindness and kissed his daughter good-bye.

It had been at no trifling sacrifice that Miss Knightly was able to call for Lesley at six thirty. Customarily she started on her long drives at nine o'clock. This morning she had to give an extra half-dollar to the man who came to curry and harness her mare. She herself got no proper breakfast, but a cold sandwich and a cup of coffee at the station lunch counter—the only eating-place open at six o'clock. Most serious of all, she must push Molly a little on the road, to land her passenger at the Wild Rose schoolhouse at nine o'clock. Such small inconveniences do not sum up to an imposing total, but we assume them only for persons we really care for.

V

It was Christmas Eve. The town was busy with Christmas "exercises," and all the churches were lit up. Hector Ferguesson was going slowly up the hill which separated the depot settlement from the town proper. He walked at no messenger-boy pace tonight, crunching under his feet the snow which had fallen three days ago, melted, and then frozen hard. His hands were in the pockets of his new overcoat, which was so long that it almost touched the ground when he toiled up the steepest part of the hill. It was very heavy and not very warm. In those days there was a theory that in topcoats very little wool was necessary if they were woven tight enough and hard enough to "keep out the cold." A barricade was the idea. Hector carried the weight and clumsiness bravely, proudly. His new overcoat was a Christmas present from his sister. She had gone to the big town in the next county to shop for it, and bought it with her own money. He was thinking how kind Lesley was, and how hard she had worked for that money, and how much she had to put up with in the rough farmhouse where she boarded, out in the country. It was usually a poor housekeeper who was willing to keep a teacher, since they paid so little. Probably the amount Lesley spent for that coat would have kept her at a comfortable house all winter. When he grew up, and made lots of money (a brakeman—maybe an engineer), he would certainly be good to his sister.

Hector was a strange boy; a blend of the soft and the hard. In action he was practical, executive, like his mother. But in his mind, in his thoughts and plans, he was extravagant, often absurd. His mother suspected that he was "dreamy." Tonight, as he trailed up the frozen wooden sidewalk toward the town, he kept looking up at the stars, which were unusually bright, as they always seem over a stretch of snow. He was wondering if there were angels up there, watching the world on Christmas Eve. They came before, on the first Christmas Eve, he knew. Perhaps they kept the Anniversary. He thought about a beautiful coloured picture tacked up in Lesley's bedroom; two angels with white robes and long white wings, flying toward a low hill in the early dawn before sunrise, and on that distant hill, against the soft daybreak light, were three tiny crosses. He never doubted angels looked like that. He was credulous and truthful by nature. There was that look in his blue eyes. He would get it knocked out of him, his mother knew. But she believed he would always keep some of it—enough to make him open-handed and open-hearted.

Tonight Hector had his leather satchel full of Christmas telegrams. After he had delivered them all, he would buy his presents for his mother and the children. The stores sold off their special Christmas things at a discount after eleven o'clock on Christmas Eve.

VI

Miss Knightly was in Lincoln, attending a convention of Superintendents of Public Instruction, when the long-to-be-remembered blizzard swept down over the prairie State. Travel and telephone service were discontinued. A Chicago passenger train was stalled for three days in a deep cut west of W—. There she lay, and the dining-car had much ado to feed the passengers.

Miss Knightly was snowbound in Lincoln. She tarried there after the convention was dismissed and her fellow superintendents had gone home to their respective counties. She was caught by the storm because she had stayed over to see Julia Marlowe (then young and so fair!) in *The Love Chase*. She was not inconsolable to be delayed for some days. Why worry? She was staying at a small but very pleasant hotel where the food was good and the beds were comfortable. She was New England born and bred, too conscientious to stay over in the city from mere self-indulgence, but quite willing to be lost to MacAlpin and X— County by the intervention of fate. She stayed, in fact, a week, greatly enjoying such luxuries as plenty of running water, hot baths, and steam heat. At that date MacAlpin houses, and even her office in the Court House, were heated by hard-coal stoves.

At last she was jogging home on a passenger train which left Lincoln at a convenient hour (it was two hours late, travel was still disorganized), when she was pleased to see Mr. Redman in conductor's uniform come into the car. Two of his boys had been her pupils when she taught in high school, before she was elected to a county office. Mr. Redman also seemed pleased, and after he had been through the train to punch tickets, he came back and sat down in the green plush seat opposite Miss Knightly and began to "tease."

"I hear there was a story going up at the Court House that you'd eloped. I was hoping you hadn't made a mistake."

"No. I thought it over and avoided the mistake. But what about you, Mr. Redman? You belong on the run west out of MacAlpin, don't you?"

"I don't know where I belong, Ma'm, and nobody else does. This is Jack Kelly's run, but he got his leg broke trying to help the train crew shovel the sleeping-car loose in that deep cut out of W—. The passengers were just freezing. This blizzard has upset everything. There's got to be better organization from higher up. This has taught us we just can't handle an emergency. Hard on stock, hard on people. A little neighbour of ours—why, you must know her, she was one of your teachers—Jim Ferguesson's little girl. She got pneumonia out there in the country and died out there."

Miss Knightly went so white that Redman without a word hunted to the end of the car and brought back a glass of water. He kept muttering that he was sorry . . . that he "always put his foot in it."

She did not disappoint him. She came back quickly. "That's all right, Mr. Redman. I'd rather hear it before I get home. Did she get lost in the storm? I don't understand."

Mr. Redman sat down and did the best he could to repair damages.

"No, Ma'm, little Lesley acted very sensible, didn't lose her head. You see, the storm struck us about three o'clock in the afternoon. The whole day it had been mild and soft, like Spring. Then it came down instanter, like a thousand tons of snow dumped out of the sky. My wife was out in the back yard taking in some clothes she'd hung to dry. She hadn't even a shawl over her head. The suddenness of it confused her so (she couldn't see three feet before her), she wandered around in our back yard, couldn't find her way back to the house. Pretty soon our old dog—he's part shepherd—came yappin' and whinin'. She dropped the clothes and held onto his hair, and he got her to the back porch. That's how bad it was in MacAlpin."

"And Lesley?" Miss Knightly murmured.

"Yes, Ma'm! I'm coming to that. Her scholars tell about how the schoolroom got a little dark, and they all looked out, and there was no graveyard, and no horses that some of them had rode to school on. The boys jumped up to run out and see after the horses, but Lesley stood with her back against the door and wouldn't let 'em go out. Told 'em it would be over in a few minutes. Well, you see it wasn't. Over four feet of snow fell in less'n an hour. About six o'clock some of the fathers of the children that lived aways off started out on horseback, but the horses waded belly-deep, and a wind come up and it turned cold.

"Ford Robertson is the nearest neighbour, you know,—scarcely more than across the road—eighth of a mile, maybe. As soon as he come in from his corral—the Herefords had all bunched up together, over a hundred of 'em, under the lee of a big haystack, and he knew they wouldn't freeze. As soon as he got in, the missus made him go over to the schoolhouse an' take a rope along an' herd 'em all over to her house, teacher an' all, with the boys leading their horses. That night Mrs. Robertson cooked nearly everything in the house for their supper, and she sent Ford upstairs to help Lesley make shakedown beds on the floor. Mrs. Robertson remembers when the big supper was ready and the children ate like wolves, Lesley didn't eat much—said she had a little headache. Next morning she was pretty sick. That day all the fathers came on horseback for the children. Robertson got one of them to go for old Doctor Small, and he came down on his horse. Doctor said it was pneumonia, and there wasn't much he could do. She didn't seem to have strength to rally. She was out of her head when he got there. She was mostly unconscious for three days, and just slipped out. The funeral is tomorrow. The roads are open now. They were to bring her home today."

The train stopped at a station, and Mr. Redman went to mend to his duties. When he next came through the car Miss Knightly spoke to him. She had recovered herself. Her voice was steady, though very low and very soft when she asked him:

"Were any of her family out there with her when she was ill?"

"Why, yes, Mrs. Ferguesson was out there. That boy Hector got his mother through, before the roads were open. He'd stop at a farmhouse and explain the situation and borrow a team and get the farmer or one of his hands to give them a lift to the next farm, and there they'd get a lift a little further. Everybody knew about the school and the teacher by that time, and wanted to help, no matter how bad the roads were. You see, Miss Knightly, everything would have gone better if it hadn't come on so freezing cold, and if the snow hadn't been so darn soft when it first fell. That family are terrible broke up. We all are, down at the depot. She didn't recognize them when they got there, I heard."

VII

Twenty years after that historic blizzard Evangeline Knightly—now Mrs. Ralph Thorndike—alighted from the last eastbound passenger at the Mac-Alpin station. No one at the station knew who she was except the station master, and he was not quite sure. She looked older, but she also looked more prosperous, more worldly. When she approached him at his office door and asked, "Isn't this Mr. Beardsley?" he recognized her voice and speech.

"That's who. And it's my guess this is, or used to be, Miss Knightly. I've been here almost forever. No ambition. But you left us a long time ago. You're looking fine, Ma'm, if I may say so."

She thanked him and asked him to recommend a hotel where she could stay for a day or two.

He scratched his head. "Well, the Plummer House ain't no Waldorf-Astoria, but the travelling men give a good report of it. The Bishop always stays there when he comes to town. You like me to telephone for an otto [automobile] to take you up? Lord, when you left here there wasn't an otto in the town!"

Mrs. Thorndike smiled. "Not many in the world, I think. And can you tell me, Mr. Beardsley, where the Ferguessons live?"

"The depot Ferguessons? Oh, they live uptown now. Ferg built right west of the Court House, right next to where the Donaldsons used to live. You'll find lots of changes. Some's come up, and some's come down. We used to laugh at Ferg and tell him politics didn't bring in the bacon. But he's got it on us now. The Democrats are sure grand job-givers. Throw 'em round for value received. I still vote the Republican ticket. Too old to change. Anyhow, all those new jobs don't affect the railroads much. They can't put a college professor on to run trains. Now I'll telephone for an otto for you."

Miss Knightly, after going to Denver, had married a very successful young architect, from New England, like herself, and now she was on her way back to Brunswick, Maine, to revisit the scenes of her childhood. Although she had never been in MacAlpin since she left it fifteen years ago, she faithfully read the MacAlpin *Messenger* and knew the important changes in the town.

After she had settled her room at the hotel, and unpacked her toilet articles, she took a cardboard box she had brought with her in the sleeping-car, and went out on a personal errand. She came back to the hotel late for lunch—had a tray sent up to her room, and at four o'clock went to the office in the Court House which used to be her office. This was the autumn of the year, and she had a great desire to drive out among the country schools and see how much fifteen years had changed the land, the pupils, the teachers.

When she introduced herself to the present incumbent, she was cordially received. The young Superintendent seemed a wide-awake, breezy girl, with bobbed blond hair and crimson lips. Her name was Wanda Bliss.

Mrs. Thorndike explained that her stay would not be long enough to let her visit all the country schools, but she would like Miss Bliss's advice as to which were the most interesting.

"Oh, I can run you around to nearly all of them in a day, in my car!"

Mrs. Thorndike thanked her warmly. She liked young people who were not in the least afraid of life or luck or responsibility. In her own youth there were very few like that. The teachers, and many of the pupils out in the country schools, were eager—but anxious. She laughed and told Miss Bliss that she meant to hire a buggy, if there was such a thing left in MacAlpin, and drive out into the country alone.

"I get you. You want to put on an old-home act. You might phone around to any farmers you used to know. Some of them still keep horses for haying."

Mrs. Thorndike got a list of the country teachers and the districts in which they taught. A few of them had been pupils in the schools she used to visit. Those she was determined to see.

The following morning she made the call she had stopped off at MacAlpin to make. She rang the doorbell at the house pointed out to her, and through the open window heard a voice call: "Come in, come in, please. I can't answer the bell."

Mrs. Thorndike opened the door into a shining oak hall with a shining oak stairway.

"Come right through, please. I'm in the back parlour. I sprained my ankle and can't walk yet."

The visitor followed the voice and found Mrs. Ferguesson sitting in a spring rocker, her bandaged right foot resting on a low stool.

"Come in, Ma'm. I have a bad sprain, and the little girl who does for me is downtown marketing. Maybe you came to see Mr. Ferguesson, but his office is—" here she broke off and looked up sharply—intently—at her guest. When the guest smiled, she broke out: "Miss Knightly! *Are* you Miss Knightly? Can it be?"

"They call me Mrs. Thorndike now, but I'm Evangeline Knightly just the same." She put out her hand, and Mrs. Ferguesson seized it with both her own.

"It's too good to be true!" she gasped with tears in her voice, "just too good to be true. The things we dream about that way don't happen." She held fast to Mrs. Thorndike's hand as if she were afraid she might vanish. "When did you come to town, and why didn't they let me know!"

"I came only yesterday, Mrs. Ferguesson, and I wanted to slip in on you just like this, with no one else around."

"Mr. Ferguesson must have known. But his mind is always off on some trail, and he never brings me any news when I'm laid up like this. Dear me! It's a long time." She pressed the visitor's hand again before she released it. "Get yourself a comfortable chair, dear, and sit down by me. I do hate to be helpless like this. It wouldn't have happened but for those slippery front stairs. Mr. Ferguesson just wouldn't put a carpet on them, because he says folks don't carpet hardwood stairs, and I tried to answer the doorbell in a hurry, and this is what come of it. I'm not naturally a clumsy woman on my feet."

Mrs. Thorndike noticed an aggrieved tone in her talk which had never been there in the old days when she had so much to be aggrieved about. She brought a chair and sat down close to Mrs. Ferguesson, facing her. The good woman had not changed much, she thought. There was a little grey in her crinkly auburn hair, and there were lines about her mouth which used not to be there, but her eyes had all the old fire.

"How comfortably you are fixed here, Mrs. Ferguesson! I'm so glad to find you like this."

"Yes, we're comfortable—now that they're all gone! It's mostly his taste. He took great interest." She spoke rather absently, and kept looking out through the polished hall toward the front door, as if she were expecting someone. It seemed a shame that anyone naturally so energetic should be enduring this foolish antiquated method of treating a sprain. The chief change in her, Mrs. Thorndike thought, was that she had grown softer. She reached for the visitor's hand again and held it fast. Tears came to her eyes.

Mrs. Thorndike ventured that she had found the town much changed for the better.

Yes, Mrs. Ferguesson supposed it was.

Then Mrs. Thorndike began in earnest. "How wonderful it is that all your sons have turned out so well! I take the MacAlpin paper chiefly to keep track of the Ferguesson boys. You and Mr. Ferguesson must be very proud."

"Yes'm, we are. We are thankful."

"Even the Denver papers have long articles about Hector and Homer and their great sheep ranches in Wyoming. And Vincent has become such a celebrated chemist, and is helping to destroy all the irreducible elements that I learned when I went to school. And Bryan is with Marshall Field!"

Mrs. Ferguesson nodded and pressed her hand, but she still kept looking down the hall toward the front door. Suddenly she turned with all herself to Mrs. Thorndike and with a storm of tears cried out from her heart: "Oh, Miss Knightly, talk to me about my Lesley! Seems so many have forgot her, but I know you haven't."

"No, Mrs. Ferguesson, I never forget her. Yesterday morning I took a box of roses that I brought with me from my own garden down to where she sleeps. I was glad to find a little seat there, so that I could stay for a long while and think about her."

"Oh, I wish I could have gone with you, Miss Knightly! (I can't call you anything else.) I wish we could have gone together. I can't help feeling she knows. *Anyhow,* we know! And there's nothing in all my life so precious to me to remember and think about as my Lesley. I'm no soft woman, either. The boys will tell you that. They'll tell you they got on because I always had a firm hand over them. They're all true to Lesley, my boys. Every time they come home they go down there. They feel it like I do, as if it had happened yesterday. Their father feels it, too, when he's not taken up with his abstractions. Anyhow, I don't think men feel things like women and boys. My boys have stayed boys. I do believe they feel as bad as I do about moving up here. We have four nice bedrooms upstairs to make them comfortable, should they all come home at once, and they're polite about us and tell us how well fixed we are. But Miss Knightly, I know at the bottom of their hearts they wish they was back in the old house down by the depot, sleeping in the attic."

Mrs. Thorndike stroked her hand. "I looked for the old house as I was coming up from the station. I made the driver stop."

"Ain't it dreadful, what's been done to it? If I'd foreseen, I'd never have let Mr. Ferguesson sell it. It was in my name. I'd have kept it to go back to and remember sometimes. Folks in middle age make a mistake when they think they can better themselves. They can't, not if they have any heart. And the other kind don't matter—they aren't real people—just poor put-ons, that try to be like the advertisements. Father even took me to California one winter. I was miserable all the time. And there were plenty more like me—miserable underneath. The women lined up in cafeterias, carrying their little trays—like convicts, seemed to me—and running to beauty shops to get their poor old hands manicured. And the old men, Miss Knightly, I pitied them most of all! Old bent-backed farmers, standing round in their shirt-sleeves, in plazas and alleyways, pitching horseshoes like they used to do at home. I tell you, people are happiest where they've had their children and struggled along and been real folks, and not tourists. What do you think about all this running around, Miss Knightly? You're an educated woman, I never had much schooling."

"I don't think schooling gives people any wisdom, Mrs. Ferguesson. I guess only life does that."

"Well, this I know: our best years are when we're working hardest and going right ahead when we can hardly see our way out. Times I was a good deal perplexed. But I always had one comfort. I did own our own house. I never had to worry about the rent. Don't it seem strange to you, though, that all our boys are so practical, and their father such a dreamer?"

Mrs. Thorndike murmured that some people think boys are most likely to take after their mother.

Mrs. Ferguesson smiled absently and shook her head. Presently she came out with: "It's a comfort to me up here, on a still night I can still hear the trains whistle in. Sometimes, when I can't sleep, I lie and listen for them. And I can almost think I am down there, with my children up in the loft. We were very happy." She looked up at her guest and smiled bravely. "I suppose you go away tonight?"

Mrs. Thorndike explained her plan to spend a day in the country.

"You're going out to visit the little schools? Why, God bless you, dear! You're still our Miss Knightly! But you'd better take a car, so you can get up to the Wild Rose school and back in one day. Do go there! The teacher is Mandy Perkins—she was one of her little scholars. You'll like Mandy, an' she loved

Lesley. You must get Bud Sullivan to drive you. Engage him right now—the telephone's there in the hall, and the garage is 306. He'll creep along for you, if you tell him. He does for me. I often go out to the Wild Rose school, and over to see dear Mrs. Robertson, who ain't so young as she was then. I can't go with Mr. Ferguesson. He drives so fast it's no satisfaction. And then he's not always mindful. He's had some accidents. When he gets to thinking, he's just as likely to run down a cow as not. He's had to pay for one. You know cows will cross the road right in front of a car. Maybe their grandchildren calves will be more modern-minded."

Mrs. Thorndike did not see her old friend again, but she wrote her a long letter from Wiscasset, Maine, which Mrs. Ferguesson sent to her son Hector, marked, "To be returned, but first pass on to your brothers."

Elevating the Ceiling

The Artist of the Beautiful

Nathaniel Hawthorne

Americans are notoriously a practical people. Much of our private and communal energies are spent solving problems, often with the help of technology, often in the service of humanitarian goals. But these practices may be in tension with less practical and more spiritual goals, such as the pursuit of artistic beauty, scientific and philosophical truth, or moral elevation. Nathaniel Hawthorne (1804–1864) was concerned that our uncritical embrace of technological progress and progressive social reform posed risks to the human spirit. In this story (1844), he delves deeply into the artistic temperament and its chances for survival in a democratic and technological age. Owen Warland, the story's protagonist, is single-mindedly bent on achieving "the Beautiful" through artistic creation. Over against him stands the useful artisan, the blacksmith Robert Danforth, a man as strong as Warland is subtle. Filling out this allegorical tale are the sneering materialist, Peter Hovenden; his daughter, Annie, who inspires the "artist of the beautiful"; and her young child—the coming generation—marked by strength, skepticism, and destructive curiosity.

What characterizes the artistic temperament as it comes to light in Owen Warland? What is the place of the "artist of the beautiful" in a problem-solving, practical-minded culture such as ours? If only "the useful" is good, but if the useful is, by definition, good as a means to an end, is there not perhaps some ultimate—useless—goal of all our efforts? What does the "artist of the beautiful"—in this story and in general—contribute to our civic life?

An elderly man, with his pretty daughter on his arm, was passing along the street, and emerged from the gloom of the cloudy evening into the light that fell across the pavement from the window of a small shop. It was a projecting window; and on the inside were suspended a variety of watches,—pinchbeck, silver, and one or two of gold,—all with their faces turned from the street, as if churlishly disinclined to inform the wayfarers what o'clock it was. Seated within the shop, sidelong to the window with his pale face bent earnestly over some delicate piece of mechanism, on which was thrown the concentrated lustre of a shade-lamp, appeared a young man.

"What can Owen Warland be about?" muttered old Peter Hovenden,—himself a retired watchmaker, and the former master of this same young man, whose occupation he was now wondering at. "What can the fellow be about? These six months past, I have never come by his shop without seeing him just as steadily at work as now. It would be a flight beyond his usual foolery to seek for the Perpetual Motion. And yet I know enough of my old business to be certain, that what he is now so busy with is no part of the machinery of a watch."

"Perhaps, father," said Annie, without showing much interest in the question, "Owen is inventing a new kind of timekeeper. I am sure he has ingenuity enough."

"Poh, child! he has not the sort of ingenuity to invent anything better than a Dutch toy," answered her father, who had formerly been put to much vexation by Owen Warland's irregular genius. "A plague on such ingenuity! All the effect that ever I knew of it, was to spoil the accuracy of some of the best watches in my shop. He would turn the sun out of its orbit, and derange the whole course of time, if, as I said before, his ingenuity could grasp anything bigger than a child's toy!"

"Hush, father! he hears you," whispered Annie, pressing the old man's arm. "His ears are as delicate as his feelings, and you know how easily disturbed they are. Do let us move on."

So Peter Hovenden and his daughter Annie plodded on, without further conversation, until, in a by-street of the town, they found themselves passing the open door of a blacksmith's shop. Within was seen the forge, now blazing up, and illuminating the high and dusky roof, and now confining its lustre to a narrow precinct of the coal-strewn floor, according as the breath of the bellows was puffed forth, or again inhaled into its vast leathern lungs. In the intervals of brightness, it was easy to distinguish objects in remote corners of the shop, and the horse-shoes that hung upon the wall; in the momentary gloom, the fire seemed to be glimmering amidst the vagueness of unenclosed space. Moving about in this red glare and alternate dusk, was the figure of the blacksmith, well worthy to be viewed in so picturesque an aspect of light and shade, where the bright blaze struggled with the black night, as if each would have snatched his comely strength from the other. Anon, he drew a white-hot bar of iron from the coals, laid it on the anvil, uplifted his arm of might, and was soon enveloped in the myriads of sparks which the strokes of his hammer scattered into the surrounding gloom.

"Now, that is a pleasant sight," said the old watchmaker. "I know what it is to work in gold, but give me the worker in iron, after all is said and done. He spends his labor upon a reality. What say you, daughter Annie?"

"Pray don't speak so loud, father," whispered Annie. "Robert Danforth will hear you."

"And what if he should hear me?" said Peter Hovenden; "I say again, it is a good and a wholesome thing to depend upon main strength and reality, and to earn one's bread with the bare and brawny arm of a blacksmith. A watchmaker gets his brain puzzled by his wheels within a wheel, or loses his health or the nicety of his eyesight, as was my case; and finds himself, at middle age, or a little after, past labor at his own trade, and fit for nothing else, yet too poor to live at his ease. So, I say once again, give me main strength for my money. And then, how it takes the nonsense out of a man! Did you ever hear of a blacksmith being such a fool as Owen Warland yonder?"

"Well said, uncle Hovenden!" shouted Robert Danforth, from the forge, in a full, deep, merry voice, that made the roof re-echo. "And what says Miss Annie to that doctrine? She, I suppose, will think it a genteeler business to tinker up a lady's watch, than to forge a horse-shoe or make a gridiron!"

Annie drew her father onward, without giving him time for reply.

But we must return to Owen Warland's shop, and spend more meditation upon his history and character than either Peter Hovenden, or probably his daughter Annie, or Owen's old schoolfellow, Robert Danforth, would have thought due to so slight a subject. From the time that his little fingers could grasp a pen-knife, Owen had been remarkable for a delicate ingenuity, which sometimes produced pretty shapes in wood, principally figures of flowers and birds, and sometimes seemed to aim at the hidden mysteries of mechanism. But it was always for purposes of grace, and never with any mockery of the useful. He did not, like the crowd of school-boy artisans, construct little windmills on the angle of a barn, or watermills across the neighboring brook. Those who discovered such peculiarity in the boy, as to think it worth their while to observe him closely, sometimes saw reason to suppose that he was attempting to imitate the beautiful movements of Nature, as exemplified in the flight of birds or the activity of little animals. It seemed, in fact, a new development of the love of the Beautiful, such as might have made him a poet, a painter, or a sculptor, and which was as completely refined from all utilitarian coarseness, as it could have been in either of the fine arts. He looked with singular distaste at the stiff and regular processes of ordinary machinery. Being once carried to see a steam-engine, in the expectation that his intuitive comprehension of mechanical principles would be gratified, he turned pale, and grew sick, as if something monstrous and unnatural had been presented to him. This horror was partly owing to the size and terrible energy of the Iron Laborer; for the character of Owen's mind was microscopic, and tended naturally to the minute, in accordance with his diminutive frame, and the marvellous smallness and delicate power of his fingers. Not that his sense of beauty was thereby diminished into a sense of prettiness. The Beautiful Idea has no relation to size, and may be as perfectly developed in a space too minute for any but microscopic investigation, as within the ample verge that is measured by the arc of the rainbow. But, at all events, this characteristic minuteness in his objects and accomplishments made the world even more incapable, than it might otherwise have been, of appreciating Owen Warland's genius. The boy's relatives saw nothing better to be done—as perhaps there was not—than to bind him apprentice to a watchmaker, hoping that his strange ingenuity might thus be regulated, and put to utilitarian purposes.

Peter Hovenden's opinion of his apprentice has already been expressed. He could make nothing of the lad. Owen's apprehension of the professional mysteries, it is true, was inconceivably quick. But he altogether forgot or despised the grand object of a watchmaker's business, and cared no more for the measurement of time than if it had been merged into eternity. So long, however, as he remained under his old master's care, Owen's lack of sturdiness made it possible, by strict injunctions and sharp oversight, to restrain his creative eccentricity within bounds. But when his apprenticeship was served out, and he had taken the little shop which Peter Hovenden's failing eyesight compelled him to relinquish, then did people recognize how unfit a person was Owen Warland to lead old blind Father Time along his daily course. One of his most rational projects was, to connect a musical operation with the machinery of his watches, so that all the harsh dissonances of life might be rendered tuneful, and each flitting moment fall into the abyss of the Past in golden drops of harmony. If a family-clock was intrusted to him for repair—one of those tall, ancient clocks that have grown nearly allied to human nature, by measuring out the lifetime of many generations—he would take upon himself to arrange a dance or funeral procession of figures across its venerable face, representing twelve mirthful or melancholy hours. Several freaks of this kind quite destroyed the young watchmaker's credit with that steady and matter-of-fact class of people who hold the opinion that time is not to be trifled with, whether considered as the medium of advancement and prosperity in this world, or preparation for the next. His custom rapidly diminished—a misfortune, however, that was probably reckoned among his better accidents by Owen Warland, who was becoming more and more absorbed in a secret occupation, which drew all his science and manual dexterity into itself, and likewise gave full employment to the characteristic tendencies of his genius. This pursuit had already consumed many months.

After the old watchmaker and his pretty daughter had gazed at him, out of the obscurity of the street, Owen Warland was seized with a fluttering of the nerves, which made his hand tremble too violently to proceed with such delicate labor as he was now engaged upon.

"It was Annie herself!" murmured he. "I should have known it, by this throbbing of my heart, before I heard her father's voice. Ah, how it throbs! I shall scarcely be able to work again on this exquisite mechanism to-night. Annie—dearest Annie—thou shouldst give firmness to my heart and hand, and not shake them thus; for if I strive to put the very spirit of Beauty into form, and give it motion, it is for thy sake alone. Oh, throbbing heart, be quiet! If my labor be thus thwarted, there will come vague and unsatisfied dreams which will leave me spiritless to-morrow."

As he was endeavoring to settle himself again to his task, the shop-door opened, and gave admittance to no other than the stalwart figure which Peter Hovenden had paused to admire, as seen amid the light and shadow of the blacksmith's shop. Robert Danforth had brought a little anvil of his own manufacture, and peculiarly constructed, which the young artist had recently bespoken. Owen examined the article, and pronounced it fashioned according to his wish.

"Why, yes," said Robert Danforth, his strong voice filling the shop as with the sound of a bass-viol, "I consider myself equal to anything in the way of my own trade; though I should have made but a poor figure at yours, with such a fist as this,"—added he, laughing, as he laid his vast hand beside the delicate one of Owen. "But what then? I put more main strength into one blow of my sledge-hammer, than all that you have expended since you were a 'prentice. Is not that the truth?"

"Very probably," answered the low and slender voice of Owen. "Strength is an earthly monster. I make no pretensions to it. My force, whatever there may be of it, is altogether spiritual."

"Well; but, Owen, what are you about!" asked his old schoolfellow, still in such a hearty volume of tone that it made the artist shrink; especially as the question related to a subject so sacred as the absorbing dream of his imagination. "Folks do say, that you are trying to discover the Perpetual Motion."

"The Perpetual Motion?—nonsense!" replied Owen Warland, with a movement of disgust; for he was full of little petulances. "It can never be discovered! It is a dream that may delude men whose brains are mystified with matter, but not me. Besides, if such a discovery were possible, it would not be worth my while to make it, only to have the secret turned to such purposes as are now effected by steam and water-power. I am not ambitious to be honored with the paternity of a new kind of cotton-machine."

"That would be droll enough!" cried the blacksmith, breaking out into such an uproar of laughter, that Owen himself, and the bell-glasses on his work-board, quivered in unison. "No, no, Owen! No child of yours will have iron joints and sinews. Well, I won't hinder you any more. Good night, Owen, and success; and if you need any assistance, so far as a downright blow of hammer upon anvil will answer the purpose, I'm your man!"

And with another laugh, the man of main strength left the shop.

"How strange it is," whispered Owen Warland to himself, leaning his head upon his hand, "that all my musings, my purposes, my passion for the Beautiful, my consciousness of power to create it—a finer, more ethereal power, of which this earthly giant can have no conception—all, all, look so vain and idle, whenever my path is crossed by Robert Danforth! He would drive me mad, were I to meet him often. His hard, brute force darkens and confuses the spiritual element within me. But I, too, will be strong in my own way. I will not yield to him!"

He took from beneath a glass, a piece of minute machinery, which he set in the condensed light of his lamp, and, looking intently at it through a magnifying glass, proceeded to operate with a delicate instrument of steel. In an instant, however, he fell back in his chair, and clasped his hands, with a look of horror on his face, that made its small features as impressive as those of a giant would have been.

"Heaven! What have I done!" exclaimed he. "The vapor!—the influence of that brute force!—it has bewildered me, and obscured my perception. I have made the very stroke—the fatal stroke—that I have dreaded from the first! It is all over—the toil of months—the object of my life! I am ruined!"

And there he sat, in strange despair, until his lamp flickered in the socket, and left the Artist of the Beautiful in darkness.

Thus it is, that ideas which grow up within the imagination, and appear so lovely to it, and of a value beyond whatever men call valuable, are exposed to be shattered and annihilated by contact with the Practical. It is requisite for the ideal artist to possess a force of character that seems hardly compatible with its delicacy; he must keep his faith in himself, while the incredulous world assails him with its utter disbelief; he must stand up against mankind and be his own sole disciple, both as respects his genius, and the objects to which it is directed.

For a time, Owen Warland succumbed to this severe, but inevitable test. He spent a few sluggish weeks, with his head so continually resting in his

hands, that the townspeople had scarcely an opportunity to see his countenance. When, at last, it was again uplifted to the light of day, a cold, dull,
nameless change was perceptible upon it. In the opinion of Peter Hovenden,
however, and that order of sagacious understandings who think that life
should be regulated, like clock-work, with leaden weights, the alteration was
entirely for the better. Owen now indeed, applied himself to business with
dogged industry. It was marvellous to witness the obtuse gravity with which
he would inspect the wheels of a great, old silver watch; thereby delighting the
owner, in whose fob it had been worn till he deemed it a portion of his own
life, and was accordingly jealous of its treatment. In consequence of the good
report thus acquired, Owen Warland was invited by the proper authorities to
regulate the clock in the church-steeple. He succeeded so admirably in this
matter of public interest, that the merchants gruffly acknowledged his merits
on 'Change; the nurse whispered his praises, as she gave the potion in the sick-
chamber; the lover blessed him at the hour of appointed interview; and the
town in general thanked Owen for the punctuality of dinner-time. In a word,
the heavy weight upon his spirits kept everything in order, not merely within
his own system, but wheresoever the iron accents of the church-clock were
audible. It was a circumstance, though minute, yet characteristic of his present
state, that, when employed to engrave names or initials on silver spoons, he
now wrote the requisite letters in the plainest possible style; omitting a variety
of fanciful flourishes that had heretofore distinguished his work in this kind.

One day, during the era of this happy transformation, old Peter Hovenden
came to visit his former apprentice.

"Well, Owen," said he, "I am glad to hear such good accounts of you from
all quarters; and especially from the town-clock yonder, which speaks in your
commendation every hour of the twenty-four. Only get rid altogether of your
nonsensical trash about the Beautiful—which I, nor nobody else, nor yourself
to boot, could never understand—only free yourself of that, and your success in life is as sure as daylight. Why, if you go on in this way, I should even
venture to let you doctor this precious old watch of mine; though, except my
daughter Annie, I have nothing else so valuable in the world."

"I should hardly dare touch it, sir," replied Owen in a depressed tone; for
he was weighed down by his old master's presence.

"In time," said the latter, "in time, you will be capable of it."

The old watchmaker, with the freedom naturally consequent on his former authority, went on inspecting the work which Owen had in hand at the
moment, together with other matters that were in progress. The artist, meanwhile, could scarcely lift his head. There was nothing so antipodal to his nature
as this man's cold, unimaginative sagacity, by contact with which everything

was converted into a dream, except the densest matter of the physical world. Owen groaned in spirit, and prayed fervently to be delivered from him.

"But what is this?" cried Peter Hovenden abruptly, taking up a dusty bell-glass, beneath which appeared a mechanical something, as delicate and minute as the system of a butterfly's anatomy. "What have we here! Owen, Owen! there is witchcraft in these little chains, and wheels, and paddles! See! with one pinch of my finger and thumb, I am going to deliver you from all future peril."

"For Heaven's sake," screamed Owen Warland, springing up with wonderful energy, "as you would not drive me mad—do not touch it! The slightest pressure of your finger would ruin me for ever."

"Aha, young man! And is it so?" said the old watchmaker, looking at him with just enough penetration to torture Owen's soul with the bitterness of worldly criticism. "Well; take your own course. But I warn you again, that in this small piece of mechanism lives your evil spirit. Shall I exorcise him?"

"You are my Evil Spirit," answered Owen, much excited—"you, and the hard, coarse world! The leaden thoughts and the despondency that you fling upon me are my clogs. Else, I should long ago have achieved the task that I was created for."

Peter Hovenden shook his head, with the mixture of contempt and indignation which mankind, of whom he was partly a representative, deem themselves entitled to feel towards all simpletons who seek other prizes than the dusty ones along the highway. He then took his leave with an uplifted finger, and a sneer upon his face, that haunted the artist's dreams for many a night afterwards. At the time of his old master's visit, Owen was probably on the point of taking up the relinquished task; but, by this sinister event, he was thrown back into the state whence he had been slowly emerging.

But the innate tendency of his soul had only been accumulating fresh vigor, during its apparent sluggishness. As the summer advanced, he almost totally relinquished his business, and permitted Father Time, so far as the old gentleman was represented by the clocks and watches under his control, to stray at random through human life, making infinite confusion among the train of bewildered hours. He wasted the sunshine, as people said, in wandering through the woods and fields, and along the banks of streams. There, like a child, he found amusement in chasing butterflies, or watching the motions of water-insects. There was something truly mysterious in the intentness with which he contemplated these living playthings, as they sported on the breeze; or examined the structure of an imperial insect whom he had imprisoned. The chase of butterflies was an apt emblem of the ideal pursuit in which he had spent so many golden hours. But, would the Beautiful Idea ever be yielded to his hand, like the butterfly that symbolized it? Sweet, doubtless, were these days, and congenial to the artist's soul. They were full of bright conceptions, which gleamed through his intellectual world, as the butterflies gleamed through the outward atmosphere, and were real to him for the instant, without the toil, and perplexity, and many disappointments, of attempting to make them visible to the sensual eye. Alas, that the artist, whether in poetry or whatever other material, may not content himself with the inward enjoyment of the Beautiful, but must chase the flitting mystery beyond the verge of his ethereal domain, and crush its frail being in seizing it with a material grasp! Owen Warland felt the impulse to give external reality to his ideas, as irresistibly as any of the poets or painters, who have arrayed the world in a dimmer and fainter beauty, imperfectly copied from the richness of their visions.

The night was now his time for the slow progress of recreating the one Idea, to which all his intellectual activity referred itself. Always at the approach of dusk, he stole into the town, locked himself within his shop, and wrought with patient delicacy of touch, for many hours. Sometimes he was startled by the rap of the watchman, who, when all the world should be asleep, had caught the gleam of lamp-light through the crevices of Owen Warland's shutters. Daylight, to the morbid sensibility of his mind, seemed to have an intrusiveness that interfered with his pursuits. On cloudy and inclement days, therefore, he sat with his head upon his hands, muffling, as it were, his sensitive brain in a mist of indefinite musings; for it was a relief to escape from the sharp distinctness with which he was compelled to shape out his thoughts, during his nightly toil.

From one of these fits of torpor, he was aroused by the entrance of Annie Hovenden, who came into the shop with the freedom of a customer, and also with something of the familiarity of a childish friend. She had worn a hole through her silver thimble, and wanted Owen to repair it.

"But I don't know whether you will condescend to such a task," said she, laughing, "now that you are so taken up with the notion of putting spirit into machinery."

"Where did you get that idea, Annie?" said Owen, starting in surprise.

"Oh, out of my own head," answered she, "and from something that I heard you say, long ago, when you were but a boy, and I a little child. But, come! will you mend this poor thimble of mine?"

"Anything for your sake, Annie," said Owen Warland—"anything; even were it to work at Robert Danforth's forge."

"And that would be a pretty sight!" retorted Annie, glancing with imperceptible slightness at the artist's small and slender frame. "Well; here is the thimble."

"But that is a strange idea of yours," said Owen, "about the spiritualization of matter!"

And then the thought stole into his mind, that this young girl possessed the gift to comprehend him, better than all the world beside. And what a help and strength would it be to him, in his lonely toil, if he could gain the sympathy of the only being whom he loved! To persons whose pursuits are insulated from the common business of life—who are either in advance of mankind, or apart from it—there often comes a sensation of moral cold, that makes the spirit shiver, as if it had reached the frozen solitudes around the pole. What the prophet, the poet, the reformer, the criminal, or any other man, with human yearnings, but separated from the multitude by a peculiar lot, might feel, poor Owen Warland felt.

"Annie," cried he, growing pale as death at the thought, "how gladly would I tell you the secret of my pursuit! You, methinks, would estimate it rightly. You, I know, would hear it with a reverence that I must not expect from the harsh, material world."

"Would I not? to be sure I would!" replied Annie Hovenden, lightly laughing. "Come; explain to me quickly what is the meaning of this little whirligig, so delicately wrought that it might be a plaything for Queen Mab. See; I will put it in motion."

"Hold," exclaimed Owen, "hold!"

Annie had but given the slightest possible touch, with the point of a needle, to the same minute portion of complicated machinery which has been more than once mentioned, when the artist seized her by the wrist with a force that made her scream aloud. She was affrighted at the convulsion of intense rage and anguish that writhed across his features. The next instant he let his head sink upon his hands.

"Go, Annie," murmured he, "I have deceived myself, and must suffer for it. I yearned for sympathy—and thought—and fancied—and dreamed—that you might give it me. But you lack the talisman, Annie, that should admit you into my secrets. That touch has undone the toil of months, and the thought of a lifetime! It was not your fault, Annie—but you have ruined me!"

Poor Owen Warland! He had indeed erred, yet pardonably; for if any human spirit could have sufficiently reverenced the processes so sacred in his eyes, it must have been a woman's. Even Annie Hovenden, possibly, might not have disappointed him, had she been enlightened by the deep intelligence of love.

The artist spent the ensuing winter in a way that satisfied any persons, who had hitherto retained a hopeful opinion of him, that he was, in truth, irrevocably doomed to inutility as regarded the world, and to an evil destiny on his own part. The decease of a relative had put him in possession of a small inheritance. Thus freed from the necessity of toil, and having lost the steadfast influence of a great purpose—great, at least to him—he abandoned himself to habits from which, it might have been supposed, the mere delicacy of his organization would have availed to secure him. But when the ethereal portion of a man of genius is obscured, the earthly part assumes an influence the more uncontrollable, because the character is now thrown off the balance to which Providence had so nicely adjusted it, and which, in coarser natures, is adjusted by some other method. Owen Warland made proof of whatever show of bliss may be found in riot. He looked at the world through the golden medium of wine, and contemplated the visions that bubble up so gayly around the brim of the glass, and that people the air with shapes of pleasant madness, which so soon grow ghostly and forlorn. Even when this dismal and inevitable change had taken place, the young man might still have continued to quaff the cup of enchantments, though its vapor did but shroud life in gloom, and fill the gloom with spectres that mocked at him. There was a certain irksomeness of spirit, which, being real, and the deepest sensation of which the artist was now conscious, was more intolerable than any fantastic miseries and horrors that the abuse of wine could summon up. In the latter case, he could remember, even out of the midst of his trouble, that all was but a delusion; in the former, the heavy anguish was his actual life.

From this perilous state, he was redeemed by an incident which more than one person witnessed, but of which the shrewdest could not explain or conjecture the operation on Owen Warland's mind. It was very simple. On a warm afternoon of spring, as the artist sat among his riotous companions, with a glass of wine before him, a splendid butterfly flew in at the open window, and fluttered about his head.

"Ah!" exclaimed Owen, who had drank freely, "Are you alive again, child of the sun, and playmate of the summer breeze, after your dismal winter's nap? Then it is time for me to be at work!"

And leaving his unemptied glass upon the table, he departed, and was never known to sip another drop of wine.

And now, again, he resumed his wanderings in the woods and fields. It might be fancied that the bright butterfly, which had come so spiritlike into the window, as Owen sat with the rude revellers, was indeed a spirit, commissioned to recall him to the pure, ideal life that had so etherealized him among men. It might be fancied, that he went forth to seek this spirit, in its sunny haunts; for still, as in the summer-time gone by, he was seen to steal gently up, wherever a butterfly had alighted, and lose himself in contemplation of it. When it took flight, his eyes followed the winged vision, as if its airy track would show the path to heaven. But what could be the purpose of the unseasonable toil, which was again resumed, as the watchman knew by the lines of lamp-light through the crevices of Owen Warland's shutters? The townspeople had one comprehensive explanation of all these singularities. Owen Warland had gone mad! How universally efficacious—how satisfactory, too, and soothing to the injured sensibility of narrowness and dullness—is this easy method of accounting for whatever lies beyond the world's most ordinary scope! From Saint Paul's days, down to our poor little Artist of the Beautiful, the same talisman had been applied to the elucidation of all mysteries in the words or deeds of men, who spoke or acted too wisely or too well. In Owen Warland's case, the judgment of his townspeople may have been correct. Perhaps he was mad. The lack of sympathy—that contrast between himself and his neighbors, which took away the restraint of example—was enough to make him so. Or, possibly, he had caught just so much of ethereal radiance as served to bewilder him, in an earthly sense, by its intermixture with the common daylight.

One evening, when the artist had returned from a customary ramble, and had just thrown the lustre of his lamp on the delicate piece of work, so often interrupted, but still taken up again, as if his fate were embodied in its mechanism, he was surprised by the entrance of old Peter Hovenden. Owen never met this man without a shrinking of the heart. Of all the world, he was most terrible, by reason of a keen understanding, which saw so distinctly what it did see, and disbelieved so uncompromisingly in what it could not see. On this occasion, the old watchmaker had merely a gracious word or two to say.

"Owen, my lad," said he, "we must see you at my house to-morrow night."

The artist began to mutter some excuse.

"Oh, but it must be so," quoth Peter Hovenden, "for the sake of the days when you were one of the household. What, my boy, don't you know that my daughter Annie is engaged to Robert Danforth? We are making an entertainment, in our humble way, to celebrate the event."

"Ah!" said Owen.

That little monosyllable was all he uttered; its tone seemed cold and unconcerned, to an ear like Peter Hovenden's; and yet there was in it the stifled outcry of the poor artist's heart, which he compressed within him like a man holding down an evil spirit. One slight outbreak, however, imperceptible to the old watchmaker, he allowed himself. Raising the instrument with which he was about to begin his work, he let it fall upon the little system of machinery that had, anew, cost him months of thought and toil. It was shattered by the stroke!

Owen Warland's story would have been no tolerable representation of the troubled life of those who strive to create the Beautiful, if, amid all other thwarting influences, love had not interposed to steal the cunning from his hand. Outwardly, he had been no ardent or enterprising lover; the career of his passion had confined its tumults and vicissitudes so entirely within the artist's imagination, that Annie herself had scarcely more than a woman's intuitive perception of it. But, in Owen's view, it covered the whole field of his life. Forgetful of the time when she had shown herself incapable of any deep response, he had persisted in connecting all his dreams of artistical success with Annie's image; she was the visible shape in which the spiritual power that he worshipped, and on whose altar he hoped to lay a not unworthy offering, was made manifest to him. Of course he had deceived himself; there were no such attributes in Annie Hovenden as his imagination had endowed her with. She, in the aspect which she wore to his inward vision, was as much a creation of his own, as the mysterious piece of mechanism would be were it ever realized. Had he become convinced of his mistake through the medium of successful love; had he won Annie to his bosom, and there beheld her fade from angel into ordinary woman, the disappointment might have driven him back, with concentrated energy, upon his sole remaining object. On the other hand, had he found Annie what he fancied, his lot would have been so rich in beauty, that, out of its mere redundancy, he might have wrought the Beautiful into many a worthier type than he had toiled for. But the guise in which his sorrow came to him, the sense that the angel of his life had been snatched away and given to a rude man of earth and iron, who could neither need nor appreciate her ministrations; this was the very perversity of fate, that makes human existence appear too absurd and contradictory to be the scene of one other hope or one other fear. There was nothing left for Owen Warland but to sit down like a man that had been stunned.

He went through a fit of illness. After his recovery, his small and slender frame assumed an obtuser garniture of flesh than it had ever before worn. His thin cheeks became round; his delicate little hand, so spiritually fashioned to achieve fairy task-work, grew plumper than the hand of a thriving infant. His aspect had a childishness, such as might have induced a stranger to pat him on the head—pausing, however, in the act, to wonder what manner of child was here. It was as if the spirit had gone out of him, leaving the body to flourish in a sort of vegetable existence. Not that Owen Warland was idiotic. He could talk, and not irrationally. Somewhat of a babbler, indeed, did people begin to think him; for he was apt to discourse at wearisome length, of marvels of mechanism that he had read about in books, but which he had learned to consider as absolutely fabulous. Among them he enumerated the Man of Brass, constructed by Albertus Magnus, and the Brazen Head of Friar Bacon; and, coming down to later times, the automata of a little coach and horses, which, it was pretended, had been manufactured for the Dauphin of France; together with an insect that buzzed about the ear like a living fly, and yet was but a contrivance of minute steel springs. There was a story, too, of a duck that waddled, and quacked, and ate; though, had any honest citizen purchased it for dinner, he would have found himself cheated with the mere mechanical apparition of a duck.

"But all these accounts," said Owen Warland, "I am now satisfied, are mere impositions."

Then, in a mysterious way, he would confess that he once thought differently. In his idle and dreamy days, he had considered it possible, in a certain sense, to spiritualize machinery; and to combine with the new species of life and motion, thus produced, a beauty that should attain to the ideal which Nature has proposed to herself, in all her creatures, but has never taken pains to realize. He seemed, however, to retain no very distinct perception either of the process of achieving this object, or of the design itself.

"I have thrown it all aside now," he would say. "It was a dream, such as young men are always mystifying themselves with. Now that I have acquired a little common sense, it makes me laugh to think of it."

Poor, poor, and fallen Owen Warland! These were the symptoms that he had ceased to be an inhabitant of the better sphere that lies unseen around us. He had lost his faith in the invisible, and now prided himself, as such unfortunates invariably do, in the wisdom which rejected much that even his eye could see, and trusted confidently in nothing but what his hand could touch. This is the calamity of men whose spiritual part dies out of them, and leaves the grosser understanding to assimilate them more and more to the things of which alone it can take cognizance. But, in Owen Warland, the spirit was not dead, nor past away; it only slept.

How it awoke again, is not recorded. Perhaps, the torpid slumber was broken by a convulsive pain. Perhaps, as in a former instance, the butterfly came and hovered about his head, and reinspired him—as, indeed, this creature of the sunshine had always a mysterious mission for the artist—reinspired him with the former purpose of his life. Whether it were pain or happiness that thrilled through his veins, his first impulse was to thank Heaven for rendering him again the being of thought, imagination, and keenest sensibility, that he had long ceased to be.

"Now for my task," said he. "Never did I feel such strength for it as now."

Yet, strong as he felt himself, he was incited to toil the more diligently, by an anxiety lest death should surprise him in the midst of his labors. This anxiety, perhaps, is common to all men who set their hearts upon anything so high, in their own view of it, that life becomes of importance only as conditional to its accomplishment. So long as we love life for itself, we seldom dread the losing it. When we desire life for the attainment of an object, we recognize the frailty of its texture. But, side by side with this sense of insecurity, there is a vital faith in our invulnerability to the shaft of death, while engaged in any task that seems assigned by Providence as our proper thing to do, and which the world would have cause to mourn for, should we leave it unaccomplished. Can the philosopher, big with the inspiration of an idea that is to reform mankind, believe that he is to be beckoned from this sensible existence, at the very instant when he is mustering his breath to speak the word of light? Should he perish so, the weary ages may pass away—the world's whole life-sand may fall, drop by drop—before another intellect is prepared to develop the truth that might have been uttered then. But history affords many an example, where the most precious spirit, at any particular epoch manifested in human shape, has gone hence untimely, without space allowed him, so far as mortal judgment could discern, to perform his mission on the earth. The prophet dies; and the man of torpid heart and sluggish brain lives on. The poet leaves his song half sung, or finishes it, beyond the scope of mortal ears, in a celestial choir. The painter—as Allston did—leaves half his conception on the canvas, to sadden us with its imperfect beauty, and goes to picture forth the whole, if it be no irreverence to say so, in the hues of Heaven. But, rather, such incomplete designs of this life will be perfected nowhere. This so frequent abortion of man's dearest projects must be taken as a proof, that the deeds of earth, however etherealized by piety or genius, are without value, except as exercises and manifestations of the spirit. In Heaven, all ordinary thought is higher and more melodious than Milton's song. Then, would he add another verse to any strain that he had left unfinished here?

But to return to Owen Warland. It was his fortune, good or ill, to achieve the purpose of his life. Pass we over a long space of intense thought, yearning effort, minute toil, and wasting anxiety, succeeded by an instant of solitary triumph; let all this be imagined; and then behold the artist, on a winter evening, seeking admittance to Robert Danforth's fireside circle. There he found the Man of Iron, with his massive substance thoroughly warmed and attempered by domestic influences. And there was Annie, too, now transformed into a matron, with much of her husband's plain and sturdy nature, but imbued, as Owen Warland still believed, with a finer grace, that might enable her to be the interpreter between Strength and Beauty. It happened, likewise, that old Peter Hovenden was a guest, this evening, at his daughter's fireside; and it was his well-remembered expression of keen, cold criticism, that first encountered the artist's glance.

"My old friend Owen!" cried Robert Danforth, starting up, and compressing the artist's delicate fingers within a hand that was accustomed to gripe bars of iron. "This is kind and neighborly, to come to us at last! I was afraid your Perpetual Motion had bewitched you out of the remembrance of old times."

"We are glad to see you!" said Annie, while a blush reddened her matronly cheek. "It was not like a friend, to stay from us so long."

"Well, Owen," inquired the old watchmaker, as his first greeting, "how comes on the Beautiful? Have you created it at last?"

The artist did not immediately reply, being startled by the apparition of a young child of strength, that was tumbling about on the carpet; a little personage who had come mysteriously out of the infinite, but with something so sturdy and real in his composition that he seemed moulded out of the densest substance which earth could supply. This hopeful infant crawled towards the new-comer, and setting himself on end—as Robert Danforth expressed the posture—stared at Owen with a look of such sagacious observation, that the mother could not help exchanging a proud glance with her husband. But the artist was disturbed by the child's look, as imagining a resemblance between it and Peter Hovenden's habitual expression. He could have fancied that the old watchmaker was compressed into this baby-shape, and was looking out of those baby-eyes, and repeating—as he now did—the malicious question:

"The Beautiful, Owen! How comes on the Beautiful? Have you succeeded in creating the Beautiful?"

"I have succeeded," replied the artist, with a momentary light of triumph in his eyes, and a smile of sunshine, yet steeped in such depth of thought that it was almost sadness. "Yes, my friends, it is the truth. I have succeeded!"

"Indeed!" cried Annie, a look of maiden mirthfulness peeping out of her face again. "And is it lawful, now, to inquire what the secret is?"

"Surely; it is to disclose it, that I have come," answered Owen Warland. "You shall know, and see, and touch, and possess, the secret! For, Annie—if by that name I may still address the friend of my boyish years—Annie, it is for your bridal gift that I have wrought this spiritualized mechanism, this harmony of motion, this Mystery of Beauty! It comes late, indeed; but it is as we go onward in life, when objects begin to lose their freshness of hue, and our souls their delicacy of perception, that the spirit of Beauty is most needed. If—forgive me, Annie—if you know how to value this gift, it can never come too late!"

He produced, as he spoke, what seemed a jewel-box. It was carved richly out of ebony by his own hand, and inlaid with a fanciful tracery of pearl, representing a boy in pursuit of a butterfly, which, elsewhere, had become a winged spirit, and was flying heavenward; while the boy, or youth, had found such efficacy in his strong desire, that he ascended from earth to cloud, and from cloud to celestial atmosphere, to win the Beautiful. This case of ebony the artist opened, and bade Annie place her fingers on its edge. She did so, but almost screamed, as a butterfly fluttered forth, and alighting on her finger's tip, sat waving the ample magnificence of its purple and gold-speckled wings, as if in prelude to a flight. It is impossible to express by words the glory, the splendor, the delicate gorgeousness, which were softened into the beauty of this object. Nature's ideal butterfly was here realized in all its perfection; not in the pattern of such faded insects as flit among earthly flowers, but of those which hover across the meads of Paradise, for child-angels and the spirits of departed infants to disport themselves with. The rich down was visible upon its wings; the lustre of its eyes seemed instinct with spirit. The firelight glimmered around this wonder—the candles gleamed upon it—but it glistened apparently by its own radiance, and illuminated the finger and outstretched hand on which it rested, with a white gleam like that of precious stones. In its perfect beauty, the consideration of size was entirely lost. Had its wings overarched the firmament, the mind could not have been more filled or satisfied.

"Beautiful! Beautiful!" exclaimed Annie. "Is it alive? Is it alive?"

"Alive? To be sure it is," answered her husband. "Do you suppose any mortal has skill enough to make a butterfly,—or would put himself to the trouble of making one, when any child may catch a score of them in a summer's afternoon? Alive? Certainly! But this pretty box is undoubtedly of our friend Owen's manufacture; and really it does him credit."

At this moment, the butterfly waved its wings anew, with a motion so absolutely lifelike that Annie was startled, and even awe-stricken; for, in spite of her husband's opinion, she could not satisfy herself whether it was indeed a living creature, or a piece of wondrous mechanism.

"Is it alive?" she repeated, more earnestly than before.

"Judge for yourself," said Owen Warland, who stood gazing in her face with fixed attention.

The butterfly now flung itself upon the air, fluttered round Annie's head, and soared into a distant region of the parlor, still making itself perceptible to sight by the starry gleam in which the motion of its wings enveloped it. The infant on the floor, followed its course with his sagacious little eyes. After flying about the room, it returned, in a spiral curve, and settled again on Annie's finger.

"But is it alive?" exclaimed she again; and the finger, on which the gorgeous mystery had alighted, was so tremulous that the butterfly was forced to balance himself with his wings. "Tell me if it be alive, or whether you created it."

"Wherefore ask who created it, so it be beautiful?" replied Owen Warland. "Alive? Yes, Annie; it may well be said to possess life, for it absorbed my own being into itself; and in the secret of that butterfly, and in its beauty—which is not merely outward, but deep as its whole system—is represented the intellect, the imagination, the sensibility, the soul, of an Artist of the Beautiful! Yes, I created it. But"—and here his countenance somewhat changed—"this butterfly is not now to me what it was when I beheld it afar off, in the day-dreams of my youth."

"Be it what it may, it is a pretty plaything," said the blacksmith, grinning with childlike delight. "I wonder whether it would condescend to alight on such a great clumsy finger as mine? Hold it hither, Annie!"

By the artist's direction, Annie touched her finger's tip to that of her husband; and, after a momentary delay, the butterfly fluttered from one to the other. It preluded a second flight by a similar, yet not precisely the same waving of wings, as in the first experiment; then, ascending from the blacksmith's stalwart finger, it rose in a gradually enlarging curve to the ceiling, made one wide sweep around the room, and returned with an undulating movement to the point whence it had started.

"Well, that does beat all nature!" cried Robert Danforth, bestowing the heartiest praise that he could find expression for; and, indeed, had he paused there, a man of finer words and nicer perception could not easily have said more. "That goes beyond me, I confess! But what then? There is more real use in one downright blow of my sledge-hammer, than in the whole five years' labor that our friend Owen has wasted on this butterfly!"

Here the child clapped his hands, and made a great babble of indistinct utterance, apparently demanding that the butterfly should be given him for a plaything.

Owen Warland, meanwhile, glanced sidelong at Annie, to discover whether she sympathized in her husband's estimate of the comparative value of the Beautiful and the Practical. There was, amid all her kindness towards himself, amid all the wonder and admiration with which she contemplated the marvellous work of his hands, and incarnation of his idea, a secret scorn; too secret, perhaps, for her own consciousness, and perceptible only to such intuitive discernment as that of the artist. But Owen, in the latter stages of his pursuit, had risen out of the region in which such a discovery might have been torture. He knew that the world, and Annie as the representative of the world, whatever praise might be bestowed, could never say the fitting word, nor feel the fitting sentiment which should be the perfect recompense of an artist who, symbolizing a lofty moral by a material trifle—converting what was earthly, to spiritual gold—had won the Beautiful into his handiwork. Not at this latest moment, was he to learn that the reward of all high performance must be sought within itself, or sought in vain. There was, however, a view of the matter, which Annie, and her husband, and even Peter Hovenden, might fully have understood, and which would have satisfied them that the toil of years had here been worthily bestowed. Owen Warland might have told them, that this butterfly, this plaything, this bridal-gift of a poor watchmaker to a black-smith's wife, was, in truth, a gem of art that a monarch would have purchased with honors and abundant wealth, and have treasured it among the jewels of his kingdom, as the most unique and wondrous of them all! But the artist smiled, and kept the secret to himself.

"Father," said Annie, thinking that a word of praise from the old watch-maker might gratify his former apprentice, "do come and admire this pretty butterfly!"

"Let us see," said Peter Hovenden, rising from his chair, with a sneer upon his face that always made people doubt, as he himself did, in everything but a material existence. "Here is my finger for it to alight upon. I shall understand it better when once I have touched it."

But, to the increased astonishment of Annie, when the tip of her father's finger was pressed against that of her husband, on which the butterfly still rested, the insect drooped its wings, and seemed on the point of falling to the floor. Even the bright spots of gold upon its wings and body, unless her eyes deceived her, grew dim, and the glowing purple took a dusky hue, and the starry lustre that gleamed around the blacksmith's hand, became faint, and vanished.

"It is dying! it is dying!" cried Annie, in alarm.

"It has been delicately wrought," said the artist calmly. "As I told you, it has imbibed a spiritual essence—call it magnetism, or what you will. In an atmosphere of doubt and mockery, its exquisite susceptibility suffers torture, as does the soul of him who instilled his own life into it. It has already lost its beauty; in a few moments more, its mechanism would be irreparably injured."

"Take away your hand, father!" entreated Annie, turning pale. "Here is my child; let it rest on his innocent hand. There, perhaps, its life will revive, and its colors grow brighter than ever."

Her father, with an acrid smile, withdrew his finger. The butterfly then appeared to recover the power of voluntary motion; while its hues assumed much of their original lustre, and the gleam of starlight, which was its most ethereal attribute, again formed a halo round about it. At first, when trans-ferred from Robert Danforth's hand to the small finger of the child, this radi-ance grew so powerful that it positively threw the little fellow's shadow back against the wall. He, meanwhile, extended his plump hand as he had seen his father and mother do, and watched the waving of the insect's wings, with infantine delight. Nevertheless, there was a certain odd expression of sagacity, that made Owen Warland feel as if here were old Peter Hovenden, partially, and but partially, redeemed from his hard skepticism into childish faith.

"How wise the little monkey looks!" whispered Robert Danforth to his wife.

"I never saw such a look on a child's face," answered Annie, admiring her own infant, and with good reason, far more than the artistic butterfly. "The darling knows more of the mystery than we do."

As if the butterfly, like the artist, were conscious of something not entirely congenial in the child's nature, it alternately sparkled and grew dim. At length, it arose from the small hand of the infant with an airy motion, that seemed to bear it upward without an effort; as if the ethereal instincts, with which its master's spirit had endowed it, impelled this fair vision involuntarily to a higher sphere. Had there been no obstruction, it might have soared into the sky, and grown immortal. But its lustre gleamed upon the ceiling; the exquisite texture of its wings brushed against that earthly medium; and a sparkle or two, as of star-dust, floated downward and lay glimmering on the carpet. Then the butterfly came fluttering down, and instead of returning to the infant, was apparently attracted towards the artist's hand.

"Not so, not so!" murmured Owen Warland, as if his handiwork could have understood him. "Thou hast gone forth out of thy master's heart. There is no return for thee!"

With a wavering movement, and emitting a tremulous radiance, the butterfly struggled, as it were, towards the infant, and was about to alight upon his finger. But, while it still hovered in the air, the little Child of Strength, with his grandsire's sharp and shrewd expression in his face, made a snatch at the marvellous insect, and compressed it in his hand. Annie screamed! Old Peter Hovenden burst into a cold and scornful laugh. The blacksmith, by main force, unclosed the infant's hand, and found within the palm a small heap of glittering fragments, whence the Mystery of Beauty had fled for ever. And as for Owen Warland, he looked placidly at what seemed the ruin of his life's labor, and which was yet no ruin. He had caught a far other butterfly than this. When the artist rose high enough to achieve the Beautiful, the symbol by which he made it perceptible to mortal senses became of little value in his eyes, while his spirit possessed itself in the enjoyment of the Reality.

The Little Man at Chehaw Station:
The American Artist and His Audience

RALPH ELLISON

The fine arts are surely central to cultural achievement. By elevating our gaze, deepening our insight, and expanding our hearts, painting, poetry, song, dance, and story lift the human spirit to realms beyond the life of daily necessity, and provide possibilities for shared, rich, communal experience. Hawthorne's story focused on the creative artist; the present selection, taken from a memoir (1977) by Ralph Ellison (1914–1994), focuses instead on artistic performance and especially on the audience for high culture—in this case, grand opera.

A talented musician in his youth, Ellison reports the advice he received from his music teacher: "You must always *play your best, even if it's only in the waiting room at Chehaw Station, because in this country there'll always be a little man hidden behind the stove" who will "know the music, and the tradition, and the standards of musicianship required for whatever you set out to perform!" Late in the memoir, Ellison has occasion to discover whether his teacher was right. Why might the teacher emphasize "in this country"? How does cultural pluralism contribute to high culture? What does Ellison's story suggest about the prospects for, and value of, lifting the ceiling in modern American life? Should we promote more appreciation of the fine arts?*

It was at Tuskegee Institute during the mid-1930s that I was made aware of the little man behind the stove. At the time I was a trumpeter majoring in music and had aspirations of becoming a classical composer. As such, shortly before the little man came to my attention, I had outraged the faculty members who judged my monthly student's recital by substituting a certain skill of lips and fingers for the intelligent and artistic structuring of emotion that was demanded in performing the music assigned to me. Afterward, still dressed in my hired tuxedo, my ears burning from the harsh negatives of their criticism, I had sought solace in the basement studio of Hazel Harrison, a highly respected concert pianist and teacher. Miss Harrison had been one of Ferruccio Busoni's prize pupils, had lived (until the rise of Hitler had driven her back to a U.S.A. that was not yet ready to recognize her talents) in Busoni's home in Berlin, and was a friend of such masters as Egon Petri, Percy Grainger, and Sergei Prokofiev. It was not the first time that I had appealed to Miss Harrison's generosity of spirit, but today her reaction to my rather adolescent complaint was less than sympathetic.

"But, baby," she said, "in this country you must always prepare yourself to play your very best wherever you are, and on all occasions."

"But everybody tells you that," I said.

"Yes," she said, "but there's more to it than you're usually told. Of course you've always been taught to *do* your best, *look* your best, *be* your best. You've been told such things all your life. But now you're becoming a musician, an artist, and when it comes to performing the classics in this country, there's something more involved."

Watching me closely, she paused. "Are you ready to listen?"

"Yes, ma'am."

"All right," she said, "you must *always* play your best, even if it's only in the waiting room at Chehaw Station, because in this country there'll always be a little man hidden behind the stove."

"A *what?*"

She nodded. "That's right," she said. "There'll always be the little man whom you don't expect, and he'll know the *music*, and the *tradition*, and the standards of *musicianship* required for whatever you set out to perform!"

Speechless, I stared at her. After the working-over I'd just received from the faculty, I was in no mood for joking. But no, Miss Harrison's face was quite serious. So what did she mean? Chehaw Station was a lonely whistle-stop where swift north- or southbound trains paused with haughty impatience to drop off or take on passengers; the point where, on homecoming weekends, special coaches crowded with festive visitors were cut loose, coupled to a waiting switch engine, and hauled to Tuskegee's railroad siding. I knew it well, and as I stood beside Miss Harrison's piano, visualizing the station, I told myself, *She has* GOT *to be kidding!*

For, in my view, the atmosphere of Chehaw's claustrophobic little waiting room was enough to discourage even a blind street musician from picking out blues on his guitar, no matter how tedious his wait for a train. Biased toward disaster by bruised feelings, my imagination pictured the vibrations set in motion by the winding of a trumpet within that drab, utilitarian structure:

first shattering, then bringing its walls "a-tumbling down"—like Jericho's at the sounding of Joshua's priest-blown ram horns.

True, Tuskegee possessed a rich musical tradition, both classical and folk, and many music lovers and musicians lived or moved through its environs, but—and my regard for Miss Harrison notwithstanding—Chehaw Station was the last place in the area where I would expect to encounter a connoisseur lying in wait to pounce upon some rash, unsuspecting musician. Sure, a connoisseur might hear the haunting, blues-echoing, train-whistle rhapsodies blared by fast express trains as they thundered past—but the classics? Not a chance!

So as Miss Harrison watched to see the effect of her words, I said with a shrug, "Yes, ma'am."

She smiled, her prominent eyes a-twinkle. "I hope so," she said. "But if you don't just now, you will by the time you become an artist. So remember the little man behind the stove."

With that, seating herself at her piano, she began thumbing through a sheaf of scores—a signal that our discussion was ended. . . .

Three years later, after having abandoned my hope of becoming a musician, I had just about forgotten Miss Harrison's mythical little man behind the stove. Then, in faraway New York, concrete evidence of his actual existence arose and blasted me like the heat from an internally combusted ton of coal.

As a member of the Federal Writers' Project, I was spending a clammy late-fall afternoon of freedom circulating a petition in support of some now long-forgotten social issue that I regarded as indispensable to the public good. I found myself inside a tenement building in San Juan Hill, a Negro district that disappeared with the coming of Lincoln Center. Starting on the top floor of the building, I had collected an acceptable number of signatures, and having descended from the ground floor to the basement level, was moving along the dimly lit hallway toward a door through which I could hear loud voices. They were male Afro-American voices, raised in violent argument. The language was profane, the style of speech a Southern idiomatic vernacular such as was spoken by formally uneducated Afro-American workingmen. Reaching the door, I paused, sounding out the lay of the land before knocking to present my petition.

But my delay led to indecision. Not, however, because of the loud, unmistakable anger sounding within; being myself a slum dweller, I knew that voices in slums are often raised in anger, but that the *rhetoric* of anger, being in itself cathartic, is not necessarily a prelude to physical violence. Rather, it is frequently a form of symbolic action, a verbal equivalent of fisticuffs. No, I hesitated because I realized that behind the door a mystery was unfolding. A mystery so incongruous, outrageous, and surreal that it struck me as a threat to my sense of rational order. It was as though a bizarre practical joke had been staged and its perpetrators were waiting for me, its designated but unknowing scapegoat, to arrive; a joke designed to assault my knowledge of American culture and its hierarchal dispersal. At the very least, it appeared that my pride in my knowledge of my own people was under attack.

For the angry voices behind the door were proclaiming an intimate familiarity with a subject of which, by all the logic of their linguistically projected social status, they should have been oblivious. The subject of their contention confounded all my assumptions regarding the correlation between educational levels, class, race, and the possession of conscious culture. Impossible as it seemed, these foulmouthed black workingmen were locked in verbal combat over which of two celebrated Metropolitan Opera divas was the superior soprano!

I myself attended the opera only when I could raise the funds, and I knew full well that opera-going was far from the usual cultural pursuit of men identified with the linguistic style of such voices. And yet, confounding such facile logic, they were voicing (and loudly) a familiarity with the Met far greater than my own. In their graphic, irreverent, and vehement criticism they were describing not only the sopranos' acting abilities but were ridiculing the gestures with which each gave animation to her roles, and they shouted strong opinions as to the ranges of the divas' vocal equipment. Thus, with such a distortion of perspective being imposed upon me, I was challenged either to solve the mystery of their knowledge by entering into their midst or to leave the building with my sense of logic reduced forever to a level of college-trained absurdity.

So challenged, I knocked. I knocked out of curiosity, I knocked out of outrage. I knocked in fear and trembling. I knocked in anticipation of whatever insights—malicious or transcendent, I no longer cared which—I would discover beyond the door.

For a moment there was an abrupt and portentous silence; then came the sound of chair legs thumping dully upon the floor, followed by further silence. I knocked again, loudly, with an authority fired by an impatient and anxious urgency.

Again silence—until a gravel voice boomed an annoyed "Come in!"

Opening the door with an unsteady hand, I looked inside, and was even less prepared for the scene that met my eyes than for the content of their loud-mouthed contention.

In a small, rank-smelling, lamplit room, four huge black men sat sprawled around a circular dining-room table, looking toward me with undisguised hostility. The sooty-chimneyed lamp glowed in the center of the bare oak table, casting its yellow light upon four water tumblers and a half-empty pint of whiskey. As the men straightened in their chairs I became aware of a fireplace with a coal fire glowing in its grate, and leaning against the ornate marble facing of its mantelpiece, I saw four enormous coal scoops.

"All right," one of the men said, rising to his feet. "What the hell can we do for *you*?"

"And we ain't buying nothing, buddy," one of the seated men added, his palm slapping the table.

Closing the door, I moved forward, holding my petition like a flag of truce before me, noting that the men wore faded blue overalls and jumper jackets, and becoming aware that while all were of dark complexion, their blackness was accentuated in the dim lamplight by the dust and grime of their profession.

"Come on, man, speak up," the man who had arisen said. "We ain't got all day."

"I'm sorry to interrupt," I said, "but I thought you might be interested in supporting my petition," and began hurriedly to explain.

"Say," one of the men said, "you look like one of them relief investigators. You're not out to jive us, are you?"

"Oh, no, sir," I said. "I happen to work on the Writers' Project . . ."

The standing man leaned toward me. "You on the Writers' Project?" he said, looking me up and down.

"That's right," I said. "I'm a writer."

"Now is that right?" he said. "How long you been writing?"

I hesitated. "About a year," I said. He grinned, looking at the others. "Y'all hear that? Ol' Home-boy here has done up and jumped on the *gravy* train! Now that's pretty good. Pretty damn good! So what did you do before that?" he said.

"I studied music," I said, "at Tuskegee."

"Hey, now!" the standing man said. "They got a damn good choir down there. Y'all remember back when they opened Radio City? They had that fellow William L. Dawson for a director. Son, let's see that paper."

Relieved, I handed him the petition, watching him stretch it between his hardened hands. After a moment of soundlessly mouthing the words of its appeal, he gave me a skeptical look and turned to the others.

"What the hell," he said, "signing this piece of paper won't do no good, but since Home here's a musician, it won't do us no harm to help him out. Let's go along with him."

Fishing a blunt-pointed pencil from the bib of his overalls, he wrote his name and passed the petition to his friends, who followed suit.

This took some time, and as I watched the petition move from hand to hand, I could barely contain myself or control my need to unravel the mystery that had now become far more important than just getting their signatures on my petition.

"There you go," the last one said, extending the petition toward me. "Having our names on there don't mean a thing, but you got 'em."

"Thank you," I said. "Thank you very much."

They watched me with amused eyes, expecting me to leave, but, clearing my throat nervously, I stood in my tracks, too intrigued to leave and suddenly too embarrassed to ask my question.

"So what'er you waiting for?" one of them said. "You got what you came for. What else do you want?"

And then I blurted it out. "I'd like to ask you just one question," I said.

"Like what?" the standing one said.

"Like where on earth did you gentlemen learn so much about grand opera?"

For a moment he stared at me with parted lips; then, pounding the mantelpiece with his palm, he collapsed with a roar of laughter. As the laughter of the others erupted like a string of giant firecrackers I looked on with growing feelings of embarrassment and insult, trying to grasp the handle to what appeared to be an unfriendly joke. Finally, wiping coal-dust-stained tears from his cheeks, he interrupted his laughter long enough to initiate me into the mystery.

"Hell, son," he laughed, "we learn it down at the Met, that's where . . ."

"You learned it *where*?"

"At the Metropolitan Opera, just like I told you. Strip us fellows down and give us some costumes and we make about the finest damn bunch of Egyptians you ever seen. Hell, we been down there wearing leopard skins and carrying spears or waving things like palm leafs and ostrich-tail fans for *years*!"

Now, purged by the revelation, and with Hazel Harrison's voice echoing in my ears, it was my turn to roar with laughter. With a shock of recognition I joined them in appreciation of the hilarious American joke that centered on the incongruities of race, economic status, and culture. My sense of order restored, my appreciation of the arcane ways of American cultural possibility was vastly extended. The men were products of both past *and* present; were both coal heavers *and* Met extras; were both workingmen *and* opera buffs. Seen in the clear, pluralistic, melting-pot light of American cultural possibility there was no contradiction. The joke, the apparent contradiction, sprang from my attempting to see them by the light of social concepts that cast less illumination than an inert lump of coal. I was delighted, because during a moment when I least expected to encounter the little man behind the stove (Miss Harrison's vernacular music critic, as it were), I had stumbled upon four such men. Not behind the stove, it is true, but even more wondrously, they had materialized at an even more unexpected location: at the depth of the American social hierarchy and, of all possible hiding places, behind a coal pile. Where there's a melting pot there's smoke, and where there's smoke it is not simply optimistic to expect fire, it's imperative to watch for the phoenix's vernacular, but transcendent, rising.

Hub Fans Bid Kid Adieu

John Updike

Kurt Vonnegut's "Harrison Bergeron" raises questions about the standing and pursuit of excellence in a society dedicated to equality. Democratic peoples are often ambivalent about people who rise above the mass, even as they cheer their heroes. But John Updike's 1960 appreciation of baseball great Ted Williams (1918–2002) calls attention to our admiration of those who aspire to be the best. What is the place of hero worship in the American character? Who are our heroes and why do they draw our devotion? What is the connection between what Updike calls "an indefensible hope" for heroic success and the ordinary hopes for the "American dream"?

Fenway Park, in Boston, is a lyric little bandbox of a ballpark. Everything is painted green and seems in curiously sharp focus, like the inside of an old-fashioned peeping-type Easter egg. It was built in 1912 and rebuilt in 1934, and offers, as do most Boston artifacts, a compromise between Man's Euclidian determinations and Nature's beguiling irregularities. Its right field is one of the deepest in the American League, while its left field is the shortest; the high left-field wall, three hundred and fifteen feet from home plate along the foul line, virtually thrusts its surface at right-handed hitters. On the afternoon of Wednesday, September 28th, 1960, as I took a seat behind third base, a uniformed groundkeeper was treading the top of this wall, picking batting-practice home runs out of the screen, like a mushroom gatherer seen in Wordsworthian perspective on the verge of a cliff. The day was overcast, chill, and uninspirational. The Boston team was the worst in twenty-seven seasons. A jangling medley of incompetent youth and aging competence, the Red Sox were finishing in seventh place only because the Kansas City Athletics had locked them out of the cellar. They were scheduled to play the Baltimore Orioles, a much nimbler blend of May and December, who had been dumped from pennant contention a week before by the insatiable Yankees. I, and 10,453 others, had shown up primarily because this was the Red Sox's last home game of the season, and therefore the last time in all eternity that their regular left fielder, known to the headlines as TED, KID, SPLINTER, THUMPER, TW, and most cloyingly, MISTER WONDERFUL, would play in Boston. "WHAT WILL WE DO WITHOUT TED? HUB FANS ASK" ran the headline on a newspaper being read by a bulb-nosed cigar smoker a few rows away. Williams' retirement had been announced, doubted (he had been threatening retirement for years), confirmed by Tom Yawkey, the Red Sox owner, and at last widely accepted as the sad but probable truth. He was forty-two and had redeemed his abysmal season of 1959 with a—considering his advanced age—fine one. He had been giving away his gloves and bats and had grudgingly consented to a sentimental ceremony today. This was not necessarily his last game; the Red Sox were scheduled to travel to New York and wind up the season with three games there.

I arrived early. The Orioles were hitting fungos on the field. The day before, they had spitefully smothered the Red Sox, 17–4, and neither their faces nor their drab gray visiting-team uniforms seemed very gracious. I wondered who had invited them to the party. Between our heads and the lowering clouds a frenzied organ was thundering through, with an appositeness perhaps accidental, "You *maaaade* me love you, I didn't wanna do it, I didn't wanna do it. . . ."

The affair between Boston and Ted Williams was no mere summer romance; it was a marriage composed of spats, mutual disappointments, and, toward the end, a mellowing hoard of shared memories. It fell into three stages, which may be termed Youth, Maturity, and Age; or Thesis, Antithesis, and Synthesis; or Jason, Achilles, and Nestor.

First, there was the by now legendary epoch when the young bridegroom came out of the West and announced "All I want out of life is that when I walk down the street folks will say 'There goes the greatest hitter who ever lived.'" The dowagers of local journalism attempted to give elementary deportment lessons to this child who spake as a god, and to their horror were themselves rebuked. Thus began the long exchange of backbiting, bat-flipping, booing, and spitting that has distinguished Williams' public relations. The spitting incidents of 1957 and 1958 and the similar dockside courtesies that Williams has now and then extended to the grandstand should be judged against this background: the left-field stands at Fenway for twenty years have held a large number of customers who have bought their way in primarily for the privilege of showering abuse on Williams. Greatness necessarily attracts debunkers, but in Williams' case the hostility has been systematic and unappeasable. His basic offense against the fans has been to wish that they weren't there. Seeking a perfectionist's vacuum, he has quixotically desired to sever the game from the ground of paid spectatorship and publicity that supports it. Hence his refusal to tip his cap to the crowd or turn the other cheek to newsmen. It has been a costly theory—it has probably cost him, among other evidences of good will, two Most Valuable Player awards, which are voted by reporters—but he has held to it. While his critics, oral and literary, remained beyond the reach of his discipline, the opposing pitchers were accessible, and he spanked them to the tune of .406 in 1941. He slumped to .356 in 1942 and went off to war.

In 1946, Williams returned from three years as a Marine pilot to the second of his baseball avatars, that of Achilles, the hero of incomparable prowess and beauty who nevertheless was to be found sulking in his tent while the Trojans (mostly Yankees) fought through to the ships. Yawkey, a timber and mining maharajah, had surrounded his central jewel with many gems of slightly lesser water, such as Bobby Doerr, Dom DiMaggio, Rudy York, Birdie Tebbetts, and Johnny Pesky. Throughout the late forties, the Red Sox were the best paper team in baseball, yet they had little three-dimensional to show for it, and if this was a tragedy, Williams was Hamlet. A succinct review of the indictment—and a fair sample of appreciative sports-page prose—appeared the very day of Williams' valedictory, in a column by Huck Finnegan in the Boston *American* (no sentimentalist, Huck):

> Williams' career, in contrast [to Babe Ruth's], has been a series of failures except for his averages. He flopped in the only World Series he ever played in (1946) when he batted only .200. He flopped in the playoff game with Cleveland in 1948. He flopped in the final game of the 1949 season with the pennant hinging on the outcome (Yanks 5, Sox 3). He flopped in 1950 when he returned to the lineup after a two-month absence and ruined the morale of a club that seemed pennant-bound under Steve O'Neill. It has always been Williams' records first, the team second, and the Sox non-winning record is proof enough of that.

There are answers to all of this, of course. The fatal weakness of the great Sox slugging teams was not-quite-good-enough pitching rather than Williams' failure to hit a home run every time he came to bat. Again, Williams' depressing effect on his teammates has never been proved. Despite ample coaching to the contrary, most insisted that they *liked* him. He has been generous with advice to any player who asked for it. In an increasingly combative baseball atmosphere, he continued to duck beanballs docilely. With umpires he was gracious to a fault. This courtesy itself annoyed his critics, whom there was no pleasing. And against the ten crucial games (the seven World Series games with the St. Louis Cardinals, the 1948 playoff with the Cleveland Indians, and the two-game series with the Yankees at the end of the 1949 season, when one victory would have given the Red Sox the pennant) that make up the Achilles' heel of Williams' record, a mass of statistics can be set showing that day in and day out he was no slouch in the clutch. The correspondence columns of the Boston papers now and then suffer a sharp flurry of arithmetic on this score; indeed, for Williams to have distributed all his hits so they did nobody else any good would constitute a feat of placement unparalleled in the annals of selfishness.

Whatever residue of truth remains of the Finnegan charge those of us who love Williams must transmute as best we can, in our own personal crucibles. My personal memories of Williams began when I was a boy in Pennsylvania, with two last-place teams in Philadelphia to keep me company. For me, "W'ms, lf" was a figment of the box scores who always seemed to be going 3-for-5. He radiated, from afar, the hard blue glow of high purpose. I remember listening over the radio to the All-Star Game of 1946, in which Williams hit two singles and two home runs, the second one off a Rip Sewell "blooper" pitch; it was like hitting a balloon out of the park. I remember watching one of his home runs from the bleachers of Shibe Park; it went over the first baseman's head and rose methodically along a straight line and was still rising when it cleared the fence. The trajectory seemed qualitatively different from anything anyone else might hit. For me, Williams is the classic ballplayer of the game on a hot August weekday, before a small crowd, when the only thing at stake is the tissue-thin difference between a thing done well and a thing done ill. Baseball is a game of the long season, of relentless and gradual averaging-out. Irrelevance—since the reference point of most individual contests is remote and statistical—always threatens its interest, which can be maintained not by the occasional heroics that sportswriters feed upon but by the players who always *care*; who care, that is to say, about themselves and their art. Insofar as the clutch hitter is not a sportswriter's myth, he is a vulgarity, like a writer who writes only for money. It may be that, compared to such manager's dreams as the manifestly classy Joe DiMaggio and the always helpful Stan Musial, Williams was an icy star. But of all team sports, baseball, with its graceful intermittences of action, its immense and tranquil field sparsely settled with poised men in white, its dispassionate mathematics, seems to me best suited to accommodate, and be ornamented by, a loner. It is an essentially lonely game. No other player visible to my generation concentrated within himself so much of the sport's poignance, so assiduously refined his natural skills, so constantly brought to the plate that intensity of competence that crowds the throat with joy.

By the time I went to college, near Boston, the lesser stars Yawkey had assembled around Williams had faded, and his rigorous pride of craftsmanship had become itself a kind of heroism. This brittle and temperamental player developed an unexpected quality of persistence. He was always coming back—back from Korea, back from a broken collarbone, a shattered elbow, a bruised heel, back from drastic bouts of flu and ptomaine poisoning. Hardly a season went by without some enfeebling mishap, yet he always came back, and always looked like himself. The delicate mechanism of timing and power seemed sealed, shockproof, in some case deep within his frame. In addition to injuries, there was a heavily publicized divorce, and the usual storms with the press, and the Williams Shift—the manuever, custom-built by Lou Boudreau of the Cleveland Indians, whereby three infielders were concentrated on the right side of the infield. Williams could easily have learned to punch singles through the vacancy on his left and fattened his average hugely. This was what Ty Cobb, the Einstein of average, told him to do. But the game had changed since Cobb; Williams believed that his value to the club and to the league was as a slugger, so he went on pulling the ball, trying to blast it through three men, and paid the price of perhaps fifteen points of lifetime average. Like Ruth before him, he bought the occasional home run at the cost of many directed singles—a calculated sacrifice certainly not, in the case of a hitter as average-minded as Williams, entirely selfish.

After a prime so harassed and hobbled, Williams was granted by the relenting fates a golden twilight. He became at the end of his career perhaps the best *old* hitter of the century. The dividing line falls between the 1956 and 1957 seasons. In September of the first year, he and Mickey Mantle were contending for the batting championship. Both were hitting around .350, and there was no one else near them. The season ended with a three-game series between the Yankees and the Sox, and, living in New York then, I went up to the Stadium. Williams was slightly shy of the four hundred at-bats needed to qualify; the fear was expressed that the Yankees pitchers would walk him to protect Mantle. Instead, they pitched to him. It was wise. He looked terrible at the plate, tired and discouraged and unconvincing. He never looked very good to me in the Stadium. The final outcome in 1956 was Mantle .353, Williams .345.

The next year, I moved from New York to New England, and it made all the difference. For in September of 1957, in the same situation, the story was reversed. Mantle finally hit .365; it was the best season of his career. But Williams, though sick and old, had run away from him. A bout of flu had laid him low in September. He emerged from his cave in the Hotel Somerset haggard but irresistible; he hit four successive pinch-hit home runs. "I feel terrible," he confessed, "but every time I take a swing at the ball it goes out of the park."

He ended the season with thirty-eight home runs and an average of .388, the highest in either league since his own .406, and, coming from a decrepit man of thirty-nine, an even more supernal figure. With eight or so of the "leg hits" that a younger man would have beaten out, it would have been .400. And the next year, Williams, who in 1949 and 1953 had lost batting championships by decimal whiskers to George Kell and Mickey Vernon, sneaked in behind his teammate Pete Runnels and filched his sixth title, a bargain at .328.

In 1959, it seemed all over. The dinosaur thrashed around in the .200 swamp for the first half of the season, and was even benched ("rested," Manager Mike Higgins tactfully said). Old foes like the late Bill Cunningham began to offer batting tips. Cunningham thought Williams was jiggling his elbows; in truth, Williams' neck was so stiff he could hardly turn his head to look at the pitcher. When he swung, it looked like a Calder mobile with one thread cut; it reminded you that since 1954 Williams' shoulders had been wired together. A solicitous pall settled over the sports pages. In the two decades since Williams had come to Boston, his status had imperceptibly shifted from that of a naughty prodigy to that of a municipal monument. As his shadow in the record books lengthened, the Red Sox teams around him declined, and the entire American League seemed to be losing life and color to the National. The inconsistency of the new super-stars—Mantle, Colavito, and Kaline—served to make Williams appear all the more singular. And off the field, his private philanthropy—in particular, his zealous chairmanship of the Jimmy Fund, a charity for children with cancer—gave him a civic presence matched only by that of Richard Cardinal Cushing. In religion, Williams appears to be a humanist, and a selective one at that, but he and the abrasive-voiced Cardinal, when their good works intersect and they appear in the public eye together, make a handsome pair of seraphim.

Humiliated by his '59 season, Williams determined, once more, to come back. I, as a specimen Williams partisan, was both glad and fearful. All baseball fans believe in miracles; the question is, how *many* do you believe in? He looked like a ghost in spring training. Manager Jurges warned us ahead of time that if Williams didn't come through he would be benched, just like anybody else. As it turned out, it was Jurges who was benched. Williams entered the 1960 season needing eight home runs to have a lifetime total of 500; after one time at bat in Washington, he needed seven. For a stretch, he was hitting a home run every second game that he played. He passed Lou Gehrig's lifetime total, and finished with 521, thirteen behind Jimmie Foxx, who alone stands between Williams and Babe Ruth's unapproachable 714. The summer was a statistician's picnic. His two-thousandth walk came and went, his eighteen-hundredth run batted in, his sixteenth All-Star Game. At one point, he hit a home run off a pitcher, Don Lee, off whose father, Thornton Lee, he had hit a home run a generation before. The only comparable season for a forty-two-year-old man was Ty Cobb's in 1928. Cobb batted .323 and hit one homer. Williams batted .316 but hit twenty-nine homers.

In sum, though generally conceded to be the greatest hitter of his era, he did not establish himself as "the greatest hitter who ever lived." Cobb, for average, and Ruth, for power, remain supreme. Cobb, Rogers Hornsby, Joe Jackson, and Lefty O'Doul, among players since 1900, have higher lifetime averages than Williams' .344. Unlike Foxx, Gehrig, Hack Wilson, Hank Greenberg, and Ralph Kiner, Williams never came close to matching Babe Ruth's season home-run total of sixty. In the list of major-league batting records, not one is held by Williams. He is second in walks drawn, third in home runs, fifth in lifetime average, sixth in runs batted in, eighth in runs scored and in total bases, fourteenth in doubles, and thirtieth in hits. But if we allow him merely average seasons for the four-plus seasons he lost to two wars, and add another season for the months he lost to injuries, we get a man who in all the power totals would be second, and not a very distant second, to Ruth. And if we further allow that these years would have been not merely average but prime years, if we allow for all the months when Williams was playing in sub-par condition, if we permit his early and later years in baseball to be some sort of index of what the middle years could have been, if we give him a right-field fence that is not, like Fenway's, one of the most distant in the league, and if—the least excusable "if"—we imagine him condescending to outsmart the Williams Shift, we can defensibly assemble, like a colossus induced from the sizable fragments that do remain, a statistical figure not incommensurate with his grandiose ambition. From the statistics that are on the books, a good case can be made that in the *combination* of power and average Williams is first; nobody else ranks so high in both categories. Finally, there is the witness of the eyes; men whose memories go back to Shoeless Joe Jackson—another unlucky natural—rank him and Williams together as the best-looking hitters they have seen. It was for our last look that ten thousand of us had come.

Two girls, one of them with pert buckteeth and eyes as black as vest buttons, the other with white skin and flesh-colored hair, like an underdeveloped photograph of a redhead, came and sat on my right. On my other side was one of those frowning chestless young-old men who can frequently be seen, often wearing sailor hats, attending ball games alone. He did not once open his program but instead tapped it, rolled up, on his knee as he gave the game his disconsolate attention. A young lady, with freckles and a depressed, dainty nose that by an optical illusion seemed to thrust her lips forward for a kiss, sauntered down into the box seat right behind the roof of the Oriole dugout. She wore a blue coat with a Northeastern University emblem sewed to it. The girls beside me took it into their heads that this was Williams' daughter. She looked too old to me, and why would she be sitting behind the visitors' dugout? On the other hand, from the way she sat there, staring at the sky and French-inhaling, she clearly was *somebody*. Other fans came and eclipsed her from view. The crowd looked less like a weekday ballpark crowd than like the folks you might find in Yellowstone National Park, or emerging from automobiles at the top of scenic Mount Mansfield. There were a lot of competitively well-dressed couples of tourist age, and not a few babes in arms. A row of five seats in front of me was abruptly filled with a woman and four children, the youngest of them two years old, if that. Someday, presumably, he could tell his grandchildren that he saw Williams play. Along with these tots and second-honeymooners, there were Harvard freshmen, giving off that peculiar nervous glow created when a sufficient quantity of insouciance is saturated with enough insecurity; thick-necked Army officers with brass on their shoulders and steel in their stares; pepperings of priests; perfumed bouquets of Roxbury Fabian fans; shiny sales-men from Albany and Fall River; and those gray, hoarse men—taxi drivers, slaughterers, and bartenders—who will continue to click through the turnstiles long after everyone else has deserted to television and tramporamas. Behind me, two young male voices blossomed, cracking a joke about God's five proofs that Thomas Aquinas exists—typical Boston College levity.

The batting cage was trundled away. The Orioles fluttered to the sidelines. Diagonally across the field, by the Red Sox dugout, a cluster of men in over-coats were festering like maggots. I could see a splinter of white uniform, and Williams' head, held at a self-deprecating and evasive tilt. Williams' conver-sational stance is that of a six-foot-three-inch man under a six-foot ceiling. He moved away to the patter of flash bulbs, and began playing catch with a young Negro outfielder named Willie Tasby. His arm, never very powerful, had grown lax with the years, and his throwing motion was a kind of mus-cular drawl. To catch the ball, he flicked his glove hand onto his left shoulder (he batted left but threw right, as every schoolboy ought to know) and let the ball plop into it comically. This catch session with Tasby was the only time all afternoon I saw him grin.

A tight little flock of human sparrows who, from the lambent and pam-pered pink of their faces, could only have been Boston politicians moved toward the plate. The loudspeakers mammothly coughed as someone huffed on the microphone. The ceremonies began. Curt Gowdy, the Red Sox radio and televi-sion announcer, who sounds like everybody's brother-in-law, delivered a brief sermon, taking the two words "pride" and "champion" as his text. It began, "Twenty-one years ago, a skinny kid from San Diego, California . . ." and ended, "I don't think we'll ever see another like him." Robert Tibolt, chairman of the board of the Greater Boston Chamber of Commerce, presented Williams with a big Paul Revere silver bowl. Harry Carlson, a member of the sports committee of the Boston Chamber, gave him a plaque, whose inscription he did not read in its entirety, out of deference to Williams' distaste for this sort of fuss. Mayor Collins, seated in a wheelchair, presented the Jimmy Fund with a thousand-dollar check.

Then the occasion himself stooped to the microphone, and his voice sounded, after the others, very Californian; it seemed to be coming, excellently amplified, from a great distance, adolescently young and as smooth as a butternut. His thanks for the gifts had not died from our ears before he glided, as if helplessly, into "In spite of all the terrible things that have been said about me by the knights of the keyboard up there . . ." He glanced up at the press rows suspended behind home plate. The crowd tittered, appalled. A frightful vision flashed upon me, of the press gallery pelting Williams with erasers, of Williams clambering up the foul screen to slug journalists, of a riot, of Mayor Collins being crushed. ". . . And they *were* terrible things," Williams insisted, with level melancholy, into the mike. "I'd like to forget them, but I can't." He paused, swallowed his memories, and went on, "I want to say that my years in Boston have been the greatest thing in my life." The crowd, like an immense sail going limp in a change of wind, sighed with relief. Taking all the parts himself, Williams then acted out a vivacious little morality drama in which an imaginary tempter came to him at the beginning of his career and said, "Ted, you can play anywhere you like." Leaping nimbly into the role of his younger self (who in biographical actuality had yearned to be a Yankee), Williams gallantly chose Boston over all the other cities, and told us that Tom Yawkey was the greatest owner in baseball and we were the greatest fans. We applauded ourselves lustily. The umpire came out and dusted the plate. The voice of doom announced over the loudspeakers that after Williams' retirement his uniform number, 9, would be permanently retired—the first time the Red Sox had so honored a player. We cheered. The national anthem was played. We cheered. The game began.

Williams was third in the batting order, so he came up in the bottom of the first inning, and Steve Barber, a young pitcher born two months before Williams began playing in the major leagues, offered him four pitches, at all of which he disdained to swing, since none of them were within the strike zone. This demonstrated simultaneously that Williams' eyes were razor-sharp and that Barber's control wasn't. Shortly, the bases were full, with Williams on second. "Oh, I hope he gets held up at third! That would be wonderful," the girl beside me moaned, and, sure enough, the man at bat walked and Williams was delivered into our foreground. He struck the pose of Donatello's David, the third-base bag being Goliath's head. Fiddling with his cap, swapping small talk with the Oriole third baseman (who seemed delighted to have him drop in), swinging his arms with a sort of prancing nervousness, he looked fine—flexible, hard, and not unbecomingly substantial through the middle. The long neck, the small head, the knickers whose cuffs were worn down near his ankles—all these cliches of sports cartoon iconography were rendered in the flesh.

One of the collegiate voices behind me said, "He looks old, doesn't he; big deep wrinkles in his face . . ."

"Yeah," the other voice said, "but he looks like an old hawk, doesn't he?"

With each pitch, Williams danced down the baseline, waving his arms and stirring dust, ponderous but menacing, like an attacking goose. It occurred to about a dozen humorists at once to shout "Steal home! Go, go!" Williams' speed afoot was never legendary. Lou Clinton, a young Sox outfielder, hit a fairly deep fly to center field. Williams tagged up and ran home. As he slid across the plate, the ball, thrown with unusual heft by Jackie Brandt, the Oriole center fielder, hit him on the back.

"Boy, he was really loafing, wasn't he?" one of the collegiate voices behind me said.

"It's cold," the other voice explained. "He doesn't play well when it's cold. He likes heat. He's a hedonist."

The run that Williams scored was the second and last of the inning. Gus Triandos, of the Orioles, quickly evened the score by plunking a home run over the handy left-field wall. Williams, who had had this wall at his back for twenty years, played the ball flawlessly. He didn't budge. He just stood still, in the center of the little patch of grass that his patient footsteps had worn brown, and, limp with lack of interest, watched the ball pass overhead. It was not a very interesting game. Mike Higgins, the Red Sox manager, with nothing to lose, had restricted his major-league players to the left-field line—along with Williams, Frank Malzone, a first-rate third baseman, played the game—and had peopled the rest of the terrain with unpredictable youngsters fresh, or not so fresh, off the farms. Other than Williams' recurrent appearances at the plate, the *maladresse* of the Sox infield was the sole focus of suspense; the second baseman turned every grounder into a juggling act, while the shortstop did a breathtaking impersonation of an open window. With this sort of assistance, the Orioles wheedled their way into a 4–2 lead. They had early replaced Barber with another young pitcher, Jack Fisher. Fortunately (as it turned out), Fisher is no cutie; he is willing to burn the ball through the strike zone, and inning after inning this tactic punctured Higgins' string of test balloons.

Whenever Williams appeared at the plate—pounding the dirt from his cleats, gouging a pit in the batter's box with his left foot, wringing resin out of the bat handle with his vehement grip, switching the stick at the pitcher with an electric ferocity—it was like having a familiar Leonardo appear in a shuffle of *Saturday Evening Post* covers. This man, you realized—and here, perhaps, was the difference, greater than the difference in gifts—really desired to hit the ball. In the third inning, he hoisted a high fly to deep center. In the fifth, we thought he had it; he smacked the ball hard and high into the heart of his power zone, but the deep right field in Fenway and the heavy air and a casual east wind defeated him. The ball died. Al Pilarcik leaned his back against the big "380" painted on the right-field wall and caught it. On another day, in another park, it would have been gone. (After the game, Williams said, "I didn't think I could hit one any harder than that. The conditions weren't good.")

The afternoon grew so glowering that in the sixth inning the arc lights were turned on—always a wan sight in the daytime, like the burning head-lights of a funeral procession. Aided by the gloom, Fisher was slicing through the Sox rookies, and Williams did not come to bat in the seventh. He was second up in the eighth. This was almost certainly his last time to come to the plate in Fenway Park, and instead of merely cheering, as we had at his three previous appearances, we stood, all of us, and applauded. I had never before heard pure applause in a ballpark. No calling, no whistling, just an ocean of handclaps, minute after minute, burst after burst, crowding and run-ning together in continuous succession like the pushes of surf at the edge of the sand. It was a sombre and considered tumult. There was not a boo in it. It seemed to renew itself out of a shifting set of memories as the Kid, the Marine, the veteran of feuds and failures and injuries, the friend of children, and the enduring old pro evolved down the bright tunnel of twenty-two summers toward this moment. At last, the umpire signaled for Fisher to pitch; with the other players, he had been frozen in position. Only Williams had moved dur-ing the ovation, switching his bat impatiently, ignoring everything except his cherished task. Fisher wound up, and the applause sank into a hush.

Understand that we were a crowd of rational people. We knew that a home run cannot be produced at will; the right pitch must be perfectly met and luck must ride with the ball. Three innings before, we had seen a brave effort fail. The air was soggy, the season was exhausted. Nevertheless, there will always lurk, around the corner in a pocket of our knowledge of the odds, an inde-fensible hope, and this was one of the times, which you now and then find in sports, when a density of expectation hangs in the air and plucks an event out of the future.

Fisher, after his unsettling wait, was low with the first pitch. He put the sec-ond one over, and Williams swung mightily and missed. The crowd grunted, seeing that classic swing, so long and smooth and quick, exposed. Fisher threw the third time, Williams swung again, and there it was. The ball climbed on a diagonal line into the vast volume of air over center field. From my angle, behind third base, the ball seemed less an object in flight than the tip of a towering, motionless construct, like the Eiffel Tower or the Tappan Zee Bridge. It was in the books while it was still in the sky. Brandt ran back to the deepest corner of the outfield grass, the ball descended beyond his reach and struck in the crotch where the bullpen met the wall, bounced chunkily, and vanished.

Like a feather caught in a vortex, Williams ran around the square of bases at the center of our beseeching screaming. He ran as he always ran out home runs—hurriedly, unsmiling, head down, as if our praise were a storm of rain to get out of. He didn't tip his cap. Though we thumped, wept, and chanted "We want Ted" for minutes after he hid in the dugout, he did not come back. Our noise for some seconds passed beyond excitement into a kind of immense open anguish, a wailing, a cry to be saved. But immortality is nontransferable. The papers said that the other players, and even the umpires on the field, begged him to come out and acknowledge us in some way, but he refused. Gods do not answer letters.

Every true story has an anticlimax. The men on the field refused to disappear, as would have seemed decent, in the smoke of Williams' miracle. Fisher continued to pitch, and escaped further harm. At the end of the inning, Higgins sent Williams out to his left-field position, then instantly replaced him with Carroll Hardy, so we had a long last look at Williams as he ran out there and then back, his uniform jogging, his eyes steadfast on the ground. It was nice, and we were grateful, but it left a funny taste.

One of the scholasticists behind me said, "Let's go. We've seen everything. I don't want to spoil it." This seemed a sound aesthetic decision. Williams' last word had been so exquisitely chosen, such a perfect fusion of expectation, intention, and execution, that already it felt a little unreal in my head, and I wanted to get out before the castle collapsed. But the game, though played by clumsy midgets under the feeble glow of the arc lights, began to tug at my attention, and I loitered in the runway until it was over. Williams' homer had, quite incidentally, made the score 4–3. In the bottom of the ninth inning, with one out, Marlan Coughtry, the second-base juggler, singled. Vic Wertz, pinch-hitting, doubled off the left-field wall, Coughtry advancing to third. Pumpsie Green walked, to load the bases. Willie Tasby hit a double-play ball to the third baseman, but in making the pivot throw Billy Klaus, an ex-Red Sox infielder, reverted to form and threw the ball past the first baseman and into the Red Sox dugout. The Sox won, 5–4. On the car radio as I drove home I heard that Williams, his own man to the end, had decided not to accompany the team to New York. He had met the little death that awaits athletes. He had quit.

Lee in the Capitol

Herman Melville

Beginning with Homer's Iliad *and* Odyssey *and Virgil's* Aeneid, *poetry has long been the form in which the deeds of heroes are remembered and passed on to succeeding generations. We Americans are a less poetic people, and our heroes have not been legendary or mythological figures from a remote past. Nonetheless, we have had poets, from Walt Whitman forward, who have attempted to shape the nation's sense of self. Not surprisingly, the crisis of the Civil War provided a dramatic occasion for poetic instruction. Herman Melville, author of perhaps the greatest American novel,* Moby-Dick, *also composed a book of Civil War poems, entitled* Battle-Pieces and Aspects of the War. *In this poem, Melville imaginatively reworks an actual event—the appearance of former Confederate general Robert E. Lee before the Reconstruction Committee of Congress early in 1866, as Congress sought to figure out how to reincorporate into the Union those eleven states that had attempted secession and been defeated on the field of battle.*

In the closing lines of his Second Inaugural, Lincoln spoke of the need "to bind up the nation's wounds" and to do so "with malice toward none, with charity for all." Why should Melville choose Lee, rather than Lincoln, to express similar sentiments? How does Lee comport himself before the congressional committee? What prompts Lee to appeal for Northern forebearance and magnanimity toward the vanquished South? What arguments does he advance for reconciliation between North and South, and what does his story of the Moor and the Christian suggest about the remaining gulf? Do you regard Lee as an American patriot? Was his audience moved? Are you? Can—does—poetry still inspire patriotic and civic attachment?

Hard pressed by numbers in his strait,
   Rebellion's soldier-chief no more contends—
Feels that the hour is come of Fate,
   Lays down one sword, and widened warfare ends.
The captain who fierce armies led
Becomes a quiet seminary's head—
Poor as his privates, earns his bread.
In studious cares and aims engrossed,
   Strives to forget Stuart and Stonewall dead—
Comrades and cause, station and riches lost,
   And all the ills that flock when fortune's fled.
No word he breathes of vain lament,
   Mute to reproach, nor hears applause—
His doom accepts, perforce content,
   And acquiesces in asserted laws;
Secluded now would pass his life,
And leave to time the sequel of the strife.
   But missives from the Senators ran;
Not that they now would gaze upon a swordless foe,
And power made powerless and brought low:
   Reasons of state, 'tis claimed, require the man.
Demurring not, promptly he comes
By ways which show the blackened homes,
   And—last—the seat no more his own,
But Honor's; patriot grave-yards fill
The forfeit slopes of that patrician hill,
   And fling a shroud on Arlington.
The oaks ancestral all are low;
No more from the porch his glance shall go
Ranging the varied landscape o'er,
Far as the looming Dome—no more.
One look he gives, then turns aside,
Solace he summons from his pride:
"So be it! They await me now
Who wrought this stinging overthrow;
They wait me; not as on the day
Of Pope's impelled retreat in disarray—
By me impelled—when toward yon Dome
The clouds of war came rolling home."
The burst, the bitterness was spent,

The heart-burst bitterly turbulent,
And on he fared.

In nearness now
He marks the Capitol—a show
Lifted in amplitude, and set
With standards flushed with a glow of Richmond yet;
Trees and green terraces sleep below.
Through the clear air, in sunny light,
The marble dazes—a temple white.

Intrepid soldier! had his blade been drawn
For yon starred flag, never as now
Bid to the Senate-house had he gone,
But freely, and in pageant borne,
As when brave numbers without number, massed,
Plumed the broad way, and pouring passed—
Bannered, beflowered—between the shores
Of faces, and the dinn'd huzzas,
And balconies kindling at the sabre-flash,
'Mid roar of drums and guns, and cymbal-crash,
While Grant and Sherman shone in blue—
Close of the war and victory's long review.

Yet pride at hand still aidful swelled,
And up the hard ascent he held.
The meeting follows. In his mien
The victor and the vanquished both are seen—
All that he is, and what he late had been.
Awhile, with curious eyes they scan
The Chief who led invasion's van—
Allied by family to one,
Founder of the Arch the Invader warred upon:
Who looks at Lee must think of Washington;
In pain must think, and hide the thought,
So deep with grievous meaning it is fraught.

Secession in her soldier shows
Silent and patient; and they feel
(Developed even in just success)

Dim inklings of a hazy future steal;
  Their thoughts their questions well express:
"Does the sad South still cherish hate?
Freely will Southern men with Northern mate?
The blacks—should we our arm withdraw,
Would that betray them? some distrust your law.
And how if foreign fleets should come—
Would the South then drive her wedges home?"
And more hereof. The Virginian sees—
Replies to such anxieties.
Discreet his answers run—appear
Briefly straightforward, coldly clear.

"If now," the Senators, closing, say,
"Aught else remain, speak out, we pray."
Hereat he paused; his better heart
Strove strongly then; prompted a worthier part
Than coldly to endure his doom.
Speak out? Ay, speak, and for the brave,
Who else no voice or proxy have;
Frankly their spokesman here become,
And the flushed North from her own victory save.
That inspiration overrode—
Hardly it quelled the galling load
Of personal ill. The inner feud
He, self-contained, a while withstood;
They waiting. In his troubled eye
Shadows from clouds unseen they spy;
They could not mark within his breast
The pang which pleading thought oppressed:
He spoke, nor felt the bitterness die.

"My word is given—it ties my sword;
Even were banners still abroad,
Never could I strive in arms again
While you, as fit, that pledge retain.
Our cause I followed, stood in field and gate—
All's over now, and now I follow Fate.
But this is naught. A People call—
A desolated land, and all

The brood of ills that press so sore,
The natural offspring of this civil war,
Which ending not in fame, such as might rear
Fitly its sculptured trophy here,
Yields harvest large of doubt and dread
To all who have the heart and head
To feel and know. How shall I speak?
Thoughts knot with thoughts, and utterance check.
Before my eyes there swims a haze,
Through mists departed comrades gaze—
First to encourage, last that shall upbraid!
How shall I speak? The South would fain
Feel peace, have quiet law again—
Replant the trees for homestead-shade.
    You ask if she recants: she yields.
Nay, and would more; would blend anew,
As the bones of the slain in her forests do,
Bewailed alike by us and you.
    A voice comes out from these charnel-fields,
A plaintive yet unheeded one:
'Died all in vain? both sides undone?'
Push not your triumph; do not urge
Submissiveness beyond the verge.
Intestine rancor would you bide,
Nursing eleven sliding daggers in your side?
Far from my thought to school or threat;
I speak the things which hard beset.
Where various hazards meet the eyes,
To elect in magnanimity is wise.
Reap victory's fruit while sound the core;
What sounder fruit than re-established law?
I know your partial thoughts do press
Solely on us for war's unhappy stress;
But weigh—consider—look at all,
And broad anathema you'll recall.
The censor's charge I'll not repeat,
The meddlers kindled the war's white heat—
Vain intermeddlers and malign,
Both of the palm and of the pine;
I waive the thought—which never can be rife—

Common's the crime in every civil strife:
But this I feel, that North and South were driven
By Fate to arms. For *our* unshriven,
What thousands, truest souls, were tried—
    As never may any be again—
All those who stemmed Secession's pride,
But at last were swept by the urgent tide
    Into the chasm. I know their pain.
A story here may be applied:
'In Moorish lands there lived a maid
    Brought to confess by vow the creed
    Of Christians. Fain would priests persuade
That now she must approve by deed
    The faith she kept. "What deed?" she asked.
"Your old sire leave, nor deem it sin,
    And come with us." Still more they tasked
The sad one: "If heaven you'd win—
    Far from the burning pit withdraw,
Then must you learn to hate your kin,
    Yea, side against them—such the law,
For Moor and Christian are at war."
"Then will I never quit my sire,
But here with him through every trial go,
Nor leave him though in flames below—
God help me in his fire!"'
So in the South; vain every plea
'Gainst Nature's strong fidelity;
    True to the home and to the heart,
Throngs cast their lot with kith and kin,
    Foreboding, cleaved to the natural part—
Was this the unforgivable sin?
These noble spirits are yet yours to win.
Shall the great North go Sylla's way?
Proscribe? prolong the evil day?
Confirm the curse? infix the hate?
In Union's name forever alienate?
From reason who can urge the plea—
Freemen conquerors of the free?
When blood returns to the shrunken vein,
Shall the wound of the Nation bleed again?

Well may the wars wan thought supply,
And kill the kindling of the hopeful eye,
Unless you do what even kings have done
In leniency—unless you shun
To copy Europe in her worst estate—
Avoid the tyranny you reprobate."

He ceased. His earnestness unforeseen
Moved, but not swayed their former mien;
   And they dismissed him. Forth he went
Through vaulted walks in lengthened line
Like porches erst upon the Palatine:
   Historic reveries their lesson lent,
   The Past her shadow through the Future sent.

But no. Brave though the Soldier, grave his plea—
   Catching the light in the future's skies,
Instinct disowns each darkening prophecy:
   Faith in America never dies;
Heaven shall the end ordained fulfill,
We march with Providence cheery still.

Yeager

from The Right Stuff

TOM WOLFE

Excellence takes many forms and is possible in many domains of life. Yet rarely does it capture the public imagination more than when found in great adventurers—explorers, scientists, inventors, entrepreneurs. In The Right Stuff *(1979), author and journalist Tom Wolfe (born 1931) pays homage to one such group of heroes, America's first astronauts. Before the space program could even be conceived, Wolfe shows in this excerpt, a prior challenge, thought by some to be impossible, had to be met: flying faster than the speed of sound. Here Wolfe profiles the first man to break the sound barrier, Charles "Chuck" Yeager. What makes possible such an accomplishment? Why do or should we esteem it? How does this form of daring compare with excellences in the arts, athletics, or education? What contribution do exploration of the unknown and the undertaking of great adventures make to our national life?*

Anyone who travels very much on airlines in the United States soon gets to know the voice of *the airline pilot* . . . coming over the intercom . . . with a particular drawl, a particular folksiness, a particular down-home calmness that is so exaggerated it begins to parody itself (nevertheless!—it's reassuring) . . . the voice that tells you, as the airliner is caught in thunderheads and goes bolting up and down a thousand feet at a single gulp, to check your seat belts because "it might get a little choppy" . . . the voice that tells you (on a flight from Phoenix preparing for its final approach into Kennedy Airport, New York, just after dawn): "Now, folks, uh . . . this is the captain . . . ummmm . . . We've got a little ol' red light up here on the control panel that's tryin' to tell us that the *land*in' gears're not . . . uh . . . *lock*in' into position when we lower 'em . . . Now . . . *I* don't believe that little ol' red light knows what it's *talk*in' about— I believe it's that little ol' red light that iddn' workin' right" . . . faint chuckle, long pause, as if to say, *I'm not even sure all this is really worth going into—still, it may amuse you* . . . "*But* . . . I guess to play it by the rules, we oughta *humor* that little ol' light . . . so we're gonna take her down to about, oh, two or three hundred feet over the runway at Kennedy, and the folks down there on the ground are gonna see if they caint give us a *vi*sual inspection of those ol' landin' gears"—with which he is obviously on intimate ol'-buddy terms, as with every other working part of this mighty ship—"and if I'm right . . . they're gonna tell us everything is copa*cetic* all the way aroun' an' we'll jes take her on in" . . . and, after a couple of low passes over the field, the voice returns: "Well, folks, those folks down there on the ground—it must be too early for 'em or somethin'—I 'spect they still got the *sleep*ers in their eyes . . . 'cause they say they caint tell if those ol' landin' gears are all the way down or not . . . But, you know, up here in the cockpit we're convinced they're all the way down, so we're jes gonna take her on in . . . And oh" . . . *(I almost forgot)* . . . "while we take a little swing out over the ocean an' empty some of that surplus fuel we're not gonna be needin' anymore—that's what you might be seein' comin' out of the wings—our lovely little ladies . . . if they'll be so kind . . . they're gonna go up and down the aisles and show you how we do what we call 'assumin' the position'" . . . another faint chuckle *(We do this so often, and it's so much fun, we even have a funny little name for it)* . . . and the stewardesses, a bit grimmer, by the looks of them, than *that voice*, start telling the passengers to take their glasses off and take the ball-point pens and other sharp objects out of their pockets, and they show them *the position*, with the head lowered . . . while down on the field at Kennedy the little yellow emergency trucks start roaring across the field—and even though in your pounding heart and your sweating palms and your broiling brainpan you *know* this is a critical moment in your life, you still can't quite bring yourself to be*lieve* it, because if it were . . . how could *the captain*, the man who knows the actual situation most intimately . . . how could he keep on drawlin' and chucklin' and driftin' and lollygaggin' in that particular voice of his—

Well!—who doesn't know that voice! And who can forget it!—even after he is proved right and the emergency is over.

That particular voice may sound vaguely Southern or Southwestern, but it is specifically Appalachian in origin. It originated in the mountains of West Virginia, in the coal country, in Lincoln County, so far up in the hollows that, as the saying went, "they had to pipe in daylight." In the late 1940s and early 1950s this up-hollow voice drifted down from on high, from over the high desert of California, down, down, down, from the upper reaches of the Brotherhood into all phases of American aviation. It was amazing. It was *Pygmalion* in reverse. Military pilots and then, soon, airline pilots, pilots from Maine and Massachusetts and the Dakotas and Oregon and everywhere else, began to talk in that poker-hollow West Virginia drawl, or as close to it as they could bend their native accents. It was the drawl of the most righteous of all the possessors of the right stuff: Chuck Yeager.

Yeager had started out as the equivalent, in the Second World War, of the legendary Frank Luke of the 27th Aero Squadron in the First. Which is to say, he was the boondocker, the boy from the back country, with only a high-school education, no credentials, no cachet or polish of any sort, who took off the feed-store overalls and put on a uniform and climbed into an airplane and lit up the skies over Europe.

Yeager grew up in Hamlin, West Virginia, a town on the Mud River not far from Nitro, Hurricane Whirlwind, Salt Rock, Mud, Sod, Crum, Leet, Dollie, Ruth, and Alum Creek. His father was a gas driller (drilling for natural gas in the coalfields), his older brother was a gas driller, and he would have been a gas driller had he not enlisted in the Army Air Force in 1941 at the age of eighteen. In 1943, at twenty, he became a flight officer, i.e., a non-com who was allowed to fly, and went to England to fly fighter planes over France and Germany. Even in the tumult of the war Yeager was somewhat puzzling to a lot of other pilots. He was a short, wiry, but muscular little guy with dark curly hair and a tough-looking face that seemed (to strangers) to be saying: "You best not be lookin' me in the eye, you peckerwood, or I'll put four more holes in your nose." But that wasn't what was puzzling. What was puzzling was the way Yeager talked. He seemed to talk with some older forms of English elocution, syntax, and conjugation that had been preserved up-hollow in the Appalachians. There were people up there who never said they disapproved of anything, they said: "I don't hold with it." In the present tense they were willing to *help* out, like anyone else; but in the past tense they only *holped*. "H'it weren't nothin' I hold with, but I holped him out with it, anyways."

In his first eight missions, at the age of twenty, Yeager shot down two German fighters. On his ninth he was shot down over German-occupied French territory, suffering flak wounds; he bailed out, was picked up by the French underground, which smuggled him across the Pyrenees into Spain disguised as a peasant. In Spain he was jailed briefly, then released, whereupon he made it back to England and returned to combat during the Allied invasion of France. On October 12, 1944, Yeager took on and shot down five German fighter planes in succession. On November 6, flying a propeller-driven P-51 Mustang, he shot down one of the new jet fighters the Germans had developed, the Messerschmitt-262, and damaged two more, and on November 20 he shot down four FW-190s. It was a true Frank Luke–style display of warrior fury and personal prowess. By the end of the war he had thirteen and a half kills. He was twenty-two years old.

In 1946 and 1947 Yeager was trained as a test pilot at Wright Field in Dayton. He amazed his instructors with his ability at stunt-team flying, not to mention the unofficial business of hassling. That plus his up-hollow drawl had everybody saying, "He's a natural-born stick 'n' rudder man." Nevertheless, there was something extraordinary about it when a man so young, with so little experience in flight test, was selected to go to Muroc Field in California for the XS-1 project.

Muroc was up in the high elevations of the Mojave Desert. It looked like some fossil landscape that had long since been left behind by the rest of terrestrial evolution. It was full of huge dry lake beds, the biggest being Rogers Lake. Other than sagebrush the only vegetation was Joshua trees, twisted freaks of the plant world that looked like a cross between cactus and Japanese bonsai. They had a dark petrified green color and horribly crippled branches. At dusk the Joshua trees stood out in silhouette on the fossil wasteland like some arthritic nightmare. In the summer the temperature went up to 110 degrees as a matter of course, and the dry lake beds were covered in sand, and there would be windstorms and sandstorms right out of a Foreign Legion movie. At night it would drop to near freezing, and in December it would start raining, and the dry lakes would fill up with a few inches of water, and some sort of putrid prehistoric shrimps would work their way up from out of the ooze, and sea gulls would come flying in a hundred miles or more from the ocean, over the mountains, to gobble up these squirming little throwbacks. A person had to see it to believe it: flocks of sea gulls wheeling around in the air out in the middle of the high desert in the dead of winter and grazing on antediluvian crustaceans in the primordial ooze.

When the wind blew the few inches of water back and forth across the lake beds, they became absolutely smooth and level. And when the water evaporated in the spring, and the sun baked the ground hard, the lake beds became the greatest natural landing fields ever discovered and also the biggest, with miles of room for error. That was highly desirable, given the nature of the enterprise at Muroc.

Besides the wind, sand, tumbleweed, and Joshua trees, there was nothing at Muroc except for two quonset-style hangars, side by side, a couple of gasoline pumps, a single concrete runway, a few tarpaper shacks, and some tents. The officers stayed in the shacks marked "barracks," and lesser souls stayed in the tents and froze all night and fried all day. Every road into the property had a guardhouse on it manned by soldiers. The enterprise the Army had undertaken in this godforsaken place was the development of supersonic jet and rocket planes.

At the end of the war the Army had discovered that the Germans not only had the world's first jet fighter but also a rocket plane that had gone 596 miles an hour in tests. Just after the war a British jet, the Gloster Meteor, jumped the official world speed record from 469 to 606 in a single day. The next great plateau would be Mach 1, the speed of sound, and the Army Air Force considered it crucial to achieve it first.

The speed of sound, Mach 1, was known (thanks to the work of the physicist Ernst Mach) to vary at different altitudes, temperatures, and wind speeds. On a calm 60-degree day at sea level it was about 760 miles an hour, while at 40,000 feet, where the temperature would be at least sixty below, it was about 660 miles an hour. Evil and baffling things happened in the transonic zone, which began at about .7 Mach. Wind tunnels choked out at such velocities. Pilots who approached the speed of sound in dives reported that the controls would lock or "freeze" or even alter their normal functions. Pilots had crashed and died because they couldn't budge the stick. Just last year Geoffrey de Havilland, son of the famous British aircraft designer and builder, had tried to take one of his father's DH 108s to Mach 1. The ship started buffeting and then disintegrated, and he was killed. This led engineers to speculate that the shock waves became so severe and unpredictable at Mach 1, no aircraft could survive them. They started talking about "the sonic wall" and "the sound barrier."

So this was the task that a handful of pilots, engineers, and mechanics had at Muroc. The place was utterly primitive, nothing but bare bones, bleached tarpaulins, and corrugated tin rippling in the heat with caloric waves; and for an ambitious young pilot it was perfect. Muroc seemed like an outpost on the dome of the world, open only to a righteous few, closed off to the rest of humanity, including even the Army Air Force brass of command control, which was at Wright Field. The commanding officer at Muroc was only a colonel, and his superiors at Wright did not relish junkets to the Muroc rat shacks in the first place. But to pilots this prehistoric throwback of an airfield became . . . shrimp heaven! the rat-shack plains of Olympus! . . .

The plane the Air Force wanted to break the sound barrier with was called the X-1 at the outset and later on simply the X-1. The Bell Aircraft Corporation had built it under an Army contract. . . .

The idea in testing the X-1 was to nurse it carefully into the transonic zone, up to seven-tenths, eight-tenths, nine-tenths the speed of sound (.7 Mach, .8 Mach, .9 Mach) before attempting the speed of sound itself, Mach 1. . . . The consensus of aviators and engineers, after Geoffrey de Havilland's death, was that the speed of sound was an absolute, like the firmness of the earth. The sound barrier was a farm you could buy in the sky. . . .

[*Yeager becomes the pilot of the X-1.*] The only trouble they had with Yeager was in holding him back. On his first powered flight in the X-1 he immediately executed an unauthorized zero-g roll with a full load of rocket fuel, then stood the ship on its tail and went up to .85 Mach in a vertical climb, also unauthorized. On subsequent flights, at speeds between .85 Mach and .9 Mach, Yeager ran into most known airfoil problems—loss of elevator, aileron, and rudder control, heavy trim pressures, Dutch rolls, pitching and buffeting, the lot—yet was convinced, after edging over .9 Mach, that this would all get better, not worse, as you reached Mach 1. The attempt to push beyond Mach 1—"breaking the sound barrier"—was set for October 14, 1947. Not being an engineer, Yeager didn't believe the "barrier" existed.

October 14 was a Tuesday. On Sunday evening, October 12, Chuck Yeager dropped in at Pancho's,* along with his wife. She was a brunette named Glennis, whom he had met in California while he was in training, and she was such a number, so striking, he had the inscription "Glamorous Glennis" written on the nose of his P-51 in Europe and, just a few weeks back, on the X-1 itself. Yeager didn't go to Pancho's and knock back a few because two days later the big test was coming up. Nor did he knock back a few because it was the weekend. No, he knocked back a few because night had come and he was a pilot at Muroc. In keeping with the military tradition of Flying & Drinking, that was what you did, for no other reason than that the sun had gone down. You went to Pancho's and knocked back a few and listened to the screen doors banging and to other aviators torturing the piano and the nation's repertoire of Familiar Favorites and to lonesome mouse-turd strangers wandering in through the banging doors and to Pancho classifying the whole bunch of them as old bastards and miserable peckerwoods. That was what you did if you were a pilot at Muroc and the sun went down.

So about eleven Yeager got the idea that it would be a hell of a kick if he and Glennis saddled up a couple of Pancho's dude-ranch horses and went for a romp, a little rat race, in the moonlight. This was in keeping with the military tradition of Flying & Drinking and Drinking & Driving, except that this was prehistoric Muroc and you rode horses. So Yeager and his wife set off on a little proficiency run at full gallop through the desert in the moonlight amid the arthritic silhouettes of the Joshua trees. Then they start racing back to the corral, with Yeager in the lead and heading for the gateway. Given the prevailing conditions, it being nighttime, at Pancho's, and his head being filled with a black sandstorm of many badly bawled songs and vulcanized oaths, he sees too late that the gate has been closed. Like many a hard-driving midnight pilot

* *Pancho's Fly Inn, "a rickety wind-blown 1930s-style establishment . . . owned, run, and bartended by a woman named Pancho Barnes," which also sported "an airstrip, a swimming pool, a dude ranch corral, and plenty of acreage for horseback riding, a big old guest house for the lodgers, and a connecting building that was the bar and the restaurant."*

before him, he does not realize that he is not equally gifted in the control of all forms of locomotion. He and the horse hit the gate, and he goes flying off and lands on his right side. His side hurts like hell.

The next day, Monday, his side still hurts like hell. It hurts every time he moves. It hurts every time he breathes deep. It hurts every time he moves his right arm. He knows that if he goes to a doctor at Muroc or says anything to anybody even remotely connected with his superiors, he will be scrubbed from the flight on Tuesday. They might even go so far as to put some other miserable peckerwood in his place. So he gets on his motorcycle, an old junker that Pancho had given him, and rides over to see a doctor in the town of Rosamond, near where he lives. Every time the goddamned motorcycle hits a pebble in the road, his side hurts like a sonofabitch. The doctor in Rosamond informs him he has two broken ribs and he tapes them up and tells him that if he'll just keep his right arm immobilized for a couple of weeks and avoid any physical exertion or sudden movements, he should be all right.

Yeager gets up before daybreak on Tuesday morning—which is supposed to be the day he tries to break the sound barrier—and his ribs still hurt like a sonofabitch. He gets his wife to drive him over to the field, and he has to keep his right arm pinned down to his side to keep his ribs from hurting so much. At dawn, on the day of a flight, you could hear the X-1 screaming long before you got there. The fuel for the X-1 was alcohol and liquid oxygen, oxygen converted from a gas to a liquid by lowering its temperature to 297 degrees below zero. And when the lox, as it was called, rolled out of the hoses and into the belly of the X-1, it started boiling off and the X-1 started steaming and screaming like a teakettle. There's quite a crowd on hand, by Muroc standards . . . perhaps nine or ten souls. They're still fueling the X-1 with the lox, and the beast is wailing.

The X-1 looked like a fat orange swallow with white markings. But it was really just a length of pipe with four rocket chambers in it. It had a tiny cockpit and a needle nose, two little straight blades (only three and a half inches thick at the thickest part) for wings, and a tail assembly set up high to avoid the "sonic wash" from the wings. Even though his side was throbbing and his right arm felt practically useless, Yeager figured he could grit his teeth and get through the flight—except for one specific move he had to make. In the rocket launches, the X-1, which held only two and a half minutes' worth of fuel, was carried up to twenty-six thousand feet underneath a B-29. At seven thousand feet, Yeager was to climb down a ladder from the bomb bay of the B-29 to the open doorway of the X-1, hook up to the oxygen system and the radio microphone and earphones, and put his crash helmet on and prepare for the launch, which would come at twenty-five thousand feet. This helmet was a homemade number. There had never been any such thing as a crash helmet before, except in stunt flying. Throughout the war pilots had used the old skin-tight leather helmet-and-goggles. But the X-1 had a way of throwing the pilot around so violently that there was danger of getting knocked out against the walls of the cockpit. So Yeager had bought a big leather football helmet—there were no plastic ones at the time—and he butchered it with a hunting knife until he carved the right kind of holes in it, so that it would fit down over his regular flying helmet and the earphones and the oxygen rig. Anyway, then his flight engineer, Jack Ridley, would climb down the ladder, out in the breeze, and shove into place the cockpit door, which had to be lowered out of the belly of the B-29 on a chain. Then Yeager had to push a handle to lock the door airtight. Since the X-1's cockpit was minute, you had to push the handle with your right hand. It took quite a shove. There was no way you could move into position to get enough leverage with your left hand.

Out in the hangar Yeager makes a few test shoves on the sly, and the pain is so incredible he realizes that there is no way a man with two broken ribs is going to get the door closed. It is time to confide in somebody, and the logical man is Jack Ridley. Ridley is not only the flight engineer but a pilot himself and a good old boy from Oklahoma to boot. He will understand about Flying & Drinking and Drinking & Driving through the goddamned Joshua trees. So Yeager takes Ridley off to the side in the tin hangar and says: Jack, I got me a little ol' problem here. Over at Pancho's the other night I sorta . . . dinged my goddamned ribs. Ridley says, Whattya mean . . . *dinged*? Yeager says, Well, I guess you might say I damned near like to . . . *broke* a coupla the sonsabitches. Whereupon Yeager sketches out the problem he foresees.

Not for nothing is Ridley the engineer on this project. He has an inspiration. He tells a janitor named Sam to cut him about nine inches off a broom handle. When nobody's looking, he slips the broomstick into the cockpit of the X-1 and gives Yeager a little advice and counsel.

So with that added bit of supersonic flight gear Yeager went aloft.

At seven thousand feet he climbed down the ladder into the X-1's cockpit, clipped on his hoses and lines, and managed to pull the pumpkin football helmet over his head. Then Ridley came down the ladder and lowered the door into place. As Ridley had instructed, Yeager now took the nine inches of broomstick and slipped it between the handle and the door. This gave him just enough mechanical advantage to reach over with his left hand and whang the thing shut. So he whanged the door shut with Ridley's broomstick and was ready to fly.

At 26,000 feet the B-29 went into a shallow dive, then pulled up and released Yeager and the X-1 as if it were a bomb. Like a bomb it dropped and shot forward (at the speed of the mother ship) at the same time. Yeager had been launched straight into the sun. It seemed to be no more than six feet in front of him, filling up the sky and blinding him. But he managed to get his bearings and set off the four rocket chambers one after the other. He then experienced something that became known as the ultimate sensation in flying: "booming and zooming." The surge of the rockets was so tremendous, forced him back into his seat so violently, he could hardly move his hands forward the few inches necessary to reach the controls. The X-1 seemed to shoot straight up in an absolutely perpendicular trajectory, as if determined to snap the hold of gravity via the most direct route possible. In fact, he was only climbing at the 45-degree angle called for in the flight plan. At about .87 Mach the buffeting started.

On the ground the engineers could no longer see Yeager. They could only hear . . . that poker-hollow West Virginia drawl.

"Had a mild buffet there . . . jes the usual instability . . ."

Jes the usual instability?

Then the X-1 reached the speed of .96 Mach, and that incredible caint-hardlyin' aw-shuckin' drawl said:

"Say, Ridley . . . make a note here, will ya?" *(if you ain't got nothin' better to do)* ". . . elevator effectiveness *regained*."

Just as Yeager had predicted, as the X-1 approached Mach 1, the stability improved. Yeager had his eyes pinned on the machometer. The needle reached .96, fluctuated, and went off the scale.

And on the ground they heard . . . that voice:

"Say, Ridley . . . make another note, will ya?" *(if you ain't too bored yet)* ". . . there's somethin' wrong with this ol' machometer . . ." (faint chuckle) ". . . it's gone kinda screwy on me . . ."

And in that moment, on the ground, they heard a boom rock over the desert floor—just as the physicist Theodore von Kármán had predicted many years before.

Then they heard Ridley back in the B-29: "If it is, Chuck, we'll fix it. Personally I think you're seeing things."

Then they heard Yeager's poker-hollow drawl again:

"Well, I guess I am, Jack . . . And I'm still goin' upstairs like a bat."

The X-1 had gone through "the sonic wall" without so much as a bump. As the speed topped out at Mach 1.05, Yeager had the sensation of shooting straight through the top of the sky. The sky turned a deep purple and all at once the stars and the moon came out—and the sun shone at the same time. He had reached a layer of the upper atmosphere where the air was too thin to contain reflecting dust particles. He was simply looking out into space. As the

X-1 nosed over at the top of the climb, Yeager now had seven minutes of . . . Pilot Heaven . . . ahead of him. He was going faster than any man in history, and it was almost silent up here, since he had exhausted his rocket fuel, and he was so high in such a vast space that there was no sensation of motion. He was master of the sky. His was a king's solitude, unique and inviolate, above the dome of the world. It would take him seven minutes to glide back down and land at Muroc. He spent the time doing victory rolls and wing-over-wing aerobatics while Rogers Lake and the High Sierras spun around below.

On the ground they had understood the code as soon as they heard Yeager's little exchange with Ridley. The project was secret, but the radio exchanges could be picked up by anyone within range. The business of the "screwy machometer" was Yeager's deadpan way of announcing that the X-1's instruments indicated Mach 1. As soon as he landed, they checked out the X-1's automatic recording instruments. Without any doubt the ship had gone supersonic. They immediately called the brass at Wright Field to break the tremendous news. Within two hours Wright Field called back and gave some firm orders. A top security lid was being put on the morning's events. That the press was not to be informed went without saying. But neither was anyone else, anyone at all, to be told. Word of the flight was not to go beyond the flight line. And even among the people directly involved—who were there and knew about it, anyway—there was to be no celebrating. Just what was on the minds of the brass at Wright is hard to say. Much of it, no doubt, was a simple holdover from wartime, when every breakthrough of possible strategic importance was kept under wraps. That was what you did—you shut up about them. Another possibility was that the chief at Wright had never quite known what to make of Muroc. There was some sort of weird ribald aerial tarpaper mad-monk squadron up on the roof of the desert out there . . .

In any case, by mid-afternoon Yeager's tremendous feat had become a piece of thunder with no reverberation. A strange and implausible stillness settled over the event. Well . . . there was not supposed to be any celebration, but come nightfall . . . Yeager and Ridley and some of the others ambled over to Pancho's. After all, it was the end of the day, and they were pilots. So they knocked back a few. And they had to let Pancho in on the secret, because Pancho had said she'd serve a free steak dinner to any pilot who could fly supersonic and walk in here to tell about it, and they had to see the look on *her* face. So Pancho served Yeager a big steak dinner and said they were a buncha miserable peckerwoods all the same, and the desert cooled off and the wind came up and the screen doors banged and they drank some more and bawled some songs over the cackling dry piano and the stars and the moon came out and Pancho screamed oaths no one had ever heard before and Yeager and Ridley roared and the old weatherbeaten bar boomed and the autographed pictures of a hundred dead pilots shook and clattered on the frame wires and the faces of the living fell apart in the reflections, and by and by they all left and stumbled and staggered and yelped and bayed for glory before the arthritic silhouettes of the Joshua trees. Shit!—there was no one to tell except for Pancho and the goddamned Joshua trees!

Address at Rice University on the Nation's Space Effort

JOHN F. KENNEDY

In May 1961, barely four months after his inauguration, President John F. Kennedy (1917–1963) delivered a special message to Congress on urgent national needs. His boldest proposal he saved for last: to land a man on the moon before the end of the decade. On September 12, 1962, at Rice University, President Kennedy delivered this major address on the nation's space effort. He links the space program to the human quest for knowledge and the impulse to explore new frontiers. Fully cognizant of the Cold War with the Soviet Union, President Kennedy also emphasizes the need to be first, the need for victory. Just seven years after this speech, on July 20, 1969, Apollo 11 astronauts Neil Armstrong and Buzz Aldrin became the first human beings to walk on the moon.

Which appeal is more compelling: to get to the moon or to get there first? What contribution has space exploration made to our national life? To our understanding of ourselves? How important is it to national greatness that we engage in great scientific and technological adventures? What are the new frontiers of today that beckon us? At what cost should we be willing to undertake them?

President Pitzer, Mr. Vice President, Governor, Congressman Thomas, Senator Wiley, and Congressman Miller, Mr. Webb, Mr. Bell, scientists, distinguished guests, and ladies and gentlemen:

I appreciate your president having made me an honorary visiting professor, and I will assure you that my first lecture will be very brief.

I am delighted to be here and I'm particularly delighted to be here on this occasion.

We meet at a college noted for knowledge, in a city noted for progress, in a state noted for strength, and we stand in need of all three, for we meet in an hour of change and challenge, in a decade of hope and fear, in an age of both knowledge and ignorance. The greater our knowledge increases, the greater our ignorance unfolds.

Despite the striking fact that most of the scientists that the world has ever known are alive and working today, despite the fact that this nation's own scientific manpower is doubling every twelve years in a rate of growth more than three times that of our population as a whole, despite that, the vast stretches of the unknown and the unanswered and the unfinished still far outstrip our collective comprehension.

No man can fully grasp how far and how fast we have come, but condense, if you will, the fifty thousand years of man's recorded history in a time span of but a half a century. Stated in these terms, we know very little about the first forty years, except at the end of them advanced man had learned to use the skins of animals to cover them. Then about ten years ago, under this standard, man emerged from his caves to construct other kinds of shelter. Only five years ago man learned to write and use a cart with wheels. Christianity began less than two years ago. The printing press came this year, and then less than two months ago, during this whole fifty-year span of human history, the steam engine provided a new source of power.

Newton explored the meaning of gravity. Last month electric lights and telephones and automobiles and airplanes became available. Only last week did we develop penicillin and television and nuclear power, and now if America's new spacecraft succeeds in reaching Venus, we will have literally reached the stars before midnight tonight.

This is a breathtaking pace, and such a pace cannot help but create new ills as it dispels old, new ignorance, new problems, new dangers. Surely the opening vistas of space promise high costs and hardships, as well as high reward.

So it is not surprising that some would have us stay where we are a little longer to rest, to wait. But this city of Houston, this state of Texas, this country of the United States was not built by those who waited and rested and wished to look behind them. This country was conquered by those who moved forward—and so will space.

William Bradford, speaking in 1630 of the founding of the Plymouth Bay Colony, said that all great and honorable actions are accompanied with great difficulties, and both must be enterprised and overcome with answerable courage.

If this capsule history of our progress teaches us anything, it is that man, in his quest for knowledge and progress, is determined and cannot be deterred. The exploration of space will go ahead, whether we join in it or not, and it is one of the great adventures of all time, and no nation which expects to be the leader of other nations can expect to stay behind in the race for space.

Those who came before us made certain that this country rode the first waves of the industrial revolutions, the first waves of modern invention, and the first wave of nuclear power, and this generation does not intend to founder in the backwash of the coming age of space. We mean to be a part of it—we mean to lead it. For the eyes of the world now look into space, to the moon and to the planets beyond, and we have vowed that we shall not see it governed by a hostile flag of conquest, but by a banner of freedom and peace. We have vowed that we shall not see space filled with weapons of mass destruction, but with instruments of knowledge and understanding.

Yet the vows of this nation can only be fulfilled if we in this nation are first, and, therefore, we intend to be first. In short, our leadership in science and in industry, our hopes for peace and security, our obligations to ourselves as well as others, all require us to make this effort, to solve these mysteries, to solve them for the good of all men, and to become the world's leading space-faring nation.

We set sail on this new sea because there is new knowledge to be gained, and new rights to be won, and they must be won and used for the progress of all people. For space science, like nuclear science and all technology, has no conscience of its own. Whether it will become a force for good or ill depends on man, and only if the United States occupies a position of preeminence can we help decide whether this new ocean will be a sea of peace or a new terrifying theater of war. I do not say that we should or will go unprotected against the hostile misuse of space any more than we go unprotected against the hostile use of land or sea, but I do say that space can be explored and mastered without feeding the fires of war, without repeating the mistakes that man has made in extending his writ around this globe of ours.

There is no strife, no prejudice, no national conflict in outer space as yet. Its hazards are hostile to us all. Its conquest deserves the best of all mankind, and its opportunity for peaceful cooperation may never come again. But why, some say, the moon? Why choose this as our goal? And they may well ask why climb the highest mountain? Why, thirty-five years ago, fly the Atlantic? Why does Rice play Texas?

We choose to go to the moon. We choose to go to the moon in this decade and do the other things, not because they are easy, but because they are hard, because that goal will serve to organize and measure the best of our energies and skills, because that challenge is one that we are willing to accept, one we are unwilling to postpone, and one which we intend to win, and the others, too.

It is for these reasons that I regard the decision last year to shift our efforts in space from low to high gear as among the most important decisions that will be made during my incumbency in the office of the presidency.

In the last twenty-four hours we have seen facilities now being created for the greatest and most complex exploration in man's history. We have felt the ground shake and the air shattered by the testing of a Saturn C-1 booster rocket, many times as powerful as the Atlas which launched John Glenn, generating power equivalent to ten thousand automobiles with their accelerators on the floor. We have seen the site where five F-1 rocket engines, each one as powerful as all eight engines of the Saturn combined, will be clustered together to make the advanced Saturn missile, assembled in a new building to be built at Cape Canaveral as tall as a forty-eight-story structure, as wide as a city block, and as long as two lengths of this field.

Within these last nineteen months at least forty-five satellites have circled the earth. Some forty of them were "made in the United States of America" and they were far more sophisticated and supplied far more knowledge to the people of the world than those of the Soviet Union.

The Mariner spacecraft now on its way to Venus is the most intricate instrument in the history of space science. The accuracy of that shot is comparable to firing a missile from Cape Canaveral and dropping it in this stadium between the forty-yard lines.

Transit satellites are helping our ships at sea to steer a safer course. Tiros satellites have given us unprecedented warnings of hurricanes and storms, and will do the same for forest fires and icebergs.

We have had our failures, but so have others, even if they do not admit them. And they may be less public.

To be sure, we are behind, and will be behind for some time in manned flight. But we do not intend to stay behind, and in this decade, we shall make up and move ahead.

The growth of our science and education will be enriched by new knowledge of our universe and environment, by new techniques of learning and mapping and observation, by new tools and computers for industry, medicine, the home as well as the school. Technical institutions, such as Rice, will reap the harvest of these gains.

And finally, the space effort itself, while still in its infancy, has already created a great number of new companies, and tens of thousands of new jobs. Space and related industries are generating new demands in investment and skilled personnel, and this city and this state, and this region, will share greatly in this growth. What was once the furthest outpost on the old frontier of the West will be the furthest outpost on the new frontier of science and space. Houston, your city of Houston, with its Manned Spacecraft Center, will become the heart of a large scientific and engineering community. During the next five years the National Aeronautics and Space Administration expects to double the number of scientists and engineers in this area, to increase its outlays for salaries and expenses to $60 million a year; to invest some $200 million in plant and laboratory facilities; and to direct or contract for new space efforts over $1 billion from this center in this city.

To be sure, all this costs us all a good deal of money. This year's space budget is three times what it was in January 1961, and it is greater than the space budget of the previous eight years combined. That budget now stands at $5,400 million a year—a staggering sum, though somewhat less than we pay for cigarettes and cigars every year. Space expenditures will soon rise some more, from forty cents per person per week to more than fifty cents a week for every man, woman, and child in the United States, for we have given this program a high national priority—even though I realize that this is in some measure an act of faith and vision, for we do not now know what benefits await us. But if I were to say, my fellow citizens, that we shall send to the moon, 240,000 miles away from the control station in Houston, a giant rocket more than three hundred feet tall, the length of this football field, made of new metal alloys, some of which have not yet been invented, capable of standing heat and stresses several times more than have ever been experienced, fitted together with a precision better than the finest watch, carrying all the equipment needed for propulsion, guidance, control, communications, food, and survival, on an untried mission, to an unknown celestial body, and then return it safely to earth, reentering the atmosphere at speeds of over twenty-five thousand miles per hour, causing heat about half that of the temperature of the sun—almost as hot as it is here today—and do all this, and do it right, and do it first before this decade is out—then we must be bold.

I'm the one who is doing all the work, so we just want you to stay cool for a minute. [*laughter*]

However, I think we're going to do it, and I think that we must pay what needs to be paid. I don't think we ought to waste any money, but I think we ought to do the job. And this will be done in the decade of the sixties. It may be done while some of you are still here at school at this college and university. It will be done during the term of office of some of the people who sit here on this platform. But it will be done. And it will be done before the end of this decade.

I am delighted that this university is playing a part in putting a man on the moon as part of a great national effort of the United States of America.

Many years ago the great British explorer George Mallory, who was to die on Mount Everest, was asked why did he want to climb it. He said, "Because it is there."

Well, space is there, and we're going to climb it, and the moon and the planets are there, and new hopes for knowledge and peace are there. And, therefore, as we set sail we ask God's blessing on the most hazardous and dangerous and greatest adventure on which man has ever embarked.

Thank you.

Preservation and Perpetuation

Old Folks' Christmas

RING LARDNER

Every society, although bent on the future, is a gift from the past. We did not make the world we inhabit; it is a monument to our ancestors. How, then, should we regard—and what do we owe—our past, our traditions, our inherited institutions, our families of origin? These enduring human questions are all the more poignant in American society, given the rapid rate of technological and social change, our embrace of youthfulness and prosperity, and our passionate devotion to "what's new."

This sad tale (1929) by Ring Lardner (1885–1933) powerfully exposes the tension between tradition and change. The overindulged young people, indifferent to tradition and heedless of family ties, care only for immediate enjoyment with their friends; the parents, heedless of the effects of social and cultural change, naively assume that their children will be like them.

What went wrong here, and why? What is "old" and what is "new"— and what is "American" and what "Christian"—in this American family's Christmas? What would you do differently, as one of the parents or as one of the young people? What are the proper attitudes toward past and future? How do you change a tradition while also preserving its meaning?

Tom and Grace Carter sat in their living-room on Christmas Eve, sometimes talking, sometimes pretending to read and all the time thinking things they didn't want to think. Their two children, Junior, aged nineteen, and Grace, two years younger, had come home that day from their schools for the Christmas vacation. Junior was in his first year at the university and Grace attending a boarding-school that would fit her for college.

I won't call them Grace and Junior any more, though that is the way they had been christened. Junior had changed his name to Ted and Grace was now

Caroline, and thus they insisted on being addressed, even by their parents. This was one of the things Tom and Grace the elder were thinking of as they sat in their living-room Christmas Eve.

Other university freshmen who had lived here had returned on the twenty-first, the day when the vacation was supposed to begin. Ted had telegraphed that he would be three days late owing to a special examination which, if he passed it, would lighten the terrific burden of the next term. He had arrived at home looking so pale, heavy-eyed and shaky that his mother doubted the wisdom of the concentrated mental effort, while his father secretly hoped the stuff had been non-poisonous and would not have lasting effects. Caroline, too, had been behind schedule, explaining that her laundry had gone astray and she had not dared trust others to trace it for her.

Grace and Tom had attempted, with fair success, to conceal their disappointment over this delayed home-coming and had continued with their preparations for a Christmas that would thrill their children and consequently themselves. They had bought an imposing lot of presents, costing twice or three times as much as had been Tom's father's annual income when Tom was Ted's age, or Tom's own income a year ago, before General Motors' acceptance of his new weather-proof paint had enabled him to buy this suburban home and luxuries such as his own parents and Grace's had never dreamed of, and to give Ted and Caroline advantages that he and Grace had perforce gone without.

Behind the closed door of the music-room was the elaborately decked tree. The piano and piano bench and the floor around the tree were covered with beribboned packages of all sizes, shapes and weights, one of them addressed to Tom, another to Grace, a few to the servants and the rest to Ted and Caroline. A huge box contained a sealskin coat for Caroline, a coat that had cost as much as the Carters had formerly paid a year for rent. Even more expensive was a "set" of jewelry consisting of an opal brooch, a bracelet of opals and gold filigree, and an opal ring surrounded by diamonds.

Grace always had preferred opals to any other stone, but now that she could afford them, some inhibition prevented her from buying them for herself; she could enjoy them much more adorning her pretty daughter. There were boxes of silk stockings, lingerie, gloves and handkerchiefs. And for Ted, a three-hundred-dollar watch, a de-luxe edition of Balzac, an expensive bag of shiny, new steel-shafted golf-clubs and the last word in portable phonographs.

But the big surprise for the boy was locked in the garage, a black Gorham sedan, a model more up to date and better-looking than Tom's own year-old car that stood beside it. Ted could use it during the vacation if the mild weather continued and could look forward to driving it around home next spring and summer, there being a rule at the university forbidding undergraduates the possession or use of private automobiles.

Every year for sixteen years, since Ted was three and Caroline one, it had been the Christmas Eve custom of the Carters' to hang up their children's stockings and fill them with inexpensive toys. Tom and Grace had thought it would be fun to continue the custom this year; the contents of the stockings— a mechanical negro dancing doll, music-boxes, a kitten that meowed when you pressed a spot on her back, et cetera—would make the "kids" laugh. And one of Grace's first pronouncements to her returned offspring was that they must go to bed early so Santa Claus would not be frightened away.

But it seemed they couldn't promise to make it so terribly early. They both had long-standing dates in town. Caroline was going to dinner and a play with Beatrice Murdock and Beatrice's nineteen-year-old brother Paul. The latter would call for her in his car at half past six. Ted had accepted an invitation to see the hockey match with two classmates, Herb Castle and Bernard King. He wanted to take his father's Gorham, but Tom told him untruthfully that the foot-brake was not working; Ted must be kept out of the garage till tomorrow morning.

Ted and Caroline had taken naps in the afternoon and gone off together in Paul Murdock's stylish roadster, giving their word that they would be back by midnight or a little later and that tomorrow night they would stay home.

And now their mother and father were sitting up for them, because the stockings could not be filled and hung till they were safely in bed, and also because trying to go to sleep is a painful and hopeless business when you are kind of jumpy.

"What time is it?" asked Grace, looking up from the third page of a book that she had begun to "read" soon after dinner.

"Half past two," said her husband. (He had answered the same question every fifteen or twenty minutes since midnight.)

"You don't suppose anything could have happened?" said Grace.

"We'd have heard if there had," said Tom.

"It isn't likely, of course," said Grace, "but they might have had an accident some place where nobody was there to report it or telephone or anything. We don't know what kind of a driver the Murdock boy is."

"He's Ted's age. Boys that age may be inclined to drive too fast, but they drive pretty well."

"How do you know?"

"Well, I've watched some of them drive."

"Yes, but not all of them."

"I doubt whether anybody in the world has seen every nineteen-year-old boy drive."

"Boys these days seem so kind of irresponsible."

"Oh, don't worry! They probably met some of their young friends and stopped for a bite to eat or something." Tom got up and walked to the window with studied carelessness. "It's a pretty night," he said. "You can see every star in the sky."

But he wasn't looking at the stars. He was looking down the road for headlights. There were none in sight and after a few moments he returned to his chair.

"What time is it?" asked Grace.

"Twenty-two of," he said.

"Of what?"

"Of three."

"Your watch must have stopped. Nearly an hour ago you told me it was half past two."

"My watch is all right. You probably dozed off."

"I haven't closed my eyes."

"Well, it's time you did. Why don't you go to bed?"

"Why don't *you*?"

"I'm not sleepy."

"Neither am I. But honestly, Tom, it's silly for you to stay up. I'm just doing it so I can fix the stockings, and because I feel so wakeful. But there's no use of your losing your sleep."

"I couldn't sleep a wink till they're home."

"That's foolishness! There's nothing to worry about. They're just having a good time. You were young once yourself."

"That's just it! When I was young, I was young." He picked up his paper and tried to get interested in the shipping news.

"What time is it?" asked Grace.

"Five minutes of three."

"Maybe they're staying at the Murdocks' all night."

"They'd have let us know."

"They were afraid to wake us up, telephoning."

At three-twenty a car stopped at the front gate.

"There they are!"

"I told you there was nothing to worry about."

Tom went to the window. He could just discern the outlines of the Murdock boy's roadster, whose lighting system seemed to have broken down.

"He hasn't any lights," said Tom. "Maybe I'd better go out and see if I can fix them."

"No, don't!" said Grace sharply. "He can fix them himself. He's just saving them while he stands still."

"Why don't they come in?"

"They're probably making plans."

"They can make them in here. I'll go out and tell them we're still up."

"No, don't!" said Grace as before, and Tom obediently remained at the window.

It was nearly four when the car lights flashed on and the car drove away. Caroline walked into the house and stared dazedly at her parents.

"Heavens! What are you doing up?"

Tom was about to say something, but Grace forestalled him.

"We were talking over old Christmases," she said. "Is it very late?"

"I haven't any idea," said Caroline.

"Where is Ted?"

"Isn't he home? I haven't seen him since we dropped him at the hockey place."

"Well, you go right to bed," said her mother. "You must be worn out."

"I am, kind of. We danced after the play. What time is breakfast?"

"Eight o'clock."

"Oh, Mother, can't you make it nine?"

"I guess so. You used to want to get up early on Christmas."

"I know, but—"

"Who brought you home?" asked Tom.

"Why, Paul Murdock—and Beatrice."

"You look rumpled."

"They made me sit in the 'rumple' seat."

She laughed at her joke, said good night and went upstairs. She had not come even within hand-shaking distance of her father and mother.

"The Murdocks," said Tom, "must have great manners, making their guest ride in that uncomfortable seat."

Grace was silent.

"You go to bed, too," said Tom. "I'll wait for Ted."

"You couldn't fix the stockings."

"I won't try. We'll have time for that in the morning; I mean, later in the morning."

"I'm not going to bed till you do," said Grace.

"All right, we'll both go. Ted ought not to be long now. I suppose his friends will bring him home. We'll hear him when he comes in."

There was no chance not to hear him when, at ten minutes before six, he came in. He had done his Christmas shopping late and brought home a package.

Grace was downstairs again at half past seven, telling the servants breakfast would be postponed till nine. She nailed the stockings beside the fireplace, went into the music-room to see that nothing had been disturbed and removed Ted's hat and overcoat from where he had carefully hung them on the hall floor.

Tom appeared a little before nine and suggested that the children ought to be awakened.

"I'll wake them," said Grace, and went upstairs. She opened Ted's door, looked, and softly closed it again. She entered her daughter's room and found Caroline semiconscious.

"Do I have to get up now? Honestly I can't eat anything. If you could just have Molla bring me some coffee. Ted and I are both invited to the Murdocks' for breakfast at half past twelve, and I could sleep for another hour or two."

"But dearie, don't you know we have Christmas dinner at one?"

"It's a shame, Mother, but I thought of course our dinner would be at night."

"Don't you want to see your presents?"

"Certainly I do, but can't they wait?"

Grace was about to go to the kitchen to tell the cook that dinner would be at seven instead of one, but she remembered having promised Signe the afternoon and evening off, as a cold, light supper would be all anyone wanted after the heavy midday meal.

Tom and Grace breakfasted alone and once more sat in the living-room, talking, thinking and pretending to read.

"You ought to speak to Caroline," said Tom.

"I will, but not today. It's Christmas."

"And I intend to say a few words to Ted."

"Yes, dear, you must. But not today."

"I suppose they'll be out again tonight."

"No, they promised to stay home. We'll have a nice cozy evening."

"Don't bet too much on that," said Tom.

At noon the "children" made their entrance and responded to their parents' salutations with almost the proper warmth. Ted declined a cup of coffee and he and Caroline apologized for making a "breakfast" date at the Murdocks'.

"Sis and I both thought you'd be having dinner at seven, as usual."

"We've always had it at one o'clock on Christmas," said Tom.

"I'd forgotten it was Christmas," said Ted.

"Well, those stockings ought to remind you."

Ted and Caroline looked at the bulging stockings.

"Isn't there a tree?" asked Caroline.

"Of course," said her mother. "But the stockings come first."

"We've only a little time," said Caroline. "We'll be terribly late as it is. So can't we see the tree now?"

"I guess so," said Grace, and led the way into the music-room.

The servants were summoned and the tree stared at and admired.

"You must open your presents," said Grace to her daughter.

"I can't open them all now," said Caroline. "Tell me which is special."

The cover was removed from the huge box and Grace held up the coat.

"Oh, Mother!" said Caroline. "A sealskin coat!"

"Put it on," said her father.

"Not now. We haven't time."

"Then look at this!" said Grace, and opened the case of jewels.

"Oh, Mother! Opals!" said Caroline.

"They're my favorite stone," said Grace quietly.

"If nobody minds," said Ted, "I'll postpone my personal investigation till we get back. I know I'll like everything you've given me. But if we have no car in working order, I've got to call a taxi and catch a train."

"You can drive in," said his father.

"Did you fix the brake?"

"I think it's all right. Come up to the garage and we'll see."

Ted got his hat and coat and kissed his mother good-by.

"Mother," he said, "I know you'll forgive me for not having any presents for you and Dad. I was so rushed the last three days at school. And I thought I'd have time to shop a little when we got in yesterday, but I was in too much of a hurry to be home. Last night, everything was closed."

"Don't worry," said Grace. "Christmas is for young people. Dad and I have everything we want."

The servants had found their gifts and disappeared, expressing effusive Scandinavian thanks.

Caroline and her mother were left alone.

"Mother, where did the coat come from?"

"Lloyd and Henry's."

"They keep all kinds of furs, don't they?"

"Yes."

"Would you mind horribly if I exchanged this?"

"Certainly not, dear. You pick out anything you like, and if it's a little more expensive, it won't make any difference. We can go in town tomorrow or next day. But don't you want to wear your opals to the Murdocks'?"

"I don't believe so. They might get lost or something. And I'm not—well, I'm not so crazy about—"

"I think they can be exchanged, too," said Grace. "You run along now and get ready to start."

Caroline obeyed with alacrity, and Grace spent a welcome moment by herself.

Tom opened the garage door.

"Why, you've got two cars!" said Ted.

"The new one isn't mine," said Tom.

"Whose is it?"

"Yours. It's the new model."

"Dad, that's wonderful! But it looks just like the old one."

"Well, the old one's pretty good. Just the same, yours is better. You'll find that out when you drive it. Hop in and get started. I had her filled with gas."

"I think I'd rather drive the old one."

"Why?"

"Well, what I really wanted, Dad, was a Barnes sport roadster, something like Paul Murdock's, only a different color scheme. And if I don't drive this Gorham at all, maybe you could get them to take it back or make some kind of a deal with the Barnes people."

Tom didn't speak till he was sure of his voice. Then: "All right, son. Take my car and I'll see what can be done about yours."

Caroline, waiting for Ted, remembered something and called to her mother. "Here's what I got for you and Dad," she said. "It's two tickets to 'Jolly Jane,' the play I saw last night. You'll love it!"

"When are they for?" asked Grace.

"Tonight," said Caroline.

"But dearie," said her mother, "we don't want to go out tonight, when you promised to stay home."

"We'll keep our promise," said Caroline, "but the Murdocks may drop in and bring some friends and we'll dance and there'll be music. And Ted and I both thought you'd rather be away somewhere so our noise wouldn't disturb you."

"It was sweet of you to do this," said her mother, "but your father and I don't mind noise as long as you're enjoying yourselves."

"It's time anyway that you and Dad had a treat."

"The real treat," said Grace, "would be to spend a quiet evening here with just you two."

"The Murdocks practically invited themselves and I couldn't say no after they'd been so nice to me. And honestly, Mother, you'll love this play!"

"Will you be home for supper?"

"I'm pretty sure we will, but if we're a little late, don't you and Dad wait for us. Take the seven-twenty so you won't miss anything. The first act is really the best. We probably won't be hungry, but have Signe leave something out for us in case we are."

Tom and Grace sat down to the elaborate Christmas dinner and didn't make much impression on it. Even if they had had any appetite, the sixteen-pound turkey would have looked almost like new when they had eaten their fill. Conversation was intermittent and related chiefly to Signe's excellence as a cook and the mildness of the weather. Children and Christmas were barely touched on.

Tom merely suggested that on account of its being a holiday and their having theatre tickets, they ought to take the six-ten and eat supper at the Metropole. His wife said no; Ted and Caroline might come home and be disappointed at not finding them. Tom seemed about to make some remark, but changed his mind.

The afternoon was the longest Grace had ever known. The children were still absent at seven and she and Tom taxied to the train. Neither talked much on the way to town. As for the play, which Grace was sure to love, it turned out to be a rehash of "Cradle Snatchers" and "Sex," retaining the worst features of each.

When it was over, Tom said: "Now I'm inviting you to the Cove Club. You didn't eat any breakfast or dinner or supper and I can't have you starving to death on a feast-day. Besides, I'm thirsty as well as hungry."

They ordered the special *table d'hôte* and struggled hard to get away with it. Tom drank six high-balls, but they failed to produce the usual effect of making him jovial. Grace had one high-ball and some kind of cordial that gave her a warm, contented feeling for a moment. But the warmth and contentment left her before the train was half way home.

The living-room looked as if Von Kluck's army had just passed through. Ted and Caroline had kept their promise up to a certain point. They had spent part of the evening at home, and the Murdocks must have brought all their own friends and everybody else's, judging from the results. The tables and floors were strewn with empty glasses, ashes and cigaret stubs. The stockings had been torn off their nails and the wrecked contents were all over the place. Two sizable holes had been burnt in Grace's favorite rug.

Tom took his wife by the arm and led her into the music-room.

"You never took the trouble to open your own present," he said.

"And I think there's one for you, too," said Grace. "They didn't come in here," she added, "so I guess there wasn't much dancing or music."

Tom found his gift from Grace, a set of diamond studs and cuff buttons for festive wear. Grace's present from him was an opal ring.

"Oh, Tom!" she said.

"We'll have to go out somewhere tomorrow night, so I can break these in," said Tom.

"Well, if we do that, we'd better get a good night's rest."

"I'll beat you upstairs," said Tom.

Everyday Use

for your grandmama

ALICE WALKER

Whether we know it or not, we carry our past with us in many ways—in the homes and families of our origin, in the names we are given, in the heirlooms we inherit. As Alice Walker (born 1944) makes clear in this story (1973), how we treat these inheritances speaks volumes about who we are and how we stand in the world. The story is narrated by an unschooled, hardworking, black woman with two daughters, one a woman of the world—stylish, sophisticated, with a new sense of self—the other a homebody—slow, timid, attached to the humble ways of her rural roots. The climax of the story concerns who shall have, and how to use, the handmade family quilts: Dee (now sporting a new African name, Wangero), who intends to hang them on her walls, or Maggie (to whom they've been promised), who would use them on her marriage bed.

In whose hands is the family's tradition better respected? What is the meaning of the quilts, and why might they matter? Is our civic inheritance something to be admired on a wall, something to wrap ourselves in, or something inside and knitted together with us? What is sacred to us? How should we honor and transmit our legacies?

I will wait for her in the yard that Maggie and I made so clean and wavy yesterday afternoon. A yard like this is more comfortable than most people know. It is not just a yard. It is like an extended living room. When the hard clay is swept clean as a floor and the fine sand around the edges lined with tiny, irregular grooves, anyone can come and sit and look up into the elm tree and wait for the breezes that never come inside the house.

Maggie will be nervous until after her sister goes: she will stand hopelessly in corners, homely and ashamed of the burn scars down her arms and legs, eyeing her sister with a mixture of envy and awe. She thinks her sister has held life always in the palm of one hand, that "no" is a word the world never learned to say to her.

You've no doubt seen those TV shows where the child who has "made it" is confronted, as a surprise, by her own mother and father, tottering in weakly from backstage. (A pleasant surprise, of course: What would they do if parent and child came on the show only to curse out and insult each other?) On TV mother and child embrace and smile into each other's faces. Sometimes the mother and father weep, the child wraps them in her arms and leans across the table to tell how she would not have made it without their help. I have seen these programs.

Sometimes I dream a dream in which Dee and I are suddenly brought together on a TV program of this sort. Out of a dark and soft-seated limousine I am ushered into a bright room filled with many people. There I meet a smiling, gray, sporty man like Johnny Carson who shakes my hand and tells me what a fine girl I have. Then we are on the stage and Dee is embracing me with tears in her eyes. She pins on my dress a large orchid, even though she has told me once that she thinks orchids are tacky flowers.

In real life I am a large, big-boned woman with rough, man-working hands. In the winter I wear flannel nightgowns to bed and overalls during the day. I can kill and clean a hog as mercilessly as a man. My fat keeps me hot in zero weather. I can work outside all day, breaking ice to get water for washing; I can eat pork liver cooked over the open fire minutes after it comes steaming from the hog. One winter I knocked a bull calf straight in the brain between the eyes with a sledge hammer and had the meat hung up to chill before nightfall. But of course all this does not show on television. I am the way my daughter would want me to be: a hundred pounds lighter, my skin like an uncooked barley pancake. My hair glistens in the hot bright lights. Johnny Carson has much to do to keep up with my quick and witty tongue.

But that is a mistake. I know even before I wake up. Who ever knew a Johnson with a quick tongue? Who can even imagine me looking a strange white man in the eye? It seems to me I have talked to them always with one foot raised in flight, with my head turned in whichever way is farthest from them. Dee, though. She would always look anyone in the eye. Hesitation was no part of her nature.

"How do I look, Mama?" Maggie says, showing just enough of her thin body enveloped in pink skirt and red blouse for me to know she's there, almost hidden by the door.

"Come out into the yard," I say.

Have you ever seen a lame animal, perhaps a dog run over by some careless person rich enough to own a car, sidle up to someone who is ignorant enough to be kind to him? That is the way my Maggie walks. She has been like this, chin on chest, eyes on ground, feet in shuffle, ever since the fire that burned the other house to the ground.

Dee is lighter than Maggie, with nicer hair and a fuller figure. She's a woman now, though sometimes I forget. How long ago was it that the other house burned? Ten, twelve years? Sometimes I can still hear the flames and feel Maggie's arms sticking to me, her hair smoking and her dress falling off her in little black papery flakes. Her eyes seemed stretched open, blazed open by the flames reflected in them. And Dee. I see her standing off under the sweet gum tree she used to dig gum out of; a look of concentration on her face as she watched the last dingy gray board of the house fall in toward the red-hot brick chimney. Why don't you do a dance around the ashes? I'd wanted to ask her. She had hated the house that much.

I used to think she hated Maggie, too. But that was before we raised the money, the church and me, to send her to Augusta to school. She used to read to us without pity; forcing words, lies, other folks' habits, whole lives upon us two, sitting trapped and ignorant underneath her voice. She washed us in a river of make-believe, burned us with a lot of knowledge we didn't necessarily need to know. Pressed us to her with the serious way she read, to shove us away at just the moment, like dimwits, we seemed about to understand.

Dee wanted nice things. A yellow organdy dress to wear to her graduation from high school; black pumps to match a green suit she'd made from an old suit somebody gave me. She was determined to stare down any disaster in her efforts. Her eyelids would not flicker for minutes at a time. Often I fought off the temptation to shake her. At sixteen she had a style of her own: and knew what style was.

I never had an education myself. After second grade the school was closed down. Don't ask me why: in 1927 colored asked fewer questions than they do now. Sometimes Maggie reads to me. She stumbles along good-naturedly but can't see well. She knows she is not bright. Like good looks and money, quickness passed her by. She will marry John Thomas (who has mossy teeth in an earnest face) and then I'll be free to sit here and I guess just sing church songs to myself. Although I never was a good singer. Never could carry a tune. I was always better at a man's job. I used to love to milk till I was hooked in the side in '49. Cows are soothing and slow and don't bother you, unless you try to milk them the wrong way.

I have deliberately turned my back on the house. It is three rooms, just like the one that burned, except the roof is tin; they don't make shingle roofs any more. There are no real windows, just some holes cut in the sides, like the portholes in a ship, but not round and not square, with rawhide holding the shutters up on the outside. This house is in a pasture, too, like the other one. No doubt when Dee sees it she will want to tear it down. She wrote me once that no matter where we "choose" to live, she will manage to come see us. But she will never bring her friends. Maggie and I thought about this and Maggie asked me, "Mama, when did Dee ever *have* any friends?"

She had a few. Furtive boys in pink shirts hanging about on washday after school. Nervous girls who never laughed. Impressed with her they worshiped the well-turned phrase, the cute shape, the scalding humor that erupted like bubbles in lye. She read to them.

When she was courting Jimmy T she didn't have much time to pay to us, but turned all her faultfinding power on him. He *flew* to marry a cheap city girl from a family of ignorant flashy people. She hardly had time to recompose herself.

When she comes I will meet—but there they are!

Maggie attempts to make a dash for the house, in her shuffling way, but I stay her with my hand. "Come back here," I say. And she stops and tries to dig a well in the sand with her toe.

It is hard to see them clearly through the strong sun. But even the first glimpse of leg out of the car tells me it is Dee. Her feet were always neat-looking, as if God himself had shaped them with a certain style. From the other side of the car comes a short, stocky man. Hair is all over his head a foot long and hanging from his chin like a kinky mule tail. I hear Maggie suck in her breath. "Uhnnnh," is what it sounds like. Like when you see the wriggling end of a snake just in front of your foot on the road. "Uhnnnh."

Dee next. A dress down to the ground, in this hot weather. A dress so loud it hurts my eyes. There are yellows and oranges enough to throw back the light of the sun. I feel my whole face warming from the heat waves it throws out. Earrings gold, too, and hanging down to her shoulders. Bracelets dangling and making noises when she moves her arm up to shake the folds of the dress out of her armpits. The dress is loose and flows, and as she walks closer, I like it. I hear Maggie go "Uhnnnh" again. It is her sister's hair. It stands straight up like the wool on a sheep. It is black as night and around the edges are two long pigtails that rope about like small lizards disappearing behind her ears.

"Wa-su-zo-Tean-o!"* she says, coming on in that gliding way the dress makes her move. The short stocky fellow with the hair to his navel is all grinning and he follows up with "Asalamalakim,† my mother and sister!" He moves to hug Maggie but she falls back, right up against the back of my chair. I feel her trembling there and when I look up I see the perspiration falling off her chin.

"Don't get up," says Dee. Since I am stout it takes something of a push. You can see me trying to move a second or two before I make it. She turns, showing white heels through her sandals, and goes back to the car. Out she peeks next with a Polaroid. She stoops down quickly and lines up picture after picture of me sitting there in front of the house with Maggie cowering behind me. She never takes a shot without making sure the house is included. When a cow comes nibbling around the edge of the yard she snaps it and me and Maggie *and* the house. Then she puts the Polaroid in the back seat of the car, and comes up and kisses me on the forehead.

Meanwhile Asalamalakim is going through motions with Maggie's hand. Maggie's hand is as limp as a fish, and probably as cold, despite the sweat, and she keeps trying to pull it back. It looks like Asalamalakim wants to shake hands but wants to do it fancy. Or maybe he don't know how people shake hands. Anyhow, he soon gives up on Maggie.

"Well," I say. "Dee."

"No, Mama," she says. "Not 'Dee,' Wangero Leewanika Kemanjo!"

"What happened to 'Dee'?" I wanted to know.

"She's dead," Wangero said. "I couldn't bear it any longer, being named after the people who oppress me."

"You know as well as me you was named after your aunt Dicie," I said. Dicie is my sister. She named Dee. We called her "Big Dee" after Dee was born.

"But who was *she* named after?" asked Wangero.

"I guess after Grandma Dee," I said.

"And who was she named after?" asked Wangero.

"Her mother," I said, and saw Wangero was getting tired. "That's about as far back as I can trace it," I said. Though, in fact, I probably could have carried it back beyond the Civil War through the branches.

"Well," said Asalamalakim, "there you are."

"Uhnnnh," I heard Maggie say.

"There I was not," I said, "before 'Dicie' cropped up in our family, so why should I try to trace it that far back?"

---

* A Swahili greeting used by Black Muslims.

† An Arabic phrase, roughly, "Peace be with you."

He just stood there grinning, looking down on me like somebody inspecting a Model A car. Every once in a while he and Wangero sent eye signals over my head.

"How do you pronounce this name?" I asked.

"You don't have to call me by it if you don't want to," said Wangero.

"Why shouldn't I?" I asked. "If that's what you want us to call you, we'll call you."

"I know it might sound awkward at first," said Wangero.

"I'll get used to it," I said. "Ream it out again."

Well, soon we got the name out of the way. Asalamalakim had a name twice as long and three times as hard. After I tripped over it two or three times he told me to just call him Hakim-a-barber. I wanted to ask him was he a barber, but I didn't really think he was, so I didn't ask.

"You must belong to those beef-cattle peoples down the road," I said. They said "Asalamalakim" when they met you, too, but they didn't shake hands. Always too busy: feeding the cattle, fixing the fences, putting up salt-lick shelters, throwing down hay. When the white folks poisoned some of the herd the men stayed up all night with rifles in their hands. I walked a mile and a half just to see the sight.

Hakim-a-barber said, "I accept some of their doctrines, but farming and raising cattle is not my style." (They didn't tell me, and I didn't ask, whether Wangero (Dee) had really gone and married him.)

We sat down to eat and right away he said he didn't eat collards and pork was unclean. Wangero, though, went on through the chitlins and corn bread, the greens and everything else. She talked a blue streak over the sweet potatoes. Everything delighted her. Even the fact that we still used the benches her daddy made for the table when we couldn't afford to buy chairs.

"Oh, Mama!" she cried. Then turned to Hakim-a-barber. "I never knew how lovely these benches are. You can feel the rump prints," she said, running her hands underneath her and along the bench. Then she gave a sigh and her hand closed over Grandma Dee's butter dish. "That's it!" she said. "I knew there was something I wanted to ask you if I could have." She jumped up from the table and went over in the corner where the churn stood, the milk in it clabber by now. She looked at the churn and looked at it.

"This churn top is what I need," she said. "Didn't Uncle Buddy whittle it out of a tree you all used to have?"

"Yes," I said.

"Uh huh," she said happily. "And I want the dasher, too."

"Uncle Buddy whittle that, too?" asked the barber.

Dee (Wangero) looked up at me.

"Aunt Dee's first husband whittled the dash," said Maggie so low you almost couldn't hear her. "His name was Henry, but they called him Stash."

"Maggie's brain is like an elephant's," Wangero said, laughing. "I can use the churn top as a centerpiece for the alcove table," she said, sliding a plate over the churn, "and I'll think of something artistic to do with the dasher."

When she finished wrapping the dasher the handle stuck out. I took it for a moment in my hands. You didn't even have to look close to see where hands pushing the dasher up and down to make butter had left a kind of sink in the wood. In fact, there were a lot of small sinks; you could see where thumbs and fingers had sunk into the wood. It was beautiful light yellow wood, from a tree that grew in the yard where Big Dee and Stash had lived.

After dinner Dee (Wangero) went to the trunk at the foot of my bed and started rifling through it. Maggie hung back in the kitchen over the dishpan. Out came Wangero with two quilts. They had been pieced by Grandma Dee and then Big Dee and me had hung them on the quilt frames on the front porch and quilted them. One was in the Lone Star pattern. The other was Walk Around the Mountain. In both of them were scraps of dresses Grandma Dee had worn fifty and more years ago. Bits and pieces of Grandpa Jarrell's paisley shirts. And one teeny faded blue piece, about the size of a penny matchbox, that was from Great Grandpa Ezra's uniform that he wore in the Civil War.

"Mama," Wangero said sweet as a bird. "Can I have these old quilts?"

I heard something fall in the kitchen, and a minute later the kitchen door slammed.

"Why don't you take one or two of the others?" I asked. "These old things was just done by me and Big Dee from some tops your grandma pieced before she died."

"No," said Wangero. "I don't want those. They are stitched around the borders by machine."

"That'll make them last better," I said.

"That's not the point," said Wangero. "These are all pieces of dresses Grandma used to wear. She did all this stitching by hand. Imagine!" She held the quilts securely in her arms, stroking them.

"Some of the pieces, like those lavender ones, come from old clothes her mother handed down to her," I said, moving up to touch the quilts. Dee (Wangero) moved back just enough so that I couldn't reach the quilts. They already belonged to her.

"Imagine!" she breathed again, clutching them closely to her bosom.

"The truth is," I said, "I promised to give them quilts to Maggie, for when she marries John Thomas."

She gasped like a bee had stung her.

"Maggie can't appreciate these quilts!" she said. "She'd probably be backward enough to put them to everyday use."

"I reckon she would," I said. "God knows I been saving 'em for long enough with nobody using 'em. I hope she will!" I didn't want to bring up how I had offered Dee (Wangero) a quilt when she went away to college. Then she had told me they were old-fashioned, out of style.

"But they're *priceless!*" she was saying now, furiously; for she has a temper. "Maggie would put them on the bed and in five years they'd be in rags. Less than that!"

"She can always make some more," I said. "Maggie knows how to quilt."

Dee (Wangero) looked at me with hatred. "You just will not understand. The point is these quilts, *these* quilts!"

"Well," I said, stumped. "What would *you* do with them?"

"Hang them," she said. As if that was the only thing you *could* do with quilts.

Maggie by now was standing in the door. I could almost hear the sound her feet made as they scraped over each other.

"She can have them, Mama," she said, like somebody used to never winning anything, or having anything reserved for her. "I can 'member Grandma Dee without the quilts."

I looked at her hard. She had filled her bottom lip with checkerberry snuff and it gave her face a kind of dopey, hangdog look. It was Grandma Dee and Big Dee who taught her how to quilt herself. She stood there with her scarred hands hidden in the folds of her skirt. She looked at her sister with something like fear but she wasn't mad at her. This was Maggie's portion. This was the way she knew God to work.

When I looked at her like that something hit me in the top of my head and ran down to the soles of my feet. Just like when I'm in church and the spirit of God touches me and I get happy and shout. I did something I had never done before: hugged Maggie to me, then dragged her on into the room, snatched the quilts out of Miss Wangero's hands and dumped them into Maggie's lap. Maggie just sat there on my bed with her mouth open.

"Take one or two of the others," I said to Dee.

But she turned without a word and went out to Hakim-a-barber.

"You just don't understand," she said, as Maggie and I came out to the car.

"What don't I understand?" I wanted to know.

"Your heritage," she said. And then she turned to Maggie, kissed her, and said, "You ought to try to make something of yourself, too, Maggie. It's really a new day for us. But from the way you and Mama still live you'd never know it."

She put on some sunglasses that hid everything above the tip of her nose and her chin.

Maggie smiled; maybe at the sunglasses. But a real smile, not scared. After we watched the car dust settle I asked Maggie to bring me a dip of snuff. And then the two of us sat there just enjoying, until it was time to go in the house and go to bed.

Farewell Address

George Washington

From the beginning, America's most thoughtful statesmen have been concerned with preserving and perpetuating our political institutions. Our nation's first president, George Washington (1732–1799), took up this topic in his farewell address (September 19, 1796). Delivered to a fledgling nation, barely launched upon the world stage, Washington's advice was geared to protecting the union and the Constitution, and thereby the independence, tranquility, peace, safety, prosperity, and, especially, liberty that Americans "so highly prize."

How important to our future flourishing are Washington's positive recommendations? How dangerous to our well-being is partisan political division? Are Washington's warnings still relevant for today's America, a long-established superpower with global commercial connections and military alliances? What is the connection between morality, religion, and the perpetuation of our institutions? How healthy is the constitutional order today?

Friends, and Fellow-Citizens:

The period for a new election of a Citizen, to Administer the Executive government of the United States, being not far distant, and the time actually arrived, when your thoughts must be employed in designating the person, who is to be cloathed with that important trust, it appears to me proper, especially as it may conduce to a more distinct expression of the public voice, that I should now apprise you of the resolution I have formed, to decline being considered among the number of those, out of whom a choice is to be made. . . .

In looking forward to the moment, which is intended to terminate the career of my public life, my feelings do not permit me to suspend the deep acknowledgment of that debt of gratitude which I owe to my beloved country, for the many honors it has conferred upon me; still more for the stedfast confidence with which it has supported me; and for the opportunities I have thence enjoyed of manifesting my inviolable attachment, by services faithful and persevering, though in usefulness unequal to my zeal. If benefits have resulted to our country from these services, let it always be remembered to your praise, and as an instructive example in our annals, that, under circumstances in which the Passions agitated in every direction were liable to mislead, amidst appearances sometimes dubious, vicissitudes of fortune often discouraging, in situations in which not unfrequently want of Success has countenanced the spirit of criticism, the constancy of your support was the essential prop of the efforts, and a guarantee of the plans by which they were effected. Profoundly penetrated with this idea, I shall carry it with me to my grave, as a strong incitement to unceasing vows that Heaven may continue to you the choicest tokens of its beneficence; that your Union and brotherly affection may be perpetual; that the free constitution, which is the work of your hands, may be sacredly maintained; that its Administration in every department may be stamped with wisdom and Virtue; that, in fine, the happiness of the people of these States, under the auspices of liberty, may be made complete, by so careful a preservation and so prudent a use of this blessing as will acquire to them the glory of recommending it to the applause, the affection, and adoption of every nation which is yet a stranger to it.

Here, perhaps, I ought to stop. But a solicitude for your welfare, which cannot end but with my life, and the apprehension of danger, natural to that solicitude, urge me on an occasion like the present, to offer to your solemn contemplation, and to recommend to your frequent review, some sentiments; which are the result of much reflection, of no inconsiderable observation, and which appear to me all important to the permanency of your felicity as a People. These will be offered to you with the more freedom, as you can only see in them the disinterested warnings of a parting friend, who can possibly have no personal motive to biass his counsel. Nor can I forget, as an encouragement to it, your endulgent reception of my sentiments on a former and not dissimilar occasion.

Interwoven as is the love of liberty with every ligament of your hearts, no recommendation of mine is necessary to fortify or confirm the attachment.

The Unity of Government which constitutes you one people is also now dear to you. It is justly so; for it is a main Pillar in the Edifice of your real independence, the support of your tranquility at home; your peace abroad; of your safety; of your prosperity; of that very Liberty which you so highly prize. But as it is easy to foresee, that from different causes and from different quarters, much pains will be taken, many artifices employed, to weaken in your minds the conviction of this truth; as this is the point in your political fortress against which the batteries of internal and external enemies will be most constantly and actively (though often covertly and insidiously) directed, it is of infinite moment, that you should properly estimate the immense value of your national Union to your collective and individual happiness; that you should cherish a cordial, habitual and immoveable attachment to it; accustoming yourselves to think and speak of it as of the Palladium of your political safety and prosperity; watching for its preservation with jealous anxiety; discountenancing whatever may suggest even a suspicion that it can in any event be abandoned, and indignantly frowning upon the first dawning of every attempt to alienate any portion of our Country from the rest, or to enfeeble the sacred ties which now link together the various parts.

For this you have every inducement of sympathy and interest. Citizens by birth or choice, of a common country, that country has a right to concentrate your affections. The name of AMERICAN, which belongs to you, in your national capacity, must always exalt the just pride of Patriotism, more than any appellation derived from local discriminations. With slight shades of difference, you have the same Religion, Manners, Habits and political Principles. You have in a common cause fought and triumphed together. The independence and liberty you possess are the work of joint councils, and joint efforts; of common dangers, sufferings and successes.

But these considerations, however powerfully they address themselves to your sensibility are greatly outweighed by those which apply more immediately to your Interest. Here every portion of our country finds the most commanding motives for carefully guarding and preserving the Union of the whole.

The *North*, in an unrestrained intercourse with the *South*, protected by the equal Laws of a common government, finds in the productions of the latter, great additional resources of Maratime and commercial enterprise and precious materials of manufacturing industry. The *South* in the same Intercourse, benefiting by the Agency of the *North*, sees its agriculture grow and its commerce expand. Turning partly into its own channels the seamen of the *North*, it finds its particular navigation envigorated; and while it contributes, in different ways, to nourish and increase the general mass of the National navigation, it looks forward to the protection of a Maratime strength, to which itself is unequally adapted. The *East*, in a like intercourse with the *West*, already finds, and in the progressive improvement of interior communications, by land and water, will more and more find a valuable vent for the commodities which it brings from abroad, or manufactures at home. The *West* derives from the *East* supplies requisite to its growth and comfort, and what is perhaps of still greater consequence, it must of necessity owe the *secure* enjoyment of indispensable *outlets* for its own productions to the weight, influence, and the future Maritime strength of the Atlantic side of the Union, directed by an indissoluble community of Interest as *one Nation*. . . .

While then every part of our country thus feels an immediate and particular Interest in Union, all the parts combined cannot fail to find in the united mass of means and efforts greater strength, greater resource, proportionably greater security from external danger, a less frequent interruption of their Peace by foreign Nations; and, what is of inestimable value! they must derive from Union an exemption from those broils and Wars between themselves, which so frequently afflict neighbouring countries, not tied together by the same government; which their own rivalships alone would be sufficient to produce, but which opposite foreign alliances, attachments and intrigues would stimulate and imbitter. Hence likewise they will avoid the necessity of those overgrown Military establishments, which under any form of Government are inauspicious to liberty, and which are to be regarded as particularly hostile to Republican Liberty: In this sense it is, that your Union ought to be considered as a main prop of your liberty, and that the love of the one ought to endear to you the preservation of the other.

These considerations speak a persuasive language to every reflecting and virtuous mind, and exhibit the continuance of the UNION as a primary object of Patriotic desire. Is there a doubt, whether a common government can embrace so large a sphere? Let experience solve it. To listen to mere speculation in such a case were criminal. We are authorized to hope that a proper organization of the whole, with the auxiliary agency of governments for the respective Sub divisions, will afford a happy issue to the experiment. 'Tis well worth a fair and full experiment. With such powerful and obvious motives to Union, affecting all parts of our country, while experience shall not have demonstrated its impracticability, there will always be reason, to distrust the patriotism of those, who in any quarter may endeavor to weaken its bands.

In contemplating the causes which may disturb our Union, it occurs as matter of serious concern, that any ground should have been furnished for characterizing parties by *Geographical* discriminations: *Northern* and *Southern*; *Atlantic* and *Western*; whence designing men may endeavour to excite a belief that there is a real difference of local interests and views. One of the expedients of Party to acquire influence, within particular districts, is to misrepresent the opinions and aims of other Districts. You cannot shield yourselves too much against the jealousies and heart burnings which spring from these misrepresentations. They tend to render Alien to each other those who ought to be bound together by fraternal affection. . . .

To the efficacy and permanency of Your Union, a Government for the whole is indispensable. No Alliances however strict between the parts can be an adequate substitute. They must inevitably experience the infractions and interruptions which all Alliances in all times have experienced. Sensible of this momentous truth, you have improved upon your first essay, by the adoption of a Constitution of Government, better calculated than your former for an intimate Union, and for the efficacious management of your common concerns. This government, the offspring of our own choice uninfluenced and unawed, adopted upon full investigation and mature deliberation, completely free in its principles, in the distribution of its powers, uniting security with energy, and containing within itself a provision for its own amendment, has a just claim to your confidence and your support. Respect for its authority, compliance with its Laws, acquiescence in its measures, are duties enjoined by the fundamental maxims of true Liberty. The basis of our political systems is the right of the people to make and to alter their Constitutions of Government. But the Constitution which at any time exists, 'till changed by an explicit and authentic act of the whole People, is sacredly obligatory upon all. The very idea of the power and the right of the People to establish Government presupposes the duty of every Individual to obey the established Government.

All obstructions to the execution of the Laws, all combinations and Associations, under whatever plausible character, with the real design to direct, controul, counteract, or awe the regular deliberation and action of the Constituted authorities are distructive of this fundamental principle and of fatal tendency. They serve to organize faction, to give it an artificial and extraordinary force; to put in the place of the delegated will of the Nation, the will of a party; often a small but artful and enterprizing minority of the Community; and, according to the alternate triumphs of different parties, to make the public administration the Mirror of the ill concerted and incongruous projects of faction, rather than the organ of consistent and wholesome plans digested by common counsels and modefied by mutual interests. However combinations or Associations of the above description may now and then answer popular ends, they are likely, in the course of time and things, to become potent engines, by which cunning, ambitious and unprincipled men will be enabled to subvert the Power of the People, and to usurp for themselves the reins of Government; destroying afterwards the very engines which have lifted them to unjust dominion.

Towards the preservation of your Government and the permanency of your present happy state, it is requisite, not only that you steadily discountenance irregular oppositions to its acknowledged authority, but also that you resist with care the spirit of innovation upon its principles however specious the pretexts. One method of assault may be to effect, in the forms of the Constitution, alterations which will impair the energy of the system, and thus to undermine what cannot be directly overthrown. In all the changes to which you may be invited, remember that time and habit are at least as necessary to fix the true character of Governments, as of other human institutions; that experience is the surest standard, by which to test the real tendency of the existing Constitution of a country; that facility in changes upon the credit of mere hypotheses and opinion exposes to perpetual change, from the endless variety of hypotheses and opinion: and remember, especially, that for the efficient management of your common interests, in a country so extensive as ours, a Government of as much vigour as is consistent with the perfect security of Liberty is indispensable. Liberty itself will find in such a Government, with powers properly distributed and adjusted, its surest Guardian. It is indeed little else than a name, where the Government is too feeble to withstand the enterprises of faction, to confine each member of the Society within the limits prescribed by the laws and to maintain all in the secure and tranquil enjoyment of the rights of person and property. . . .

Of all the dispositions and habits which lead to political prosperity, Religion and morality are indispensable supports. In vain would that man claim the tribute of Patriotism, who should labour to subvert these great Pillars of human happiness, these firmest props of the duties of Men and citizens. The mere Politician, equally with the pious man ought to respect and to cherish them. A volume could not trace all their connections with private and public felicity. Let it simply be asked where is the security for property, for reputation, for life, if the sense of religious obligation *desert* the oaths, which are the instruments of investigation in Courts of Justice? And let us with caution indulge the supposition, that morality can be maintained without religion. Whatever may be conceded to the influence of refined education on minds of peculiar structure, reason and experience both forbid us to expect that National morality can prevail in exclusion of religious principle.

'Tis substantially true, that virtue or morality is a necessary spring of popular government. The rule indeed extends with more or less force to every species of free Government. Who that is a sincere friend to it can look with indifference upon attempts to shake the foundation of the fabric?

Promote then as an object of primary importance, Institutions for the general diffusion of knowledge. In proportion as the structure of a government gives force to public opinion, it is essential that public opinion should be enlightened.

As a very important source of strength and security, cherish public credit. One method of preserving it is to use it as sparingly as possible: avoiding occasions of expence by cultivating peace, but remembering also that timely disbursements to prepare for danger frequently prevent much greater disbursements to repel it; avoiding likewise the accumulation of debt, not only by shunning occasions of expence, but by vigorous exertion in time of Peace to discharge the Debts which unavoidable wars may have occasioned, not ungenerously throwing upon posterity the burthen which we ourselves ought to bear. The execution of these maxims belongs to your Representatives, but it is necessary that public opinion should co-operate. To facilitate to them the performance of their duty, it is essential that you should practically bear in mind, that towards the payment of debts there must be Revenue; that to have Revenue there must be taxes; that no taxes can be devised which are not more or less inconvenient and unpleasant; that the intrinsic embarrassment inseparable from the selection of the proper objects (which is always a choice of difficulties) ought to be a decisive motive for a candid construction of the Conduct of the Government in making it, and for a spirit of acquiescence in the measures for obtaining Revenue which the public exigencies may at any time dictate.

Observe good faith and justice towards all Nations. Cultivate peace and harmony with all. Religion and morality enjoin this conduct; and can it be that good policy does not equally enjoin it? It will be worthy of a free, enlightened, and, at no distant period, a great Nation, to give to mankind the magnanimous and too novel example of a People always guided by an exalted justice and benevolence. Who can doubt that in the course of time and things the fruits of such a plan would richly repay any temporary advantages which might be lost by a steady adherence to it? Can it be that Providence has not connected the permanent felicity of a Nation with its virtue? The experiment, at least, is recommended by every sentiment which ennobles human Nature. Alas! is it rendered impossible by its vices?

In the execution of such a plan nothing is more essential than that permanent, inveterate antipathies against particular Nations and passionate attachments for others should be excluded; and that in place of them just and amicable feelings towards all should be cultivated. The Nation, which indulges towards another a habitual hatred, or a habitual fondness, is in some degree a slave. It is a slave to its animosity or to its affection, either of which is sufficient to lead it astray from its duty and its interest. . . .

The Great rule of conduct for us, in regard to foreign Nations is in extending our commercial relations to have with them as little *political* connection as possible. So far as we have already formed engagements let them be fulfilled, with perfect good faith. Here let us stop. . . .

If we remain one People, under an efficient government, the period is not far off when we may defy material injury from external annoyance; when we may take such an attitude as will cause the neutrality we may at any time resolve upon to be scrupulously respected; when belligerent nations, under the impossibility of making acquisitions upon us, will not lightly hazard the giving us provocation; when we may choose peace or war, as our interest guided by our justice shall Counsel. . . .

'Tis our true policy to steer clear of permanent Alliances, with any portion of the foreign world. . . .

Taking care always to keep ourselves, by suitable establishments, on a respectably defensive posture, we may safely trust to temporary alliances for extraordinary emergencies.

Harmony, liberal intercourse with all Nations, are recommended by policy, humanity and interest. But even our Commercial policy should hold an equal and impartial hand: neither seeking nor granting exclusive favours or preferences; consulting the natural course of things; diffusing and deversifying by gentle means the streams of Commerce, but forcing nothing; establishing with Powers so disposed; in order to give to trade a stable course, to define the rights of our Merchants, and to enable the Government to support them; conventional rules of intercourse, the best that present circumstances and mutual opinion will permit, but temporary, and liable to be from time to time abandoned or varied, as experience and circumstances shall dictate; constantly keeping in view, that 'tis folly in one Nation to look for disinterested favors from another; that it must pay with a portion of its Independence for whatever it may accept under that character; that by such acceptance, it may place itself in the condition of having given equivalents for nominal favours and yet of being reproached with ingratitude for not giving more. There can be no greater error than to expect, or calculate upon real favours from Nation to Nation. 'Tis an illusion which experience must cure, which a just pride ought to discard.

In offering to you, my Countrymen, these counsels of an old and affectionate friend, I dare not hope they will make the strong and lasting impression, I could wish; that they will controul the usual current of the passions, or prevent our Nation from running the course which has hitherto marked the Destiny of Nations: But if I may even flatter myself, that they may be productive of some partial benefit, some occasional good; that they may now and then recur to moderate the fury of party spirit, to warn against the mischiefs of foreign Intriegue, to guard against the Impostures of pretended patriotism; this hope will be a full recompence for the solicitude for your welfare, by which they have been dictated.

How far in the discharge of my Official duties, I have been guided by the principles which have been delineated, the public Records and other evidences of my conduct must Witness to You and to the world. To myself, the assurance of my own conscience is, that I have at least believed myself to be guided by them. . . .

Though in reviewing the incidents of my Administration, I am unconscious of intentional error, I am nevertheless too sensible of my defects not to think it probable that I may have committed many errors. Whatever they may be I fervently beseech the Almighty to avert or mitigate the evils to which they may tend. I shall also carry with me the hope that my Country will never cease to view them with indulgence; and that after forty five years of my life dedicated to its Service, with an upright zeal, the faults of incompetent abilities will be consigned to oblivion, as myself must soon be to the Mansions of rest.

Relying on its kindness in this as in other things, and actuated by that fervent love towards it, which is so natural to a Man, who views in it the native soil of himself and his progenitors for several Generations; I anticipate with pleasing expectation that retreat, in which I promise myself to realize, without alloy, the sweet enjoyment of partaking, in the midst of my fellow Citizens, the benign influence of good Laws under a free Government, the ever favourite object of my heart, and the happy reward, as I trust, of our mutual cares, labours, and dangers.

Manhood and Statehood

from The Strenuous Life

THEODORE ROOSEVELT

We are prone to take for granted the privileges America offers us, forgetting how we got where we are. As our twenty-sixth president, Theodore Roosevelt (1858–1919), puts it in this selection, "It is a law of our intellectual development that the greatest and most important truths, when once we have become thoroughly familiar with them, often because of that very familiarity grow dim in our minds." Can our natural forgetfulness of the past imperil our future? Can a certain kind of conservatism in fact contribute to progress? Celebrating the quarter-centennial of Colorado's statehood, in August 1901, Roosevelt (then vice president) reminds us of the great achievements of our ancestors. He summons us to continue what they began and to preserve the national spirit and character responsible for past success.

What are the qualities of "manhood" that Roosevelt celebrates? What relation does he see between "manhood" and "statehood"? What does he mean by "moral purpose" and "moral sense," and what do they add to courage, strength, and intellect? What are the foundations, according to Roosevelt, of good citizenship, and how might these foundations be preserved? Do you agree?

This anniversary, which marks the completion by Colorado of her first quarter-century of Statehood, is of interest not only to her sisters, the States of the Rocky Mountain region, but to our whole country. With the exception of the admission to Statehood of California, no other event emphasized in such dramatic fashion the full meaning of the growth of our country as did the incoming of Colorado.

It is a law of our intellectual development that the greatest and most important truths, when once we have become thoroughly familiar with them, often because of that very familiarity grow dim in our minds. The westward spread of our people across this continent has been so rapid, and so great has been their success in taming the rugged wilderness, turning the gray desert into green fertility, and filling the waste and lonely places with the eager, thronging, crowded life of our industrial civilization, that we have begun to accept it all as part of the order of Nature. Moreover, it now seems to us equally a matter of course that when a sufficient number of the citizens of our common country have thus entered into and taken possession of some great tract of empty wilderness, they should be permitted to enter the Union as a State on an absolute equality with the older States, having the same right both to manage their own local affairs as they deem best, and to exercise their full share of control over all the affairs of whatever kind or sort in which the nation is interested as a whole. The youngest and the oldest States stand on an exact level in one indissoluble and perpetual Union.

To us nowadays these processes seem so natural that it is only by a mental wrench that we conceive of any other as possible. Yet they are really wholly modern and of purely American development. When, a century before Colorado became a State, the original thirteen States began the great experiment of a free and independent Republic on this continent, the processes which we now accept in such matter-of-course fashion were looked upon as abnormal and revolutionary. It is our own success here in America that has brought about the complete alteration in feeling. The chief factor in producing the Revolution, and later in producing the War of 1812, was the inability of the mother country to understand that the freemen who went forth to conquer a continent should be encouraged in that work, and could not and ought not to be expected to toil only for the profit or glory of others. When the first Continental Congress assembled, the British Government, like every other government of Europe at that time, simply did not know how to look upon the general question of the progress of the colonies save from the standpoint of the people who had stayed at home. The spread of the hardy, venturesome backwoodsmen was to most of the statesmen of London a matter of anxiety rather than of pride, and the famous Quebec Act of 1774 was in part designed with the purpose of keeping the English-speaking settlements permanently east of the Alleghenies, and preserving the mighty and beautiful valley of the Ohio as a hunting-ground for savages, a preserve for the great fur-trading companies; and as late as 1812 this project was partially revived.

More extraordinary still, even after independence was achieved, and a firm Union accomplished under that wonderful document, the Constitution adopted in 1789, we still see traces of the same feeling lingering here and there in our own country. There were plenty of men in the seaboard States who looked with what seems to us ludicrous apprehension at the steady westward growth of our people. Grave Senators and Representatives expressed dire foreboding as to the ruin which would result from admitting the communities growing up along the Ohio to a full equality with the older States; and when Louisiana was given Statehood, they insisted that that very fact dissolved the Union. When our people had begun to settle in the Mississippi Valley, Jefferson himself accepted with equanimity the view that probably it would not be possible to keep regions so infinitely remote as the Mississippi and the Atlantic Coast in the same Union. Later even such a stanch Union man and firm believer in Western growth as fearless old Tom Benton of Missouri thought that it would be folly to try to extend the national limits westward of the Rocky Mountains. In 1830 our then best-known man of letters and historian, Washington Irving, prophesied that for ages to come the country upon which we now stand would be inhabited simply by roving tribes of nomads.

The mental attitude of all these good people need not surprise anybody. There was nothing in the past by which to judge either the task before this country, or the way in which that task was to be done. As Lowell finely said, on this continent we have made new States as Old World men pitch tents. Even the most far-seeing statesmen, those most gifted with the imagination needed by really great statesmen, could not at first grasp what the process really meant. Slowly and with incredible labor the backwoodsmen of the old colonies hewed their way through the dense forests from the tide-water region to the crests of the Alleghanies. But by the time the Alleghanies were reached, about at the moment when our national life began, the movement had gained wonderful momentum. Thenceforward it advanced by leaps and bounds, and the frontier pushed westward across the continent with ever-increasing rapidity until the day came when it vanished entirely. Our greatest statesmen have always been those who *believed in the nation*—who had faith in the power of our people to spread until they should become the mightiest among the peoples of the world.

Under any governmental system which was known to Europe, the problem offered by the westward thrust, across a continent, of so masterful and liberty-loving a race as ours would have been insoluble. The great civilized and colonizing races of antiquity, the Greeks and the Romans, had been utterly unable to devise a scheme under which when their race spread it might be possible to preserve both national unity and local and individual freedom. When a Hellenic or Latin city sent off a colony, one of two things happened. Either the colony was kept in political subjection to the city or state of which it was an offshoot, or else it became a wholly independent and alien, and often a hostile, nation. Both systems were fraught with disaster. With the Greeks race unity was sacrificed to local independence, and as a result the Greek world became the easy prey of foreign conquerors. The Romans kept national unity, but only by means of a crushing centralized despotism.

When the modern world entered upon the marvelous era of expansion which began with the discoveries of Columbus, the nations were able to devise no new plan. All the great colonizing powers, England, France, Spain, Portugal, Holland, and Russia, managed their colonies primarily in the interest of the home country. Some did better than others,—England probably best and Spain worst,—but in no case were the colonists treated as citizens of equal rights in a common country. Our ancestors, who were at once the strongest and the most liberty-loving among all the peoples who had been thrust out into new continents, were the first to revolt against this system; and the lesson taught by their success has been thoroughly learned.

In applying the new principles to our conditions we have found the Federal Constitution a nearly perfect instrument. The system of a closely knit and indestructible union of free commonwealths has enabled us to do what neither Greek nor Roman in their greatest days could do. We have preserved the complete unity of an expanding race without impairing in the slightest degree the liberty of the individual. When in a given locality the settlers became sufficiently numerous, they were admitted to Statehood, and thenceforward shared all the rights and all the duties of the citizens of the older States. As with Columbus and the egg, the expedient seems obvious enough nowadays, but then it was so novel that a couple of generations had to pass before we ourselves thoroughly grasped all its features. At last we grew to accept as axiomatic the two facts of national union and local and personal freedom. As whatever is axiomatic seems commonplace, we now tend to accept what has been accomplished as a mere matter-of-course incident, of no great moment. The very completeness with which the vitally important task has been done almost blinds us to the extraordinary nature of the achievement.

You, the men of Colorado, and, above all, the older among those whom I am now addressing, have been engaged in doing the great typical work of our people. Save only the preservation of the Union itself, no other task has been so important as the conquest and settlement of the West. This conquest and settlement has been the stupendous feat of our race for the century that has just closed. It stands supreme among all such feats. The same kind of thing has been in Australia and Canada, but upon a less important scale, while the Russian advance in Siberia has been incomparably slower. In all the history of mankind there is nothing that quite parallels the way in which our people have filled a vacant continent with self-governing commonwealths, knit into one nation. And of all this marvelous history perhaps the most wonderful portion is that which deals with the way in which the Pacific Coast and the Rocky Mountains were settled.

The men who founded these communities showed practically by their life-work that it is indeed the spirit of adventure which is the maker of commonwealths. Their traits of daring and hardihood and iron endurance are not merely indispensable traits for pioneers; they are also traits which must go to the make-up of every mighty and successful people. You and your fathers who built up the West did more even than you thought; for you shaped thereby the destiny of the whole Republic, and as a necessary corollary profoundly influenced the course of events throughout the world. More and more as the years go by this Republic will find its guidance in the thought and action of the West, because the conditions of development in the West have steadily tended to accentuate the peculiarly American characteristics of its people.

There was scant room for the coward and the weakling in the ranks of the adventurous frontiersmen—the pioneer settlers who first broke up the wild prairie soil, who first hewed their way into the primeval forest, who guided their white-topped wagons across the endless leagues of Indian-haunted desolation, and explored every remote mountain-chain in the restless quest for metal wealth. Behind them came the men who completed the work they had roughly begun: who drove the great railroad systems over plain and desert and mountain pass; who stocked the teeming ranches, and under irrigation saw the bright green of the alfalfa and the yellow of the golden stubble supplant the gray of the sage-brush desert; who have built great populous cities—cities in which every art and science of civilization are carried to the highest point—on tracts which, when the nineteenth century had passed its meridian, were still known only to the grim trappers and hunters and the red lords of the wilderness with whom they waged eternal war.

Such is the record of which we are so proud. It is a record of men who greatly dared and greatly did; a record of wanderings wider and more dangerous than those of the Vikings; a record of endless feats of arms, of victory after victory in the ceaseless strife waged against wild man and wild nature. The winning of the West was the great epic feat in the history of our race.

We have then a right to meet to-day in a spirit of just pride in the past. But when we pay homage to the hardy, grim, resolute men who, with incredible toil and risk, laid deep the foundations of the civilization that we inherit, let us steadily remember that the only homage that counts is the homage of deeds—not merely of words. It is well to gather here to show that we remember what has been done in the past by the Western pioneers of our people, and that we glory in the greatness for which they prepared the way. But lip-loyalty by itself avails very little, whether it is expressed concerning a nation or an ideal. It would be a sad and evil thing for this country if ever the day came when we considered the great deeds of our forefathers as an excuse for our resting slothfully satisfied with what has been already done. On the contrary, they should be an inspiration and appeal, summoning us to show that we too have courage and strength; that we too are ready to dare greatly if the need arises; and, above all, that we are firmly bent upon that steady performance of every-day duty which, in the long run, is of such incredible worth in the formation of national character.

The old iron days have gone, the days when the weakling died as the penalty of inability to hold his own in the rough warfare against his surroundings. We live in softer times. Let us see to it that, while we take advantage of every gentler and more humanizing tendency of the age, we yet preserve the iron quality which made our forefathers and predecessors fit to do the deeds they did. It will of necessity find a different expression now, but the quality itself remains just as necessary as ever. Surely you men of the West, you men who with stout heart, cool head, and ready hand have wrought out your own success and built up these great new commonwealths, surely you need no reminder of the fact that if either man or nation wishes to play a great part in the world there must be no dallying with the life of lazy ease. In the abounding energy and intensity of existence in our mighty democratic republic there is small space indeed for the idler, for the luxury-loving man who prizes ease more than hard, triumph-crowned effort.

We hold work not as a curse but as a blessing, and we regard the idler with scornful pity. It would be in the highest degree undesirable that we should all work in the same way or at the same things, and for the sake of the real greatness of the nation we should in the fullest and most cordial way recognize the fact that some of the most needed work must, from its very nature, be unremunerative in a material sense. Each man must choose so far as the conditions allow him the path to which he is bidden by his own peculiar powers and inclinations. But if he is a man he must in some way or shape do a man's work. If, after making all the effort that his strength of body and of mind permits, he yet honorably fails, why, he is still entitled to a certain share of respect because he has made the effort. But if he does not make the effort, or if he makes it half-heartedly and recoils from the labor, the risk, or the irksome monotony of his task, why, he has forfeited all right to our respect, and has shown himself a mere cumberer of the earth. It is not given to us all to succeed, but it is given to us all to strive manfully to deserve success.

We need then the iron qualities that must go with true manhood. We need the positive virtues of resolution, of courage, of indomitable will, of power to do without shrinking the rough work that must always be done, and to persevere through the long days of slow progress or of seeming failure which always come before any final triumph, no matter how brilliant. But we need more than these qualities. This country cannot afford to have its sons less than men;

but neither can it afford to have them other than good men. If courage and strength and intellect are unaccompanied by the moral purpose, the moral sense, they become merely forms of expression for unscrupulous force and unscrupulous cunning. If the strong man has not in him the lift toward lofty things his strength makes him only a curse to himself and to his neighbor. All this is true in private life, and it is no less true in public life. If Washington and Lincoln had not had in them the whipcord fiber of moral and mental strength, the soul that steels itself to endure disaster unshaken and with grim resolve to wrest victory from defeat, then the one could not have founded, nor the other preserved, our mighty federal Union. The least touch of flabbiness, of unhealthy softness, in either would have meant ruin for this nation, and therefore the downfall of the proudest hope of mankind. But no less is it true that had either been influenced by self-seeking ambition, by callous disregard of others, by contempt for the moral law, he would have dashed us down into the black gulf of failure. Woe to all of us if ever as a people we grow to condone evil because it is successful. We can no more afford to lose social and civic decency and honesty than we can afford to lose the qualities of courage and strength. It is the merest truism to say that the nation rests upon the individual, upon the family—upon individual manliness and womanliness, using the words in their widest and fullest meaning.

To be a good husband or good wife, a good neighbor and friend, to be hardworking and upright in business and social relations, to bring up many healthy children—to be and to do all this is to lay the foundations of good citizenship as they must be laid. But we cannot stop even with this. Each of us has not only his duty to himself, his family, and his neighbors, but his duty to the State and to the nation. We are in honor bound each to strive according to his or her strength to bring ever nearer the day when justice and wisdom shall obtain in public life as in private life. We cannot retain the full measure of our self-respect if we cannot retain pride in our citizenship. For the sake not only of ourselves but of our children and our children's children we must see that this nation stands for strength and honesty both at home and abroad. In our internal policy we cannot afford to rest satisfied until all that the government can do has been done to secure fair dealing and equal justice as between man and man. In the great part which hereafter, whether we will or not, we must play in the world at large, let us see to it that we neither do wrong nor shrink from doing right because the right is difficult; that on the one hand we inflict no injury, and that on the other we have a due regard for the honor and the interest of our mighty nation; and that we keep unsullied the renown of the flag which beyond all others of the present time or of the ages of the past stands for confident faith in the future welfare and greatness of mankind.

Speech on the Occasion of the 150th Anniversary of the Declaration of Independence

CALVIN COOLIDGE

The Fourth of July, the date of the signing of the Declaration of Independence, is annually celebrated as the birthday of the United States of America, marked with parades, marching bands, and fireworks. In earlier times, the day was also marked by specially prepared orations that commemorated our founding principles. A wonderful example of this at once celebratory and reflective genre can be found in the present selection, a speech that President Calvin Coolidge (1872–1933) delivered in 1926 in honor of the Declaration's sesquicentennial. Here President Coolidge affirms the enduring veracity of human equality, inalienable rights, and the consent of the governed—"those old theories and principles which time and the unerring logic of events have demonstrated to be sound." By locating our abstract creed (see Chapter 2) in its historical, cultural, and religious contexts, he argues against the idea that the American Republic was founded on thought alone, and insists on the importance of our religious heritage. What specifically are his arguments, and what is his evidence? How does this speech affect your own perception of the American Republic? How does it affect your understanding of the Fourth of July and the ways it should be celebrated?

We meet to celebrate the birthday of America. The coming of a new life always excites our interest. Although we know in the case of the individual that it has been an infinite repetition reaching back beyond our vision, that only makes it the more wonderful. But how our interest and wonder increase when we behold the miracle of the birth of a new nation. It is to pay our tribute of reverence and respect to those who participated in such a mighty event that we annually observe the fourth day of July. Whatever may have been the impression created by the news which went out from this city on that summer day in 1776, there can be no doubt as to the estimate which is now placed upon it. At the end of 150 years the four corners of the earth unite in coming to Philadelphia as to a holy shrine in grateful acknowledgement of a service so great, which a few inspired men here rendered to humanity, that it is still the preeminent support of free government throughout the world.

Although a century and a half measured in comparison with the length of human experience is but a short time, yet measured in the life of governments and nations it ranks as a very respectable period. Certainly enough time has elapsed to demonstrate with a great deal of thoroughness the value of our institutions and their dependability as rules for the regulation of human conduct and the advancement of civilization. They have been in existence long enough to become very well seasoned. They have met, and met successfully, the test of experience.

It is not so much then for the purpose of undertaking to proclaim new theories and principles that this annual celebration is maintained, but rather to reaffirm and reestablish those old theories and principles which time and the unerring logic of events have demonstrated to be sound. Amid all the clash of conflicting interests, amid all the welter of partisan politics, every American can turn for solace and consolation to the Declaration of Independence and the Constitution of the United States with the assurance and confidence that those two great charters of freedom and justice remain firm and unshaken. Whatever perils appear, whatever dangers threaten, the Nation remains secure in the knowledge that the ultimate application of the law of the land will provide an adequate defense and protection.

It is little wonder that people at home and abroad consider Independence Hall as hallowed ground and revere the Liberty Bell as a sacred relic. That pile of bricks and mortar, that mass of metal, might appear to the uninstructed as only the outgrown meeting place and the shattered bell of a former time, useless now because of more modern conveniences, but to those who know they have become consecrated by the use which men have made of them. They have long been identified with a great cause. They are the framework of a spiritual event. The world looks upon them, because of their associations of one hundred and fifty years ago, as it looks upon the Holy Land because of what took place there nineteen hundred years ago. Through use for a righteous purpose they have become sanctified.

It is not here necessary to examine in detail the causes which led to the American Revolution. In their immediate occasion they were largely economic. The colonists objected to the navigation laws which interfered with their trade, they denied the power of Parliament to impose taxes which they were obliged to pay, and they therefore resisted the royal governors and the royal forces which were sent to secure obedience to these laws. But the conviction is inescapable that a new civilization had come, a new spirit had arisen on this side of the Atlantic more advanced and more developed in its regard for the rights of the individual than that which characterized the Old World. Life in a new and open country had aspirations which could not be realized in any subordinate position. A separate establishment was ultimately inevitable. It had been decreed by the very laws of human nature. Man everywhere has an unconquerable desire to be the master of his own destiny.

We are obliged to conclude that the Declaration of Independence represented the movement of a people. It was not, of course, a movement from the top. Revolutions do not come from that direction. It was not without the support of many of the most respectable people in the Colonies, who were entitled to all the consideration that is given to breeding, education, and possessions. It had the support of another element of great significance and importance to which I shall later refer. But the preponderance of all those who occupied a position which took on the aspect of aristocracy did not approve of the Revolution and held toward it an attitude either of neutrality or open hostility. It was in no sense a rising of the oppressed and downtrodden. It brought no scum to the surface, for the reason that colonial society had developed no scum. The great body of the people were accustomed to privations, but they were free from depravity. If they had poverty, it was not of the hopeless kind that afflicts great cities, but the inspiring kind that marks the spirit of the pioneer. The American Revolution represented the informed and mature convictions of a great mass of independent, liberty-loving, God-fearing people who knew their rights, and possessed the courage to dare to maintain them.

The Continental Congress was not only composed of great men, but it represented a great people. While its members did not fail to exercise a remarkable leadership, they were equally observant of their representative capacity. They were industrious in encouraging their constituents to instruct them to support independence. But until such instructions were given they were inclined to withhold action.

While North Carolina has the honor of first authorizing its delegates to concur with other Colonies in declaring independence, it was quickly followed by South Carolina and Georgia, which also gave general instructions broad enough to include such action. But the first instructions which unconditionally directed its delegates to declare for independence came from the great Commonwealth of Virginia. These were immediately followed by Rhode Island and Massachusetts, while the other Colonies, with the exception of New York, soon adopted a like course.

This obedience of the delegates to the wishes of their constituents, which in some cases caused them to modify their previous positions, is a matter of great significance. It reveals an orderly process of government in the first place; but more than that, it demonstrates that the Declaration of Independence was the result of the seasoned and deliberate thought of the dominant portion of the people of the Colonies. Adopted after long discussion and as the result of the duly authorized expression of the preponderance of public opinion, it did not partake of dark intrigue or hidden conspiracy. It was well advised. It had about it nothing of the lawless and disordered nature of a riotous insurrection. It was maintained on a plane which rises above the ordinary conception of rebellion. It was in no sense a radical movement but took on the dignity of a resistance to illegal usurpations. It was conservative and represented the action of the colonists to maintain their constitutional rights which from time immemorial had been guaranteed to them under the law of the land.

When we come to examine the action of the Continental Congress in adopting the Declaration of Independence in the light of what was set out in that great document and in the light of succeeding events, we can not escape the conclusion that it had a much broader and deeper significance than a mere secession of territory and the establishment of a new nation. Events of that nature have been taking place since the dawn of history. One empire after another has arisen, only to crumble away as its constituent parts separated from each other and set up independent governments of their own. Such actions long ago became commonplace. They have occurred too often to hold the attention of the world and command the admiration and reverence of humanity. There is something beyond the establishment of a new nation, great as that event would be, in the Declaration of Independence which has ever since caused it to be regarded as one of the great charters that not only was to liberate America but was everywhere to ennoble humanity.

It was not because it was proposed to establish a new nation, but because it was proposed to establish a nation on new principles, that July 4, 1776, has come to be regarded as one of the greatest days in history. Great ideas do not burst upon the world unannounced. They are reached by a gradual development over a length of time usually proportionate to their importance. This is especially true of the principles laid down in the Declaration of Independence. Three very definite propositions were set out in its preamble regarding the nature of mankind and therefore of government. These were the doctrine that all men are created equal, that they are endowed with certain inalienable rights, and that therefore the source of the just powers of government must be derived from the consent of the governed.

If no one is to be accounted as born into a superior station, if there is to be no ruling class, and if all possess rights which can neither be bartered away nor taken from them by any earthly power, it follows as a matter of course that the practical authority of the Government has to rest on the consent of the governed. While these principles were not altogether new in political action, and were very far from new in political speculation, they had never been assembled before and declared in such a combination. But remarkable as this may be, it is not the chief distinction of the Declaration of Independence. The importance of political speculation is not to be under-estimated, as I shall presently disclose. Until the idea is developed and the plan made there can be no action.

It was the fact that our Declaration of Independence containing these immortal truths was the political action of a duly authorized and constituted representative public body in its sovereign capacity, supported by the force of general opinion and by the armies of Washington already in the field, which makes it the most important civil document in the world. It was not only the principles declared, but the fact that therewith a new nation was born which was to be founded upon those principles and which from that time forth in its development has actually maintained those principles, that makes this pronouncement an incomparable event in the history of government. It was an assertion that a people had arisen determined to make every necessary sacrifice for the support of these truths and by their practical application bring the War of Independence to a successful conclusion and adopt the Constitution of the United States with all that it has meant to civilization.

The idea that the people have a right to choose their own rulers was not new in political history. It was the foundation of every popular attempt to depose an undesirable king. This right was set out with a good deal of detail by the Dutch when as early as July 26, 1581, they declared their independence of Philip of Spain. In their long struggle with the Stuarts the British people asserted the same principles, which finally culminated in the Bill of Rights deposing the last of that house and placing William and Mary on the throne. In each of these cases sovereignty through divine right was displaced by sovereignty through the consent of the people. Running through the same documents, though expressed in different terms, is the clear inference of inalienable rights. But we should search these charters in vain for an assertion of the doctrine of equality. This principle had not before appeared as an official political declaration of any nation. It was profoundly revolutionary. It is one of the corner stones of American institutions.

But if these truths to which the declaration refers have not before been adopted in their combined entirety by national authority, it is a fact that they had been long pondered and often expressed in political speculation. It is generally assumed that French thought had some effect upon our public mind during Revolutionary days. This may have been true. But the principles of our declaration had been under discussion in the Colonies for nearly two generations before the advent of the French political philosophy that characterized the middle of the eighteenth century. In fact, they come from an earlier date. A very positive echo of what the Dutch had done in 1581, and what the English were preparing to do, appears in the assertion of the Rev. Thomas Hooker of Connecticut as early as 1638, when he said in a sermon before the General Court that—

"The foundation of authority is laid in the free consent of the people."

"The choice of public magistrates belongs unto the people by God's own allowance."

This doctrine found wide acceptance among the nonconformist clergy who later made up the Congregational Church. The great apostle of this movement was the Rev. John Wise, of Massachusetts. He was one of the leaders of the revolt against the royal governor Andros in 1687, for which he suffered imprisonment. He was a liberal in ecclesiastical controversies. He appears to have been familiar with the writings of the political scientist, Samuel Pufendorf, who was born in Saxony in 1632. Wise published a treatise, entitled "The Church's Quarrel Espoused," in 1710, which was amplified in another publication in 1717. In it he dealt with the principles of civil government. His works were reprinted in 1772 and have been declared to have been nothing less than a textbook of liberty for our Revolutionary fathers.

While the written word was the foundation, it is apparent that the spoken word was the vehicle for convincing the people. This came with great force and wide range from the successors of Hooker and Wise. It was carried on with a missionary spirit which did not fail to reach the Scotch-Irish of North Carolina, showing its influence by significantly making that Colony the first to give instructions to its delegates looking to independence. This preaching reached the neighborhood of Thomas Jefferson, who acknowledged that his "best ideas of democracy" had been secured at church meetings.

That these ideas were prevalent in Virginia is further revealed by the Declaration of Rights, which was prepared by George Mason and presented to the general assembly on May 27, 1776. This document asserted popular sovereignty and inherent natural rights, but confined the doctrine of equality to the assertion that "All men are created equally free and independent." It can scarcely be imagined that Jefferson was unacquainted with what had been done in his own Commonwealth of Virginia when he took up the task of drafting the Declaration of Independence. But these thoughts can very largely be traced back to what John Wise was writing in 1710. He said, "Every man must be acknowledged equal to every man." Again, "The end of all good government is to cultivate humanity and promote the happiness of all and the good of every man in all his rights, his life, liberty, estate, honor, and so forth. . . ." And again, "For as they have a power every man in his natural state, so upon combination they can and do bequeath this power to others and settle it according as their united discretion shall determine." And still again, "Democracy is Christ's government in church and state." Here was the doctrine of equality, popular sovereignty, and the substance of the theory of inalienable rights clearly asserted by Wise at the opening of the eighteenth century, just as we have the principle of the consent of the governed stated by Hooker as early as 1638.

When we take all these circumstances into consideration, it is but natural that the first paragraph of the Declaration of Independence should open with a reference to Nature's God and should close in the final paragraphs with an appeal to the Supreme Judge of the world and an assertion of a firm reliance on Divine Providence. Coming from these sources, having as it did this background, it is no wonder that Samuel Adams could say, "The people seem to recognize this resolution as though it were a decree promulgated from heaven."

No one can examine this record and escape the conclusion that in the great outline of its principles the Declaration was the result of the religious teachings of the preceding period. The profound philosophy which Jonathan Edwards applied to theology, the popular preaching of George Whitefield, had aroused the thought and stirred the people of the Colonies in preparation for this great event. No doubt the speculations which had been going on in England, and especially on the Continent, lent their influence to the general sentiment of the times. Of course, the world is always influenced by all the experience and all the thought of the past. But when we come to a contemplation of the immediate conception of the principles of human relationship which went into the Declaration of Independence we are not required to extend our search beyond our own shores. They are found in the texts, the sermons, and the writings of the early colonial clergy who were earnestly undertaking to instruct their congregations in the great mystery of how to live. They preached equality because they believed in the fatherhood of God and the brotherhood of man. They justified freedom by the text that we are all created in the divine image, all partakers of the divine spirit.

Placing every man on a plane where he acknowledged no superiors, where no one possessed any right to rule over him, he must inevitably choose his own rulers through a system of self-government. This was their theory of democracy. In those days such doctrines would scarcely have been permitted to flourish and spread in any other country. This was the purpose which the fathers cherished. In order that they might have freedom to express these thoughts and opportunity to put them into action, whole congregations with their pastors had migrated to the colonies. These great truths were in the air that our people breathed. Whatever else we may say of it, the Declaration of Independence was profoundly American.

If this apprehension of the facts be correct, and the documentary evidence would appear to verify it, then certain conclusions are bound to follow. A spring will cease to flow if its source be dried up; a tree will wither if its roots be destroyed. In its main features the Declaration of Independence is a great spiritual document. It is a declaration not of material but of spiritual conceptions. Equality, liberty, popular sovereignty, the rights of man—these are not elements which we can see and touch. They are ideals. They have their source and their roots in the religious convictions. They belong to the unseen world. Unless the faith of the American people in these religious convictions is to endure, the principles of our Declaration will perish. We can not continue to enjoy the result if we neglect and abandon the cause.

We are too prone to overlook another conclusion. Governments do not make ideals, but ideals make governments. This is both historically and logically true. Of course the government can help to sustain ideals and can create institutions through which they can be the better observed, but their source by their very nature is in the people. The people have to bear their own responsibilities. There is no method by which that burden can be shifted to the government. It is not the enactment, but the observance of laws, that creates the character of a nation.

About the Declaration there is a finality that is exceedingly restful. It is often asserted that the world has made a great deal of progress since 1776, that we have had new thoughts and new experiences which have given us a great advance over the people of that day, and that we may therefore very well discard their conclusions for something more modern. But that reasoning can not be applied to this great charter. If all men are created equal, that is final. If they are endowed with inalienable rights, that is final. If governments derive their just powers from the consent of the governed, that is final. No advance, no progress can be made beyond these propositions. If anyone wishes to deny their truth or their soundness, the only direction in which he can proceed historically is not forward, but backward toward the time when there was no equality, no rights of the individual, no rule of the people. Those who wish to proceed in that direction can not lay claim to progress. They are reactionary. Their ideas are not more modern, but more ancient, than those of the Revolutionary fathers.

In the development of its institutions America can fairly claim that it has remained true to the principles which were declared 150 years ago. In all the essentials we have achieved an equality which was never possessed by any other people. Even in the less important matter of material possessions we have secured a wider and wider distribution of wealth. The rights of the individual are held sacred and protected by constitutional guaranties, which even the Government itself is bound not to violate. If there is any one thing among us that is established beyond question, it is self-government—the right of the people to rule. If there is any failure in respect to any of these principles, it is because there is a failure on the part of individuals to observe them. We hold that the duly authorized expression of the will of the people has a divine sanction. But even in that we come back to the theory of John Wise that "Democracy is Christ's government." The ultimate sanction of law rests on the righteous authority of the Almighty.

On an occasion like this a great temptation exists to present evidence of the practical success of our form of democratic republic at home and the ever-broadening acceptance it is securing abroad. Although these things are well known, their frequent consideration is an encouragement and an inspiration. But it is not results and effects so much as sources and causes that I believe it is even more necessary constantly to contemplate. Ours is a government of the people. It represents their will. Its officers may sometimes go astray, but that is not a reason for criticizing the principles of our institutions. The real heart of the American Government depends upon the heart of the people. It is from that source that we must look for all genuine reform. It is to that cause that we must ascribe all our results.

It was in the contemplation of these truths that the fathers made their declaration and adopted their Constitution. It was to establish a free government, which must not be permitted to degenerate into the unrestrained authority of a mere majority or the unbridled weight of a mere influential few. They undertook to balance these interests against each other and provide the three separate independent branches, the executive, the legislative, and the judicial departments of the Government, with checks against each other in order that neither one might encroach upon the other. These are our guaranties of liberty. As a result of these methods enterprise has been duly protected from confiscation, the people have been free from oppression, and there has been an ever-broadening and deepening of the humanities of life.

Under a system of popular government there will always be those who will seek for political preferment by clamoring for reform. While there is very little of this which is not sincere, there is a large portion that is not well informed. In my opinion very little of just criticism can attach to the theories and principles of our institutions. There is far more danger of harm than there is hope of good in any radical changes. We do need a better understanding and comprehension of them and a better knowledge of the foundations of government in general. Our forefathers came to certain conclusions and decided upon certain courses of action which have been a great blessing to the world. Before we can understand their conclusions we must go back and review the course which they followed. We must think the thoughts which they thought. Their intellectual life centered around the meeting-house. They were intent upon religious worship. While there were always among them men of deep learning, and later those who had comparatively large possessions, the mind of the people was not so much engrossed in how much they knew, or how much they had, as in how they were going to live. While scantily provided with other literature, there was a wide acquaintance with the Scriptures. Over a period as great as that which measures the existence of our independence they were subject to this discipline not only in their religious life and educational training, but also in their political thought. They were a people who came under the influence of a great spiritual development and acquired a great moral power.

No other theory is adequate to explain or comprehend the Declaration of Independence. It is the product of the spiritual insight of the people. We live in an age of science and of abounding accumulation of material things. These did not create our Declaration. Our Declaration created them. The things of the spirit come first. Unless we cling to that, all our material prosperity, overwhelming though it may appear, will turn to a barren sceptre in our grasp. If we are to maintain the great heritage which has been bequeathed to us, we must be like-minded as the fathers who created it. We must not sink into a pagan materialism. We must cultivate the reverence which they had for the things that are holy. We must follow the spiritual and moral leadership which they showed. We must keep replenished, that they may glow with a more compelling flame, the altar fires before which they worshiped.

In Our Youth Our Hearts Were Touched with Fire

Oliver Wendell Holmes Jr.

Holidays are, among other things, commemorations, days for renewing memories. The Fourth of July renews the memory of the birth of the nation; Memorial Day renews the memory of those who gave their lives "that that nation might live." Originally called Decoration Day, it was first instituted by the Grand Army of the Republic on May 30, 1868, "for the purpose of strewing with flowers or otherwise decorating the graves of comrades who died in defense of their country during the late rebellion, and whose bodies now lie in almost every city, village, and hamlet churchyard in the land." After World War I, Memorial Day was expanded to commemorate the lives of all those who have died in service to our country.

As personal memories of these conflicts fade, people—especially young people—may wonder why Memorial Day matters. Just such a question is the point of departure for this Memorial Day address that Oliver Wendell Holmes Jr. (1841–1935) delivered on May 30, 1884, in Keene, New Hampshire. Holmes, a Civil War veteran and later a distinguished justice of the United States Supreme Court (1902–1935), provides, as he puts it, "an answer which should command the assent of those who do not share our memories, and in which we of the North and our brethren of the South could join in perfect accord." What is that answer? Does it persuade you? What is the meaning of the title? What is the proper way for us, the living, to honor those who made the supreme sacrifice in service to their country?

Not long ago I heard a young man ask why people still kept up Memorial Day, and it set me thinking of the answer. Not the answer that you and I should give to each other—not the expression of those feelings that, so long as you and I live, will make this day sacred to memories of love and grief and heroic youth—but an answer which should command the assent of those who do not share our memories, and in which we of the North and our brethren of the South could join in perfect accord.

So far as this last is concerned, to be sure, there is no trouble. The soldiers who were doing their best to kill each other felt less of personal hostility, I am very certain, than some who were not imperiled by their mutual endeavors. I have heard more than one of those who had been gallant and distinguished officers on the Confederate side say that they had had no such feeling. I know that I and those whom I knew best had not. We believed that it was most desirable that the North should win; we believed in the principle that the Union is indissoluable; we, or many of us at least, also believed that the conflict was inevitable, and that slavery had lasted long enough. But we equally believed that those who stood against us held just as sacred convictions that were the opposite of ours, and we respected them as every man with a heart must respect those who give all for their belief. The experience of battle soon taught its lesson even to those who came into the field more bitterly disposed. You could not stand up day after day in those indecisive contests where overwhelming victory was impossible because neither side would run as they ought when beaten, without getting at last something of the same brotherhood for the enemy that the north pole of a magnet has for the south—each working in an opposite sense to the other, but each unable to get along without the other. As it was then, it is now. The soldiers of the war need no explanations; they can join in commemorating a soldier's death with feelings not different in kind, whether he fell toward them or by their side.

But Memorial Day may and ought to have a meaning also for those who do not share our memories. When men have instinctively agreed to celebrate an anniversary, it will be found that there is some thought of feeling behind it which is too large to be dependent upon associations alone. The Fourth of July, for instance, has still its serious aspect, although we should no longer think of rejoicing like children that we have escaped from an outgrown control, although we have achieved not only our national but our moral independence and know it far too profoundly to make a talk about it, and although an Englishman can join in the celebration without a scruple. For, stripped of the temporary associations which gave rise to it, it is now the moment when by common consent we pause to become conscious of our national life and to rejoice in it, to recall what our country has done for each of us and to ask ourselves what we can do for the country in return.

So to the indifferent inquirer who asks why Memorial Day is still kept up we may answer, It celebrates and solemnly reaffirms from year to year a national act of enthusiasm and faith. It embodies in the most impressive form our belief that to act with enthusiasm and faith is the condition of acting greatly. To fight out a war you must believe something and want something with all your might. So must you do to carry anything else to an end worth reaching. More than that, you must be willing to commit yourself to a course, perhaps a long and hard one, without being able to foresee exactly where you will come out. All that is required of you is that you should go somewhither as hard as ever you can. The rest belongs to fate. One may fall—at the beginning of the charge or at the top of the earthworks—but in no other way can he reach the rewards of victory.

When it was felt so deeply as it was on both sides that a man ought to take part in the war unless some conscientious scruple or strong practical reason made it impossible, was that feeling simply the requirement of a local majority that their neighbors should agree with them? I think not: I think the feeling was right—in the South as in the North. I think that as life is action and passion, it is required of a man that he should share the passion and action of his time at peril of being judged not to have lived.

If this be so, the use of this day is obvious. It is true that I cannot argue a man into a desire. If he says to me, Why should I wish to know the secrets of philosophy? Why seek to decipher the hidden laws of creation that are graven upon the tablets of the rocks, or to unravel the history of civilization that is woven in the tissue of our jurisprudence, or to do any great work, either of speculation or of practical affairs? I cannot answer him; or, at least my answer is as little worth making for any effect it will have upon his wishes as if he asked, why should I eat this or drink that? You must begin by wanting to. But, although desire cannot be imparted by argument, it can be by contagion. Feeling begets feeling, and great feeling begets great feeling. We can hardly share the emotions that make this day to us the most sacred day of the year and embody them in ceremonial pomp without in some degree imparting them to those who come after us. I believe from the bottom of my heart that our memorial halls and statues and tablets, the tattered flags of our regiments gathered in the Statehouses, and this day with its funeral march and decorated graves, are worth more to our young men by way of chastening and inspiration than the monuments of another hundred years of peaceful life could be.

But even if I am wrong, even if those, who come after us are to forget all that we hold dear, and the future is to teach and kindle its children in ways as yet unrevealed, it is enough for us that this day is dear and sacred.

Accidents may call up the events of the war. You see a battery of guns go by at a trot, and for a moment you are back at White Oak Swamp or Antietam or on the Jerusalem Road. You hear a few shots fired in the distance, and for an instant your heart stops as you say to yourself, The skirmishers are at it, and listen for the long roll of fire from the main line. You meet an old comrade after many years of absence; he recalls the moment when you were nearly surrounded by the enemy, and again there comes up to you that swift and cunning thinking on which once hung life and freedom—Shall I stand the best chance if I try the pistol or the sabre on that man who means to stop me? Will he get his carbine free before I reach him, or can I kill him first? These and the thousand other events we have known are called up, I say, by accident, and, apart from accident, they lie forgotten.

But as surely as this day comes round we are in the presence of the dead. For one hour, twice a year at least—at the regimental dinner, where the ghosts sit at table more numerous than the living, and on this day when we decorate their graves—the dead come back and live with us.

I see them now, more than I can number, as once I saw them on this earth. They are the same bright figures, or their counterparts, that come also before your eyes; and when I speak of those who were my brothers the same words describe yours.

I see a fair-haired lad, a lieutenant, and a captain on whom life had begun somewhat to tell, but still young, sitting by the long mess-table in camp before the regiment left the State, and wondering how many of those who gathered in our tent could hope to see the end of what was then beginning. For neither of them was that destiny reserved. I remember, as I awoke from my first long stupor in the hospital after the battle of Ball's Bluff, I heard the doctor say, "He was a beautiful boy," and I knew that one of those two speakers was no more. The other, after passing harmless through all the previous battles, went into Fredericksburg with strange premonition of the end and there met his fate.

I see another youthful lieutenant as I saw him in the Seven Days, when I looked down the line at Glendale. The officers were at the head of their companies. The advance was beginning. We caught each other's eye and saluted. When next I looked he was gone.

I see the brother of the last—the flame of genius and daring in his face—as he rode before us into the wood of Antietam, out of which came only dead and deadly wounded men. So, a little later, he rode to his death at the head of his cavalry in the Valley.

In the portraits of some of those who fell in the civil wars of England, Vandyke has fixed on canvas the type who stand before my memory. Young and gracious figures, somewhat remote and proud, but with a melancholy and sweet kindness. There is upon their faces the shadow of approaching fate and the glory of generous acceptance of it. I may say of them, as I once heard it said of two Frenchmen, relics of the *ancien régime*, "They were very gentle. They cared nothing for their lives." High breeding, romantic chivalry—we who have seen these men can never believe that the power of money or the enervation of pleasure has put an end to them. We know that life may still be lifted into poetry and lit with spiritual charm.

But the men, not less, perhaps even more, characteristic of New England, were the Puritans of our day—for the Puritan still lives in New England, thank God! and will live there so long as New England lives and keeps her old renown. New England is not dead yet. She still is mother of a race of conquerors. Stern men, little given to the expression of their feelings, sometimes careless of the graces, but fertile, tenacious, and knowing only duty. Each of you, as I do, thinks of a hundred such that he has known. I see one—grandson of a hard rider of the Revolution and bearer of his historic name—who was with us at Fair Oaks, and afterwards for five days and nights in front of the enemy the only sleep that he would take was what he could snatch sitting erect in his uniform and resting his back against a hut. He fell at Gettysburg.

His brother, a surgeon, who rode, as our surgeons so often did, wherever the troops would go, I saw kneeling in ministration to a wounded man just in rear of our line at Antietam, his horse's bridle round his arm—the next moment his ministrations were ended. His senior associate survived all the wounds and perils of the war, but, not yet through with duty as he understood it, fell in helping the helpless poor who were dying of cholera in a Western city.

I see another quiet figure of virtuous life and silent ways, not much heard of until our left was turned at Petersburg. He was in command of the regiment as he saw our comrades driven in. He threw back his left wing and the advancing tide of defeat was shattered against his iron wall. He saved an army corps from disaster, and then a round shot ended all for him.

There is one who on this day is always present to my mind. He entered the army at nineteen, a second lieutenant. In the Wilderness, already at the head of his regiment, he fell, using the moment that was left him of life to give all of his little fortune to his soldiers. I saw him in camp, on the march, in action. I crossed debatable land with him when we were rejoining the Army together. I observed him in every kind of duty, and never in all the time that I knew him did I see him fail to choose that alternative of conduct which was most disagreeable to himself. He was indeed a Puritan in all his virtues without the Puritan austerity; for, when duty was at an end, he who had been the master and leader became the chosen companion in every pleasure that a man might honestly enjoy. In action he was sublime. His few surviving companions will never forget the awful spectacle of his advance alone with his company in the streets of Fredericksburg. In less than sixty seconds he would become the focus of a hidden and annihilating fire from a semicircle of houses. His first platoon had vanished under it in an instant, ten men falling dead by his side.

He had quietly turned back to where the other half of his company was waiting, had given the order, "Second Platoon, forward!" and was again moving
on, in obedience to superior command, to certain and useless death, when
the order he was obeying was countermanded. The end was distant only a
few seconds; but if you had seen him with his indifferent carriage, and sword
swinging from his finger like a cane, you would never have suspected that he
was doing more than conducting a company drill on the camp parade ground.
He was little more than a boy, but the grizzled corps commanders knew and
admired him; and for us, who not only admired but loved, his death seemed
to end a portion of our life also.

There is one grave and commanding presence that you all would recognize, for his life has become a part of our common history. Who does not
remember the leader of the assault at the mine of Petersburg? the solitary
horseman in front of Port Hudson, whom a foeman worthy of him bade his
soldiers spare, from love and admiration of such gallant bearing? Who does
not still hear the echo of those eloquent lips after the war teaching reconciliation and peace? I may not do more than allude to his death, fit ending of his
life. All that the world has a right to know has been told by a beloved friend
in a book wherein friendship has found no need to exaggerate facts that speak
for themselves. I knew him; and I may even say I knew him well; yet, until
that book appeared, I had not known the governing motive of his soul. I had
admired him as a hero. When I read, I learned to revere him as a saint. His
strength was not in honor alone but in religion; and those who do not share
his creed must see that it was on the wings of religious faith that he mounted
above even valiant deeds into an empyrean of ideal life.

I have spoken of some of the men who were near to me among others very
near and dear, not because their lives have become historic, but because their
lives are the type of what every soldier has known and seen in his own company. In the great democracy of self-devotion private and general stand side
by side. Unmarshaled save by their own deeds, the armies of the dead sweep
before us, "wearing their wounds like stars." It is not because the men I have
mentioned were my friends that I have spoken of them, but, I repeat, because
they are types. I speak of those whom I have seen. But you all have known
such; you, too, remember!

It is not of the dead alone that we think on this day. There are those still
living whose sex forbade them to offer their lives, but who gave instead their
happiness. Which of us has not been lifted above himself by the sight of one
of those lovely, lonely women, around whom the wand of sorrow has traced
its excluding circle—set apart, even when surrounded by loving friends who
would fain bring back joy to their lives? I think of one whom the poor of a

great city know as their benefactress and friend. I think of one who has lived not less greatly in the midst of her children, to whom she has taught such lessons as may not be heard elsewhere from mortal lips. The story of these and of their sisters we must pass in reverent silence. All that may be said has been said by one of their own sex:

> But when the days of golden dreams had perished,
> And even despair was powerless to destroy;
> Then did I learn how existence could be cherished,
> Strengthened, and fed without the aid of joy.
>
> Then did I check the tears of useless passion,
> Weaned my young soul from yearning after thine;
> Sternly denied its burning wish to hasten
> Down to that tomb already more than mine.

Comrades, some of the associations of this day are not only triumphant but joyful. Not all of those with whom we once stood shoulder to shoulder—not all of those whom we once loved and revered—are gone. On this day we still meet our companions in the freezing winter bivouacs and in those dreadful summer marches where every faculty of the soul seemed to depart one after another, leaving only a dumb animal power to set the teeth and to persist—a blind belief that somewhere and at last there was rest and water. On this day, at least, we still meet and rejoice in the closest tie which is possible between men—a tie which suffering has made indissoluble for better, for worse.

When we meet thus, when we do honor to the dead in terms that must sometimes embrace the living, we do not deceive ourselves. We attribute no special merit to a man for having served when all were serving. We know that if the armies of our war did anything worth remembering, the credit belongs not mainly to the individuals who did it, but to average human nature. We also know very well that we cannot live in associations with the past alone, and we admit that if we would be worthy of the past we must find new fields for action or thought and make for ourselves new careers.

But, nevertheless, the generation that carried on the war has been set apart by its experience. Through our great good fortune, in our youth our hearts were touched with fire. It was given to us to learn at the outset that life is a profound and passionate thing. While we are permitted to scorn nothing but indifference, and do not pretend to undervalue the worldly rewards of ambition, we have seen with our own eyes beyond and above the gold fields the snowy heights of honor, and it is for us to bear the report to those who come after us. But above all, we have learned that whether a man accepts from Fortune her spade, and will look downward and dig, or from Aspiration her axe and cord, and will scale the ice, the one and only success which it is his to command is to bring to his work a mighty heart.

Such hearts—ah me, how many!—were stilled twenty years ago; and to us who remain behind is left this day of memories. Every year—in the full tide of spring—at the height of the symphony of flowers and love and life—there comes a pause, and through the silence we hear the lonely pipe of death. Year after year lovers wandering under the apple boughs and through the clover and deep grass are surprised with sudden tears as they see black veiled figures stealing through the morning to a soldier's grave. Year after year the comrades of the dead follow with public honor, procession and commemorative flags and funeral march—honor and grief from us who stand almost alone, and have seen the best and noblest of our generation pass away.

But grief is not the end of all. I seem to hear the funeral march become a paean. I see beyond the forest the moving banners of a hidden column. Our dead brothers still live for us, and bid us think of life, not death—of life to which in their youth they lent the passion and glory of the spring. As I listen, the great chorus of life and joy begins again, and amid the awful orchestra of seen and unseen powers and destinies of good and evil our trumpets sound once more a note of daring, hope, and will.

Thanksgiving Proclamation

GEORGE WASHINGTON

After the Fourth of July, Thanksgiving Day is our most observed national holiday. The tradition harks back to the colonists of Plymouth Plantation, Massachusetts, who, after their first harvest, held a celebratory feast in the fall of 1621—a three-day celebration in which local Native American chiefs and tribesmen participated. But the first national Thanksgiving, authorized by the federal government, took place in 1789, the first year of George Washington's presidency. President Washington issued this proclamation recognizing November 26 as "a day of public thanksgiving and prayer."*

What, according to Washington's proclamation, are the blessings for which the earliest citizens of the United States should have been grateful? What list of blessings would a modern-day proclamation include? Can the giving of thanks be commanded—should it be commanded—by governmental authority? In the eighteenth century, thanksgiving days were observed by prayer and fasting; do today's ritual feasting and drinking alter in any way the intended purpose of the holiday? How does Thanksgiving Day matter to your identity as an American citizen?

By the President of the United States of America. A Proclamation.

Whereas it is the duty of all Nations to acknowledge the providence of Almighty God, to obey his will, to be grateful for his benefits, and humbly

---

* *The initiative for this proclamation came from the House of Representatives, but support was hardly unanimous. Some representatives objected that such imitations of European practices would make a mockery of genuine expressions of prayer and thanksgiving, while others objected that expressions of gratitude are private matters that the federal government has no business mandating. But a majority favoring a presidential proclamation prevailed.*

to implore his protection and favor, and Whereas both Houses of Congress have by their joint Committee requested me "to recommend to the People of the United States a day of public thanks-giving and prayer to be observed by acknowledging with grateful hearts the many signal favors of Almighty God, especially by affording them an opportunity peaceably to establish a form of government for their safety and happiness."

Now therefore I do recommend and assign Thursday the 26th. day of November next to be devoted by the People of these States to the service of that great and glorious Being, who is the beneficent Author of all the good that was, that is, or that will be. That we may then all unite in rendering unto him our sincere and humble thanks, for his kind care and protection of the People of this country previous to their becoming a Nation, for the signal and manifold mercies, and the favorable interpositions of his providence, which we experienced in the course and conclusion of the late war, for the great degree of tranquillity, union, and plenty, which we have since enjoyed, for the peaceable and rational manner in which we have been enabled to establish constitutions of government for our safety and happiness, and particularly the national One now lately instituted, for the civil and religious liberty with which we are blessed, and the means we have of acquiring and diffusing useful knowledge and in general for all the great and various favors which he hath been pleased to confer upon us.

And also that we may then unite in most humbly offering our prayers and supplications to the great Lord and Ruler of Nations and beseech him to pardon our national and other transgressions, to enable us all, whether in public or private stations, to perform our several and relative duties properly and punctually, to render our national government a blessing to all the People, by constantly being a government of wise, just and constitutional laws, discreetly and faithfully executed and obeyed, to protect and guide all Sovereigns and Nations (especially such as have shown kindness unto us) and to bless them with good government, peace, and concord. To promote the knowledge and practice of true religion and virtue, and the encrease of science among them and Us, and generally to grant unto all Mankind such a degree of temporal prosperity as he alone knows to be best.

Two Thanksgiving Day Gentlemen

O. HENRY

Maintaining traditions in America is neither easy nor always welcome. Times change. Rituals ossify. Their meanings become obscured. For those who are down and out or who live alone, even our most beloved holidays can be depressing. More deeply, upholding traditions may be at odds with our devotion to progress or self-interest. These issues are humorously but powerfully exposed in this short story (1905) by O. Henry (pseudonym for William Sydney Porter [1862–1910]), who casts an ironic and irreverent eye on Thanksgiving Day—perhaps on institutionalized ritual altogether. Every Thanksgiving for the past nine years, Stuffy Pete, a homeless man, has been summoned from his bench in New York's Union Square by an "Old Gentleman," who takes him to a restaurant, orders up a sumptuous dinner, and sits by watching Stuffy eat. This year, however, Stuffy is interrupted on his way to the park when "two old ladies of ancient family" invite him into their home and serve him a meal more sumptuous than his traditional fare. By the time he meets the old gentleman at the familiar bench, Stuffy is already stuffed to the gills. The sequel raises poignant questions about Thanksgiving and about American traditions in general.

What is the meaning of the story's title? Are the "traditions" reported in this story praiseworthy? Does the outcome of the story vindicate the narrator's seeming irreverence for tradition? In what spirit, and in what manner, should we celebrate Thanksgiving? Other holidays?

There is one day that is ours. There is one day when all we Americans who are not self-made go back to the old home to eat saleratus biscuits and marvel how much nearer to the porch the old pump looks than it used to. Bless the day. President Roosevelt gives it to us. We hear some talk of the Puritans, but don't just remember who they were. Bet we can lick 'em, anyhow, if they try to land again. Plymouth Rocks? Well, that sounds more familiar. Lots of us have had to come down to hens since the Turkey Trust got its work in. But somebody in Washington is leaking out advance information to 'em about these Thanksgiving proclamations.

The big city east of the cranberry bogs had made Thanksgiving Day an institution. The last Thursday in November is the only day in the year on which it recognizes the part of America lying across the ferries. It is the one day that is purely American. Yes, a day of celebration, exclusively American.

And now for the story which is to prove to you that we have traditions on this side of the ocean that are becoming older at a much rapider rate than those of England are—thanks to our git-up and enterprise.

Stuffy Pete took his seat on the third bench to the right as you enter Union Square from the east, at the walk opposite the fountain. Every Thanksgiving Day for nine years he had taken his seat there promptly at one o'clock. For every time he had done so things had happened to him—Charles Dickensy things that swelled his waistcoat above his heart, and equally on the other side.

But to-day Stuffy Pete's appearance at the annual trysting place seemed to have been rather the result of habit than of the yearly hunger which, as the philanthropists seem to think, afflicts the poor at such extended intervals.

Certainly Pete was not hungry. He had just come from a feast that had left him of his powers barely those of respiration and locomotion. His eyes were like two pale gooseberries firmly imbedded in a swollen and gravy-smeared mask of putty. His breath came in short wheezes; a senatorial roll of adipose tissue denied a fashionable set to his upturned coat collar. Buttons that had been sewed upon his clothes by kind Salvation fingers a week before flew like popcorn, strewing the earth around him. Ragged he was, with a split shirt front open to the wish-bone; but the November breeze, carrying fine snowflakes, brought him only a grateful coolness. For Stuffy Pete was overcharged with the caloric produced by a super-bountiful dinner, beginning with oysters and ending with plum pudding, and including (it seemed to him) all the roast turkey and baked potatoes and chicken salad and squash pie and ice cream in the world. Wherefore he sat, gorged, and gazed upon the world with after-dinner contempt.

The meal had been an unexpected one. He was passing a redbrick mansion near the beginning of Fifth Avenue, in which lived two old ladies of ancient family and a reverence for traditions. They even denied the existence of New York, and believed that Thanksgiving Day was declared solely for Washington Square. One of their traditional habits was to station a servant at the postern gate with orders to admit the first hungry wayfarer that came along after the hour of noon had struck, and banquet him to a finish. Stuffy Pete happened to pass by on his way to the park, and the seneschals gathered him in and upheld the custom of the castle.

After Stuffy Pete had gazed straight before him for ten minutes he was conscious of a desire for a more varied field of vision. With a tremendous effort he moved his head slowly to the left. And then his eyes bulged out fearfully, and his breath ceased, and the rough-shod ends of his short legs wriggled and rustled on the gravel.

For the Old Gentleman was coming across Fourth Avenue toward his bench.

Every Thanksgiving Day for nine years the Old Gentleman had come there and found Stuffy Pete on his bench. That was a thing that the Old Gentleman was trying to make a tradition of. Every Thanksgiving Day for nine years he had found Stuffy there, and had led him to a restaurant and watched him eat a big dinner. They do those things in England unconsciously. But this is a young country, and nine years is not so bad. The Old Gentleman was a stanch American patriot, and considered himself a pioneer in American tradition. In order to become picturesque we must keep on doing one thing for a long time without ever letting it get away from us. Something like collecting the weekly dimes in industrial insurance. Or cleaning the streets.

The Old Gentleman moved, straight and stately, toward the Institution that he was rearing. Truly, the annual feeding of Stuffy Pete was nothing national in its character, such as the Magna Charta or jam for breakfast was in England. But it was a step. It was almost feudal. It showed, at least, that a Custom was not impossible to New Y—ahem!—America.

The Old Gentleman was thin and tall and sixty. He was dressed all in black, and wore the old-fashioned kind of glasses that won't stay on our nose. His hair was whiter and thinner than it had been last year, and he seemed to make more use of his big, knobby cane with the crooked handle.

As his established benefactor came up Stuffy wheezed and shuddered like some woman's over-fat pug when a street dog bristles up at him. He would have flown, but all the skill of Santos-Dumont could not have separated him from his bench. Well had the myrmidons of the two old ladies done their work.

"Good morning," said the Old Gentleman. "I am glad to perceive that the vicissitudes of another year have spared you to move in health about the beautiful world. For that blessing alone this day of thanksgiving is well proclaimed to each of us. If you will come with me, my man, I will provide you with a dinner that should make your physical being accord with the mental."

That is what the Old Gentleman said every time. Every Thanksgiving Day for nine years. The words themselves almost formed an Institution. Nothing could be compared with them except the Declaration of Independence.

Always before they had been music in Stuffy's ears. But now he looked up at the Old Gentleman's face with tearful agony in his own. The fine snow almost sizzled when it fell upon his perspiring brow. But the Old Gentleman shivered a little and turned his back to the wind.

Stuffy had always wondered why the Old Gentleman spoke his speech rather sadly. He did not know that it was because he was wishing every time that he had a son to succeed him. A son who would come there after he was gone—a son who would stand proud and strong before some subsequent Stuffy, and say: "In memory of my father." Then it would be an Institution.

But the Old Gentleman had no relatives. He lived in rented rooms in one of the decayed old family brownstone mansions in one of the quiet streets east of the park. In the winter he raised fuchsias in a little conservatory the size of a steamer trunk. In the spring he walked in the Easter parade. In the summer he lived at a farmhouse in the New Jersey hills, and sat in a wicker armchair, speaking of a butterfly, the ornithoptera amphrisius, that he hoped to find some day. In the autumn he fed Stuffy a dinner. These were the Old Gentleman's occupations.

Stuffy Pete looked up at him for a half minute, stewing and helpless in his own self-pity. The Old Gentleman's eyes were bright with the giving-pleasure. His face was getting more lined each year, but his little black necktie was in as jaunty a bow as ever, and his linen was beautiful and white, and his gray mustache was curled gracefully at the ends. And then Stuffy made a noise that sounded like peas bubbling in a pot. Speech was intended; and as the Old Gentleman had heard the sounds nine times before, he rightly construed them into Stuffy's old formula of acceptance.

"Thankee, sir. I'll go with ye, and much obliged. I'm very hungry, sir."

The coma of repletion had not prevented from entering Stuffy's mind the conviction that he was the basis of an Institution. His Thanksgiving appetite was not his own; it belonged by all the sacred rights of established custom, if not by the actual Statute of Limitations, to this kind old gentleman who had preëmpted it. True, America is free; but in order to establish tradition some one must be a repentend—a repeating decimal. The heroes are not all heroes of steel and gold. See one here that wielded only weapons of iron, badly silvered, and tin.

The Old Gentleman led his annual protégé southward to the restaurant, and to the table where the feast had always occurred. They were recognized.

"Here comes de old guy," said a waiter, "dat blows dat same bum to a meal every Thanksgiving."

The Old Gentleman sat across the table glowing like a smoked pearl at his corner-stone of future ancient Tradition. The waiters heaped the table with holiday food—and Stuffy, with a sign that was mistaken for hunger's expression, raised knife and fork and carved for himself a crown of imperishable bay.

No more valiant hero ever fought his way through the ranks of an enemy. Turkey, chops, soups, vegetables, pies, disappeared before him as fast as they could be served. Gorged nearly to the uttermost when he entered the restaurant, the smell of food had almost caused him to lose his honor as a gentleman, but he rallied like a true knight. He saw the look of beneficent happiness on the Old Gentleman's face—a happier look than even the fuchsias and the ornithoptera amphrisius had ever brought to it—and he had not the heart to see it wane.

In an hour Stuffy leaned back with a battle won.

"Thankee kindly, sir," he puffed like a leaky steampipe; "thankee kindly for a hearty meal."

Then he arose heavily with glazed eyes and started toward the kitchen. A waiter turned him about like a top, and pointed him toward the door. The Old Gentleman carefully counted out $1.30 in silver change, leaving three nickels for the waiter.

They parted as they did each year at the door, the Old Gentleman going south, Stuffy north.

Around the first corner Stuffy turned, and stood for one minute. Then he seemed to puff out his rags as an owl puffs out his feathers, and fell to the sidewalk like a sunstricken horse.

When the ambulance came the young surgeon and the driver cursed softly at his weight. There was no smell of whiskey to justify a transfer to the patrol wagon, so Stuffy and his two dinners went to the hospital. There they stretched him on a bed and began to test him for strange diseases, with the hope of getting a chance at some problem with the bare steel.

And lo! an hour later another ambulance brought the Old Gentleman. And they laid him on another bed and spoke of appendicitis, for he looked good for the bill.

But pretty soon one of the young doctors met one of the young nurses whose eyes he liked, and stopped to chat with her about the cases.

"That nice old gentleman over there, now," he said, "you wouldn't think that was a case of almost starvation. Proud old family, I guess. He told me he hadn't eaten a thing for three days."

6

Making One Out of Many

Immigration and Assimilation

True Americanism

Theodore Roosevelt

America, it is rightly said, is the world's first cosmopolitan nation. Our fellow citizens come from every corner of the earth. A small few may still trace their origins to the original settlers, but most of us are children or grandchildren of immigrants. What, then, do we have in common, and what unites us as Americans? Today, questions of identity are often discussed under the heading of multiculturalism: people are viewed and view themselves as members of racial and ethnic subcultures, as hyphenated Americans (for example, African-, Mexican-, Chinese-, etc.). Yet this entire volume assumes that notwithstanding our enriching differences, there are deep beliefs, sentiments, and practices that do and should unite us as American citizens.

Questions about our identity are not new. They were especially prominent in the late nineteenth and early twentieth centuries, as European immigrants, not always warmly welcomed, flooded the American shores. In this essay (1894), Theodore Roosevelt (1858–1916) addresses the question of immigration and American identity. What criteria does he suggest for becoming and being American? Are they sufficient to make one out of many? Considering the even greater ethnic and religious heterogeneity of modern-day America, how might you modify Roosevelt's suggestions regarding "True Americanism"?

Patriotism was once defined as "the last refuge of a scoundrel"; and somebody has recently remarked that when Dr. Johnson gave this definition he was ignorant of the infinite possibilities contained in the word "reform." Of course both gibes were quite justifiable, in so far as they were aimed at people who use noble names to cloak base purposes. Equally of course the man shows little wisdom and a low sense of duty who fails to see that love of country is one of the elemental virtues, even though scoundrels play upon it for their own selfish ends; and, inasmuch as abuses continually grow up in civic life as in all other kinds of life, the statesman is indeed a weakling who hesitates to reform these abuses because the word "reform" is often on the lips of men who are silly or dishonest.

What is true of patriotism and reform is true also of Americanism. There are plenty of scoundrels always ready to try to belittle reform movements or to bolster up existing iniquities in the name of Americanism; but this does not alter the fact that the man who can do most in this country is and must be the man whose Americanism is most sincere and intense. Outrageous though it is to use a noble idea as the cloak for evil, it is still worse to assail the noble idea itself because it can thus be used. The men who do iniquity in the name of patriotism, of reform, of Americanism, are merely one small division of the class that has always existed and will always exist,—the class of hypocrites and demagogues, the class that is always prompt to steal the watchwords of righteousness and use them in the interests of evil-doing. . . .

But we must never let our contempt for these men blind us to the nobility of the idea which they strive to degrade.

We Americans have many grave problems to solve, many threatening evils to fight, and many deeds to do, if, as we hope and believe, we have the wisdom, the strength, the courage, and the virtue to do them. But we must face facts as they are. We must neither surrender ourselves to a foolish optimism, nor succumb to a timid and ignoble pessimism. Our nation is that one among all the nations of the earth which holds in its hands the fate of the coming years. We enjoy exceptional advantages, and are menaced by exceptional dangers; and all signs indicate that we shall either fail greatly or succeed greatly. I firmly believe that we shall succeed; but we must not foolishly blink the dangers by which we are threatened, for that is the way to fail. On the contrary, we must soberly set to work to find out all we can about the existence and extent of every evil, must acknowledge it to be such, and must then attack it with unyielding resolution. There are many such evils, and each must be fought after a fashion; yet there is one quality which we must bring to the solution of every problem,—that is, an intense and fervid Americanism. We shall never be successful over the dangers that confront us; we shall never achieve true greatness, nor reach the lofty ideal which the founders and preservers of our mighty Federal Republic have set before us, unless we are Americans in heart and soul, in spirit and purpose, keenly alive to the responsibility implied in the very name of American, and proud beyond measure of the glorious privilege of bearing it. There are two or three sides to the question of Americanism, and two or three senses in which the word "Americanism" can be used to express the antithesis of what is unwholesome and undesirable. In the first place we wish to be broadly American and national, as opposed to being local or sectional. We do not wish, in politics, in literature, or in art, to develop that unwholesome parochial spirit, that over-exaltation of the little community at the expense of the great nation, which produces what has been described as the patriotism of the village, the patriotism of the belfry. . . . Indeed, there is, all through our life, very much less of this parochial spirit than there was formerly. Still there is an occasional outcropping here and there; and it is just as well that we should keep steadily in mind the futility of talking of a Northern literature or a Southern literature, an Eastern or a Western school of art or science. Joel Chandler Harris is emphatically a national writer; so is Mark Twain. They do not write merely for Georgia or Missouri or California any more than for Illinois or Connecticut; they write as Americans and for all people who can read English. St. Gaudens lives in New York; but his work is just as distinctive of Boston or Chicago. It is of very great consequence that we should have a full and ripe literary development in the United States, but it is not of the least consequence whether New York, or Boston, or Chicago, or San Francisco becomes the literary or artistic centre of the United States.

There is a second side to this question of a broad Americanism, however. The patriotism of the village or the belfry is bad, but the lack of all patriotism is even worse. There are philosophers who assure us that, in the future, patriotism will be regarded not as a virtue at all, but merely as a mental stage in the journey toward a state of feeling when our patriotism will include the whole human race and all the world. This may be so; but the age of which these philosophers speak is still several aeons distant. In fact, philosophers of this type are so very advanced that they are of no practical service to the present generation. It may be, that in ages so remote that we cannot now understand any of the feelings of those who will dwell in them, patriotism will no longer be regarded as a virtue, exactly as it may be that in those remote ages people will look down upon and disregard monogamic marriage; but as things now are and have been for two or three thousand years past, and are likely to be for two or three thousand years to come, the words "home" and "country" mean a great deal. Nor do they show any tendency to lose their significance. At present, treason, like adultery, ranks as one of the worst of all possible crimes.

One may fall very far short of treason and yet be an undesirable citizen in the community. The man who becomes Europeanized, who loses his power of doing good work on this side of the water, and who loses his love for his native land, is not a traitor; but he is a silly and undesirable citizen. He is as emphatically a noxious element in our body politic as is the man who comes here from abroad and remains a foreigner. Nothing will more quickly or more surely disqualify a man from doing good work in the world than the acquirement of that flaccid habit of mind which its possessors style cosmopolitanism.

It is not only necessary to Americanize the immigrants of foreign birth who settle among us, but it is even more necessary for those among us who are by birth and descent already Americans not to throw away our birthright, and, with incredible and contemptible folly, wander back to bow down before the alien gods whom our forefathers forsook. . . .

It is because certain classes of our people still retain their spirit of colonial dependence on, and exaggerated deference to, European opinion, that they fail to accomplish what they ought to.

It is precisely along the lines where we have worked most independently that we have accomplished the greatest results; and it is in those professions where there has been no servility to, but merely a wise profiting by foreign experience, that we have produced our greatest men. Our soldiers and statesmen and orators; our explorers, our wilderness-winners, and commonwealth-builders; the men who have made our laws and seen that they were executed; and the other men whose energy and ingenuity have created our marvelous material prosperity—all these have been men who have drawn wisdom from the experience of every age and nation, but who have nevertheless thought, and worked, and conquered, and lived, and died, purely as Americans; and on the whole they have done better work than has been done in any other country during the short period of our national life.

On the other hand, it is in those professions where our people have striven hardest to mold themselves in conventional European forms that they have succeeded least; and this holds true to the present day, the failure being of course most conspicuous where the man takes up his abode in Europe; where he becomes a second-rate European, because he is over-civilized, over-sensitive, over-refined, and has lost the hardihood and manly courage by which alone he can conquer in the keen struggle of our national life. Be it remembered, too, that this same being does not really become a European; he only ceases being an American, and becomes nothing. . . .

The third sense in which the word "Americanism" may be employed is with reference to the Americanizing of the newcomers to our shores. We must Americanize them in every way, in speech, in political ideas and principles, and in their way of looking at the relations between Church and State. We welcome the German or the Irishman who becomes an American. We have no use for the German or Irishman who remains such. We do not wish German-Americans and Irish-Americans who figure as such in our social and political life; we want only Americans, and, provided they are such, we do not care whether they are of native or of Irish or of German ancestry. We have no room in any healthy

American community for a German-American vote or an Irish-American vote, and it is contemptible demagogy to put planks into any party platform with the purpose of catching such a vote. We have no room for any people who do not act and vote simply as Americans, and as nothing else. Moreover, we have as little use for people who carry religious prejudices into our politics as for those who carry prejudices of caste or nationality. We stand unalterably in favor of the public-school system in its entirety. We believe that English, and no other language, is that in which all the school exercises should be conducted. We are against any division of the school fund, and against any appropriation of public money for sectarian purposes. We are against any recognition whatever by the State in any shape or form of State-aided parochial schools. But we are equally opposed to any discrimination against or for a man because of his creed. We demand that all citizens, Protestant and Catholic, Jew and Gentile, shall have fair treatment in every way; that all alike shall have their rights guaranteed them. The very reasons that make us unqualified in our opposition to State-aided sectarian schools make us equally bent that, in the management of our public schools, the adherents of each creed shall be given exact and equal justice, wholly without regard to their religious affiliations; that trustees, superintendents, teachers, scholars, all alike shall be treated without any reference whatsoever to the creed they profess. We maintain that it is an outrage, in voting for a man for any position, whether State or national, to take into account his religious faith, provided only he is a good American....

The mighty tide of immigration to our shores has brought in its train much of good and much of evil; and whether the good or the evil shall predominate depends mainly on whether these newcomers do or do not throw themselves heartily into our national life, cease to be Europeans, and become Americans like the rest of us. More than a third of the people of the Northern States are of foreign birth or parentage. An immense number of them have become completely Americanized, and these stand on exactly the same plane as the descendants of any Puritan, Cavalier, or Knickerbocker among us, and do their full and honorable share of the nation's work. But where immigrants, or the sons of immigrants, do not heartily and in good faith throw in their lot with us, but cling to the speech, the customs, the ways of life, and the habits of thought of the Old World which they have left, they thereby harm both themselves and us. If they remain alien elements, unassimilated, and with interests separate from ours, they are mere obstructions to the current of our national life, and, moreover, can get no good from it themselves. In fact, though we ourselves also suffer from their perversity, it is they who really suffer most. It is an immense benefit to the European immigrant to change him into an American citizen. To bear the name of American is to bear the most honorable titles; and whoever does not so believe has no business to bear the name at all, and, if he comes from Europe, the sooner he goes back there the better. . . . We freely extend the hand of welcome and of good-fellowship to every man, no matter what his creed or birthplace, who comes here honestly intent on becoming a good United States citizen like the rest of us; but we have a right, and it is our duty, to demand that he shall indeed become so and shall not confuse the issues with which we are struggling by introducing among us Old-World quarrels and prejudices. . . . But I wish to be distinctly understood on one point.

Americanism is a question of spirit, conviction, and purpose, not of creed or birthplace. The politician who bids for the Irish or German vote, or the Irishman or German who votes as an Irishman or German, is despicable, for all citizens of this commonwealth should vote solely as Americans; but he is not a whit less despicable than the voter who votes against a good American, merely because that American happens to have been born in Ireland or Germany. Know-nothingism, in any form, is as utterly un-American as foreignism. It is a base outrage to oppose a man because of his religion or birthplace, and all good citizens will hold any such effort in abhorrence. A Scandinavian, a German, or an Irishman who has really become an American has the right to stand on exactly the same footing as any native-born citizen in the land, and is just as much entitled to the friendship and support, social and political, of his neighbors. . . .

We Americans can only do our allotted task well if we face it steadily and bravely, seeing but not fearing the dangers. Above all we must stand shoulder to shoulder, not asking as to the ancestry or creed of our comrades, but only demanding that they be in very truth Americans, and that we all work together, heart, hand, and head, for the honor and the greatness of our common country.

O K*A*P*L*A*N! My K*A*P*L*A*N!

from The Education of H*Y*M*A*N K*A*P*L*A*N

Leonard Q. Ross

Huge numbers of European immigrants once entered the United States at Ellis Island, today a treasured monument to their arrival. Across from Ellis Island stands the Statue of Liberty, erected in 1896, to whose pedestal is affixed Emma Lazarus's poem "The New Colossus," which concludes with the words: "Give me your tired, your poor, / Your huddled masses yearning to breathe free, / The wretched refuse of your teeming shore. / Send these, the homeless, tempest-tossed to me, / I lift my lamp beside the golden door!" Once here, the new immigrants struggled not only to make a living in a foreign land but also to learn the language and ways of their adopted country. Many of them, after a long day's work, took evening classes to prepare for citizenship. A humorous yet touching (fictional) portrait of immigrant adult education is presented in this selection (1937) by Leo Rosten (using the pseudonym Leonard Q. Ross [1908–1997]), a noted humorist and journalist who was himself an immigrant from Poland. Mr. Kaplan, an irrepressible student in the beginners' class at the American Night Preparatory School for Adults—who insists on spelling his name with stars inserted between each of the letters—operates with a zany logic and a profound indifference to the promptings of his teacher, Mr. Parkhill. But his zeal for his new language and his new country are heartfelt and absolutely winning.

What does this selection reveal about Hyman Kaplan's attitude toward the English language? Toward America? Is there any serious point to be made for Mr. Kaplan's triumvirate of Washington, Lincoln, and Jake Popper? What about his final endorsement of what he calls "dat dip American idea, 'Business bafore pleasure!'"? Can you imagine yourself in Mr. Kaplan's shoes? Which is more important to Americanization: getting the

*facts straight and the ideas right, or having the right sentiments and atti-
tudes? Can humor and laughter contribute to making one out of many?*

Mr. Parkhill was not surprised when the first three students to participate in Recitation and Speech practice delivered eloquent orations on
"Abraham Lincoln," "Little George and the Sherry Tree," and "Wonderful U.S.,"
respectively. For the activities of the month of February had injected a patriot
fervor into the beginners' grade, an *amor patriae* which would last well into
March. There was a simple enough reason for this phenomenon: Mr. Robinson,
principal of the school, did not allow either Lincoln's or Washington's Birthday
to pass without appropriate ceremonies. On each occasion the whole student
body would crowd into Franklin Hall, the largest of the five rooms occupied
by the school, to commemorate the nativity of one of the two great Americans.

At the Lincoln assembly, Mr. Robinson always gave a long eulogy entitled
"The Great Emancipator." ("His name is inscribed on the immortal roll of
history, in flaming letters of eternal gold!") A "prize" student from the gradu-
ating class delivered a carefully corrected speech on "Lincoln and the Civil
War"—a rather short speech. Then Miss Higby recited "O Captain! My Captain!" to an audience which listened with reverently bated breath.

For the Washington convocation, the order of things was much the same.
Mr. Robinson's address was entitled "The Father of His Country." ("First in
war, first in peace, and first in the hearts of his countrymen—his name burns
in the hearts of true Americans, each letter a glowing ember, a symbol of
his glorious achievement!") The prize student's speech was on "Washington
and the American Revolution." And Miss Higby recited "My Country, 'Tis
of Thee." (Miss Higby often remarked that it was a sad commentary on our
native bards that there was no poem as *perfectly* appropriate for Washington
as "O Captain! My Captain!" was for Lincoln.)

The result of these patriotic rites was that for weeks afterward, each year, the
faculty would be deluged with compositions on Lincoln, even little poems on
Lincoln or Washington. Night after night, the classrooms echoed with the hallowed phrases "1776," "Father of His Country," "The Great Emancipator," "The
Civil War," "Honest Abe," "Valley Forge." Mr. Parkhill found it a nerve-sapping
ordeal. He thought of this annual period as "the Ides of February and March."

"I will spik ona Garibaldi," announced Miss Caravello, the fourth student
to face the class.

Mr. Parkhill felt a surge of gratitude within him. It was, however, short-
lived.

"Garibaldi—joosta lak Washington! Firsta da war, firsta da peace, firsta da
heartsa da countrymens!"

In the middle of the front row, Mr. Hyman Kaplan printed his name aimlessly for the dozenth time on a large sheet of foolscap, and sighed. Mr. Kaplan had been sighing, quite audibly, throughout each of the successive historico-patriotic declamations. Mr. Parkhill felt a distinct sense of comradeship with Mr. Kaplan.

"Hisa name burns, lak Mist' Principal say. Da 'g,' da 'a,' da 'r,' da 'i,' . . ."Miss Caravello articulated the letters with gusto. Mr Norman Bloom sharpened his pencil. Miss Schneiderman stared into space, vacantly. Miss Moskowitz rounded out the latest of a lengthy series of yawns. Mr. Parkhill frowned.

"Horray Washington! Viva Garibaldi!"

In a fine Latin flush, Miss Caravello resumed her seat. Mr. Kaplan sighed again, rather publicly. E*N*N*U*I was stamped in Mr. Kaplan's features.

"Corrections, please," Mr. Parkhill announced, trying to be as cheery as possible.

The zest of competition animated the class for a few brief moments. Miss Mitnick began the discussion, commenting on Miss Caravello's failure to distinguish between the past and present tenses of verbs, and her habit of affixing mellifluous "a"s to prosaic Anglo-Saxon words. Mr. Pinsky suggested, with a certain impatience, that it was "foist *in* war, foist *in* peace, foist *in* the hots his countryman."

"How you can comparink a Judge Vashington mit a Gary Baldy?" Mr. Kaplan remarked with icy scorn. "Ha!"

Mr. Parkhill quickly spread oil on the troubled nationalistic waters. To avoid an open clash (Miss Caravello had long ago allied herself with the Mitnick forces in the Kaplan-Mitnick vendetta), and in an effort to introduce a more stimulating note into Recitation and Speech, Mr. Parkhill said, "Er—suppose *you* speak next, Mr. Kaplan." Mr. Parkhill had learned to respect the catalytic effect of Mr. Kaplan's performances, oral or written.

Mr. Kaplan's ever-incipient smile burst into full bloom. He advanced to the front of the room, stuffing crayons into his pocket. Then he buttoned his coat with delicate propriety, made a little bow to Mr. Parkhill, and began, "Ladies an' gantleman, faller-students, an' Mr. Pockheel." He paused for the very fraction of a moment, as if permitting the class to steel itself; then, in a dramatic voice, he cried, "JUDGE VASHINGTON, ABRAM LINCOHEN, AN' JAKE POPPER!"

The class was galvanized out of its lassitude. Other students, less adventurous students, might undertake comments on Lincoln *or* Washington, but only Mr. Kaplan had the vision and the fortitude to encompass Lincoln *and* Washington—to say nothing of "Jake Popper."

"Er—Mr. Kaplan," suggested Mr. Parkhill anxiously. "It's *George* Washington, not 'Judge.' And Abra*ham* Lin*coln*, not 'Abram Lin*cohen*.' Please try it again." (Mr. Parkhill could think of nothing relevant to say in regard to "Jake Popper.")

"JAWDGE VASHINGTON, ABRAHAM LINCOLLEN, AN' JAKE POPPER!" Mr. Kaplan repeated, with renewed ardor. "Is dat right, Mr. Pockheel?"

Mr. Parkhill decided it might be best to let well enough alone. "It's—er—*better.*"

"Hau Kay! So foist abot Jawdge Vashington. He vas a fine man. Ectually Fodder fromm His Contry, like dey say. Ve hoid awreddy, fromm planty students, all abot his movvellous didds. How, by beink even a leetle boy, he chopped don de cherries so he could ensswer, 'I cannot tell lies, Papa. I did it mit mine leetle hatchik!' But ve shouldn't forgat dat Vashington vas a beeg ravolutionist! He was fightink for Friddom, against de Kink Ingland, Kink Jawdge Number Tree, dat tarrible autocrap who—"

"'Auto*crat*'!" Mr. Parkhill put in, but too late.

"—who vas puddink stemps on *tea* even, so it tasted bed, an' Jawdge Vashington trew de tea in Boston Hobber, drassed op like a Hindian. So vas de Ravolution!"

The class, Mr. Parkhill could not help observing, hung on Mr. Kaplan's every word, entranced by his historiography.

"Jawdge Vashington vas a hero. A foist-cless hero! In de meedle de coldest vedder he crossed de ice in a leetle boat, he should cetch de Bridish an' de missionaries—"

"'*Merce*naries,' Mr. Kaplan, '*mer*cenaries'!"

"—foolink around, not mit deir minds on de var!" Mr. Kaplan, having finished the sentence, said, "Podden me, '*Moisinaries*' I mant!" and, with scarcely a break in his stride, continued. "So efter de Ravolution de pipple said, 'Jawdge Vashington, you our hero an' lidder! Ve elactink you Prazident!' So he vas elected Prazident U.S.—anonymously!"

Mr. Parkhill's "'Unanimously'!" was lost in Mr. Kaplan's next words.

"An' like Mr. Robinson said, 'In Vashington's name is itch ladder like a coal, boinink ot his gloryous achivmants!'"

Mr. Kaplan ended the peroration with a joyous sweep of the arm.

"Mr. Kaplan!" Mr. Parkhill took the occasion to interrupt firmly. "You *must* speak more slowly, and—er—more carefully. You are making too many mistakes, far too many. It is *very* difficult to correct your English." Mr. Parkhill was aware that "Abraham Lincollen an' Jake Popper" were still to come.

Mr. Kaplan's face fell as he recognized the necessity of smothering the divine fire which flamed within him. "I'll try mine bast," he said. In a gentler mood, he continued. "Vell, I said a lot of fine tings abot Jawdge Vashington. But enyho, is Abraham Lincollen more *close* to me. Dat Abraham Lincollen! Vat a sveet man. Vat a fine cherecter. Vat a hot—like *gold!* Look!" Mr. Kaplan pointed dramatically to the lithograph of the Great Emancipator which hung on the back wall; the heads of the students turned. "Look on his face! Look his ice, so sad mit fillink. Look his mot, so full goodness. Look de high forehat—dat's showink smotness, *brains!*" Mr. Kaplan's invidious glance toward Miss Caravello left no doubt that this high quality was missing in "Gary Baldy." "Look de honest axpression! I esk, is it a *vunder* dey vas callink him 'Honest Abie'?"

"'Honest Abe'!" Mr. Parkhill exclaimed with some desperation, but Mr. Kaplan, carried away by the full, rich sweep of his passion, had soared on.

"No, it's no vunder. He vas a poor boy, a voodchopper, a rail-splinter like dey say. But he made de Tsivil Var! Oh my, den vas tarrible times! Shoodink, killink, de Naut Site U.S.A. aganst de Sot Site U.S.A. Black neegers aganst vhite, brodder fightink brodder, de Blues mit de Grays. An' who von? *Who?* Ha! Abraham Lincollen von, netcherally! So he made de neegers should be like vhite. Ufcawss, Lincollen didn't change de *collars,*" Mr. Kaplan footnoted with scholarly discretion. "Dey vas still *black.* But *free* black, not slafe black. Den"—Mr. Kaplan's voice took on a pontifical note—"Lincollen gave ot de Mancipation Prockilmation. Dat vas, dat all men are born an' created *in de same vay!* So he vas killed."

Exhausted by this mighty passage, Mr. Kaplan paused. Mrs. Moskowitz chose the opportunity to force down a yawn.

"Vell, vat's got all dis to do mit Jake Popper?" Mr. Kaplan asked suddenly. He had taken the question out of the very mouths of Miss Mitnick, Mr. Bloom, *et al.* It was a triumph of prescience. "Vell, Jake Popper vas also a fine man, mit a hot like gold. Ve called him 'Honest Jake.' Ufcawss, Jake Popper vasn't a beeg soldier; he didn't make Velley Fudges or free slafes. Jake Popper had a dalicatessen store." (The modest shrug which accompanied this sentence made it live and breathe: "Jake Popper had a dalicatessen store.") "An' in his store could even poor pipple mitout money, alvays gat somtin to eat—if dey vas honest. Jake Popper did a tremandous beeg business—on cradit. An' averybody loved him.

"Vun day vas 'Honest Jake' fillink bed. He had hot an' cold vaves on de body by de same time; vat ve call a fivver. So averybody said, 'Jake, lay don in bad, rast.' But did Jake Popper lay don in bad, rast? No! He stayed in store, day an' night. He said, 'I got to tink abot mine *customers!*' Dat's de kind high sanse *duty* he had!"

Whether from throat strain or emotion, a husky tone crept into Mr. Kaplan's voice at this point.

"Den de doctor came an' said, 'Popper, you got bronxitis!' So Jake vent in bad. An' he got voise an' voise. So de doctor insulted odder doctors—"

"'*Cons*ulted' other—"

"—an' dey took him in Mont Sinai Hospital. He had double demonia! So dere was special noises, an' fromm all kinds maditzins de bast, an' an oxen tant, he should be able to breed. Even blood confusions dey gave him!"

"'*Trans*fusions,' Mr. Kaplan!" It was no use. Mr. Kaplan, like a spirited steed, was far ahead.

"An' dey shot him in de arm, he should fallink aslip. Dey gave him *epidemics*." Mr Parkhill estimated his speed and made no protest. "An' efter a vhile 'Honest Jake' Popper pest avay."

Mr. Kaplan s face was bathed in reverence, suffused with a lofty dignity. Mrs. Moskowitz yawned no more; she was shaking her head sadly, back and forth, back and forth. (Mrs. Moskowitz wore her heart on her sleeve.)

"So in Jake Popper's honor I made dis leettle spitch. An' I vant also to say for him somting like 'O Ceptin! My Ceptin!'—dat Miss Higby said abot Abraham Lincollen. I got fromm her de voids." Mr. Kaplan took a piece of paper out of an inner vest pocket, drew his head up high, and, as Mr. Parkhill held his breath, read:

"O hot! hot! hot!
O de bliddink drops rad!
Dere on de dack
Jake Popper lies,
Fallink cold an' dad!"

Celestial wings fluttered over the beginners' grade of the American Night Preparatory School for Adults, whispering of the grandeur that was Popper.

"Isn't dat beauriful?" Mr. Kaplan mused softly, with the detachment of the true artist. "My!"

Mr. Parkhill was just about to call for corrections when Mr. Kaplan said, "Vun ting more I should say, so de cless shouldn't fill *too* bed abot Jake Popper. It's awreddy nine yiss since he pest avay!"

Mrs. Moskowitz shot Mr. Kaplan a furious look: her tender emotions had been cruelly exploited.

"An' *I* didn't go to de funeral!" On this strange note, Mr. Kaplan took his seat.

The class hummed, protesting against this anticlimax which left so much to the imagination.

"*Why you didn't?*" cried Mr. Bloom, with a knowing nod to the Misses Mitnick and Caravello.

Mr. Kaplan's face was a study in sufferance. "Becawss de funeral vas' de meedle of de veek," he sighed. "An' I said to minesalf, 'Keplen, you in America, so tink like de *Americans* tink!' So I tought, an' I didn' go. Becawss I tought of dat *dip* American idea, '*Business bafore pleasure!*'"

Aria

from Hunger of Memory: The Education of Richard Rodriguez

RICHARD RODRIGUEZ

In the previous selection, we considered a humorous account of the process by which an immigrant becomes Americanized, primarily through schooling. In the present selection, we consider the often more poignant case of children of immigrants, caught between two worlds: public life conducted in English and private intimacy conducted in the language of the home. In his memoir, Hunger of Memory *(1981), writer and cultural critic Richard Rodriguez (born 1944) presents a thoughtful account of his journey from "minority student," who began school knowing but fifty words of English, to accomplished student of English literature and published author. Rodriguez makes vivid the price he has paid for his successful assimilation: a painful alienation from his origins, his family, and the immediate intimacies of his Spanish-speaking home. At the same time, he celebrates his Americanization and insists that the gain of a place in our public life has been worth the price and pain.*

What is the difference between "public language" and "private language"? How is that distinction related to the difference, emphasized by Rodriguez, between listening to sounds and listening to words—and why, given this difference, might Rodriguez call this chapter "Aria"? What is the relation between language and the possibility of intimacy? Of citizenship? Is Rodriguez right about bilingual education in schools (or bilingualism in voting and other civic activities)? If you were an immigrant parent, would you regard the Americanization of your child more with pride or with sorrow?

I remember to start with that day in Sacramento—a California now nearly thirty years past—when I first entered a classroom, able to understand some fifty stray English words.

The third of four children, I had been preceded to a neighborhood Roman Catholic school by an older brother and sister. But neither of them had revealed very much about their classroom experiences. Each afternoon they returned, as they left in the morning, always together, speaking in Spanish as they climbed the five steps of the porch. And their mysterious books, wrapped in shopping-bag paper, remained on the table next to the door, closed firmly behind them.

An accident of geography sent me to a school where all my classmates were white, many the children of doctors and lawyers and business executives. All my classmates certainly must have been uneasy on that first day of school—as most children are uneasy—to find themselves apart from their families in the first institution of their lives. But I was astonished.

The nun said, in a friendly but oddly impersonal voice, "Boys and girls, this is Richard Rodriguez." (I heard her sound out: *Rich-heard Road-ree-guess.*) It was the first time I had heard anyone name me in English. "Richard," the nun repeated more slowly, writing my name down in her black leather book. Quickly I turned to see my mother's face dissolve in a watery blur behind the pebbled glass door.

Many years later there is something called bilingual education—a scheme proposed in the late 1960s by Hispanic-American social activists, later endorsed by a congressional vote. It is a program that seeks to permit non-English-speaking children, many from lower-class homes, to use their family language as the language of school. (Such is the goal its supporters announce.) I hear them and am forced to say no: It is not possible for a child—any child—ever to use his family's language in school. Not to understand this is to misunderstand the public uses of schooling and to trivialize the nature of intimate life—a family's "language."

Memory teaches me what I know of these matters; the boy reminds the adult. I was a bilingual child, a certain kind—socially disadvantaged—the son of working-class parents, both Mexican immigrants.

In the early years of my boyhood, my parents coped very well in America. My father had steady work. My mother managed at home. They were nobody's victims. Optimism and ambition led them to a house (our home) many blocks from the Mexican south side of town. We lived among *gringos* and only a block from the biggest, whitest houses. It never occurred to my parents that they couldn't live wherever they chose. Nor was the Sacramento of the fifties bent on teaching them a contrary lesson. . . . But despite all they achieved, perhaps because they had so much to achieve, any deep feeling of ease, the confidence of "belonging" in public was withheld from them both. They regarded the people at work, the faces in crowds, as very distant from us. They were the others, *los gringos*. That term was interchangeable in their speech with another, even more telling, *los americanos*. . . .

During those years when I was first conscious of hearing, my mother and father addressed me only in Spanish; in Spanish I learned to reply. By contrast, English (*inglés*), rarely heard in the house, was the language I came to associate with *gringos*. I learned my first words of English overhearing my parents speak to strangers. At five years of age, I knew just enough English for my mother to trust me on errands to stores one block away. No more.

I was a listening child, careful to hear the very different sounds of Spanish and English. Wide-eyed with hearing, I'd listen to sounds more than words. First, there were English (*gringo*) sounds. So many words were still unknown that when the butcher or the lady at the drugstore said something to me, exotic polysyllabic sounds would bloom in the midst of their sentences. Often, the speech of people in public seemed to me very loud, booming with confidence. The man behind the counter would literally ask, "What can I do for you?" But by being so firm and so clear, the sound of his voice said that he was a *gringo*; he belonged in public society.

I would also hear then the high nasal notes of middle-class American speech. The air stirred with sound. Sometimes, even now, when I have been traveling abroad for several weeks, I will hear what I heard as a boy. In hotel lobbies or airports, in Turkey or Brazil, some Americans will pass, and suddenly I will hear it again—the high sound of American voices. For a few seconds I will hear it with pleasure, for it is now the sound of *my* society—a reminder of home. But inevitably—already on the flight headed for home—the sound fades with repetition. I will be unable to hear it anymore.

When I was a boy, things were different. The accent of *los gringos* was never pleasing nor was it hard to hear. Crowds at Safeway or at bus stops would be noisy with sound. And I would be forced to edge away from the chirping chatter above me.

I was unable to hear my own sounds, but I knew very well that I spoke English poorly. My words could not stretch far enough to form complete thoughts. And the words I did speak I didn't know well enough to make into distinct sounds. . . . But it was one thing for *me* to speak English with difficulty. It was more troubling for me to hear my parents speak in public: their high-whining vowels and guttural consonants; their sentences that got stuck with "eh" and "ah" sounds; the confused syntax; the hesitant rhythm of sounds so different from the way *gringos* spoke. I'd notice, moreover, that my parents' voices were softer than those of *gringos* we'd meet.

I am tempted now to say that none of this mattered. In adulthood I am embarrassed by childhood fears. And, in a way, it didn't matter very much that my parents could not speak English with ease. Their linguistic difficulties had no serious consequences. My mother and father made themselves understood at the county hospital clinic and at government offices. And yet, in another way, it mattered very much—it was unsettling to hear my parents struggle with English. Hearing them, I'd grow nervous, my clutching trust in their protection and power weakened. . . .

But then there was Spanish. *Español*: my family's language. *Español*: the language that seemed to me a private language. I'd hear strangers on the radio and in the Mexican Catholic church across town speaking in Spanish, but I couldn't really believe that Spanish was a public language, like English. Spanish speakers, rather, seemed related to me, for I sensed that we shared—through our language—the experience of feeling apart from *los gringos*. It was thus a ghetto Spanish that I heard and I spoke. Like those whose lives are bound by a barrio, I was reminded by Spanish of my separateness from *los otros, los gringos* in power. But more intensely than for most barrio children—because I did not live in a barrio—Spanish seemed to me the language of home. . . . It became the language of joyful return.

A family member would say something to me and I would feel myself specially recognized. My parents would say something to me and I would feel embraced by the sounds of their words. Those sounds said: *I am speaking with ease in Spanish. I am addressing you in words I never use with* los gringos. *I recognize you as someone special, close, like no one outside. You belong with us. In the family.*

(*Ricardo.*)

At the age of five, six, well past the time when most other children no longer easily notice the difference between sounds uttered at home and words spoken in public, I had a different experience. I lived in a world magically compounded by sounds. I remained a child longer than most; I lingered too long, poised at the edge of language—often frightened by the sounds of *los gringos*, delighted by the sounds of Spanish at home. I shared with my family a language that was startlingly different from that used in the great city around us. . . .

Supporters of bilingual education today imply that students like me miss a great deal by not being taught in their family's language. What they seem not to recognize is that, as a socially disadvantaged child, I considered Spanish to be a private language. What I needed to learn in school was that I had the right— and the obligation—to speak the public language of *los gringos*. The odd truth is that my first-grade classmates could have become bilingual, in the conventional sense of that word, more easily than I. Had they been taught (as upper-middle-class children are often taught early) a second language like Spanish or

French, they could have regarded it simply as that: another public language. In my case such bilingualism could not have been so quickly achieved. What I did not believe was that I could speak a single public language.

Without question, it would have pleased me to hear my teachers address me in Spanish when I entered the classroom. I would have felt much less afraid. I would have trusted them and responded with ease. But I would have delayed—for how long postponed?—having to learn the language of public society. I would have evaded—and for how long could I have afforded to delay?—learning the great lesson of school, that I had a public identity.

Fortunately, my teachers were unsentimental about their responsibility. What they understood was that I needed to speak a public language. So their voices would search me out, asking me questions. Each time I'd hear them, I'd look up in surprise to see a nun's face frowning at me. I'd mumble, not really meaning to answer. The nun would persist, "Richard, stand up. Don't look at the floor. Speak up. Speak to the entire class, not just to me!" But I couldn't believe that the English language was mine to use. (In part, I did not want to believe it.) I continued to mumble. I resisted the teacher's demands. (Did I somehow suspect that once I learned public language my pleasing family life would be changed?) Silent, waiting for the bell to sound, I remained dazed, diffident, afraid.

Because I wrongly imagined that English was intrinsically a public language and Spanish an intrinsically private one, I easily noted the difference between classroom language and the language of home. At school, words were directed to a general audience of listeners. ("Boys and girls.") Words were meaningfully ordered. And the point was not self-expression alone but to make oneself understood by many others. The teacher quizzed: "Boys and girls, why do we use that word in this sentence? Could we think of a better word to use there? Would the sentence change its meaning if the words were differently arranged? And wasn't there a better way of saying much the same thing?" (I couldn't say. I wouldn't try to say.)

Three months. Five. Half a year passed. Unsmiling, ever watchful, my teachers noted my silence. They began to connect my behavior with the difficult progress my older sister and brother were making. Until one Saturday morning three nuns arrived at the house to talk to our parents. Stiffly, they sat on the blue living room sofa. From the doorway of another room, spying the visitors, I noted the incongruity—the clash of two worlds, the faces and voices of school intruding upon the familiar setting of home. I overheard one voice gently wondering, "Do your children speak only Spanish at home, Mrs. Rodriguez?" While another voice added, "That Richard especially seems so timid and shy."

That Rich-heard!

With great tact the visitors continued, "Is it possible for you and your husband to encourage your children to practice their English when they are home?" Of course, my parents complied. What would they not do for their children's well-being? And how could they have questioned the Church's authority which those women represented? In an instant, they agreed to give up the language (the sounds) that had revealed and accentuated our family's closeness. The moment after the visitors left, the change was observed. "*Ahora*, speak to us *en inglés*," my father and mother united to tell us.

At first, it seemed a kind of game. After dinner each night, the family gathered to practice "our" English. . . . Laughing, we would try to define words we could not pronounce. We played with strange English sounds, often over-anglicizing our pronunciations. And we filled the smiling gaps of our sentences with familiar Spanish sounds. But that was cheating, somebody shouted. Everyone laughed. In school, meanwhile, like my brother and sister, I was required to attend a daily tutoring session. I needed a full year of special attention. I also needed my teachers to keep my attention from straying in class by calling out, *Rich-heard*—their English voices slowly prying loose my ties to my other name, its three notes, *Ri-car-do*. Most of all I needed to hear my mother and father speak to me in a moment of seriousness in broken— suddenly heartbreaking—English. The scene was inevitable: One Saturday morning I entered the kitchen where my parents were talking in Spanish. I did not realize that they were talking in Spanish however until, at the moment they saw me, I heard their voices change to speak English. Those *gringo* sounds they uttered startled me. Pushed me away. In that moment of trivial misunderstanding and profound insight, I felt my throat twisted by unsounded grief. I turned quickly and left the room. But I had no place to escape to with Spanish. (The spell was broken.) My brother and sisters were speaking English in another part of the house.

Again and again in the days following, increasingly angry, I was obliged to hear my mother and father: "Speak to us *en inglés*." (*Speak.*) Only then did I determine to learn classroom English. Weeks after, it happened: One day in school I raised my hand to volunteer an answer. I spoke out in a loud voice. And I did not think it remarkable when the entire class understood. That day, I moved very far from the disadvantaged child I had been only days earlier. The belief, the calming assurance that I belonged in public, had at last taken hold.

Shortly after, I stopped hearing the high and loud sounds of *los gringos*. A more and more confident speaker of English, I didn't trouble to listen to *how* strangers sounded, speaking to me. And there simply were too many English-speaking people in my day for me to hear American accents anymore. Conversations quickened. Listening to persons who sounded eccentrically pitched voices, I usually noted their sounds for an initial few seconds before I concentrated on *what* they were saying. Conversations became content-full. Transparent. Hearing someone's *tone* of voice—angry or questioning or sarcastic or happy or sad—I didn't distinguish it from the words it expressed. Sound and word were thus tightly wedded. At the end of a day, I was often bemused, always relieved, to realize how "silent," though crowded with words, my day in public had been. (This public silence measured and quickened the change in my life.)

At last, seven years old, I came to believe what had been technically true since my birth: I was an American citizen.

But the special feeling of closeness at home was diminished by then. Gone was the desperate, urgent, intense feeling of being at home; rare was the experience of feeling myself individualized by family intimates. We remained a loving family, but one greatly changed. No longer so close; no longer bound tight by the pleasing and troubling knowledge of our public separateness. Neither my older brother nor sister rushed home after school anymore. Nor did I. When I arrived home there would often be neighborhood kids in the house. Or the house would be empty of sounds. . . .

Matching the silence I started hearing in public was a new quiet at home. The family's quiet was partly due to the fact that, as we children learned more and more English, we shared fewer and fewer words with our parents. Sentences needed to be spoken slowly when a child addressed his mother or father. (Often the parent wouldn't understand.) The child would need to repeat himself. (Still the parent misunderstood.) The young voice, frustrated, would end up saying, "Never mind"—the subject was closed. Dinners would be noisy with the clinking of knives and forks against dishes. My mother would smile softly between her remarks; my father at the other end of the table would chew and chew at his food, while he stared over the heads of his children. . . .

The silence at home, however, was finally more than a literal silence. Fewer words passed between parent and child, but more profound was the silence that resulted from my inattention to sounds. At about the time I no longer bothered to listen with care to the sounds of English in public, I grew careless about listening to the sounds family members made when they spoke. Most of the time I heard someone speaking at home and didn't distinguish his sounds from the words people uttered in public. I didn't even pay much attention to my parents' accented and ungrammatical speech. At least not at home. Only when I was with them in public would I grow alert to their accents. Though, even then, their sounds caused me less and less concern. For I was increasingly confident of my own public identity. . . .

Today I hear bilingual educators say that children lose a degree of "individuality" by becoming assimilated into public society. (Bilingual schooling was popularized in the seventies, that decade when middle-class ethnics began to resist the process of assimilation—the American melting pot.) But the bilingualists simplistically scorn the value and necessity of assimilation. They do not seem to realize that there are *two* ways a person is individualized. So they do not realize that while one suffers a diminished sense of *private* individuality by becoming assimilated into public society, such assimilation makes possible the achievement of *public* individuality.

The bilingualists insist that a student should be reminded of his difference from others in mass society, his heritage. But they equate mere separateness with individuality. The fact is that only in private—with intimates—is separateness from the crowd a prerequisite for individuality. (An intimate draws me apart, tells me that I am unique, unlike all others.) In public, by contrast, full individuality is achieved, paradoxically, by those who are able to consider themselves members of the crowd. Thus it happened for me: Only when I was able to think of myself as an American, no longer an alien in *gringo* society, could I seek the rights and opportunities necessary for full public individuality. The social and political advantages I enjoy as a man result from the day that I came to believe that my name, indeed, is *Rich-heard Road-ree-guess*. It is true that my public society today is often impersonal. (My public society is usually mass society.) Yet despite the anonymity of the crowd and despite the fact that the individuality I achieve in public is often tenuous—because it depends on my being one in a crowd—I celebrate the day I acquired my new name. Those middle-class ethnics who scorn assimilation seem to me filled with decadent self-pity, obsessed by the burden of public life. Dangerously, they romanticize public separateness and they trivialize the dilemma of the socially disadvantaged.

My awkward childhood does not prove the necessity of bilingual education. My story discloses instead an essential myth of childhood—inevitable pain. If I rehearse here the changes in my private life after my Americanization, it is finally to emphasize the public gain. The loss implies the gain: The house I returned to each afternoon was quiet. Intimate sounds no longer rushed to the door to greet me. There were other noises inside. The telephone rang. Neighborhood kids ran past the door of the bedroom where I was reading my schoolbooks—covered with shopping-bag paper. Once I learned public language, it would never again be easy for me to hear intimate family voices. More and more of my day was spent hearing words. But that may only be a way of saying that the day I raised my hand in class and spoke loudly to an entire roomful of faces, my childhood started to end. . . .

Making more and more friends outside my house, I began to distinguish intimate voices speaking through *English*. I'd listen at times to a close friend's confidential tone or secretive whisper. Even more remarkable were those instances when, for no special reason apparently, I'd become conscious of the fact that my companion was speaking only to me. I'd marvel just hearing his voice. It was a stunning event: to be able to break through his words, to be able to hear this voice of the other, to realize that it was directed only to me. After such moments of intimacy outside the house, I began to trust hearing intimacy conveyed through my family's English. Voices at home at last punctured sad confusion. I'd hear myself addressed as an intimate at home once again. Such moments were never as raucous with sound as past times had been when we had had "private" Spanish to use. (Our English-sounding house was never to be as noisy as our Spanish-speaking house had been.) Intimate moments were usually soft moments of sound. My mother was in the dining room while I did my homework nearby. And she looked over at me. Smiled. Said something— her words said nothing very important. But her voice sounded to tell me (*We are together*) I was her son.

(*Richard!*)

Intimacy thus continued at home; intimacy was not stilled by English. It is true that I would never forget the great change of my life, the diminished occasions of intimacy. But there would also be times when I sensed the deepest truth about language and intimacy: *Intimacy is not created by a particular language; it is created by intimates.* The great change in my life was not linguistic but social. If, after becoming a successful student, I no longer heard intimate voices as often as I had earlier, it was not because I spoke English rather than Spanish. It was because I used public language for most of the day. I moved easily at last, a citizen in a crowded city of words. . . .

My city seems silent until some ghetto black teenagers board the bus I am on. Because I do not take their presence for granted, I listen to the sounds of their voices. Of all the accented versions of English I hear in a day, I hear theirs most intently. They are *the* sounds of the outsider. They annoy me for being loud—so self-sufficient and unconcerned by my presence. Yet for the same reason they seem to me glamorous. (A romantic gesture against public acceptance.) Listening to their shouted laughter, I realize my own quiet. Their voices enclose my isolation. I feel envious, envious of their brazen intimacy.

I warn myself away from such envy, however. I remember the black political activists who have argued in favor of using black English in schools. (Their argument varies only slightly from that made by foreign-language bilingualists.) I have heard "radical" linguists make the point that black English is a complex and intricate version of English. And I do not doubt it. But neither do I think that black English should be a language of public instruction. What makes black English inappropriate in classrooms is not something *in* the language. It is rather what lower-class speakers make of it. Just as Spanish would have been a dangerous language for me to have used at the start of my education, so black English would be a dangerous language to use in the schooling of teenagers for whom it reenforces feelings of public separateness.

This seems to me an obvious point. But one that needs to be made. In recent years there have been attempts to make the language of the alien public language. "Bilingual education, two ways to understand . . . ," television and radio commercials glibly announce. Proponents of bilingual education are careful to say that they want students to acquire good schooling. Their argument goes something like this: Children permitted to use their family language in school will not be so alienated and will be better able to match the progress of English-speaking children in the crucial first months of instruction. (Increasingly confident of their abilities, such children will be more inclined to apply themselves to their studies in the future.) But then the bilingualists claim another, very different goal. They say that children who use their family language in school will retain a sense of their individuality—their ethnic heritage and cultural ties. Supporters of bilingual education thus want it both ways. They propose bilingual schooling as a way of helping students acquire the skills of the classroom crucial for public success. But they likewise insist that bilingual instruction will give students a sense of their identity apart from the public.

Behind this screen there gleams an astonishing promise: One can become a public person while still remaining a private person. At the very same time one can be both! There need be no tension between the self in the crowd and the self apart from the crowd! Who would not want to believe such an idea? Who can be surprised that the scheme has won the support of middle-class Americans? If the barrio or ghetto child can retain his separateness even while being publicly educated, then it is almost possible to believe that there is no private cost to be paid for public success. Such is the consolation offered by any of the current bilingual schemes. Consider, for example, the bilingual voters' ballot. In some American cities one can cast a ballot printed in several languages. Such a document implies that a person can exercise that most public of rights—the right to vote—while still keeping apart, unassimilated from public life.

It is not enough to say that these schemes are foolish and certainly doomed. Middle-class supporters of public bilingualism toy with the confusion of those Americans who cannot speak standard English as well as they can. Bilingual enthusiasts, moreover, sin against intimacy. An Hispanic-American writer tells me, "I will never give up my family language; I would as soon give up my soul." Thus he holds to his chest a skein of words, as though it were the source of his family ties. He credits to language what he should credit to family members. A convenient mistake. For as long as he holds on to words, he can ignore how much else has changed in his life.

It has happened before. In earlier decades, persons newly successful and ambitious for social mobility similarly seized upon certain "family words." Working-class men attempting political power took to calling one another "brother." By so doing they escaped oppressive public isolation and were able to unite with many others like themselves. But they paid a price for this union. It was a public union they forged. The word they coined to address one another could never be the sound (*brother*) exchanged by two in intimate greeting. In the union hall the word "brother" became a vague metaphor; with repetition a weak echo of the intimate sound. Context forced the change. Context could not be overruled. Context will always guard the realm of the intimate from public misuse.

Today nonwhite Americans call "brother" to strangers. And white feminists refer to their mass union of "sisters." And white middle-class teenagers continue to prove the importance of context as they try to ignore it. They seize upon the idioms of the black ghetto. But their attempt to appropriate such expressions invariably changes the words. As it becomes a public expression, the ghetto idiom loses its sound—its message of public separateness and strident intimacy. It becomes with public repetition a series of words, increasingly lifeless.

The mystery remains: intimate utterance. The communication of intimacy passes through the word to enliven its sound. But it cannot be held by the word. Cannot be clutched or ever quoted. It is too fluid. It depends not on word but on person.

From *Land of Lincoln: Adventures in Abe's America*

Andrew Ferguson

For Richard Rodriguez, Americanization was a matter mainly of language; for the Thai family featured in this selection, Americanization involves reverence for Abraham Lincoln and all that he represents. Journalist Andrew Ferguson, himself born (in 1956) into a Lincoln-worshipping family, tells the story of how the Esche family, which arrived in Chicago from Thailand in the early 1970s, came to learn of and appreciate Lincoln. Lincoln himself, in an 1858 speech in Chicago, described how the immigrants of his day (German, Irish, French, and Scandinavian) reacted to reading the Declaration of Independence's assertion of human equality: "They feel that that moral sentiment taught in that day evidences their relation to those men, that it is the father of all moral principle in them, and that they have a right to claim it as though they were blood of the blood, and flesh of the flesh of the men who wrote that Declaration." The Esches experience that same patriotic identification through Lincoln and his teaching about equality.

For the Esches, how does reverence for the greatness of Lincoln—as Mrs. Esche says, "He's the head man in history"—fit with devotion to Lincoln's teaching that "no man is better than any other man"? How do they square the elements of their Thai culture, such as ancestor worship and ritual expressions of gratitude, with their Americanism? Think about the historical sites that you have visited: What effect, if any, have they had on your patriotic attachment to the United States? Are there any sites that you will want your children and grandchildren to visit?

I was on my way to meet Oscar Esche, who had a Lincoln statue of his own I wanted to see. I'd read about Esche and his statue in a wonderful book called *Never a City So Real*, by Alex Kotlowitz, about the difficulties immi-

grants face in Chicago these days, now that "Americanization," both the word
and the ideal, seems so weirdly quaint—a phrase not just from another time
but almost another language, a civic language that's as dead as Babylonian. Mr.
Esche owns the Thai Little Home Café, in the city's Albany Park neighborhood.
To get there you take Lincoln Avenue from where it starts at the southern tip
of Lincoln Park, by the Saint-Gaudens Lincoln statue, and you drive north for
several miles, past the Lincoln restaurant and the Lincoln National Bank and
the Lincoln Life Insurance office, till you get to Lincoln Square, where you turn
left, and pretty soon you're in polyglot Chicago. Mr. Esche's restaurant is on a
stretch of Kedzie Avenue, tucked in among the Casablanca Hair Salon, the Arab
Jewelry Outlet, a Super Mercado, Marbello's Bakery, Desayumos Burrito, and
the storefront office of Al-Muhaseb Bookkeeping. And a Starbucks.

The Thai Little Home Café is a converted storefront, too. But inside it's
neat and homey. Exuberant plants hang in the window and rise festively from
urns on the floor. The walls are papered in travel posters from Asia, washed
out by years of afternoon sun pouring through the plate glass. At two o'clock
the place was supposed to be closing for the afternoon, but several customers,
Asian and Anglo and Latin, lounged over coffee. Soft rock—a Norah Jones–
type singer who might have been Norah Jones—purred from a CD player near
the back by the bar.

A young woman came to greet me and I asked to see Oscar Esche, and she
brought me to the back, where an elderly man sat with a woman of similar
vintage at a table covered in ledger books and piles of silverware. The woman
was rolling forks and knives in paper napkins for the evening rush.

Mr. Esche is tall and handsome, in his late seventies, I'd guess, with sharp
features and large black Buddy Holly glasses. He looked at me and nodded. I
told him I'd read about him in Kotlowitz's book.

"Oh, I'm just in there for two, three lines," he said, in uncertain English.

I said I was intrigued by what Kotlowitz had written about him and Abraham Lincoln, and would he mind telling me a little more?

He didn't say anything but turned instead to the old woman at the table.
He spoke to her for a minute or two, in Thai. I heard him say the word "Lee-
cone," and her face suddenly broke into a smile. She rose from her seat. She
was very short, scarcely five feet, but commanding, with a wide, friendly face;
humorous and shrewd. She extended a soft hand for me to shake. With Oscar,
who was a foot taller than she but still very deferential, we went into an adja-
cent dining room. Their every move was a courtesy, to each other and to me.
Oscar pulled out the chair for me, then for his wife, before he sat down.

Mr. Esche said, "We first hear of Mr. Lincoln"—Lee-cone—"when we
move here from Thailand."

His wife spoke to him in Thai. He listened patiently, then turned to me.

"My wife says, we move here in 1973," he said. "We open the third Thai restaurant in Chicago."

She spoke again, in Thai, at some length, and at length he turned back to me.

"My wife sees the license plate on all the cars after we move here to Chicago. 'Land of Lincoln,' they say. She wonders, 'Who is this Lincoln?' So she gets a book from a friend to read about Lincoln."

She spoke again; he turned back to me again.

"She says, in our country it is our custom that we pay respect to the person who is in charge of the country. And here it is Lincoln's country. He's the head man in history. You see him everywhere. Everyone loves him.

"My wife reads the book, and we realize, we must go pay respects to this man. He is a very great man. He helps the poor. He tells everyone that they are equal, that no man is better than any other man. This is very important. Everyone is equal. Everyone have same right. This is what he says, and he makes sure the country is this way."

She spoke another paragraph.

"We went to Springfield," Mr. Esche said, after she's finished. "We want to pay respects for Lincoln. We go to his grave site with our children. Very young then. We go to this temple"—I figured he meant Lincoln's tomb in the cemetery at Springfield—"and on the roof has a big, tall . . . I don't know the word . . ."

"Obelisk?" I said.

He looked at me a moment, then smiled and shrugged. "Okay," he said. "And we bring flowers, and when we are there, we sit, all the family, and we sit by his grave and we pray to him, to give him thanks for such a wonderful country. We just want to show thanks."

His wife seemed to follow his every word, nodding once in a while. She spoke again, and he listened carefully.

"This is the thing," he said at last. "All people, poor people and rich people, they are equal in their rights. This is what Lincoln teach. My wife hear this and she bought a—what?" He made a box with his long fingers. Neither could remember the word. In his frustration, he beckoned me to the bar. On it was an ivory reproduction of the Daniel Chester French sculpture of Lincoln, the one that sits in the Lincoln Memorial in Washington, D.C.

"Like this," he said.

Statue, I said.

"Yes, statue. We bought a statue, to show our respect, and we put this here, and ever since that time we have statue, our business never go down. Always the business goes up, never down, no matter what. Lincoln does this. And for many years, every year we do the same—drive in the car with the children, go down in morning, come back at night. We see his house and we see his grave and we pray and give thanks and we come home."

I ask about the Esches' children—when they were younger, did they learn about Lincoln in school? Mr. Esche translated the question to Mrs. Esche. She shrugged.

"We don't know," he said. "We make sure the children know what we tell them. We make sure they understand Lincoln and be grateful to him for our country and for letting us live here and bringing us this good life he make for us. We pass this down to them. They will pass it down too. The way we are brought up, we must look to him and respect him, every generation, old people, young people, everybody."

Beginning in 1976, the Esche family made their Springfield pilgrimage— that's the right word, isn't it—in the spring. Now two of their three kids are married, one with children, and driving is getting to be a problem for Mr. Esche, especially at night. So he and Mrs. Esche haven't made the trip the past few years. But the children go every year, as they hope their children will when they have children of their own. "We must remember and respect," he said.

Mr. Esche showed me a plate of chicken satay behind the Lincoln statue. As a final form of commemoration, every morning he and his wife set out a meal for Lincoln in the restaurant, next to his statue.

"It's full meal—everything, entrée, dessert, appetizer, drink also," Mr. Esche said. "We change the meal every day, so it's always different. We serve him everything."

Mrs. Esche interrupted.

"Yes," Mr. Esche said. "Everything but no pork."

Oh?

"We do not want to be disrespectful."

I guess Mr. Esche saw my puzzled look.

"He is *Abraham* Lincoln, yes?" he said, with special emphasis. "Jewish people, they don't eat pork."

Songs for Free Men and Women

The Star-Spangled Banner

Daniel Mark Epstein

The United States of America, a most unusual nation, has a most unusual national anthem. Compared with the anthems of other nations—for example, Great Britain's "God Save the Queen," France's "Marseillaise," and Canada's "O Canada"—our anthem is hard to sing, hard to scan, and even hard to understand. Moreover, it became our anthem, by an act of Congress, only in 1931, more than a century after it was written, and only after much debate. What is special about this anthem—its words, its music? In this essay from his collection Star of Wonder *(1986), poet and essayist Daniel Epstein (born 1948) reviews the story behind its selection and makes the case in its defense. What, according to Epstein, is to be said for "The Banner"? Which, if any, of his arguments do you find persuasive? What is the purpose of a national anthem? Of this national anthem?*

"The Star-Spangled Banner" is a sublime anthem, democratic and spacious, holding at least one note for every American, but too many for any solitary singer. The tune is a test pattern, not only for the voice, but for the human spirit. The soul singer, the rock star, and the crooner—all are humbled by the anthem. We have heard world-famous tenors and sopranos choke upon the low notes, and cry out in pain at the high ones. We have seen the great Mahalia Jackson tremble.

It is unlikely that our worst enemy would have written a melody with a range more challenging to the solo performer. The melody *was* in fact given to us, like the Trojan horse, by our worst enemy at the time, the English. John Stafford Smith, an Englishman, composed the tune to which Francis Scott Key penned his lyrics a few days after the British set fire to our capital in 1814. The capital was rebuilt but the melody remains exactly as we received it—an inspiration and a terror. The anthem perfectly suits our collective spirit, our ambition and national range. So it ought to be sung by a crowd of Americans, who may guarantee that all of the notes will be covered.

You may wonder how the national anthem achieved its election in the first place. And why, since the tune is so uncooperative, we can't impeach and throw the anthem out of office, like any other incompetent or mischievous official? If you are thinking such thoughts you are in good patriotic company. The House Resolution 14, which legalized the national anthem, was voted down when it was first introduced in 1929, and hotly debated in 1931, when it did pass. Every few years since, there has been an uprising, with newspaper editorials, petitions against the song, and insurgents campaigning to replace "The Banner" with "America" or "This Land Is Your Land."

If you are fond of "The Star-Spangled Banner," as most of us are, the way folks will love a cantankerous grandfather, you may rest assured there are no new arguments likely to unseat or reform the anthem. Everything that could be said on the subject was said, over and over, during those debates of more than fifty years ago. Congressmen brought dire charges against "The Star-Spangled Banner." They denounced its ancestry, its birth and character. They dug up all the song's dirtiest secrets, ancient indiscretions, the follies of a wild and adventurous youth. They dragged "The Star-Spangled Banner" through the mud.

First of all there was that embarrassing business about the Anacreontic Society. We know that Francis Scott Key did not get his tune from a virgin inspiration. He wrote only the words; the melody had been married before, to the lyrics of an English song called "To Anacreon in Heaven," which made a very different kind of anthem indeed. The ancient Greek poet Anacreon delighted in wine and lovemaking above all else. In the 1770s, the London "gentlemen" of the Anacreontic Society chose the poet for their patron, and spent nights reviving his spirit with songs, and tippling, and unspecified merrymaking.

There were other problems as well. The congressmen against the "Banner" claimed that the song was useless on the parade and battle grounds because our soldiers cannot march to it. To this charge there seems to be no answer. Yet John Philip Sousa, who should have known, once told Teddy Roosevelt that "The Star-Spangled Banner" was dandy for marching. Perhaps the soldiers had not tried hard enough. After all, any fool army could march to the "Marseillaise" or "God Save the Queen," but who but an American army could get in step to "The Star-Spangled Banner"? And finally, if our soldiers cannot march to "The Star-Spangled Banner," they cannot dance to it either. Better that it does not lend itself to any kind of frivolity. In fact you can do little with the anthem but listen to it, and only with great difficulty, since the song is nearly impossible to sing.

This brings us to the next argument against "The Star-Spangled Banner": that it is too difficult for school children to sing. An editorial in the New York *World* of March 31, 1930, answered this charge with logic and eloquence: "What if school children could sing it? We should be so sick of it by now that we could not endure the sound of it, as the French are sick of the 'Marseillaise.' The virtues of 'The Star-Spangled Banner' are that it does require a wide compass, so that school children cannot sing it, and that it is in three-four time so that parades cannot march to it. So being, it has managed to remain fresh, not frayed and worn, and the citizenry still hear it with some semblance of a thrill, some touch of reverence."

To the *World's* persuasive comments, we can only add that the school children of the Third Reich had an anthem they could sing and march to with the greatest of ease. It did them no good. An amusing irony of the congressional debates is that, while some lawmakers complained the "Banner" was unmarchable, others thought the lyrics were too warlike. A close reading of all four stanzas should reassure the doves. Far from advocating war, Key's words express the utmost horror of it, suiting the occasion that brought the song into being.

As for the occasion, the bombardment of Fort McHenry in 1814, a few congressmen suggested this was too paltry a background for our national anthem. They had not read their history. If the British had gotten into Baltimore, only a few days after burning down our capital, no one can say where they might have stopped. Who would have stopped them? George Washington had been dead fifteen years. Andrew Jackson was in New Orleans. If the British navy's offensive had not foundered at Fort McHenry we might be singing "God Save the Queen" instead of not singing "The Star-Spangled Banner."

So, a half century ago, our anthem stood proud and unflinching and unrepentant while the lawmakers weighed it, prodded it and leered at it, examining its teeth and moral record. Perhaps the best argument against the House Resolution is that it was unnecessary, and therefore impertinent, rather like electing the turkey to be the Official Entrée of Thanksgiving. Way back in the nineteenth century Admiral Dewey designated "The Star-Spangled Banner" as the anthem for all Navy ceremonies. And when advisers asked what song should accompany state functions in 1916, President Wilson automatically replied, "The Banner." Everybody knew it was the national anthem.

But Americans do not like to be told what to eat, or drink, or sing. Though they have eaten hot dogs and drunk beer and sung "The Star-Spangled Banner" in baseball parks for generations, try to pass a law to that effect and Congress will never hear the end of it. That is the American way, and a good way. When Representative J. C. Linthicum of Maryland agitated to make "The Star-Spangled Banner" our *official* anthem, he might have foreseen he would be subjecting the "Banner" to a scrutiny usually reserved for presidential candidates. The final vote to give the song official status as our national anthem, despite its vocal challenges, unmarchability, and checkered past, is a gesture of American affection without precedent or parallel.

"The Star-Spangled Banner" deserves it. That insuperable anthem remains the purest example of unpremeditated, inspired genius in American history. Remember that Francis Scott Key, the lawyer poet, was more lawyer than poet. Apart from the lyrics of "The Banner" Key never wrote a line of memorable verse, . . . excepting "Lord with Glowing Heart I'd Praise Thee," a hymn infrequently sung in churches. Francis Scott Key was tone deaf. If anyone had told him early in September of 1814 that he was about to write the most famous song in America, the lawyer poet would have laughed, with a modesty rare in poets, and gone about his business.

Key's business in September of 1814 was a matter of life and death. America had declared war upon slender pretexts the lawyer poet condemned as a cover for imperialism. American privateers were looting British ships, and our troops had set Toronto on fire in the interest of annexing Canada. Not to be outdone, the British burned down Washington, D.C. Key was a gentle soul, so unsuited to conflict he could never bring himself to run for political office. Yet he fought dutifully in the defense of Washington. And when the British took away a civilian prisoner, Dr. William Beanes, Key begged for President Madison's commission to sail after them, and plead for the doctor's release.

Key sailed down the Chesapeake in a small cartel ship, under the white flag of truce. He found the British fleet lying at anchor in the mouth of the Potomac. Admiral George Cockburn was about to hang Dr. Beanes from the ship's yardarm for his inhospitality to English soldiers as they passed through Upper Marlboro. The doctor had been having a garden party to celebrate the town's escape from burning, when a few straggling dragoons came into his yard and made bold to steal the punch. Dr. Beanes had been court-martialed for not giving them any, among other discourtesies.

With the passion and eloquence of a great lawyer poet, Francis Scott Key pleaded for Dr. Beanes's life. The lawyer suggested that the strictest guardians of etiquette did not require a host to serve punch to the army of the occupation. Then he argued that the detaining of civilians outraged all principles of civilized warfare; if great nations cannot agree upon the principles of warfare, what on earth *could* they agree upon? Admiral Cockburn was unmoved. What finally swayed him were certain letters from his wounded soldiers, showing what tender care Dr. Beanes had taken of them. Key produced these letters from his satchel. After a heated conference the British officers announced they would release the ill-mannered doctor the next morning.

Key's mission was badly timed for all purposes but the creation of our anthem. That very night the British fleet received orders to attack Baltimore. Since they could not conceal this from Key, they insisted that he accept their hospitality until the battle was over, making him an offer he could not refuse. The British entertained the lawyer poet on his own cartel ship. From there he had an excellent view of the contest, being right in the middle of it.

Now let us pay tribute to Key's inspiration, which came in a moment bearing a song that must outlive every American. We have all known some inspiration, whether we write, or paint, or teach, or build houses. Inspiration is, above all, emotion. What was Francis Scott Key *feeling* as he watched the rockets' red glare, and the bombs bursting in air, and then saw the banner waving? He jotted notes on the back of an envelope. Later the lawyer poet would admit: "If it had been a hanging matter to make a poem, I must have made it." The reference to execution is not careless. It is more than likely that the gentle Key, in making his poem, was as terrified a lawyer poet as ever held a quill in his hand.

You singers who have been honored with an invitation to perform the anthem for a crowd, remember Key's terror and be comforted. Whatever indignities you may suffer from bungling "The Star-Spangled Banner," you are not likely to die from it. But in 1814, the rockets' red glare and bombs bursting in air were neither poetic fantasies nor Fourth of July fireworks. They were real, live bombs, screaming, and whistling, and exploding around the poet. Dr. Beanes, who had joined Key on the cartel's deck, must have thought he had been saved from hanging only to be blown up.

The British rocket, a kind of primitive guided missile, was an awesome innovation in 1814. Key had watched his own men panic under bombardment from those rockets during the defense of Washington, and probably figured the Baltimoreans would do the same. The lawyer poet must have had wildly mixed emotions as the British ships, and his country's own boat, approached the shore, beautifully lighted by rockets so that his fellow Americans could take better aim at him with their cannons. We could hardly blame Key if he had prayed for a swift surrender. He did not. He wrote a poem instead, and prayed for a sight of the flag.

A word about the flag. It is not just any flag, the one that flew above Fort McHenry in 1814. It is arguably the largest battle flag ever flown, thirty-six feet long by twenty-nine feet wide, one hundred forty square yards of red, white and blue bunting. The flag was made to order for the defense of Fort McHenry, as well as the creation of our anthem. What else would possess General Stricker and Commodore Barney, otherwise reasonable men, to order such a gigantic banner? They wanted to be sure that Key would see it. Although the seamstress Mary Pickersgill snipped the stripes and stars in her tiny workroom, she could not stitch them together there. Mary and her little daughter worked on their hands and knees, by daylight and lamplight, stitching together the star-spangled banner on the malthouse floor of Claggett's brewery. They finished their sewing just as the British fleet was nearing the Baltimore harbor.

The flag is surrealistically large. If you do not believe this, then go and look at it, hanging like a dinosaur in the Smithsonian Institution's Museum of American History. That flag, flying above Fort McHenry, must have made the fort, and the city behind it, look like a child's sand castle. What was the author of our anthem feeling, after the long night of rockets and bomb blasts and horror, what was he feeling when he saw that titanic flag flying weirdly above his miniature homeland? Some would say relief. But it was too soon for Key to feel relief—he was still a prisoner of war. Some would say pride. But Key was famous for nothing but his humility; he was anecdotally humble. And besides, pride does not spring readily in one's breast so soon after courage has been shaken. After a night of unspeakable terror, with every reason to believe that America would surrender in the glare of the rockets, Francis Scott Key's emotion upon spying that bizarre flag must have been utter amazement.

Wonder is a better word. Key could not believe his eyes, and his lyrics reproduce in us that sense of wonder. Remember, the refrain that closes the first stanza is a question:

> O! say does that star-spangled banner yet wave,
> O'er the Land of the free, and the home of the brave?

When we sing the anthem in the ballpark, or in school, or before the fireworks display on July 4, it is altogether fitting that we sing no more of the lyrics after that question. The birth and survival of this nation remains one of the wonders of the world. This was never more evident than it was to the lawyer poet on that cloudy morning in 1814. The flag was amazing but undeniable. Key knew exactly how brave *he* was, having so recently been measured for bravery. Yet he still had sensible doubts about his freedom. That is the American way, and it is a good way.

The Star-Spangled Banner

Words by Francis Scott Key

As we learn from the previous selection, Francis Scott Key (1779–1843), Washington lawyer and amateur poet, was inspired to pen the verses of "The Star-Spangled Banner" by the unlikely success of American troops resisting the British attack on Baltimore's Fort McHenry on September 13, 1814, two days after the burning of the capital. Nearly all American schoolchildren are taught the words of Key's first stanza, now our national anthem, and for the rest of their lives they hear it sung on patriotic holidays and at sporting events. Rarely, however, do we attend to the words. Many whose hearts are stirred by hearing the anthem sung probably could not tell you what it literally means or what Key intended to convey.

What is the meaning of the poem's opening question: "O! say can you see by the dawn's early light / What so proudly we hailed at the twilight's last gleaming"? How does it differ from the question that concludes the first stanza: "O! say does that star-spangled banner yet wave / O'er the land of the free and the home of the brave?" Why, according to the song, is the waving banner important? Why sing a song about a flag? The last stanza turns from the present war to the future. For what does it call? What relation does the song suggest between the flag and the motto "In God is our trust"? How does singing the song make you feel? Does thinking about the anthem's words alter those feelings?

O! say can you see by the dawn's early light
What so proudly we hailed at the twilight's last gleaming;
Whose broad stripes and bright stars thro' the perilous fight,
O'er the ramparts we watched were so gallantly streaming?
And the rockets' red glare, the bombs bursting in air,

Gave proof through the night that our flag was still there.
O! say does that star-spangled banner yet wave
O'er the land of the free and the home of the brave?

On the shore, dimly seen through the mists of the deep,
Where the foe's haughty host in dread silence reposes,
What is that which the breeze, o'er the towering steep,
As it fitfully blows, half conceals, half discloses?
Now it catches the gleam of the morning's first beam,
In full glory reflected now shines in the stream:
'Tis the star-spangled banner! O! long may it wave
O'er the land of the free and the home of the brave!

And where is that band who so vauntingly swore
That the havoc of war and the battle's confusion
A home and a country should leave us no more!
Their blood has washed out their foul footsteps' pollution.
No refuge could save the hireling and slave
From the terror of flight, or the gloom of the grave:
And the star-spangled banner in triumph doth wave
O'er the land of the free and the home of the brave!

O! thus be it ever, when freemen shall stand
Between their loved home and the war's desolation!
Blest with vict'ry and peace, may the heav'n rescued land
Praise the Power that hath made and preserved us a nation.
Then conquer we must, when our cause it is just,
And this be our motto: "In God is our trust."
And the star-spangled banner in triumph shall wave
O'er the land of the free and the home of the brave!

My Country, 'Tis of Thee

Words by Samuel F. Smith

Until it was officially replaced by "The Star Spangled-Banner" in 1931, "My Country, 'Tis of Thee" served as our de facto national anthem. It was written in 1831 by Samuel Francis Smith (1808–1895), Baptist minister, journalist, and author. Though it is set to the music of Britain's national anthem, Smith came to it by way of a German song. Also known as "America," this song was first performed in public on July 4, 1831, at a children's Independence Day celebration at Park Street Church in Boston.

What is it about "My Country" that the song primarily celebrates? Several verses explicitly refer to the Divine: for what reasons and for what purposes? Several verses speak about education and school: what role do they play in the nation's story? What, according to the song, do we owe to our ancestors? To what—ancestors, or schools, or God, or something else—are we indebted for "Sweet Freedom"? How does singing this song make you feel?

My country, 'tis of thee,
Sweet Land of Liberty
Of thee I sing;
Land where my fathers died,
Land of the pilgrims' pride,
From every mountain side
Let Freedom ring!

My native country, thee,
Land of the noble free,
Thy name I love;
I love thy rocks and rills,

Thy woods and templed hills;
My heart with rapture thrills,
Like that above.

Let music swell the breeze,
And ring from all the trees
Sweet Freedom's song;
Let mortal tongues awake;
Let all that breathe partake;
Let rocks their silence break,
The sound prolong.

Our fathers' God, to Thee,
Author of Liberty,
To Thee we sing.
Long may our land be bright
With Freedom's holy light;
Protect us by Thy might
Great God, our King.

America the Beautiful

Words by Katharine Lee Bates

This popular and eminently singable song was written by Katharine Lee Bates (1859–1929), an English professor at Wellesley College. The poem, originally called "Pikes Peak," was inspired by the sights Bates had seen on a train ride to and from Colorado Springs, especially by the vista she beheld from the top of Pikes Peak. As she explained, "Near the top we had to leave the wagon and go the rest of the way on mules. I was very tired. But when I saw the view, I felt great joy. All the wonder of America seemed displayed there, with the sea-like expanse." Bates's poem, published on July 4, 1895, was eventually combined with music written by church organist and choirmaster Samuel A. Ward (1847–1903), becoming popular around 1910. Like the other patriotic songs, "America the Beautiful" is mostly known by its first stanza, which begins by celebrating America's natural gifts and ends with a plea (or is it a prayer?) for brotherhood. What do the other stanzas celebrate, and what do they call for? How would you summarize the teaching and ideals of this poem? How does singing this song make you feel?

O beautiful for spacious skies,
For amber waves of grain,
For purple mountain majesties
Above the fruited plain!
America! America!
God shed His grace on thee,
And crown thy good with brotherhood
From sea to shining sea!

O beautiful for pilgrim feet
Whose stern impassion'd stress
A thoroughfare of freedom beat
Across the wilderness.
America! America!
God mend thine every flaw,
Confirm thy soul in self-control,
Thy liberty in law.

O beautiful for heroes prov'd
In liberating strife,
Who more than self their country loved
And mercy more than life.
America! America!
May God thy gold refine
Till all success be nobleness
And ev'ry gain divine.

O beautiful for patriot dream
That sees beyond the years
Thine alabaster cities gleam
Undimmed by human tears.
America! America!
God shed His grace on thee
And crown thy good with brotherhood
From sea to shining sea.

The Battle Hymn of the Republic

WORDS BY JULIA WARD HOWE

"The Battle Hymn of the Republic" was written in 1861 as an abolitionist song by Julia Ward Howe (1819–1910), a prominent American abolitionist and social activist. While witnessing a review of Union troops in Washington, D.C., Howe heard the Union army marching song "John Brown's Body" set to a tune written by William Steffe (1830–1890). The stirring tune inspired her to write new lyrics: this poem came to her in the middle of the night and she scrawled the verses in the dark, using an old stump of a pen. It became a popular Union song during the rest of the Civil War and after.

The song is called a hymn: is there a difference between a hymn and an anthem? What is a battle hymn? The song seems to offer an interpretation of the Civil War: what is its teaching? Other songs collected here also make reference to God and speak of His relation to our national affairs: how does this one differ from the others? The second-to-last line of stanza five originally read, "As He died to make men holy, let us die to make men free": what do you make of the substitution of "live" for "die"? How can what was a partisan Union song become a song of the entire nation? How does singing this song make you feel?

Mine eyes have seen the glory of the coming of the Lord:
He is trampling out the vintage where the grapes of wrath are stored;
He hath loosed the fateful lightning of His terrible swift sword:
　　His truth is marching on.

(Chorus)
　　Glory, glory Hallelujah!
　　Glory, glory Hallelujah!

Glory, glory Hallelujah!
   His truth is marching on.

I have seen Him in the watch-fires of a hundred circling camps,
They have builded Him an altar in the evening dews and damps;
I can read His righteous sentence by the dim and flaring lamps:
   His day is marching on.

(Chorus)
   Glory, glory Hallelujah!
   Glory, glory Hallelujah!
   Glory, glory Hallelujah!
     His day is marching on.

I have read a fiery gospel writ in burnished rows of steel:
"As ye deal with my contemners, so with you my grace shall deal;
Let the Hero, born of woman, crush the serpent with his heel,
   Since God is marching on."

(Chorus)
   Glory, glory Hallelujah!
   Glory, glory Hallelujah!
   Glory, glory Hallelujah!
     Since God is marching on.

He has sounded forth the trumpet that shall never call retreat;
He is sifting out the hearts of men before His judgment-seat:
Oh, be swift, my soul, to answer Him! be jubilant, my feet!
   Our God is marching on.

(Chorus)
   Glory, glory Hallelujah!
   Glory, glory Hallelujah!
   Glory, glory Hallelujah!
     Our God is marching on.

In the beauty of the lilies Christ was born across the sea,
With a glory in his bosom that transfigures you and me:

As he died to make men holy, let us die* to make men free,
   While God is marching on.

(Chorus)
   Glory, glory Hallelujah!
   Glory, glory Hallelujah!
   Glory, glory Hallelujah!
      While God is marching on.

He is coming like the glory of the morning on the wave,
He is wisdom to the mighty, He is succour† to the brave;
So the world shall be His footstool, and the soul of Time‡ His slave,
   Our God is marching on.

(Chorus)
   Glory, glory Hallelujah!
   Glory, glory Hallelujah!
   Glory, glory Hallelujah!
      Our God is marching on.

---

* *In today's version, "live" is usually substituted for the original "die."*

† *In today's version, "honor" is usually substituted for the original "succour."*

‡ *In today's version, "wrong" is usually substituted for the original "Time."*

God Bless America

Irving Berlin

Composer and lyricist Irving Berlin, born Israel Baline (1888–1989), immigrated with his family to the United States in 1893 to escape the pogroms against the Jews in his native Russia. In 1918, while serving in the Army, Berlin wrote "God Bless America," taking its title from the phrase his mother often used to indicate that "without America, her family would have had no place to go." In 1938, around the twentieth anniversary of the end of World War I, the popular singer Kate Smith asked Berlin for a song. Concerned about the war clouds gathering in Europe, he tried writing a few songs about the United States, but then remembered this one, which had sat in a drawer for twenty years. Berlin revised the song and Smith introduced it on her Armistice Day 1938 radio broadcast.* On September 11, 2001, following the terrorist attacks on the World Trade Center and the Pentagon, this was the song that members of the House of Representatives solemnly sang on the steps of the Capitol.

The introduction speaks of allegiance, gratitude, and prayer: what exactly is their connection, one to another? The song is said to be a prayer: for what exactly do we pray? Is this a song only for times of crisis? How does singing this song make you feel?

(Spoken Introduction)
While the storm clouds gather
Far across the sea,
Let us swear allegiance

---

* *Berlin also provided the spoken introduction to the song, which Smith used regularly but which is rarely heard now.*

To a land that's free;
Let us all be grateful
For a land so fair,
As we raise our voices
In a solemn prayer.

(Song)
God bless America,
Land that I love,
Stand beside her and guide her
Through the night with a light from above.
From the mountains, to the prairies,
To the oceans white with foam.
God bless America,
My home sweet home.
God bless America,
My home sweet home.

This Land Is Your Land

WOODY GUTHRIE

Not everybody took to "God Bless America." Songwriter, folk singer, and radical political activist Woody Guthrie (1912–1967) wrote this popular folk song in 1940 as an answer to Irving Berlin and Kate Smith. Troubled by many scenes of poverty and desolation that he had witnessed on his travels during the Great Depression, Guthrie wrote "This Land Is Your Land" in a populist egalitarian and antiestablishment spirit.*

What is celebrated in this song? What does Guthrie mean in his claim "This land was made for you and me"? Is this a patriotic song? Is there anything particularly American about its message? How does singing this song make you feel?

(Chorus)
This land is your land, this land is my land,
From California to the New York island;
From the redwood forest, to the Gulf Stream waters,
This land was made for you and me.

As I was walking that ribbon of highway,
I saw above me that endless skyway;
I saw below me that golden valley:
This land was made for you and me.

(Repeat Chorus)

---

* *The song caught on right away, after Guthrie expunged a couple of his overtly Marxist verses.*

I've roamed and rambled and I followed my footsteps
To the sparkling sands of her diamond deserts;
And all around me a voice was sounding:
This land was made for you and me.

(Repeat Chorus)

When the sun came shining, and I was strolling,
And the wheatfields waving and the dust clouds rolling,
As the fog was lifting a voice was chanting:
This land was made for you and me.

(Repeat Chorus)

As I went walking, I saw a sign there,
And on the sign it said "No Trespassing."
But on the other side it didn't say nothing,
That side was made for you and me.

(Repeat Chorus)

In the shadow of the steeple I saw my people,
By the relief office I seen my people;
As they stood there hungry, I stood there asking
Is this land made for you and me?

(Repeat Chorus)

Symbols

The Great Seal of the United States

*Most nations have national seals, signifying their status as sovereign nations, bearing mottoes and emblems dear to them, and used to mark the most important official documents. Our national seal is widely seen yet little noticed. Most Americans, in fact, hold it in their hands on a daily basis: images of its two sides appear on the back of every one-dollar bill.**

---

* *The seal is even older than the Constitution. On the day the Declaration of Independence was signed, July 4, 1776, a committee comprising Benjamin Franklin, John Adams, and Thomas Jefferson was appointed to design the seal for the newly independent United States of America. The task proved more difficult than expected, requiring six years, two more committees, and the combined efforts of fourteen men before it was completed. The final version, the Great Seal of the United States, combining features suggested by each of the three committees, was designed by Charles Thomson of Philadelphia (1729–1824), secretary of the Continental Congress. On June 20, 1782, Congress adopted the seal and also Thomson's accompanying "Remarks and Explanations":*

> *The Escutcheon [shield] is composed of the chief [upper part of shield] & pale [perpendicular band], the two most honorable ordinaries [figures of heraldry]. The Pieces, paly [alternating pales], represent the several states all joined in one solid compact entire, supporting a Chief, which united the whole and represents Congress. The Motto alludes to this union. The pales in the arms are kept closely united by the Chief and the Chief depends on that union & strength resulting from it for its support, to denote the Confederacy of the United States of America & the preservation of their union through Congress.*
>
> *The colours of the pales are those used in the flag of the United States of America; White signifies purity and innocence, Red, Hardiness & valour, and Blue, the colour of the Chief signifies vigilance, perseverance & justice The Olive branch and arrows denote the power of peace & war which is exclusively vested in Congress. The Constellation denoted a new State taking its place and rank among other sovereign powers. The Escutcheon is born on the breast of an American Eagle without any other supporters to denote that the United States of America ought to rely on their own Virtue [power].*

Like the republic it represents, the Great Seal bears the marks of its origin in democratic deliberation. Each of its various details was hotly debated, including, on its obverse (or front), the bald eagle and the bundle of arrows and olive branch in the eagle's talons, and, on its reverse (or back), the unfinished pyramid, the Roman numerals at the pyramid's base, and the eye of Providence above. And, to complicate things further, not one but three mottoes were affixed to the seal. Each is in Latin: E Pluribus Unum *(Out of many, one),* Annuit Coeptis *(He has approved of our undertakings), and, borrowed from Virgil,* Novus Ordo Seclorum *(A new order of the ages).*

Many subscribe to the adage "A picture is worth a thousand words." Is this the case with the Great Seal of the United States? Can you weave a coherent story from the images affixed on it? Or, are the images—and mottoes—in tension? Why are the mottoes of the United States in Latin rather than English, and what difference does that make? How does the obverse differ from the reverse, and what picture of the nation does each side convey? What feelings do the images evoke in you?

Reverse. The pyramid signifies Strength and Duration: the Eye over it and the Motto allude to the many signal interpositions of providence in favour of the American cause. The date underneath is that of the Declaration of Independence and the words under it signify the beginning of the New American Era, which commences from that date.

The American Eagle: Two Poems

Whereas the Great Seal is laden with the complex symbolism of the ancient art of heraldry, the symbol of the nation is simpler. But in selecting an animal to inspirit the nation, not everyone was convinced that the eagle was the right choice. Benjamin Franklin, for one, preferred a more democratic, less imperial symbol, one that would better exemplify American—rather than Roman—virtues. In a pseudonymous article published in late 1775, he made the case for the American rattlesnake, which had become an early symbol of colonial unity and independence; the image of a coiled rattlesnake, along with the motto "Don't Tread on Me," achieved prominence during the Revolution, appearing on the Gadsden flag and elsewhere. Franklin's article, entitled "The Rattle-Snake as a Symbol of America," traced the animal's admirable and appropriate attributes.* Despite other contenders, the American bald eagle was chosen as the symbol of America, first for the Great Seal (1782), then as the nation's official bird (1789). It is often displayed atop the standard bearing the national flag.

The following two poems demonstrate the increased power of symbols to inspire and instruct when they become the subject of song.

---

* *Later, in a 1784 letter to his daughter, Franklin privately criticized the eagle as lazy, predatory, and cowardly, and expressed his preference for the turkey, "a much more respectable Bird, and withal a true original Native of America . . . [a] Bird of Courage [who] would not hesitate to attack a Grenadier of the British Guards, who should presume to invade his Farm Yard with a red Coat on."*

Song of the American Eagle

AUTHOR UNKNOWN

In this recital poem for young people, the symbol of the nation, the eagle, delivers his song to an American audience. Although traditionally the eagle was considered the king of the air, just as the lion was king of the jungle, this poem reenvisions the eagle's meaning, associating him not with rule and authority but with liberty: he is "a type of the sons of Liberty." In the poem's last four stanzas, the far-seeing eagle delivers a warning to future generations: we freeborn can lose our heritage of freedom if we allow ourselves to descend into luxury and voluptuousness. Materialism breeds cowards. By the end of the poem, liberty is reconnected to rule, but it is vigilant self-rule rather than rule over others. Should we disgrace ourselves, the eagle threatens to attack that other symbol of the nation, the flag, tearing the stars and stripes from us.

Imagine yourself tasked to memorize this poem—better yet, actually memorize it—what effect does it have on your attitudes toward your country and your life choices? Is it a duty of citizenship to see to it that your own soul is not enchained? Do we, both individually and collectively, have to be worthy of our symbols? What activities and virtues does the eagle model for us?

I build my nest on the mountain's crest,
Where the wild winds rock my eaglets to rest,
Where the lightnings flash, and the thunders crash,
And the roaring torrents foam and dash;
For my spirit free henceforth shall be
A type of the sons of Liberty.

Aloft I fly from my aërie high,
Through the vaulted dome of the azure sky;
On a sunbeam bright take my airy flight,
And float in a flood of liquid light;
For I love to play in the noontide ray,
And bask in a blaze from the throne of day.

Away I spring with a tireless wing,
On a feathery cloud I poise and swing;

I dart down the steep where the lightnings leap,
And the clear blue canopy swiftly sweep;
For, dear to me is the revelry
Of a free and fearless Liberty.

I love the land where the mountains stand,
Like the watch-towers high of a Patriot band;
For I may not bide in my glory and pride,
Though the land be never so fair and wide,
Where Luxury reigns o'er voluptuous plains,
And fetters the free-born soul in chains.

Then give to me in my flights to see
The land of the pilgrims ever free!
And I never will rove from the haunts I love
But watch, from my sentinel-track above,
Your banner free, o'er land and sea,
And exult in your glorious Liberty.

O, guard ye well the land where I dwell,
Lest to future times the tale I tell,
When slow expires in smoldering fires
The goodly heritage of your sires,
How Freedom's light rose clear and bright
O'er fair Columbia's beacon-hight,
Till ye quenched the flame in a starless night.

Then will I tear from your pennon fair
The stars ye have set in triumph there;
My olive-branch on the blast I'll launch,
The fluttering stripes from the flagstaff wrench,
And away I'll flee; for I scorn to see
A craven race in the land of the free!

The Eagle of the Blue

Herman Melville

This poem originally appeared in Herman Melville's collection Battle-Pieces
and Aspects of the War. *In an attached note, Melville explained that some
regiments during the Civil War carried live eagles with them:*[*]

> *The bird commemorated here was, according to the account, borne
> aloft on a perch beside the standard; went through successive battles
> and campaigns; was more than once under the surgeon's hands; and at
> the close of the contest found honorable repose in the capital of Wiscon-
> sin, from which state he had gone to the wars.*

*Traditionally, the eagle was associated with strength, courage, farsight-
edness, and immortality. Melville highlights each of these characteristics. If
the eagle is a symbol of the nation, how is the eagle—now "chained" and
"anchored"—faring? What does it mean that he "exulteth in the war"? What
effect does the living emblem of the nation have even upon the rebels? How
much power can a symbol have? To which of the three main national symbols
(the Great Seal, the eagle, and the flag) do you most respond and why? Had
we chosen a different bird or other animal, would your answer be different?*

Aloft he guards the starry folds
   Who is the brother of the star;
The bird whose joy is in the wind
   Exulteth in the war.

No painted plume—a sober hue,
   His beauty is his power;
That eager calm of gaze intent
   Foresees the Sibyl's hour.

Austere, he crowns the swaying perch,
   Flapped by the angry flag;

---

[*] *Roman legions did the same. A special post of great honor, called the Aquilifer, bore the eagle.
Thus, the original standard-bearer was in fact the eagle-bearer.*

The hurricane from the battery sings,
   But his claw has known the crag.

Amid the scream of shells, his scream
   Runs shrilling; and the glare
Of eyes that brave the blinding sun
   The vollied flame can bear.

The pride of quenchless strength is his—
   Strength which, though chained, avails;
The very rebel looks and thrills—
   The anchored Emblem hails.

Though scarred in many a furious fray,
   No deadly hurt he knew;
Well may we think his years are charmed—
   The Eagle of the Blue.

The Flag

The preeminent symbol of the United States, as with every nation, is its national flag. It is displayed from public buildings, private homes, ships at sea, and embassies abroad, always in a manner governed by defined protocol. It is saluted on ceremonial occasions and celebrated annually on Flag Day (June 14); it is lowered to mark the deaths of national leaders and to mourn national tragedies; it drapes the coffins of those who have fallen in the nation's defense. The American flag—"The Stars and Stripes"—has additional and exceptional significance: it is the subject of our national anthem (see the previous section); it, and "the Republic for which it stands," is the object of our Pledge of Allegiance; and, in its very composition, it symbolically reflects the idea and ideal of E Pluribus Unum, as well as something of our national history.*

But knowing the meaning of the symbol does not reveal the symbol's power—how it affects the hearts and minds of American citizens. The idea of "one out of many" symbolized by the flag is about making one nation out of many states; can the flag also help forge one nation out of many—and

---

* *The thirteen stripes, alternating red and white, stand for the thirteen original colonies and states; each of the fifty stars, white on a field of blue, stands for one of the fifty states; the constellation of the fifty stars stands for the United States as a whole. As the Union has grown from thirteen to fifty states, the flag has evolved in parallel: with each addition to the Union, the number of stars increased to reflect the new state added, but the thirteen stripes and the overall structure and colors have (almost always) remained constant. In fact, there have been twenty-seven different versions of the American flag, from the so-called Betsy Ross flag of 1777, to the fifteen star–fifteen stripe flag (the only flag not to have thirteen stripes; used from 1795 to 1818) about which Francis Scott Key wrote his poem, to the current and longest-used flag, adopted on July 4, 1960, after Hawaii was admitted to the Union.*

highly diverse—citizens? Can it contribute to a felt sense of American iden-
tity? Here, a good story may be worth a hundred arguments.

The Namesake

Willa Cather

This anthology began with the question of national identity and with Edward
Everett Hale's story "The Man without a Country," about an American sol-
dier who is permanently exiled at sea from his native land, in accordance
with his wish never again to hear the name of the United States. We conclude
the anthology with this story (1907) by Willa Cather (1873–1947), about
how an American expatriate discovers the meaning of his home country.
Lyon Hartwell, the son of an American artist, born abroad and now himself
a sculptor living in Paris, habitually entertains his fellow Americans, all the
while working on a memorial statue of his late uncle, his namesake, who was
killed in the Civil War while still in his teens.

    Cather's story describes a rare episode of self-revelation, as Hartwell
tells his compatriots of his epiphany about American identity. How does
Hartwell's insight come? What does he discover? Crucial to his experience
is his encounter with his namesake's copy of Virgil's Aeneid, *inside of which*
his uncle drew the federal flag and inscribed the opening two lines of "The
Star-Spangled Banner." How and why is Hartwell moved by this encounter?
What, for Hartwell, is the relation of the flag to the Republic for which it
stands? What is the relation of the flag to our—and to your—American
identity?

Seven of us, students, sat one evening in Hartwell's studio on the Boulevard
St. Michel. We were all fellow-countrymen; one from New Hampshire, one
from Colorado, another from Nevada, several from the farm lands of the Middle West, and I myself from California. Lyon Hartwell, though born abroad,
was simply, as every one knew, "from America." He seemed, almost more than
any other one living man, to mean all of it—from ocean to ocean. When he
was in Paris, his studio was always open to the seven of us who were there that
evening, and we intruded upon his leisure as often as we thought permissible.

    Although we were within the terms of the easiest of all intimacies, and
although the great sculptor, even when he was more than usually silent, was
at all times the most gravely cordial of hosts, yet, on that long remembered

evening, as the sunlight died on the burnished brown of the horse-chestnuts below the windows, a perceptible dullness yawned through our conversation.

We were, indeed, somewhat low in spirit, for one of our number, Charley Bentley, was leaving us indefinitely, in response to an imperative summons from home. To-morrow his studio, just across the hall from Hartwell's, was to pass into other hands, and Bentley's luggage was even now piled in discouraged resignation before his door. The various bales and boxes seemed literally to weigh upon us as we sat in his neighbor's hospitable rooms, drearily putting in the time until he should leave us to catch the ten o'clock express for Dieppe.

The day we had got through very comfortably, for Bentley made it the occasion of a somewhat pretentious luncheon at Maxim's. There had been twelve of us at table, and the two young Poles were thirsty, the Gascon so fabulously entertaining, that it was near upon five o'clock when we put down our liqueur glasses for the last time, and the red, perspiring waiter, having pocketed the reward of his arduous and protracted services, bowed us affably to the door, flourishing his napkin and brushing back the streaks of wet, black hair from his rosy forehead. Our guests having betaken themselves belated to their respective engagements, the rest of us returned with Bentley—only to be confronted by the depressing array before his door. A glance about his denuded rooms had sufficed to chill the glow of the afternoon, and we fled across the hall in a body and begged Lyon Hartwell to take us in.

Bentley had said very little about it, but we all knew what it meant to him to be called home. Each of us knew what it would mean to himself, and each had felt something of that quickened sense of opportunity which comes at seeing another man in any way counted out of the race. Never had the game seemed so enchanting, the chance to play it such a piece of unmerited, unbelievable good fortune.

It must have been, I think, about the middle of October, for I remember that the sycamores were almost bare in the Luxembourg Gardens that morning, and the terrace about the queens of France were strewn with crackling brown leaves. The fat red roses, out the summer long on the stand of the old flower woman at the corner, had given place to dahlias and purple asters. First glimpses of autumn toilettes flashed from the carriages; wonderful little bonnets nodded at one along the Champs-Elysées; and in the Quarter an occasional feather boa, red or black or white, brushed one's coat sleeve in the gay twilight of the early evening. The crisp, sunny autumn air was all day full of the stir of people and carriages and of the cheer of salutations; greetings of the students, returned brown and bearded from their holiday, gossip of people come back from Trouville, from St. Valery, from Dieppe, from all over Brittany and the Norman coast. Everywhere was the joyousness of return, the taking up again of life and work and play.

I had felt ever since early morning that this was the saddest of all possible seasons for saying good-by to that old, old city of youth, and to that little corner of it on the south shore which since the Dark Ages themselves—yes, and before—has been so peculiarly the land of the young.

I can recall our very postures as we lounged about Hartwell's rooms that evening, with Bentley making occasional hurried trips to his desolated workrooms across the hall—as if haunted by a feeling of having forgotten something—or stopping to poke nervously at his *perroquets*, which he had bequeathed to Hartwell, gilt cage and all. Our host himself sat on the couch, his big, bronze-like shoulders backed up against the window, his shaggy head, beaked nose, and long chin cut clean against the gray light.

Our drowsing interest, in so far as it could be said to be fixed upon anything, was centered upon Hartwell's new figure, which stood on the block ready to be cast in bronze, intended as a monument for some American battlefield. He called it "The Color Sergeant." It was the figure of a young soldier running, clutching the folds of a flag, the staff of which had been shot away. We had known it in all the stages of its growth, and the splendid action and feeling of the thing had come to have a kind of special significance for the half dozen of us who often gathered at Hartwell's rooms—though, in truth, there was as much to dishearten one as to inflame, in the case of a man who had done so much in a field so amazingly difficult; who had thrown up in bronze all the restless, teeming force of that adventurous wave still climbing westward in our own land across the waters. We recalled his "Scout," his "Pioneer," his "Gold Seekers," and those monuments in which he had invested one and another of the heroes of the Civil War with such convincing dignity and power.

"Where in the world does he get the heat to make an idea like that carry?" Bentley remarked morosely, scowling at the clay figure. "Hang me, Hartwell, if I don't think it's just because you're not really an American at all, that you can look at it like that."

The big man shifted uneasily against the window. "Yes," he replied smiling, "perhaps there is something in that. My citizenship was somewhat belated and emotional in its flowering. I've half a mind to tell you about it, Bentley." He rose uncertainly, and, after hesitating a moment, went back into his workroom, where he began fumbling among the litter in the corners.

At the prospect of any sort of personal expression from Hartwell, we glanced questioningly at one another; for although he made us feel that he liked to have us about, we were always held at a distance by a certain diffidence of his. There were rare occasions—when he was in the heat of work or of ideas—when he forgot to be shy, but they were so exceptional that no flattery was quite so seductive as being taken for a moment into Hartwell's confidence. Even in the matter of opinions—the commonest of currency in our circle—he was niggardly and prone to qualify. No man ever guarded his mystery more effectually. There was a singular, intense spell, therefore, about those few evenings when he had broken through this excessive modesty, or shyness, or melancholy, and had, as it were, committed himself.

When Hartwell returned from the back room, he brought with him an unframed canvas which he put on an easel near his clay figure. We drew close about it, for the darkness was rapidly coming on. Despite the dullness of the light, we instantly recognized the boy of Hartwell's "Color Sergeant." It was the portrait of a very handsome lad in uniform, standing beside a charger impossibly rearing. Not only in his radiant countenance and flashing eyes, but in every line of his young body there was an energy, a gallantry, a joy of life, that arrested and challenged one.

"Yes, that's where I got the notion," Hartwell remarked, wandering back to his seat in the window. "I've wanted to do it for years, but I've never felt quite sure of myself. I was afraid of missing it. He was an uncle of mine, my father's half-brother, and I was named for him. He was killed in one of the big battles of Sixty-four, when I was a child. I never saw him—never knew him until he had been dead for twenty years. And then, one night, I came to know him as we sometimes do living persons—intimately, in a single moment."

He paused to knock the ashes out of his short pipe, refilled it, and puffed at it thoughtfully for a few moments with his hands on his knees. Then, settling back heavily among the cushions and looking absently out of the window, he began his story. As he proceeded further and further into the experience which he was trying to convey to us, his voice sank so low and was sometimes so charged with feeling, that I almost thought he had forgotten our presence and was remembering aloud. Even Bentley forgot his nervousness in astonishment and sat breathless under the spell of the man's thus breathing his memories out into the dusk.

"It was just fifteen years ago this last spring that I first went home, and Bentley's having to cut away like this brings it all back to me.

"I was born, you know, in Italy. My father was a sculptor, though I dare say you've not heard of him. He was one of those first fellows who went over after Story and Powers,—went to Italy for 'Art,' quite simply; to lift from its native bough the willing, iridescent bird. Their story is told, informingly enough, by some of those ingenuous marble things at the Metropolitan. My father came over some time before the outbreak of the Civil War, and was regarded as a renegade by his family because he did not go home to enter the army. His half-brother, the only child of my grandfather's second marriage, enlisted at fifteen and was killed the next year. I was ten years old when the news of his death reached us. My mother died the following winter, and I was sent away to a Jesuit school, while my father, already ill himself, stayed on at Rome, chipping away at his Indian maidens and marble goddesses, still gloomily seeking the thing for which he had made himself the most unhappy of exiles.

"He died when I was fourteen, but even before that I had been put to work under an Italian sculptor. He had an almost morbid desire that I should carry on his work, under, as he often pointed out to me, conditions so much more auspicious. He left me in the charge of his one intimate friend, an American gentleman in the consulate at Rome, and his instructions were that I was to be educated there and to live there until I was twenty-one. After I was of age, I came to Paris and studied under one master after another until I was nearly thirty. Then, almost for the first time, I was confronted by a duty which was not my pleasure.

"My grandfather's death, at an advanced age, left an invalid maiden sister of my father's quite alone in the world. She had suffered for years from a cerebral disease, a slow decay of the faculties which rendered her almost helpless. I decided to go to America and, if possible, bring her back to Paris, where I seemed on my way toward what my poor father had wished for me.

"On my arrival at my father's birthplace, however, I found that this was not to be thought of. To tear this timid, feeble, shrinking creature, doubly aged by years and illness, from the spot where she had been rooted for a lifetime, would have been little short of brutality. To leave her to the care of strangers seemed equally heartless. There was clearly nothing for me to do but to remain and wait for that slow and painless malady to run its course. I was there something over two years.

"My grandfather's home, his father's homestead before him, lay on the high banks of a river in Western Pennsylvania. The little town twelve miles down the stream, whither my great-grandfather used to drive his ox-wagon on market days, had become, in two generations, one of the largest manufacturing cities in the world. For hundreds of miles about us the gentle hill slopes were honeycombed with gas wells and coal shafts; oil derricks creaked in every valley and meadow; the brooks were sluggish and discolored with crude petroleum, and the air was impregnated by its searching odor. The great glass and iron manufactories had come up and up the river almost to our very door; their smoky exhalations brooded over us, and their crashing was always in our ears. I was plunged into the very incandescence of human energy. But, though my nerves tingled with the feverish, passionate endeavor which snapped in the very air about me, none of these great arteries seemed to feed me; this tumultuous life did not warm me. On every side were the great muddy rivers, the ragged mountains from which the timber was being ruthlessly torn away, the vast tracts of wild country, and the gulches that were like wounds in the earth; everywhere the glare of that relentless energy which followed me like a searchlight and seemed to scorch and consume me. I could only hide myself in the tangled garden, where the dropping of a leaf or the whistle of a bird was the only incident.

"The Hartwell homestead had been sold away little by little, until all that remained of it was garden and orchard. The house, a square brick structure, stood in the midst of a great garden which sloped toward the river, ending in a grassy bank which fell some forty feet to the water's edge. The garden was now little more than a tangle of neglected shrubbery; damp, rank, and of that intense blue-green peculiar to vegetation in smoky places where the sun shines but rarely, and the mists form early in the evening and hang late in the morning.

"I shall never forget it as I saw it first, when I arrived there in the chill of a backward June. The long, rank grass, thick and soft and falling in billows, was always wet until midday. The gravel walks were bordered with great lilac-bushes, mock-orange, and bridal-wreath. Back of the house was a neglected rose garden, surrounded by a low stone wall over which the long suckers trailed and matted. They had wound their pink, thorny tentacles, layer upon layer, about the lock and the hinges of the rusty iron gate. Even the porches of the house, and the very windows, were damp and heavy with growth: wistaria, clematis, honeysuckle, and trumpet vine. The garden was grown up with trees, especially that part of it which lay above the river. The bark of the old locusts was blackened by the smoke that crept continually up the valley, and their feathery foliage, so merry in its movement and so yellow and joyous in its color, seemed peculiarly precious under that somber sky. There were syca-mores and copper beeches; gnarled apple-trees, too old to bear; and fall pear-trees, hung with a sharp, hard fruit in October; all with a leafage singularly rich and luxuriant, and peculiarly vivid in color. The oaks about the house had been old trees when my great-grandfather built his cabin there, more than a century before, and this garden was almost the only spot for miles along the river where any of the original forest growth still survived. The smoke from the mills was fatal to trees of the larger sort, and even these had the look of doomed things—bent a little toward the town and seemed to wait with head inclined before that on-coming, shrieking force.

"About the river, too, there was a strange hush, a tragic submission—it was so leaden and sullen in its color, and it flowed so soundlessly forever past our door.

"I sat there every evening, on the high veranda overlooking it, watching the dim outlines of the steep hills on the other shore, the flicker of the lights on the island, where there was a boat-house, and listening to the call of the boatmen through the mist. The mist came as certainly as night, whitened by moonshine or starshine. The tin water-pipes went splash, splash, with it all evening, and the wind, when it rose at all, was little more than a sighing of the old boughs and a troubled breath in the heavy grasses.

"At first it was to think of my distant friends and my old life that I used to sit there; but after awhile it was simply to watch the days and weeks go by, like the river which seemed to carry them away.

"Within the house I was never at home. Month followed month, and yet I could feel no sense of kinship with anything there. Under the roof where my father and grandfather were born, I remained utterly detached. The somber rooms never spoke to me, the old furniture never seemed tinctured with race. This portrait of my boy uncle was the only thing to which I could draw near, the only link with anything I had ever known before.

"There is a good deal of my father in the face, but it is my father transformed and glorified; his hesitating discontent drowned in a kind of triumph. From my first day in that house, I continually turned to this handsome kinsman of mine, wondering in what terms he had lived and had his hope; what he had found there to look like that, to bound at one, after all those years, so joyously out of the canvas.

"From the timid, clouded old woman over whose life I had come to watch, I learned that in the backyard, near the old rose garden, there was a locust-tree which my uncle had planted. After his death, while it was still a slender sapling, his mother had a seat built round it, and she used to sit there on summer evenings. His grave was under the apple-trees in the old orchard.

"My aunt could tell me little more than this. There were days when she seemed not to remember him at all.

"It was from an old soldier in the village that I learned the boy's story. Lyon was, the old man told me, but fourteen when the first enlistment occurred, but was even then eager to go. He was in the court-house square every evening to watch the recruits at their drill, and when the home company was ordered off he rode into the city on his pony to see the men board the train and to wave them good-by. The next year he spent at home with a tutor, but when he was fifteen he held his parents to their promise and went into the army. He was color sergeant of his regiment and fell in a charge upon the breastworks of a fort about a year after his enlistment.

"The veteran showed me an account of this charge which had been written for the village paper by one of my uncle's comrades who had seen his part in the engagement. It seems that as his company were running at full speed across the bottom lands toward the fortified hill, a shell burst over them. This comrade, running beside my uncle, saw the colors waver and sink as if falling, and looked to see that the boy's hand and forearm had been torn away by the exploding shrapnel. The boy, he thought, did not realize the extent of his injury, for he laughed, shouted something which his comrade did not catch, caught the flag in his left hand, and ran on up the hill. They went splendidly up over the breastworks, but just as my uncle, his colors flying, reached the top of the embankment, a second shell carried away his left arm at the arm-pit, and he fell over the wall with the flag settling about him.

"It was because this story was ever present with me, because I was unable to shake it off, that I began to read such books as my grandfather had collected upon the Civil War. I found that this war was fought largely by boys, that more men enlisted at eighteen than at any other age. When I thought of those battlefields—and I thought of them much in those days—there was always that glory of youth above them, that impetuous, generous passion stirring the long lines on the march, the blue battalions in the plain. The bugle, whenever I have heard it since, has always seemed to me the very golden throat of that boyhood which spent itself so gaily, so incredibly.

"I used often to wonder how it was that this uncle of mine, who seemed to have possessed all the charm and brilliancy allotted to his family and to have lived up its vitality in one splendid hour, had left so little trace in the house where he was born and where he had awaited his destiny. Look as I would, I could find no letters from him, no clothing or books that might have been his. He had been dead but twenty years, and yet nothing seemed to have survived except the tree he had planted. It seemed incredible and cruel that no physical memory of him should linger to be cherished among his kindred,—nothing but the dull image in the brain of that aged sister. I used to pace the garden walks in the evening, wondering that no breath of his, no echo of his laugh, of his call to his pony or his whistle to his dogs, should linger about those shaded paths where the pale roses exhaled their dewy, country smell. Sometimes, in the dim starlight, I have thought that I heard on the grasses beside me the stir of a footfall lighter than my own, and under the black arch of the lilacs I have fancied that he bore me company.

"There was, I found, one day in the year for which my old aunt waited, and which stood out from the months that were all of a sameness to her. On the thirtieth of May she insisted that I should bring down the big flag from the attic and run it up upon the tall flagstaff beside Lyon's tree in the garden. Later in the morning she went with me to carry some of the garden flowers to the grave in the orchard,—a grave scarcely larger than a child's.

"I had noticed, when I was hunting for the flag in the attic, a leather trunk with my own name stamped upon it, but was unable to find the key. My aunt was all day less apathetic than usual; she seemed to realize more clearly who I was, and to wish me to be with her. I did not have an opportunity to return to the attic until after dinner that evening, when I carried a lamp up-stairs and easily forced the lock of the trunk. I found all the things that I had looked for; put away, doubtless, by his mother, and still smelling faintly of lavender and rose leaves; his clothes, his exercise books, his letters from the army, his first boots, his riding-whip, some of his toys, even. I took them out and replaced them gently. As I was about to shut the lid, I picked up a copy of the *Æneid*, on the fly-leaf of which was written in a slanting, boyish hand,

Lyon Hartwell, January, 1862.

He had gone to the wars in Sixty-three, I remembered.

"My uncle, I gathered, was none too apt at his Latin, for the pages were dog-eared and rubbed and interlined, the margins mottled with pencil sketches— bugles, stacked bayonets, and artillery carriages. In the act of putting the book down, I happened to run over the pages to the end, and on the fly-leaf at the back I saw his name again, and a drawing—with his initials and a date—of the Federal flag; above it, written in a kind of arch and in the same unformed hand:

'Oh, say, can you see by the dawn's early light
What so proudly we hailed at the twilight's last gleaming?'

It was a stiff, wooden sketch, not unlike a detail from some Egyptian inscription, but, the moment I saw it, wind and color seemed to touch it. I caught up the book, blew out the lamp, and rushed down into the garden.

"I seemed, somehow, at last to have known him; to have been with him in that careless, unconscious moment and to have known him as he was then.

"As I sat there in the rush of this realization, the wind began to rise, stirring the light foliage of the locust over my head and bringing, fresher than before, the woody odor of the pale roses that overran the little neglected garden. Then, as it grew stronger, it brought the sound of something sighing and stirring over my head in the perfumed darkness.

"I thought of that sad one of the Destinies who, as the Greeks believed, watched from birth over those marked for a violent or untimely death. Oh, I could see him, there in the shine of the morning, his book idly on his knee, his flashing eyes looking straight before him, and at his side that grave figure, hidden in her draperies, her eyes following his, but seeing so much farther— seeing what he never saw, that great moment at the end, when he swayed above his comrades on the earthen wall.

"All the while, the bunting I had run up in the morning flapped fold against fold, heaving and tossing softly in the dark—against a sky so black with rain clouds that I could see above me only the blur of something in soft, troubled motion.

"The experience of that night, coming so overwhelmingly to a man so dead, almost rent me in pieces. It was the same feeling that artists know when we, rarely, achieve truth in our work; the feeling of union with some great force, of purpose and security, of being glad that we have lived. For the first time I felt the pull of race and blood and kindred, and felt beating within me things that had not begun with me. It was as if the earth under my feet had grasped and rooted me, and were pouring its essence into me. I sat there until the dawn of morning, and all night long my life seemed to be pouring out of me and running into the ground."

Hartwell drew a long breath that lifted his heavy shoulders, and then let them fall again. He shifted a little and faced more squarely the scattered, silent company before him. The darkness had made us almost invisible to each other, and, except for the occasional red circuit of a cigarette end traveling upward from the arm of a chair, he might have supposed us all asleep.

"And so," Hartwell added thoughtfully, "I naturally feel an interest in fellows who are going home. It's always an experience."

No one said anything, and in a moment there was a loud rap at the door,—the concierge, come to take down Bentley's luggage and to announce that the cab was below. Bentley got his hat and coat, enjoined Hartwell to take good care of his *perroquets*, gave each of us a grip of the hand, and went briskly down the long flights of stairs. We followed him into the street, calling our good wishes, and saw him start on his drive across the lighted city to the Gare St. Lazare.

Acknowledgments

We each wish to acknowledge, with deep gratitude, the help and support of individuals and institutions that contributed to the preparation of this volume.

This anthology grew out of a series of seminars, using many of these readings, conducted by Amy Kass at the Hudson Institute: "Appreciating American Identity" (Winter 2008) and "Making American Citizens: Dispositions and Sensibilities for Civic Life" (Winter 2009). Amy Kass is indebted to all the participants in the seminars, who enthusiastically and thoughtfully demonstrated the value of this approach to civic education and who helped the editors refine the questions and issues in need of attention: Elizabeth Barringer, Darren Beattie, James Bowman, Karlyn Bowman, William Dennis, Laura Drinkwine, Francis DuVinage, Matt Glover, Adam Keiper, Rita Koganzon, Nelly Forbes Lambert, Walker Lambert, Kevin Laskowski, Yael Levin, Yuval Levin, Haven Ley, McKenzie Lock, Jacqueline Pfeffer Merrill, Cheryl Miller, Caitrin Nicol, Virginia Rice, Christy Robinson, Mary Rose Ryback, Sharon Schambra, William Schambra, Krista Shaffer, Anne Snyder, Evan Sparks, Juliet Squire, Jean Weicher, John Weicher, Thomas Wilburn, Will Wilson, and Robert Zarate. Some participants also offered additional assistance: Kevin Laskowski, Adam Keiper, Darren Beattie, and Matthew Glover did bibliographical research and found suitable stories for discussion and inclusion; William Schambra of Hudson Institute's Bradley Center for Philanthropy and Civic Renewal offered unflagging support of the project and invaluable conversations on many of the selected stories; and Krista Shaffer provided superb logistical support and hospitality for the seminar series, from scanning readings to setting up the nourishing delectables that were always at hand. Amy Kass would also like to thank her colleagues at the Hudson Institute: Kenneth Weinstein, the institute's chief executive officer, for providing a most hospitable home for this project, start to finish; Lewis Libby for recommending the stories of Stephen Crane; and John Walters for suggesting the subtitle of our volume. Finally, she is most grateful to the following individuals and institutions who provided generous financial support of the project in its various stages: Roger Hertog, John Wohlstetter and the Billy Rose Foundation, Leslie Lenkowsky and the Achelis and Bodman Foundations, Frank Hanna, Montgomery Brown and the Earhart Foundation, and Keith Whitaker and the Fred Fund.

Leon Kass wishes to thank Arthur Brooks and the American Enterprise Institute for their support and encouragement of this project; Kimberly Hudson for scanning some of the readings and converting them into Word documents; Keriann Hopkins for rendering excellent help securing permissions to reprint the various selections and preparing the bibliography; and Gordon and Adele Binder for a generous grant that defrayed the publishers' fees for permission to reprint.

Diana Schaub would like to thank Lucas Morel for story suggestions and Lauren Weiner for invaluable help at each stage of the project. She is grateful to Jill and Boyd Smith for their generous sponsorship of the Hoover Institution's Task Force on the Virtues of a Free Society, which provided support and encouragement for this anthology.

Finally, we would all like to thank Jed Donahue of ISI Books for his enthusiasm for the book, his wise advice about selections, and his superb editorial comments on our introductory materials. The book has been much improved as a result of his fine efforts.

Sources and Credits

Author Unknown. "The American Eagle." Available at http://www. apples4theteacher.com/holidays/flag-day/poems-rhymes/song-of-the-american-eagle.html.

Antin, Mary. *The Promised Land.* Cambridge: Houghton Mifflin Company, The Riverside Press, 1912, 180–81, 184–88, 197–98, 202–5, 221–31.

Ballou, Sullivan. "Letter to Sarah." In Ballou, Adin, *An Elaborate History and Genealogy of the Ballous in America.* Providence, RI: A. and L. W. Ballou, 1888.

Bates, Katharine Lee. "America the Beautiful," lyrics written between 1895 and 1910. Available at http://en.wikipedia.org/wiki/America_the_Beautiful.

Bellow, Saul. "A Father-to-Be." In Bellow, Saul, *Mosby's Memoirs and Other Stories.* Copyright © 1951, 1954, 1955, 1957, 1967, 1968 by Saul Bellow. Used by permission of Viking Penguin, a division of Penguin Group (USA) Inc.

Benét, Stephen Vincent. "The Devil and Daniel Webster." Illustrated by Harold Denison. New York: Farrar & Rinehart, 1937. Copyright © 1936 by Stephen Vincent Benét. Copyright renewed © 1964 by Thomas C. Benét, Stephanie B. Mahin, and Rachel Benét Lewis. Used by permission of Brandt & Hochman Literary Agents, Inc.

Berlin, Irving. "God Bless America." Copyright © 1938, 1939 by Irving Berlin. Copyright renewed © 1965, 1966 by Irving Berlin. Copyright © Assigned the Trustees of the God Bless America Fund. International copyright secured. All rights reserved. Reprinted by permission.

Cather, Willa Silbert. "The Best Years." In *Willa Cather: Stories, Poems, and Other Writings.* New York: Literary Classics of the United States, Inc., 1992, 728–57.

_____. "The Namesake." In *Willa Cather: Stories, Poems, and Other Writings*. New York: Literary Classics of the United States, Inc., 1992, 52–63.

Crane, Stephen. "The Blue Hotel." In *Stephen Crane: Poetry and Prose*. New York: Literary Classics of the United States, Inc., 1996, 799–828.

_____. "The Open Boat." In *Stephen Crane: Poetry and Prose*. New York: Literary Classics of the United States, Inc., 1996, 885–909.

_____. "The Veteran." In *Stephen Crane: Poetry and Prose*. New York: Literary Classics of the United States, Inc., 1996, 666–70.

Coolidge, Calvin. "Speech on the Occasion of the 150th Anniversary of the Declaration of Independence." July 5, 1926. Available at http://teachingamericanhistory.org/library/index asp?documentprint=41.

The Declaration of Independence. Available at http://www.archives.gov/exhibits/charters/declaration_transcript.html.

Douglass, Frederick. "Why Should a Colored Man Enlist?" *Douglass' Monthly*. April 1863. Reprinted in *The Life and Writings of Frederick Douglass*, edited by Philip S. Foner. New York: International Publishers, 1975, III. 340–44.

_____. "The Last Flogging." From *My Bondage and My Freedom*. In *Frederick Douglass: Autobiographies*. New York: Literary Classics of the United States, Inc., 1994, 277–87.

DuBois, W. E. B. "The Talented Tenth." In *W. E. B. DuBois: Writings*. New York: Literary Classics of the United States, Inc., 1986, 842–48, 852–56, 861 (excerpted).

Ellison, Ralph. "In a Strange Country." In Ellison, Ralph, *Flying Home and Other Stories*, edited by John F. Callahan. New York: Vintage International, 1996, 137–46. Copyright © 1996 by Fanny Ellison; Introduction copyright © 1996 by John F. Callahan. Used by permission of Random House, Inc.

_____. "The Little Man at Chehaw Station: The American Artist and His Audience." In Ellison, Ralph, *Going to the Territory*. New York: Vintage Books, a Division of Random House, 1986, 2–5, 32–38. Copyright © 1986 by Ralph Ellison. Used by permission of Random House, Inc.

Epstein, Daniel Mark. "The Star-Spangled Banner." In Epstein, Daniel Mark, *Star of Wonder: American Stories and Memoirs*. New York: The Overlook Press, 1986, 49–57. Copyright © 1986 by Daniel Mark Epstein. All rights reserved. www.overlookpress.com. Used with permission.

Ferguson, Andrew. From *Land of Lincoln: Adventures in Abe's America*. New York: Atlantic Monthly Press, 2007, 72–76. Reprinted with permission of the author.

Franklin, Benjamin. From "The Autobiography." In *Benjamin Franklin: Writings*. New York: Literary Classics of the United States, Inc., 1987, 1383–94 (excerpted).

Glaspell, Susan. "A Jury of Her Peers." In *The Best American Short Stories of the Century*, edited by John Updike. Boston/New York: Houghton Mifflin, 1999, 18–37. (First appeared in *Every Week*, 1917.) Copyright ©1917 by the Crowell Publishing Company; Copyright © 1918 by Susan Glaspell Cook.

The Great Seal of the United States. Shutterstock Images, www.shutterstock.com.

Guthrie, Woodrow ("Woody") Wilson. "This Land Is Your Land." Words and Music by Woody Guthrie. TRO—Copyright © 1956 (Renewed), 1958 (Renewed), 1970 (Renewed), 1972 (Renewed), Ludlow Music, Inc., New York, NY. International copyright secured. Made in U.S.A. All rights reserved including public performance for profit. Used by permission.

Hale, Edward Everett. "The Man without a Country." *The Atlantic Monthly*, Vol. XII, December 1863, No. LXXIV, 665–79.

Hawthorne, Nathaniel. "The Artist of the Beautiful." In *Nathaniel Hawthorne: Tales and Sketches*. New York: Literary Classics of the United States, Inc., 1982, 907–31.

———. "The May-Pole of Merry Mount." In *Nathaniel Hawthorne: Tales and Sketches*. New York: Literary Classics of the United States, Inc., 1982, 360–70.

Henry, O. "Two Thanksgiving Day Gentlemen." In *The Complete Works of O. Henry*. Garden City, NY: Doubleday & Co., 1953.

Hickam, Homer. "Dosie, of Killakeet Island." In *The Best Christian Short Stories*, edited by Bret Lott. WestBow Press, Division of Thomas Nelson, 135–52. Copyright © 2006 Bret Lott. Used by permission. Thomas Nelson Inc., Nashville, Tennessee. All rights reserved.

Holmes, Oliver Wendell, Jr. "In Our Youth Our Hearts Were Touched with Fire" ("Memorial Day Address," 1884). In *American Speeches: Political Oratory from Abraham Lincoln to Bill Clinton*. New York: Literary Classics of the United States, Inc., 2006, 89–97.

Howe, Julia Ward. "The Battle Hymn of the Republic." Lyrics written in 1861. Available at http://en.wikipedia.org/wiki/The_Battle_Hymn_of_the_Republic.

James, Henry. "Pandora." In *Henry James: Complete Stories 1874–1884*. New York: Literary Classics of the United States, Inc., 1999, 816–64 (abridged).

Jefferson, Thomas. From "Notes on the State of Virginia." In *The Portable Thomas Jefferson*, edited by Merrill D. Peterson. New York: Viking Penguin, 1975, 193–94, 198.

_____. From "Report of the Commissioners for the University of Virginia." In *The Portable Thomas Jefferson*, edited by Merrill D. Peterson. New York: Viking Penguin, 1975, 333–35.

_____. "Letter to Isaac McPherson." In *The Portable Thomas Jefferson*, edited by Merrill D. Peterson. New York: Viking Penguin, 1975, 529–30.

Kelly, John F. "Veterans Day Speech to the Semper Fi Society of St. Louis" (abridged). Available at http://www.marines.mil/unit/marforres/CMFR/blog/CMFR101113.aspx.

Kennedy, John F. "Address at Rice University on the Nation's Space Effort, Houston Texas, September 12, 1962." Available at http://www.jfklibrary.org/Research/Ready-Reference/JFK-Speeches/Address-at-Rice-University-on-the-Nations-Space-Effort-September-12-1962.aspx.

Key, Francis Scott. "The Star-Spangled Banner." Written in 1814. Available at http://en.wikipedia.org/wiki/The_Star-Spangled_Banner.

King, Martin Luther, Jr. "Letter from Birmingham Jail." In King, Martin Luther, Jr., *Why We Can't Wait*. New York: The New American Library, 2000, 64–84. Copyright © 1963, Dr. Martin Luther King Jr.; copyright renewed 1991, Coretta Scott King. Reprinted by arrangement with the Heirs to the Estate of Martin Luther King Jr., c/o Writers House as agent for the proprietor, New York, NY.

Lardner, Ring. "Contract." In *The Ring Lardner Reader*, edited by Maxwell Geismar. New York: Charles Scribner's Sons, 1963, 379–91.

_____. "Old Folks' Christmas." In Lardner, Ring, *The Best Short Stories of Ring Lardner*. New York: A Scribner Classic, Collier Books, Macmillan Publishing Company, 1957, 139–48.

Le Guin, Ursula K. "The Ones Who Walked Away from Omelas." In Le Guin, Ursula K., *The Wind's Twelve Quarters*. New York: Harper and Row, 1975. (First appeared in *New Dimensions 3*.) Copyright © 1973, 2001 by Ursula K. Le Guin. Reprinted by permission of the author and the author's agents, the Virginia Kidd Agency, Inc.

Lincoln, Abraham. "Address to the Young Men's Lyceum of Springfield, Illinois." In *Abraham Lincoln: Speeches and Writings, 1832–1858*. New York: Literary Classics of the United States, Inc., 1989, 28–36.

_____. "Gettysburg Address." *In Abraham Lincoln: Speeches and Writings, 1859–1865*. New York: Literary Classics of the United States, Inc., 1989, 536.

_____. "Second Inaugural Address." In *Abraham Lincoln: Speeches and Writings, 1859–1865*. New York: Literary Classics of the United States, Inc., 1989, 686–87.

London, Jack. "To Build a Fire." In *Jack London: Novels and Stories*. New York: Literary Classics of the United States, Inc., 1982, 462–78.

Malamud, Bernard. "Idiots First." In Malamud, Bernard, *Idiot's First.* New York: Farrar, Straus & Giroux, Inc., 1961. Copyright © 1963 by Bernard Malamud. Copyright renewed 1991 by Ann Malamud. Reprinted by permission of Farrar, Straus and Giroux, LLC.

Mayflower Compact. From Bradford, William, *Of Plymouth Plantation, 1620–1647,* edited by Samuel Eliot Morison. New York: Knopf, 1952, 75–76.

McCain, John (with Mark Salter). "On Roy Benavidez." From McCain, John (with Mark Salter), *Why Courage Matters: The Way to a Braver Life.* New York: Ballantine Books Mass Market Edition, 2008, 3–12. Copyright © 2004 by John McCain and Marshall Salter. Used by permission of Random House, Inc.

Melville, Herman. "Bartleby, The Scrivener: A Story of Wall-Street." In *Herman Melville: Pierre, or, The Ambiguities; Israel Potter: His Fifty Years of Exile; The Piazza Tales; The Confidence Man: His Masquerade; Uncollected Prose; Billy Budd, Sailor (An Inside Narrative).* New York: Literary Classics of the United States, Inc., 1984, 635–72.

_____. "The Eagle of the Blue." From Melville, Herman, *Battle-Pieces and Aspects of the War: Civil War Poems.* Originally published New York: Harper and Brothers, 1866, 122–23. Reprinted Amherst, NY: Prometheus Books, 2001, 132.

_____. "Lee in the Capitol." From Melville, Herman, *Battle-Pieces and Aspects of the War: Civil War Poems.* Originally published New York: Harper and Brothers, 1866, 229–37. Reprinted Amherst, NY: Prometheus Books, 2001, 213–19.

O'Connor, Flannery. "The Artificial Nigger." In *The Complete Stories of Flannery O'Connor.* New York: Farrar, Straus & Giroux, 1979, 249–70. Originally published in O'Connor, Flannery, *A Good Man Is Hard to Find and Other Stories.* New York: Harcourt, Brace and Company, 1955. Copyright © 1955 by Flannery O'Connor and renewed 1983 by Regina O'Connor. Reprinted by permission of Houghton Mifflin Harcourt Publishing Company.

Province, Charles, M. "The Famous Patton Speech." From Province, Charles M., *The Unknown Patton* (self-published). Available at http://www.pattonhq.com/speech.html. With permission of Charles M. Province, the General George S. Patton Jr. Historical Society.

Publius. "Federalist No. 10." From *The Federalist: A Commentary on the Constitution of the United States.* New York: The Modern Library, Random House, 1941.

Rodriguez, Richard. "Aria." From *Hunger of Memory: The Education of Richard Rodriguez.* Boston: David R. Godine, Publisher, Inc., 1981, 11–16, 19–23,

25, 26–28, 31–36. Reprinted by permission of David R. Godine, Publisher, Inc. Copyright © 1981 by Richard Rodriguez.

Roosevelt, Theodore. "Manhood and Statehood: Address at the Quarter-Centennial Celebration of Statehood in Colorado, at Colorado Springs, August 2, 1901." In Roosevelt, Theodore, *The Strenuous Life.* Stilwell, KS: Digireads.com Publishing, 2008, 73–77.

———. "True Americanism." From Roosevelt, Theodore, *American Ideals and Other Essays: Social and Political.* New York: G. P. Putnam's Sons, 1897, 15–34 (abridged). Available also at http://teachingamericanhistory.org/library/index.asp?document=672.

Ross, Leonard Q. "O K*A*P*L*A*N! My K*A*P*L*A*N!" From Ross, Leonard, *The Education of Hyman Kaplan.* New York: Harcourt, Inc. 1965, 76–85. Copyright © 1937 by Harcourt, Inc., and renewed 1965 by Leo C. Rosten. Reprinted by permission of Houghton Mifflin Harcourt Publishing Company.

Roth, Philip. "Defender of the Faith." In Roth, Philip, *Goodbye Columbus.* Boston: Houghton Mifflin Company, 1959, 116–43. Copyright © 1959, renewed 1987 by Philip Roth. Reprinted by permission of Houghton Mifflin Harcourt Publishing Company. All rights reserved.

Rustin, Bayard. "Twenty-Two Days on a Chain Gang." In *Time on Two Crosses: The Collected Writings of Bayard Rustin.* San Francisco: Cleis Press Inc., 2003, 31–57 (abridged). Reprinted by permission of the Estate of Bayard Rustin.

Shaara, Michael. "Chamberlain." From Shaara, Michael, *The Killer Angels.* New York: Ballantine Books, 1974, 17–32. Copyright © 1974 by Michael Shaara, copyright renewed 2002 by Jeff M. Shaara and Lila E. Shaara. Used by permission of Ballantine Books, a division of Random House, Inc.

Smith, Samuel Francis. "My Country, 'Tis of Thee." Lyrics written in 1831. Available at http://en.wikipedia.org/wiki/My_Country,_'Tis_of_Thee.

Stegner, Wallace Earle. "The Traveler." In *The Collected Stories of Wallace Stegner.* New York: Penguin Group USA, Inc., 2006, 3–11. Copyright © 1990 by Wallace Stegner. Used by permission of Random House, Inc.

———. "He Who Spits at the Sky." In *The Collected Stories of Wallace Stegner.* New York: Penguin Group USA, Inc., 2006, 487–511. Copyright © 1990 by Wallace Stegner. Used by permission of Random House, Inc.

Twain, Mark. "The Man That Corrupted Hadleyburg." From *Mark Twain: Tales, Sketches, Speeches, and Essays 1891–1910.* New York: Literary Classics of the United States, Inc., 1992, 390–438.

Updike, John. "The Deacon." In Updike, John, *Museums and Women and Other Stories*. New York: Vintage, 1972, 41–48. Copyright © 1972 by John Updike. Used by permission of Alfred A. Knopf, a division of Random House, Inc.

_____. "Hub Fans Bid Kid Adieu." Originally published in *The New Yorker*, October 22, 1960. Reprinted in Updike, John, *Assorted Prose*. New York: Alfred A. Knopf, 1965. Copyright © 1960 by John Updike. Used by permission of Alfred A. Knopf, a division of Random House, Inc.

Vonnegut, Kurt, Jr. "Harrison Bergeron." From Vonnegut Jr., Kurt, *Welcome to the Monkey House*. New York: The Dial Press, 1968, 7–14. Copyright © 1961 by Kurt Vonnegut Jr. Used by permission of Dell Publishing, a division of Random House, Inc.

Washington, Booker T. "Democracy and Education." In *African-American Social and Political Thought 1850–1920*, edited by Howard Brotz. New Brunswick, NJ: Transaction Publishers, 1992, 362–71 (abridged).

Washington, George. "Farewell Address." In *George Washington: Writings*. New York: Literary Classics of the United States, Inc., 1997, 962–77 (abridged).

_____. "To the Hebrew Congregation in Newport, Rhode Island." In *George Washington: Writings*. New York: Literary Classics of the United States, Inc., 1997, 766–67.

_____. "Thanksgiving Proclamation (1789)." In *George Washington: A Collection*, edited by W. B. Allen. Indianapolis: Liberty Classics, 1988, 534–35.

Walker, Alice. "Everyday Use." In *Major American Short Stories* (3rd edition), edited by A. Walton Litz. New York: Oxford University Press, 1994, 805–13. Originally published in Walker, Alice, *In Love and Trouble: Stories of Black Women*. New York: Harcourt Brace Jovanovich, 1967. Copyright © 1973 by Alice Walker. Reprinted by permission of Houghton Mifflin Harcourt Publishing Company.

Wolfe, Tom. "Yeager." From Wolfe, Tom, *The Right Stuff*. New York: Farrar, Straus & Giroux, Inc, 1979, Bantam Paperback edition 1983, 35–40, 41–42, 42–48. Copyright © 1979 by Tom Wolfe. Reprinted by permission of Farrar, Straus and Giroux, LLC.